IRONSIDE

IRONSIDE

THE AUTHORISED BIOGRAPHY OF FIELD MARSHAL LORD IRONSIDE

EDMUND IRONSIDE
WITH ANDREW BAMFORD

To my beloved wife Audrey and to my family, who inspired
me to bring to life my father's diaries and give context to the
life of this extraordinary man and his contribution to British
military history.

First published 2018

The History Press
The Mill, Brimscombe Port
Stroud, Gloucestershire, GL5 2QG
www.thehistorypress.co.uk

© Edmund Ironside, 2018

The right of Edmund Ironside to be identified as the Author
of this work has been asserted in accordance with the
Copyright, Designs and Patents Act 1988.

All rights reserved. No part of this book may be reprinted
or reproduced or utilised in any form or by any electronic,
mechanical or other means, now known or hereafter invented,
including photocopying and recording, or in any information
storage or retrieval system, without the permission in writing
from the Publishers.

British Library Cataloguing in Publication Data.
A catalogue record for this book is available from the British Library.

ISBN 978 0 7509 6379 4

Typesetting and origination by The History Press
Printed in India by Thomson Press

Contents

	Foreword by General the Lord Richards of Herstmonceux GCB CBE DSO	7
	List of Maps	11
	Introduction	13
1	Early Days	19
2	Undercover Subaltern	36
3	The Making of a Staff Officer	51
4	Apprenticeship to Command	69
5	Holding the Line	91
6	Polar Mission	106
7	Spring Relief, Autumn Homecoming	124
8	Temporary Commands	140
9	Persia on the Carpet	154
10	From Cairo to Camberley	172
11	Modernising Commandant	183
12	Command at Home	199
13	The Raj that Was	223
14	Eastern Command	246
15	In Sight of the War Office	263
16	On Call at the Rock	280
17	Waiting in the Wings	293
18	CIGS	309
19	Scandinavian Sideshow	330
20	Desperate Days	347
	Epilogue	376
	Notes	382
	Select Bibliography	404
	Index	407

Foreword

by General the Lord Richards of Herstmonceux GCB CBE DSO

The more I got stuck into this engrossing book, the more fascinated I became by its subject, Field Marshal the Lord Ironside. Like the field marshal, I too am a 'Gunner'. Through proud regimental folklore I had long been aware that the Royal Regiment of Artillery had produced two of the three chiefs of the Imperial General Staff (CIGS) that served this country during the Second World War, one being Field Marshal the Lord Alanbrooke. Everyone seemed to know of Alanbrooke but few people outside the regiment appeared to be aware of the other, 'Tiny' Ironside. What made Ironside tick? What was his background and character? How did he reach such exalted rank at such a critical time and what happened to him?

Almost uniquely, Ironside kept a diary through much of his life so the author, his son, uses it with great authority to explain all this and much more. In my judgement, Baron Ironside does so most successfully. The book is highly readable, well-constructed, simply expressed and yet full of important detail. He captures, in a delightfully understated way, the challenges and variety of the era in which his father lived. An era for which Tiny Ironside was tailor-made and one in which he clearly prospered, yet was marginalised at the height of his influence and power.

Born in Edinburgh, the son of an army surgeon who died in 1881, Ironside was brought up by his widowed mother. Educated at Tonbridge School and RMA Woolwich, he was commissioned into the Royal Artillery in 1899. His first operational posting was to the Boer War where, amongst other roles, working with John Buchan, he spied on the Germans in South West Africa. It is said that Buchan modelled John Hannay of *The Thirty-Nine Steps* fame on Ironside, so taken was he by the latter's character and bravery. In the period before the First World War, he had a pretty conventional career but exceptionally played rugby for Scotland and won the army heavyweight boxing championship. Clearly here is a young officer with courage and, at 6ft 4in height, considerable physical prowess. As his career progressed, it was these 'extras' that increasingly distinguished Ironside from most of his peers. During the First World War, this included the award of no less than six Mentions in Despatches; a DSO; command first in the Machine Gun Corps and then of an infantry brigade, both of which were out of the ordinary for a Gunner;

a posting to North Russia, and at the war's end a knighthood and promotion to substantive major general at the tender age of 39. Clearly Ironside had had a 'good war' and no doubt was already marked out as an officer of exceptional promise by the military secretary's office.

The variety and demands of Ironside's interwar career follow in the same mould. It includes being commandant of the Staff College Camberley. Here he advocated Boney Fuller's radical doctrines, a brave line in an era when many members of the Army Board considered Fuller a dangerous eccentric. He commanded 2nd Division in Aldershot and Meerut District in India before being promoted to lieutenant general and, after a period on half pay, returning to India as QMG (quartermaster general). In 1936, he was promoted general and appointed GOC-in-C (general officer commanding-in-chief) Eastern Command.

In 1938 Ironside became governor of Gibraltar, a job that conventionally presaged retirement. In his case this was not to be. My experienced eye wonders what changed No. 1 Board's collective mind. The threat of war with Germany certainly would have focused their attention on the need for genuine talent in the top jobs, if necessary at the expense of orthodoxy. 'Tiny' Ironside clearly met their criteria and was ordered back to the UK to take up the post of inspector general of overseas forces and commander designate of the field force due to go to France in the event of war.

That this did not happen, the CIGS Lord Gort himself taking the post, must have been a considerable blow to a man of Ironside's character and instincts. His consolation prize was that he was appointed the CIGS. But this was a post for which, of his own account, he was 'not suited in temperament', a feeling for which I have much empathy! And the historical consensus is that Ironside's self-analysis was typically perceptive. His nine months as CIGS were mixed at best. The author explains this most challenging of times well and I am not going to reach a judgement here. Suffice to say, Ironside could not have been in this vital post at a tougher time, politically or militarily. It is interesting to speculate if any CIGS would have survived this period with his reputation intact. My instinct is not; whoever was CIGS during this period was not destined to be in the post for too long, as the nation, its political leaders and the army settled down for the long haul ahead.

This captivating book describes the life of an exceptional officer, and his journey through a remarkable series of overseas postings and commands, even by the standard of the day. Clearly his own man, Ironside served his country bravely and imaginatively at a time when orthodoxy was the order of the day. He was, most importantly, a soldier's soldier and I cannot do better in concluding this short foreword than quoting from Ironside's obituary in the *Glasgow Herald* of 26 September 1959:

Ironside, his troops felt, was an ideal leader, a big man physically as well as in character. In his Arctic kit and thigh boots he was an impressive figure, and he had the common touch which is part of the gift of leadership. A famous military historian wrote of him that he might well become a national hero; while that forecast was not fulfilled, he certainly made his own legend with those who served under him.

This is high praise indeed and is the type of judgement that matters most to all good officers, not least Tiny Ironside. This sympathetic but perceptive biography is historically important and will usefully correct some unwarranted myths and misjudgements.

List of Maps

1	Southern Africa in the first decade of the twentieth century	29
2	The Western Front	64
3	The assault on Vimy Ridge	81
4	North Russia	110
5	Persia and Mesopotamia	156
6	Anti-invasion deployments, May–June 1940	361
7	Anti-invasion deployments, July 1940	374

Introduction

In the history of the British Army in the last century, the name Ironside seems to be mentioned only infrequently. Yet my father, Field Marshal William Edmund Ironside, 1st Baron Ironside, had one of the most active careers imaginable for a general officer of his day, serving in three major wars, rising through the ranks to eventually hold the post of CIGS, and ending his active career as the man directly responsible for defending Britain against a German invasion which, in 1940, seemed all too imminent. It must be questioned, therefore, why so little has been written about the man and his career, to the extent that his name is often passed over, even in histories dealing with events with which he was heavily involved.

The answer, I suspect, stems from the fact that he made few friends amongst his contemporaries and peers, and it has been around the stories of these men – the likes of Gort, Dill and Alanbrooke – and of the younger generation of generals who followed them after 1940, that much of our understanding of events before and during the Second World War has been shaped. My father recognised from an early age that successful service in the British Army depended on falling into line with your superiors and stepping out of line with your equals. Opportunity and good fortune allowed him to display his talents at an early age, which led to rapid promotion but did little to endear him to those over whose heads he jumped in the process. This biography, therefore, sets out to redress the balance and tell my father's story from his own point of view, and to bring to life a character who is too often written off with the briefest of pen portraits.

His real story is not only worth telling to redress the historical balance and give him his rightful place amongst Britain's military leaders of the twentieth century, but also because, as life stories go, it is as eventful as anything one might find in fiction. Indeed, while my father gained a fictional counterpart in John Buchan's Richard Hannay, it is doubtful whether even Hannay managed to pack quite so much into his life as did my father. He was blessed by a number of attributes that set him up for a career as a soldier. His physical stature was there for all to see, although army humour being what it is, he inevitably acquired the nickname 'Tiny'. Coupled with this was the ability to get on well with the men under his command and win their support, and, if he jarred in his relationships with his peers, he was generally able to impress his superiors, thanks to a mind that was quick-thinking both in front of the enemy and behind a desk. Above all, he had a natural ability with languages which, cultivated throughout his youth, rendered him proficient in French, Dutch, Russian, German and Afrikaans amongst others. This skill took him across the world as an intelligence officer and spy, and as peacemaker and peacekeeper.

Although there were times when peacetime cutbacks found him placed on half pay, my father's military career was one of steady progress, and he mastered in turn the three steps needed to reach the highest office. The first, after distinguished service as a subaltern of artillery in the Second Boer War, was from the regiment to the staff. The second, after graduating from the Staff College in 1914 as chief staff officer of 4th Canadian Division, was from staff to command, as a brigadier on the Western Front and then an independent command in North Russia. Having flown his flag as C-in-C afloat in the White Sea, he returned home to a knighthood at the age of 39, and was thereafter entrusted with diplomatic action by Prime Minister David Lloyd George, to supervise the departure of the Romanian Army from Hungary and the Turkish Army from the Izmir Peninsula.

He went on to perform a military-diplomatic sleight of hand in clearing away the Russian officer influence in Persia from the bodyguard at the court of the Shah. This highly important exploit was instrumental in keeping the gateway to India properly defended and made way for Winston Churchill, then colonial secretary, to take him under his wing with a view to giving him a senior command in Mesopotamia. In this he was thwarted by injuries sustained in a plane crash, which brought him home to recover. This, however, turned out to be the watershed in his professional career and served to line him up as commandant of the Staff College Camberley, which allowed him to make the third major step into a position where he could actively influence the future development of the army. In this role, he championed aviation and mechanisation, working with the likes of 'Boney' Fuller to turn out a new generation of staff officers, many of whom would go on to high command in the 1940s.

After Camberley, peacetime stagnation slowed his rise, but rise he continued to do, commanding a division at Aldershot and a district in India before being selected to work hand in hand with the viceroy and GOC-in-C India as quartermaster general to modernise the Indian Army.

Returning home, he made the final step to high office with an appointment to head Eastern Command, during which time he gained some astonishing insights into the power of a resurgent Germany when he was invited to attend the German combined manoeuvres in 1937 as the personal guest of

Generalfeldmarschal von Blomberg. For a moment, it seemed as if this might be the pinnacle of his career as, with the retirement clock ticking towards the age of 60, he found himself seemingly sidelined to the governorship of Gibraltar. Even this proved no sinecure, with the Spanish Civil War in its final stages, and carried with it the implicit promise of appointment as C-in-C Middle East had war broken out. In the event, after less than a year on the Rock he returned to the War Office as inspector general of overseas forces to prepare the British Army for war, and on 3 September 1939 he was appointed CIGS. After retirement in 1940, he was made a field marshal, and created a peer of the United Kingdom by Winston Churchill as his reward for organising the defence of Calais as a shield for the British Expeditionary Force's (BEF) withdrawal from Dunkirk, and for his final service as C-in-C Home Forces when the threat of invasion was at his highest.

Undoubtedly, then, the story of his life and career is worth telling. What I believe makes this book exceptional, however, is the fact that it is possible to tell the story using so many of my father's own words, ideas and opinions. From an early age, he was an inveterate diarist, and his collected writings fill an entire case with beautifully bound foolscap volumes. In his retirement, my father began using these papers to prepare a memoir of his career, filling in those gaps when circumstances during his early life had prevented him maintaining a daily diary. For this reason, his recollections up to 1918 take the form of a memoir, and contain his later reflections as well as his impressions of the times. Further memoirs, covering his command in North Russia and his overseas missions during the early 1920s, have already seen publication; the first in his own lifetime, the second – edited for completion by myself – after his death. Also published is a selection of extracts from his later diaries, covering the period 1937–40 and edited by his former staff officer, the late Colonel Roderick Macleod, and Denis Kelly. This published selection, however, represents only a tiny fraction of the surviving diaries, which run from late 1918 to the year of my father's death. This book is the first study to use this source in full, and I believe that the insights contained within the diaries will add much to our understanding of the man and his times.

Nevertheless, it would be folly to base any biography on a single source, and many other important original sources have also been employed. My father's papers contain many letters to him from leading figures of the day, and I have been fortunate to have access to the substantial correspondence between himself and his good friend, the broadcaster Christopher Stone. It is clear he realised that a word or two from the lips of the media man of the time was likely to improve his prospects of advancement: as a diarist, my father knew that he was writing for himself, but his correspondence with Stone – who had served with him during the First World War and been awarded a DSO – indicated those views that he wished to receive a more public airing. It has therefore been intriguing for me to have an insight into his two modes of expression: research which, I am sure, will help to make this a fitting memorial for my father's military mindset. I am grateful to Stone's late daughter Felicity for her gesture of goodwill, following her father's death, in returning to me all those letters written to my father.

A substantial amount of material relating to my father is now contained in the National Archives at Kew and this has been used to help fill some of the gaps in my father's own narrative or to add another angle to the story. For the same reason, the diaries and memoirs of several of his contemporaries have also been drawn upon – it is, after all, as important to know what others thought of my father as it is to know what he thought of them.

Lastly, it is both a necessity and my pleasure to acknowledge the assistance of a number of individuals without whose assistance this book would never have seen publication. Special thanks are due to my late wife Audrey, whose constant support and encouragement over many years has made this book possible. I offer my grateful thanks to Wendy Sanford, who typed out the entire manuscript with cheer and efficiency.

Despite a long acquaintance and many changes of tack, the decision of Michael Leventhal, formerly with The History Press but now with his family firm, Greenhill Books, was an act of faith, which has resulted in my father's story being published as a readable piece of military history. I owe him and his team a great debt of gratitude. Mervyn Bassett, the Beadle of the Skinners' Company, also deserves my sincere thanks for his unceasing ability to transform problems into solutions.

I would like to thank the Royal Artillery and all its regimental resources for their record searches and Major General John Moore-Bick, when he was head of United Kingdom Support Command Germany, for his assistance in accessing German Army records relating to German South West Africa, the scene of one of my father's early exploits as an intelligence officer. I would also like to thank Gerhardt von Estorff for his kindness in providing access to his great-uncle's biography covering his colonial service, during which time, unbeknownst to him, he engaged my father as his transport adviser when in charge of operations in German South West Africa.

General Lord Richards, former Chief of the Defence Staff, deserves particular thanks for having done me the honour of writing the excellent foreword to this book. Most of all I am indebted to the late Dr Anthony Holmes-Walker, Senior Past Master of the Worshipful Company of Skinners who acted as my literary agent. Deserving of special thanks is the military historian Dr Andrew Bamford who has carried out much of the important archival work for the project. He has worked with skill and imagination to put my father's words of military wisdom into context for the present-day reader. Both Anthony and Andrew have proved an invaluable source of additional research which has helped to ensure this book will serve as a fitting memorial to my father's military mindset. Final responsibility for all content and opinions, however, remains mine alone.

1

Early Days

Genealogists tell us that the Ironside name, in its Scots form, comes either from Ironside in Aberdeenshire, or Earnside in Fife, and is a parallel evolution to its English homonym made famous by the Anglo-Saxon king, Edmund Ironside. My father, for his part, preferred to believe in our reputed descent from Margaret, granddaughter of King Edmund Ironside, who was born during the family's exile to Hungary and who eventually married Malcolm Canmore, King of Scots, in 1068.[1]

In either event, tracing the family's more recent line of descent in Scotland is difficult, following the destruction of most of the records in fires at critical times in the public record offices in both Edinburgh and London, but, with the help of the Poll Books and Church Records, my father was able to trace our more recent family history back to his own great-great-grandfather who farmed at Lonehead, Old Rayne, in Aberdeenshire and was born in March 1733.

His son, William, also a farmer, was born on 21 October 1766. William's wife, born Elspeth Mitchell, bore him four girls and five boys. The three middle sons died without issue, and the youngest remained all his life on the family farm. The eldest, also William, lived until 1843 and in November 1806 fathered another William, my great-grandfather, who married Grizeal Garden and died in August 1879.

My grandfather, yet another William, was one of five children. He was born in 1836 and sadly died after contracting pneumonia following a fishing trip on 16 January 1881, aged 45, while he was a surgeon major in the Royal Artillery serving as army medical commandant in Edinburgh, leaving my grandmother widowed for fifty years and more, after a married life of only nine years. At the time of his own father's untimely death, my father, the subject of this biography, was less than a year old, having been born on 6 May 1880.

My grandfather's unexpected death in 1881 brought a year of sadness to the Ironside family and, being newly widowed, my grandmother had to make up her mind where to live after losing her entitlement to army quartering. She decided to settle in Scotland at St Andrews, rather than in England at Rochester and near to her sister. So, with a small inherited income from her father and an army means-tested compassionate allowance, she was able to employ a nursemaid and to rent a large flat at Lockhart Place in the middle of town, which allowed her to enjoy trips by boat with her family from Leith to Antwerp to visit favourite haunts in the Ardennes on the back of highly profitable holiday lets to visiting golfers.

My father attended St Salvator's School as a day boy, which overlooks the first tee at the Royal and Ancient and, like all boys of his age, he learned to play golf there. The ritual was, after doffing their caps for a moment to the monument of the protestant martyrs, Patrick Hamilton and George Wishart, facing the school gates, they would play a few holes before breakfast each morning. With the most expensive club costing 4s 6d and a ball at 6d, the citizens of the town had the privilege of playing for free. The boys swam from the Step Rock near the school and played football as juniors, before going on to play rugby football in their last two years as seniors at the school. They also boxed and learned to ride.

During my father's six years at St Salvator's it was only in his last year that he began to think seriously about the future. A civic visit of the Channel Fleet to St Andrews Bay allowed him to go on board HMS *Camperdown* to see what life at sea was like, but the Royal Navy held no attraction for him. It perhaps did not help the senior service's cause that this same battleship had been involved in the collision that had led to the sinking of HMS *Victoria* while on exercises in the Mediterranean, a scandal that was still fresh in the public mind. So, he was not persuaded to join the Royal Navy and in due course opted instead for entry to the Royal Military Academy at Woolwich and then to become a Gunner.

This preference for the Royal Artillery no doubt owed more than a little to the influence of his two godfathers, both of whom were officers of that corps and who together inspired my father to seek a commission with the regiment that stood on the 'right of the line'. One of them, Major General Stuart James Nicholson, CB, had for many years commanded the Chestnut Troop and the other, Major General Sir John Ramsay Slade, KCB, had distinguished himself at the Battle of Maiwand in Afghanistan and had taken part in the march from Kabul to Kandahar. On his death in 1913 he bequeathed the star of his knighthood to one of his godchildren and his three medals to my father, his other godchild. They are the Khedive's Star, Ashanti Star and Kabul to Kandahar Star, which I have in my possession now.

I think the greatest impression that arises out of accounts of my father's boyhood is his gift for learning and speaking foreign languages, which grew through the foreign trips shared with his mother, and showed itself long before he went to St Salvator's School. He was clearly blessed with a good ear for a foreign tongue, but he developed a system for increasing his vocabulary whereby he sought a colloquial translation for the first half a dozen thoughts that came into his head each morning, thus quickly developing a familiarity with the everyday use of an unfamiliar language. With respect to the northern European languages, he also felt that he had an advantage in that Dutch and Flemish, early command of which gave him in turn an easy route into learning Afrikaans, shared something in terms of accent with the Scots dialect that he had grown up with. This skill was developed over successive trips abroad with his mother. Although my father's many and varied overseas appointments in his career as a soldier did not depend upon his ability to speak the appropriate foreign language, nevertheless it is clear that he achieved so much more by being able to do so when he was a subaltern in South Africa, and again as a general officer successively in Russia, on mission in Hungary, commanding in Iran and, much later, as governor of Gibraltar.

For very good reasons, having been through the English educational mill herself and having an intimate knowledge of what such a grounding had done for her seven older brothers, my grandmother wanted a public school education for her son in England. For her to be able to afford to send him as boarder, however, scholarship backing was crucial and attempts to make the grade at Wellington, Bradfield and Bedford all ended in disappointment. Fortunately, her sister came to the rescue: her own son, Robert Arnold, had been to Tonbridge School and, on her advice, my grandmother applied for a foundation place there for my father by taking up residence within the 10-mile qualifying reach of the parish church, at Cage Green Farm.

My father arrived at Tonbridge School three weeks after the start of the 1894 Lent term and vividly described the first two days of class removes which paved the way for many more leaps up the classroom ladder. Armed with his admission papers, which marked him out as destined for the 16–18-year-old entry to the Royal Military Academy, he was ushered into the headmaster's study by the school porter, arrayed in his livery and top hat. After a brief interview with the headmaster, which revealed my father's shortcomings in Latin and Greek, he was assigned to 'Modern F' and sent to his new classroom:

> The form-master was the Rev. William Rashleigh, a very famous Kent County bat at that time who appeared to be giving a German lesson. All the boys in the class quite naturally turned their eyes on me, glad to see something to relieve the boredom of the lesson. The Rev. William nodded and pointed to a seat at the back of the room. Within a minute of sitting down I realised by his accent that he knew no German and my attention soon wandered, but I was suddenly brought back to life by hearing my name being called. As I had always been taught, I answered in German, saying that I had not quite caught the sense of the question. Suddenly there was a deadly silence and again everybody stared at me. Rashleigh paused for a moment and then moved on to question some other boy. After the lesson was over he questioned me and I told him that I spoke three languages fluently, including German. All he said was, 'This is no place for you. Come back after lunch and I will tell you where to go.' When I came back I found I had been given a double remove to 'Modern D' next door, run by a man called Pattison. The class was doing French repetition and the boys were repeating by heart the lines that they had just learnt. When I repeated my lines in a truly French accent,

it created roars of laughter and I was told to catch up on the work that I had missed. [...] The next morning I repeated what had been done over the previous three weeks, which was not greeted with any pleasure by the rest of the class. After the lesson was over, I was told that I was a prig – which was probably true – and as I had spoilt the market, I was to appear in a fight with gloves on to have the stuffing knocked out of me. I didn't have any idea of how to box and when my opponent came running at me I clipped him on both ears and gave him an uppercut on the chin. He collapsed on the ground and the boys watching looked at me in astonishment. I was never molested again, but had learnt my lesson and didn't spoil any more markets.[2]

In retrospect, my father's size and power as a fully grown man, which must have been apparent in him even as a youth, suggest that the attempt by his new fellows to administer physical chastisement was decidedly unwise!

Notwithstanding his prowess at modern languages, my father lagged behind in Latin and Maths and some other subjects; he nevertheless moved up to Modern C for the 1894 summer term, which brought him into contact with Edward Goldberg, who was the head of the Modern side of the school and spoke French and German like a native. My father kept in touch with him after leaving Tonbridge, and later said:

Seldom could a school have found such a good foreign language master as Edward Goldberg. In French and German his accent was without fault. Curiously enough, he kept his French up to a higher state than his German. Long after I came back from my wanderings in South Africa I found him starting to learn Russian, so I lent him my dictionary and grammar. I don't think he ever learnt to speak the language fluently, but well enough for reading.[3]

For his summertime sport my father chose, instinctively perhaps, to shoot and to join the school Volunteer Corps, thereby being able to excuse himself from the cricket field on which the school's sporting reputation had largely been built. Even though he did not take to cricket, records show that, still being under 14 in April 1894, he competed in the broad and long jump heats and was placed first in the 100 yards sprint. In the 1894 Michaelmas term he took naturally to rugby football and 'Sapper Ironside' was seen shooting for the school against St Paul's in December of that year.

All in all, my father could look back with some pride on his first months at Tonbridge; but, in looking ahead, he realised that it was important to make sure that his curriculum was tailored towards the entry requirements for the Royal Military College (RMC) as opposed to the needs of university entrance or commercial qualification. So far, he had advanced rapidly up the Modern side of the school, but he realised that if he was to make the grade for a Regular Army career, he had to change course. Goldberg, who was now his form master, promised to put things right and for the summer term he found that he had been moved up another peg to Modern B. But, despite his unique position in the school, being the only boy wanting to read for the RMC entry, he still felt the pressures on him to delay sitting the exam and fall in line with the general pattern of school life. As this was spoiling his plans to win the coveted army cadetship at the earliest opportunity, he went on badgering his form master to put things right.

Equally, after joining the school Volunteer Corps and putting so much of his energies into shooting, attending drills and camping, he did not want to see his army career ambitions being thwarted by a trivial curriculum deficiency. In the Lent term of 1896, still under 16, he found he had been moved up to the top of the Modern side of the school into Modern A; he was also selected for the 2nd XV school rugger team, and won the Volunteer Corps first prize for achievement.

Nevertheless, there was still no change in the teaching timetable. This drove him and his mother to visit that famed faculty of last resort, a 'crammer' called James, Carlisle & Gregson in London's Lexham Gardens, to seek help from the redoubtable Captain James to ensure a successful placing in the RMC entry examinations. The answer was simply and plainly put – 'If he comes at once I will guarantee to get him into Woolwich. If he delays, I cannot promise.' This put the seal of approval on 'Jimmies'. On returning to Tonbridge, he and his mother confronted Goldberg with her decision to withdraw my father from Tonbridge School immediately:

> My mother's statement almost knocked him out. He was struck dumb for several minutes. Then he began by saying he could not understand how we could be so rash. I was throwing away all the advantages of my last year at a public school. What would we do about payment of fees, if I didn't go back? I had been promised trial exams and nothing had happened. Nothing but promises, never fulfilled ... I didn't go back for the next term and nobody sued us for the term's fees.[4]

So, my father's schooling at Tonbridge was brought to an abrupt halt after nine terms. Certainly, he made the most of his time at the school and I believe that his entry plans for the RMC would have been frustrated, together with his army career prospects, had he stayed on. He felt that the school had done well in teaching him languages and mathematics, but had failed with respect to the humanities. When he reflected in 1957 on what happened, he said:

> The truth is that schools do not like to specialise. They like to have a boy up to age of 18 and then send him on to university. That is easy for them and does

not take them out of their stride. They are oblivious to the wishes of the parents and reply that they do not like their curriculum being pushed out of its stride.[5]

No school, he felt, could compete with such a place as Jimmies in preparing boys for a service that had a stiff and highly competitive entry exam.

At Jimmies, still under 17, my father found that he was not alone in his struggle to qualify for the RMC. As well as potential candidates seeking entry to Woolwich, Jimmies was also geared to helping officers pass their promotion exams and preparing them for entry to the Staff College at Camberley. While a specialised training to prepare candidates for Woolwich was no bad thing, the idea of cramming to pass these latter exams served to rather defeat the object of the Staff College, which had been established as 'an institution devoted to the instruction of the future leaders of the army after they had been commissioned'.[6] My father would in due course attend as a student and later head the college as commandant.

All this was yet in the future, however, and so having taken up lodgings nearby in Eardley Crescent, he started at Jimmies by having his timetable tailored to his exam needs. His daytime studies were not onerous, but were clearly focused on the single purpose of winning one of the forty coveted cadetships, selected from some 400 applicants openly competing for entry. In the winter months, he found time to play rugger for the London Scottish at Richmond and in the summer to play golf. As sitting the exam meant sacrificing a week of tuition, his teachers preferred him to skip his first entry shot to shorten the odds of winning at either the second or final attempt. The outcome of his first sitting was to qualify in fifty-first place, followed by taking forty-first place on his final sitting. This, sadly, seemed to indicate that he had missed out on selection by one place: then, to his astonishment, it was announced that a revised contingency plan to take account of the ongoing expansion of the army had led to an increase in the number of places to sixty-six. To his great delight he was at last gazetted a gentleman cadet: inwardly he exclaimed, 'Gosh and good fortune!'

A hangover from the days when the ordnance remained separate from the rest of the army, the Royal Military Academy at Woolwich, known to all Gunners as 'the Shop', was the well-respected feeder college for future officers of the Royal Artillery and Royal Engineers, and remained so until closure in 1939. Unlike the more rarefied ideals of the Staff College, the purpose of Woolwich was to provide a 'sound scientific education' for the future officers of the army's most technically demanding branches.[7] Gentleman Cadets of the RMC spent eighteen months at Woolwich before being commissioned as 2nd lieutenants within their designated or chosen branches of service.

The fees being charged in January 1898 when my father joined were £200 per year, but my grandmother, as a surgeon major's widow, only had to pay £40. A cadet's pay was 3s per day, all found, which was enough to cover all incidental costs. In my father's first term as a 'snooker', he shared a room with three others and most of the time was spent on small-arms drill and exercises. Academically, he did well in every subject except for higher maths, but with extra private tuition he was still able to 'accelerate' in his second term to pass out with all his friends in three months, thereby gaining six months' seniority.

As a ready reader of military history, he felt that the greatest blot on the teaching curriculum was the lack of military history studies. He always supposed that this was a continuation of the methods of the old ordnance days, when an artillery officer was first and foremost a technician who did not need to know anything about military history and was not generally eligible for the command of mixed forces. In passing, it should be noted that it was while at Woolwich that he acquired the nickname 'Tiny' – a mocking compliment to his 6ft 4in and 17 stone – which stuck with him for the rest of his military life.

Discipline at the Shop, like discipline in any cadet establishment, was centred on timing and turnout, which meant that punishments were designed to remedy the cause. So, a failure to deliver on time was invariably penalised by a time-consuming dressing down drill, while a lack of turnout was usually penalised by some pointless dressing up task. Such perils notwithstanding, my father always looked back happily at the months he spent at the Shop, especially after all his exertions at school to realise his ambition of winning an entry into the army.

In fact, he records that he only had one bad encounter with authority, but it was one that very nearly killed off all his ambitions to make a life for himself in the army. Unexpectedly, in his last term, he was confronted by the Shop subaltern, Charles Vereker, with the prospect of his being commissioned into the Royal Garrison Artillery (RGA). This was at a time when the Royal Artillery was in the process of being split into two corps, separating the static heavy guns from the mobile batteries comprising the Royal Horse Artillery (RHA) and Royal Field Artillery (RFA). Naturally, service in the latter branch was far more appealing for, aside from including – rather oddly – the batteries of mountain guns, the RGA was restricted to siege and fortress work.

The role of the Shop subaltern was to oversee the daily lives of the cadets and, as such, Vereker – who had himself come from the Garrison Artillery service, and may not have viewed it in quite such a negative light as my father – was in no real position to influence my father's eventual appointment. Nevertheless, when my father retorted that he would turn down such an appointment as Vereker was proposing, he was accused of insubordination! The incident was regarded seriously enough for him to be brought before the assistant commandant to explain himself, as a result of which he pondered over the prospect of resigning and seeking an alternative career in the colonial police service, going so far as to enquire for details and complete, but not post, an application to the London office of the Cape Police and the Bechuanaland Border Police:

The little Colonel reasoned with me that I might be ruining my whole life by refusing a commission. I told him that I was certain I should be ruining my whole life if I did join the RGA. I wasn't going to be forced. I thanked him for being so kind to me and for having had patience with me. I told him that I had already decided upon what I should do if I were not posted to the Mounted Branch. I had already made all my preparations to go out and join the Bechuanaland Border Police as a Pte. Again they held up their hands in despair at having no power to make me change my mind. […] I have often looked back on this little struggle I had had with Military Authority. I am sure that I was right. Had I given in, I would have resigned my unwanted Commission in the Garrison Artillery within six months & thus have been so many months behind in my new career. I should have been quite happy as a Police Officer in Africa.[8]

While one can sympathise with my father's preference for a life of dash and adventure in the Field or Horse Artillery, not to mention the far better prospects for promotion associated with that branch, it seems most likely that Vereker was using the threat of a possible posting to fortress duty as a reaction to a stroppy cadet, in the hope that the threat of relegation to a less appealing branch of service would put a stop to further unruly behaviour. Quite possibly, it was said only to test my father's reaction. Certainly, his response showed considerable strength of character, but it also served to blow the whole affair somewhat out of proportion and it is rather unlikely that it was truly the case, as he seems to have believed, that it was only his robust response that saved him from an unwanted posting. In all events, though, he need not have worried, for when his commission duly came through on 25 June 1899, it was as a 2nd lieutenant in the RFA.

Second Lieutenant Ironside's first posting, effective from 1 July 1899, was to 44th Field Battery, stationed at Colchester. Here he joined a garrison consisting of a cavalry regiment, two field batteries and two battalions of infantry, under the overall command of Major General Sir William Gatacre. Having just turned 19, his first taste of regimental life must have been very frustrating for the newly joined junior subaltern as he was immediately sidelined as a spectator in the battery's visit to Okehampton Artillery Practice Camp on Dartmoor because it was feared that his inexperience might spoil his battery's chances of making a favourable showing.

However, if the change from the busy cadet routine to boring barrack life had its disappointments, there were strong rumours of impending war, and the prospect of service in South Africa served as a spur that kept my father's career ambitions moving. Thoughts of a more financially rewarding life in the Bechuanaland Border Police were still lingering in the back of his mind, but were finally put aside for good when 44th Battery was mobilised on 24 December 1899. This, I believe, was the first watershed in his army career, when he discovered the excitement of command, coupled with his ability to take responsibility for the men under him.

For himself, though, my father realised that active service would shorten his path to promotion and bring greater financial reward in the meantime. There was little margin for play in making ends meet on a junior subaltern's pay of under £12 per month, but for the time being all thoughts of switching careers evaporated. In the short term, though, mobilisation brought with it substantial costs, as there were bills for khaki uniform, helmets, new boots and, to cap it all, a subscription to campaign messing to ensure that the five battery officers did not suffer in isolation because they were too few to mess on their own. Exceptionally, the only extravagance he allowed himself was to keep a pet bulldog called Bill, who stayed at his heels throughout his subaltern days in South Africa, remaining with him even when he was detached on special service in German South West Africa, until Bill's death some six years later in Ambala.

Leading 44th Battery to the South African War was Major Bernard Francis Drake, aged 39, a horse master who seemed to think more of his horses than of his men and who had plenty of foreign service to his credit. The fact that he had married a girl from Natal while serving there some fifteen years earlier, and knew exactly what the South African *veldt* was like, was only revealed after arrival in Cape Town. As a subaltern, he had survived anti-rabics injections after being bitten by a mad dog, and later his son had been killed in a hunting accident, so he was not the easiest sort of character for his fellow officers to befriend.

His second in command, replacing Captain C.C. Owen who had held the post while the battery was at Colchester, was Captain Dalrymple 'Dally' Arbuthnot, aged 32 and another veteran of foreign service. He was the only man in the battery wearing a campaign medal, which had been awarded for taking part in the relief of Chitral in 1895. Arbuthnot, who eventually retired as a lieutenant colonel in 1916, was later himself replaced by Captain A.H.N. Devenish for the later stages of 44th Battery's time in South Africa. The other two subalterns, together with my father each responsible for a two-gun section when the battery went into action, were H.A.L. Mundy, aged 22, who became the lame duck of the battery through failing to pass his promotion exams, and Barton B. Crozier, son of the Archbishop of Armagh, who was the most likeable and popular man and who rose to be a major general. He remained a lifelong regimental friend.

When 44th Battery set off from Colchester on 21 January 1900 by train bound for Woolwich Docks to embark for South Africa, the bands played and the whole garrison turned out to say farewell. Transporting a mounted battery by sea to an overseas base may have been a commonplace exercise for the army at the turn of the nineteenth century, but my father's description of the voyage does shed some interesting light on what life on board a horse transport was like. The troopship *St Andrew*, which left harbour the next day, was one of the western ocean ships designed to take large cargoes of horses, mules and cattle across the seas in all kinds of weather with little or no creature comforts, and for this voyage had embarked the horses and men of two artillery batteries and one ammunition column. Horses stood on a concrete-surfaced floor laid with coconut matting, in stalls set up between decks so that they could not sway about in rough seas. Each one had a sling under its belly, just touching, to prevent a fall, and all shoes had been removed. In front of the stalls, a coconut-matted track ran all around the ship and every horse was led by its groom for exercise lasting at least an hour every day. After passing through the Bay of Biscay, the horses were all clipped to get their coats ready for the southern summer weather: luckily, Major Drake, who had been on a troopship with horses before, had the forethought to bring several pairs of clippers with him.

The twenty-one-day voyage was uneventful in every way and daily stable duties lasted for five hours or more. There were only four fatal casualties to the horses on board and the vet kept the stalls well aired to avoid cases of pneumonia in the climate change en route. At Las Palmas, the ship stopped to take on fresh water and passed by the wreck of a steamer which had been shipping traction engines to South Africa for trials by the Royal Engineers. At Walvis Bay, they passed the wreck of the troopship that had carried 63rd Battery to Cape Town earlier, in which all the horses were lost.

On any voyage, it is always hard to keep up the tempo of everyday working life, and this voyage was no exception, especially as there were few incentives to get out into the open air on the upper deck. Instruction took place on fixing tents and packing saddle wallets, and there was practise firing revolver shots at towed kites. All personnel were given newly developed enteric fever inoculations. The only fun time had by all was during the traditional crossing-the-line ceremony, which helped to relieve some of the boredom of the journey. But what my father, as a junior subaltern, felt was most lacking during the trip was a failure to familiarise everybody with the wartime conditions in South Africa and to say what was expected of them.

There is no denying that such a briefing would have been invaluable to the officers and men of 44th Battery and, indeed, to those of other units heading out to join the growing conflict. The fact remains, however, that the early months of fighting the Boers showed that the British Army of the day was very much out of step with modern warfare in general and with its application to the terrain of southern Africa in particular. Much that was held as dogma would be proved, through bloody experience, to be flawed, and only by trying and failing were the correct lessons being learned, albeit at the price of losing men and horses. Quite simply, the means did not exist to pass on the lessons of the early battles – which, in any case, were still being fully absorbed – back to troops on their way to join. Only when the battery joined the forces in the field could the process of relearning how to fight a modern war begin.

By the time the *St Andrew* arrived in Cape Town on 12 February 1900, the war had been underway for four months. In its opening weeks, the Boers of the

Orange Free State and Transvaal had opted for attack as the best form of defence, striking hard against the British frontier posts in Natal and Cape Colony, where much of the available British forces had unwisely been concentrated. The majority of the Natal Field Force was shut up in Ladysmith, while in Cape Colony smaller garrisons were cut off at Kimberley and Mafeking. Thus, when General Sir Redvers Buller brought his newly mobilised army corps to the theatre he could not strike against the Boer capitals of Bloemfontein and Pretoria because political pressure required that he first relieve the besieged garrisons. This in turn required him to split his forces between the Natal and Kimberley fronts, and forced him and his subordinates to attack the Boers on ground of the latter's choosing. The result was a series of battles that were either pyrrhic tactical victories won at great cost, or out-and-out defeats for the British.

Buller, who had led the offensive in Natal, found himself sacked as commander-in-chief and relegated to command in that province, with overall charge being taken by Field Marshal Lord Roberts who arrived on 23 December 1899 with the backing of substantial reinforcements and with Major General Lord Kitchener as his Chief of Staff. Roberts and Kitchener then mounted a ponderous but ultimately successful offensive that would in due course relieve Kimberley, three days after 44th Battery landed, and then go on to capture Bloemfontein on 13 March.

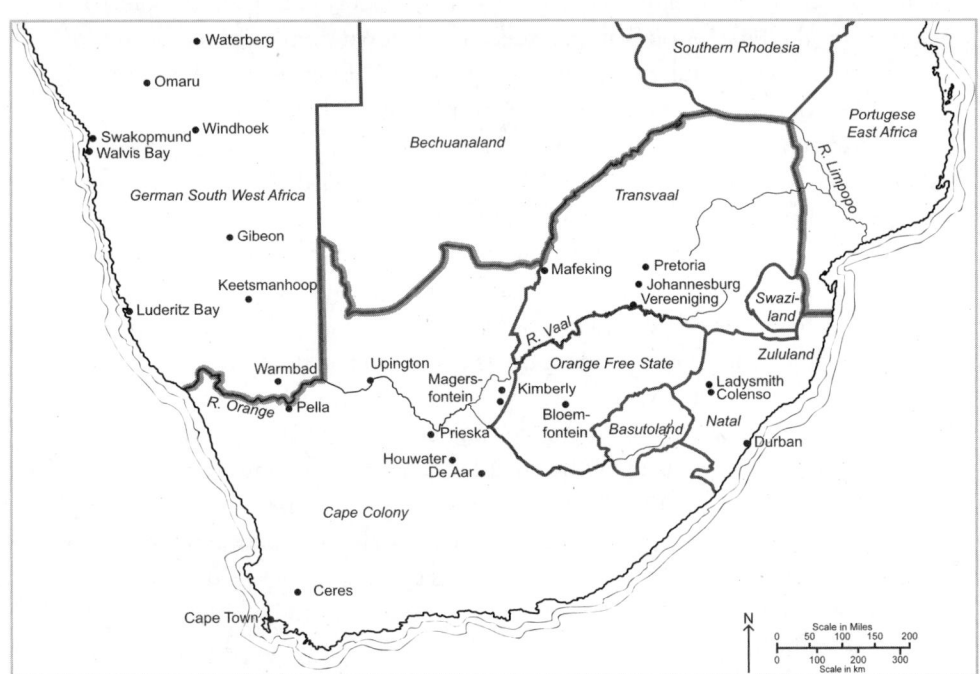

Southern Africa in the first decade of the twentieth century.

Isolated Mafeking would be left a little longer, but was finally relieved in May. Meanwhile, Buller had applied the lessons learned in his previous defeats and successfully fought his way across the Tugela River and to the gates of Ladysmith, which were reached on 1 March.

On the face of it, therefore, the war was seemingly a good way towards being won, with only the capture of the Transvaal capital, Pretoria, required to complete the job. However, the British commanders had failed to take account of the Boers – who they had mistakenly written off as demoralised after their series of reverses – resuming the offensive. This, however, is what happened, and just as the British Army and its leaders had begun to master the techniques of modern pitched battle, they now found themselves faced with a new and very different challenge. The younger and more active Boer field commanders, men like De Wet, De La Rey and Smuts, had quickly grasped that they could no longer fight the British in the field and hope to win. Instead, they threw their energies into a guerrilla campaign that would serve to drag out the conflict for months to come, and give it a bitter quality that had largely been lacking from its earlier exchanges. It was this war that my father and his battery would find themselves embroiled in when they completed their disembarkation.

At the time of the Second Boer War, there was no permanent organisational element of artillery above the battery level. Batteries were grouped, generally by threes, under the command of a lieutenant colonel, to form a brigade division. Later, in time for the First World War, the title was cut down simply to brigade, but the function, to provide artillery support to an infantry division, remained the same. By the time 44th Battery arrived in South Africa, however, all the divisions of the field forces had guns enough of their own and although 44th Battery was grouped with 2nd and 8th Batteries to constitute XIII Brigade Division, this remained essentially a paper formation and the component units found themselves split up amongst the various columns sent out to try and curtail the activities of the Boer commandos. In the case of 44th Battery, my father was told that plans were in hand to move up country by train to the Cape Colony border with Griqualand West and to be ready to resist the incursions of marauding Boers coming across from the Transvaal.

First stop after landing was the Maitland Base Camp, which was just as wretched for the horses as it was for the men. Nothing could have been so badly chosen as the open stretch of grassland by the coast for quartering mounted troops with its exposure to the sandblasting offshore winds mixed with the stench of seaweed. To keep the horses quiet, special headrope tie lines stretched between limbers had to be rigged, instead of the usual heelrope ties secured to pickets driven into the ground. At the same time, a mass of surplus harness had to be returned to store, together with the officers' swords. Thus, the patterns of good practice taught at Woolwich and put into place at Colchester had to be redrawn to suit the needs of the mounted Gunner in the new war on the *veldt*. A new landscape and climate, new inhabitants with their own language, all contributed to the uncertainties in the minds of many of the soldiers. Although they were achieving success in the field, Roberts and Kitchener had failed to make adequate arrangements for supply, commissariat and the rear areas, and my father's first glimpses of the dockside at Cape Town were enough to show him just a few of the many shortcomings. In due course, he would begin to absorb the more subtle lessons that the staff and command network were already learning about their new enemy from all the skirmishes that had already taken place in the opening months of hostilities.

After dockside cranes had unloaded the guns, limbers and wagons, along with all the rest of the gear, many hours were then spent – wasted, my father felt – in matching wheels to platforms before the newly shod horses were landed, all looking extremely fit after their long voyage from England. On 18 February, they were all put into trucks for the train journey to De Aar and packed tightly to stop them falling and breaking their necks, which they might have done if tied to a halter and headrope. Any fallen horses could then easily be picked up at one of the halts. My father spent the journey in a rather more pleasant and productive way:

> We sat in our trucks with our legs dangling out of the doors as we watched the country. On the way at a tiny platform someone would put in a bunch of grapes and wish us a good journey. Even the Dutch did this. I had sworn to myself that I would learn the language properly. I was already supplied with an extensive vocabulary and all I had to do was to listen to the pronunciation and to learn which words were current in 'Afrikaans' and which were not. No one in the Battery thought it was peculiar that I could already make myself understood. No one ever asked me how I had been able to pick the language up.[9]

At De Aar on 21 February, 44th Battery set up camp close to the desolate railway junction and after enduring a tropical downpour in the night awoke to the news of an approaching Boer commando some 300 strong. Talking to people in the *winkel*, or local store, my father heard rumours that a force of Transvaal Boers was making its way south from Griqualand, commandeering meat and fodder. Although militarily insignificant, the appearance of this force had facilitated a rebellion by pro-Boers within Cape Colony, with its centre in the Prieska district, bringing to life one of the main nightmares of Britain's high commissioner in South Africa, Sir Alfred Milner. Milner, in turn, leant upon the army to act swiftly against the twin threat posed by Boers and rebels, whose combined force amounted to 600 men with two pieces of field artillery. Direction of these operations was given to Lord Kitchener, who in turn divided the available troops into several smaller columns. My father, along with the rest of 44th Battery, was assigned to the column commanded by Colonel John Adye, an artilleryman who was a Kitchener protégé from Egypt and lacked any experience of command. The remainder of this force was composed of detachments from the City Imperial Volunteers (CIV), a recently arrived volunteer unit, and of Regular mounted infantry.

Intending to make a reconnaissance in force, Adye made plans to attack the Boers at Houwater, some 15 miles north of Britstown, on 7 March 1900. After a three-week voyage from England and within a week of landing, the very unfit CIVs had to struggle with a 30-mile, or two-day, march in the hot weather from De Aar to Britstown and were then called upon to fight the enemy without any rest. They were, of course, in no condition to do this so the mounted infantry had to march on some 15 miles further with 44th Battery in advance of them to shell the Boer positions from a line of *kopjes* (hills). My father described what happened after the first ranging shots were fired at the enemy:

> Suddenly, in a small saddle or nek as the Dutch called it came a small gun with four horses pulling it came out and came into action. It fired a round and to our immense surprise it was firing smoky powder. The whole Battery burst into roars of laughter. The Major ordered my Section to fire a couple of rounds of shrapnel which landed on the [gun] team and knocked it out.[10]

He then went on to explain how the exhausted CIVs arrived in the early afternoon, 'but when they reached their jumping off point, they lay there incapable of going forward another yard'. With his troops in no fit condition to make an attack, Adye found himself at the mercy of the Boers and was compelled to retreat. 44th Battery was assigned to cover the withdrawal back to Britstown, with the Boers soon remounting and moving in pursuit. My father recorded how the Gunners 'gave them some twenty rounds of shrapnel a mile away, which drove them back helter-skelter'. No doubt, subalterns through the centuries have always known better than their commanders, but on this occasion the analysis of the raw 2nd Lieutenant Ironside, thinking back over his first time in action, has a ring of truth and sense to it:

> Even to my untutored eye the whole manoeuvre had been a miserably amateurish show. Our casualties except amongst the MI amounted to nothing. We had never looked like doing anything. The Reconnaissance in Force was busted.[11]

In view of Adye's failure to dislodge the Boers from Houwater, Kitchener came back a few days later with a larger force of Regular troops, determined to chase the Boers completely out of Cape Colony. This he achieved, with the Boer commandos driven back across the Orange River and the Cape rebellion nipped in the bud by the application of overwhelming military force.[12]

His mission accomplished, Kitchener left the area on 21 March. Thereafter, 44th Battery were left at the little *dorp* (village) of Prieska on peacekeeping duties, along with a Yeomanry company and part of the locally raised Nesbitt's Horse, working up as far as Upington where the Orange River turns towards the sea. With nothing much to do, my father was given the task of going out on reconnaissance with the natives who came into the camp with snippets of news and to monitor what was happening in the area. As he had improved his grasp of Afrikaans so that he could speak the *taal* with some fluency, he reasoned that he could make better use of his time by going out with one of the battery's cape boy wagon drivers to gain specific intelligence about Boer movements, but his proposal was turned down by Major Drake.

Nevertheless, even if he felt thwarted in his military ambitions, it is clear that he had fallen in love with Africa:

> From the moment we left Maitland Camp I began to revel in South Africa. I liked the air and the bright sun. The broad open *veldt*. For years we slept in the open under a wagon or Cape Cart with a waterproof sheet against the wheel to keep the cold out. […] I turned to smoking Boer baccy, which one carried in a little bag which shut with a string. It was dry stuff and only fit for a dry country. One had to have a longish deep-bowled pipe to take the baccy. […] I mixed with the Boers in the Colony because I could speak their language. I blessed the day that had made me do this, which gave me power over them. I realised how one gained in strength if one could speak to a man in his own language.[13]

This last realisation was an important one, something that would stand him in good stead in years to come, but which for the moment set him to redouble his efforts to master foreign tongues. The interest in and taste for intelligence work, first awakened by his dealings with the local Basuto scouts but for the time being supressed by Major Drake, would also become a key element of his future career, but not quite yet: for the moment, there remained a war to be won.

Duty at Prieska was a waiting game for 44th Battery. The *dorp* at the railway halt was made up of a dozen or so houses grouped round the Dutch Reformed Church with two local stores, and Major Drake had set up an officers' mess in one of the houses used by all detachments. The battery camp was about a mile away and that was where the subalterns slept, out in the open. Prieska was also known as a river crossing place, which had its own 'pont' – a flat-bottomed pontoon – for carrying ox wagons and beasts across the Orange River. A large pulley wheel on a line attached to the pont ran along a wire rope strung across the water between concrete posts, so that it could shuttle back and forth on demand. In the dry summer season, the water level was usually low enough for animals to walk across, but the pont became indispensable in the winter months when the rains from the Transvaal and the Orange Free State could make the level rise 40ft.

The six-week camping break at Prieska gave 44th Battery time to adapt its stable routines to fit in with the South African climate, as the peacetime practices put in place by Major Drake needed considerable revision to match up with the demands of trekking and fighting on the *veldt*. In May, after idling away their time for more than a month in camp at Prieska, news was received that some 300 Boers had come out of Griqualand and had taken up post on the far side of the river, some 80 miles away at Kleis Drift. This time they had no guns with them, but they were commandeering stock and fodder in their usual manner and pressganging supporters as they moved along. Colonel Adye still had charge of the mounted infantry column, including 44th Battery, and immediately decided to move north to Tesobe Drift, 10 miles from the Boer position.

The river was low and a man on horseback could easily cross the 200-yard stretch of water. The colonel's plan was to position his artillery to cover the river between the two drifts, making a feint attack at Kleis Drift and his main attack with the mounted infantry crossing the river at Tesobe Drift and moving along under the ridge on the far bank to attack the Boer *laager* (encampment). Adye had clearly learned from his earlier failure at Houwater, for the operation was highly successful and practically everybody in the commando was captured. British casualties were six killed and twenty wounded. All the stolen livestock, including some good riding horses, were recovered together with all the wagons and 278 prisoners. Nesbitt's Horse were left to sweep up what was left and hand over to the police.

The army's traditionally held suspicion of putting artillery officers in command of mixed forces may have been allayed on this occasion by Adye's dispositions, as all the detachments were mounted and the operation depended on the effective positioning of the guns above Kleis Drift. For my father, this operation again saw his obvious tendency to think for himself bring him into conflict with the authority of Major Drake. The battery's subalterns had found that on an early morning watering parade their lines of horses would only sniff at the surface and curl up their lips at the thought of drinking any water at that hour of the day in South Africa, because it was too cold for their palates. When my father pointed this out to Major Drake, the battery commander insisted that he would not give in to the opinion of any subaltern and he was told, perhaps as a lesson, to take the watering order at dawn after their arrival at Tesobe Drift. So, my father having filed his horses away after their refusal to drink, his section came under heavy rifle fire from the other side of the river causing the horses to bolt. Luckily, the low-lying mist on the surface of the water just about concealed him, so he avoided being shot and managed to escape into the bush after lifting two wounded men onto his own horse and helping them to get away.

Although 44th Battery remained in the theatre for the remainder of the war, this action was the last occasion in which my father and his comrades were actively engaged. They had taken no part in the war's major battles and sieges, but they had taken an active part in several important minor operations and experienced both defeat and victory. My father certainly recognised the value, so far as his own career was concerned, of having been blooded in this way and his reflections on his war service reveal how determined he became to pursue his career in the army and how much he enjoyed himself on active service in South Africa:

> War had become a habit to me and I liked it. I had few expenses and could not only live within my income but I could save a little. I had no money with which to enjoy myself at home with hunting and shooting. I didn't want the war to stop. My brief experience of soldiering at home had not made me like it very much and I didn't want to return to that. I liked Africa and the free and easy life out there and I intended to stay there if I could. There could doubtless be other wars and that was what I wanted.[14]

2

Undercover Subaltern

As even the most resolute of the Boer leaders came to accept that they no longer had any hope of obtaining any sort of favourable settlement by further resistance, a favourable response was at last received to the peace feelers that Britain had for some time been putting out. Accordingly, talks were arranged at Vereeniging, and safe conduct was promised to those Boer delegates who attended to represent the two former republics, both now annexed as Crown colonies. One such delegate who received a free pass was Jan Smuts who, like my father, would one day obtain the baton of a British field marshal. The despatch of Captain James Jardine to find Smuts and bring him in caused my father to again reflect on the lack of use that the army had thus far made of his own linguistic skills and local knowledge:

> Jardine in the 5th Lancers was chosen to go out with a White Flag and see if he could get in touch with Smuts and give him Kitchener's message. I never thought about it at the time, but here was I who spoke Cape Dutch fluently and I was never once employed where my Dutch could have been of any use. I had a mild sort of desire to be in Intelligence, but I was so proud of my Section of Artillery, an independent command, that I never bothered much about it. Intelligence in war is a curious business. It is very much a laborious piecing together of scraps of news that have filtered in from various sources. But, a knowledge of the people with whom one is dealing gives one a much better chance of drawing conclusions. Our Intelligence never seems to draw these conclusions. I believe that I could have become a very capable Intelligence Staff Officer but I never got the chance. Fate ruled otherwise. Luckily for me. Anyway, I would have given a lot to have gone out with Jardine.[1]

The assembly at Vereeniging, which would in due course culminate in the signing of the peace treaty on 31 May 1902, was only just the beginning of a long trek to union in South Africa, but it did at least bring peace to the British colonies and the Boer Republics. My father's wartime service qualified for the award of the Queen's South Africa Medal with 'Cape Colony', 'Transvaal' and 'Orange Free State' clasps, as well as the King's South Africa Medal: the latter decoration, as well as recognising the accession of King Edward VII, was intended to help iron out the differences between the trekkers on the *veldt* and the heroes of Kimberley, Mafeking, Ladysmith and the famous early battles of the war. To qualify for a campaign medal, one simply had to be present during the operations in question: however, my father also received a formal Mention in Despatches as someone who had 'rendered special and meritorious service', a clear mark that he had already been identified by his superiors as someone to watch.[2]

My father was now obliged to consider what he might do next, for he had some years still to serve as a subaltern before he could expect further promotion, and in the back of his mind other opportunities still vied with his military ambitions. As a personality, he had moved on from being a spirited schoolboy and stroppy cadet to being a pushy subaltern, and I think it becomes clear that his superiors had a bit of a problem containing his energies without damping his enthusiasm for a long-term career in the army.

Guidance at length came via a long talk about his future with his one-time column commander, Colonel Charles Callwell, a fellow artilleryman, who advised him to stay on and serve in South Africa until he was promoted and could qualify for the Staff College as, in his opinion, he was destined for the top.

Callwell was not the only one who had appreciated my father's talents: another who did so, at this time and later, was the author and academic John Buchan, private secretary to the high commissioner, who was heading up negotiations with Smuts. The two men struck up a friendship, but the full extent of Buchan's interest in my father's activities did not become apparent until *The Thirty-Nine Steps* was published in 1915.

Buchan had employed him as an interpreter at the time of the Vereeniging Conference to listen in to the Boer deliberations. As my father later explained, unbeknown to the Boers, early versions of Marconi recording equipment had been installed in the tents. Effectively, the proceedings had been bugged, and Buchan needed someone by his side who was more than just an interpreter, when he was in discussion with Smuts and his associates. Specifically, he needed someone who not only knew the language but someone with an intimate understanding of the way the Boers lived and thought, who was able to judge their reactions to proposals made across the negotiating table. My father fitted the bill perfectly and his insights aided Buchan's negotiations by enabling the latter to foster an atmosphere of trust between the negotiating parties, with the odds running in favour of the High Commission.

The peace conference over, and with Callwell's advice in mind, my father got himself fitted out with a new uniform in Cape Town and met up again with Major Hugh Jeudwine, who he had met when Jeudwine was serving as assistant quartermaster general for Cape Colony, and asked for his help in finding a job to help fill in the years of waiting before he might hope to get a more interesting appointment. Help was not long in coming and he was called in to see Major General Sir Henry Settle in Cape Town. It was clear that the general was quite aware that my father spoke the *taal* like a native and used to lead his section so effectively while trekking in the *veldt*.

Settle then outlined the job he had in mind for him and asked him whether he was prepared to tour the isolated districts either side of the Orange River to search out the *Bittereinders*, the embittered Boers unprepared to accept the Vereeniging settlement, who were refusing to take an oath of allegiance to the Crown. By passing word around that they could return to their farms with a free pardon, the authorities thought that they could buy off further trouble. My father's role would be to make a tour around the countryside, passing himself off as a Boer, to discreetly and officially advise any of the 600 or so *Bittereinders* to mend their ways without suffering any penalty.

The remaining Boer holdouts were mostly destitute and hungry and wanted to go home, but were afraid of going to the police to seek asylum: instead, they were pestering all the farmers for food and facilities. My father recognised that trying to bring any of these desperate men in would be a tough and daring assignment, but after twenty-four hours to think it over and plan his way of working, he accepted the job. He already had the knowledge and experience of trekking in the Cape Colony border country where the bandit Boers were roaming, but he did not realise that his new work would lead him into the unmapped and lawless territory along little-trodden tracks on the borders of the Bechuanaland Protectorate and German South West Africa, having to continually judge the situation for himself and act on his own initiative. No time limits had been set, but he recognised that if the situation changed, he could always break off and return to civilisation whenever he wanted.

He arranged to pose as a travelling trader with two natives in a cape cart – a two-wheel carriage – with four mules and two riding horses, all to be supplied and maintained at public expense. His army pay was remitted to an account in Cox's Bank in London and 45*s* a day was paid into the Nederlandsche Bank in Cape Town by a Dutch paymaster with no British connections. At his own expense, he stocked himself up with goods for sale and stood to gain or lose by his trading them.

It took him a fortnight to prepare for his trek and he arranged to send his reports back to headquarters via a retired doctor from the Indian Medical Service who had settled in Africa and ran a practice in Upington in the Northern Cape. As the doctor was sending documents weekly to Cape Town, he included any of my father's reports with his own correspondence. The cape cart, together with the native drivers and animals, was delivered to a young farmer at Ceres, about 70 miles north of Cape Town, and picked up from there. For his Boer disguise my father went to a store on the outskirts of Cape Town and bought a longish coat with large pockets, bell-bottomed corduroy trousers, a wide-brimmed felt hat with crepe band stuck with ostrich feathers, Veldtschoen (specially stitched boots), two flannel suits, two cotton shirts, a couple of *karosses* – native sheepskin cloaks – for himself and his bulldog Bill, and two navy blue seamen's jerseys. No socks were needed and little underwear, as water for washing was scarce in the *veldt*.

For protection, he armed himself with a combined Mannlicher rifle cum 16-bore ejector shotgun and ammunition. On the advice of a local Jewish pedlar he stocked up with a mixed collection of cloth, beads, knives, tinderboxes, tobacco, buttons, cotton, needles and miscellaneous trinkets for trading. He arranged to sleep on a mattress on the floor of the wagon with two long lockable boxes each side for stowing his goods, and he bought four canvas bottles for keeping drinking water cool as they hung in the open air at the side of the wagon.

His identification papers, written on old paper in faded ink, belonged to a deceased Transvaaler who had been born on a farm in the northern Transvaal. My father's new alter ego had been educated for three or four years in Holland and had spoken Dutch and the *taal* with equal ease. Finally, to cover his tracks, he went to a small, out of the way Cape Town hotel to make an orderly changeover from Briton to Boer by undressing to shut out the old in one room and dressing up to bring in the new in the room next door. Ready for action, Lieutenant W.E. Ironside, RFA – alias Piet van der Westhuizen – set off, along with Bill the bulldog, who had escaped all the dressing-up process.

It has not proved possible to put a precise date on the change from battery officer to Boer, and as the assignment was supposed to be an undercover operation it is not surprising that there is no record of my father's departure in 44th Battery's paperwork. However, the inferences are that he must have set off during September 1902 after he had taken all the necessary precautions to hide his real identity, even going so far as to remove a family signet ring from his little finger.

With all the talk focusing on resettlement and settling down to peacetime pursuits, no one seemed to notice his being called away, officially on a mapping project. In fact, between September 1902 and his posting to 'I' Battery RHA on 13 June 1904, deliberate steps were taken by the authorities in Cape Town to conceal his movements. Only those with a need to know could make contact with him and, even then, they could only find him through his accommodation address in Upington. So, for a period of twenty-one months, the inner secrets of his undercover life have remained a public mystery.

When the day came to set off, my father took a train to Ceres Road to meet up with his farmer friend, who had the wagon ready with four bay mules and the cape boys with the two *schimmel* (roan or dapple grey) horses, both of which rode well and seemed to be well trained in spite of their uncared-for appearance. The cape boys did not impress him, speaking poor Afrikaans and looking sullen and dirty; furthermore, they were only willing to travel part of the way north.

Equipped with all the means for survival, he stayed for a few days at Ceres to get used to his new way of life and to make sure that he had all the right gear with him and that everything worked properly. Having already got used to trekking in the *veldt*, speaking and thinking in the *taal*, he felt that acting the Boer would come naturally, but above all he had to talk and behave like one and avoid making any giveaway gestures. The only uncertainty in his mind was guarding against a lapse into English if he became ill or was suddenly caught unawares. There was, of course, a risk of being recognised, but this seemed to be worth taking in such remote outlying areas where the population density was less than one person per square mile.

The *Bittereinders* were reported to be lurking around the most northerly Gordonia District of Cape Colony and menacing the farmers in the areas bordering on Bechuanaland and German South West Africa. As he knew this part of the *veldt* intimately from his wartime activities, my father decided to aim for Upington to touch base with his feeder, the retired doctor practising there at what became his accommodation address for the foreseeable future. So, working his way north through Clanwilliam, Van Rijnsdorp and Springbok to the remote settlement at Pella on the Orange River frontier with German South West Africa, he checked in first with the priests at the Roman Catholic mission there, who could be relied upon to reveal all the latest asylum trading news.

The daytime trekking routine started at 06.00, with pitstops every hour, covering 30 miles or more by nightfall, depending on conditions. The night-time routine was different, starting at 17.00 and outspanning after two hours to feed and water the animals. This was followed by pitstops every hour until daylight, before setting up camp in any shady place that could be found, until it was time to set off again. When camping, the rule was to string up cans of pebbles around the camp to sound off the alarm in case of intruders, which often included lions and even leopards. Bill was with him and he was always the first to raise the alarm.

During the trek to Upington, food and water were readily available in the *winkels*, but he had to change his cape boys twice, first at Clanwilliam and then at Pella. As cape boys chose their masters, they easily found substitutes each time, which spoke well of my father's handling of them, notwithstanding his reservations about the original duo. Each pair was better than the last and he finally ended up with two Basuto brothers, Seiso and Motho, who spoke excellent Afrikaans and, in return, taught him to speak Sesotho. They had worked for a German copper company and had been sacked after falling out with the overseer. They had managed to escape across the Orange River with nothing but their lives and, after my father fitted them out with clothes like his own, they stayed on with him for the rest of his assignment.

At Pella, he was welcomed in French by the priests of the mission station there. My father responded in Flemish and broken French, passing himself off as a Belgian, and was then treated to a hearty breakfast. The priests, who were suffering from the *cafard*, or desert blues, were eager for news from their home country and introduced him to the bishop, who had been installed in 1898. It soon became clear why the *Bittereinders* were behaving as they were: most of them were well-rooted Transvaalers or Freestaters, and their resentment of British rule stemmed largely from their own history book, *The History of our Land in the Language of our People*, which portrayed them as peaceful, law-abiding and well-behaved inhabitants of the *veldt*, and attached all the blame on the British for the way in which they had been persecuted. Their refusal to accept constitutional change, which would blend the Boer beliefs with British rule, had turned them into a mix and match of travellers seeking the right to live according to their own rulebook and settlers seeking asylum from oppressions of their own making.

Gaining a greater understanding of the *Bittereinders* was certainly useful, but fell far short of meeting them face to face and spelling out the error of their ways. Fortunately, the bishop revealed that he knew places where they were hiding out either side of the Orange River and agreed to co-operate by passing on the message of a free pardon, whenever they sought sanctuary at the mission.

As he drove on towards the river, my father had his own first encounter with his quarry. This particular *Bittereinder* had lost all his possessions when his wagon had broken down during his search for new farming land in German South West Africa and he was making his way back on horseback to the mission at Pella to seek sanctuary. He was wet, exhausted and at the end of his tether. After venting his feelings about British rule and having a good meal and rest in camp for the night, he calmed down and gave my father the names of several others sheltering in German territory, who were ready to give themselves up as well. Further on, at Skerrit Drift, he encountered two more, with only their Khoikhoi boys – my father in his diary called them Hottentots – and stock of goats left, who agreed to give themselves up to the police in Upington. At the Aughrabies Falls, where the river waters fall spectacularly down into a narrow gorge, he was able to persuade others to turn themselves in and spread the word around. By the time he had reached the Dutch Reformed Church Mission in Kakamus he had persuaded more to surrender and it appeared that his propaganda campaign was working well.

When he reached Upington, being a newcomer, the eyes of all the other traders were upon him in case he turned out to be a potential threat to their own livelihoods. The local Cape Police Force had few resources and very little control over what happened in this part of the colony, so my father relied on Seiso and Motho with their *assegais* (spears) to protect him and had them keeping watch all the time to defend his interests. In fact, this became necessary after he was approached in camp by two English-born strangers and warned to leave town. When they returned at night to attack him for ignoring their warnings, he subdued them with the help of Seiso and Motho and handed them over to the Cape Police.

He easily found his feeder, the doctor, and queued as a visiting outpatient to be able to deal with the postbag from Cape Town within the privacy of his contact's consulting room. It soon became clear that, having won over nearly 500 of the

Boer misfits in face-to-face encounters and leaking the word of pardon, he had been altogether too successful for his own purposes, for if he brought his mission to a speedy conclusion then he would be obliged to give up his lucrative pastime as a trader and return to the monotony of a subaltern's life in Cape Town. So, when reports came in to show that the remaining diehards were likely to respond to the German Army bids for wagons and trek oxen to service their emergency transport needs, he decided to seek permission from the staff in Cape Town to offer his own services to the German Army, as a way of finding out how they deployed and supported their troops and conducted their military operations.

In the meantime, while he awaited a response to his proposal, he planned to trek further north to Rietfontein, located in far northern Cape Colony on the 20° meridian, in a finger of territory squeezed between Bechuanaland and the German South West African border. His purpose was to assess the rising tensions on the border and monitor the Boer wagon movements at the frontier post. To cope with the waterless desert conditions, he returned to Kakamas to exchange his mules for a span of oxen and, having replenished his range of goods for sale, set off on the first 40-mile leg of his trek north to the bed of the Molopo River, taking careful note of frontier movements and water reserves on the way.

Trekking was mostly by night through the moving sand dunes, and constant watch was needed when camping within the magic circle strung with alarm cans. Groups of bushmen were encountered and sometimes police patrols mounted on their camels. Armed groups of Bondelszwarts tribesmen were seen criss-crossing the border at will, unchecked by the corporal and two patrolmen that he met on the German side. Neither of them could speak *Khoikhoi* or the *taal* and he had to converse with them in Low German. In any case, all natives on the German side of the border were expected to speak German.

My father spent three days at Rietfontein, meeting and talking to many different people who managed to exist in this remote settlement. He met more Boer outlaws, most of whom were ready to jump at any opportunity for resettlement and took his advice to return to their farms. Intelligence reports showed that they had had their eyes on farms in German South West Africa, and some of them had been given land in return for stealing and handing over wagons and trek oxen to the German Army. More ominously, events pointed to an impending rising by the native population in the German colony, provoked by a combination of racial tensions, enforced resettlement of the Herero people and unforeseen consequences to the Credit Ordinance of 1 November 1903, which had been intended to write off long-term debts owed by Africans, but which instead led to white creditors attempting to obtain payment in kind by force. At Rietfontein, the well-armed and mounted Bondelszwarts were boasting that they could easily overcome the company of German troops stationed at Warmbad, adding to my father's expectations that matters would soon come to a head.

In this he was not mistaken, and by early 1904 the German colonial authorities were facing a substantial revolt. Once it was clear that the native insurrection had started, my father made his way back to Upington again to restock his wagon, where he found a letter giving him permission to cross the German frontier and offer his services to the German Army as a wagon driver. The letter was addressed to his Dutch name, care of the doctor, and ended with a handwritten postscript saying, 'Have a care'.

He was thrilled at having this news, but electing to enter a foreign country while in the service of your own and masquerading in all respects as a citizen of a third took him from military intelligence to out-and-out espionage and I wonder if he really knew what he was trekking into when he crossed the border at Rietfontein. With his existing experience under his belt, it is not surprising that at the age of 22 he felt that this way of life had more to offer than life on the barrack square.

Luckily, the German attempts to contract out their transport services across the border were seen by the Boers as an open invitation to seek asylum, and he judged that in the German Army's desperate haste to sign up wagon teams, they would not vet the bidders too thoroughly. Also, he had decided to offer a fully-manned wagon package at immediate readiness and knew that they would have difficulty in turning down his offer. Nevertheless, negotiations with the recruiting officer and his Boer assistant still took two days to complete.

Finally, after some hard bargaining my father obtained a signed and stamped authority, which secured the services of his four wagons and spans of trek oxen with his assistant and drivers for six months in a buyback deal, whatever the outcome, at the daily rate of £3 per wagon – £2 for himself, £1 for his assistant – all found at German ration levels for men and animals.

Germany had been a late entrant to the business of African empire building, and the colony of German South West Africa was only two decades old when my father took service with its military establishment. The German hold was hardly secure, with limited infrastructure and a small garrison of colonial *Schutztruppen* to protect the settlers and establish German control over the indigenous Herero and Nama peoples. Already, back in the early 1890s, there had been a major rising, and in late 1903 the Nama rose again against the colonists. The catalyst was a preventative measure by which the tribesmen were required to register their firearms; this was interpreted as a way of starting to disarm them and fighting broke out on 26 October 1903, in which some German soldiers were killed.

By early 1904, the Herero had joined the revolt, over 100 settlers had been killed and the *Schutztruppen* – less than 1,000 strong, including native auxiliaries – were hard pressed. With so weak a force at his disposal, it is hardly surprising that the German commander, *Major* Theodor Leutwein, had to hire Boer wagon men to give his army the mobility that it required to operate in 300,000 square miles of roadless and desert-like territory. Bereft of a staff or much in the way of administrative services, the German commander's only advantage was the lack of co-operation between the Nama under Hendrik Witbooi in the south and the Herrero under Samuel Maherero in the north.

A relief force of 14,000 men under *Generalleutnant* Lothar von Trotha was on its way from Germany, and once the reinforcements were in the field a battlefield victory over the Herero was won at Waterberg on 11 August. Thereafter, a policy of extermination was pursued, but even the resultant genocide did not immediately restore German control, which was not fully established until 1908 after the loss of over 100,000 African lives.

Having crossed the border, my father was instructed to trek 100 miles westward to Keetmanshoop, which was the headquarters for the troops being deployed against an armed and mounted group of 500 Bondelswartz tribesmen. On arrival, he presented himself with his string of wagons to the *leutnant* in charge of transport, who was struggling to assemble wagon teams without any real understanding of what was required. At the briefing for Boer operators in the local bar, the *leutnant* nervously opened discussions with my father by admiring the studded collar on his bulldog Bill and the dreaded moment came when he caught sight of the nametag still bearing the name 'Lt Ironside, RFA'. With a bit of quick thinking, my father said that he had stolen it from a British officer's dog during the war and luckily the *leutnant* did not pursue the point, but went on to tell him that he had added another four wagons to his string. This gave him time to turn the collar round to hide the tag and after the briefing he took the first opportunity to remove it and bury it in the ashes of his camp fire. Looking back on his carefully laid plans to mask his identity, he had of course forgotten to put Bill through the screening process in Cape Town.

Even though he tried to keep a low profile in these mixed and unsettled circumstances, my father could not avoid being called on by the inexperienced transport *leutnant* to advise Leutwein about transport requirements on the *veldt*. In particular, arrangements had to be made for the field company based at Omaru under *Hauptmann* Franke to be moved south to support the garrison at Keetmanshoop. However, after a four-day forced march of 300 miles to Gibeon, Franke was ordered back to Windhoek on 12 January 1904 to assist in quelling the spreading violence in the north now that the Herero had taken advantage of the governor's absence from their homeland to join the rebellion.

Pushed into returning to the capital, *Major* Leutwein quickly went out in a cape cart to meet the chieftain of the Bondelszwarts to stitch up a temporary deal, before taking a circuitous journey back to his headquarters in Windhoek, via Lüderitz Bay and by sea to Swakopmund, so as to take charge of operations in the north. In fact, it was only through the determined efforts of *Hauptmann* Franke to march his men from Omaru to Gibeon and back to Windhoek that turned the scales of battle in favour of the German forces. My father recalled that he saw Franke many weeks later and described him as 'a small, modest and unassuming little man'.

The astonishing fact was that he left Gibeon on 15 January with his men and horses and completed the 300-mile trek to Windhoek in four days, the last two in a tropical downpour. After pausing for a day's rest on 20 January, he entered the capital and the Herreros dispersed. Furthermore, after picking up more men and a field gun, he set off again and recaptured Okahandja on 27 January and Omaru on 3 February. While the governor was away, the north had been left without a military staff officer in charge over the crucial period of the uprising and, in my father's view, Franke had shown himself to be a fine and courageous leader of men, who was directly responsible for the Herrero defeat.

Amongst the first batch of reinforcements to arrive by troopship from Hamburg was a *Major* Ludwig Gustav Adolph von Estorff of the German General Staff and, after some weeks of trekking in hot weather, my father was assigned to work under him. The *major* had been put in charge of a column operating with the main force in the west of Herreroland, alongside *Major* Glasenapp, who took charge of a column in the east to prevent the Herreros retreating across the frontier into the Bechuanaland Protectorate.

Working for a German staff officer in such circumstances was a unique and at times unnerving experience for a British officer, aged 23, masquerading as a Boer, and it would not have been possible for my father to have acted the part of Piet van der Westhuizen unless he had absolute confidence in his ability to think and speak in Dutch and Afrikaans and hold his tongue in front of German officers in their own language. He could easily conceal any nuances of speech amongst the people he met, as Dutch and Afrikaans were well mixed in with the Bantu-speaking tribes in the north and the Nama-speaking ones in the south, punctuated by the clicking of the Khoisan speakers thereabouts, although the governor and his administrators attempted to force the use of German onto the population. Just as long as he feigned an inability to speak any German, he had no difficulty in understanding what was being said or making himself understood without giving any secrets away.

Major von Estorff was 44 at the time he was appointed a column commander in the South West African *Schutztruppen* and most certainly had been chosen because he had served with them previously as a subaltern and also as a *major* on the staff in East Africa. Furthermore, by permission of Lord Kitchener he had travelled through South Africa during the Boer War to take up one of his earlier appointments in German South West Africa. After a distinguished career as an infantry officer, he retired as a *generalleutnant* in 1920 to manage his estates and write a family history. He was further honoured by being made a *general der infanterie* in 1939 and died on 5 October 1943, aged 83.

In my father's view, his experiences of serving covertly with the German Army showed up many of the shortcomings of a military administration that lacked the traditions of colonial service, even though the *Schutztruppen*, at the outbreak of the rebellion, formed an excellent military unit. Its companies were highly mobile and capable of operating for long periods away from their bases. Its officers and men knew the country well, but the arrival of reinforcements, encumbered by bureaucratic machinery, destroyed most of this mobility and took away most of their initiative. When he was asked afterwards what it felt like trekking for an undermanned and overstretched garrison force for six months virtually as a vassal of the German Reich, my father said that he was held in respect by most of the young servicemen as he was larger than they were, but it was hard to stomach being called 'a dirty bloody Dutchman' by the officers, who did not know otherwise. On one occasion, when he had been summoned to a transport meeting at the Million Mark Haus in Keetmanshoop and was waiting outside, a *Schutztruppen* commander named *Major* von Deimling galloped to a halt in front of him, throwing the reins over his horse's head in Boer fashion, as he jumped off his mount and said, 'Here, you damned Dutchman, hold this horse for me!'

But, however patronising the German Army attitudes may have been towards their Boer transport staff, my father did command a degree of recognition as *oberkonductor* in the eyes of *Major* von Estorff, his column commander, who was twice his age. The logistical problems of maintaining a mobile force in the roadless and practically rail-less deserts of South West Africa were formidable. The trails that did exist were for the most part barely marked paths through the heavy sands, into which the wheels of the wagons would sink, making it difficult for the trek oxen to haul them along.

As von Estorff became more familiar with the wagon routines he came to understand the value of my father's services and gradually put more trust and responsibility into his hands for sorting out the day-to-day problems arising mainly from the ignorant and overbearing behaviour of the junior *leutnants* towards their Boer *konductors*, which proved to be highly disruptive. So much so, that at one point my father had to get the *major* to harangue his own men in order to preserve discipline and prevent them from deserting. After that, von Estorff bypassed his own junior staff and dealt directly with my father. Nevertheless, the latter could still sense the *major*'s lasting annoyance at having to accept practices that were being forced on him by circumstances, and his reluctance to accept the Boer *konductors* and their native drivers as equals of his own men or to show any outward signs of friendliness towards them.

Indeed, at least initially, my father was even made to feel his own inferiority. At his first meeting with *Major* von Estorff he was brought into his camp tent for interview by the transport *leutnant*, who described him as *oberkonductor*. Laid back in his chair, the *major* made no attempt to move or say anything, but merely looked him up and down through half-closed eyes, while my father was left standing shiftily in front of him for a while – an unnerving experience for someone living between falsehood and fact. The *major* was a smallish, middle-aged man with fair hair growing grey at the edges. His moustache curled up at the ends and he was dressed in uniform, wearing the standard leather gaiters worn by all ranks. Then, in curt and slowly spoken German, questions were fired at my father about who he was, where he came from, what his military service was and why he had enlisted with the German Army. Answering in Dutch with German words thrown in, he told the *major* that he had been to military college and had been mobilised for commando service. Realising he could be understood, the *major* talked more rapidly, told him that the *leutnant* had spoken well of him, before dismissing him with a brief word of approbation.

My father stayed on with *Major* von Estorff's column throughout the time he spent in German South West Africa, trekking into Herreroland, where he was involved with a number of successful skirmishes in February 1904. Having secured the *major*'s trust he recalled that he constantly had to be aware of the risks in giving himself away if he showed too much enthusiasm for his work and became overconfident. Also, he had to pretend to learn German, however well he already spoke it, and take care not to use the Hanoverian accent in which he had been taught it. Only one risky incident occurred, when he found two natives tied to a wagon wheel for a beating on a trumped-up charge as a lesson to others. He threatened to report the incident to the *major* if they were not released immediately and had to face the wrath of a young cavalry *leutnant* who tried to threaten him with beating if he continued to interfere. This incited him to answer back in German and, when he realised what he had done, he quickly reverted to Afrikaans. Fortunately, the *leutnant* was so enraged that he failed to notice the sudden switch to German and although he had the natives released he was then severely reprimanded by von Estorff, who sided with my father and ordered the *leutnant* back to Germany. The *major* thanked my father for his actions and the matter was never mentioned again.

Insofar as the intelligence element of my father's activities was concerned, he sent his reports back to Cape Town concealed as letters to his wife, via different Boer operators on their way home through Walvis Bay, who then passed them to the British Consul for posting on. Amongst the recipients of his intelligence reports was John Buchan, still serving on the staff of the high commissioner. This material, pasted together with my father's earlier exploits, helped Buchan shape the character make-up he needed for his fictional hero Richard Hannay, many aspects of whose character and career are based upon my father. This, however, was all in the future, for Buchan did not start work on what would become *The Thirty-Nine Steps* until he was back in England in 1914, convalescing from treatment in hospital.

The parallels only go so far: Hannay, for example, was not a Regular Army officer, although his later military career does bear some resemblance to that of my father; nor, conversely, did my father's intelligence work take him to half the places that the fictional Hannay visited in the course of his adventures. Nevertheless, I was assured by Buchan's son, the 2nd Lord Tweedsmuir, that it was an open secret in his family that Hannay was modelled in the image of my father, but my father probably did not become aware of this until it became public knowledge amongst his friends and contemporaries after the First World War.

As the fighting in German South West Africa progressed, my father witnessed the way that *Major* von Estorff's tactics succeeded in breaking down the Herrero defences to such an extent that he was able to get the better of his opponents. Imitating the chanting of the Herrero women in support of their warrior folk fighting at Okahandja, who shrieked out, 'Who owns Herreroland? – We own Herreroland!', he was able to proclaim to his own men, 'To whom belongs this place? To whom? This place belongs to us!' After that, he was publicly praised by the Kaiser for all his efforts, no doubt in part to help hide from the public eye the series of defeats suffered by the garrison during the months of March and April 1904, before the main influx of reinforcements from Germany. Clearly, the *major*'s achievements boosted his standing in the eyes of the governor, which softened his manner noticeably towards the Boer *konductors*. He became more agreeable to my father, who had always made sure that the supply lines delivered the ammunition and victuals to him as required.

As the build-up of German forces continued after the arrival of von Trotha, my father had to face being dragged into the German colonial administration or sticking to his original plan of terminating his contract with the German Army and returning to Cape Town to pursue his career ambitions with the British Army. After a little thought, he decided that it was time to pull out of the dangerous and demanding life of a spy and make his way back to Cape Town. His resolve to do this was confirmed and justified one day when he was withdrawing money from the local bank. He overheard a German officer telling the bank cashier that there was a suspected British agent working with the German forces.

Such risks aside, he judged that his work in evaluating the German military presence in South West Africa to assess their strengths and weaknesses was complete and that it was time to leave. So, at the beginning of May, he requested an interview with *Major* von Estorff and was greeted cordially enough. He explained that all his savings were locked up in the German colony and that he had to return to his farm in the Transvaal to get married. He asked the German Army to redeem their pledge of buying back his wagons and trek oxen so that he could depart with his two cape boys and leave Gert de Wet, his capable assistant, to take his place. Finally, he finished by saying how honoured he was to serve under such a distinguished officer as the *major*, who had personally done so much to bring peace to the colony. To his surprise the *major* listened attentively to what he had said and endeavoured to make him change his mind about leaving by offering him the post of Chief of Transport to the *Schutztruppen*, working under an expert from Germany. My father steadfastly refused to change his plans and was told to wait a day for the governor to approve his contract settlement.

When he met the *major* on the following day, the accounting officer was there to present him with the cheque for the wagons, which he could cash at the Dutch bank in Cape Town. Seiso and Motho were included in the pay-out. Finally, before setting off, the *major* invited him to supper in his rooms at Okahandja, where he made a last plea to encourage him to stay, by offering him German nationality and a secure future in the German colony. For a moment, he marvelled at the idea, but turned it down at once. Then, for the first time, the *major* shook hands with him and said, '*Auf wiedersehen*' pleasantly, before dismissing him.

My father never knew what thoughts were really running through the *major's* mind, as he perceived that von Estorff had only a superficial understanding of the Boers and their affairs. Even so, he thought that he was a staff officer of high repute and far above the average for his rank, as well as being an able field commander who won the respect of his men. Von Estorff later became commander of the *Schutztruppen* in 1907, before returning to Germany in 1911.

My father departed for Swakopmund in the first part of May, armed with his discharge papers, before the arrival of General von Trotha's staff on 20 May 1904. At Swakopmund he hired an ox cart to take himself and his cape boys to the border post at Walvis Bay and they all crossed into British territory without fuss. He immediately called on the British Consul, who arranged for a launch to take them out to the cruiser HMS *Forte*, lying at anchor in the bay. A dirty looking Boer, accompanied by two Basutos with their *assegais*, received little acclamation as passengers for the voyage back to Cape Town, but Bill the bulldog instantly became a favourite with the ship's crew. Back at Cape Town, my father set off to re-join 44th Battery in Natal, before being posted, on 13 June 1904, to 'I' Battery RHA at Ambala in India. Having fought in the front line of one army and trekked behind the front line of another, his record of active service had already given him a good grounding for further advancement in due course.

On 19 March 1907, the Kaiser signed a decree authorising the issue of the South West Africa Commemorative Medal to all German military personnel serving there, and the governor was given permission to recommend foreigners for the award in either bronze for combatants or steel for non-combatants. By that time the newly promoted *Oberstleutnant* von Estorff was commanding officer of the *Schutztruppen* and was most probably able to nominate people for the award who had served under him at the time of the Herrero Uprising: as my father told me that he had received the award at that time, it is evident that the services of Piet van der Westhuizen had been officially recognised by the German authorities and that only von Estorff could have nominated him.

An issue of these medals to members of the Cape Mounted Police was made en bloc, and the medals given to the Governor of Cape Colony for distribution.[3] This would seem to imply that any earlier awards made to foreigners must have been distributed in the same way, so it is feasible that von Estorff nominated my father for the Bronze Medal in mid-1907, which was then issued to him via the Cape Governor's Office. This would have meant that he received it while serving as a staff officer at Roberts Heights in South Africa sometime after he was posted there in August 1907, following his return from India. Certainly, whenever it was that the medal reached him, it must have given him great satisfaction that he had deceived the Germans for so long. There is no evidence in von Estorff's memoirs that he had any suspicions about the real identity of his *oberkonductor*, though he must have been very pleased to have had such a resourceful person working for him.[4]

3

The Making of a Staff Officer

My father's service in India with 'I' Battery lasted from August 1904 until February 1906, when the unit was ordered back to England. He found service there monotonous and was thankful to leave the subcontinent. His only regret was that he had missed out on serving with a mountain battery; ironically, these units, as earlier noted, were administratively part of the Royal Garrison Artillery, the thought of service with which had filled him with thoughts of resignation.

Upon 'I' Battery's return from India, it was stationed first at Ipswich and then at Manchester, but little is known about what he did or how he amused himself during the year he spent as a subaltern on home service. He was a stranger to both places and when he had leave he used it to visit his mother, who lived in Rochester at a house in the cathedral precincts called 'The Vines'. Otherwise, when able to escape from military duties, I believe that he usually travelled to the Continent to practise his languages. He was even able to join the temporary workforce of *Fabrique Nationale* in Belgium to earn a little pocket money and gain some military intelligence about their activities.

With four years of fighting and undercover service behind him, backed by fluency in five or more languages and dialects, it is not hard to imagine that the boredom of barrack life did not match up to the expectation of an accomplished RHA lieutenant in his mid-twenties looking for excitement. Increasingly, therefore, his eyes were drawn to South Africa and the possibility of renewed service in a theatre that he knew, and where his abilities were widely recognised. Besides that, he was strongly aware that being a master linguist was not seen in the eyes of his superiors in England as being such a shining example of military achievement as that which was reflected off the polished boots and brass work at Ipswich and Manchester.

With the new Liberal Government planning defence cuts following their landslide victory in the 1906 general election, my father felt that any officer who elected to remain in the UK was starved of opportunity to advance his career. He must have sensed that the odds were stacked against him unless he went overseas. In particular, the opportunities were lacking for the sort of staff service that would enhance his career prospects and help him secure a place at the Staff College.

That being so, the logical conclusion all round was that South Africa was the best place for him. Luckily, he was able to arrange an exchange with Lieutenant C.T. Lawrence, effective on 27 August 1907, and secured an assisted passage to Cape Town to take up a posting with 'Y' Battery, which brightened up his outlook on life and gave him the military opportunity he wanted.

By the time my father returned to South Africa, the results of the Vereeniging peace settlement were beginning to be felt. The former Boer Republics had successfully transitioned into Crown colonies, and had been granted internal self-government as part of the Liberal policy of peace and retrenchment. Talks were already under way for the formation of what would become the Union of South Africa, although that entity would not come into being until 1910. There was little opportunity for either active service or a return to intelligence work, but my father was at least serving again at a station in which he felt at home, and where his talents were appreciated. By contrast, most senior officers disliked being posted to South Africa in its unsettled political state and not all the subalterns were thrilled by the prospect either, but my father was exceptional.

There is little record of how my father spent his time with 'Y' Battery, at Roberts Heights, Pretoria, where he came under the command of the Hon. Francis Bingham, third son of the 4th Earl of Lucan, who later rose to be a major general and Deputy Director of Artillery at the War Office during the First World War. This posting lasted until my father's promotion to captain came through on 18 February 1908, after which he was appointed to command 90th Battery at Standerton in the Transvaal.

Although this appointment gave him his first unit command, it was short-lived as, on 24 September, he was posted as staff captain to the Cavalry Brigade at Potchefstroom, 100 miles south-west of Johannesburg.[1] It was here that he met and became friendly with 2nd Lieutenant Arthur H.L. Soames of the 3rd Hussars, who in due course would be the best man at his wedding. This appointment was again of less than a year's duration, for on 2 June 1909 he was posted back to Roberts Heights to serve as brigade major on the staff of the Transvaal District, headquartered at Pretoria. The district was commanded by Brigadier General Sir Robert Colleton CB, and it was Colleton who, in due course, recommended my father for the Staff College at Camberley when he left Roberts Heights after three years in the post.

During the four years of his peacetime service in South Africa, he was probably as much in demand for his extra-professional skills as his military ones. As the years went by these two sides of his character began to merge, instead of growing apart as they had been doing prior to 1902. His appointments as staff captain and brigade major helped turned him from being a gifted and rather unsettled personality into someone well on the way to becoming an accomplished and highly respected staff officer.

As well as the coveted recommendation for the Staff College, my father won two other honours during his time in South Africa. The first of these was fourth prize in the 1909 South African Amateur Golf Championship. The second was the heart of Miss Mariot Ysobel Cheyne.

Following her eighteenth birthday in 1908, using a £50 grant from her late father's army pension rights, my mother had travelled with her cousin, Eileen O'Brien, to stay with the latter's father, Colonel Edmund D.J. O'Brien, who was commanding at Potchefstroom. For her, it must have been a trip of a lifetime, especially as she met my father, who had acquired an almost Bond-like image for his daring deeds as a spy. Her father, Charles Cheyne, had died of tuberculosis at Denver, Colorado when she was 6 years old. As my paternal grandfather had succumbed to pneumonia when my father was just a year old, they shared a common sadness of growing up without getting to know their fathers. My maternal grandmother, Eva Alice Cheyne, married Dr Lawrence Duckworth on 16 September 1902, who became professor of anatomy and anthropology at Cambridge University and later, master of Jesus College. So, my mother had plenty of opportunity to meet people of her own age amongst the Cambridge undergraduates, but my father was the one who caught her eye.

It is clear from the O'Brien family papers that the colonel was instrumental in trying to improve relationships with the Boer community, and he was later officially commended for his expert handling of the uprisings which broke out in Johannesburg as a result of the union settlement. As my father was serving nearby, he could readily accept invitations to attend parties at the O'Brien residence to meet some of the prominent Boers, using these contacts to help to build up better relationships with them through his knowledge and experience of their language and way of life. One letter to Eileen O'Brien from Louis Botha, turning down an invitation to play tennis, illustrates that he was a welcome local guest at her father's tennis parties. It was surely at one of these affairs that father first met my mother and where they formed an attachment for each other, although they did not actually become engaged until 1912, just before he returned to England to join the 1913 Staff College course.

From his appointment to the staff of the Cavalry Brigade at Potchefstroom in September 1908 until he was given a brigade command of his own on the Western Front nearly a decade later, my father's military career was entirely focused on staff work, either serving as a staff officer or else as a student at the Staff College. It is, therefore, worth breaking off for a moment from the main narrative to look at the structure of the British Army's staff in the early twentieth century, and explore its ways and means of working and the functions and responsibilities of the various types of staff officer.

The army's staff organisation became more complex the higher up the chain of command and the more important the formation concerned. Staffs at all levels also expanded greatly once Britain entered the First World War, with a plethora of new posts being created to fill specialist roles in the new divisions, corps and armies being fielded to meet the demands of the Western Front. As a result of this expansion, officers with pre-war staff experience could be assured of rapid promotion, and my father was fortunate to benefit in this way in due course.

At the brigade level, which is where my father gained his initial staff experience in South Africa, the brigade commander – in peacetime at least – had only two officers to assist him. These were the brigade major and the staff captain, although, as we have already seen with respect to my father having held both appointments while having the substantive regimental rank of captain, these posts were job titles rather than ranks. Nevertheless, as the name implied, the brigade major was the senior of the two posts, and in wartime this individual had responsibility for all operational staff work.

The staff captain, by contrast, also doubled as an aide-de-camp (ADC) to the brigade commander – tending, for this reason, to be the latter's personal choice – and in wartime had responsibility for administrative and logistical staff work. Similar staff functions existed within the artillery chain of command, but it is a telling sign of my father being groomed for the top that he was assigned to posts, while in South Africa, that enabled him to gain additional experience of cavalry and infantry service. This grounding, along with his subsequent Staff College training, helped ensure that he was fit to serve on the staff of, and later command, large formations of multiple arms.

Until the nineteenth century, staff work had been a largely ad hoc affair, with officers receiving no specialist training. Failings in the Crimea led to a recognition of the value of effective staff work, as did observation of the Prussian Army, and in 1870 the Staff College, which had started life as the senior department of the Royal Military College, became an independent institution and began a process of expansion. Even then, however, there was a strong anti-intellectual streak in the late-Victorian army, and the value of attending the course, which entitled the successful student to the initials 'psc' next to his name in the Army List, was not always appreciated. Nor was the situation helped by officers gaining a place by means of 'crammers' such as that which my father earlier attended to help improve his chances of getting into Woolwich. Such officers may have been able to bluff their way through the entry exams, but rarely did well thereafter.

By 1913, of course, my father had long since dispensed with the need for cramming, and was assured a place thanks to his recommendation from South Africa and his considerable linguistic skills which had by now gained him 1st Class Interpreterships in six languages and, surprisingly, only a 2nd Class Interpretership in French, despite having mastered it during his schooldays.[2]

After the Second Boer War had exposed the deficiencies of the British Army's ability to organise itself for a major war, the Staff College again achieved a greater level of respect, with a grudging realisation that an officer with psc after his name had not been wasting his time away from his regimental duties. Following the eventual victory in South Africa, plans were set afoot to raise the profile of the college and increase the number of students, although it was necessary to resist moves that would have turned it into an institution devoted purely to developing military skills to the detriment of other attributes – notably foreign languages – that would help produce a more rounded graduate.

More pertinent, insofar as the prospects of the college's graduates were concerned, the Elgin Commission's report into the Boer War led to the decision to create for the first time a General Staff for the British Army, and with it the post of Chief of the General Staff – from 1909 renamed Chief of the Imperial General Staff (CIGS). The staff system that was created never had the power, or influence, of Germany's Greater General Staff as honed by Moltke and von Schlieffen, and nor was it the case in Britain that Staff College graduates henceforth had their own career paths separate from the rest of the army. Rather, men who had obtained the coveted psc were expected to rotate between regimental and staff postings as their careers progressed – staff postings being graded according to rank.

A post requiring a General Staff Officer Grade One (GSO1) would be filled by a lieutenant colonel; a major's billet would be GSO2, and a captain's GSO3. The three grades equated to the three main posts on a division staff, and were frequently used as shorthand for these posts, but GSO1 roles, for example, also existed as subordinate positions in corps and army staffs, where the chief staff officer would hold general rank. Again, unlike the German system, these various staff officers had no command role and were not part of the chain of command per se – at least in theory, although it was certainly possible for a staff man to steer his commander in the right direction on occasion. For example, if a divisional commander were to become a casualty, his place would be taken by his senior brigade commander, not by the divisional Chief of Staff. Fundamentally, it grew to be the case that Staff College graduates went on to positions of influence and frequently to the highest rank, such that 'if there was a "Brain of the Army" capable of producing a "School of Thought", it was to be found at Camberley in the Staff College, and nowhere else'.[3]

Back in England in the autumn of 1912, my father wrote to Colonel O'Brien to give him news about the Aldershot scene and let him know that he had finally come to an agreement with his future mother-in-law about marrying her daughter and that he was planning for the marriage to take place at the end of 1914. He then joined the rest of his fellow students at Camberley in time for the beginning of his time at the Staff College. There were 104 students on the 1913 course, eighteen of whom were Gunners like my father. Except for seven majors and four lieutenants, they were all captains and included eighteen holders of the DSO.

Amongst them were Captain J.G. Dill of the Leinster Regiment and Captain H.C.T. Dowding, Royal Artillery; together with my father, these men would form the trio sharing responsibility for the defence of Britain in 1940, serving respectively as CIGS, air officer commanding Fighter Command and GOC-in-C Home Forces. A year behind, joining as part of the 1914 intake, was Captain J.F.C. Fuller, who would go on to become a noted and influential military theorist, and who will also feature again in this narrative.

The directing staff also included a substantial number of names who had distinguished themselves in South Africa, many of whom would go on to do so again during the First World War. A posting as an instructor at Camberley was seen as a useful step towards a divisional command or a senior post as Chief of Staff to a higher formation. The tone of the college in the years prior to my father's arrival had been set by a very distinguished succession of commandants: Colonel Sir Henry Rawlinson from 1903 to 1906, followed by Brigadier General Henry Wilson through to 1910 and then Major General William Robertson, who was still in post when my father arrived as a student. Rawlinson would later command Fourth Army on the Western Front, while Wilson and Robertson would both later rise to field marshal and CIGS; Robertson, famously, becoming the first and only man to rise from private soldier to the very top of the military hierarchy. When Robertson departed in autumn 1913, he was replaced by Brigadier General Launcelot Kiggell, then another rising star but later vilified for his perceived inadequacies as Haig's chief staff officer in the second half of the First World War.

Naturally, successive commandants had their own style and focus. Wilson had been an innovator, exposing his students to the political element of their trade, bringing in experts to lecture on the military applications of aviation and borrowing ideas from the contemporary French staff under Foch as part of a growing realisation that Britain would very likely find herself fighting her next war in France and Belgium alongside the armies of those powers. Robertson, for his part, was far more practical, believing that it was the primary job of the Staff College to fit its graduates for the more junior posts that they would fill immediately after leaving Camberley, and focusing on how to deal with defeat and withdrawal as well as with successful operations. Robertson was also keen to inculcate an ethos of the staff sharing the hardships of the troops; no doubt a reaction to the old music hall joke that if bread was the staff of life, the life of the staff was one long loaf.

In general terms, however, the two-year course was structured so that the first year was devoted primarily to obtaining knowledge of staff work and the second to practising its application. Within this, the syllabus focused on the following main areas:

- Military history, geography, strategy and tactics.
- The principles of imperial defence, including offensive and defensive operations and the armies against which it might be necessary to mount them.

- Systems of transport and supply.
- The medical and ordnance services, insofar as they concerned staff and command responsibilities.

Where funds permitted, staff tours also formed part of the curriculum. Assessment was by classification, agreed upon by the directing staff in conference.

In 1921, as a major general with five years of experience in France and North Russia to his credit, my father looked back critically at the time he spent at the Staff College, not then realising that he was virtually writing his own job description for a return to Camberley as commandant. Having spent four years in staff jobs preparing for entry to the college, he was one of the few who had not had to cram in order to qualify for it. Besides that, he had acquired a much more cosmopolitan attitude to army affairs. Although he enjoyed the lectures, he nevertheless felt that much of their content was not relevant to the war that it looked increasingly likely Britain was going to have to fight, and he no doubt made little secret of this, going on to reflect that he was likely considered insubordinate as a result. His mindset, one feels, would have made him far more at home under Henry Wilson's more liberal and free-thinking regime, than under Wilson's two successors as commandant.

One area in which my father's insubordinate streak made itself apparent was with respect to the mobilisation roles to which all Camberley students were assigned in the event of war. The idea was that, upon hostilities, the college would close and its students would join the BEF in a predefined role. Naturally, the junior pupils, who were those in their first year of studies, were assigned the lesser roles, moving on to more responsible assignments in the second year of their course. My father's mobilisation role during his first year at Camberley, which he would have taken up had war broken out in 1913, was to oversee and supervise the loading of machinery on board ships at Avonmouth Docks. This, naturally, was not to his taste, and he railed against the injustice of it:

> I can well remember my rage and despair at being given such a pedestrian task. I had been a Staff officer for nearly five years and had served with the Cavalry, Infantry and Transport, as well as with the Artillery. I had five years' war service out of twelve years total and spoke French, Dutch, Afrikaans, Danish, Norwegian, Urdu and Flemish fluently and knew these countries intimately. Surely one could have been given something more suited to one's attainments?[4]

In the event, by the time that war did come, he had been reassigned to a mobilisation role with No. 3 Base at Boulogne, but he still felt that the initial Avonmouth assignment had been inappropriate for someone who had spent so long equipping himself with the linguistic and other skills that he felt would be needed in the coming war. He was self-aware enough to realise that such ideas could make him appear bumptious, writing that he was afraid that he 'was regarded by many of the Instructors as being distinctly swollen-headed', but confessing at the same time that he 'regarded them as distinctly stupid in not discriminating between the individuals under their schooling'.[5]

There is no denying that my father had every right to be proud of his own abilities. Nevertheless, his response to the Avonmouth assignment – which, it should be remembered, was a vital job that needed doing by someone or other and was really no more degrading than the sorts of postings assigned to his classmates – was rather akin to his earlier fit of pique at Woolwich when he was threatened with a posting to the RGA. It seems not to have occurred to him that he was only one of over 100 young officers who had been collectively picked out as the rising stars of the British Army, and that, to the army's administrators, he was no better or worse than his classmates until he had proven otherwise.

He had been very lucky that he had, to a considerable extent, been able during his first decade of service to choose his own postings, or at least have some influence over them. So, this assignment should perhaps have served as a reminder that a large part of service in the army required one to do as one was told, unpleasant as this could sometimes be. This time, unlike during the Woolwich incident, there were no thoughts of resignation, so it may be assumed that this unpalatable lesson had been swallowed. Nevertheless, there is no denying that he was far happier when his mobilisation role was changed to the Boulogne posting, which remained his assignment in the fateful summer of 1914.

When the 1914 summer term came to an end, my father was about to join his fiancée on holiday with his mother, who had rented a house by the seaside at Selsey. Instead, he was told to remain at Camberley to await the probability of war. Sure enough, Britain declared war on Germany on 4 August, but the first consequence of war that he had to deal with was personal rather than professional:

> My fiancée was desperately keen that we should be married at once, but I couldn't agree to this, as one had no right to take on these responsibilities at such a moment. The nature of the war to come was quite unknown and, as a soldier, one had no right to neglect one's duty in such a crisis. In the light of events I'm sure that it was the right thing to do.[6]

For the moment, my mother's entreaties were to no avail, and my father was soon on his way to join the British Expeditionary Force in France. Duly gazetted psc, he received orders to proceed to No. 3 Base at Boulogne as per his assigned mobilisation role. As he departed for Southampton, he found time to drop a line to his fiancée, who was living with her mother at East House in Cambridge, saying, 'Just off. Enthusiasm unbounding!'

In professional terms, being a Staff College graduate was at times both a blessing and a curse over the years of the war. The numbers admitted to the two-year course at Camberley were designed to fulfil the needs of the peacetime army, with sufficient surplus to provide a staff for the planned BEF of seven divisions – six infantry and one cavalry. Yet, as newly appointed secretary of state for war, Lord Kitchener realised from the start that this conflict had every likelihood of being a long war of attrition in which a vast influx of manpower would be needed. This led to the famous appeal for volunteers and, in due course, to the expansion of the British Army to a force of over seventy infantry divisions, plus a further ten from the Dominions, and a multi-division cavalry corps.

Each of these divisions, and the corps and armies of which they formed part, needed trained staff officers who were in short supply. It was therefore not felt possible to deploy newly qualified staff officers in non-staff duties, which, in turn, meant that the chance of men like my father being appointed to a position of command was unlikely in the extreme. Then again, the rate of attrition amongst Regular officers serving with the BEF in 1914 was extremely heavy. Those who lived to see the war progress often rose with great speed, but they left behind many comrades who did not make it through the vital early battles in which the old Regular Army held the line until first the Territorials and then the first of Kitchener's Volunteers could begin to take the strain. From a practical point of view, too, so far as my father and his newly graduated colleagues were concerned, there was some sense in letting the new crop of 'Camberley Captains' cool their heels for a time, as the retreat from Mons had upset the divisional chains of command and they could then be placed at the front where they were most needed, while serving an important rear-echelon role in the meantime. Certainly, my father performed to great satisfaction in this role, which brought him the distinction of another Mention in Despatches. In all events, he did not have to wait long to go to the front, as he was promoted to major on 30 October 1914 and posted to 6th Division as GSO3.

The formation to which my father was posted was one of the divisions of the original BEF but, as it happened, the last of them to arrive on the Continent on account of its having been held back to assist with defence at home until the Territorial force had completed its mobilisation. The division was also one of the strongest then in the line: not only had it missed the earliest battles, which had cut swathes through the formations engaged, but it had four brigades of infantry rather than the usual three, having incorporated the stray 19th Infantry Brigade – formed from lines-of-communication troops as an emergency measure during the retreat from Mons, and heavily engaged during the retreat and subsequent battles – along with the three brigades with which it had initially deployed.

When my father joined it near Armentières, 6th Division together with the 4th formed part of III Corps commanded by Lieutenant General Sir William Pulteney, known to his own staff as 'Old Putty'. Pulteney had previously been general officer commanding (GOC) 6th Division until his elevation to higher command. Pulteney's replacement as GOC, who had overseen the mobilisation of the division and now led it to war, was an artilleryman, Major General Jack Keir. My father described him thus:

> Jack Keir was an extraordinary man, who hardly knew what was going on. He didn't bother himself about any detail, and couldn't show the line on the map. He afterwards became very violent in temper and eventually had to go home. I think the strain of things was rapidly driving him off his head. He came into the J.S. Office just before the King's visit and I showed him where the line was and gave him all the details. When the King came, Keir showed him the 4th Division line as the one held by us and they discussed it for some time. Naturally the King didn't know and the mistake was never discovered. I thought this pretty good for the commander of a Division.[7]

Keir later went on to a corps command, only to be relieved and sent back to Britain following a spat with General Edmund Allenby, a man with a temper even more volcanic than his own.

At the time that my father joined it as GSO3, the divisional order of battle stood as follows:

Table I: 6th Division Order of Battle, October 1914

GOC: Major General J.L. Keir
16th Infantry Brigade: Brig. Gen. E.C. Ingouville-Williams
    1st Buffs (East Kent Regiment)
    1st Leicestershire Regiment
    1st King's Shropshire Light Infantry
    2nd York and Lancaster Regiment
17th Infantry Brigade: Brig. Gen. W.R.B. Doran
    1st Royal Fusiliers
    1st North Staffordshire Regiment
    2nd Leinster Regiment
    3rd Rifle Brigade
18th Infantry Brigade: Brig. Gen. W.N. Congreve
    1st West Yorkshire Regiment
    1st East Yorkshire Regiment

2nd Sherwood Foresters
   2nd Durham Light Infantry
19th Infantry Brigade: Brig. Gen. Hon. F. Gordon
   2nd Royal Welch Fusiliers
   1st Cameronians
   1st Middlesex Regiment
   2nd Argyle and Sutherland Highlanders
Divisional Artillery: Brig. Gen. W.H. Paget
   II Brigade RFA
   XXIV Brigade RFA
   XXXVIII Brigade RFA
   XII (Howitzer) Brigade RFA
   24th Heavy Battery RGA

Of course, this structure did not remain constant. Brigade commanders came and went, and from the spring of 1915 each brigade had a battalion from the Territorial force attached as a reinforcement. This measure was intended to give the latter some experience while bringing the old Regular divisions back up to strength, and temporarily raised the brigades to five battalions each. Once whole divisions of Territorials were ready to take the field, these battalions were returned to their parent formation; the last having gone by early 1916.

Back in May 1915, 19th Brigade was taken out and posted to the newly formed 27th Division, taking 6th Division back to its standard three-brigade organisation. Finally, when the first New Army divisions reached the Western Front, it was arranged that brigades would be redistributed to stiffen some of the new divisions with more experienced troops, the old Regular divisions receiving a New Army brigade in return. For 6th Division, this meant 17th Brigade leaving in October 1915 and being replaced by 71st Brigade. An exchange of battalions then took place between the new arrivals and the two remaining original brigades, and this created the following order of battle which was in force during my father's later service with the division.

Table II: 6th Division Order of Battle, February 1916

GOC: Major General C. Ross
16th Infantry Brigade: Brig. Gen. E.C. Ingouville-Williams
   1st Buffs (East Kent Regiment)
   8th Bedfordshire Regiment
   1st King's Shropshire Light Infantry
   2nd York and Lancaster Regiment
   16th Machine Gun Company

18th Infantry Brigade: Brig. Gen. R.J. Bridgford
  1st West Yorkshire Regiment
  11th Essex Regiment
  2nd Durham Light Infantry
  14th Durham Light Infantry
  18th Machine Gun Company
71st Infantry Brigade: Brig. Gen. M.T. Shewen
  9th Norfolk Regiment
  9th Suffolk Regiment
  1st Leicestershire Regiment
  2nd Sherwood Foresters
  71st Machine Gun Company
Divisional Artillery: Brig. Gen. G. Humphreys
  II Brigade RFA
  XXIV Brigade RFA
  XXXVIII Brigade RFA
  XII (Howitzer) Brigade RFA

The division also had its own organic support units of Royal Engineers, Royal Army Service Corps, signals, veterinary and medical troops, and at various times had detachments of cavalry and cyclists attached as well. Total strength, assuming all units were at full establishment, was in excess of 18,000, but rarely reached that level once the war was underway. It is telling, with that figure in mind, to note that 6th Division suffered over 14,000 casualties during my father's service with it.

Of the four original 1914 brigadiers, my father sketched a series of pen portraits, capturing a very disparate set of characters. Edward Ingouville-Williams, known by the nickname 'Inky Bill' and later killed by a stray shell when serving as GOC 34th Division on the Somme, he described as 'a small nervous-looking man, always on springs', whose command was 'the best Brigade in the Division, manned by good old County fighting Battalions'. Walter Doran, notwithstanding being the most senior brigadier, 'was a gloomy individual, always grousy', while, by contrast, Walter Congreve VC was 'undoubtedly our best Brigadier', whose brigade was always in good order. Congreve would, in due course, replace Keir as GOC when Keir was moved up to command a corps.

The last of the quartet was Brigadier General Hon. Frederick Gordon, who initially led 19th Brigade but later left for a divisional command of his own. He was 'a dour old bird, often very sarcastic to us on the Divisional Staff. A good fighting man and very good at heart. His Brigade Major, Hayward [sic], was a Guardsman who had been at the Staff College with me and was the life and soul of the Brigade.'[8]

These differing perceptions are particularly interesting in that they show a good appreciation of the merits and demerits of each individual, something that it was vital for a good staff officer to acquire if he was to do his job to the best of his ability. It is telling, too, that my father made a distinction between the best brigadier and the best brigade, and that he recognised the vital, if unsung, role that the staff officer – in this case his friend Heywood, another rising star – could play in serving as the real directing force of a formation, something that he would find himself doing later in the war.

For the moment, however, he was in little position to influence anything, and was the most junior officer on the divisional staff, working under the GSO1, Colonel William Furse. Furse was later replaced as GSO1 by Lieutenant Colonel J.M. Shea, and he in turn by Lieutenant Colonel G.F. Boyd. In the breakdown of jobs, the GSO1 oversaw operations, the GSO2 oversaw training and the GSO3 had responsibility for intelligence, although as the junior man my father also found that he picked up all the duties that the others did not fancy. Quite apart from being the normal lot of a divisional GSO3, the intelligence assignment was certainly one that played to my father's strengths and experience.

Unfortunately, there were times when there was little for him to do, with only a few prisoners – mostly deserters – to interrogate. To my father, it was second nature to use his German, French and Dutch speaking ability to learn as much as he could about his enemy and what was happening in the front line, but he felt that this view was not shared and he became increasingly critical of the way that the BEF organised its intelligence-gathering activities, eventually coming to conclude – perhaps with the benefit of post-war hindsight – that they had been unduly optimistic in their assessments of the situation on the Western Front. Still, with the additional technological advantages that had been added to the military repertoire in the decade since he had last seen active service against the Boers, he was able to develop a complete and much more thorough appreciation of the enemy on the Western Front by making the most of aerial reconnaissance, propaganda, interrogation and subterfuge.

The build-up of the Western Front into a continuous line of trenches extending virtually from the Channel to the Swiss border engendered a deep sense of frustration into everybody serving in the BEF, which, in common with the other armies of the day, had been trained for mobile warfare. Inevitably, there were delays in coming to terms with just what this new form of warfare entailed, and the different organisational and logistical demands that it placed upon the armies. These matters, of course, were for the staff to sort out, for planning had not taken place for a war of this nature and it was necessary to evolve a system of reliefs to enable the troops to rotate between the forward trenches and camps to the rear where hot baths and other necessary elements of logistical support needed to be established. Nevertheless, 6th Division may have had some advantage over its sister formations in being based for much of the time around Armentières, leading to them acquiring the nickname of 'The Mademoiselles'. During this hard winter, on 17 February 1915, my father was appointed as divisional GSO2.

As the New Year progressed and the number of British troops on the Western Front increased, changes were in order, to find commanders and staff for the increasing number of higher formations. As already noted, Keir left the division to command the new VI Corps, and Congreve was promoted to major general to replace him as GOC. Keir, however, took his old division with him as part of his new corps, and this meant a shift to the Ypres Salient. The Second Battle of Ypres had been fought while 6th Division was holding the line further south, but there was still heavy shelling in the salient when the division moved to take over the line previously held by 29th Division, and the consequences of the earlier battles were immediately apparent – 'Ypres was in a state of ruins and nobody was living in it except the troops who inhabited cellars in various places. The town had an indescribable smell about it – dead bodies, gas, powder and general decay.'[9]

The 6th Division Headquarters were established in a large château at Vlamertinghe, 2 miles west of Ypres. Initial operations were in a supporting role, and this enabled my father to obtain leave to get married. The wedding took place on 26 June 1915 at Jesus College Chapel, Cambridge, with Arthur

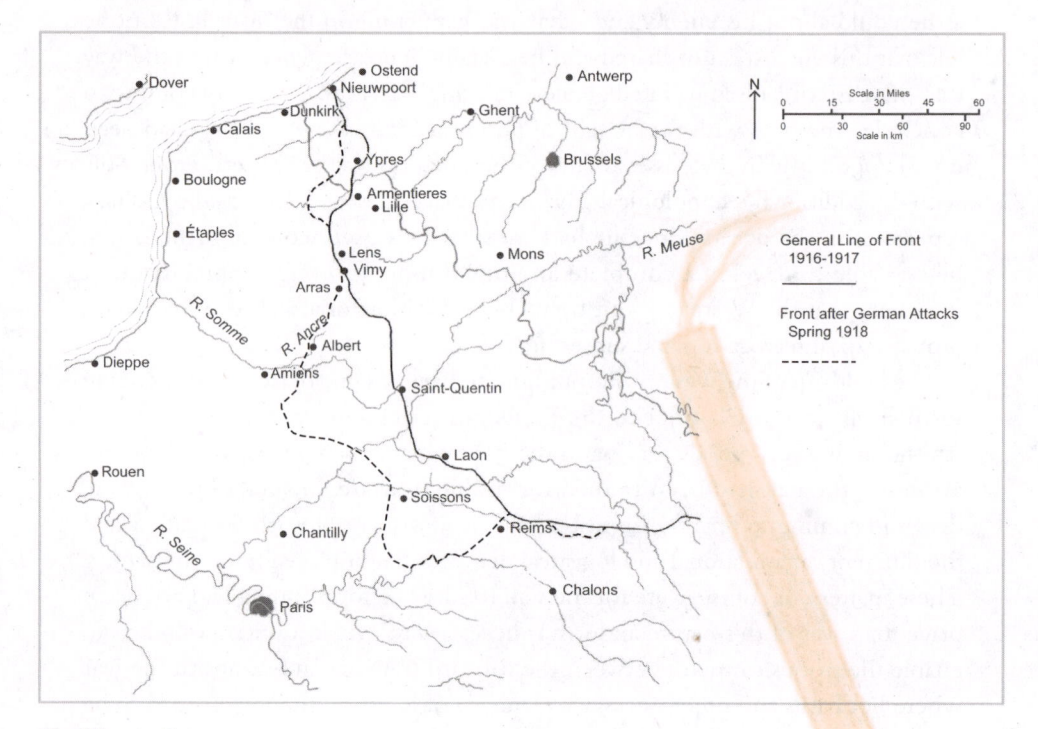

The Western Front.

Soames, now a captain attached to the Royal Flying Corps and sporting one of the first Military Crosses to be awarded, as best man. Sadly, Soames would be killed shortly afterwards in an accident while inspecting some bombs.

My parents spent their honeymoon in Devon at a house lent to them by a friend of my mother's; for my father, it was an all too brief respite before returning to France. There were few wedding presents, but the staff of 6th Division clubbed together to give him a large silver tea tray inscribed to 'Tulip', the nickname he had acquired through being perceived by his fellow officers as being tall and big-headed. A few days after his wedding he received two more gifts courtesy of the War Office when his name appeared in the *London Gazette*s of 22 and 23 June 1915: the first of these conferred the third of the six Mentions in Despatches that he would ultimately obtain during the First World War, and the second confirmed the award of the DSO.[10]

On his return to the Ypres Salient he found that the Germans had made an attack in the Hooge sector on 30 July using flamethrowers – *Flammenwerfer* – for the first time, which had panicked elements of the New Army 14th Division into withdrawing into the woodlands. This was the response to the British detonation of a large mine – containing a ton and a half of ammonal – directly under the German trenches, which had created a huge crater and thereafter became a key feature in this part of the battlefield. The Germans were able to seize the crater in the aftermath of the *Flammenwerfer* attack, and it was therefore imperative to regain the initiative by getting it back. As part of the process of attempting to recapture the crater, and to make good the territory lost as a consequence of Second Ypres, a series of counter-attacks were planned for early August 1915, which would see 6th Division committed to a major offensive for the first time.

In preparation for its part in the attack, 6th Division was taken out of the line on 2–3 August, taking up its new front on the 6th of the month. Three days were then allowed for the divisional artillery to bombard the enemy positions before the main attack went in on 9 August. The attack was to be made by 16th and 18th Brigades, and was scheduled to begin at 03.15. An important part of the plan was that it included a co-ordinated artillery barrage to give close support to the attacking troops. This was not the 'creeping barrage' introduced later in the war – the techniques for that were still being developed – but called for a heavy bombardment of the German front-line trenches to begin at zero hour, under the cover of which the attacking infantry were to move out into no man's land. Thereafter, the barrage would shift to the German support trenches, allowing the British attack to go in without fear of losses from their own guns, while preventing the Germans bringing up reserves.

Another feature of the artillery plan was the support of two batteries of French 75mm guns firing phosphorous shells. Unfortunately, the one thing that the Allied artillery could not do was neutralise the German guns, and the division lost a total of seventy officers and 1,700 other ranks, largely as a result of very heavy shellfire directed against the right flank of the attacking troops. Nevertheless, the overall result was a striking success, not only retaking all the ground lost on 30 July but also seizing an important spur dominating the ground to the north of the Menin Road. As such, it was widely hailed as 'a model of really close cooperation between infantry and artillery',[11] and as a key member of the divisional staff my father must share some of the credit for this.

As is clear from his own narrative of events, his role did not end with the conception of the attack. He was actively involved in making sure that things went as planned, even when not all of those around him were able to cope as well as he could with the near-constant shelling and the strain of command. Brigadier General H.S. Ainslie, who had replaced Congreve at the head of 18th Brigade when the latter took over the division, 'came to Congreve and said that he couldn't carry on any more & that it would be murder to send the Brigade into action against the Enemy under him'.[12] Thus, at the last minute it was necessary to reassign command of the brigade to its senior battalion commander, Lieutenant Colonel Francis Towsey of 1st West Yorkshire Regiment, who led it in the attack.

It was 18th Brigade, on the right of the divisional frontage, that suffered most heavily from the German shelling, and when my father made his way to the front to aid in the consolidation of the captured ground it was clear that the heavy casualties had taken their toll, not helped by the fact that the Allied bombardment had completely obliterated the German front-line trenches and thus, in effect, deprived the brigade both of its objective and of any cover. As communications with 18th Brigade became increasingly difficult, Congreve sent my father up to re-establish contact and find out what had happened:

I arrived at the Bde HQ about 4 p.m. They were in a hut in Zouave Wood. The whole show had collapsed with the exception of Morgan-Grenville the signal officer. The Commander, Towsey, was sitting with his head in his hands and moaning. He could say nothing but 'Oh those Guns' & I could get no sense out of him. The others were all asleep. No one had been down the line and no arrangements made to run the Show. I told Boyd [the GSO1] on the telephone that things were bad & I was going up to take charge. He said that he would send up 2 Bns of the 17th Brigade to take over the next day. I went round the line and found everything in hopeless confusion. The only man with any sense in his head was [Lieutenant Colonel Michael] Goring-Jones, the CO of the Durhams. He at least was trying to do something but had no knowledge. I personally got the men in position and thinned out the line & pushed the machineguns into the line. We arranged telephone and runners communications & then went back to the Bde HQ. I commanded the whole night and then handed over to [Brevet Lieutenant] Colonel Price of the Royal Fusiliers. The show was really too disgraceful. Towsey was quite incapable of command & should really have been court-martialled. As it was, he was sent off to get fit again. Nothing was ever said of the whole episode nor known to no one except the immediate actors.[13]

It may be noted that the Hon. Thomas Morgan-Grenville, then a junior officer in the Rifle Brigade, would much later become my father-in-law.

In the aftermath of the action, a number of changes were made within the division, for the most part allowing younger men to take over. Congreve was quite ruthless with those who were perceived to have had failed so badly, although the unfortunate Towsey suffered more than anything for having had the command thrust upon him so unexpectedly. Ainslie, whose nerve had failed him, was later reassigned to a battalion command but was clearly unable to cope with the pressures of leading a brigade. My father, by contrast, was forced by circumstances to take on a command role, even while the army continued to keep him back in a staff position.

It must not be assumed, however, that he was able to maintain a complete detachment from the tension, nor that he was completely free of fear himself. Those fears, however, were for the most part for the safety of his canine companion for, as in South Africa, he again had a pet with him on active service:

> My old bull dog, Gibby, was a great comfort in these days. He used to go everywhere with me and was never frightened of any shells whatever. He hated the duck-boards that we used to put in the trenches, for his toes used to get caught in them. He then took to walking outside the trenches, which frightened me, for I was afraid he would be sniped. He had the most wonderful 'homing' sense and if ever he missed me he used to go off straight home and never used to miss his way. Harrison, my servant, used to tell me that he used to arrive all panting and out of breath.[14]

Gibby was unfortunate enough to be slightly gassed at 6th Division's HQ at Vlamertinghe at the time of one of the earliest gas attacks in 1916, which was subsequently reported in the Canadian and US newspapers. This earned him a reward from a small girl living in Hertford, Connecticut, whose guardian sent Prime Minister David Lloyd George a $1 cheque on 5 August 1917 to buy Gibby a proper gas mask.

As GSO2 of 6th Division, my father survived all the shelling in the Ypres Salient and only suffered two minor wounds. All this time he hammered away for command, but was always held back because he could not be spared from the staff. As the staff pool was seen in army circles as the fount of command capability, it was not surprising that there was a strong sense of brotherhood and competitive spirit at play amongst the Camberley graduates as they crossed each other's paths in their advances to higher rank. It was to their great advantage that they had a taste of all the staff duties if they were to succeed in moving higher up the ladder, and as the war went on my father never missed an opportunity for making his desire for command known to visiting senior officers.

Congreve, in his turn, left the division to command a corps, and his post as GOC was taken by Major General Charles Ross. The division was taken out of the line in late October and placed in rest around Houtkerque and Poperinghe, but was still obliged to furnish working parties for the front-line troops. Furthermore, and giving a very relative value to the term 'rest', planning was undertaken and training carried out using dummy trenches for a mooted attack on Pilckem Ridge. In the event, this operation did not take place, for the focus of the war had shifted south in preparation for the planned offensive on the Somme, but in 1917 the plans were dusted off and the attack carried out with great success by other troops. Again, as a key member of the divisional staff, a share of the credit must here go to my father. Indeed, his contributions to the success of 6th Division's operations were recognised at the time for, after being replaced as GSO2 on 29 February 1916, my father was gazetted temporary lieutenant colonel three days later. This cleared his way to higher rank and greater responsibility, but still not to command.

4

Apprenticeship to Command

For a newly promoted lieutenant colonel with my father's background and training, two obvious potential appointments presented themselves. The first was a GSO1 post on the staff; the second was command of an infantry battalion. True, he remained a Gunner by cap badge and, as such, might also have had cause to expect an appointment to command an artillery brigade, which was also a lieutenant colonel's posting. In practical terms, however, it was nearly a decade since he had last served with the guns and artillery warfare had changed greatly in the intervening years, so that such an appointment does not seem to have been an option.[1]

Of the other two possibilities, there is no doubt that he would have preferred the command of an infantry battalion; not just for the command itself, but because such a posting was the usual prerequisite for selection for an infantry brigade command and thus a stepping stone to further promotion. Indeed, even before his lieutenant colonelcy came through, he had sought to obtain such an appointment by writing to William Furse, the original GSO1 of 6th Division, who had since been promoted to the rank of major general and was serving as GOC 9th (Scottish) Division. Furse, a fellow artilleryman, was quite amenable, but things were not so straightforward:

> He offered me the command of the 7th Seaforths, if he could get me & I jumped at it. He very nearly got me but was defeated by Wigram on the Staff who refused to let me go. Here one was tied to the wheel of the staff and the best officers in the Army were kept to bolster up the incompetents. [...] Every Staff Officer worth his salt wanted to get off.[2]

Having been so closely connected with the development of successful trench warfare practices with 6th Division, and having demonstrated his ability to take charge of front-line operations at battalion level after the breakdown of command in the actions at the Hooge crater, there is no doubt that my father had the skills and experience to command a battalion, in the Seaforths or any other regiment. Equally, with so few Staff College graduates available, it is hardly to be wondered that the army wished to place them where their skills could be best used. One can therefore see the army's logic, but it certainly did nothing to take the sting out of losing this appointment when, six months later, the man who was appointed to command 7th Seaforth Highlanders was promoted again to command a brigade.

Although clearly disappointed to miss out on getting a battalion, my father nevertheless recognised that his temporary lieutenant colonelcy was in itself a mark of the high regard in which he was held for his work as a staff officer, noting that he had received the promotion some way ahead of any of his Staff College contemporaries. He recognised too that such an appointment was an important stepping stone to higher rank for, once his temporary rank had been confirmed by brevet (as it was by gazette of 3 June 1916), the regulations governing promotions ensured that he could expect to automatically become a full colonel four years later.[3] Such a policy of widespread brevet promotions for Camberley graduates, he felt, was the army's recognition that trained staff officers required some form of compensation for their being kept back from command posts so that they could instead provide trained support for senior officers who, in many cases, had been very rapidly promoted to the command of formations far larger and more complex than they had ever led in peacetime.

For an ambitious career soldier, these were important considerations, but the more pertinent consideration in the short term was what posting he might be given in his new rank. It having been made clear that he could not expect a command appointment, much as he would have wished for one, the obvious next best thing would have been to remain with 6th Division as GSO1. Instead, however, my father found that he was posted back to Britain to assume the duties of GSO1 in the newly formed 4th Canadian Division, and thus left the Western Front after a spell of service that had lasted a little over eighteen months and had carried him two rungs up the army's promotion ladder.

My father's first reaction to his posting was not positive. Indeed, he confessed that it came as 'a nasty shock', and the prospect of returning home to put the Canadians through their training was doubly disheartening. While he could not entirely discount the fact that he was being sent home for a rest from trench warfare, the thought of a break made him feel that he might lose his touch and prevent him from picking up the threads of front-line fighting again very easily.

By the end of the First World War, the men of the Canadian Expeditionary Force (CEF) would come to be ranked as some of the most effective troops under British command, but in 1916 this reputation was still largely to be earned and my father's perception of the men of the first three Canadian divisions already serving in France was of troops who were gallant enough, but undisciplined. This was, perhaps, something of an exaggeration, but it was perfectly true that the CEF was lacking, due to the extremely small size of the pre-war Canadian Regular forces, in anything like the number of trained and experienced officers who were required to fill its senior command and staff postings. As a result, hand-picked British officers were brought into the CEF from the outset, with 1st Canadian Division going to war in February 1915 under the command of a British GOC, Lieutenant General E.A.H. Alderson.

The arrival in France of 2nd Canadian Division in September of that year allowed the formation of a Canadian Corps under Alderson's command, which was later further increased by the formation of the 3rd Canadian Division early the following year. Although the brigade and divisional command positions now increasingly passed to Canadians, the majority of the staff and specialist command posts within the corps remained in the hands of British officers.[4] My father's two eventual successors as CIGS during the Second World War were both Canadian Corps staff officers in the 1st, underlining the fact that some of the most promising British staff officers were selected for these posts. In some Canadian quarters, however, this British presence was resented, something that served to colour both events at the time and their historical interpretation in the intervening years.

One of the main opponents to the posting of British staff officers to CEF formations was the man who had been primarily responsible for its creation and organisation, Canada's minister of militia and defence, Major General Sir Sam Hughes. Hughes had long held an interest in military matters, and had taken a break from his political career to serve in South Africa during the Boer War, following which he repeatedly sought the award of the Victoria Cross for what he – but, insofar as can be established, no one else – believed to be actions of great heroism.

Given the portfolio of the minister of militia and defence in 1911, Hughes had hoped to create a distinctly national army for Canada, based on a nation in arms embodied in the Canadian Militia rather than building on the small existing permanent force of Regular troops already in existence. War in 1914 gave him the chance to develop his concept on a scale beyond his wildest dreams, and he worked tirelessly to raise over 30,000 recruits in the first months of the conflict.

However, Hughes had thrown out all existing plans to do so, causing much confusion, and the training camp that he set up at Valcartier, Québec, was poorly managed. A politician to the core, Hughes gave senior appointments to friends, family and political allies, while indulging his own prejudices to promote erstwhile militiamen over the heads of Canadian Regulars. The result was that some – but by no means all – of the first crop of senior Canadian officers lacked the skills and experience for their posts, thus underlining the requirement for British help. Hughes, however, repeatedly protested over the assignment of British officers to CEF staffs, and after the formation of 3rd Canadian Division fumed that 'Staff College Recruits' had been given plum jobs, as befitted the War Office's 'pets'.[5]

Later he claimed that 'the men who fought so well at St. Julien and Festubert require no staff college theorists to direct them', seemingly forgetting that

Canadian success in those early battles was down, at least in part, to the fact that the troops had benefited from just such direction.[6] Histories more sympathetic to Hughes' ideas, if not to the man himself, and in particular those written when it was fashionable to denigrate the quality of British command and control on the Western Front more generally, accordingly tend at best to ignore the role of men like my father in turning the Canadian Corps into the elite formation that it had become by 1918.

In fact, by the time that my father received his posting to 4th Canadian Division, Hughes' time was nearly up. As well as incompetent officers, he had also foisted upon the men of the CEF inadequate or unsuitable equipment such as the Ross Rifle and MacAdam Shield-Shovel, which had proved unfit for trench conditions. The men of the Canadian Corps had also come to realise the value of British assistance, ultimately forging an identity that took British military traditions and knowledge but superimposed them on a distinctly Canadian military mentality that eschewed 'bull' for a freer, more informal approach to command.

In such an environment, Hughes found that he had fewer and fewer allies, a situation in which he did himself no favours with his continued attempts to meddle in officer appointments, thereby bringing upon his head the wrath of General Sir Douglas Haig and Lieutenant General the Hon. Julian Byng, who in May 1916 replaced Alderson as GOC Canadian Corps. Eventually, in November 1916, Hughes was forced to resign as Minister of Militia and Defence, but in the last months of his tenure he remained as interfering as ever. Accordingly, my father soon discovered that the formation and organisation of 4th Canadian Division had become a political battleground.

My father's first intimation that things were not as they should be came when he travelled back from France in the company of Brigadier General Lord Brooke, previously commander of 4th Canadian Brigade, who was then the senior officer – and apparent GOC designate – of the still partially formed 4th Canadian Division.

With the division still not yet organised, Brooke sent my father on leave, but the latter used this time to acquaint himself with the senior Canadian authorities in London, beginning with Hughes' personal representative, Major General John Wallace Carson, who had charge of CEF administrative affairs. My father's impression was of 'an oldish man, sixty-five or so, dressed in khaki [who] wore *pince-nez* and looked more like a professor than a Major General'. Carson recommended that my father visit Hughes in person, as well as Sir Max Aitken – the future Lord Beaverbrook, who was then in charge of the Canadian War Record Office – and the high commissioner, Sir George Perley.

This my father did, finding them all helpful, but forming a decidedly mixed impression of the mercurial minister. He certainly recognised that Hughes had done great things in creating an army corps effectively from nothing, but deplored the man himself and his methods, considering that he had made two great mistakes in abandoning Canada's pre-war militia system and in allowing his prejudices as a fervent Orangeman to blind him to the value of the French Canadian population as potential recruits.

After an initial meeting in London conducted amidst a hubbub of staff officers and stenographers, my father met Hughes several times during the division's training in England:

> I came to the conclusion that the man had served his time and was past his usefulness. He clogged things with his political graft and patronage. He forced a bad rifle – the Ross – upon the Canadian Army and made money out of it. He appointed his family to positions which they could not fill. He began to think himself a Napoleon and infallible. He rubbed up the military authorities in England and France and he did his best to upset the unity of the Canadian Corps.[7]

My father's conclusion was that 'one simply couldn't like the man'. No doubt, considering Hughes' distaste for British staff officers being foisted upon him, the dislike was mutual.

In the same way that Hughes had no time for British staff officers, it is hardly surprising that he had no time for the idea of Lord Brooke as GOC 4th Canadian Division and soon ensured that the division would go to war under a Canadian officer of his choosing. Instead of Brooke, Brigadier General David Watson, commanding 5th Canadian Brigade in France, was promoted to major general and brought across to be GOC of the new division, with Brooke relegated to a brigade command. In the interim, however, the composition of the division needed to be sorted out, for it remained incomplete and in something of a mess.

The four battalions of 10th Canadian Brigade were largely fit for service, lacking only a brigade commander, and 38th Battalion had spent some time in garrison on Bermuda so was at least trained, even if the men had never seen action, but the material from which the rest of the division was to be constituted was rather less promising:

> [W]e had some twenty Battalions of different kinds, which had been enlisted and brought to England under the men who had enlisted them with a promise that they would not be broken up on arrival. Their training was being neglected and none of them had any war experience.[8]

This mix-up was largely Hughes' doing, having cheerfully made impossible promises to those engaged in raising the new battalions, but it took much further politicking, in which my father was able to use his new acquaintanceship with Sir Max Aitken to good effect, to break up sufficient units to bring the remainder up to strength and finally get the division – which was officially embodied on 26 April 1916 – properly established.

While it was undergoing training, the division was stationed at Bramshott, forming part of the Aldershot Command, and my parents rented the nearby Mill House from Lord Redesdale, fully furnished. My father was allocated a Canadian servant named Duncan Campbell from Vancouver, and had a Russian émigré groom, named Piskoff, to look after his two horses.

For the division to be a success required the development of an effective partnership between the GOC, David Watson, and my father as GSO1. On the face of it, the two men had little in common: Watson, born in 1869, was not even a professional soldier. Orphaned at a young age, and lacking much by the way of schooling, he had risen through the ranks of the *Quebec Chronicle* to manage both the newspaper and its publisher. His military experience prior to 1914 was restricted to the militia, in which he was a lieutenant colonel when war came. He was, however, also a friend of Sam Hughes, and this ensured that he kept his rank in the CEF and was given command of the 2nd Battalion. Thereafter, he learned on the job and learned well: his battalion was soon famed as the 'Iron 2nd', and it was his fighting record as much as his connections that carried him to brigade and then divisional command.

Whatever their difference in background, therefore, both GOC and GSO1 came to their posts with a reputation as fighting soldiers, and this no doubt helped the two men get off to a good start, as my father later recorded:

> He was as anxious as I was to get out to France with his new Division and I was able to make up a programme of training that forced us to work at high pressure. I warned him that unless we got to France soon, the other three Divisions might stop us by demanding our men as reinforcements.
>
> He knew nothing about training, but accepted the papers that I drew up for him. He could not understand at first why I didn't mind his 'cribbing' my work as he called it. I told him that that was what I had been sent to do, that I was a trained officer and could make plans of simple nature, which were easy to learn. And so he and I got on very well. I never had a row with him and never would have had one.[9]

Watson had learned through experience how to command in the front line, but as a battalion and brigade commander he had not gained the same insight into higher operations that my father had picked up as a divisional staff officer. To his credit, Watson seems to have recognised this and their early co-operation seems to have set a precedent for their future relationship, with my father as the Staff College professional serving at times as much military adviser as Chief of Staff in the conventional sense.

My father recognised that this unusual relationship was a good thing, giving him far greater responsibility than he would have exercised as GSO1 of a British division. Of Watson, he observed, 'His knowledge of war was nothing and I soon found that his nerve was none too good. I may truthfully say that I commanded the 4th Canadian Division from the moment we went to France to the moment I left it after Passchendaele.'[10]

We might here expect to make some allowance for my father's ever high self-opinion, and indeed, it was standard practice across the British Army that the bulk of divisional orders be formulated by the GSO1 and go out under his signature, so in that sense my father would always have had a substantial command role by virtue of his position. Nevertheless, his eventual special place within the division was recognised more widely: Lieutenant E.L.M. Burns, the divisional signals officer, for example, recorded that Watson's 'personality was rather put in the shade by that of his General Staff Officer Grade 1 – Lieutenant Colonel E. Ironside. The general opinion was that Ironside was the real commander of the division.'[11] To set against this, it should be stressed that there is also evidence that Watson took decisions on his own when he needed to, albeit with mixed results. He did not always follow my father's advice, and was by no means relegated to a cypher. Still, as we shall see, my father's intervention in a direct-command role was at times of decisive importance in the success of the division's operations, and this intervention would become increasingly necessary as time went on.

In bringing the new 4th Canadian Division up to readiness for action, Watson and my father found that they had good material to work with, and this in turn gave my father confidence that the training regime he had devised, and Watson and the brigadiers were implementing, would prove successful:

> I never had any anxiety as to whether we would turn out a good Division or not. We had far more of the Canadian born lads than the other three Divisions and fewer of the old British soldiers. Each month we increased the pace of our training programme until we could go no faster.[12]

The process was helped by the fact that the brigade command posts all went to veterans. Lord Brooke we have already encountered and, notwithstanding my father's poor opinion of him, he had at least already served as a brigade commander in action. The other two brigadiers, William St Pierre Hughes – brother of Sir Sam – and Victor Odlum, were both newly promoted, having made their names leading Canadian battalions during the earlier battles of the war.

Odlum, in particular, would be recognised as one of Canada's best home-grown commanders, although his strictly teetotal views did not endear him to his troops, and Watson had to intervene to restore the brigade's rum rations after Odlum sought to replace them with hot pea soup. Another strong character, Odlum was one man over whom my father was able to exert little control, as we shall see, and was a competing influence on Watson. Hughes, he eventually came to dismiss as being all show and no substance, noting after the division's first actions on the Somme that he 'had done about as badly as a man could do'.[13] Hughes was replaced before the Vimy fighting. On the staff side, my father had as his GSO2 another British professional, the Hon. Thomas Morgan-Grenville, my future father-in-law, now promoted to major. He had impressed my father at Hooge, and subsequently followed him across from 6th Division.

The training of 4th Canadian Division quickly progressed, and my father found that his expectation that the process would take in the region of five months had in fact been unduly pessimistic. By August 1916 the division was ready to deploy to France, lacking only its artillery component which was to be added later by reassigning units already on the Continent. My father was concerned that although the divisional standard of musketry was high, they would be encumbered by the unsuitable Ross Rifle, but in the event many of the men soon unofficially replaced their Rosses with British Lee–Enfields once they were in France.

On 25 August, the division entered the line for the first time as part of the Second Army in the Ypres Salient, taking part in several trench raids to accustom the men to active service. In one of these minor actions, Lord Brooke was wounded and obliged to relinquish command of his brigade. Official sanction was also received during this time to replace the last remaining Ross Rifles and re-equip the whole division with Lee–Enfields. After this successful blooding, and with its infantry carrying a rifle they could trust not to let them down in the mud of the Western Front, the division then entrained on 2–3 October for redeployment as part of Reserve Army (later redesignated Fifth Army) on the Somme.

The original three divisions of the Canadian Corps had already been heavily engaged on the Somme, and were on the point of being pulled out of the line when 4th Division arrived at the front. For its first battle, therefore, the division would come under the command of Lieutenant General Sir Claude Jacob's II Corps alongside three British divisions. My father had a good opinion of Jacob, but a poor one of Lieutenant General Sir Hubert Gough, commanding Reserve Army, who he believed to be overconfident and ignorant of conditions at the front.

When a post-war committee was given the job of retrospectively naming the battles of the Western Front, they dignified the operations in question as the Battle of the Ancre Heights, but so far as 4th Canadian Division was concerned their primary objective was to take and hold the German position code named Regina Trench. Earlier attacks by the Canadian Corps had failed to take this position. Rather than trying to take the objective in one attempt, there were to be a linked series of assaults with co-ordinated artillery support and an additional barrage provided by indirect machine-gun fire over the heads of the attacking troops.

Notwithstanding these measures — the latter being very much the latest in new thinking — the Germans were able to man their defences in time to resist the attacking troops, and the assault on 21 October succeeded only with heavy losses. This secured the western part of the objective, but the division thereafter had to endure a series of heavy counter-attacks over the succeeding days before rain brought operations to a close. Only after a cold snap set in was the ground hard enough to permit further movement, which, in turn, enabled 4th Canadian Division to stage a carefully orchestrated attack on the night of 10–11 November. This time, the artillery plan — a two-day preparatory bombardment followed by a brief but extremely heavy barrage timed to cover the passage of the attacking troops across no man's land — worked perfectly and the objective was taken with only light losses.

Following the success of these operations, the offensive was planned which would later be dignified as the Battle of the Ancre. 4th Canadian Division — still part of II Corps — was initially deployed only in a supporting role, but on 18 November was again put into the line, attacking into driving rain and sleet. Odlum's 11th Canadian Brigade, which had done well in the Regina Trench fighting, was again successful but 10th Canadian Brigade, which had taken heavy losses in the earlier fighting, did less well. Nevertheless, the division as a whole was able to advance nearly half a mile on a 2,000-yard front, taking 600 prisoners in the process but at the cost of 1,250 casualties. By the following day, the weather having again closed in, further active operations were cancelled and thus the final phase of the Somme battles came to an end.

My father had little to say about these actions, which he considered an unnecessary result of Gough not knowing when to call an end to operations that had no chance of leading to a breakthrough. He was pleased, however, with the progress made by the newly formed division, writing of the Regina Trench fighting, 'Our men did very well indeed and we were all proud of 11th and 12th Brigades'.[14] Certainly, these operations were considered to have successfully blooded 4th Canadian Division, which was deemed to have won its spurs and earned a place alongside the veteran divisions of the Canadian Corps.

Even as the last gasps of the 1916 offensive petered out in the mud and sleet along the Ancre, plans were afoot for the next series of attacks in the New Year. The new French commander-in-chief, Robert Nivelle, had great hopes for an advance across the River Aisne into Champagne country, but this in turn required support from the British to the north, who would therefore mount an attack around Arras with General Sir Edmund Allenby's Third Army. The success of the Arras Offensive, however, was in turn conditional on the recapture of Vimy Ridge, which dominated the lower land to the south over which the main attack was to be made. Vimy Ridge was therefore an important objective, and it was a telling complement to the men of Canadian Corps that General Sir

Henry Horne, commanding First Army with responsibility for the Vimy Sector, assigned them the task of taking it. All four Canadian divisions would take part in the main attack, a single British division being temporarily attached to function as a corps reserve, and 4th Canadian Division was assigned the far left of the attacking line.

At the time of the battle, the organisation of the division stood as follows:

Table III: 4th Canadian Division Order of Battle, April 1917

GOC: Major General D. Watson
10th Canadian Infantry Brigade: Brig. Gen. E. Hilliam
    44th (Manitoba) Battalion
    46th (Regina and Moose Jaw) Battalion
    47th (British Columbia) Battalion
    50th (Calgary) Battalion
    10th Canadian Light Trench Mortar Battery
    10th Canadian Machine Gun Company
11th Canadian Infantry Brigade: Brig. Gen. V. Odlum
    54th (Kootenay) Battalion
    75th (Mississauga) Battalion
    87th Battalion (Canadian Grenadier Guards)
    102nd (Northern British Columbia) Battalion
    11th Canadian Light Trench Mortar Battery
    11th Canadian Machine Gun Company
12th Canadian Infantry Brigade: Brig. Gen. J. H. MacBrien
    38th (Ottawa) Battalion
    72nd Battalion (Seaford Highlanders of Canada)
    73rd Battalion (Royal Highlanders of Canada)
    78th Battalion (Winnipeg Grenadiers)
    12th Canadian Light Trench Mortar Battery
    12th Canadian Machine Gun Company
Un-brigaded:
    85th Battalion (Nova Scotia Highlanders)[15]
    67th Canadian Pioneer Battalion
    124th Canadian Pioneer Battalion

As well as the two pioneer battalions, there were also three companies of engineers; altogether a far more generous engineer component than would be found in an equivalent British formation. The division still lacked its own artillery, but was loaned British artillery brigades, detached from the 2nd and Lahore Divisions, under the temporary command of Brigadier General G.H. Sanders. Additional heavy guns from Canadian Corps and the First Army reserve artillery would also provide supporting fire. Altogether, it was said that some 42,500 tons of shells were amassed for the softening up of enemy positions with creeping barrages to clear the way for infantry attack. The gun count along the 7,000-yard front amounted to one field gun every 10 yards and one heavy gun every 20 yards.

During the planning for the offensive, careful note was taken of the lessons that had been learned in previous fighting in the sector, and also elsewhere on the Western Front. As well as the extremely heavy artillery support made available to the attacking troops, the attack itself was carefully co-ordinated, with set objectives and with provision for supporting troops to leapfrog the initial wave of attackers and push past them to maintain the momentum of the advance. In order to help secure surprise, and to minimise pre-battle casualties, a complete network of underground subways was constructed to provide safe passage and secure communications for the troops moving up to the front line. Finally, aerial reconnaissance ensured that every movement made by the enemy was observed.

Probably the biggest problem facing the Canadian Corps was the state of the winter weather, which caused havoc amongst the horses and mules that provided the only means of transport for vital ammunition supplies through the quagmire of the battlefield. Notwithstanding these privations, however, my father recognised that morale in the corps remained high as a result of the thorough preparations:

> The Germans had beaten the French off the Ridge by continually mining underneath them and driving them steadily back into the valley. However, the Canadians had very good Engineer Companies, treble the size of ours and they included a Battalion of miners, which helped to prepare the way for our famous victory. I remember seeing the Colonel of the Mining Battalion and learning about his plan to undermine the Germans and blow up their workings. Within a month we drove them out and they ceased work altogether. Our mining had succeeded beyond all our hopes and the whole Canadian Corps were on top of the world.[16]

When the Canadian Corps took over the Vimy front, it was felt important to gain an advantage over the enemy in all possible ways, to gain the best possible footing from which to launch the planned attack. The mining operations formed one part of this, but another crucial element was trench raids. Of varying sizes, ranging from small patrols to brigade-level attacks, these were intended to test the ground over which the attack was to be made, and to upset enemy defensive arrangements. Successful raids would also give the attacking troops a moral ascendancy over their enemy when they went over the top in earnest.

If anything, the policy was too aggressive – indeed, it was recognised as such by the post-war Kirke Report which analysed the lessons of the Western Front – and certainly it led on occasion to disaster, when the largest of all the pre-Vimy raids was mounted on 1 March.

The greatest exponent of raiding in 4th Canadian Division, and the mastermind of this operation, was Victor Odlum of 11th Canadian Brigade, which was to employ two battalions in a 'reconnaissance in force' combined with a gas attack. The latter element was not a success, as my father related:

> We installed gas cylinders and let them off, meaning to follow the gas up. The enemy had got wind of the gas or the wind was not favourable. In any case, the attack was easily met and repulsed. I think myself that the contour of the hill took the gas over the German front line and that any casualties it did inflict were far back. The Vimy Ridge was most unsuitable for this kind of attack had we but known as much about things as we do now.[17]

Matters were made worse when enemy shelling blew open two of the cylinders, gassing some of the attacking troops. Odlum and my father were already at odds, as was perhaps inevitable for the two most dominant personalities amongst the division's senior leadership, and the failure of the 1 March raid reinforced the breach between the two men. Even without the failed gas attack, there had been much controversy over Odlum's plan, with the commanders of both attacking battalions protesting against the risks. When the plan remained unchanged, both COs insisted on leading their men into action, and both were killed. This, my father felt, greatly harmed Odlum's credibility within his brigade but he retained his command, only for his insistence on doing things in his own way to cause yet further problems when the main offensive got under way.

After this initial setback, the Battle of Vimy Ridge started in earnest on 20 March 1917 with the bombardment of enemy positions prior to the main attack which was launched before dawn on Easter Monday, 9 April. Naturally, as GSO1 my father was heavily involved in the detailed staff work necessary to implement the complex plan of attack, but once the fighting was underway he found himself again obliged to act in a direct command role. The fact that he was obliged to do so, however, indicates the limitations of the influence that he was able to bring to bear during the planning process for, as he related, several of the problems that the division encountered during its attack represented threats that he had himself identified but which had been discounted when the final orders were prepared.

The primary objective of 4th Canadian Division was Hill 145, the highest point on the ridge and thus a key to the successful occupation of the whole position. Odlum's 11th Canadian Brigade, on the right of the divisional advance, was to attack Hill 145 itself, with MacBrien's 12th Canadian Brigade advancing on its left – and thus forming the left flank of the entire attack – with the twin objectives of covering Odlum's advance and capturing the German trench lines to the

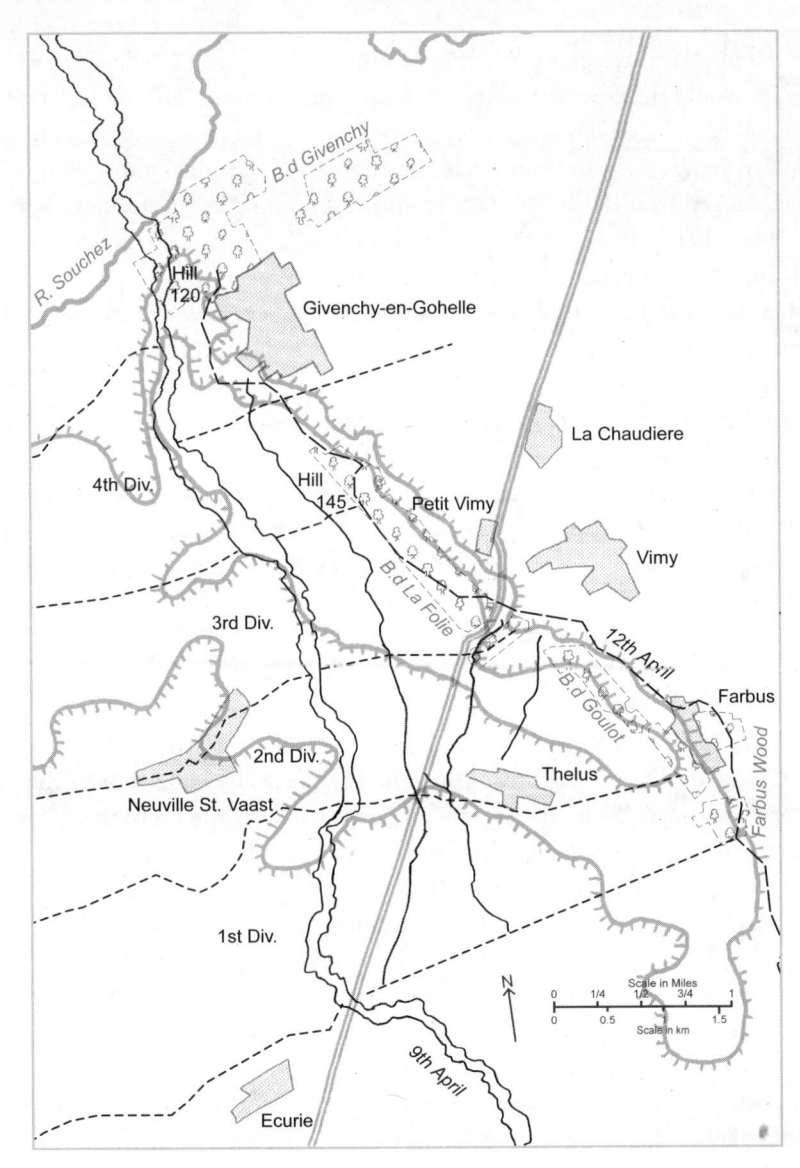

The assault on Vimy Ridge.

north-west of the hill. Hill 145, where the Canadian Monument today stands, was clearly a tough nut to crack and, in the case of Odlum's brigade, it did not help that the men would be attacking over the same ground that they had tried and failed to capture during the previous month's ill-fated raid. Naturally, it seemed logical to my father that these troops be supported as best as possible. Unfortunately, however, circumstances prevented his views being reflected in the eventual plan of attack.

In the plan, as it was put into action on the morning of 9 April, both attacking brigades would be exposed to fire from a position to their left, on the extremity of Vimy Ridge, marked on military maps as Hill 120 but commonly known as the Pimple, which is what my father had hoped to avoid. Originally this position was to be attacked by a British brigade from the adjoining 24th Division, but then plans were changed and it instead became a secondary objective for 4th Canadian Division. 10th Canadian Brigade, the divisional reserve formation, was now assigned to storm the Pimple, but not until *after* the other two brigades had made their attacks. My father was not convinced of the logic of this arrangement:

> I had had the most heated arguments with the Corps Staff as to being able to include the left end of the line of the Ridge, nick-named the Pimple. [...] We were ordered to take the summit and find a flank to the Pimple but not to take it. [...] I had pointed out that the men I had to use as a flanking force would in themselves be sufficient to take the Pimple but I was overruled. All the other Divisions in the Corps had to go a good deal further than we had & I suppose the Corps could find no other reserve.[18]

My father seems to have remained unconvinced, although he recognised that the choice lay between two equally poor alternatives, the other being to send 10th Canadian Brigade directly against the Pimple at the same time as the other two brigades made their attacks, which would have left the division with only a single raw battalion in reserve. Whichever way one looks at it, the corps-level plan left 4th Canadian Division very thinly stretched indeed, which explains why it ultimately took the formation longer to achieve its objectives than its three sister divisions attacking to the south. It also explains, in conjunction with the leadership issues already identified within 4th Canadian Division, why my father ultimately found himself forced to intervene in a command role to help ensure success.

At 05.30 on 9 April, mines that had been tunnelled under the German defences as part of the preparatory phase of the operation were detonated and the massed Allied artillery began the first stage of the fire-support plan. To the south, the other three divisions stormed forward and, despite losses, were soon well on their way to gaining their initial objectives. On the front of 4th Canadian Division, MacBrien's attack was equally successful, rushing the German first-line trenches while their shocked defenders were still recovering from the mine explosions, with Captain T.W. MacDowell of the 38th Battalion winning the VC for his part in the capture of over seventy Germans. However, the attack of Odlum's 11th Canadian Brigade was far less successful and, indeed, had all but collapsed before the troops were properly out of their trenches.

The problem highlighted another flaw in the planning process, and also emphasised the limitations inherent in the role of GSO1 even when the post was filled by an officer as experienced and forceful as my father. The cause of the disaster to Odlum's brigade was that a portion of the German trenches had been deliberately left un-bombarded at the request of the commanding officer of 87th Battalion which was slated to attack it. The logic for this was that, once captured, the trench could then be used as a strongpoint by the Canadians, but instead it became a strongpoint for the Germans and completely checked the advance both of 87th Battalion and of the units assigned to support it.

The brigade was badly cut up, and it proved very hard to restore any momentum to the attack. This was partly because the troops had now lost their artillery support, which had moved on to other objectives as part of the phased fire-support plan, but also because, at Odlum's insistence, none of the brigade's battalions had ever been withdrawn from the front to undertake unit-level training; instead, companies within the battalions had been rotated in and out of the line, which proved far less effective. It may safely be assumed that my father's experience would have caused him to council against these counter-intuitive and ultimately flawed methods, but Odlum was a brigadier general and my father a colonel, so the former had rank on his side and this evidently was what counted for Watson when the GOC accepted the proposals.

Thanks to the failure of 11th Canadian Brigade's initial attack and 12th Canadian Brigade also being held up, due to very poor ground condition and machine-gun fire from the Pimple, it was not until nightfall, and not until Hilliam's 10th Canadian Brigade had been redirected to support the other two, that the division was able to gain a lodgement on Hill 145. It was the following day before the Germans were finally evicted from the position. Because of the redirection of Hilliam's men, however, the Pimple still remained in German hands.

After two days of fighting, 11 April was a day for consolidation, but on the 12th the battle entered its final phase with a renewed attack on the Pimple by Hilliam's 10th Canadian Brigade. In the interim, the position had been reinforced, the Germans deploying, amongst other units, the elite Prussian *5. Garde-Regiment zu Fuß*. Two of Hilliam's battalions, the 44th and 50th, had already taken heavy losses when they were brought to the aid of Odlum's men in the initial attack, so for the assault on the Pimple they were joined by the fresh men of 46th Battalion.

A substantial concentration of artillery was deployed in support of the attack, and the troops were grimly determined as they prepared to go over the top. In 50th Battalion, out for revenge for their casualties two days previously, the acting CO had ordered that no prisoners were to be taken. The attack was timed for dawn on 12 April, but when dawn came the weather had closed in and visibility was right down. In these circumstances, with command and communications increasingly disjointed, my father found himself obliged to intervene to prevent a disaster:

> During the afternoon [of 11 April] my clerk Duncan Campbell came to me & said that Watson was talking to the Brigadier who had to do the attack & I

reached the office in time to hear Watson say, 'The weather is too bad. Never you mind what Ironside says, don't do the attack if you don't want to.' I waited until he had gone back to his dugout and then rang up the Brigadier and told him that I was coming down to see him and that the attack must take place. If I found that he didn't propose to do it, I should find someone else to do it. The Brigadier promised. I then went and tackled Watson. His nerve had completely gone and he was cowering in his dugout in no fit state to command anything. I told him that he had very nearly upset everything. If he wanted his orders cancelled, the only thing to do was tell me & I would issue the orders. I warned him at the same time that if he cancelled the attack on the Pimple he would ruin everything. The poor devil gave in as he always did & I went off to the Brigadier leaving orders with Duncan to ring me up if Watson did anything. I found the Brigadier had succumbed to a good deal of liquor & that his B[rigade] M[ajor] a regular officer was in despair. I stayed until the show began. The morning was one of the most awful I have ever seen in the war. It was blowing a hurricane against the Germans and snowing heavily. I had slowed up the barrage considerably but was terrified that the conditions would be too much for the men to surmount. The Germans had crammed the hill with men and they suffered heavily in the short bombardment & could not see or stand up against our men when they came on. More men were bayonetted in that fight than I have seen anywhere. It must have been slow going.

As soon as I saw the show had gone well I telephoned for Watson to come down to Brigade HQ & we started up the hill to see things. Watson had got over his funk and was trying to pull himself together. I am afraid I must have been a sore trial to him, for he knew that I knew his innermost feelings. Still, in war there is no place for a physical or moral coward in any position & certainly not in high command. I realised fully that he was not a soldier and that he was breaking up & one had no time for pity when it was question of men's lives.

The hill was a terrible sight. We saw German trench-mortar and machine-gun crews lying dead around their guns, bayonetted by our people. In one place there was a Canadian & a German both transfixed with each other's bayonets and quite dead, though standing up & leaning on each other.[19]

Hilliam's lapse was neither reported nor repeated, and he continued in command of his brigade, eventually rising to the rank of major general. At the time of the attack he was very newly promoted to brigade command, and caught in a struggle between Watson on the one hand and my father on the other. Like the unfortunate Lieutenant Colonel Towsey at Hooge, the responsibility seems for a time to have overwhelmed him. My father, meanwhile, had in helping restore the situation also cemented his position as the real direction behind the command of 4th Canadian Division.

Taking the Pimple allowed the British 24th Division to extend the attack to the north, driving the Germans back to the outskirts of Lens, with elements of 4th Canadian Division providing support as the British went forward. That night, their work done, the Canadians were relieved by the British 5th Division, which took over the line and allowed them to withdraw into billets. Many visitors came to scrutinise the scene after the capture of the ridge, amongst whom was Sir William Robertson, now a lieutenant general and CIGS since December 1915, who shook my father warmly by the hand, greeting him in his usual down-to-earth ex-ranker style by saying, 'I see you ain't got no smaller!' But what caught the eyes of the photographers who accompanied the visitors was my father's bulldog Gibby, whose presence in the front line had never been questioned and who now proudly wore the ribbon of the Mons Star around his collar.

The capture of Vimy Ridge successfully eliminated any threats to the main Allied offensives further south, although in the event Nivelle's French attack ended in disaster and the thrust around Arras by Allenby's Third Army also became bogged down. Needing to take pressure off his French allies, whose forces were close to collapse, Sir Douglas Haig now shifted his attention to the German lines in Flanders, where the BEF was far better placed to engage the enemy. In the meantime, the Canadian Corps remained on hold at Vimy Ridge, now under the command of the Canadian-born Lieutenant General Sir Arthur Currie, who had replaced Byng when the latter was in turn moved to take over Third Army from Allenby in June 1917.

For the rest of the war, even during the German attacks of 1918, the line in the Vimy Sector remained static, although a number of small-scale attacks were mounted over the summer in order to keep the Germans on their toes, and to tie down enemy forces. My father was nevertheless extremely busy during this time, working out defensive schemes to secure the ground that had been taken during the great attack.

There was, however, time to rest and relax as well, when the troops were out of the line, and my father learned to play baseball from his Canadian counterparts. He also had the opportunity for an occasional day's leave within France:

> As an amusement one often had a run down to Boulogne in a car, bringing back some fresh fish & every time a car went down to fetch any one coming home on leave, we used to send down a clerk. I remember one time taking my servant Harrison and Campbell & Gibby & lying in the sun on the beach the whole day.[20]

Thus, as the fighting and dying continued elsewhere on the Western Front, the Canadian Corps rested and built up its strength. Only after some months was the corps moved north into the Ypres Salient, where the new offensive, initially successful at Messines Ridge, had now bogged down in the mud and blood of Passchendaele.

Writing four decades later, with the benefit of hindsight, my father felt that it was a mistake to commit the Canadian divisions to this sector when, as he saw it, there was more profitable employment for them elsewhere at Cambrai where the first big tank attack was being planned. Hindsight would certainly indicate that the Cambrai attack might have achieved more had sufficient troops been available to follow it up, and resources could have been employed far more profitably there than around Ypres. At the time, however, my father was not even aware – as he himself admitted – that the great tank attack was planned. In all events, the fact of the matter was that Canadian Corps moved north from Vimy in the autumn of 1917 to play their part in the battle that has become synonymous with all that was horrific about the trenches of the Western Front.

By the time that my father and his comrades reached the salient, the original offensive that had begun in late summer had petered out due to the appalling conditions, but pressure was being maintained by a series of smaller attacks. Although the original offensive in Flanders had been intended to have wide-ranging strategic consequences, these had long been abandoned and the focus now was on winding down the Flanders operations to free up resources for the Cambrai attack and also for redeployment to help keep a faltering Italy in the war.

In order to bring matters on the Ypres front to conclusion, however, the village of Passchendaele itself remained to be taken, and this was the task assigned to Canadian Corps. The corps was assigned to General Sir Herbert Plumer's Second Army, and was put into line to relieve the exhausted II ANZAC. The basic operational plan called for three successive assaults, each having limited objectives, to be mounted on 26 and 30 October, and 6 November, with the intervening time set aside for relieving the attacking troops and securing the ground that had been taken. These 'bite-and-hold' attacks were the trademark of Plumer's generalship, and were to be supported by additional attacks by I ANZAC on the right of the Canadians, and by elements of Fifth Army to their left.

In preparation for the attacks, 4th Canadian Division was to take over the portion of line held by 3rd Australian Division. My father had, of course, served in the Ypres Salient before, earlier in the war, but even this did not prepare him for the horrors that now awaited him:

When we emerged from the Menin gate it was as if we had come into another world. Mud reigned supreme. The whole area from the ramparts to the Roulers Ridge was pitted with shell-holes filled with mud and water, and so close together that their outer rims met. For the first two miles up to the gun line a beaten track had been maintained, more or less along what had been the old pavé road. Along this we joined an endless stream of artillery horses, each laden with four rounds of field artillery ammunition and led in pairs by an artillery driver. Day and night this stream never stopped, so that the means to keep up our

> terrific barrages might be maintained. This track was kept open by large working parties, filling up ever-renewed shell-holes and throwing up the débris on either side. In the months of this long battle this track had become a sunken lane, with banks composed of broken carts, dead horses and equipment of every kind. The stench of death was almost overpowering. Before us in the distance stood the menacing Ridge, from which the enemy could look right into the very innards of our back area.[21]

My father eventually made it through to the headquarters of one of the Australian brigades that were to be relieved, which was situated in a captured pillbox. From here, the Australian brigadier briefed him on the situation further forward, but even at this point, 2 miles back from the fighting, the scene was horrific:

> The pillbox was crammed with men to overflowing & around the place lay several men, orderlies, telephonists, and the commander of the Reserve Coy with a weak Coy. They lay in the open and as I waited I looked round at these men, two were sitting in front of the pill box, in front of a small wood fire. One was leaning forward with a pannikin of tea in his hand, just as if he were about to drink. Their rifles lay on the ground beside them. Both were dead, killed only a few minutes before by the shock of a shell which burst close to them. The shelling never ceased day or night and yet the men lay or sat sleeping or waiting and watching the bursts, paid little attention to the state of affairs.[22]

The Australians has managed to get their patrols into Passchendaele itself during the earlier fighting, but were now in no fit condition to push on any further. My father therefore had to orchestrate their relief by the well-rested Canadians, but this was no easy task when the advanced positions were so close to the German lines and the intervening terrain so badly cut up by the shelling:

> Each mud-crater was a trap from which no man could have escaped unaided, and we encountered bodies around these craters which had been lying there for days. I made up my mind then and there that we could not risk a night advance. The men would have to be filtered up in daylight, and some place would have to be found close to the top of the ridge, where they could spend their time unseen until zero hour. They would then be in good heart for the daylight attack the next morning.[23]

The one advantage that the Canadians were able to employ was that all four divisions were lavishly endowed with engineer and pioneer units, these troops amounting almost to the strength of a fourth brigade within each division. It was therefore possible to build new ways forward, shored up with duckboards, and to get the troops into their attacking positions relatively easily in the way that my father first envisaged.

During these operations, my father was forced to do far more in an active command role than ever before, exercising more control over the planning as well as the execution of the division's operations. This expanded responsibility was due to what he saw as the increasing incapacity of Major General Watson, who he believed had suffered some sort of collapse following Vimy which even a spell of relative rest had not been able to shake off. Notwithstanding the problems identified by my father, Watson, who was knighted in 1918, remained in his post as GOC 4th Canadian Division for the remainder of the war but finished the conflict in poor health and died in 1922. It is clear, however, that my father had a far greater role in the planning and execution of 4th Canadian Division's main attack on 30 October than he had in the Vimy operations, even if, as at Vimy, not all of his ideas were adopted in the final scheme.

Perhaps because he felt that his own contributions to the planning had been slighted, my father's account is extremely critical of the senior officers involved in the Passchendaele operations. Unaware that Passchendaele was the final objective, he worried that the attack was being made on too narrow a front which would prevent subsequent exploitation. He also observed that neither Haig nor Plumer had actually been to the front lines to make a reconnaissance, and that the same could be said for the new corps commander, Currie, and his chief staff officer Brigadier General Percy Radcliffe.

My father, who had been in the front-line trenches from the outset as we have seen, sought to shape 4th Canadian Division's planning in order to reflect this, producing a detailed and defiant report which he contrasted favourably with that produced by his opposite number with 3rd Canadian Division, 'which outlined the frightful condition of the terrain, but made absolutely no suggestions on how to overcome it'. Sadly, my father's poor opinion of the planning by 3rd Canadian Division was reflected when that formation began the corps' offensive on 26 October. Notwithstanding support by 4th Canadian and 1st Australian Divisions, this attack failed to take all its objectives due to imperfect co-operation with the Australians as well as vigorous enemy counter-attacks. This now meant that an attack on the 30th, which was intended to capture the ground that would provide the final jumping-off position for the attack on Passchendaele itself, was all the more important.

My father's narrative of the detailed planning process for this attack indicates the sort of issues that he had to deal with, emphasises the difficulty of co-ordinated planning between the two attacking divisions and also suggests that the amount of influence my father was able to exert within 4th Canadian Division had increased considerably since the Vimy Ridge operations. His initial thoughts were recorded during his first visit to the front, when the lines were still held by the Australians:

As I sat and watched the scene with men wandering about on either side and no definite obstacle to take when we attacked, it seemed to me that our attack was wrong. Given that we could have our men up to the cover we had found and could attack in daylight, why did we not do so as a surprise in daylight. No one had ever done anything but attack at dawn. The enemy could go nap that we were going to do so again. Of course I could not vouch for what the 3rd Division on our left flank could do and we had to make our attacks a common one. I wanted the attack to be a real surprise & to be executed with lightly loaded men going all out to arrive at the top of the enemy ridge in record time. Or to do it in two lines. One to take an imaginary line, say half way to the ridge and then the second attack to follow at once, jumping over the men holding the first objective. I saw a very good chance of surprise. By this time, our barrages were far greater than any fire put up by the Germans in return. I even hoped that we might make a smoke attack. That would also be a surprise to the Germans, who had never seen us attack with smoke on a large scale.[24]

Once back behind the lines, after a hair-raising journey during which he had to extricate his servant, Campbell, from a shell hole, he was able to report to Watson and begin serious planning:

I explained the position to Dave Watson & he understood what we had to face. We issued orders for the duckboards and the white tape marking lines that we wanted & then drove off to tell our story to Currie, the Corps Commander & the B[rigadier] G[eneral] S[taff] at that time, an old Gunner friend, Percy Radcliffe. Both understood that all depended on what the 3rd Division had discovered. On being sent for, they had to admit that they had to bring up their men during the night before the attack, just as all the other Divisions who failed had done. They thought that they could be certain of being able <u>to be certain</u> [*sic*; emphasis as original] that they could follow their barrage. But any question of a surprise attack with them was out of the question.

There was nothing to be done about it. Dawn it would have to be. But our men would be fitter than the 3rd Div ones when they attacked & I was certain that we could do a lot of camouflaging our men during the hours of daylight. I was also hoping that during the day preceding the dawn attack we might be able to obtain air superiority over the enemy for many of the hours of waiting.

Our attack was a success and our casualties were very small.[25]

As my father states, 4th Canadian Division, spearheaded by MacBrien's 12th Canadian Brigade, carried out a textbook attack, which in fact exceeded its objectives and briefly secured a lodgement in Passchendaele village itself only to be obliged to give this up to conform to the line attained by 3rd Canadian

Division, which had again failed to take all its assigned objectives. The attack had, nevertheless, secured the necessary ground from which 1st and 2nd Canadian Divisions would successfully attack on 6 November, taking Passchendaele and bringing the campaign to an end.

After helping to bring the operations in the Ypres Salient to a successful conclusion, Canadian Corps was again assigned to the Vimy Sector where it was to refit and absorb replacements for the 15,654 casualties that it had sustained during its deployment to Flanders. My father's time with the corps, however, was almost up. In part, this was due to an ongoing process of appointing Canadians to senior positions within the corps, now that there were sufficient Canadian officers with the relevant qualifications and experience. Also my father's own enhanced experience made him eligible for more senior roles and on 7 January 1918 he received an appointment, with the rank of temporary colonel, to command the Small Arms School. His replacement as GSO1 was a Staff College counterpart, Edouard Panet, whose French-Canadian background ensured that he was acceptable on all levels for the post.

As well as the two Mentions in Despatches that he been awarded during his time with 4th Canadian Division, not to mention the promotion that came when he left it, my father also received the praise of the corps commander, Currie, who wrote a letter 'thanking me for all I had done for the 4th Division'. For his part, my father wrote that he 'look[ed] back on my time with the Canadians as two of the happiest war years that I had spent'.

The war, however, was still not over, and it now remained for the experience that he had gained as staff officer to be put to good use once a command appointment was at last in his grasp.

5

Holding the Line

My father's new posting took him to the headquarters of the Machine Gun Corps at Camiers, one of the many subcamps that formed part of the BEF's huge base depot at Étaples. The Machine Gun Corps had only been formed in late 1915, as part of a move to centralise control of the heavy Vickers Guns that had initially been parcelled out in small numbers amongst the infantry battalions and cavalry regiments. Thereafter, these guns had been grouped into companies, one of which was assigned to every brigade, but now it was felt that more flexibility could be obtained if these companies were in turn grouped into battalions.

Each division had, since late 1917, already had been assigned a fourth machine gun company to supplement those belonging to its three brigades, but now all the Vickers Guns were to be consolidated at divisional level. In this way, larger concentrations of fire could be massed against particular targets if required, leaving immediate support of the infantry to the new, lighter, Lewis Guns which now formed an integral part of every platoon.

However, although the material to form the new battalions was readily available since the men and guns were already in the field as part of the independent machine gun companies, the fifty-odd new battalions needed officers to command them. It was to train these men that my father had been appointed.

The men selected to command the new battalions were a mixed body, amongst whose numbers my father found men drawn from as varied sources as the Household Cavalry, the Indian Army and cyclist battalions. Nevertheless, he found the job, which mostly consisted of passing on the latest methods and thinking, to be 'a task after my own heart',[1] and as winter turned into spring the first of the new battalions began to be activated and take their place in the divisional orders of battle. My father was proud of what had been achieved in so short a time:

> I had worked hard at the tactical doctrine for MGs and I had several high-class instructors to help me. I was able to infuse something of a real feeling in the men of what might happen with plenty of tanks & a general forgetting of trench warfare.[2]

His only regret was that his role placed him in a purely training capacity and he itched for a chance to exercise command in battle. In fact, such a chance was looming, for the German Army was preparing its last great offensive of the war and every man and gun would soon be needed in the front line.

Although it was generally accepted by March 1918 that a major German attack was imminent, now that enemy forces had been redeployed from the Eastern Front and before American reinforcements had begun to arrive in France in appreciable numbers, an attitude of complacency still existed within parts of the Allied command. At a strategic level, the problems facing the BEF were fully understood. Sir Douglas Haig found himself obliged to take on responsibility for a larger extent of the Western Front than ever before, shifting the Fifth Army south to take over the line south of the Somme that was previously held by the French. At the same time, government concerns that the war would likely go on into 1919 meant that manpower was being husbanded by politicians who no longer trusted Haig not to squander his resources in the sort of futile attacks that had been seen at Passchendaele. The result of this was that Haig had had to thin down his infantry divisions, reducing the number of battalions in each and trusting to technology to make up the shortfall. But, for years, the BEF had operated almost exclusively on the offensive at both the strategic and operational level, and a shift to defensive warfare proved problematic. Some thought had been given to how best to resist the new German storm tactics, which had already been seen in action at Riga and Caporetto, but the evaluation of these lessons had been flawed, and even such doctrine as had been developed was only imperfectly and intermittently applied. Thus, when the storm broke on 21 March 1918, the results quickly threatened to become catastrophic.

Directed by the architect of the German war effort, *General der Infanterie* Erich Ludendorff, the Michael Offensive, also known as the *Kaiserschlacht*, was targeted against Byng's Third and Gough's Fifth Armies on the southern extremity of the British front. Although the grand strategic objective was to cripple the Anglo-French forces before the Americans could intervene, thus potentially ending the war, Ludendorff's immediate focus remains unclear. Indeed, it has been suggested that the whole series of 1918 offensives, of which this was the first and most dangerous, represented opportunism rather than the pursuit of a specific strategic goal.

Third Army was initially to have received the brunt of the attack but, in the event, the fact that Fifth Army quickly crumbled opened up a new opportunity for the Germans, with a serious risk developing that Gough's battered formations might lose contact with either Third Army on their left, the French on their right, or both.

My father had already been called down to the threatened sector prior to the opening of the offensive, acting as a representative of General Headquarters. He described his role and findings as follows:

I was to make sure that the order concerning MGs was to be carried out. It was that 50% of the available MGs must be in Second Reserve lines when the expected German attack took place. The new technique of attack was expected to be a complete destruction of our front and even second lines by a bombardment from guns & mortars, firing gas & other missiles. Anything in these first lines would not be available for the battle after the preliminary bombardment was over. I was to impress upon Sir Hubert Gough that it would be better if he kept more than 50% in the reserve lines, for it was there that the main infantry attack would strike our forces. We must be ready there to resist. The weaker we were in the front lines the stronger we would be behind.

I had a long interview with Sir Hubert Gough [...]. He told me that he had only lately had his sector increased in size and that he was holding it with very few troops. He must keep a large part of his MGs in the front or the enemy would walk in. He seemed to fail to realise what this first bombardment was going to be like. Better to reduce the men & machines in the forward lines, I told him, than lose his MGs for ever. But he refused to be guided by what I said & I told him that after I had seen the positions of the MGs in front in 2 Divisions, I would have to return to report to Sir Douglas Haig. He acknowledged that it was my duty to do this.[3]

My father's report — delivered on 20 March, the day before the storm broke — caused some concern over the suitability of the Fifth Army's dispositions. Since by this time there were growing indications that the Germans were massing against that sector of the front, my father received orders to return to Camiers and to collect as many machine guns as possible, along with their ammunition, and bring them and their crews by lorry to form a mobile reserve. In all, he was able to collect no less than 400 machine guns. However, by this time, the initial German attack had swamped the forward positions of Fifth Army and Gough's men were in retreat. This created the dangerous situation already outlined above, and my father was ordered into the fray with his ad hoc detachment:

I was told to proceed to the right of the 3rd Army line near Foncquevillers & there I met Walter Braithwaite in command of a division [Major General Walter Braithwaite, GOC 62nd Division]. On his right the gap began. With the capture of a horse I saw to the long stream of MGs going up to the line of ridges, near which the withdrawing men of the 5th Army were struggling. There seemed to be no opposition to the reported steady advance of the German patrols. It seemed to be a race between myself & the Germans to see who could reach the line of ridges first. In many cases, my men began shooting at 800–1,200 yards at the approaching infantry patrols. There appeared to be no Cavalry operating on either side.[4]

My father used his lorries to rapidly deploy his men, placing pairs of machine guns every 400 yards, doubling up to place four guns at key spots. The mobility afforded by having wheeled transport available was clearly decisive, but he had difficulty integrating his ad hoc force into the local command structure:

> No one had heard that I was coming & except one Gunner Brigadier and one Infantry Brigadier I never had converse with any Superior Officer of the 5th Army.
>
> To everyone I saw I said that they ought to close on the line I was laying out at the moment, no matter what they were. If I could get some formed bodies into position I should be happy. I had a dreadful altercation with the Gunner Brigadier. He rode up to me & ordered me to evacuate my line I had laid out. I told him my orders straight from GHQ [General Headquarters] but he would have none of it. He had chosen to meet the Germans with fire on the hill I had chosen for my MGs. He became so menacing that he made several motions to ride at me. I dodged him and caught his collar as he went by. His horse galloped away from between his legs & I let him drop to the ground. I galloped off to continue my line making knowing that it would take him some time to get his guns firing at my line of hills. I never knew who he was or where he came from.[5]

By nightfall my father had established a defensive line extending beyond Albert, where he was able to link up with elements of the newly arrived Australian Corps, sent to help plug the gap and restore the line. What he had in effect created with his rapid deployment of machine gun sections was a sort of reserve or stop-line, which would prevent further infiltration by patrols of German stormtroops. He recorded hearing 'several busts of fire' from the guns he had emplaced, but also that the Germans were unable to bring any artillery into action against the positions that he had created. For the most part, this was because the German advance had carried them across the old Somme battlefield of 1916, so that the ground over which they had to move was horribly cut up with old trenches, craters and the like.

The point that my father had chosen for his defensive line thus coincided with the point where the German advance began to run out of steam; his actions, therefore, cannot in themselves be given credit for checking the enemy offensive, but they did undoubtedly help in the re-establishment of a new Allied defensive line. It was evidently with some surprise that he noted in his unpublished memoirs, 'I have never seen mention of my force in any history of the German attack', before going on to give his opinion that 'the MG Corps did a fine effort in the first action of its life'.[6]

Again, as at Hooge and Vimy Ridge, my father had demonstrated that he was able to maintain a cool head even in a desperate situation, and was fully prepared to risk the wrath of a senior officer if he felt himself obstructed in what he saw as his duty. It would seem, however, that he had already been selected for further promotion, as he was to find out the following morning:

> I was standing talking to Walter Braithwaite when a despatch-rider on a motor bike rode up to me to ask if I were General Ironside. I told him that I was Colonel Ironside. With that he delivered me a message and he gave me a message to hand over the line of machine guns to General Braithwaite's Division & proceed at once to take over command of the 99th Infantry Brigade of the 2nd Division.[7]

There was surely not time for my father's actions of the previous day to have influenced his selection for this new appointment, so it must be inferred that he had already been identified as a candidate for brigade command. He had at last achieved the command posting that he had been yearning for ever since the war had started, and would hold command of 99th Infantry Brigade from 27 March until 19 September 1918, during some of the most active and eventful fighting of the whole war on the Western Front. When he took command, however, it was to join a brigade and a division that had been through some of the worst of the retreat in the face of the German offensive, and his new command was decidedly battered and shrunken.

It was some measure of the seriousness of the German Spring Offensive, and of the heavy fighting that had ensued when the Allied line was broken, that the man who my father was to replace, Brigadier General Randle Barnett Barker, had been killed in action during the retreat after brigade headquarters came under artillery bombardment. So much for the popular idea of First World War generalship taking place in châteaux safely behind the lines!

Even the strongest of the brigade's three battalions had a bare half of its established strength when my father arrived to take up his new posting, and the other two were weaker still. Indeed, that there were three battalions in the brigade, rather than the four that would have been typical earlier in the war, was itself due to the wider manpower shortage that had led to the reduction of battalions in each division from thirteen to ten, through the expedient of taking one from each brigade.[8] My father, it may be noted, considered that this had been a mistaken concept, recognising that it was better to have a smaller number of up-to-strength battalions, but believing that these should have been concentrated in a reduced number of full-strength divisions. This, he believed, would have reduced the number of staff and command posts and enabled those that remained to be filled by the most effective officers.[9] However, for the generals and politicians the priority was to keep the maximum number of divisions in the line, even if those divisions were weaker than they once had been and were therefore stretched all the thinner to be able to cover the same frontages with three battalions less.

The state and composition of my father's new command gave some indication of the way in which the British Army on the Western Front had been shaken up by the reorganisation. 2nd Division, to which the brigade belonged, was one of the original Regular Army divisions sent to France in 1914, but 99th Brigade had begun life as part of 33rd Division, a New Army formation made up of Pals battalions raised from the area around London. The brigade had been transferred into 2nd Division in November 1915 as part of an effort to intermix veterans with new troops, and by March 1918 only one of the original New Army battalions remained – 23rd Royal Fusiliers (1st Sportsman's Battalion), which had originally been raised from noted cricketers and other sportsmen. Alongside it were two Regular battalions, 1st Royal Berkshire Regiment and 1st King's Royal Rifle Corps (KRRC), transferred across from 6th Brigade in 1915, and a brigade trench mortar battery.

Total strength in the infantry battalions was forty-eight officers and 1,392 other ranks, which was so low that the effective manpower was temporarily reorganised into a single provisional battalion, with 1st Royal Berkshires providing manpower for two companies, and the other battalions sufficient for one company apiece. The division as a whole mustered 136 officers and 3,899 other ranks when my father joined it, having lost 207 and 3,721 respectively during the German offensive, and was commanded by Major General Cecil Pereira, a Grenadier Guardsman, who offered my father a warm welcome.

My father would hold command of 99th Brigade for six months, during a period of hard and – by the standards of the Western Front – fluid fighting as the Allies grappled with a succession of German offensives. After the initial attack against Third and Fifth Armies had run its course, but drawn Allied reserves to the Amiens Sector, Ludendorff shifted the German efforts to the north, where the Georgette Offensive during early April secured significant gains around Ypres, wiping out the Allied gains around Passchendaele and coming close to pinching out the salient completely.

During May and June, the Blücher-Yorck and Gniesenau Offensives drove towards Paris, creating a dangerous bulge in the Allied lines but, as with Georgette, failed to break through. German losses were now mounting, particularly amongst the irreplaceable stormtroops, whereas Allied resistance was stiffening as reinforcements were brought to bear and new counter-attack tactics developed. Accordingly, on 15 July 1918, Ludendorff launched the *Friedensturm*, or Peace Offensive, designed as a last-gasp effort to break the Allied line.

The Germans attacked the French east of Rheims, but the attack failed to make serious gains and once the French began to put in counter-attacks the Germans were even obliged to withdraw from much of the territory captured during the Blücher-Yorck operations. The initiative now passed back to the Allies and on 8 August Haig was able to launch a major offensive in the Amiens

Sector which eliminated much of the gains made back in March by the initial German attacks.

The Battle of Amiens marked the beginning of the Hundred Days Offensive which, in a series of attacks by the combined Allied forces, would drive the Germans back first to the Hindenburg Line and then, after that line was broken in late September, back towards the Rhine. By the time of these final attacks, my father had left the Western Front, but 99th Brigade under his leadership would play an important role in the equally vital early fighting, winning him plaudits from his superiors and the respect and admiration of those who served under his command.

In the first instance, though, what the whole of 2nd Division needed was chance to rest, recuperate and absorb much-needed replacements for the men who had fallen during the retreat. Although the pressure of the renewed German attacks during April meant that another spell in the line was required to free more effective formations for the fighting in the north, by May the division had been pulled back into VI Corps reserve to facilitate the training and integration of reinforcement drafts. Their arrival meant that by June the divisional strength had more than doubled and the battalions of 99th Brigade again had sufficient manpower to resume their proper identities.

The brigade War Diary indicates that my father was extremely busy during this time, reconnoitring the line and getting to know his new command through formal inspections and informal visits, but also attending conferences through which the lessons to be learned from the March collapse were established and the appropriate solutions developed. These lessons were then passed on to the senior officers of the brigades through staff rides, and to the troops in a series of battalion tactical exercises. In the case of 99th Brigade, these were devised and run by my father.

The document outlining the objectives of the battalion exercises is worth quoting at length because it outlines what he, and the British Army, had learned over the past four years of warfare. My father stated his aims and objectives as follows:

> The Exercise has been devised with the objective of impressing upon all ranks the following:
> (a) Wood fighting, as in all close country fighting, must be carried out by Units advancing each in close order as regards itself.
> (b) Consequently, the importance of communications being maintained between these Units.
> (c) Every unit is responsible for its own security. Scouts and Sentries must be pushed forward in front of each Section if the view is restricted.
> (d) The importance of bombing straights in all trenches. In this Exercise the impossibility of attacking one directly will be demonstrated.

(e) Use of Smoke-Bombs and Rifle Grenades for attack of Strong Points.
(f) Co-operation of Stokes Mortars.
(g) Use of Light Signals to denote progress when working in close country.
(h) Impossibility of always being able to turn a nasty situation.
(i) With the absence of Artillery support the most intense S[mall] A[rms] covering fire must be developed from a flank and overhead if possible, so that the attack will not be delayed until Artillery can be brought up.
(j) This is the first Battalion Exercise that has been carried out, and it is intended to try and make the work deliberate and correct.
(k) The system to be adopted for the setting of the exercise was as follows:
  (i) The Brigadier walked round with each Battalion Commander, showed him the ground available, and the lessons he wished taught, with the general direction of the Attack.
  (ii) The Battalion Commanders then prepared a General and Special idea and told off their Companies to various duties.
  (iii) Reconnaissance of ground was then carried out by the King's Royal Rifle Corps Company Commanders by themselves and by the 23rd Royal Fusiliers with the battalion Commander.[10]

As well as the practical lessons, of which point (i) surely owes something to his time at Camiers with the Machine Gun Corps, the inclusion of point (h) is particularly interesting, reflecting a clear acknowledgement of the limits to which men could be pushed both in attack and in defence.

Later exercises also accepted that there would be occasions in which British troops would be forced to yield ground, and sought to develop tactics in which the troops could be withdrawn in good order and the penetration of enemy forces could be minimised. No doubt drawing upon his theoretical grounding from the training job at Camiers and his actual experience helping stem the German advance back in March, my father stressed above all else the effective employment of machine guns under these circumstances.

Also during this time, United States forces were rotated through 2nd Division formations in order to introduce them to the nature of warfare on the Western Front. 99th Brigade played host to officers and senior NCOs from the US 307th and 308th Infantry Regiments. Subsequently the 3rd Battalion of the 308th was temporarily attached to the brigade, being met by my father in person upon detraining and welcomed by the band and pipes of the 23rd Royal Fusiliers. Later, on 16 May, my father personally delivered a lecture to the US battalion, which was temporarily broken up and its companies attached to the British battalions of the brigade.

As was the norm, after having absorbed its replacement manpower, 2nd Division was then put back into the line in early June to acclimatise the new troops through small-scale operations and trench raids. 3/308th US Infantry remained attached to the brigade during the first part of this spell in the line, later being replaced by a similar detachment from 3/319th US Infantry. My father recorded that the inexperienced Americans 'showed great keenness and took their full share of holding the line, patrolling and other duties'.[11]

The sector that was occupied was near Monchy-au-Bois, between Arras and Albert, facing the northern flank of the German salient that had been left after the Spring Offensives. Both sides were particularly active in their raiding at this time, as the Germans sought to maintain the initiative, and the Allies to re-exert their dominance of no man's land and wear down the enemy forces prior to the coming Amiens Offensive. Nevertheless, the brigade was not so heavily engaged as to prevent my father spending a few days in England (leaving on 27 June and returning on 2 July) to attend a conference on honours and awards.

On 22 July, a major raid was mounted by 1st Royal Berkshires, which, thanks to several days of detailed preparations, was a marked success that obtained important information about the nature of the German defences as well as capturing five prisoners and a machine gun. Another raid, by 1st KRRC on 14 August, produced similar results and gave an early indication that the Germans, by now under heavy pressure now that the Amiens Offensive was in full swing, were making preparations to fall back.

It was increasingly clear that 2nd Division was fully recovered in both strength and combat readiness and was now ready to be committed to a major operation again, and this was confirmed by the army commander, Byng, when my father conducted him around 99th Brigade's positions. It must have come as little surprise when notification was received on 16 August that a major attack was to be made in the sector, in which 2nd Division would play an important role. Over the following days, the division was therefore relieved from its front-line duties in order to prepare for its part in the offensive.

Building on the successes scored at Amiens, a new offensive was planned on the Somme to recover the last of the ground that had been lost in March. In effect, this new attack, which would become known as the Battle of Albert, meant advancing over the same ground that had been fought over in 1916 and, as such, provides an instructive look at how far the British Army had progressed in the intervening two years. The attack was made by Byng's Third Army of three corps, of which Lieutenant General Sir Aylmer Haldane's VI Corps included 2nd Division, along with two corps from Rawlinson's Fourth Army. Tank and air support was integrated into the attack plan, and the infantry were well supported both by Vickers Guns in the divisional Machine Gun Corps battalions that my father had helped train, and by the more mobile Lewis Guns carried by the infantrymen themselves.

Only limited time was available to prepare for the attack, and my father, his staff and the battalion commanders had an eventful week of it as they completed the necessary arrangements in time for zero hour at 04.55 on 21 August. 99th Brigade was to open 2nd Division's assault, supported by a company apiece from 2nd Machine Gun Battalion and 12th Tank Battalion – the latter fielding nine tanks – working in conjunction with elements of the Guards Division to the north and 37th Division to the south. The objective was to gain the line of the Arras–Albert railway, north of the Ancre.

Although the tanks began to move into position around midnight, this did not draw down any adverse attention, and enemy shelling was, if anything, lighter than normal although some casualties were incurred by 23rd Royal Fusiliers as they formed up for the attack. The barrage opened exactly on time, and a heavy ground mist further aided the attackers by offering concealment from the enemy. Unfortunately, however, this would prove a double-edged sword as the poor visibility impeded effective co-operation between the infantry and tanks. The damp still air also prevented the dispersal of pockets of gas which, lingering, effectively drenched the long grass through which the troops were advancing. 23rd Royal Fusiliers, on the left of the brigade advance, eventually sustained a total of 383 casualties, mostly from gas, and had to be pulled out of the line and replaced by 1st KRRC which had begun the attack as the brigade's reserve battalion.

Notwithstanding this setback, however, the attack swiftly attained its objectives and captured some 200 prisoners. It is a telling comment on my father's effective training of his command that he did not need to intervene personally in the conduct of the attack, only joining the front-line troops to oversee the establishment of new positions once the advance was complete. By this time, it was evening. Cavalry and Whippet light tanks were moving up to exploit the success, and the brigade's work was complete. Accordingly, the two remaining battalions were relieved during the course of the night.

Unfortunately for the Allied planners, however, thoughts of exploitation turned out to be premature. Although the ground up to the Arras–Albert railway line had been gained as planned, doing so revealed that the railway marked the enemy's main defensive line. Accordingly, renewed attacks were planned for 23 and 24 August, with 99th Brigade tasked to capture the village of Ervillers and consolidate in a position a further 200 yards to the east of that place. This attack was launched at 15.30 on 24 July.

In order to make up for the losses sustained earlier by 23rd Royal Fusiliers, the remnants of which had been reformed into a single consolidated company, 1st King's Liverpool Regiment was attached to my father's command for this operation. When the attack went in, it was met with heavy machine-gun fire which caused a temporary check before 1st KRRC, with tank support, was able to gain a flanking position and take the objective from the rear. This secured Ervillers and some 400 prisoners, allowing the brigade to move forward and consolidate as per the plan.

Finally, on the following day, one last attack was ordered in which the brigade was to take the Mory Copse position. An initial attempt by 1st King's Liverpool was unsuccessful, but a renewed attack by 1st Royal Berkshires captured the copse along with 100 prisoners from five different enemy regiments. This objective taken, 99th Brigade was pulled back into reserve for a well-earned respite.

Throughout this series of operations, the brigade's War Diary indicates that my father was extremely active, not only in directing his own troops but in liaising with neighbouring formations in order to better co-ordinate the actions of his brigade. It is clear that his long apprenticeship had produced a first-class tactical commander, and his success and that of his brigade was recognised by both divisional and corps commanders. As the War Diary noted, 'Apparently the only adverse comment made by the Corps Commander was on the Brigadier wearing "shorts".' Evidently the extremely warm August weather had tempted my father into a return to the attire of the *veldt*.[12]

From 26 August until 1 September, the whole division was pulled back out of the line and into corps reserve. Even then, however, any concept of rest was illusory, for there were more replacements to be absorbed and a continued training program to carry through. Within three days of coming out of the line after the Battle of Albert, 99th Brigade War Diary could report, 'Battalions commenced serious training devoting their attention entirely to "open warfare"'.[13]

With the Battle of Amiens having broken the back of the German forces on the Western Front, and set in motion the climactic Hundred Days that would end with November's Armistice, it was clear that any respite would be brief and, indeed, it was just under a week before the division was back in action. The offensive to which 2nd Division was now committed was part of what would become known as the Battle of Drocourt-Quéant Line, the eponymous line representing the northernmost extremity of the Hindenburg Line, the main German defensive position on the Western Front. 2nd Division was to return to the line on the night of 2–3 September, relieving 62nd Division.

Even before this relief took place, however, my father received notice that his time with 99th Brigade was very likely almost up and he had been ordered 'to report at the War Office immediately on completion of the operations then in progress, with a view to going to RUSSIA on special service'.[14] In preparation for such a move, the faithful Gibby was sent back down to the base depot, and Brigadier General A.E. McNamara, a Staff College contemporary of my father's, joined the division to be on hand to take over as soon as my father received positive orders to depart.

Having become aware of the supposed move, my father sought to find out the truth behind what seemed initially to be confused rumours, and was buoyed by the fact that his superiors seemed keen to keep him in France. Indeed, as he later discovered, VI Corps Commander Lieutenant General Sir Aylmer Haldane had already put his name forward for a divisional command as and when one should become vacant. It seemed a harsh blow indeed that the staff should exert its pull upon him once more just as his skills in command were gaining recognition, but orders were orders and there was little that my father or his superiors could do once the recall was confirmed.

In the interim, while everything was sorted out, however, there was still a battle to be fought. 99th Brigade put in its last attack under my father's command at 05.20 on 3 September 1918, with 1st KRRC and 23rd Royal Fusiliers up front and 1st Royal Berkshires in brigade reserve, with 6th Brigade going forward on their right supported by half a dozen Whippet light tanks. Enemy resistance was limited, and the attacking infantry advanced quickly under cover of an effective barrage. Two days' hard fighting then followed as the brigade struggled to hold the ground that had been taken while the rest of the division pushed on with the attack.

The advance had now entered the coal-mining country around Lens, and good use was made of a slag heap as a defensive feature, from where the ground could be covered by fire from Vickers and Lewis Guns. This operation was still in progress on the morning of 6 September when, at 11.00, my father received positive instructions that he was to hand over command of the brigade to McNamara and to report as ordered to the War Office. His departure, we are informed by the War Diary, 'was keenly regretted by the whole Brigade',[15] a sentiment echoed after the war by the published history of 2nd Division.

Since his recall to London marked the end of my father's service on the Western Front, it is worth considering what effect the past four years had had upon him and his career. Having begun the war as a captain, he was now a substantive major, a brevet lieutenant colonel and a temporary brigadier general. He had served on the staff as a logistician, an intelligence officer and an operational planner, filling all roles with distinction and obtaining the praise of his superiors in doing so. Thanks to his unique relationship with David Watson, he had at times functioned as the de facto commander of 4th Canadian Division, and had then distinguished himself as both a trainer and leader of men during his service with the Machine Gun Corps and in command of 99th Brigade.

The brigade level of command, he later reflected, was in many ways the ideal one because it allowed the exercise of higher responsibility without losing touch with the men under command, so that 'as a B[riga]de Major's job is the best thing on the Staff, so the Command of a Brigade of Infantry is the best command a man can have'. To leave for something certain would have been one thing, but to give it all up for something unknown was anathema, the more so since the war seemed at last to be approaching its conclusion. 'I had known that the Germans were done months ago and I dearly wanted to be in at the end. Here I was going to lose it all & the march to Berlin.'[16] That said, the dangers of the Western Front even for senior officers were brutally underlined during my father's final farewell and handover of command, during which a heavy German bombardment hit 99th Brigade Headquarters, causing my father, his replacement McNamara and Brigadier General Arthur 'Jumbo' Goschen, commanding 2nd Division's artillery, to all dive for cover in the same shell hole. The sight of three brigadier generals, none of them small men, thus making use of such clearly insufficient cover must have offered some quiet amusement to any watching troops, and perhaps reminded my father that there were some things about France that need not be remembered with quite such affection.

My father left the Western Front at least having the comfort that he had received written testimonials from his corps commander, Haldane, and his army commander, Byng, assuring him of the value that they placed upon his services. It was only when he reached London, however, that he obtained some hard facts to back up the rumours surrounding his recall. Upon attending the War Office on 21 September, where he was met by Major General Arthur Lynden-Bell, Director of Staff Duties, he at last received formal notice that he was to be sent out to North Russia as Brigadier General, General Staff, to Major General Frederick Poole, who was commanding at Archangel. Commonly abbreviated to BGGS, the post signified the Chief of Staff to a large formation and was, in effect, an expanded version of the sort of duties that fell to a GSO1 at divisional level.

Poole had initially been sent to Archangel to manage shipments of heavy artillery to the Russian Front, but as events had escalated following the Russian Revolution he had ended up as the head of an international force which was trying to keep open the Arctic supply line to Russia in the vain hope of resurrecting an Eastern Front against the Germans, while at the same time hopefully checking the excesses of Bolshevism. It was a vague, confused mission that had grown in size and scope without the commensurate growth of a command and support network for the growing numbers of Allied troops being sent out, and matters were not helped by the reported inadequacies of Poole's existing staff, who were, as my father was given to understand, weak and in need of a shake-up:

> Apparently, they had all been dissatisfied with what was going on in Russia and especially the administrative people who were having frightful trouble with Poole's indents. The staff out at Archangel were all amateurs and had to be strengthened. They had all been told to write down the name of an officer to go out and put things right and some 9 out of 15 at the table had put my name down. Such it is to have a reputation. I cannot get out of it.[17]

That he had been selected in such a way was a testament to the regard in which my father's abilities were held, but it was still unclear whether he had been handed a poisoned chalice.

The first duty of any officer taking up a senior staff appointment on foreign soil that has never been a battlefield on which British troops have fought is to brief himself thoroughly for the task. My father spoke Russian as well as the other Scandinavian and neighbouring European languages, had experience of command on the Western Front and had the reputation of being resourceful. But beyond that, he had to rely on suspect briefings and hearsay from War Office officials, who sat well back from the main theatre of operations in France and were only required to know that Archangel was the principal port of entry into Russia for weapons and supplies being shipped out to the Eastern Front.

There was no history of British Army exposure to Arctic fighting operations. In fact, the sixteenth-century merchant adventurers trading out of London into Muscovy were probably far better briefed about the hazards of the White Sea than the twentieth-century staff in Whitehall. Nevertheless, my father sought to make the best of things, and spent a frantic few days briefing himself as best he could about what to expect in Archangel and making sure that he obtained all the cold weather clothing that he could lay his hands on for life in the Arctic Circle.

My mother and grandmother both came to London to see him off and to enjoy themselves briefly shopping and going to the theatre. Before finally departing from London, he visited the Canadian Headquarters off Regent Street and arranged for his Russian-born groom, Piskoff, to be posted to XVI Brigade, Canadian Field Artillery, which was to form part of the reinforcement being sent out to North Russia. Two Canadian intelligence officers were also posted to his staff, as was another familiar face in the shape of my future father-in-law, who by this stage in the war had obtained a further promotion to lieutenant colonel.

During his briefing sessions, he was told by Director of Military Operations, Percy Radcliffe, whom he knew well from Radcliffe's previous posting as Chief of Staff to the Canadian Corps, what the main purpose of the British presence in North Russia was:

> Radcliffe says that our job is to stop the Germans from reaching Murmansk and Archangel and then establishing submarine bases. The origin of the Force was to collect any Russians who were ready to join us and oppose the Germans, because the Kerensky Government has disappeared and the Soviets and Bolsheviks have made friends with the Germans & might even have invited the Germans up to Murmansk and Archangel if we hadn't gone there. No one seems to know what conditions are likely to be, except that it is dark & damned cold.[18]

On the evening of 25 September, the men who were going out to Russia with my father all assembled at King's Cross Station to entrain for Dundee. They made a varied and multinational contingent, with Canadian and French artillerymen, 'bearded Russian officers in khaki jackets and baggy light blue britches with broad red stripes down their sides', more French soldiers from the colonial infantry, and assorted liaison officers and Allied representatives, including the incongruous figure of 'a Japanese colonel in a blue braided jacket, trailing a long sword behind his small figure'. My mother accompanied him to the station, both aware that this could represent a long separation, but with my father by his own admission also looking forward to a new adventure and having 'already quite forgotten my disappointment at being reverted to the Staff'.[19]

During the First World War, shipping movements posting the departure dates for the Arctic Circle ports were high on the list of closely guarded secrets. The loss of Lord Kitchener on his ill-fated mission to Russia, drowned when HMS *Hampshire* was mined off the Orkneys, was a grim reminder to my father and all those with him on board the SS *Stephen* of the real danger from German U-boats operating in the North Sea, as they left the port of Dundee on their four-day passage to Archangel on 26 September 1918.

6

Polar Mission

The roots of Bolshevism, which lay in the disorderly growth of revolutionary sentiments across the ranks of the underprivileged Russian majority, were first expressed at the Second Congress of the Russian Social Democratic Labour Party held in Brussels and London in 1903. It was from there that Lenin developed the doctrines of Bolshevism, breaking away from more moderate Social Revolutionaries.

The moment of truth for the Allies did not come until well after Lenin had arrived in Petrograd in April 1917, in the wake of the February Revolution, where the Provisional Government had been vacillating between parliamentary rule and dictatorship while the old Imperial Russian Army largely fell apart with much political unrest amongst the demoralised troops. Having returned to Russia with German aid, Lenin was able to capitalise on the situation in Petrograd to launch the October Revolution and establish Bolshevik control over the organs of government.

Decrees to resume peaceful diplomatic relations with other nations, abolish private ownership of land and introduce worker control into industry were swiftly issued. In due course, this policy would lead to the Brest-Litovsk settlement with Germany which would allow the Central Powers to redeploy their forces from the Eastern to the Western Front, the consequences of which we have seen in the previous chapter. Meanwhile, as unrest spread and a variety of local flashpoints brought about an onset of fighting, Russia began to descend into civil war. Bolshevism has come and gone, but its history remains, and my father lived and worked under its pervasive and proletarian shadows for a whole year, providing a shield for Social Revolutionary reform in North Russia.

The port and town of Archangel – Russian Arkhangelsk – has long been a centre of trade with Britain and the maritime nations of northern Europe. Indeed, as an Old Tonbridgian, my father must have known that he was travelling in the wake of the school's founder, Sir Andrew Judde, who had been one of the Tudor merchants responsible for helping open the port to western trade. In both world wars, Archangel and its northern but ice-free neighbour Murmansk were vital conduits for supplies being sent to Russia by her allies.

In the post-Revolution chaos, it was feared that the Germans were planning to use Archangel as a submarine base, which would have been bad enough in itself but would have also meant the huge quantities of heavy munitions stored there falling into enemy hands. Accordingly, Archangel was occupied on 31 July 1918 by a British-led naval squadron under Rear Admiral T.W. Kemp, flying his flag in the cruiser HMS *Attentive* in company with the seaplane carrier HMS *Nairana* and the French cruiser *Amiral Aube*, each carrying a contingent of French infantry. In addition, there were 100 Royal Marines embarked on the French cruiser, and the squadron was also accompanied by a US patrol vessel.

In theory, this was a straightforward operation, but the shifting political situation in post-Revolution Russia meant that nothing was so simple. While the Allies were seeking to evict Bolshevik forces from Archangel, they were also reliant on Bolshevik assistance in resisting attack from the 55,000-strong German forces in Finland, who were then in the process of helping the Finns to win freedom from their Russian overlords. In effect, therefore, the Allies were simultaneously in league with the Bolsheviks in Murmansk while precipitating their flight out of Archangel.

This made it difficult for the War Office to find out exactly what was happening and conduct a successful campaign against an enemy in one place, who was simultaneously an ally elsewhere. Thus, Major General Frederick Poole, the RGA officer who had been in charge of shifting heavy munitions to the Russian Front, found himself being propelled out of an essentially administrative role into a fighting command for which he was totally unsuited. Poole's growing command, to which my father was appointed chief staff officer, was a decidedly multinational body, as had been apparent from the mixed collection of reinforcing troops who travelled out on the SS *Stephen*.

Poole, as senior officer present, was required to command the coalition forces and stand alone in an uncongenial and desolate foreign region at a time when public feeling in Britain was running strongly against the government prolonging hostilities by incurring further open-ended expenditure on sending more troops overseas to battle with Bolshevism. In sending my father out to stiffen Poole's resolve and provide him with someone who could provide both administrative and operational assistance, the War Office no doubt hoped to facilitate the main objective of providing a peacekeeping force in North Russia throughout the winter, so that a White Russian force could be trained to take over this duty in 1919.

When my father was briefed at the War Office, it was made clear that he was to prepare for a winter campaign, but that the ultimate goal was to hand over to local troops as soon as possible. In working towards this objective, my father had the facility of speaking the principal languages of the participating Allied nations fluently and was acceptable to their various governments; he was also, of course, fluent in Russian. He had established an excellent and widely recognised battlefield reputation for himself and any hesitation about his being given command from the outset likely arose from his age and seniority by comparison with any of the other possible candidates for the post. Whether there was an expectation all along that he would, in due course, succeed to the command cannot be proven, although I strongly suspect this to be the case, but as BGGS there was never any doubt that he would have to play a significant role in all aspects of the Allied operations.

After the flight of the Bolsheviks from Archangel in July 1918 following the arrival of Allied forces, the undercurrents of revolt still swirled around the mixed society populating the town and, with so many pockets of political reform trying to make their voices heard across the Russian heartlands, it was natural enough for the motors of revolution to be working overtime to pick up support wherever they could find it. In the main, the Bolsheviks were taking the lead and keeping it by various ways and means in most of the districts where they were waving the Red Flag. In Archangel, however, those countries who had most to gain from keeping a presence in the area maintained diplomatic contacts with the politically moderate Provisional Government in North Russia. These nations included Great Britain, France, USA, Italy, Serbia, China and Japan, and had been largely responsible for winning over local opinion in support of the Provisional Government and hastening the Bolshevik exit from the town.

Unfortunately, the members of the Provisional Government became the target of a *coup d'état* by elements whose leanings and loyalties were still tsarist. It happened on the night of 5 September 1918, when they kidnapped President Tchaikovsky and his Cabinet and had them impounded in the monastery on Solevetsky Island in the middle of the White Sea. Major General Poole was forced by the ambassadors to have them released, but the whole affair had left a dirty mark on his authority, as it emerged that the plot had been engineered by Captain George Chaplin, a Russian naval officer who had been attached to Poole's staff. My father, learning on his arrival of the failed coup, believed that this more than anything had served to sour relations between the various factions and interests operating within Archangel.

Also prior to my father's arrival, open hostilities between the Allies and the Bolsheviks had commenced in earnest when elements of the 6th Royal Marine Light Infantry had come under fire while attempting to secure communications between Archangel and Murmansk. What was worse, after two actions in which a number of the battalion's senior officers were killed or wounded, a mutiny took place in which a whole company refused to take part in further attacks. Heavy sentences were passed against its ringleaders, only to later be reduced by the authorities at home. In all respects – the political infighting, the mixed military fortunes and the clear evidence of demoralisation and war-weariness amongst the Allied troops – the events of August and September 1918 would set the tone for the course of things after my father's arrival.

The four-day voyage of the SS *Stephen* to Archangel was uneventful, giving my father time to measure up some of the people who would be serving with him in North Russia. Being the senior officer aboard, he invited his French counterpart, Major Lucas, who expected to be appointed Governor of Archangel, to sit at his table.

When the ship dropped anchor on 1 October, he was immediately taken to meet Poole at the latter's headquarters, situated in one of the merchant's houses on the Troitsky Prospekt:

> His first conversations with me was cordial, though one could see that he hadn't asked for me to come out & it was evident that he had not the slightest idea of the value of a Staff. I don't suppose he has ever used one. I told him that I had been ordered to report on the situation and that I should naturally do so through him. He smiled and said, 'All I ask you is to be kind to my present staff, who have done me very well'. I didn't hesitate to let him know that the War Office was distinctly uneasy about the situation. Poole pooh-poohed the whole thing and kept saying 'We're as right as anything here'. He explained to me that he was more of a swash-buckler than a soldier. He certainly isn't a trained soldier.[1]

Trained or not, Poole was able to give my father a briefing on the local situation that was rather more thorough and up to date than anything that he had been given in London. In basic terms, the situation stood as follows. The Dvina, Onega, Pinega and Vaga Rivers determined the bounds of the Allied presence around Archangel, embracing a population of some 40,000, which was seen as an adequate recruiting base for White – that is, anti-Bolshevik – Russian forces. In due course, it might be sensible for the Allies to push southwards in company with Russian troops, before the Bolsheviks got there, provided they could protect their rear as they advanced. The main axes of advance to the south were along the Dvina, or overland by way of the railway line to Volgda and points south. As well as a scratch force of British units, many of them formed from second-rate manpower sources and of which 2/10th Royal Scots formed the major element, the Allied troops included the French and Canadian forces that had come out with my father on the *Stephen* and an American contingent built around the 339th US Infantry, along with an attached battalion of engineers.

Having brought himself up to date with the situation, my father promptly set about his new duties. In case anybody had failed to get the message that their new BGGS meant business, he made certain that his stamp of authority was quickly and firmly impressed on all commanders by crossing the river to see Brigadier General Robert Gordon-Finlayson at his headquarters in Isa Gorka. He found his colleague 'trying to run a small force up the Dwina [sic] a distance of one hundred and fifty miles and a force up the Rly 100 miles away'. This was clearly

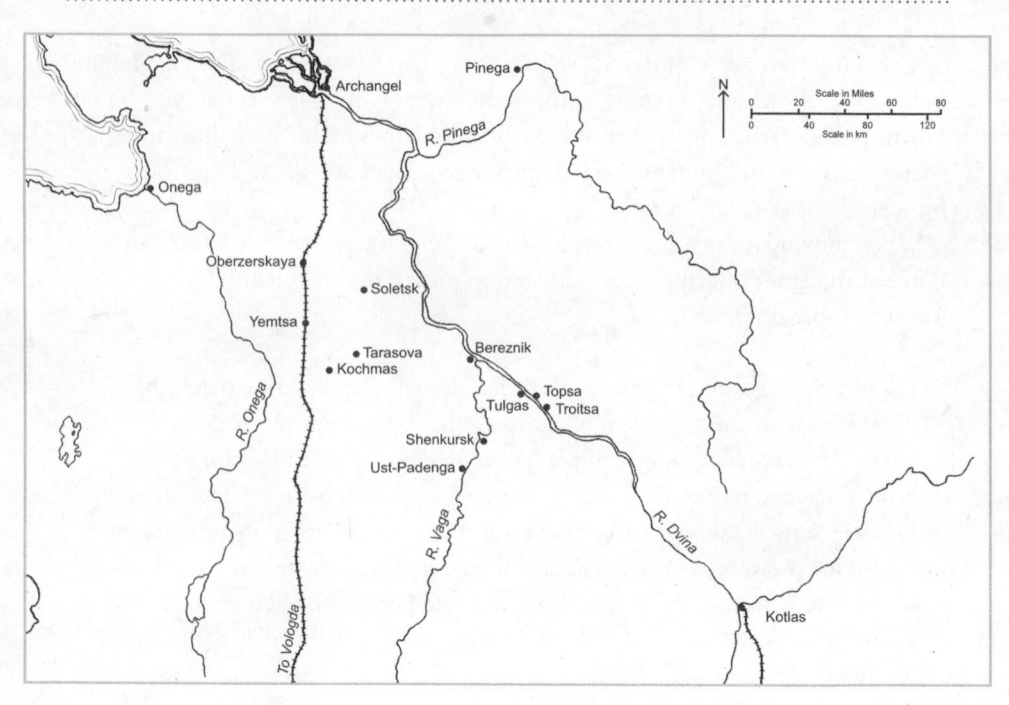

North Russia.

too much for one man to co-ordinate and my father told him so, remarking nevertheless that he 'had to be very careful not to create trouble, as he is the same rank as I am, though I am senior to him actually'.[2] Although my father had to tread carefully, recognising that as BGGS he had no direct-command responsibility, he was nevertheless able to persuade Gordon-Finlayson, who was an old friend and another former artilleryman, to concentrate his attentions on the Dvina front while my father took direct responsibility for the fighting along the line of the railway.

New orders were drafted that limited Gordon-Finlayson from advancing beyond his winter positions and ordered him to have all his stores sent up by river to Bereznik. Having agreed the delineation of the commands, my father set off for Oberzerskaya on 4 October to see the railway front defences and to assure himself that the best mix of coalition columns and commanders was in place to preserve morale and fighting efficiency throughout the darkness and intense cold of the winter months.

The British Government was responsible for administration and the commanders of all the national contingents were committed to putting Allied interests before their own, leaving the diplomats to resolve any differences which stood in the way of furthering the aims and objectives of the expeditionary force. However, as precedence habitually played a part in the diplomatic arena, there was always the possibility that petty grievances might be aired to gain national advantage, as in the case of the Italian ambassador, who felt affronted at the lack of respect being shown to his country even though there were only twenty-five Italian soldiers in the expeditionary force. It therefore behove my father to develop a good relationship with the diplomats of all nations, although he naturally began by introducing himself to Sir Francis Lindley, who was the Foreign Office representative and who chaired the local council of ministers:

> He is a gentleman at least and I gather is not very much in love with Poole who has been fighting with him. He impressed upon one how important it was for the soldiers not to mix themselves up in politics and then poured the whole story of the landing out to me. Poole has always set himself up as a kind of arch-dictator, above all the ambassadors and rightly or wrongly is under suspicion of having interfered with the general policy of the Allied Nations.[3]

My father felt able to confide in Lindley his fears that Poole was too political a soldier to be effective, but also stated that once Poole had returned from the impending leave that was due to him he, my father, expected to depart rather than remain in Russia under a commander for whom he did not care. Lindley's French counterpart, M. Noullens, also brought up the matter of Poole's impending leave, congratulating my father at having been appointed to replace him. My father stated that this was not so, only to receive a cryptic reply from the Frenchman, who perhaps knew more than he was letting on. At all events, the courtesy that my father had shown to Major Lucas on the voyage out was repaid by good initial relations with the French.

On 6 October, Major General Poole received permission to travel back to England and leave my father in command, although he did not sail home until the 14th on board HMS *Attentive*. In the interim, a curious limbo prevailed, with my father bemoaning that he was 'hopelessly hampered by not being in charge of this show. Poole moons around doing nothing and agrees to everything I say.'[4] The departure of the cruiser that would take Poole home was part of a general withdrawal by the naval forces operating in the White Sea, which would have become icebound had they remained much longer in the area. However, the departure of the shallow-draught monitors, whose heavy guns had been providing much-needed fire support up the Dvina, placed the troops in that sector at an even greater disadvantage and, notwithstanding Gordon-Finlayson's desire for continued offensive operations, eventually necessitated a withdrawal.

Only after Poole's departure could my father take stock and properly grasp the reins of command, something that came as a definite relief:

> I was glad to see him go, as I am now in command, though temporarily. I at least have the full authority which I didn't have before. His last words were that he would be back in a month. I can hardly fancy myself in his position nipping off like that when there is serious fighting going on. He simply doesn't understand

that it is all serious. He smiles, & I can't make out whether his mind is a blank or too lazy to work.[5]

However, the supposedly temporary nature of his command meant that my father had some difficulty exerting his authority. Gordon-Finlayson, under pressure on the Dvina, had requested reinforcements. There had been stiff fighting on both banks of the river in which the British and US troops had done well, but my father nevertheless felt that his subordinate had brought his predicament upon himself and was, therefore, not entirely sympathetic:

> He is now reaping the result of his thoughtless advance. There are no more troops. I have told London that I must have some more and they have told Murmansk that they must be supplied from there. Maynard won't like that. He has already shown restlessness at being placed under me even temporarily. I must see that I don't create a spirit of trouble by being too drastic after Poole's departure. Everybody thinks he has gone for good.[6]

Nevertheless, although my father did his best to tread carefully, it became apparent that the view that Poole was not coming back, and that my father would be permanently appointed to the command, was more widely held than he had assumed. Four days after Poole's departure came another meeting with Sir Francis Lindley:

> Lindley tells me quite openly that he has wired to the Foreign Office, asking that Poole shall not return. I discussed the matter quite openly with him and I find that Poole was even more disliked by the Diplomatic Corps than I thought. He was always interfering in politics. I told him that Poole was hopeless as a soldier. I don't know what will come of it.[7]

It was not until 19 October, however, that my father formally received notice that Poole would not be returning, and that he was himself appointed to the command with the temporary rank of major general.

Being sealed in to Archangel for the winter, with few of the regular comforts and amusements normally expected by servicemen, was an exercise of mind over body for most of the troops and their officers, but more a test of will for my father, upon whose shoulders the success or failure of the expedition rested. During the five months of constant sub-zero cold and Arctic twilight, he clocked up more than 1,500 miles of sleigh riding through the roadless forests, survived an assassination attempt, personally suppressed mutinies in the ranks of the British, French and Russian troops, and continued to engage the Bolsheviks as and when he could.

With the exception of Brigadier General Henry Needham, the chief administrative officer, and Lieutenant Colonel Morgan-Grenville, he had to place his trust in a staff that was entirely inherited from Poole. Almost all the officers at his headquarters were untrained for the work of supporting fighting forces in the field and he frequently found himself carrying out staff duties himself to ensure that his objectives were achieved. Nevertheless, as things settled down he quickly established himself in his new role, his authority unquestioned now that his promotion had come through, and after a month he was able to tell his friend Christopher Stone that he was having 'a most happy time in my first actual command'. In the same letter, he noted that he had learned a lot from Cecil Pereira during his service under him in 2nd Division, but went on to conclude that, everything considered, things had worked out better for him than if he had remained on the Western Front. 'I really am more lucky than at having got a division in France as I may get a chance of doing things here and the great time is to be the cock on the dunghill, however small a dunghill it maybe [sic].'[8]

My father felt that it was essential for him to inspect the various sectors that came under his command and now that he had full authority the way was clear for him to inspect all the battlefronts in person. His first trip was made to Oberzerskaya with the intention of making his presence felt in the isolated columns under the overall command of the Frenchman Lucas, whose performance had not measured up to my father's initial good opinion of him. These expeditions were effective insofar as their primary purpose was concerned, but his absences from Archangel caused some upset, as he recorded in his diary after returning from one of his early trips:

> I arrived back to find some wild excitements. They haven't yet got used to my departures to see the columns. The Diplomats have been particularly bad and have given the staff not a minute's rest asking what has happened to me and had I been lost and when was I coming back. It shows really that I have them in the hollow of my hand and they won't dare to make any trouble if things become serious. [...] I cannot get a decent ADC amongst all this crowd. I must have someone to go about with me on these journeys in the winter, but I must have a boy who will do the work and who will also have a stout heart. I have a sort of Orderly officer called Meise, a Russian of German extraction who speaks French and English.[9]

Meise he later characterised as 'useless', and a drunkard to boot, so that the problem of finding a worthwhile aide remained.

To obtain better speed, he utilised one of the light country sleighs for his travels, without a hood, and had it harnessed with a horse team rather than a single pony. Hay for the horses was stowed under the sleigh and this also provided some insulation, and blankets and sleeping bags were liberally employed. However, my father's substantial frame caused some difficulties, with an NCO who served under him later recalling that 'he required two ordinary sleeping bags sewn up to make one which would accommodate him'.[10] The question of personal protection on these sleigh rides was always a worry for those he was visiting, but he preferred to travel anonymously.

Initially he was only accompanied on these trips by the groom, Piskoff, but soon also acquired a second assistant:

> I had a most delightful boy called Constantine driving my sleigh. He came from somewhere down on the Dvina and had been up since the beginning of the snow. He was always roaring with laughter and singing away to his pony. When we had come back in to Seletskoe again he asked me if I were the Commandant on the railway and would I give him work. I gave him my name on a bit of paper and told him to call on me in Archangel and I would make him my sleigh driver in the town with a pair of ponies. He had a bright red face and looked more like a Scandinavian than a Russian.[11]

My father thought no more of this meeting but then, just before Christmas, he was surprised by an old peasant with a long beard, who came to see him with Constantine:

> I had forgotten all about it, but the father has brought the boy in. Dressed in all sorts of funny old sheepskin coats and tattered *valenkis*. The father is a fairly well-to-do peasant in the Kholmogori district and has three boys. This is the middle one. I asked the boy if he wanted to stay and take service in the Mess and he said yes. I explained that he would have to join up in the Slavo-British Legion and do what he was told. His name is Constantine Ossipov. I gave the father some tobacco and he trekked off again leaving Constantine in the hands of [Sergeant] Harrison to train. Both father and son seemed quite calm about it and the tobacco seemed to console him for the loss of the boy who must be about seventeen. I have told Harrison to get him washed and clothed.[12]

This was the opening of a long engagement in service by Constantine, who soon acquired the nickname of 'Kosti', but the new servant proved his worth almost immediately when he helped foil an attempt on his new master's life. As my father laconically recorded on 25 January 1919, 'to add to my troubles they tried to assassinate me today'. He went on to explain what had happened:

> I was walking down to the office with Kosti following me when a man ran out of a side-street and opened [fire] on me with an automatic pistol. As usual I couldn't get at my own pistol if I actually had it. I ran on and dodged a bit and really didn't

know what to do. What can one do? It would have been stupid to sit down and wait to be hit. Luckily, Kosti kept his head and actually shot the man before he had let off more than five shots. Really providential as he is only a boy & only had a revolver for a few days. The man actually hit me in the clothes with three bullets though he never touched me. What is one to do? One cannot always lark about with an escort & if a man really wished to assassinate one, he would do it, escort or no escort. Kosti is frightfully pleased with himself. He certainly is a good boy & I shall stick to him now & take him away from Russia when I go. A damnable experience. I am glad to say that I don't feel upset in any way. It all sums up that the Russians are combining. I still have a good deal of the winter with which to compete.[13]

The cold affected every aspect of living, working and fighting. If the ice prevented the use of monitors and gunboats on the Dvina, it did not prevent either side from using the air, provided they had serviceable machines and pilots to fly them. Allied forces amounted to three Slavo-British squadrons manned by a mixture of Russian pilots and attached officers from the newly constituted RAF. Operating from their bases at Oberzerskaya, Bereznik and Bakaritsa, the enemy that they feared the most was not the Bolsheviks but the cold.

My father had great admiration for the pilots serving under his command, and for the mechanics who kept the aircraft serviceable in all weathers. By contrast, it was widely believed that Russian officers flying for the Bolsheviks lived in greater fear of losing their wives and children, who were being held as hostages for their good behaviour, than of the enemy or the elements. Many of the RAF pilots and officers were from the Dominions and the commanding officer was Lieutenant Colonel Kenneth van du Spuy, who later became a major general and led the South African Military Mission to Britain in 1939. During his service in North Russia, van du Spuy was taken prisoner by the Bolsheviks after a crash landing near Bereznik and only released in 1920.

My father's comments on aviation matters show a considerable degree of mechanical understanding beyond the superficial knowledge required of a theatre commander which, although perhaps natural for someone with his technical mindset, prefigured a lengthy and informed involvement in military aviation that would continue for the remainder of his career.

Cameras, bombsights and radio communications were rudimentary and phosphor bombs were unsuccessfully used in attempts to start forest fires to burn the Bolsheviks out of their strongholds. Air Gunners had to fire machine-gun bursts every few minutes to prevent the oil freezing in the mechanisms and putting their guns out of action. As there was little wind at Archangel during the summer months and never from the north, the 'M' Type gas bombs, designed for ground use, could not be used effectively against the Bolshevik positions, so my father arranged for 2,000 of them to be adapted for air drops. On striking, the bombs emitted a dense cloud of smoke, but as the vapour condensed in the deep cold of winter, they could not be used in those conditions and he reserved them for use as a final *bonne bouche* for the Bolsheviks when he withdrew during the summer months.[14]

Despite the problems caused by the climate, my father remained active and was able to continue to exert his authority over his disparate and widespread command. With the backing of the Diplomatic Corps, and with delegated authority to oversee the reform of the White forces, his personal authority in preserving the military of power in favour of the Allies in North Russia was conclusive. By having his train and his sleds on call he had no trouble in reaching the outposts and did so frequently to exercise his control over the columns in the field and to keep up their morale.

When morale faltered or there was trouble, he was there to restore order and, if necessary, to discipline the culprits, whatever their nationality. The most serious incident occurred on 11 December, following his written orders to General Marushevsky, commanding the anti-Bolshevik forces, to send the first batch of his newly mobilised troops to the front to take over a section of the line. Marushevsky, who my father had entertained to dinner the night before but who he found 'a funny little man' and 'quite impossible' to work with, predicted that trouble would ensue, but my father deemed it better to force the issue there and then, to which the Russian commander agreed.[15] My father then recorded what happened on the 11th, which he characterised as 'a long, but not happy day':

> The Coy. of the 1st Archangel Regiment was to have paraded for me at 11 a.m., but at 10 a.m. I was told that the whole of the men in the Alexander Nevski Barracks, some 2,000, had refused to come out to parade and had shut all the doors & that Red Flags were waving everywhere. I ordered the town to be quartered and the Barracks to be surrounded which was done in a few minutes. I then went up to the street leading towards the barracks and found Marushevsky rushing about shouting to burn the barracks down. I seized him and explained that I wanted the men and that it could only be a few ringleaders who had led away the vast majority of the boys who had been mobilised. As he wouldn't keep quiet I sent him into a house near and went down to the scene of action. The great long white building was full of men & any number of Red flags were hanging out & a desultory fire going on the direction of our MG School some hundreds of yards away. The whole place was surrounded by piquets behind houses at an average distance of 200 yards. Everybody was under cover and very few civilians anywhere. The British Colonel in charge of the Alexander Nevski area came up and reported saying that all the Russians were in the building and that none of the Russian officers had been harmed in any way. I told the Colonel to get a Lewis gun into action against a window and then to summon the men to come out.

The Lewis gun started on the window & fired some five bursts, breaking it up altogether. The only result was that there was a good deal more spasmodic firing in every direction and a good many many more Red flags shown. I remember wondering how it was that they had so many pieces of red cloth all ready for the occasion and considered whether they came from petticoats. I then ordered up the young Russian officer class of Stokes mortars and ordered them to fire a couple of rounds at the Alexander Nevski Barracks from behind one of the new huts. The first round went too far and, as we found out later, burst on the stones in the quadrangle in the centre. The noise was deafening. The second round landed on top of the flat roof about the centre and burst with a terrific crash. Before a third could be fired, the door burst open and the men came tearing out with their hands over their heads and shouting that they surrendered. As if by magic, the Red flags fell from the windows and the shooting ceased. I really couldn't help laughing at the hopeless imbecility of their mutiny. In a most orderly fashion, they then fell in without arms by companies and were then formed in close order on the grass parade ground in front of the barracks. I shouted for the ringleaders of the mutiny to fall out and about 13 or 14 men fell out. When I asked if there were any more, all the 13 shouted out together that there were not, which was repeated by the others. It was really all most weird.[16]

It would seem, in fact, that a little more persuasion was needed than my father here admits for, as British eyewitness CSM Frederick Neesham recorded, there was no initial response when my father asked for the ringleaders to step forward, whereupon 'he ordered every tenth man to step forward and told them that they would be shot if they didn't hand over the guilty ones. They talked, and thirteen men were rounded up.'[17] As Neesham's account confirms and, indeed, as my father makes clear in his diary, the guilty men were shot that afternoon following a trial by their own officers.

However, when he published his account of his Russian adventures in 1953, my father stated that he had the sentences commuted and that the men were later released: this was not the case, and it is as well to set the record straight. At the time, certainly my father had no doubt that the response had been the correct one, being 'quite sure that the 13 men I shot were really guilty' and that, since the ringleaders were all mature men, 'the example to the recruits was salutary'.[18]

M. Noullens, the French ambassador, congratulated him as being responsible for being the first person to successfully quell a mutiny since the Revolution.

In addition to the thirteen men who were shot, it was found that one civilian agitator had been killed by the mortar fire; a subsequent crackdown on civilians found around the barracks area brought in a number of other Bolshevik agents. Meanwhile, after being given a day to cool off, during which no further mutinous activity took place, the Russians were sent by train to the front, being informed that they would receive their arms back when they reached the lines and warned that any further misconduct would be met with the utmost severity.

The need for the Russians and any other reinforcements that could be sent up, including a Polish detachment, was due to the worsening conditions on the Dvina, where the Bolshevik Sixth Red Army under General N.N. Kuzmin had mounted an offensive. Unbeknownst to my father, Kuzmin had fewer troops than he did – notwithstanding its grandiose name, Kuzmin's command was more like an under-strength division – but the Bolsheviks were a homogenous force rather than the ragtag mixture at my father's disposal, and they could concentrate their forces to attack, whereas my father's command was strung out in an extensive cordon, trying to block all the various axes of advance.

The Bolshevik offensive on the Dvina was held off only after considerable fighting in which 2/10th Royal Scots were distinguished, as were the Canadian Gunners, but it was clear that more could be expected from the same quarter once the enemy had regrouped. The shortage of effective commanders for the dispersed Allied forces became even more acute when Lieutenant Colonel Morgan-Grenville was obliged to report himself sick: my father had pulled him from his staff duties to act as a column commander, but his health had broken down under the strain and he had to go home.

Nevertheless, my father was still able to derive some amusement from the situation and from his allies, pasting Marushevsky's following General Order into his diary in full:

Order No 100 to the Forces of the Northern Region at Archangel
27th December 1918

Madame Botchkareva arrived from Shenkursk and reported to me on 26th December. She wore officers' uniform of a Caucasian pattern with officers' shoulder straps and was accompanied by Lieutenant Filipov, whom she called her Adjutant. Madame Botchkareva offered me her services in regard to organisation of the Russian Army.

I do not undertake to estimate the merits of Madame Botchkareva in respect of formation of the Russian Army and I consider that her work for her country and the shedding of her blood will be finally appreciated by the Central Government and Russian history.

I only consider it my duty to declare that within the limits of the Northern Region, thank God, the time has already come for quiet creative Government work and I think that the summoning of women for military duties, which are not appropriate to their sex, would be a heavy reproach and disgraceful stain on the whole population of the Northern Region.

I order that Madame Botchkareva will take off her uniform and that Lieutenant Filipov will immediately report to the Administration of the Commander of

Forces for registration and be detailed for duties or to the reserve for work in accordance with his rank and calling.

The carrying out of this order is placed under the supervision of the Town Commandant and a copy of this order is to be sent to the Government Commissionary under my order as General Governor, that he is also to take part in the carrying out of the above.[19]

This lady warrior had previously commanded the infamous 1st Women's Battalion, but Marushevsky evidently had no time for her services. That his allies could devote such attention to trivialities was a real trial for my father, and it was impossible for him to take Marushevsky and his colleagues seriously: as he noted in his diary below the pasted extract, 'they really are too funny for anything'.

Funny or not, the White forces around Archangel were growing steadily in numbers. By 31 December 1918, 4,358 men had been mobilised for service in Archangel, and by the end of January this had increased to 5,878, of whom 2,500 were doing duty with various columns at the fronts. This was all to the good, for events in Britain meant that there was now little hope of reinforcements from home even when the ice lifted in the spring.

London was the scene of action for British soldiers seeking demobilisation, and protesters could be seen crowding into Whitehall to call for their peace dividend, but little of this news reached the shores of the White Sea at Archangel and then only infrequently by way of the Samoyed-led sleigh runs from Murmansk. As there was no direct line of communication with Major General Alfred Knox, the liaison officer with the White Russian Government in Siberia led by Admiral Kolchak, any news from the rest of Russia only reached my father after it had been suitably edited by the War Office. As my father saw it, and as he explained it to the representatives of the Provisional Government, there was no opportunity to mount a counter-offensive against the Bolsheviks, but the Allies should hold their ground and use the winter months to build up a credible force ready for operations in the spring. He continued to assume that the Bolsheviks had more troops than they did, but he was correct in the belief that White forces would continue to expand: by the end of February, there were 11,750 of them on the rolls.

All fronts were being subjected to desultory shelling, and patrol encounters were frequent. My father had identified the Dvina front as the most important sector, and troops there were relieved at regular intervals. However, the sector lacked a Regular commander due to the departure, on health grounds, of Gordon-Finlayson. As a temporary measure, Colonel Sharman of the Canadian Field Artillery had the command, but my father wanted a permanent replacement and set his eye on Gordon-Finlayson's former staff officer, Colonel C.A.L. Graham. However, Graham was currently commanding at Shenkursk on the Vaga, where an advanced post had been set up and expanded into a sizeable base. Due to its exposed location, however, the post became a major target for Bolshevik attacks, and my father decided to make a visit in person and assess the situation on both fronts.

Sharman on the Dvina reported that the level of shelling had increased but that he did not anticipate a major attack, and that he also doubted that Shenkursk was at risk. However, after spending the night at the headquarters of the American detachment in this sector, my father found that Piskoff and another of his entourage had spent the night sleeping outside his door as bodyguards. Their contact with the locals had informed them that there had been much talk of getting rid of the foreigners – hence their immediate concern for my father's safety – and that a major attack against Shenkursk was imminent.

My father accordingly set off to visit Graham's command and see for himself whether a viable defence of the outpost on the Vaga was possible. His major concern was that should the Bolsheviks succeed in turning the flanks of the Allied positions there, Graham and his troops were likely to be cut off and my father left with the onus of mounting a relief expedition. Such was his shortage of effective troops and commanders that he doubted such an expedition would be viable and the Shenkursk garrison, if surrounded, would likely fall. This, of course, was an unacceptable risk.

On the other hand, as my father discovered when he arrived at Shenkursk, the 400 local conscripts who had been undergoing training there were all in good spirits and close to being ready for deployment to active duty. To pull out now, at the mere rumour of an attack, would likely have a bad effect on their morale and undo much of the good work that had been done in training them. My father therefore decided to leave Graham to hold Shenkursk for the moment, but with discretionary orders to evacuate if attacked. He then returned to Sharman's headquarters at Bereznik and left him with orders to be prepared to aid Graham if the latter was attacked.

As he later admitted in his memoir of the campaign, the desire to stay at Shenkursk, share the dangers of his subordinates and control operations himself was strong. But as the commander of the whole theatre, he had to remain at a remove from the individual fronts and delegate responsibility to the commanders on the spot. His recognition of this, and his exercise of the self-discipline necessary to act against his natural instinct, marks an important point in his development from a fighting soldier into a commander.

Piskoff's intelligence was correct, and a major Bolshevik attack was indeed in preparation. On the morning of 19 January, multiple columns advanced both directly along the line of the Vaga, where they drove in the outpost at Ust-Padenga, and through the snow-covered country to either side of the river, where their skirmishers adopted white camouflage to better infiltrate the Allied positions. US infantry under Captain Odgaard inflicted a severe check on the attackers, who were stopped by machine gun and rifle fire, but the steady Bolshevik pressure forced

Graham to plan for a retreat, which was managed by steadily pulling detachments out of the fighting to maintain the line of escape northwards along the river.

On the night of 24–25 January, the evacuation of both troops and civilian refugees was set in motion. There were substantial desertions from the Shenkursk Battalion, which my father was forced to admit was only natural when the men were being asked to leave their wives and families behind to the mercy of the Bolsheviks, but otherwise the retreat was made in good order. It was doubtless with much relief that he was able to record in his diary entry for 26 January:

> Graham is safely out and his casualties have been about one hundred, including a Captain in the Canadian Artillery, who can ill be spared. Sharman has practically collapsed under the strain & I propose to put Graham in charge & one of the new Lt. Colonels I have will be put in charge of the Vaga. Graham reports that the Bolsheviks came on very well and lost between four hundred and five hundred. They attacked over the snow in white coats & looked very weird, almost as if they were gliding. Think if they had had skis! I should have been back with the remainder of my men in the inner defences.[20]

Graham's good service in extricating his command from this trap increased his standing in my father's eyes and confirmed him for the command on the Dvina, but in making the appointment my father also recorded his concern over the way in which the operational situation was developing:

> I have managed to keep things going for 3 months [of] winter and have another 3 to go. The Shenkursk business is evidently the beginning of the Bolsheviks' winter effort. They have proved themselves better than we are at carrying out an offensive & have surprised me with their growing efficiency.[21]

However, the evacuation of Shenkursk did mean that the Allied positions on the Dvina and Vaga were now much closer together and able to offer mutual support. Patrols from both commands could link up with each other, and thus a loose cordon was maintained between the two defensive positions which would hopefully prevent an enemy thrust isolating the one from the other.

Nevertheless, the Bolshevik pressure was maintained all along the outposts and my father had to continue to juggle his available forces to meet the potential threats. What was more, he now did so in the knowledge that new priorities at home meant that he was to plan for an evacuation during the summer of 1919, pending the successful handover to White forces. In order to facilitate this withdrawal and handover, fresh troops would be sent out from home in the form of the North Russia Relief Force, comprising several brigades of volunteer troops who would cover the evacuation.

War-weariness was not just confined to Britain and the other Allied powers were also making plans to withdraw their contingents. Accordingly, my father asked Sir Francis Lindley to let it be known amongst the Allied ambassadors that the Allied contingents could not be evacuated before May or June and that he expected by that time to have built up the anti-Bolshevik forces to 20,000 men who would be well armed, clothed and moderately well trained.

The training of the Russian levies was given an apparent boost by the arrival on 7 February of a new commander in the shape of General Yevgeny Miller. The selection of the Allied Council in Paris, Miller had begun the war as a staff officer and had risen to an army command at the time of the February Revolution. Attacked by his men after he tore red ribbons from their uniforms, he had been packed off to Rome as military attaché and thereby missed the October Revolution, something that had very likely saved his life. He was optimistic about the chances of defeating the Bolsheviks and he and my father were able, on the whole, to co-operate effectively, notwithstanding the fact that my father entertained significant doubts as to some of Miller's political views. In particular, my father felt that Miller was in error for not supporting the granting of autonomy, or even independence to minority national groups such as the Balts and Finns, in return for support against the Bolsheviks. Miller would continue in command of the anti-Bolshevik forces right up to the White collapse, whereupon he became a leading light of the Russian exile community in Paris. Sadly, however, he eventually fell victim to NKVD kidnappers in 1937, being smuggled back to Russia for trial and execution.

Playing the waiting game between himself and his staff, the War Office, General Miller and his own subordinate commanders, as well as with the forces of nature, exercised all my father's powers of authority and persuasion to keep the wheels of war spinning until the relief force arrived. War-weariness was spreading, and was particularly prevalent in some of the most recently arrived British battalions, which had been formed from decidedly mixed manpower sources.

Matters came to a head in the ranks of the 13th Green Howards and my father, who had already faced down a mutiny amongst the Russian levies, now found himself face to face with one from his own British troops. The battalion, commanded by Lieutenant Colonel H.E. Lavie, who was on secondment from the Durham Light Infantry, had initially been posted to Murmansk, and had been brought down overland to reinforce my father's command. This journey, during the middle of winter, had been extremely taxing and brought to the surface internal problems caused by the fact that the unit, though nominally a Yorkshire battalion, had been made up to strength with men drafted from anywhere that they could be found.

My father's initial impression of the battalion had nevertheless been good, and they were ordered into the line near Selestkoe to relieve some of the US Infantry. However, on 26 February, elements of the battalion refused to march out when ordered to do so and Lieutenant Colonel Lavie was confronted by two sergeants who informed him that the battalion would do no more fighting. Keeping his nerve, the CO had the two men placed under close arrest, so that when my father arrived the following day the crisis had passed and the battalion had taken its place in the line. The sergeants were tried by court martial and sentenced to death. My father noted that the two men had been transferred from the Pay Corps and had not seen action prior to this point; he also recorded that the sentences were later commuted to life imprisonment.[22]

Notwithstanding the rapid quelling of the mutiny in the Green Howards, the threat soon spread and elements of both the French and US contingents also showed signs of unrest, up to and including men refusing to obey orders. It was clear that the long winter had taken its toll and the arrival of the relief force was of the utmost importance. The collapse in Allied morale also indicated better than anything how futile it would have been to attempt to continue operations beyond the already agreed withdrawal date. Quite simply, such political will as remained for a crusade against Bolshevism did not extend down anywhere near as far as the men who would have to carry it out.

With time dragging, my father found himself counting the days until the spring thaw which would, he knew, temporarily bring all active operations to a standstill. The increase in the number of effective White forces also enabled him to hand over responsibility for the Pinega front to the Russians, although their first independent operations in this sector did not meet with a deal of success. It did, however, further permit the concentration of the other Allied forces along the southern axes of approach to Archangel. The only problem sector that remained was along the line of the Vologda railway, where the senior French officer, Lucas, had failed to live up to the promise that my father had initially detected in him. Operations under his command did not go well, but my father was spared the diplomatic difficulty of relieving him when the Frenchman was obliged to report himself sick with frostbite after being left out in the open for twenty-four hours following a Bolshevik ambush. Sadly, his replacement, Major Aarchen, proved to be just as unsatisfactory. Thus, with continued alarums and excursions but no major change to the operational situation, did matters continue until the thaw finally brought about a temporary halt to the fighting.

7

Spring Relief, Autumn Homecoming

The spring thaw, which brought with it the promise of reinforcements, allowed both a breathing space and an opportunity to reassess Allied strategy. This revealed two, apparently mutually exclusive, priorities. On the one hand, all the non-Russian forces were slated for withdrawal before the ice closed in again; on the other, major offensive operations were necessary if the forces operating out of Archangel were to effect a junction with those operating in Siberia under Admiral Kolchak.

On 25 April, my father received a detailed appraisal of the situation as understood by the War Office, delivered to him in person by his new BGGS, Frederick Walshe, who had travelled out via Murmansk and arrived at Archangel overland. The appraisal did not make for happy reading, as it related the withdrawal of Allied forces from the Black Sea ports and the removal from the scene of the Czech Legion previously operating in Siberia, which it had been hoped would form a part of any future Allied operations. From Russian sources, my father knew that Kolchak's offensive in the south had failed, but that some progress had been made in the north. Planning therefore now focused on an advance up the Dvina to Kotlas, thence continuing southwards by way of the railway line from that place, but all this was conditional on Kolchak's troops being able to continue their offensive. My father made his plans, allowing that the Allied troops might be used to break the Bolshevik lines but that any further exploitation would necessarily be left to Miller and his Russians, and these were sent to the War Office for approval.

Meanwhile, after the ice on the lower Dvina had been dynamited to open up the waterway, Archangel was again opened to access by sea and the way was clear for the first elements of the relief force – 238th Special Brigade under the command of Brigadier General George Grogan – to join my father's command. He was on hand on 27 May to greet the new arrivals, who were given the traditional Russian welcome with bread and salt by the Mayor of Archangel:

> Grogan, I found a funny little round-faced man with chubby cheeks. He was probably a little bit older than I was, I thought. A good many orders on his chest, including the VC. His Brigade Major also had the VC, and one of his Colonels, Sherwood Kelly, also a VC. Curious that they put a non-regular like that into the

command of a Regular Bn. Little Grogan said that his men were young regulars, all very keen, but not too well trained. The number of VCs almost makes one think they painted too vivid a picture of all the dangers in the Arctic North.[1]

The brigade comprised two infantry battalions, 2nd Hampshire Regiment and 1st Oxfordshire & Buckinghamshire Light Infantry, plus a signals detachment and a battery of Mountain Artillery. At my father's insistence, the formation was henceforth referred to not by its number but as Grogan's Brigade.

It was, unfortunately, not long before my father began to detect a problem with the commander of the 2nd Hampshires, Lieutenant Colonel John Sherwood Kelly. Born in South Africa in the same year as my father, Kelly had begun his military career as a 16-year-old volunteer in Matabeleland and had later served with the Cape Mounted Police during the Boer War and the 1906 Zulu Rebellion. He obtained a commission in the Territorial Force and served throughout the First World War, both at Gallipoli, where he won the DSO, and on the Western Front, where he won the VC at Cambrai while commanding 1st Royal Inniskilling Fusiliers. My father's first impression of him was not good, although it was also somewhat inaccurate:

[A] great big Irishman. Must be somewhere about 50 I fancy. Enlisted as a Pte and got his VC at Gallipoli for bomb throwing, I think. He is a fine looking man, but uneducated & I should say the worst possible man to put in charge of a Regular Bn.[2]

The following day, he went on to record a further 'disillusionment' with the South African:

One saw at once that he had no pretensions to being a gentleman and that his sole claim to be a Lt. Colonel was his energy & bravery. I sent down a message to say that I should look at the Bn. in fatigue dress just outside their barracks & was met by Kelly who threw a devil of a salute and then stood behind me whilst I spoke to the Bn. I told the men what Bolshevism meant to the world and why they had been sent out to North Russia. All the time I was speaking Kelly was applauding audibly with 'Good, that's the stuff to give them', 'That's what they want' until I turned round and told him to be quiet.

After I had spoken to the officers I went off to my car & as I had asked Kelly to lunch I offered him a lift. When we had gone a little way down the Troitsky Prospekt Kelly espied a platoon of his men in fatigue dress going down to bathe with towels in their hands. He seized the handle of the door & shouted to the chauffeur to stop & then jumped out & damned the Corporal in charge for allowing the men to smoke in the street. I really didn't know what to do I was so annoyed. As a matter of fact I told Grogan afterwards of the whole affair and said that he must speak to him. A man so unbalanced as Kelly was not fit to command a Bn. and that Regular soldiers were not to be treated in that way. I was for turning him off at once, but Grogan begged for a reprieve which I reluctantly gave, chiefly because I found that the 2nd in Command of the Hants had been a prisoner all the war & really didn't know what war was like.

A man like Kelly may be all very well in trench warfare where he is close under the eye of the Brigadier and where all the administration is done for him in the Brigade, but he can't be any good here despite the VC.[3]

The whole incident caused my father to reflect on the effect that a high award for gallantry could have on one's career, remarking that:

We are a curious people. If one of our officers gets a VC, he is made for life. The gaining of a VC depends upon many chances and in most cases merely denotes that a recipient is a very brave man. With us, as often as not, he is promoted to high rank as a result of the VC & in most cases proves himself to be quite useless as a Commander or as a Staff officer. I presume that Stewart, the American Colonel, is much about the same. He has no attributes which make him a Colonel and yet his Congressional Medal has brought the rank to him.[4]

George E. Stewart, the commander of the 339th US Infantry and senior US officer under my father over the previous winter, had won the Congressional Medal of Honor as a junior officer in the Philippine–American War, having previously been commissioned from the ranks. He had failed to co-operate effectively with my father, much to the annoyance of the latter, although this was in no small part down to extremely restrictive orders from Washington that limited the role of his troops. Insofar as Kelly was concerned, Grogan's intervention had won him a reprieve, but my father clearly considered him a marked character from hence forward and was on the alert for any further displays of military inadequacy.

Following the disembarkation of Grogan's men, the next contingent of reinforcements arrived a little over a week later in the form of a brigade under the command of Brigadier General Lionel Warren de Vere Sadleir-Jackson. A former cavalryman, the new brigadier was known to my father from when the two men had served together as brigade majors in South Africa, but he was amused to note that his scruffy opposite number from Potchefstroom was now a smartly attired *beau idéal* of military tailoring.

Sadleir-Jackson's command was formed of hostilities-only personnel, including a sizeable Australian contingent, who had volunteered to extend their service and go to Russia for which purpose they had been organised as the 45th and 46th Battalions of the Royal Fusiliers and the 201st Machine Gun Battalion. There was also a similar range of supporting units as had been sent with Grogan. The brigade lacked an official number, but it was in any case immediately incorporated into the enlarged Dvina Force, where it was earmarked to play a leading role in the projected offensive. First, however, my father had first to clarify the nature of Sadleir-Jackson's appointment:

> He seemed to have an idea that he was commanding the North Russian Relief Force, something quite separate from anything else and that he was in a sense relieving me. I disabused him of that at once and told him that unless I had an undertaking from him that I should have no more trouble I should send him home there and then. This he gave me after a little thought. He is a great dandy, with curled hair and moustache but he is certainly a driver of men and knows his own mind. I think he must have got a swollen head in some way or other and, being theatrical he liked to make a show. He is a regular leader of men of the Murat type – vain and intemperate, but full of courage and energy. His two Colonels are both Dominion men and their men are all good & fit and above all are volunteers for the job they are doing. All my staff are in a deal of a rage with S-J for his airs and graces and I expect that he treated them in an off-hand way. I have had some difficulty in calming them down and have pointed out that they must put up with any insult rather than stop the show from running. I have promised that I shall deal with him properly but that I must have time to deal with him in my own way. I propose to put him in to do the fighting and I must humour him a little in consequence.[5]

As well as humouring the man on whom he would have to rely to command the offensive, my father had to humour the men who would be obliged to pick it up once Sadleir-Jackson's men had broken the Bolshevik lines. To try and give the Russian levies a sense of achievement, he ordered Dyer's Battalion in the Slavo-British Legion to parade for the King's birthday on 1 June and for inspection by General Miller, combined with the presentation of colours and blessing by the priests. Miller was apparently impressed but it left my father wondering what would become of these men after the Allied withdrawal:

> I can't help feeling that this half-hearted espousal of the White Russian cause is wrong. Either we should do the thing thoroughly or not at all. We cannot do the thing properly as the country is against it. Thus, all we are doing is making the Bolshevik movement a national movement, which it was not before. The resistance of Bolshevism is certainly hardening. We cannot hope for much. Up here the peasants have never seen Bolshevism in operation or they would rise up and put it down. They simply don't care and you cannot do anything with a nation that doesn't care.
>
> I shall be able to get Dyer's Bn. up country very shortly and I must put them with a British Regt. for training.[6]

Unfortunately, it would soon become apparent that General Miller's confidence in Dyer's men had been misplaced, and that my father's concerns about the strengthening Bolshevik hold over Russia were all too prescient.

As he dealt with new men and new problems, many of the units that had been the mainstay of my father's command over the winter months were preparing to depart. The French contingent had left and the Americans were preparing to go. Although my father had received a French decoration, he refused to recommend either of the French commanders, Lucas and Aarchen, for a British honour since he felt that neither deserved such an award. The American Colonel Stewart he dismissed in much the same way, but for the departure of the US troops it was not Stewart but his successor, the newly arrived Brigadier General Wilds P. Richardson, with whom my father had to deal.

The Americans wanted to use their departure as an occasion for self-congratulation and my father was railroaded into taking part. As my father had discovered when it became clear to what extent Colonel Stewart had been confined in his activities by orders from Washington, the USA under President Woodrow Wilson was not inclined to become involved in the Russian intervention, even as they were sending troops to Archangel. With no prospect of democracy in sight, they were perhaps guided more by the articles in the treaty of 6 July 1918 between the Murmansk Soviet and the representatives of Great Britain, France and the United States: in particular, Articles 7 to 14, which catered for the supply of food for the whole population of the region, together with free importation of manufactured goods and which, in US eyes, made no distinction between true Russian citizens and Bolsheviks.

On the day that the US contingent embarked from Point Economy, my father inspected them and addressed them from a platform specially set up by Brigadier General Richardson. My father delivered the speech as required, managing to steer a fine line between acknowledging the harsh climatic conditions under which the Americans had served but not going so far as to give direct praise for, as he wrote, 'it is so very difficult to say that you are pleased when you are not. Luckily I was able to confine myself to those who have given their lives, and after all a man cannot give more than that.'[7] Although he had a low opinion of the US officer corps generally, when he came to write his Russian memoirs later in life he acknowledged that he had made friends from amongst their numbers and found praise for the brave Captain Odgaard who had helped hold off the Bolsheviks long enough for Graham to complete the evacuation of Shenkursk back in January.

On the other hand, my father had nothing but praise for the men of 2/10th Royal Scots when their turn came to embark a few days later. Whereas the US troops who had – in my father's eyes, at least – done so little were all of first-class physique, the Scottish battalion had been formed almost entirely from Category C men who were never intended for active service and had yet fought hard and well throughout the winter:

> The Royal Scots have come down to Archangel and I had a parade to say goodbye. They have improved out of all knowledge. Early in October 1918 they were a measly lot of devils with no physique. Many of them had been rejected from other units and all of them had defects of sorts physically. Over 30% of them wore glasses and one of the first things that I had to do was to see that these glasses were all covered up with felt or leather in order to prevent the metal causing frostbite. What an administrative complication! Who would have thought of choosing only men without glasses? The physical health of the men has improved 50% all round. Those that have survived – and there has been little sickness – go back very much better men than they came. The Colonel, Skiel, is a schoolmaster from Glasgow with an accent you can cut with a knife. I was able to say how pleased I had been and how I could tell them that they had done their duty well under very difficult conditions. They gave me three very hearty cheers and I am sure they leave the country with a good taste in their mouths.[8]

With the last of the departures overseen, it was now time to look in earnest at the possibilities for the offensive. However, this was not without its problems for the Dvina had fallen to its lowest level for fifty years and was only navigable with flat-bottomed boats. This curtailed the activities of the Royal Navy, whose river monitors had returned to support the troops now that the ice had melted. A constant watch had to be kept on the water levels, but, even so, two of the five monitors were eventually trapped by the falling waters at the time of the final evacuation and had to be scuttled to prevent them falling into enemy hands – such was the price paid by the flotilla for the close support it was able to afford the Allied troops.

My father's plans had been approved by the War Office, in no small part down to the endorsement given of him by Sir Francis Lindley, who gave it as his opinion to the prime minister and to Sir Henry Wilson (the CIGS) that my father was 'a man of sober sense and good judgement'. Lloyd George was particularly concerned by my father having in one telegram discussed the circumstances in which it might be necessary for British troops to move south of Kotlas, and instructed Wilson to make two points quite clear when issuing instructions to my father:

> [F]irst, that under no circumstances whatever was he to get himself so embroiled that it would be necessary to send an expedition to pull him out, because no expedition would be sent; and secondly under no circumstances whatever was he to run any chance of not being able to withdraw the whole of his force anyway.[9]

Wilson assured Winston Churchill, secretary of state for war and a driving force behind the Russian intervention, that my father was fully aware of these restrictions but, in any case, sent a telegram reasserting them. All this left my father with some concerns as to whether it would be deemed appropriate for him to use the relief force troops in offensive operations, but felt that to do otherwise would be to place the evacuation at risk. What mattered most to my father was that every man under his command should be evacuated from the port in a safe and orderly manner, and this would not be possible if the Bolsheviks were able to press the Allied troops as they fell back.

In order to co-ordinate the offensive, my father made his way upriver along with his senior staff, so as to be better placed to respond to events. The main blow was still to be struck by Sadleir-Jackson's command, but my father authorised Graham, now a brigadier general and in command on the Dvina, to mount a preliminary attack 'to give S-J a good jump-off for his effort'.[10]

This attack was to be made by Lieutenant Colonel Kelly's 2nd Hampshires in conjunction with a Russian brigade under Colonel Prince Mourousi, and opened on 20 June. The objective was to take the high ground overlooking the Dvina around Troitsa, from where the Bolsheviks were using the vantage point to direct their long-range artillery fire. This attack was to be delivered by Mourousi's Russians, supported by the fire of the shallow-draught gunboats HMS *Cockchafer* and HMS *Glowworm* and by a supporting advance on the opposite bank of the river. Kelly, with two companies of his own battalion and a pair of light mountain howitzers, was to make a more circuitous advance to arrive in the rear of the Bolshevik positions at the same time as the main attack went home.

The Russian part of the operation went off without a hitch, with the 3rd North Russian Rifles under Colonel Voulichevitch storming the Bolshevik positions around Topsa, inflicting at least 100 casualties and taking around 500 prisoners. Although the attacking troops also incurred substantial losses this was, as my father was pleased to note, the first successful Russian offensive operation that he had witnessed since his arrival. Unfortunately, the operation was marred by the ineffective performance of Kelly's flanking attack, which caused my father to erupt with rage at what he perceived to be the cowardice of the battalion commander:

> Sherwood Kelly actually carried out the march and then, hearing nothing of the Russian attack, which in fact was some few minutes late, Kelly lost his head and thought he was surrounded. Although he had a telephone at the moment in touch with Graham's Headquarters he marched the 2 Coys. back again and took no part in the fight. The whole of the Bolshevik troops in the front area must have been in the bag had he waited there with nearly 400 Regular troops and 2 mountain guns. The 2nd in command of the Hants was a poor miserable creature who had been a prisoner since the early days of the war and who knew

nothing of war and who had not the guts to protest. I believe that the Regt. was furious.

I landed and interviewed Grogan who had also heard the details & then I sent for Kelly. I gave him hell for twenty minutes and brought tears to his eyes. Weakly, I gave in to the supplications of Grogan and did not take the Bn. out of the line there and then. One could see plainly that the man had lost his nerve beyond recall and I should have sent him down country at once. Grogan seems to have a fellow VC feeling for Kelly. When once his courage had gone, Kelly was quite useless.[11]

This would not be the end of my father's trouble with Kelly but, considering that Kelly had proven himself to be an argumentative, outspoken and awkward character with little time for any of his superiors, the fact that Grogan still elected to defend him does suggest that there was more to the failure of the Hampshires' attack than my father had assumed.

Kelly had been extremely active in conducting reconnaissance operations ahead of the attack and may well have been exhausted when he led the operation; the fact that my father had believed him to be around 50 when they met, when the two men were in fact of an age, does suggest that he was not in the best state of physical fitness and this is hardly to be wondered at when one considers the number of wounds that he had incurred during the previous five years. An error of judgement under such circumstances is more understandable than cowardice and explains, even if it does not excuse, Kelly's incorrect decision. That said, Kelly himself did not believe that he had acted wrongly, citing difficult terrain, lack of communications and heavier than anticipated Bolshevik resistance to justify his withdrawal.

The rights and the wrongs of the matter can be argued at great length, but so far as his future was concerned Kelly most certainly did not help himself in his post-battle insistence to Graham that he had been 'shamefully let down', nor his direct refusal to renew the attack at Graham's request – particularly if he did indeed cast aspersions on Graham's and my father's military capabilities in the process, as the latter was later informed had been the case. Kelly also made it plain that he considered it his primary duty to bring his battalion home with the minimum of casualties, believing that the mission on which they had been sent – that is to say, the whole operation to assist the White Russians, not just the advance on Troitsa – was a fool's errand.[12] So far as my father was concerned, Kelly had now had two reprieves and he had no intention of allowing him a third.

Notwithstanding that one of the reasons for the strong resistance at Troitsa had been the warning given by one of Mourousi's men who had deserted to the Bolsheviks, the success of the 3rd North Russian Rifles encouraged my father to press on with his plans for bringing more of these regiments into the front line. As he was dependent on the Russian successes at the front for his own disengagement plans, this move was essential in any case, and he still strongly believed that a successful offensive on the Dvina would completely break up the Bolshevik lines in that sector and buy at least a two-month window in which the evacuation could then proceed unmolested. Whether anything more than that was possible, however, remained open to question.

In public, for Russian consumption, he remained positive but, in private, he entertained strong doubts as to the viability of Allied grand strategy even as he continued to brief his key subordinates on their roles in its implementation:

> I have told S-J that we intend to advance to Kotlas and join up with the Siberians, but I really have little hope of doing this now. I cannot go and put my head right into the middle of Russia with no prospect of the movement becoming a national one. It isn't national and there is no use trying to hide the fact. I have no real idea that we will get to Kotlas, but I think it good for the Russians to begin to think of an offensive.[13]

After the position had been secured, patrols were able to push up the Dvina for some 10 miles beyond Troitsa without meeting significant resistance: a further advance of any sort proved impossible until the river had been cleared of mines.

In the event, although the minesweeping was eventually completed after much hard and risky work by the officers and men of the Dvina flotilla, Troitsa would prove to be the high-water mark of the advance. On 1 July, a new strategic appreciation reached my father from the War Office in which the real situation on the Siberian front was at last fully revealed. As much through incompetence and infighting as through Bolshevik action, Kolchak's forces were in disarray and in no fit state to carry out an offensive. Indeed, their right wing, far from being in a position to link up with my father and Miller at Kotlas, was 'carrying out a slow retirement almost without resisting'.[14]

My father's fears had been realised, but he resolved to keep the news secret for the moment while he flew to Archangel to confer with Miller. The latter, naturally enough, was despondent at the changed situation and hoped to persuade my father to allow some British troops to remain behind as volunteers to continue the fight; this my father could of course not permit, and from now on his sole priority became the successful extrication of his British troops.

As if to underline the unrealistic expectations that had underpinned the now aborted Kotlas offensive, on 7 July a mutiny took place in Dyer's Battalion in the Slavo-British Legion in which five of the unit's British officers were murdered and around 100 men successfully went over to the Bolsheviks. This was one of the units that would have been responsible for supporting Sadleir-Jackson in the main offensive, and was the same battalion in which General Miller had expressed such confidence when he and my father had reviewed it back at Archangel in the spring.

With such troops in support, it is hard to see how any drive on Kotlas could have succeeded, even if there had been any Siberians there to link up with.

Following the mutiny in Dyer's Battalion, another more general mutiny took place in the Russian forces on the Onega front in which, again, a number of men were able to go over to the Bolsheviks after murdering their officers, while others simply took advantage of the confusion to desert. This confirmed my father in his desire to complete the evacuation as swiftly as could be managed, and a new plan was developed in which Sadleir-Jackson would make a spoiling attack on the Dvina front to buy time for Miller to establish his forces in the positions around Bereznik that had been held over the winter. This would then enable the British forces to withdraw on Archangel and embark.

My father delegated full tactical command of this operation to Sadleir-Jackson, who opened his attack on 10 August and comprehensively defeated the Bolshevik forces, inflicting some 3,000 casualties for the loss of only 145 of his own men. Sadleir-Jackson would ultimately be rewarded for his services with a Mention in Despatches and a brevet colonelcy, while the gallantry shown in the attack would see two of his men receive the VC. My father, however, had been singled out for an honour even before this attack put the seal on his successful execution of the campaign.

On 1 August, a day which would bring more than its share of surprising news, a telegram was received from the secretary of state for war informing him that he was to receive a knighthood:

> It really came as the most wonderful surprise. In my wildest dreams I should never have thought of such a thing. I wonder if they have even given such an honour to a mere Major before. Winston Churchill is responsible for it all. The wire he sent to me announcing the fact was curious and also very characteristic:
>
> 'On my recommendation, His Majesty has been graciously pleased to create you a Knight Commander of the Bath.'
>
> I was really so astonished that I could hardly believe it and it really came to me as the most wonderful surprise. The first thing that struck me was that I could hardly go back to Regtl. duty, as I can imagine what a nuisance I should be in a Bde of Artillery.[15]

That Churchill, who would remain a leading figure in government for much of the next decade, had noticed my father and singled him out for attention was an important development that would pay dividends for my father in the years to come. In the meantime, as if news of his knighthood was not enough, the same day brought notification from the War Office that General Sir Henry Rawlinson, erstwhile commander of Fourth Army on the Western Front, was coming out to

North Russia to co-ordinate the withdrawal. It was, however, made clear to my father that the appointment of 'Rawly' in his place was no reflection on him or his powers of command and was simply because the War Office could not any longer control things directly from Whitehall and wanted to have someone on the spot.

Notwithstanding his being superseded in command, my father would remain at Archangel as GOC, taking day-to-day charge while Rawlinson, whose command also extended over Maynard's troops at Murmansk, co-ordinated the evacuation. The new commander left Newcastle on 4 August on board HMT *Czaritsa*, accompanied by a huge staff, something that struck my father as an unnecessary luxury. He also had his doubts over the sort of briefing that Rawlinson would have received, and speculated that he would have to 'try and get out of the officers if I know any of them what the War Office actually said about things when they were called for'.[16]

Although he had his doubts over Rawlinson's staff, he had no reservations about serving under so distinguished an officer and, indeed, recognised the advantages inherent in having a commander of unquestionable seniority to co-ordinate the Murmansk and Archangel forces:

> One or two of my people have been inclined to say to me that it is a shame to send Rawly out at the last minute to get all the credit, but I do not look on it in that way at all. I think that he will save me a great deal in negotiations with the Russians and I certainly do not want to fall into any squabbles with our sick friend Maynard. Maynard is my senior and I could not have been put over his head. Personally, I am looking forward very much to seeing Rawly, whose reputation I have heard discussed so often. Now I shall know him and I hope that our relations will be happy.[17]

As a result of getting to know Rawlinson in Russia, they both corresponded regularly until the former's death in 1925 while serving as C-in-C India. Meanwhile, nothing interrupted my father's plans for the withdrawal, which remained unaltered.

The *Czaritsa* reached the harbour bar on 11 August and he immediately presented himself on board, finding Rawlinson:

> [F]ull of life with a sort of twinkle in his eye. He has a jumpy sort of way of talking, but is quite at home with everybody at once. He took me warmly by the hand, standing with his feet well apart and his head slightly drawn back. He congratulated me on what we had done and said he quite understood the situation. He was smiling and cheery all the time. [...] I took Rawly ashore and then brought General Miller to my office to be introduced. The talk had to be in English, as Rawly's French was too horrible. I was astounded to find that a man

of his education could not speak French better. However, whenever Miller failed, he gave me a French or Russian word and I explained. Rawly informed Miller that he had come out to superintend the withdrawal of the British. I think Miller had been hoping against hope that it might be possible to retain us here. Rawly put it very clearly to Miller, so that there could not be a shadow of doubt. Miller said that he had decided to hold on to Archangel after we had gone.[18]

After overcoming the major hurdle of establishing a working relationship with Miller and achieving an agreement on the terms under which the evacuation would be carried out and stores transferred to Russian control, Rawlinson accompanied my father on an inspection tour of the Dvina front before leaving for Murmansk. My father, therefore, oversaw the final evacuation as GOC Archangel and all was successfully managed on the Dvina front where Sadleir-Jackson was able to disengage and fall back with minimal casualties: the only major loss, as already noted, was of the two monitors that were trapped in the river by the low water.

On the railway front, however, there was a final contretemps in which Lieutenant Colonel Kelly, who had been transferred there after incurring my father's displeasure at Troitsa, finally pushed his luck too far and found himself relieved of command. The issue this time was over the gas bombs, which it was proposed to use as part of a major raid scheduled for 17 August. Kelly protested the whole operation – not just the use of gas which, as it turned out, was not possible due to the wind conditions – and was relieved on the spot by the local commander, Brigadier General John Turner, and sent down to Archangel. There, after interviews with my father and Rawlinson, Kelly found himself unceremoniously ordered home. Unfortunately, this was not the end of the story and Kelly's attempts to redress his perceived grievances would cause my father further upset and embarrassment.

On his return to Britain, Kelly wrote several letters to protest about the conduct of operations. These were published by the *Daily Express*, which used them to mount a stinging indictment of Churchill's policy towards Russia. This landed him in front of a court martial, but his stance won considerable support from a war-weary public. Certainly, notwithstanding speeches made by Churchill in the Commons and by my father to the assembled troops as they prepared to take ship from Archangel, it was hard to disguise the fact that intervention in Russia had indeed failed to do anything to set back the spread of Bolshevism and that the dissatisfaction that Kelly had voiced was shared by at least some of the officers and men under my father's command. Furthermore, when Kelly's trial took place his plea for mitigation consisted largely of an attempt to defend himself against the damning report that my father had penned concerning his fitness to command a battalion.[19]

Even if a defence can be offered with respect to Kelly's conduct at Troitsa, it is evident from his other escapades and outbursts that my father had correctly judged Kelly's fitness for his post, and no doubt he bitterly regretted not having relieved him earlier when he had the chance. It is tempting, too, to think that my father's own adroit use of contacts with the press in years to come stemmed from the lessons of this incident. Earlier he had written to Christopher Stone, protesting that the latter had used information from private letters as the basis of journalistic articles, telling him:

> I had no intention that you should write articles about what I write to you. I merely send them to you as I know you are interested & because we were such good friends in France. I am not for publicity, so if you do write anything, hide it up without names.[20]

As his career progressed, however, he would use his connections with Stone to far better effect.

If the Kelly affair highlighted the strategic futility of Britain's attempt to aid the anti-Bolshevik forces, it is nevertheless difficult to question my father's handling of the Archangel front at an operational level, and this solid performance was maintained right up until the end, with Brigadier General Needham, the chief administrative officer, working tirelessly to oversee the details of the evacuation.

On 22 September, my father dined General Miller at his house and drank his health silently, wishing him success. Sadleir-Jackson came back into Archangel on the 23rd, and everything in the town became weirdly quiet with the men back in their barracks by 22.00. As the transport ships went down the channel, Rear Admiral Sir John Green, commanding the White Sea flotilla, had armed sailors standing by the pilots on the bridges in case they suddenly refused their services, but my father had ensured that the men were paid double rates which he felt was more important than any other inducements. Some 6,000 Russians who had been accepted as refugees embarked along with the troops, covered by the newly arrived 2nd Highland Light Infantry, sent down by Rawlinson from Murmansk. By evening on 26 September, with nothing more to do in his office, he finally cleared out his desk and, after checking with intelligence that the coast was clear, he waited until 18.00 and then went to dine with the admiral, without whose effective co-operation he readily acknowledged the evacuation could never have been so well conducted.

There can be no better description of his feelings at the end of a crucial year in his career than that contained in his diary entry on his last day in North Russia, at the end of a campaign that had marked him down as someone who had more to offer than just command capability. My father was aboard the admiral's yacht, on which he was allowed to hoist the C-in-C's flag for the final time:

Miller has ordered people to keep in their homes until the afternoon. I should have said quite unnecessary.

We had a certain amount of trouble with Sadleir-Jackson and Altham up river. They spent so long monkeying around saluting each other and making ceremonious visits of goodbye that the Admiral tickled them up with a couple of messages. I think he was quite glad to come & see them go past us and salute all correct. All in complete silence.

At noon exactly Miller came down in a motor-car with his ADC and stayed a few minutes. He had tears in his eyes as he took me by the hand for the last time and I can hardly blame him.

Not a sign of man woman or child in the street.

The tugs came up and delivered one man picked up on the quay at Bakaritsa and went off again. The report of this man was most amusing. He was seen sitting quite alone on an officer's kit in the middle of the great quay and when hailed he replied: 'Beg pardon Sir, but I am Mr Snodgrass's servant and he told me to wait here.' We laughed to think that the British Tommy hadn't altered and also that the name of Snodgrass still existed. I thought that it had become historical long ago.

Off we went about 12:30 p.m. the last in the long line. Not a sign of life anywhere. All past the empty timber factories and fishing boats and then to the rendezvous just as it was beginning to get dusk.

I took many a look back and saw the golden church towers shining in the sun & thought of the day a year ago all but two days when I came out and saw them in the morning sun. There didn't seem quite the same sign of life. One felt older somehow or other.

A launch came alongside the Admiral's Yacht and I said goodbye before going down the rickety rope ladder into the swaying launch. As I stepped on board the little Admiral shouted out for three cheers and the sailors gave us a good send-off. And so to the troopship and away.[21]

There is a rather impressionistic, almost lyrical, quality to my father's closing observations, quite unlike his usual matter-of-fact recording. Undoubtedly, his experiences in Russia were an important part of his life, furthering his career but also clearly impacting upon him on a personal level. Of his two Russian companions, the groom Piskoff had left along with the rest of the Canadian troops, but Kosti remained with him until the end and chose to accompany him to England and remain in his service out of a desire to see the world.

My father had some initial reservations about assuming what was, in effect, full charge of a youth of 17, remarking that 'he might turn to the bottle or any other kind of iniquity and I should be responsible for him'.[22] In due course, however, he agreed to take him and was rewarded with two decades of loyal service, following which Kosti, now a British subject, enlisted in the Royal Tank Corps during the

Second World War and finished that conflict as an intelligence officer in Berlin. As my father justly recorded in his Russian memoir, 'A more level-headed, loyal and dependable man I have never met'.[23]

Saying farewell to Russia, however, also meant facing an uncertain future back home, and as the convoy made its way out of the White Sea my father's thoughts not unnaturally turned to his potential prospects:

> Everything seems so quiet on board and I am not in command of the ship, so that I have no responsibility at all. I try to analyse my feelings a little and I think that I am a little sorry that is all over. I am glad to be rid of the responsibility for a bit, but I am rather dreading unemployment.
>
> What an extraordinary difference in my prospects during the last year! I can hardly believe it even now as I look back on it all. If they promote me a pukka Major General [that is to say, permanent rank] I shall have made almost a record for quick promotion. I can hardly hope that they will and yet I have commanded an independent Army in the field. If this Archangel campaign had come at a time when there was no other war going on, what an excitement it would have created. Now it has actually passed by with little comment except from a small section of the public which has steadily tried to stop the whole thing. When I think of the number of times that I have been laughed at in my service for working, it makes me feel that I ought to bless the Scots spirit that was bred in me and forced me to go on. I did prepare myself for my chance and I managed to take it when it came. I also had the luck never to be knocked out badly in the war. That kept me going strong. So many people got to the top of the ladder, only to be hit and knocked down to the bottom again. Even if they lost their health and went to England they were forgotten and the war went so fast that they were out of it all in six months and had to learn new tricks instead of the old ones.
>
> Peace soldiering will be pretty boring if one has to deal with routine. There is nothing I like better than dealing with men, but I really could not stay slinging ink around in some office.[24]

There was also his home life to consider. After marrying him in 1915, my mother had spent most of her married life living with her mother in Cambridge. Although she had contemplated making a trip to Archangel to be with my father, this had never come to fruition, but now at last there seemed to be an opportunity to pick up a proper married life. In one of his letters to Christopher Stone from Archangel, my father said:

> My wife tells me that she enjoyed herself immensely during May week, dancing round the clock for the whole week. I don't know whether she was pleased or otherwise when someone said to her unbelievably, 'How well your father is doing

in Russia.' I think she must have been going back to the days when her friends were undergraduates – though she is not very old even now. She has had a bad time of it all, for we have only been together for a few days in five years and I think women feel these things more than men. I often wonder how I shall find a married establishment suits me or rather how I shall suit it. I suppose it comes easily enough in the end.[25]

8

Temporary Commands

Upon his return to Britain, my father was left with little choice but to settle down to family life for the first time. As well as my mother, that family now also included my sister, Elspeth, born in 1917, and the three of them set up home in a rented furnished house at High Wycombe in Buckinghamshire. His rank as temporary major general was converted to a permanent appointment which was announced in the *London Gazette* of 3 February 1920, with seniority backdated to 11 November 1919; this was explicitly noted as recognising his services at Archangel, but it did not open the way to further active service. Indeed, it was made clear to my father by the military secretary, Lieutenant General Sir Philip Chetwode, that he could not expect a permanent appointment in his new rank for some time due to the great number of men who had received accelerated promotion to general rank during the late war, and for whom there were insufficient appointments in the reduced peacetime establishment. Nevertheless, Chetwode also informed him that he would be considered for temporary appointments that might arise due to particular circumstances, pending which he would, however, have to go on half pay. This he did, but even with the joys of his family to distract him and the opportunity to further improve his language skills, time at High Wycombe soon began to drag and he feared that his career, which had shown such promise, might yet stagnate.

In the event, however, he had no cause to worry, for the following years saw him undertake a series of overseas postings that kept him fully occupied up until 1922 when he received his first permanent appointment in his new rank. He wrote extensively about this time in the second volume of his memoirs, which I edited for publication after his death under the title *High Road to Command*. It would be impossible in the space that is available here to convey any more than a fraction of the experiences and insights that are contained within that book, and so rather than attempt to condense it all here I have chosen to focus in these chapters on those aspects that are most interesting, or that played a major part in my father's rise to higher things in the years that followed.

The first of these missions took my father to Hungary, where he was one of three representatives of the Allied Supreme Council tasked with overseeing the departure of Romanian troops from Hungarian soil. Romania, having backed the

Allies during the war, had already been granted a portion of Hungarian territory as part of the ongoing peace negotiations that sought to bring some order and a permanent settlement to the chaos that had been left by the collapse of the old Habsburg dual monarchy. However, Romanian troops had then advanced further into Hungary to help crush the Communist forces that had seized power there under Béla Kun: this had been achieved and a stable Hungarian Government was established under Admiral Miklós Horthy, who ruled under the title of regent. Although, as a successor state to one of the defeated Central Powers, Hungary could expect to be forced to accept territorial concessions as part of the peace settlement, there was now no longer a need to have foreign troops on her soil. The Romanians, however, were in no hurry to leave, which explained the need for my father and his colleagues to oversee their departure.

In fact, and in some part down to my father having had the sense to break his journey at Versailles and there obtain the co-operation of the Romanian Prime Minister Alexandru Vaida-Voevod, the mission was a success and the departure of the Romanian troops went off without a hitch. The trip was more remarkable for my father's adventurous overland journey, made in the company of Kosti and two recently demobilised ex-RAF drivers in a pair of second-rate ex-army cars. The journey was an eye-opener as to the state of post-war Europe, where currencies in the former Central Powers depreciated drastically even over the course of my father's trip.

His time in Hungary also gave my father a chance to visit the sites associated with the Hungarian exile of his supposed royal ancestors nine centuries previously, and to strike up an acquaintance with Regent Horthy. Of the latter, mocked by some as an admiral without a navy and a regent without a king, my father remarked that there were few men to whom he had ever taken a more immediate liking. He compared him to Jan Smuts, an honourable foe who had later become a friend of the British, and respected his attempts to restore order to his nation. He retained this view even after the Second World War, in which Horthy became an unwilling ally of the Third Reich and was eventually deposed in favour of a Nazi puppet.

The evacuation complete, my father travelled into Romania itself, where he was present in Bucharest when Vaida-Voevod and his government were dismissed and replaced by the military dictatorship under General Averescu and where he later enjoyed an audience with King Carol. His mission accomplished, he returned home by way of Italy, thence over the Alps and up through France where he took the time to revisit the battlefields of the Western Front.

Upon his return, my father was refused an audience with the foreign secretary, Lord Curzon, who did not wish to be distracted by a personal report, but it is evident that others in high office continued to appreciate his merits as it would not be long before he was again sent overseas. In the meantime, however, he was urged by many friends to consider leaving the army while he was still young enough to make a new career in civilian life. Surely, it was suggested to him, there would be no more active soldiering for him now that peace had been restored. Weighing things up, however, he reflected:

> [F]rom what I had seen in Eastern Europe I thought that the world was very far from being peaceful. Some of the offers of employment were tempting enough, but I always came back to the thought that I must be true to my salt. I loved the Army and had been very happy during my service in it. And how could I tell whether I should be happy in civilian life? I simply could not contemplate leaving the Army for good.[1]

After a pleasant late summer spent at High Wycombe with his family, my father found that his path to further active duty was being smoothed by Winston Churchill, who at this point still retained the twin portfolios of secretary of state for war and secretary of state for air. The two men dined together at Aldershot in July 1920 as guests of Lord Rawlinson, and Churchill commented at the time that although my father was still at the bottom of the list of major generals, the list was likely to soon become a lot shorter. Later that same month, my father was summoned to London in response to a request from General Sir George Milne, commanding British forces deployed around the Black Sea littoral, for 'a young fighting Major General' who was able to speak French.[2] My father was deemed to fit the bill and was asked if he was willing to go out to Constantinople. To this he readily agreed, not just for the chance of active employment but because he had a great deal of respect for Milne, who had commanded Salonika Army during the war, as a fellow Scot and a fellow Gunner. Although, as my father pointed out in his memoir, Milne was the only wartime army commander not to have received a peerage, he was nevertheless a man whose career was still in the ascendancy and, as it turned out, someone whose influence would cast a long shadow over the interwar British Army.

Prior to his departure, my father spent some time with the Intelligence Branch to bring himself up to date with events in Turkey, and had an interview with Prime Minister David Lloyd George, who he had not previously met and from whom he gained the impression that the government was taking a decidedly pro-Greek stance in the ongoing border dispute between that nation and Turkey. Greece naturally expected some rewards for having backed the winning side in the war, but her ambitions had rapidly grown out of control and there was a strong movement for the re-establishment of a Greek Empire that would encompass parts of Asia Minor.

Thus, although the British had, along with the French, supported the initial Greek landings at Smyrna in May 1919, they were in no way prepared to become involved in the further offensive operations that the Greeks were now undertaking, nor to enter into a full-scale war with the resurgent Turkish nationalist forces under

Mustafa Kemal. The main British priority was to secure the adaptation of the provisions of the Treaty of Sèvres, which would confirm the British and French mandates over the former Ottoman holdings in the Middle East as well as formalise the Greek seizure of Smyrna and the bulk of what remained of European Turkey including the Gallipoli Peninsula and the northern shores of the Sea of Marmora. In the interim, pending the signing of the treaty, British forces held a neutral zone centred on Constantinople and extending some way into the hinterland south of the Sea of Marmora.

When my father reached Constantinople, he was invited by Milne to stay at his home on the Bosphorus, which had once been occupied by Krupp. Milne's job required that he oversaw Britain's interests in the dismemberment of the Ottoman Empire, which meant that he spent most of his time eyeing intelligence sources and keeping on top of the French, whose primary purpose was seemingly to look after their own interests in Syria:

> I had known Milne before in France as the 4th Division, when I was next door on the GS [General Staff] of the 6th Division. He had [then] just been made a Major General. I found him looking much the same, though tired after his long campaigning in the Near and Middle East without leave. Thinner & greyer. The same eye-glass screwed into his one good eye. A type of East Coast Scot with a strong Aberdeenshire accent. He was nicknamed 'Bulldog' chiefly on account of his old-fashioned rugged face. He had a hard dour character which brought him into conflict at once with the French. [...] He could not speak a word of French and seemed to go quite crazy when he saw one.
>
> I found Milne's temper distinctly bad. The army was a one man show. He was secretive to the extreme & his staff knew little or nothing of his intentions. The staff was bad and acted in these difficult circumstances with little intelligence. All in watertight compartments.[3]

If he was to be judged by his temperament in Constantinople, then it can readily be appreciated why Milne had not been rewarded for his services to the nation, but keeping the realigned frontiers intact, though a trial at the time, proved in the long term to be a reward as it paved the way for 'Uncle George' to eventually climb to the top of the tree. Nevertheless, peacekeeping was a costly and unwanted burden for the Allied governments to bear just at a time when demobilisation was in full swing: all the powers were worn out from years of fighting, and the officers and men under Milne's command at Constantinople were for the most part serving out their time for pensions.

A substantial number of the field-rank officers were ex-prisoners of war, but Constantinople had been one of the few places where lack of fighting experience was not regarded as a drawback. Unfortunately, however, the growing Turkish nationalist movement was proving increasingly aggressive and was pushing back with force not only against the Greeks in Smyrna but against the British too. On 15 June, the British positions at Ismid came under heavy attack and a substantial number of casualties were inflicted. This led to concerns as to whether the town, situated at the head of the gulf of the same name, 60 miles east of Constantinople, could be held. If it could not, and Turkish nationalist forces were able to gain control of the Ismid Peninsula – bounded to its south by the eponymous Gulf, to its north by the Black Sea and to its west by the Bosphorus – it was feared that the British hold on Constantinople would become most precarious.

It was after the June attack incident that Sir George Milne had called for help from the War Office, and my father's new posting was to command the Ismid Force, composed of British and Indian troops. When my father appeared on the scene, Milne put his command yacht at his disposal to use as a mobile headquarters and gave him a free hand to take charge of the fighting in the Ismid sector. The troops at his disposal consisted of two infantry brigades under Brigadier Generals Emery and Montague-Bates, along with the 20th Hussars – who had on 13 July carried out what was arguably the last mounted charge ever conducted by British cavalry, during the defence of the Ismid perimeter against Turkish forces – and some detachments of artillery and engineers.

It seemed to my father that this was an unnecessarily large force, and he also had doubts about his two chief subordinates. Emery had been a senior captain in the Royal Artillery when my father was a subaltern, and had not aged well. Francis Montague-Bates was a younger, more active, officer, yet it was he who had been in command on the spot during the June fighting and so his record was to some extent tarnished in my father's eyes by his conduct then and since.

My father wasted no time in getting by train to Ismid and on arrival he took up residence in a commandeered Turkish palace. He immediately inspected the town and was amazed to find that a relatively small Turkish force had caused such disarray amongst the defenders:

The wretched Montague-Bates must have lost his head after this minor disaster, details of which I haven't heard, as he has now had an enormous wire fence round the town up in the hills and all the troops inside peering into the distance & not a sign of a damned Turk to be seen anywhere. No Intelligence outside & everybody expecting to be attacked at a moment's notice. A horrible position. Some 8,000 and some 300 possible Turks in front. I have rated them all. Poor Bates nearly had a fit when I ordered the Regts. to take down great bits in the wire and send out patrols. Day & night. I have seldom seen people more frightened of shadows than these. I have ordered a column of a Bn., a Bty. & the 20th Hussars squadron to go out for an outing tomorrow. How Milne, Wilson & Croker can have allowed a position like this to arise, I don't know. A Battleship standing by in the Gulf behind Ismid to fire over the wire. Maddening. All regular Bns. including the Gordons.[4]

My father did at least have some good staff officers to assist him, including Lavie of the DLI who had been with him in North Russia, but he noted a sense of déjà vu with respect to the attitudes surrounding him. To his way of thinking, operations at Ismid had been brought to a standstill by an almost total lack of direction:

> Over and over again do I find the same thing. If troops sit down and voluntarily give up the initiative, they lose their morale at once. You must always get them on the move and into action, but I suppose they all think that I'm mad.[5]

Accordingly, he personally set about shaking them out of their torpor. He had an airstrip constructed near the town, mechanised the Indian work parties, sent patrols across to the Black Sea coastline and arranged for Royal Navy launches to support operations along the River Sarkaria.

In restoring activity to his command, he was aided by an unexpected reinforcement in the shape of a Greek regiment, which arrived on 23 July:

> A Cretan Regt, of black avised Scoundrels. Well-dressed, but badly booted. The 16th Hellenic Regiment looks as if it could fight. I had to interview the Colonel in French, which he spoke very badly. Mad keen to get at the Turk & to obey any orders given by me. They had two or three Evzanoi trumpeters in their white kilts, who blew a salute for me and shouted '*Strategos*!' – the term for General.
>
> They go in to Ismid and are off across the Peninsula to Shilé tomorrow [24 July] with a squadron of 20th Hussars.[6]

This drive across the peninsula was the first of a series of sweeps against the Turkish forces, and was a marked success. However, the number of Greek troops in the area was growing and although the Greek commanders, like the colonel of the 16th, were keen for the British to fight alongside them long term, my father knew that this was not possible. Britain's sympathies might have been with the Greeks, but even had the political will remained the logistical means to support a sustained offensive by my father's troops or any other part of Milne's command simply did not exist.

As July turned to August and my father awaited a final decision as to what would become of his command, he found himself obliged to send Montague-Bates back to Constantinople after the brigadier staged an unauthorised sortie across the River Sarkaria to drive the Turks away from the Ismid perimeter. The brigadier had been sent out with a column of troops, but had failed to keep in active communication with my father at Ismid, who was at one point obliged to send out air patrols to establish just where Montague-Bates had got to. He recorded some sympathy with his errant subordinate, noting that when the force was broken up, Montague-Bates would revert to his substantive rank and be left commanding a company in his old regiment. It was therefore of little wonder that he sought to make the most of his temporary general rank when he had it, and one wonders too if there was a desire to make up for his perceived inadequacies during the operations prior to my father taking command.

There was a stormy interview when the column returned:

> I think he had some idea that he was being independent by not communicating with me. I had it out with him and explained what I wanted – and what I wanted was to be or else he would go elsewhere. I found him a little bit inclined to be truculent and refer to Milne & I put him right at once.[7]

My father also issued a rebuke to Montague-Bates' brigade major, but he felt that the underlying problem was the fact that the army was insufficiently used to mobile operations after so many years of trench warfare.

Shortly afterwards, Montague-Bates was sent down to Constantinople and Brigadier General H.A.V. Cummins arrived to take over 242nd Brigade in his stead. Cummins was a senior Indian Army officer for whom my father had little time, believing that the two years that he had spent in captivity after the fall of Kut had rendered him unfit for modern war (although it must be noted that he had done well during the June defence of Ismid when he had been in command of the 24th Punjabis). By then, however, a decision had finally been reached and the Allies were preparing to pull out. The French and Italians had already left, and the British Government was preparing to hand over Constantinople to the Greeks: the only alternative would have been to abandon the city entirely and leave the inhabitants to face an uncertain future. Staff officers were dropping out fast and lines of communication were hardly able to function.

On 10 August, my father was formally notified that the Ismid Force was to be disbanded and that his command was at an end. This development did not, however, necessarily mean a return to England, for Milne informed him that Lieutenant General Sir Aylmer Haldane, GOC Mesopotamia, had for some time been wiring both Milne and the War Office to request my father's services in his command; my father was now told that he was at liberty to go to Mesopotamia if he so wished. Taken aback, he asked for twenty-four hours to consider his options.

Acknowledging to himself that he could hardly hope for a permanent peacetime job at home, where 'all the other old birds must be served first',[8] he had nevertheless entertained some hopes of a command in India where Rawlinson, with whom he knew himself to be in good standing, was now commander-in-chief. However, he recognised that, in putting appointments like this in his way, the War Office were doing their best to be helpful and a rejection of this help would not be good for his prospects. He therefore elected to accept Haldane's offer. In retrospect, although he had no way of knowing it at the time, his move from Ismid to Mesopotamia can be seen as the critical watershed in his career, which set him on the road towards being in a position to seriously influence both political events and military policy for the first time.

Killing time as the operations at Ismid were wound down, he had plenty of time to sleep on all the ideas that had been flooding through his head but which he had never had the chance to get down on paper since 1914. As a thinking soldier, he saw the need for military men to keep themselves informed as to political developments, noting points of risk and whether these were likely to develop into conflict. In a 4,000-word paper covering the issues affecting the growth of nations and how they had built security around their cities, ports and key resources, he noted the importance of freedom of language, as used in British conquest and colonisation practices, which had led to self-determination. Looking ahead in Europe, which he feared had been Balkanised by the events of the previous decade, he visualised a customs union as being the most favourable outcome.

His second piece of literary accomplishment during the voyage was an equally well thought out monograph on the prerequisites for motivating the minds of junior officers, so that they would not be taken by surprise at the start of a future war. In this, he emphasised the necessity of junior officers being given a full picture of events so as to be able to form their own judgements, and emphasised that the post-war army should not be taken by surprise by the growing power inherent in military aviation.

Although he did not know it at the time, with many of these concepts he had virtually written his own brief for his future billet as Staff College commandant. For the moment, however, he had a different role in mind for himself:

> I wonder that they do not make me into a kind of European Liaison Officer, working with the DMI. I could help them a good deal and in the proper way. That would be asking too much liberty, and I presume we have started our military attaches again. They are supposed to do all the work of that sort. I remember when my ambition was to get into Intelligence at the War Office and to be a Military Attaché in Berlin. I have now been defeated in both. I never got even the meanest job in Intelligence and I am now too senior to be an Attaché. Even Paris won't come my way. Intelligence was a dead end and I must bless my stars that I never got pushed into either. When it came to fighting and commanding I made a good show of it & there was there no dead-end. I must devote myself to training and commanding. I wonder if I shall? What we have to do is to see that all the experience we have does not go lost. We must see that the new idea has something definite to chew and that it chews in the right way.[9]

As both Milne in Constantinople and Haldane in Mesopotamia had plans up their sleeves for keeping my father on hold in the Middle East by shipping him from the Black Sea to the Caspian, the farewell scene was not inspiring although my father felt that this was primarily down to Milne's great social shyness, as the shy and awkward general could not 'bring himself to be genial for fear of making an exhibition of himself'.[10] But, in contrast to his fellow officers, the commander of the Greek contingent at Ismid wrote to him effusively and sincerely:

Dear General,
   Great sorrow was felt by my officers, soldiers and myself when we heard about your departure.
   We are losing one of the most gallant Generals of Great Britain, under whose orders we served for a very short time.
   We found in you a fatherly administration, noble sentiments, courage, bravery and great sympathy to us and the Hellenic Nation, that we represent at Ismid.
   We take this opportunity of thanking you heartily for your support and of wishing you to add new pages of Glory to the Glorious History of the Great British Nation.[11]

My father hauled down his flag at the palace in Ismid on 18 August and sailed off from Constantinople in a small British India vessel, the *Katorian*, bound on a roughish sea journey for Port Said.

As no ship bound for Bombay was expected at Port Said for several days, my father passed the time waiting in Cairo, which had become the clearing house for Middle East movements. There, amongst many other friends from the past, he was able to meet his one-time divisional commander in France, Sir Walter Congreve, who was now GOC Middle East. Also, he tried to persuade Air Vice Marshal Sir Geoffrey Salmond, AOC Middle East, who had been a friend of his since their time as Woolwich cadets, to fly him direct from Cairo to Baghdad, but the rebellious state of Iraq rendered this out of the question. Thus, my father's journey to Baghdad, which could have been a 250-mile hop by air, turned into a one-month voyage by sea, which tested the patience of all those on board as they set off on 1 September in the P&O liner *Delta* for Bombay and Basra.

On board the *Delta*, my father found that he was travelling with Sir Percy Cox, who had been minister to Persia at the time of the signing of the secret Anglo-Persian Agreement, before the signing of the Versailles Peace Treaty:

He is supposed to know more about the Persian Gulf than any person. He doesn't look to me like a man of action. He was the Chief Political Officer in Mesopotamia during the latter part of the war and so he ought to be well up in all the problems. The Arabs are supposed to have a great opinion of him and call him 'Cockus'. He has a funny fat old wife with him, usually known as Bertha. She is always with him wherever he goes and has done many hot weathers in awful places around the Persian Gulf. The old woman looks fit on it too.

These 'Politicals' have a bad name in the Indian Army. They are always attached to a General, & though they have no control of military operations, they have a good say in all dealings with the enemy. The idea, of course, is that we are peace-making and preparing for peace and the soldier is popularly supposed to think of nothing but war. I have never had any dealings with these 'Politicals', a purely Indian product, so I cannot speak personally of what they are like. Cox has been made an honorary Major General, which seems quite unnecessary, as he left the Indian Army at the age of 27 as a Captain. I think we should keep a civilian a civilian and he will have more authority than dressed as a pseudo-officer.[12]

Cox, along with others who my father encountered on his journey, voiced the belief that he was being sent out to replace Haldane, and this belief was also current at Bombay, where he arrived on 13 September.

The local newspapers were not slow in picking up my father's movements, with the implication that he was on his way to supersede Haldane in the Mesopotamian command. Even Colonel Sydney Muspratt, a member of Lord Rawlinson's inner Cabinet, was under the same impression when he came to brief my father on 15 September. 'He gave me about the situation as far as he knew it in Mespot. There has been a complete lack of liaison between India & Mespot & India is aggrieved. I was asked to represent this to Haldane and to try and put this right.'[13]

This grievance was deep-seated, as all troops in Mesopotamia came from India and the Indian Army had no mandate for the defence of Iraq. The British Government were expected to pay twice over for the privilege of using Indian troops; a standing charge for each battalion and another for its deployment outside India. If this payment for a 'blank file' system was denied, there was more than a probability that recruits for the Indian Army would either not come forward or they would refuse the obligation of foreign service.

In Bombay, my father stayed at the Taj Mahal Hotel for a few days to await the arrival of a troopship to take him, with Kosti and his ADC, to Basra. To fill in time, he visited Thackers, the bookseller, to buy a copy of Sykes' two-volume *History of Persia*:

Curiously enough, when I got back to the hotel I found that I was destined to go to North Persia to command there. Haldane had been wiring for me for months and Milne had refused to part with me. I am more than relieved that I shall have a more or less independent Command. I have always wanted to see Persia. Almost prophetic my buying a copy of its history.

I had an amusing incident *en route*. I was walking along in my khaki drill – with my jodhpurs and rather civilian-looking Hawkes topee – when up behind me came a small red-faced Captain who shouted out at me 'You aren't allowed to turn your trousers up in the Western Command!' I was so flabbergasted that I could hardly answer when I turned round to look at him, so I took hold of him by the elbows & lifted him up, saying, 'Look at my shoulders!' I saw his little face turning redder than it was before & when I put him down he just took to his heels and fled without uttering a word. My mind is full of wars and rumours of wars, but it seemed to me typical of India that they should bother whether jodhpurs were turned up or down.[14]

To my father, this farcical scene was indicative of the attitudes prevalent amongst the senior command in India, and he expressed the hope that Rawlinson's energy and ability would change things now that he had been made commander-in-chief.

My father set sail for Basra on 17 September in the troopship *Coconada*, with a break in the voyage at the hot and unpleasant port of Bushire. Also on board were two battalions of infantry, 2nd East Yorkshire Regiment and 2nd Duke of Cornwall's Light Infantry (DCLI), on their way to reinforce Haldane's command. Upon arrival at Basra after a week on board ship, orders were received to proceed by river steamer to Kut with the East Yorks, while the DCLI stayed at Basra. As he made his way north to Baghdad, my father's thoughts on the situation in a post-Ottoman Middle East, the shape and character of which would inevitably exert a considerable influence over his own command, began to crystallise:

> Whatever form of Govt. we set up in Iraq it must be one that can resist the efforts of the Turks to re-assert themselves in Arabia. It seems to me that this will be a big business. How will Arabs behave themselves[?] I don't suppose they were ever a nation in the European sense of the word, but they have now been split up into various mandates under different nations. Lawrence's idea of a Great Arabia that he preached in the war to get the rising along will never be brought into being. Never intended either.
>
> The political business is as follows:
>
> (i) Set up an Arab Government in Iraq including the villayet of Mosul. To ensure peace and to prevent raids by Turkish Nationalists. We can then withdraw our own Forces to just North of Baghdad, leaving gendarmerie and police under our instructions to keep the Mosul villayet in order.
> (ii) To propagand [*sic*] against Bolshevism with all our energy. To make Kutchik Khan, the rebel Persian on the Caspian, into an enemy of the Soviet and not its friend. To maintain the Teheran Government.

> The question of the withdrawal from Persia is complicated by the fact that the Shah's Govt. would probably fall if we went.[15]

Clearly, what he had already said about Iraq could not be read in isolation from what he had to say about Persia, the country in which he expected to operate. Although a sovereign state, under the rule of Ahmad Shah Qajar since 1909, Persia was caught in the middle of the Anglo-Russian 'Great Game' that had been played out through the course of the nineteenth century, and both powers had done their best to exert their influence at the expense of the other.

Britain's 1907 Accord with the Tsarist Government had divided Persia into two spheres of influence; the Russian sphere being bounded by an imaginary line drawn between Kermanshah in the west, through the ancient capital of Isfahan and Yazd to Zulficar in the east, to the point at which the borders of Persia, Turkmenistan and Afghanistan trifurcated. The British sphere was bounded by a line running from the port of Bandar Abbas on the Straits of Hormuz, northwards to Kirman, Birjand and then east to the Afghan border. This left a curiously shaped buffer zone between the two, stretching along the whole of the border with Iraq and along the Persian Gulf coastline in the west and funnelling down to a 100-mile strip along the Afghan border.

The 1919 Anglo-Persian Agreement conceived by Lord Curzon was intended to tidy up the state of affairs after the Russian Revolution by quashing the 1907 Accord and providing Persia with the means and wherewithal to create an army of its own. To bring it into fruition, this involved a £2 million loan, tariff concessions on trade with Great Britain and expert military assistance: as a quid pro quo, Britain would obtain exclusive access to Persian oil reserves.

As the treaty terms were expected to be agreed before the Versailles Peace Conference had been signed, there were no compelling reasons for Lord Curzon to seek international approval until it had been ratified in Teheran by the *Mejlis* – the Persian Parliament. Unfortunately, the treaty had fallen apart and Persia's Prime Minister Moshir od-Dowleh, had to renegotiate the terms to appease his recalcitrant supporters amongst the strongly anti-foreign tribal leaders in the north. So, to bring an end to Persian procrastinations, Curzon gave Moshir od-Dowleh four months' notice to convene a session of the *Mejlis* to allow the terms of the treaty to be varied and ratified or face losing the loan.

My father had reservations that the treaty would ever be ratified, observing:

> It seems doubtful whether the Mejlis will ratify the Agreement. It was made by Curzon and Cox at a time when Denikin was doing well and when there was no fear of the Bolsheviks. It was made in secret and if the truth were told, we bribed some of the Persian Ministers. Perhaps that is putting it too baldly. Earnest money was given. That is better. I don't see what other alternative remains to

the Persian Govt. but ratification. Our subsidy comes to an end & the Persian Government is bankrupt. Still, Eastern countries have means of living that we wot [know] not of.[16]

Before addressing the state of Persia, however, it was necessary for my father to visit Baghdad and mark his card with Haldane and the rest of the great and good of Mesopotamia.

Baghdad in 1920 was noticeable because of its growing importance as a stopping-off place across the desert for road, rail and air traffic. The Turks, obviously inspired by their German advisers, had opened up the main street by cutting ruthlessly through everything that got in their way and it had become a passable thoroughfare. Quite the most important building in the town was the British Residency, which looked out on to the river. Adjacent to it was Haldane's headquarters, where as well as the general my father first encountered the noted orientalist Gertrude Bell:

> [Bell was] employed by Cox as a kind of Oriental Secretary. Has lived a long time amongst the Arabs and knows them intimately. She is very democratic and talks wildly about Arab dominion and parliaments. Oldish and unmarried. Judgement is a bit warped. A flattish face with freckles. A sandy sort of fringe & antiquated clothes. She is said to have a great power in the land.[17]

Miss Bell, for her part, thought my father to be:

> [A] remarkable creature, being in the first place one of the biggest men I've ever seen and in the second having a pretty sound knowledge of affairs from Archangel to the Black Sea. A major general at thirty-seven, a first class interpreter in seven languages – and that's not nothing. But above all he is a man, a sex for which useful employment can be found in North Persia.[18]

Haldane, perhaps pleased to find a brother Scot to confide in, was happy to bring my father up to date and to take him out for a boat ride on the Tigris to get away from some of the heat and dust of the city, during which the two men shared stories of their Boer War service. The fact that the two men got on so well may also have had something to do with the glowing reference that the CIGS had provided to Haldane:

> I do not know if you know Ironside, but you will find him an absolute pillar of strength. He is beyond question one of the most rising, if not the most rising, of the young fellows in the Army, a very fine headpiece, wonderful linguist, great physical strength, and infinite courage and resource.[19]

Unfortunately, the quality of Haldane's staff did not impress my father at all and he found them to be unhelpful, verging on resentful, with altogether too much of the old Indian Army attitudes about them. When my father took his leave, he still had no formal written orders but he did have Haldane's word that the latter would do everything he could to support him. At 01.00 on 1 October 1920, my father set off by train for Persia.

9

Persia on the Carpet

The background to my father's new command, at least so far as internal Persian politics were concerned, was not so much a power struggle as a power vacuum into which my father was thrust to command the North Persian Force. The coming months would see dramatic changes within Persia, culminating in the overthrow of the Qajar dynasty, and various historical accounts published in the intervening years have sought to cast my father in a variety of roles ranging from unwitting bystander to active participant in the plotting that led to the coup and ultimately to the establishment of the Pahlavi dynasty. Since many of these accounts have failed even to draw information from *High Road to Command*, let alone from my father's other papers, it is therefore important to put on record the true story of the role he played and how he played it, so that all historians in future are able to judge more accurately what happened and how the change to Persian rule came about.

My father's immediate command, which had its headquarters at Kazvin, was not a particularly powerful force, numbering only around 6,000 all ranks. However, it constituted one of only a small number of effective bodies of troops in the area. As such it, and its commander, could exercise an influence that was out of proportion to its actual military strength. As my father recorded, his command stood as follows:

Table IV: North Persia Force (Norperforce) Order of Battle, October 1920

Infantry (36th Indian Brigade)
    2nd York and Lancaster Regiment
    1st Royal Berkshire Regiment
    2nd Gurkha Rifles
    42nd Deoli Regiment
    122nd Rajput Regiment

Other troops
>   The Guides Cavalry
>   A Battery RHA
>   31st Indian Pack Battery
>   15th Light Armoured Motor Battery

The last-named unit was an armoured car company with a total of sixteen vehicles available; a detachment of the RAF was also subordinate to my father's command, in the form of a detached flight from 30 Squadron with four DH9as.[1]

As for the other bodies of formed troops in the region, these comprised the Persian Cossack Brigade, nominally loyal to the Shah but with White Russian officers, and the pro-Bolshevik rebel forces of Kutchik Khan. The latter were, in my father's opinion, being used as a stalking horse by the Bolsheviks, enabling them to test the water in Persia by supplying the indigenous rebels with arms, money and military advice but not committing troops of their own.

The bigger threat posed by the Bolsheviks was their propaganda, which could place them as the supporters of Persian liberty in the shape of Kutchik Khan while casting the British as an occupying foreign army. This was certainly a problem, but in many ways the more dangerous force, due to the political complications it brought in its train, was the one that was nominally allied to the British, in the shape of the Persian Cossack Brigade. Its commander was Colonel Vsevolod Dmitryevich Starosselsky, whose loyalties were only loosely aligned to the Shah who he nominally served:

> He openly looks upon these Cossacks as a White Russian Force and intends to keep things warm for the return of Czarist Russia. Therein, he is opposed to the British. But, he is anti-Bolshevik and requires all the help he can get to defeat them. Therein he is friendly to us. He encourages our Regular troops, for these must ultimately be withdrawn, but he is bitterly opposed to any British Mission to make an Army. Starosselsky is an astute man and influences both the Shah and the Mejlis. He is the main prop of the Shah and has promised to see that he remains on the throne so long as he keeps his job. The Shah cannot make up his mind what to do, but is inclined to trust the devil he knows to the devil he doesn't know. The Bolsheviks say that Starosselsky is a danger to the Soviet and demand his departure. A great deal of the pressure the Soviet is exerting against the Persians is really against at Starosselsky and Russian Officers. This is all very curious as the money for the pay of Starosselsky and his troops is found by us, as is the pay of all the other foreign officials — Swedes in the gendarmerie, Belgians in the Customs and French in the Public Institutions. To put it vulgarly, we are left with the baby once more.[2]

The delay in having to wait for the 1919 Treaty to be ratified by the Mejlis meant that most members of the British Military Mission, who had come out to Persia to organise and nurture the new army, had gone away disgusted, leaving no one to offer the Shah an alternative voice on military matters.

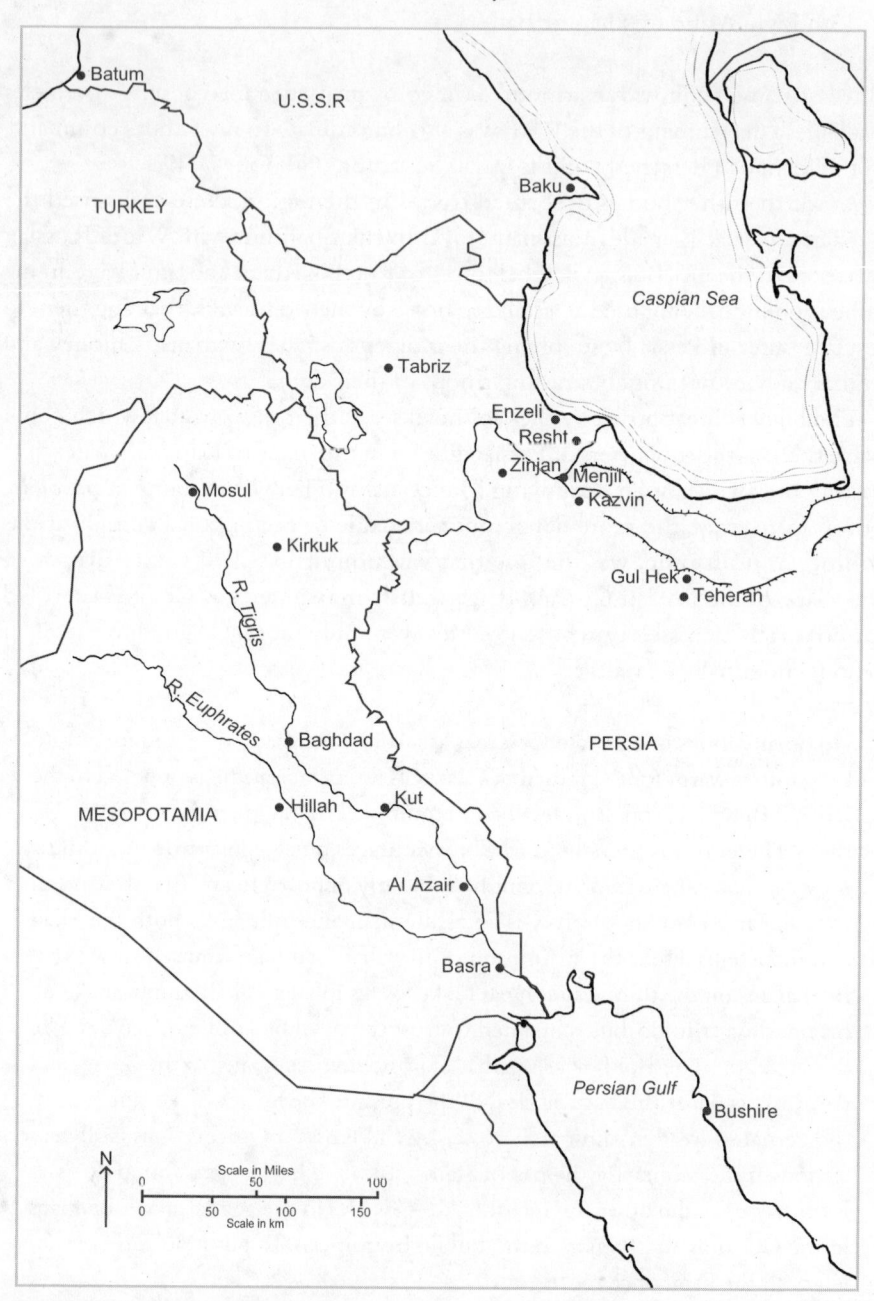

Persia and Mesopotamia.

In the first instance, however, the priority was dealing neither with Kutchik Khan nor with Colonel Starosselsky, but rather the far more mundane one of establishing effective logistical support for his troops. My father realised, drawing on his North Russian experience of working in an inhospitable and trackless theatre, that there was little choice in Persia but to make the best use of the few roads across his front lines and the mountainous interior to keep his base at Kazvin functioning. This was where his command was centred, although there was a strong garrison – denominated Menjcolumn, or Menjcol – holding the Menjil Pass where the road from the Caspian Sea crossed the mountains, and a detached battalion at Zinjan.

What mattered most was keeping the 450-mile route to Baghdad open in a climate which was politically as well as naturally hostile. From the outset, he was obliged to rely on aircraft and motor transport for communication purposes: although this was simply a practical response to the situation he was faced with, it served to further increase his familiarity with, and appreciation for, the tools of modern mechanised warfare. There was also an additional priority for keeping communications open, which was that he had been informed that Persia was to be evacuated in March 1921 and that he was being sent there to supervise the withdrawal.

Unfortunately, because the force was slated for withdrawal, logistical arrangements had been skimped so that no preparations had been made for the construction of huts at Kazvin, where a garrison that was already weakened by malaria was now settling down to overwinter in the mountains. This cost cutting was not the only problem that had existed prior to my father taking command. British troops had also failed to act when Bolshevik forces had landed at Enzeli, on the Caspian Sea, where they had established themselves in support of the rebel Kutchik Khan. These forces were now being observed by Starosselsky and his Cossacks, who had fallen back inland to the town of Resht.

Understandably, this lacklustre performance had done nothing for Britain's credibility with the Persians and, in my father's opinion, had all but killed the chances of getting Lord Curzon's agreement ratified by the Mejlis. Although my father considered that the poor response to the Bolshevik advance had largely been down to conflicting political instructions, he also placed a portion on the blame on the shoulders of the man he was to relieve, Brigadier General Hugh Bateman-Champain, who he described as:

> A handsome very worn-looking man. He has spent his time as a military secretary and an ADC and I should say is very weak. He has his wife, an English nurse, and two little girls. The Bolshevik invasion caught him on the hop, so to speak, and having no orders he did nothing. I believe his withdrawal was nothing short of scandalous. He has evidently found the responsibility too much for him & has broken up badly.[3]

Rather than place this unfavourable view in print, my father claimed in his memoir of the campaign that he did not meet Bateman-Champain in person, but in fact the handover of command did take place face to face and the brigadier then accompanied him on the 100-mile car journey to Teheran to introduce him to the British Minister Plenipotentiary to Persia Herman Norman.

My father stayed as Norman's guest at the legation's residence at Gulhek, just north of Teheran, where the minister, who he considered 'a funny little effeminate looking bachelor, very fussy and old-maidish', did his best to bring him up to speed on the situation as it now stood:

> He at once told me that he had had a bad time with Champain, who never did anything on his own and refused to assume any kind of responsibility. I told him that he needn't fear that with me. All I wanted to know was the policy and then to be left alone to carry it out. An ineffective little man. I was not impressed with his powers of forcing anything. He came down to dinner in a plum-coloured dinner jacket and trousers. He is very well off and has a French chef and an English valet. His name is Hermann so I see he must have some Bosche blood in his veins. We sat talking of the situation well into the night and I came away with a sense of futility. Curzon wants to assume the role of protector all over Persia now that the Russians are gone. He sent Cox out to arrange the Anglo-Persian Agreement and Cox fixed it up with Ministers, whom he is reported to have bribed by giving them a dollop of the subsidy in advance. Then Cox went away and Norman was sent out to see the Agreement ratified by the Mejlis or Persian Parliament. Why Cox left before he had done his job, I don't know. Bad diplomacy on his part. The bribes have grown cold and the Ministers who received it are now unwilling or unable to get the thing through the Mejlis. Poor Norman has never had a chance. Cox got all the credit and really left an impossible position. Rather what I should have expected from the look of the men. The Shah and his Ministers are famous procrastinators. None know better how to play with a so-called parliament and to hoodwink us. They want an independent Persia. That has been their ambition for centuries. Ever since the struggle for ascendancy between us and the Russians began, a struggle which finished in 1907 by a virtual division of the country into two spheres, Persia has wanted freedom. She doesn't care in the least that her institutions are inefficient. She just wants to hobble along in her old way as she likes. Even Russian spasmodic efficiency is abhorrent to her. Norman seemed to me to be rather helpless and spent his time sending memoranda to the Shah and dispatches to England. Curzon is said to be very autocratic. He once came to Persia many years ago and wrote a standard book on it. He still thinks that he is *au-fait* with Persian affairs and ignores the fact that there has been a war and that the world has changed considerably, especially in the East. He will not listen to that pest 'the man on the spot'.[4]

The fact quickly struck my father that both Norman and Champain had been altogether too much in awe of Colonel Starosselsky and his Cossacks, and that they believed the White Russian to be far more trustworthy than did my father. On 7 October, a conference took place attended by Norman, my father and the head of the British Military Mission, Brigadier General William E.R. Dickson. My father used the opportunity to stress the following points:

(i) That Norperforce would be withdrawn in April 1921 for certain. That it would take me 3 months to carry out the withdrawal.
(ii) If Starosselsky were still in power when we went, it would be difficult for the British Mission to get the Persian Army organised.
(iii) That immediate efforts should be made to get Starosselsky out and a Persian Commander put in.
(iv) Both the War Office and Foreign Office should be informed, so that they might consider things.[5]

My father's belief in the need to remove Starosselsky was further reinforced when a wire was received later that day reporting a success against the Bolshevik-backed rebels. Such successes were accompanied by considerable looting by the Cossacks and their officers, and it was understood that the Shah was a personal beneficiary of the proceeds. It was also the case, as my father was reminded when he enjoyed an audience with the prime minister, that the Shah viewed the Cossack Brigade very much as a personal bodyguard and considered it an advantage to retain its White Russian officers as they had no other loyalties and nowhere else to turn for employment.

Of course, it was also necessary to retain in mind the anti-British feeling amongst the Persians, which stemmed from the sudden withdrawal of British troops from Enzeli and which could not be wished away overnight. But, such was the corruption surrounding Starosselsky and his officers that it seemed to him that their removal would ultimately be in the Persian as well as the British interest.

His two-day visit to Teheran allowed him to scrutinise every aspect of the workings of the stalled Anglo-Persian Treaty and the prospects for the military mission that was supposed to accompany it, which he dismissed as minimal due to its overambitious goals and the apparent lack of military spirit amongst the Persians. His visit also gave him a complete understanding of the quality of the ambassadorial staff and what was left of the British Military Mission, so that when he returned to Kazvin on 8 October, he knew exactly what he wanted to do and how to set about doing it. He was now resolved to remove Starosselsky from power and to put a Persian in command of the Cossacks, before the British troops were withdrawn.

The return journey to Kazvin was a rough one; he would have preferred to have flown, but there was then no aerodrome at Teheran so the journey had to be made by car. His first week in Persia had opened his eyes to the primitive means of the people and the realisation that he would have to force change upon the Shah and his ministers through his personal insistence on Norman playing a forceful diplomatic hand.

On arriving back in Kazvin, he immediately set to work on his own staff, who were the instruments of his own security. With the approach of winter, he realised that he would be cut off from his source of supplies until the snows melted. Rather than risk a refusal, he solved the hutting problem by authorising the construction of housing for two battalions and a battery, presenting the expenditure to Baghdad as a fait accompli. He also brought Haldane up to date on the politico-military situation and his plans to resolve it, emphasising two key points which he later summarised in his diary:

(i) Russian and other foreign influence must be eliminated.
 The Russian influence is the most antagonistic to us and the most important in the Country. The few Swedes left in the gendarmerie can easily be dealt with. The question of Russian influence is immediate. It consists of:
 56 Russian Officers
 66 Russian NCOs
(ii) A start with the British controlled Persian Army must be made while Norperforce is here.

The Mission have put in a very big scheme, envisaging an Army which could never be paid for by such a country as Persia. All to supply themselves with highly paid jobs. War Office & Cadet School and intricate machinery can wait until the dhow is going.

It seems that a fresh start should be made and that the Persian Cossacks should be allowed to die away as such I don't think we should take them over lock, stock and barrel.[6]

My father went on to observe that he had 'written some scathing remarks on the Mission's paper. They want a good scallywag soldier to command and another to do the business part of the show.'[7]

The insistence on providing proper winter accommodation was closely linked to these objectives, for unless all the troops in Norperforce could be made fighting fit again, there was little chance of achieving either of his objectives. In due course, the hoped for reply was received, although not before my father had to pay a personal visit to Baghdad for more discussion with Haldane and Cox. He was to act with tact and firmness against Starosselsky, while taking political direction from

HM minister in Teheran. Reading between the lines it can be inferred that the War Office were confident that he would not only get rid of Starosselsky, but make sure that HM Minister delivered an ultimatum to the Shah.

On 23 October, he set in motion the train of events to bring an end to the Russian influence at the Imperial Court of the Shah in Teheran, although even on this momentous day he still had time for more mundane matters:

> To Teheran in a Ford. Had lunch with the Minister, who agreed with me about the dismissal of Starosselsky. In the evening my column reported the Cossacks tumbling through them. Norman will see the Shah tomorrow & get him to dismiss Starosselsky. I should like to see his face. Fancy being asked to send away your chief hope of safety. Poor little devil. I want to get the Russians removed constitutionally.[8]

The next day was spent with the prime minister and minister of war. As is evident from my father's account of the meeting with the Persian ministers, he had evidently been able to inspire Norman into taking a more assertive role and, indeed, it was Britain's Minister Plenipotentiary who broke the news to the minister of war of Starosselsky's corruption. Meanwhile, my father tackled the prime minister himself, so that the ultimatum was seen as coming from both men; a shrewd move that maintained, at least on paper, military subordination to a diplomatic initiative. Nevertheless, the reality was that it was my father who was setting the pace, insisting on Starosselsky being immediately dismissed and being brought to account for his corruption and peculations.

My father made it clear to the prime minister that Starosselsky was to be 'recalled, dismissed, and called upon to render an account of the money he had spent in his so-called campaign'. Such news, delivered so bluntly, did not sit well with the Persian:

> The wretched man was up against it. He wriggled in his chair like an eel at the end of a line. He said that his head would be chopped off if he went to the Shah and asked for the dismissal of his own special favourite. He suggested the substitution of the drunken Swedish General of Gendarmerie and several other names. Anything to escape. I felt like a bulldog cornered with a small dog in front of me. I was told that to institute British control in the Persian Cossacks now would make the Agreement impossible. I told him he made no effort to make it possible and that I had no intention of instituting British control. I merely refused to have British money embezzled and wasted by the Russians. He said he must consult the Shah and his colleagues. I let myself go and said that Starosselsky used our money to propagand [sic] against ourselves and used the rest to make a nest-egg in Paris.

> The Prime Minister wept and wrung his hands, and short of kneeling at my feet he did everything to attempt me to change. I left him exhausted, but not too impolite to forget the departure coffee. Norman tells me that I frightened him thoroughly & that he will get Starosselsky dismissed. There may be a few more arguments but he will engage to see that the dismissal takes place.[9]

My father returned immediately to Kazvin, being followed closely by M. Bonin, the French minister, whose country's influence at the court of the Shah was also at stake.

Intelligence reports showed that the Cossacks were in disarray after a renewed Bolshevik offensive and heading towards Kazvin. By instructing 2nd Gurkha Rifles to keep a day ahead of them as all parties fell back, he was able to prevent them from re-forming and – for the moment, at least – prevent Starosselsky returning to Teheran and attempting to use political means to retain his post. On 27 October, as he monitored the movements of the Cossacks, the Bolsheviks stepped up their shelling of the British positions at Gunjan. The pace of the diplomatic dispute in Teheran also quickened, but my father was pleased to see that Norman was sticking to his guns. This was all well and good, for my father now had a serious Bolshevik push on his hands, which sent Starosselsky's Cossacks streaming back from through the Menjil Pass. This left the British positions there exposed to the fire of the Bolshevik artillery, and it became necessary to ascertain the true extent of the enemy force:

> Menjcolumn has sent out a reconnaissance, which arrived back at 5:30 p.m. They estimate the enemy at about 1,200 to 1,500 with four field guns. Also 300 cavalry. Our casualties 2 killed and 9 wounded, all 122 Rajputs. Armoured cars had good targets and report some 40 enemy casualties. Airoplane reconnaissance in very bad weather by Robinson reports that some transport some 5,000yds from our position. I have ordered up 250 of the Berks under Francis, who will take command. An experienced officer with guts. All in motor transport. I got off 350 Gurkhas, too.
>
> I don't believe that there are many Russians against us. Mostly Kutchik Khan's men, stiffened by some Bolos.[10]

Even under pressure, however, he recognised that the situation could be turned to the political advantage, observing, 'If I give the Bolos a good knock, the British Minister can force their hand by saying that we are saving Persia after the complete failure of their own armed forces'.

Unfortunately, on 28 October the negotiations in Teheran suffered a setback thanks to an intervention by the Shah who, at a meeting with Norman, rather neatly threw Britain's pretence of enforcing democracy back in the minister's face. Even my father had to admit that he was impressed:

Norman saw the Shah, who was loud in his protestations of good feeling towards the British. He very rightly said that he had done his best, but our method of democratic Government, which he had been bringing in, didn't allow the Agreement to be signed. Had he been as he was the thing would have been signed months ago. Damned good reply. The rotten little brute scored. He openly said he was frightened of sacking Starosselsky.[11]

Meanwhile, the desultory shelling of the Menjil positions continued, but the offensive had lost much of its impetus now that British and Indian troops were coming into action and my father began to prepare plans for a counter-offensive to recover Resht.

As the Cossacks completed their retreat, they were shepherded into cantonments at Aga Baba, some miles outside Kazvin. There was still some doubt as to how the Russian officers could be separated from their men, but Starosselsky now played into my father's hands by setting out for Teheran to see the Shah. Up until now, this intervention might have been fatal, but at so late a stage it was too late for an intervention by the Shah to alter my father's plans.

Since a British wire-tapping detachment controlled the telegraph system, it was possible first to prevent Starosselsky notifying the Shah that he was on his way and then, once the Russian had reached Teheran and learned of his dismissal, prevent him from regaining contact with the Cossacks at Aga Baba. He was picked up by an armoured car patrol as he attempted to get back to his men; meanwhile, the Russian officers and NCOs had been rounded up and placed in temporary custody. As my father wrote in his memoir, carrying things off in such a high-handed fashion 'might have led to a nasty scene with some shooting, but they were so sure of their position that they never dreamt of falling into such a trap'.[12]

The Cossack rank and file came in quietly and my father placed the brigade under the temporary jurisdiction of Lieutenant Colonel R.C. Smyth, an officer from the British Military Mission. The Cossacks themselves 'were in a pitiable condition, being dirty and many with rags and tatters on. All their boots were in a terrible state. I think that they were glad to get in to Kazvin. Obviously all very nervous, but they behaved like lambs on seeing the Guides Cavalry.'

The situation was also good in Teheran, from where Norman reported by telegram that 'the Shah in the end accepted things quietly. He expressed a wish to give pensions to some of the junior officers, "who had not been able to enrich themselves like their seniors".'[13] Norman also confirmed that a Persian officer would be appointed to take over the Cossack Brigade. The officer in question turned out to be Ghassem Khan Vali, Sardar Homayoun, an aristocrat whose experience was in the diplomatic rather than the military sphere. The new commander, who freely admitted that he was no soldier, did not impress my father.

Conversely, both he and Smyth noted the effective state of Tabriz *Otryad*, or troop, under the command of a captain by the name of Reza Khan, and marked him as a promising officer ideally suited for leadership of the brigade.

My father's resourcefulness in engineering Starosselsky's removal so rapidly and smoothly left the War Office without a proper policy for their future operations in Persia, and he had to be careful to quash a suggestion from Haldane that the Cossack Brigade be incorporated into Norperforce. In this he had the agreement of the War Office, but at the same time no one at Horse Guards wanted to see the Cossacks subordinated to the British Military Mission either, leaving him to speculate that this was due to a distrust of its head, Dickson, who was an Indian Army appointee. Things would be much simpler, he felt, if the various ministries could only co-operate, but there seemed little sign of this coming to pass:

> Norman is depending upon the British officers of the Mission to carry out the reorganisation. The W[ar] O[ffice] say that nothing can be done till spring, when Norperforce departs. They evidently don't want to touch Persia. Another example of F[oreign] O[ffice] not having the military means to carry out their Schemes. I don't blame the WO, which has evidently been ignored by the FO in this project designed to exert influence in Persia permanently. H[enry] W[ilson]'s policy is to get back to essentials and look to the defence of the British Empire.[14]

Lord Curzon was reportedly furious that Norman and my father had acted without consulting him, taking out his ire on the unfortunate Norman, and at the same time the War Office was no less anxious about the effects of Starosselsky's summary dismissal:

> War Office perturbed by a wire from Norman to the FO, saying that I guaranteed the Persian Capital against attack from the North. I can quite see their idea. I had told Norman that I could not see any large Bolshevik Force arriving from the North, say Astarabad, and that I guaranteed to stop Menjil. I suppose the WO is terrified of becoming involved in any further adventures. I have wired to reassure them that I am not involved, that I merely took precautions in case the Cossacks fell down and that I can release the Persian Cossacks under their Persian Commander at any moment. I considered that the elimination of the White Russian Element in North Persia as being the most beneficial thing that could happen for ourselves and for Persia, which I considered secondary in importance from our point of view.[15]

Starosselsky, meanwhile, after a stormy interview with my father, was sent down to Teheran with his family. In due course, he emigrated to the United States and lived out the rest of his life in exile.

On New Year's Day in Kazvin, an air of suspense hung over Norperforce as the Diplomatic Corps in Teheran watched and waited for signs that the evacuation of British troops from Persia had been sanctioned by the Foreign Office. My father's immediate task was to ensure that the evacuation of British forces was carried out in an orderly fashion to avoid any last-minute panics, following the same procedures that he had used in the evacuation of Archangel. As he said to Christopher Stone, 'Having carried out two evacuations in the face of the Bolsheviks in two successive years, I ought to be an expert at it by now.'[16]

It was not an easy exercise to move troops with all their paraphernalia from the north of Persia to Baghdad when heavy snowfalls had made all the roads impassable and the Persian labourers were not inclined to exert themselves in clearing the way in such icy weather. Notwithstanding the problems, he started to move the Indian troops out first, in anticipation of the Foreign Office instructions, but thankfully on 5 January a message came through from Haldane to say that the Cabinet had put off the evacuation until April.

It seemed to my father that the diplomats were still hoping for some sort of settlement, but as soon as the Foreign Office had sanctioned the evacuation of all women and children the news broke out over the Bolshevik radio and the British plans could no longer be concealed. My father's reaction was intuitive and his response was clear: the army would not foot the bill on behalf of the Foreign Office and there would be no last-minute grants for transport to anybody, as demands for such had seriously compromised the last stages of the Archangel evacuation, when civilians who had insisted on staying put suddenly awoke to the Bolshevik threat.

If there was a case for a British military presence in Persia in 1919 to guard the gateway to India, then by 1921 it had evaporated. The Shah's authority had been undermined and his government had not only despaired of the British presence, but their coffers were empty and they had seemingly sided with the Bolsheviks:

> We have been defeated and thoroughly outwitted by the Soviet, who have now underbid us by proclaiming that they require nothing from Persia & make her a present of all Russian Institutions, buildings, and roads in the country. All debts are cancelled. How can we compete with this? They naturally think that they can get it all back when they have a Soviet in Persia. They are prepared to give away a sprat to catch a whale.
>
> I interviewed the Prime Minister & told him that I quite understood that he wished to be free of either the British or Russians sitting on his neck as an old man of the sea. But, did he really believe the protestations of the Bolsheviks? I also asked him how it was possible to arrange a treaty with the Soviet without submitting it to the Mejlis, when the Anglo-Persian Treaty had to be so submitted. He naively replied, '*Mais nous avons bien peur des Bolsheviques.*'[17]

By 17 January he had received orders to start moving on 1 April, provided no decision had been taken to evacuate Mesopotamia by the end of the year. He was informed that Churchill, now secretary of state for the colonies, was paying a visit to the ex-Turkish mandates in March, and would formally order the evacuation then.

The only downside to this delay was that he learned from Rawlinson in India that no district commands were due to fall vacant. Clearly having a return of the doubts about his future that had beset him at earlier points, he unburdened himself to Christopher Stone, speculating that it might do as well to ask Churchill at the Colonial Office for a governorship in Africa rather than continue with the peacetime army.

Even though he wondered what the future held in store for him, he did not idle away his time while being snowed in at Kazvin and spent the next four weeks liaising with the various legations in Teheran in order that the evacuation might be managed with the least possible difficulty. As he judged the situation, the Bolsheviks would likely restrict themselves to giving support to Kutchik Khan rather than mounting a full-scale invasion, and under such circumstances there would be no need to evacuate the foreign diplomats. Lord Curzon was still saying that if the Persian Government would sign the Anglo-Persian Agreement the British Government would do their best to 'help them through', but it was clear to those at the scene of action that he was out of touch with the events. *The Times* rightly asked whether General Ironside was to be instructed to strew leaves from a Persian rose garden in the path of the Reds, should they advance before the Persian Cossacks could again take the field. In the House of Lords, Curzon made no attempt to justify his actions or to deny the possibilities of being at war with the Soviet Government in Persia.

Meanwhile, something needed to be done about the future of the Persian Cossack Brigade, which was under the temporary supervision of Colonel Smyth. Neither Smyth nor my father had received any clear instruction as to what was to be done about these troops who, even in their poor state, would by default become a dominant force in northern Persia once the British had gone. This brings us to one of the key decisions that my father would take during his career, one which, albeit inadvertently, would cast him as a kingmaker and a shaper of Persia's dynastic future.

What must be understood, therefore, is his actions were from beginning to end motivated by purely military concerns, albeit that he had at the same time a pretty shrewd idea of the likely political consequences of his actions, at least in broad terms. After a long discussion with Smyth, he considered his options in a diary entry of 14 January:

> If I let go the Cossacks before I go I can perhaps control the situation – even though I cannot go to Teheran with a force. If I let them go as I disappear from Kazvin they may have a go at me, which would be very annoying because I

would have to turn and fight them. I would be wrong to kill any of them. Also, they may rush over to Teheran and make a revolution. Personally I am of opinion that we ought to let these people go before I depart. I told Smyth that I thought they could do little harm. In fact a military dictatorship would solve our troubles and let us out of the country without any trouble at all.[18]

It was this last remark that would prove most prescient, but the fact that he welcomed the idea of a strong man taking control of the country should not be taken as implying, as some historians have chosen to, that he deliberately conspired to bring such a situation about. Nor, however, did he exert himself to prevent it, attempting to convince Norman, the Minister Plenipotentiary, of the wisdom of giving the Cossack officers their heads:

He couldn't make up his mind. I told him that he would have to make it up, as I should have to act and that I did not mean to ask for instructions at the last minute. I said quite plainly that I thought we ought to let the Cossacks go and chance a Military Dictatorship. It would be in our favour. It might stop the Shah flying. The poor little man was terrified when I asked him not to tell anybody about the possibility of my letting the Cossacks go. He is unable to act without his Soviet. He is almost as bad a procrastinator as the Persians.[19]

In the event, Norman's indecision created a vacuum in which the British hand was effectively forced, and on 29 January he recorded that Sardar Homayoun had left his post at the head of the brigade and that Reza Khan, who had by now been promoted to the rank of lieutenant colonel, had assumed all his responsibilities. It is not clear to what extent this change had been engineered by Smyth, for my father went on to note, 'Smyth and Reza are great friends',[20] nor to what extent Smyth had been encouraged by my father's clear desire for the Cossack Brigade, and more particularly its officers, to play a key role in shaping the country's future. Certainly, however, both Smyth and my father agreed that Reza Khan was the obvious contender for an indigenous commander for the Cossacks to replace Sardar Homayoun.

My father had few reservations about the change of command, and his impression of Reza Khan, when he interviewed him at length on 31 January in the company of Colonel Smyth, was largely positive. At the same time, he recognised that there was little that he, or anyone else in British service, could do once the new commander of the Cossack Brigade was in place, but he did at least attempt to impress upon Reza Khan the consequences of attempting to play false while there were British troops still in the theatre, and to extract a promise concerning the limits of his future aspirations. It was one thing for a military dictator to assume control and restore order in Persia under the nominal suzerainty of the Shah, but dynastic regime change had never been part of my father's agenda:

Reza is a hard-looking creature with rather a big nose. One might almost call him Jewish-looking, but the Persian nose is not so bulbous as that of the Jew. Hair turning a little grey. He wishes to get on with some work and frets at not being involved. He talks only Persian and my classical Persian must have surprised him. They tell me that he was a *Syce* [groom] in Tabriz. All the more power to him if he was. He certainly is the most manly Persian that I have yet struck.[21]

On 12 February, my father confirmed Reza Khan's appointment to command the Cossacks, informing him that British command was to be gradually withdrawn and that Reza would need to co-ordinate his actions with Smyth in order to successfully oppose the Bolsheviks. Naturally, certain undertakings were required in return:

I wondered if I ought to have anything in writing, but I decided in the end that writing would be no good. If Reza wants to play false, he will & he will merely say that any promises he made were made under duress and that he needn't fulfil them.

I made two things clear to Reza when I agreed to let him go:

(i) That he must make no attempt to shoot me up behind as he goes or as I go. That would lead to his annihilation & good to nobody except the Revolutionary Party.
(ii) That the Shah must on no account be deposed.

Reza promised glibly enough and I shook hands with him. I have told Smyth to let go of control gradually. I don't really mind when he goes.[22]

In the first instance, the priority was holding the Menjil Pass against the threat that Kutchik Khan's Persian Revolutionary Army would press southwards once the British had withdrawn, and in this role my father was left with no doubt that the Cossacks under their new commander would more than hold their own against a force that was predominately composed of Persian rebels with very little by way of Russian stiffening.

Then, out of the blue, my father was forced to shift his focus. On Valentine's Day in Kazvin, as if by magic carpet, father received no billet-doux but, instead, a wire from Haldane telling him to reach him in Baghdad by the 20th at the latest and to be prepared for a short sea journey. He was left to speculate on what might have prompted this, but it was clear that his departure was to be permanent, for his successor, Major General George Cory, was already on his way to relieve him.

Of course, with the winter conditions as they were, getting from Kazvin to Baghdad was no easy task. It would have to be a flight, but even that was by no means straightforward with the weather being so inclement. Before leaving, my father needed to pay farewell visits to his own minister and to the Shah. From the latter, he was to receive the Persian Order of the Lion and Sun, which was conferred by the Shah in person at an audience on the 15th.

Herman Norman accompanied him to the audience, and he still did not know whether his releasing control of the Cossacks and putting Reza Khan in command had the minister's approval or not. By informing him prior to the audience, he was able to force the minister's hand and ensure that there was no going back. For the benefit of his successor, he recommended to Norman that the Cossack Brigade be formally released from British service a month prior to the departure of the British forces. What took place at the award ceremony itself did nothing at all to improve my father's already poor opinion of Ahmad Shah. The audience took place in a huge room, decorated with a carpet depicting Adam and Eve and the Tree of Knowledge:

> The Shah sat right up towards the top of the tree and we sat together at the bottom. We each had a little table & the Shah a table to himself. He was quite a long way from us, which seemed peculiar. After bowing we were asked to sit down & then Chamberlain came in with a cushion upon which was the Order of the Lion & Sun which he proposed to present to me. The scene became rather farcical when I approached to receive the sash and the star. As the Chamberlain lifted it up to hand to the Shah, the lion fell out of the sun. The Chamberlain was not to be beat for he lifted it up & stuck it in again. I found afterwards that it was a very common piece of enamel fitted into a kind of steel star – probably made in the bazaar. The sash is a beautiful green. I can imagine how good this order must have been in the old days when they were covered with jewels.
>
> We then got to business. The Minister told the Shah that he had lost patience over the Treaty. Nobody seemed to be making any attempt to ratify the Treaty. No more money would be forthcoming. The wretched little Shah, very fat and dressed in a black frock coat & Persian close-fitting black hat. He also wore black kid gloves. I am told that he has a horror of being assassinated by some kind of poison and so he never touched anything directly. The wretched little man was very nervous and told us that he was in a cleft stick. He wanted to ratify the Treaty at once and would have done so at once had he been an autocrat as he used to be. But, we had introduced democratic ideas into Persia – which he considered out of place in the East – and now he could do nothing to influence anybody. The Mejlis would not do what he told them to do and he was in despair. He was told by his Ministers that he was disloyal to his country by listening to orders from us. I thought it was rather a knock for us and our democratic methods.
>
> Coffee was brought to us in priceless Sèvres cups, each one his own cup & little pot. The Shah himself had his coffee out of a gold cup. A eunuch came in

and had to try every thing himself before the Shah tried. I noticed that the Shah watched the eunuch very carefully every time he had to try anything.

The routine is that you are given coffee a short time after arriving for an interview. Then, when the Shah wishes to conclude the interview he sends for another lot of coffee. You drink this & clear out as soon as possible afterwards.

The Shah said that we had sent away the Russian officers in his Service, and he was sure that the Mejlis would never allow British officers to take the place of the Russians. Their view was that the British were just as bad as the Russians for sitting on their hands. He suggested that any other neutral Power should be asked to supply the officers. I pointed out that we were not likely to supply money for other officers to steal – as I said Starosselsky had been doing. I saw a very wry smile on the face of the Shah when I said this.

The Shah then impressed us with the appalling happenings that would arise in Mesopotamia & India if there was a Bolshevik Persia close to us. He prayed me to keep the troops in Persia as long as I could, as we constituted his only hope. I told him that he must do something with Reza Khan, but I noticed that the Shah didn't seem to want to have anything to do with him.

Then the Shah became very ingratiating and asked me to do him a favour. He said that he had a sum of money that he wished to transfer out of the country. He enlarged upon the difficulties of getting money away & how the British Lines of Communication were always safe. I asked him why he didn't arrange for a transfer with the Imperial Bank & he replied that the head of the Bank – McMurray – was unsympathetic. I asked him how much the sum was & arrived at the fact that it was ¾'s of a million and was in silver tomans. These were enormous great pieces & the weight would have been colossal. I began to get a bit cross & so I said to him 'But, Your Majesty, how is it that you are now shipping money out of the country, when we are trying to consolidate the finances?' The Shah made his sickly smile and replied at once 'Mais, mon général, au fond tout le monde est égoiste [everyone is selfish]'. Pretty thick, in so bare-faced a way.

I naturally refused to have anything to do with such a transaction and told McMurray later. He said that the Shah had been transferring money by every possible means to Europe. He took bills of exchange from any merchant on Bombay. He reckoned that he had got away a good deal. This was the last lot & perhaps not the biggest.

His last effort was to try and get us to scrap the agreement altogether & to get the Mejlis to put another in front of us.

We must have been talking for 2½ hours before the second lot of coffee arrived.

An interesting interview, all conducted in very good French. Norman very punctilious all the time, but I am afraid I became a little short at times. The Shah was a pitiable object, in terror of being assassinated. His one idea was to get out of the country as quickly as possible. I fancy he thinks that Reza will stop him from going.[23]

His audience complete, my father had to wait until the 18th before it was clear to fly south to Baghdad. The planes were fit, but the weather was not. A frozen oil pipe brought them down well short of their destination, causing the pilot, Flight Lieutenant Kidd, to crash-land. Thankfully, they had been following the road and were quickly picked up, but it took several days of unpleasant travelling to reach the railhead at Quraitu from where the journey was completed by train.

The delay did, however, mean that Kosti, who had been in a second aircraft accompanying Kidd's, was able to return to Kazvin and re-join my father overland with all his heavy kit. Thus reunited with his baggage and servant, my father was able to complete his journey to Baghdad. There, he learned that Reza Khan had launched a *coup d'état* in Persia on the very day that my father had departed. He had led a 2,000-strong force of Cossacks and Gendarmerie to Teheran, which fell without bloodshed on 21 February.

The coup was directed not against the Shah but against the government, which was removed and replaced by a new administration under the reforming journalist Seyyed Zia'eddin Tabatabaee. Reza Khan became commander-in-chief of the Persian armed forces, thus positioning himself as the military dictator that my father recognised as being necessary to bring security to the country. Governors and other officials who refused to accept the coup were replaced by trusted military officers.

True to his oath, however, Reza Khan did not act against the Shah, who remained upon the throne for the moment, albeit as little more than a puppet. My father was, for the most part, content with this knowledge, writing:

> They are going to have no truck with the Bolsheviks and I fancy he has established a kind of dictatorship, sacking all the useless Ministers, who would do nothing but procrastinate and make money. So far so good. It will be all to our own good if Reza Khan has order in Persia.[24]

For the historical record, it is important to clarify my father's position with respect to the coup. Then and since, it has been implied that he had a greater or lesser role in events, and he himself followed the above observations by noting, 'I fancy that everybody thinks that I engineered the *coup d'état*. I suppose I did strictly speaking.' While I hesitate to question his own analysis of events, it seems that it would be fairer to say that his actions engineered not the coup itself but the situation from where Reza Khan was in a position to launch a coup, which is not quite the same thing.

10

From Cairo to Camberley

Upon his arrival in Baghdad, my father learned that his ultimate destination was Cairo. Here, a special conference had been called under the auspices of the Colonial Office and at the behest of Winston Churchill, to settle a common British policy for the future of the Middle East.

Following the defeat and collapse of the Ottoman Empire at the end of the First World War, Britain and France had together inherited the responsibility for the former Turkish lands in the Middle East, which were to be governed as mandates. Various schemes, promises and treaties were in place, some of them dating from before the Ottoman collapse, and part of the purpose of the conference was to agree upon a common path going forward. Borders needed to be settled, as did the demarcation between the British and French mandates, and local claims for authority over particular territories needed to be assessed and agreed upon. More pertinently for my father's role in events, Britain also needed to find a solution to her military responsibilities in the area, which remained considerable. Thanks to the lack of a clear policy as to how the area was to be governed, and a failure to recognise the claims of those who had fought alongside the British against the Turks, much of this territory was in revolt against the British occupation.

In order to restore the situation, a key proposal to be finalised at the conference was the ceding of power to members of the Hashemite dynasty, who had long been championed by T.E. Lawrence, thanks to the aid that they had given in his desert campaigns. This proposal would, amongst other things, place the Emir Faisal bin Hussein, up until now a central figure in the resistance to British and French rule, upon the throne of a new Kingdom of Iraq.

Even if successor states could be established to fill the void left by the Ottoman collapse, as was expected to be the case in Trans-Jordan and Arabia as well as Mesopotamia/Iraq, they would need British financial aid and military assistance until they were fully established and had their own police institutions and armed forces in place. Therefore, a key element of what was to be discussed at the conference was the scheme put forward by Air Marshal Sir Hugh Trenchard, Chief of the Air Staff, which called for the use of air power to take over the imperial policing role and thereby release the greater part of the troops currently deployed in the region. Such a garrison as remained would, per this scheme, function essentially as guards for a series of fortified airfields from which the RAF would deter any unrest.

Trenchard's proposal was based in theory on the successful application of air power during the 1920 revolt in Somaliland, but it also came at a very convenient moment for the RAF, which was struggling to carve out a role for itself alongside the two established services. One of the upshots of Trenchard's proposal was that, if it were to be adopted and the Mesopotamian garrison reduced, there was no need for a GOC as senior as Haldane and, expecting to be superseded, that officer suspected that my father would be appointed to replace him:

> Haldane has turned down the scheme uncompromisingly and now thinks that I shall be put in to run it. He doesn't seem to bear me any grudge. Stupid if he did. He said that my being brought along was a kind of threat to him, but he will not change his views or be forced into anything that he doesn't believe in. I believe he will do exactly as Winston says if he is rewarded enough. I don't believe in his strong will. He knows Winston well & doesn't trust him.[1]

Cox, my father observed, was also against the scheme.

For my father's part, although he still had hopes of a post in India as and when one should become vacant, he saw advantages in taking on the running of the scheme, but also entertained substantial doubts about its merits and the difficulties inherent in enacting it:

> There is no General in the Army who is as well known in the Air Force as I am. They may have chosen me on account of that. The old Air Force is run on very extravagant lines at present and, as they have no experienced Commanders and no Staff Officers. We shall have to train them all.
>
> If I do take on things I shall have to be given a free hand and will have hard work – and plenty of flying. Sufficient unto the day is the evil thereof.[2]

He embarked for Cairo in the Royal Indian Marine troopship *Hardinge* on 26 February, using the voyage to work his way through the papers put forward by Air Vice Marshal Sir Geoffrey Salmond for the defence of the 'Posts of Refuge'. These, according to the RAF scheme, were to be the fortified airfields from which the flyers would deal out retribution to anyone who prevailed in rebellion against either the British or whichever client they installed in Baghdad.

The role of the army in all this would essentially be as a sedentary garrison to protect the bases of the RAF. There were to be five large bases, each capable of holding out for at least a month, and four smaller ones. Understandably, this concept did not appeal to my father for it suggested that Salmond, an old friend and a former Gunner, had lost sight of the tactical lessons that they had both been taught at Woolwich in respect of the best use of ground troops. Salmond's paper also seemed to assume rather too much too soon from the local levies that were to form the new Iraqi Army. Most significantly, and having wider implications beyond the immediate problem at hand, the proposal tended to emphasise how far apart the army and the RAF had drifted in their concept of integrating air and ground operations, something that my father identified as a point that required redressing.

As the conference progressed, my father began to develop his own counter-proposals, based on employing light mobile columns of motorised infantry: undoubtedly this would have been a more effective policy from a purely military viewpoint, but it would not have delivered the cost-cutting measures that Churchill, who had one eye on the chancellorship of the Exchequer, was expecting to be able to deliver.

Having armed himself with the weaponry needed to defend himself from verbal onslaughts at the conference, he was able to make the most of the friendly encounters with all the other principal players on board. Some of these, including Haldane, Sir Percy Cox and Gertrude Bell, he already knew. Others, including Jafar Pasha al-Askari, who would ultimately end up in command of the Iraqi Army, he had met for the first time at Baghdad. Jafar would be one of only two Arab delegates at the conference, the other being Faisal, and it was from him that my father learned of the proposed new kingdom that was to be carved from Mesopotamia. Jafar gave my father further ammunition to deploy against the RAF scheme, convincing him that once an effective indigenous army had been created, only limited British support would be needed to maintain order and certainly no large garrison of any sort – airborne or ground based.

At Aden, the ship stopped off to pick up Geoffrey Archer, the governor of British Somaliland, who brought with him a couple of lion cubs with their chains and leather collars, being led to the zoo by a sergeant from the Kings African Rifles. As the voyage continued, my father continued to try and get the measure of his fellow delegates. Haldane, who seemed increasingly jumpy as the voyage went on, he thought to be 'looking forward to a Command at home as a reward for his quelling of the rebellion, but I think that the authorities know that he called for too many troops and had a panic'.[3] Of Gertrude Bell, meanwhile, an increasingly negative perception replaced the initially favourable view that he had developed when they first met, finding her outspoken support for Arab nationalism to be almost un-British. He worried about her influence over Cox, and did his best to avoid her, writing on 8 March:

> Old Gertrude Bell tried to tackle me for a talk in a corner but I escaped. I don't like the woman. She may know a lot about the Arabs, but she is not looking at things from an Imperial point of view. She has not seen very much of the rest of

the Empire and her point of view is bounded by the coast of Arabia – a woman's definite limitation. She told me today that she had been brought up by her father to enter into all the discussions and arguments of her brothers and had always been treated more as a man than a woman. I must say that I don't like her.[4]

The voyage ended on 11 March at Suez, from where the passengers went on by train to Cairo to register at the Semiramis Hotel to start the conference on 12 March. With all the celebrities assembled and seated – other important delegates, already in Cairo by the time that the *Hardinge* contingent disembarked, included Sassoon Eskell, finance minister in the provisional administration of Mesopotamia; Field Marshal Sir Edmund Allenby, now high commissioner for Egypt and Sudan; Herbert Samuel, high commissioner of Palestine; Air Marshall Sir Hugh Trenchard, author of the scheme; and, of course, Churchill – work commenced.

From the outset, Churchill made no bones about the fact that economy was the object at hand, citing for example the fact that an Indian Battalion in Mesopotamia was in effect being paid for twice, for there was also a necessity to pay for the relief battalion filling its place back in India. 'Winston plaintively said that it was difficult to economise under circumstances like these.'[5]

On the second day of the conference, Churchill emphasised his determination to carry the RAF programme through and to cast the army's objections aside. Particularly resistant to this was Cox, who seemed even more inflexible on military points than the soldiers, and appeared:

[W]eighed down by the cares and responsibilities that are being forced on him. He really is a little bureaucrat – not a big man, as I said before. He is niggling over little things in the way of reductions & shouts for Inf. Bns. all without transport. I tried to explain what a mobile force meant, but he couldn't listen or understand.[6]

Then, on the third day the detailed schemes began to take shape and were cut down to size to fit his budget. This, in turn, led to a definite offer with respect to my father's role in the new plans:

Winston has asked me definitely whether I will take over the Levies and get them started and then take over from Haldane & 'ready' the show for the RAF to take over in 1 or 2 years time. Haldane would go in September. Why the old man wants to stay another hot weather, I don't know. Winston took my arm confidentially & walked me up and down the ball-room saying, 'You stay & work with me and we shall have some good times together, before we are done'. He has the enthusiasm of a boy. I told him that I would certainly come, but that I must have a definite proposition and definite pay.

Winston runs these Conferences very well indeed. He is wonderfully quick in catching the importance of a thing & elaborates on it in a minute.

I went to bed dreaming of Mespot and the work that I shall have to do there. It will mean a lot of flying about & I must see if I can get a regular pilot of my own, as I cannot put myself at the mercy of a different pilot every time I fly.[7]

As a forerunner to the final statement, provisional proposals for swingeing financial reductions were issued to commence in or after October 1921, and my father was instructed to be prepared to take over command in September or October. In the meantime, he was to go back to Iraq to start the levies on their way and then to take leave in England before returning to formally relieve Haldane.

My father reviewed the conclusions of the conference as a whole, insofar as the future of Mesopotamia was concerned, in his memoirs. These were issued on 18 March:

1. Immediate reduction to twenty-three battalions.
2. Immediate formation of the following local forces
   a) Arab Army under Jafar Pasha
   b) Levies under British officers.
3. Reduction in September, 1921, to twelve battalions and six squadrons RAF.
4. Reduction during 1922–23 to either
   a) A smaller army with six squadrons RAF
   b) Four battalions with eight squadrons RAF.[8]

He concluded this summary by observing that Churchill had put through his economies in a masterly way, with mild protests on the part of the army authorities.

Apart from all the wining and dining, the conference was now virtually over and the government had achieved what it wanted in shifting the military expenditure in Mesopotamia and Palestine off the army estimates and on to the Colonial Office accounts. The farewell exchanges in the saloons and dining rooms of the Semiramis Hotel added the finishing touches to the gathering and had polished up my father's image greatly in the eyes of the secretary of state for the colonies and those of Eric Kennington, the popular society portrait painter who happened to be staying in the hotel and sketched him to attract further business. Today, I have this portrait in my possession, which was greatly admired by my mother.

The one person that he had not managed to win over, however, was Sir Percy Cox, and this was a significant problem as it was Cox, first as high commissioner and then as ambassador, who would be the power behind Faisal's new Iraqi throne for some time to come. Gertrude Bell outlined her concerns in a letter to her own father, written during the return journey from Cairo to Baghdad, via Basra. Arguments aboard the *Hardinge* remained heated as to exactly how the Iraqi levies were to be organised and constituted, and while my father remained at odds with Bell, she, for her part, retained a good opinion of his abilities and was concerned over the differences that had arisen between my father and her own chief:

> The only thing that disturbs me is that my Chief and General Ironside don't seem to be coming together. Now General Ironside is essential for the vital part of our programming, namely our promise to take over in two months' time the Mosul outposts — north and east of Mosul in the Hills — with Kurdish levies which are non-existent until General Ironside creates them. If it weren't he I should say out of hand that the task is impossible; but to do it he must be given a straight run and that's what Sir Percy shows no sign of doing. He's a difficult man to tackle, is my Chief. He won't stand opposition unless it's very cleverly veiled and he likes to direct things he doesn't know about as much as things he knows about. I expect there will be some pretty hard knocks between these two but I hope that General Ironside will get his way.[9]

Had my father had the chance to work through the tussles that would have inevitably ensued between himself and Cox in Iraq, it would likely not only have been good for British policy in the new kingdom but would also have given my father some useful practise in dealing with politicians and civil servants that would have stood him in good stead later in his career. Instead, however, fate now took a hand and caused his future to proceed down a very different path.

From Basra, now eagerly looking forward to flying around Iraq to launch the levies, he decided to make a start at Shaiba and fly from there to Baghdad, but when he arrived on time to take off at 09.00 he found that both the pilot and the plane were out of service and he did not get away until much later in the morning. The aircraft in which he finally took off was a DH9a, a two-seat light bomber of wartime vintage, and my father had to squeeze his sizeable frame into the rear cockpit. Being restricted by the ring mounting for the Lewis gun that would normally be carried when on an offensive patrol, he was unable to strap himself in:

> A strong south wind and I expected a good journey, but the wind changed in half-an-hour to the north & blew strongly & then at 12 noon a thickish dust-storm. After 2 hours flying, the pilot signalled that he must come down. We had gone up to 11,000ft & down to 50ft, but couldn't get away from the dust. The wind blew a hurricane and we could hardly see anything. I think the pilot had lost his bearings and also his head a little. If I had known as much about dust-storms as I do now, I should have made him go on, but as it was I signalled to him that he could come down. He eventually saw the railway line & I saw a hut. He flew round & round two or three times, looking for a landing place & how to land. I saw two or three people come out of the little hut on the line. The sand was as bad as ever

and the wretched pilot apparently missed something for he landed down wind. I distinctly remember two bumps & then a third & then a complete somersault & as far as I could judge at about 60 miles or so an hour. I must have come to almost immediately & found myself some 60 yards from the machine & lying on the ground on my back. I must have been slung out of the back of the machine as the great tail of the plane turned over. I remember feeling very stupid and sick, but I had no pain of any sort of kind. I managed to turn over & get into a sitting position & looked at the plane. The plane was clean upside down & the pilot still in his seat, strapped in. I always refused to be strapped in & to this fact I owe my life, because I would have otherwise banged my head on the ground when the plane hit. I am too big really for the observer's seat in these planes.

I looked at the machine & gradually made up my mind that I must go & get the pilot out. I had been badly concussed in the fall, though I didn't know it. I got up & stood upright & commenced to move to the machine. I must have shuffled along, for when I looked down I saw that my right leg was not right & that the heel was facing the front. I didn't in the least know what was wrong. I worked away and reached the machine. I can distinctly remember the pilot upside down with his long hair hanging down. He was evidently one of those who brushed his hair back over his head. I pulled him by the hair & eventually must have loosened him from his straps because he came away & I began to drag him away from the machine. I distinctly remember the drip-drip of the petrol & my one idea was to get away. Why the plane did not burst into flames, I don't know.[10]

The two men were eventually carried to the railway hut by the linesmen there, who had seen them come down. Once the storm had abated, an RAF surgeon was flown in to attend to their injuries and, at length, they were taken to Basra by train:

I had crashed at 1 p.m. By 7 p.m. my leg was in a splint & by 4 a.m. the train arrived & I was in hospital at Basra by 5 p.m. on the 9th. A long enough time & everybody surprised that I had no pain. A catheter relieved me on arrival, but the wind still kept on.[11]

Once he had been examined, it was revealed that there were two breaks to his right leg and multiple fractures to his left. This ultimately resulted in a slight shortening to both legs by the time that everything had been set and the bones had knitted back together. This, however, would take some months and for the first few weeks he was flat on his back, albeit suffering little pain.

On his birthday – 6 May – he reflected on what had happened to him and, in the company of his ADC, he celebrated with a drink to the future and a realisation that if the accident had tipped the scales in the wrong direction, his weighty reputation was helping to tip them back again the way he wanted. With calliper and crutches, he hobbled back aboard *Hardinge* on 26 May, only for the ship to run aground the following day as she made her way to sea. This necessitated a change of plans and he eventually sailed for home on board the Bibby liner, SS *Yorkshire*, disembarking at Tilbury on 8 July.

Having fought for his life when he was pitched out of the DH9a, he found that he now had to fight for his future as well as his rights. He was released from the Millbank Hospital in London on sick leave and was placed on half pay from the date of his landing in England, even though he had informed the CIGS that he would be ready and fit to return to Iraq by 1 November.

Back at home outside High Wycombe, he spent his time visiting all his friends and colleagues in London to keep in touch with the mood of things in the army and to assess what his standing was in the eyes of the CIGS. It was clear that Winston Churchill was anxious to secure my father's services to push on with his plans for reordering the defences of the Middle East and whatever the hang-ups were in finding a job for him, his reputation stood out above others more senior to him. Also, there was no doubt that the army did not want to lose him merely because he had to wait for a vacancy to occur in the list of general officers filling in their time to retirement in the home commands. As 'The Elephant in the Corridors of Whitehall', his persistency all but forced the War Office to come to terms with the situation and confirm his new appointment.

He received the news that would resurrect his career and secure his future in a personal interview with Sir Henry Wilson:

> I went up to see the CIGS. An eventful day. I was ushered into old HW's sanctum & there I found him surrounded by papers & cursing the heat in London. He started off at once by saying, 'How would you like your name sent in for …?' He then stopped with one of his old monkeyish gestures and went on to talk about all kinds of subjects & left me in absolute ignorance as to what he intended to say. After a bit he said, 'Alright you are to go to the Staff College'. Of all the things that I had thought, that was the most unexpected. I really had no inkling that they could choose me for such a thing. I told him that I was sure that I could make the show a human one. He said to me that I was one of the few people in the Army who had the chance of rising to the highest rank. I had plenty of experience in commanding, but that the other side was necessary. The job is to go vacant in April 1922, when Hastings Anderson goes away elsewhere. It means a certain time on ½ pay, which is always lean. I shall get a house for 4 years in which to settle up.
>
> HW asked me if I had engaged myself to Winston to go to Mespot & I told him that I had been done in over my pay & didn't see why I should go. Indeed I wasn't fit. He promised to write & fix the thing up with Winston. Very good of him.
>
> Thinking the thing over, professionally I could not have been offered a greater honour, especially when one thinks that my immediate predecessors have been

Rawlinson, Henry Wilson, Robertson, Kiggell and then Anderson. I am being offered the appointment at from 10 to 15 years earlier in proportion than they got it. It will give one just the time necessary to digest all the stuff I have been accumulating during the war. I could not have borne a job at the WO unless it had been a high one, because of the indoor work. I am too young to give up exercise. Now I shall get plenty of outdoor work and plenty of time for thought. I hope I shall fill the bill well. It is a great responsibility to have the training of future generations of soldiers upon my shoulders. I shall have a good try at keeping the place human and not like a school. I have a feeling that I have not served my apprenticeship in vain. My luck has been with me.[12]

Churchill, on being acquainted with his new appointment, wrote a very gracious letter in which he regretted that he could no longer make use of his services with the Iraqi levies and wished him luck in his new posting, remarking that he could not have sent him to Mesopotamia at the cost of his professional advancement and assuring him, 'I regard your career as a matter of high importance to the Army'.[13]

My father's new appointment as commandant of the Staff College ensured that he would have an important role in shaping the future of the army at a time when new technology, on the one hand, and money and manpower shortages on the other, created an awkward situation where it was necessary to develop the methods for fighting future wars while stretching the available budget to cover Britain's extensive imperial commitments.

Inevitably, debates would rage across the coming years over mechanisation and the development of the equipment and tactics that went with it, and the need to reform the army as a whole in the long term while still retaining an effective force of imperial garrisons in the short. Throughout the interwar era, these debates, and the tensions that they created, would shape much of my father's career; he, in turn, would do his part in shaping the course of those debates.

On some issues, he was a passionate advocate of change; on others, a moderate supporter of reform. On some points, indeed, he even acquired the tag of 'reactionary', something that can be seen in his advocacy of a strong Imperial Reserve operating out of India and able to influence events in the Middle East, even as the political centre of gravity shifted increasingly back to Europe. Even then, however, while clinging to the old idea of a strong force in India as an imperial strategic reserve, he deplored the inflexibility of the old Cardwell System by which the British element of that force was maintained, and sought to modernise and reform the Indian Army during his two tours of duty on the subcontinent between 1928–31 and 1933–36, as we shall see in the following chapters. All this was still to come, but his four years as commandant at Camberley gave him the chance to develop and settle his own ideas and to inculcate them with the new generation of bright young staff officers who, though none of them could know it, would form Britain's high command in the next war.

News of my father's appointment was quick to spread and invitations to lunch and to lecture or dine came flooding in, so he had to combine his time spent in advancing his own interests with shaping up the Staff College regime. He spoke to the Senior Officers' School – a then relatively new institution designed to improve the professional education of middle-ranking officers of all three services – about his time at Archangel and in Persia, and as his legs continued to improve he began to play a little golf and to shoot again. By December, he was passed fit for service and had progressed to relearning to ride, feeling very clumsy due to his shortened legs. But the fact remained that there was only so much that he could do to fill the remainder of his convalescence, and time had begun to drag as 1921 turned to 1922 and months remained before he took up his new post at Camberley.

It was therefore a considerable relief, and a useful professional opportunity, to receive on 3 January 1922 an invitation from Admiral Sir Charles Madden, commanding the Atlantic Fleet, to join him aboard his flagship for a spring cruise to Gibraltar and the Mediterranean. Madden, who would go on to serve as First Sea Lord, was a distinguished veteran of the Grand Fleet, having served as Chief of Staff to Jellicoe at Jutland and then as second in command under Sir David Beatty. He clearly had inter-service co-operation on his mind, for his invitation expressed the hope that a chance to learn more about the Royal Navy, and in particular about the fleet at sea, would be of great benefit to my father once he got to Camberley. My father recognised that this would indeed be essential, accepting that his existing knowledge of the senior service was small indeed:

> I had read a good deal of naval history, and as a student at the Staff College I had taken part in many combined exercises on paper. Towards the end of the South African War, a cruiser and a gunboat had helped put ashore at Port Nolloth, close to the mouth of the Orange River, the mobile column with which I was serving. As a staff officer at Boulogne in 1914 I had seen the Expeditionary Force carried over to France without a mishap. I had also read the reports of the major naval engagements during the War, but like many another Army officer I had been too busy with Trench-warfare to give them much thought. Of practical experience with the Fleet I had none. I had, in fact, taken the Navy very much for granted.[14]

The cruise on which he now embarked, aboard Madden's flagship HMS *Queen Elizabeth*, consisted of a series of exercises. The first saw the Atlantic Fleet's three battleships attempt to escort a convoy to Gibraltar while the faster Battlecruiser Squadron sought to intercept them; my father was particularly impressed with the speed of the latter, and marked both the value and limitations of the sole aircraft carrier under Madden's command, the experimental converted liner HMS *Argus*.

At Vigo, where the fleet put in for a courtesy call after the completion of the first exercise, he transferred to the battlecruiser flagship HMS *Hood* for the passage to Gibraltar, renewing a Boer War acquaintance with Vice Admiral Sir Walter Cowan, who he had first met twenty-odd years before when Cowan was naval ADC to Lord Kitchener. After some time anchored in the shadow of the famous Rock, during which time my father familiarised himself with the Gibraltar defences, little knowing that he would one day command them as governor, Madden's forces now sailed as one body for a full-scale fleet exercise with their counterparts of the Mediterranean Fleet.

These operations, which my father observed from the light cruiser HMS *Curacao*, were expressly intended to assess the role of naval aviation in fleet actions, pitting the aircraft from the *Argus* against those of the Mediterranean Fleet's seaplane carrier HMS *Pegasus*. Madden had already stressed to my father the value of aircraft at sea, and expressed his fears that the RAF would argue for the battle fleet being obsolete. In much the same way that my father had expressed concerns that senior officers of the new RAF, including his old friend Salmond, were pursuing inter-service politics at the expense of their military education, Madden feared for the future of naval aviation if – as was currently the case, and would remain so until 1939 when the Fleet Air Arm was returned to Admiralty control – aviation personnel aboard carriers were all provided by the RAF. After taking passage aboard the *Argus* himself and seeing this bizarre dual control first hand, my father came to fully agree that the development of aviation was thereby being hindered, and that the RAF's policy 'violated the principle that the user must have the final say in the makings of the weapons he has to use'.[15]

After a month at Malta, the fleet returned to British ports with a final exercise during the passage up-Channel during which a simulated attack was made against the battleships by land-based torpedo bombers of the RAF. Notwithstanding Madden's expressed intent to make it as difficult as possible for the attacking pilots, the aircraft pressed home their attack and made a favourable impression upon my father.

Due to poor weather conditions, the senior observers sent by the RAF to view the exercise were unable to do so, and my father was therefore asked by Sir Hugh Trenchard to furnish a report – 'from the point of view of a layman' – on what he had seen. My father quite happily did so, although, as he remarked in his memoir, 'after all my years of fighting and commanding large forces of aircraft I felt that I was least of all a layman!'[16] This exchange, however, opened up a correspondence with Trenchard that would continue for some years and, along with his cruise with the fleet, ensured that he would begin his new job with not only a quarter of a century of experience in his own profession but with a good working knowledge of the other two services as well. Few incoming commandants can have taken up their appointments at Camberley so well informed and so well placed to influence events.

11

Modernising Commandant

My father assumed his new duties as commandant in May 1922, replacing Major General Hastings Anderson who had re-established the Staff College after its closure between 1914 and 1919. Directly after being notified of his impending appointment, he observed to Christopher Stone, 'It really means the training of all the future brains of the Army'. He saw a key part of his role as the dissemination of the lessons that he himself had learned during the previous decade, but saw that this process would be useful for himself as well, telling Stone, 'I can also digest what has been happening in the war. A thing I have never been able to do yet.'

From a personal perspective, he also acknowledged that the posting would allow him to resume a proper family life, but at the same time he saw that there would be a great deal of hard work involved if he were to succeed in applying his own philosophy to the role of commandant:

> I know I can humanise the place and prevent it falling into a School job, which is a great thing, but I really have doubts about taking on such a great responsibility and it has been altogether out of my line so far. It really does make one laugh. To think that I was a very unruly student there only seven years ago.[1]

With a reduced peacetime army, constrained by a national unwillingness for conflict and by the financial limitations inherent in the newly adopted Ten Year Rule, it was all the more important that the best officers be brought forward as leaders. Although this applied very much to the students of the new post-war intakes, the same could be said of the instructors, who formed a particularly distinguished group, many of whom would also go on to great things. Some of them, such as Lieutenant Colonel Lord Gort VC, had themselves only had the chance to attend as students after the college reopened in 1919, having missed their proper turn due to the war, and were thus well placed to combine both practical and theoretical instruction. Indeed, the first two years after the college reopened in 1919 were taken up by courses for specially nominated mid-ranking officers like Gort, who would have otherwise missed out on any formal staff training, and it was only in 1921 that the conventional intake of captains and majors resumed. As such, my father was the first commandant to be in a position to seriously shape the post-war character of the college.

Working under my father from 1923 as Director of Studies was Colonel J.F.C. Fuller, the army's great exponent of armoured warfare, in whom my father found a fellow modernising spirit. Indeed, it was at my father's request that Fuller was posted to Camberley, something that did much to advance the latter's standing and gave him a further opportunity to develop his ideas. It will be recalled that Fuller and my father had first met when they coincided as students at Camberley before the war. Undoubtedly, Fuller courted my father's patronage upon learning of his appointment as commandant, but it is clear that he was pushing at an open door.

On 24 April, my father recorded receiving:

> ... a long letter from Fuller, the author of the 'Tanks'. He is at the War Office in the Staff Duties office. He is regarded as a mad theorist by many people, but he has a great brain and is one of the most advanced officers we have in the Army. I think that properly controlled, he is the man we want at the Staff College. I shall certainly try to get him there later on. At present there is rather an outcry against him owing to his advanced writings. Both he and I are agreed that the course we went through at the Staff College was a really bad one. All the teaching was directed to the study of old campaigns and we never got any further than that.[2]

Between my father's wholehearted endorsement of air power and Fuller's visions for the development of the tank, the two of them were already looking ahead to the type of battles that we would see in the Second World War, and from the perspective of historical enquiry it is interesting to see how the two men borrowed from each other's ideas as the new doctrines of mechanised warfare were developed.

Unfortunately, however, Camberley was something of an exception in terms of modern thinking within an army that, on an institutional level, had seemingly decided that the First World War was an aberration and what was now required was a return to 'proper soldiering' of the type seen before 1914. This, it seemed, consisted of as little intellectual activity as possible, a focus on sports and recreation over training, and a prioritisation, insofar as military matters were concerned, upon preparation for duties in India and in the small wars of Empire. Added to this was the problem caused by a proliferation of senior officers who had risen to high rank during the war years and who now filled the army's senior posts, at worst by rotation and at best in the form of an extremely slow game of musical chairs.

When my father became commandant, he was eighty-ninth on the list of major generals and after six months at Camberley he had moved up to seventy-fifth place on a slightly smaller grouping, but there were still many more of them than there were jobs for their ranking. Those who were unemployed were placed on half pay until they found themselves in retirement, but this did nothing to speed up the rise of their juniors. If this was stifling enough for a man of my father's seniority, who had at least obtained substantive general rank through his wartime and immediate post-war services, the crushing effect on those who had risen to temporary high rank in the war and now reverted to their substantive regimental rank can only be imagined.

On 21 May, my father and mother dined with the king at the Royal Pavilion in Aldershot, having already taken tea with Sir Henry and Lady Wilson. Wilson had stepped down as CIGS that February, to be replaced by General the Earl of Cavan, who had commanded the British forces in Italy during the last months of the First World War. Cavan's term as CIGS coincided almost exactly with my father's tenure at Camberley and their relationship would be a good one, with their correspondence highlighting a progressive attitude that is at odds with the popular characterisation of Cavan as 'an amiable but unimaginative guards officer'.[3] Of his talk with the king, my father wrote that they had spoken at length:

> He told me that I mustn't vegetate too long at Camberley, which would have amused the people at the War Office if they knew that the Staff College had been described like that. He said he was sure that a General College of War for training all arms was necessary and I agreed thoroughly with him.

He also remarked that my mother had seemed to enjoy herself, and that all present 'seemed quite natural'.[4]

Most of June gave him time to clear his mind on the agenda for a conference meeting with the CIGS to review the background to staff training:

> Cavan is very clear and concise and we got down to work at once. Broadening the education. Three students each year to be chosen to be sent to a University for a year. Cavan was most impressed by the breadth of teaching at West Point in America and wished to emulate things. I agreed. We cannot broaden things too much. I suggested that my job was to turn out good young Staff officers and that I could do it in a year. Many officers were not fitted to go on with the course for more than one year & one was not likely to broaden their minds at all.
>
> All this cannot be considered until 1923, so we have plenty of time to formulate things.[5]

My father had already developed ideas of his own on how the lecturing might be improved upon, based in part on his observations of how the existing course was being taught. On his first impressions, he had no doubt as to the quality of the students, but clearly entertained some reservations as to the methods by which they were instructed:

I addressed the students in the large lecture hall, which is a really fine room and the hundred and more students assembled looked really as if they were just a few. I told them briefly that I did not intend to be a 'new broom' but that later on I hoped to have some effect on the situation. They listened with very wrapt [*sic*] attention. They naturally are all looking to see what manner of man I was. They certainly should be a good class of audience.

I then attended my first lecture of the Senior Division given by [Lieutenant Colonel Ernest] Lewin upon Imperial Communications. It was well delivered, but in a very pompous form & with a professorial manner. There were far too few '<u>nuts</u>' concealed in verbiage. I came away with little concrete idea in my head as to what the lecturer wished to convey – we were backward as regarded the French and the Marconi people were having a row with the Norman Commission and that thereby the Empire was suffering. The whole lecture was a padded wordy indefinite picture. No wonder they consider that lecturing is the worst form of tuition. That kind of lecturing is.[6]

The eighteen members of the directing staff were all placed under notice to open their eyes to the wider world of imperial defence and to tailor their courses accordingly. Many of them already knew of my father's reputation in the field of command and had served under him, which of course helped considerably.

As he could only make marginal changes to the system at the start of his posting, he was dependent on waiting for the Senior Division to qualify before he could remodel the course for the new arrivals in 1923 and set about having instructors of his own choosing. He was also keen to bring in outside expertise where appropriate, and to place the course material in its appropriate political context. With this in mind, he sought to assist Colonel Nugent, the instructor assigned to organise the Middle East lectures, by passing all the Colonial Office correspondence to him to engage the speakers. To my father's way of thinking, and contrary to the methods that he had seen employed by instructors such as Lewin, the lectures should serve the purpose of getting the audience reading and thinking on the right lines, and to this end it was no bad thing if the lecturer could speak from first-hand knowledge.

Even more so than colonial matters, the aspect of the course that was closest to my father's heart, and which clearly needed specialist input if it was to be adequately incorporated into the syllabus, was the role of aviation in modern warfare. Having asked for a senior RAF officer to lecture to his students, my father was ultimately successful in securing Trenchard's co-operation in developing the air aspect of the lecture program henceforth. This drew an immediate response from the CIGS:

I hear from Trenchard that you have asked him to send a senior officer to lecture to your Junior Division. He has shown me his answer, in which you will see that the lecturer will enlarge on two hypothetical cases – one in which the Army is predominant and the Air the auxiliary, and the other in which the air is predominant and the Army the auxiliary.

This may seem rather startling to the younger officers, but I should like you to accept whole-heartedly a lecturer on those terms, as although we may not agree with everything that the lecturer says, it is obviously right for them to put their view forward. My policy is to arrive at co-operation with the Air Force as close and as friendly as that between us and the Navy.[7]

My father was extremely pleased to have won the CIGS over to his way of thinking, writing, 'Cavan is a man to give approval at once to anything one starts. The policy he lays down is the only possible one.'[8]

In the absence of its own air service, the army had to find an effective way of working with the RAF, and he continued to develop his ideas on this front throughout his time at Camberley. Quite quickly he developed the theory that the best solution would be to institute a single combined ministry for all three services, so as to do away with so much counter-productive rivalry: as early as October 1922 he was discussing the idea with Sir Charles Madden.[9] As may be divined from the fact that Madden was not in agreement, this was extremely advanced thinking for the times – some of the ideas expressed being more akin to those later credited to Fuller than to my father – but it will be noted that as far back as 1919, when still in North Russia, my father had rhetorically asked of his diary, 'Who will sit down and work out the new organisation for the Army? We shall certainly have Tank units and I think that it would be very unadvisable to do away with the Machine Gun Corps. Shall we have our own Air units?'[10]

Undoubtedly, my father's views on these topics matured and changed as time went on and he was exposed to new ways of thinking, but it is clear that he was already thinking on these lines long before his close association with Fuller and other modernisers. If his focus for much of the 1920s was on aircraft rather than tanks, this should be understood in the context of his considerable personal involvement in the development of air power for imperial policing, his observations on naval aviation during his cruise with the fleet and, of course, to the ongoing political tussles with the new RAF over the control of military aviation.

The political currency of these latter points, and growing concerns over the role of air power as a strategic as well as a tactical weapon, made air warfare the primary concern in the immediate post-war era, at a time when the proponents of mechanisation on land were still overcoming the technical and tactical issues surrounding their new equipment. Nevertheless, he did not let his enthusiasm for air warfare blind him to the ongoing inter-service problems caused by the RAF's highly politicised commitment to the defence of Mesopotamia where, as he had feared, the savings in the ground forces were nowhere as large as had been hoped.

However, it was still possible to find a silver lining, as he eventually noted later in the year:

> The military side of the [Mesopotamian] question is that we are giving the RAF a chance to learn how to command and test their theories of running small campaigns. The experience we gain will be great and we shall be so much advanced over other nations when the next war comes.[11]

Meanwhile, although he was able to enjoy the Name Day Feast at Corpus Christi College, and the Old Tonbridgian Dinner at the Connaught Hotel, the month of June 1922 was overshadowed by the murder of Field Marshal Sir Henry Wilson in the street just outside his Eaton Square House in London on the 21st of the month. In common with the rest of the establishment, my father's reaction was one of shock:

> Poor Lady Wilson will be in a dreadful state about it all and will not be left any too well off. Two men have been arrested but that does not do much good. It is certain to create a sensation & will make dealing with the Irish question more and more difficult. [...] Being an Ulsterman he naturally had that cause very much at heart and it is presumably Sinn Féin who have murdered him. He was looking so exceedingly well last Saturday when he visited us and I had lent my car over to him on Monday to take him to inspect his Regt. the Ulster Rifles.[12]

Knowing Wilson well, my father had no difficulty believing that the field marshal had drawn his sword in his defence. Whether this rumour was true, what certainly was true was that my father had lost a good friend, to whom he owed his appointments to command in Russia and at Camberley.

In July, my father settled down to broadening his own mind by studying Bolshevik literature about the Russian 1914 campaign in East Prussia to prepare himself for his visit to Tannenberg, where he proposed to make a study of the first great German victory of the war on the Eastern Front. However, his plans were temporarily delayed when he was suddenly taken ill on 21 July after enduring a night of pain and sickness:

> By the time Scott [the Medical Officer] came in the morning I was all tied up in knots after a very short consultation between Scott and Goodwin, they told me that I ought to get into the hands of a Surgeon at once, so I ordered my car & packed off at once. [...] Apparently I had been suffering from a 'fulminating appendix' sufficiently awe-inspiring name. Anyway they operated just in time & the amount of filth taken out of my inside was I believe colossal. Extraordinary how quickly these things come on & quite without warning of any kind.[13]

He was up and about after fourteen days and by the middle of August he was able to visit the War Office and show himself off again to his superiors. Locally, he attended the unveiling of the Camberley and Frimley War Memorial by the Duke of Connaught, which had been erected just outside the Staff College gates. Also, his own memories of the Great War were brought back to life by a letter from General Viscount Byng of Vimy, who was then currently Governor General of Canada, congratulating him on his appointment and informing him that one of Byng's ADCs, Major George Vanier, was shortly to join as a student – only the second French Canadian to do so, after my father's friend and wartime colleague, Edouard Panet.[14] George Vanier did extremely well at Camberley and in the end also became Governor General of Canada.

On 1 September my father, together with Christopher Stone, set off on the boat train from Victoria Station to visit East Prussia and to see for himself the battlefield of Tannenberg with the intention of writing his own informed account of the military encounters between the German and Russian Armies that took place during the first month of the Great War. From my father's point of view the Tannenberg Campaign, which had been so-named by General Ludendorff to turn the 1440 defeat into a 1914 victory, was of particular interest to the British Army because it showed what a small well-trained force could achieve in the face of numerical strength. Pursuing this logic to its obvious conclusion, the advent of new weapons that had not been available to the commanders of 1914 led my father to accordingly assert that the army that had most thoroughly adopted mechanisation, and could therefore use this advantage to economise on its manpower, would in all likelihood enjoy success.

For my father, the Continental tour was inspiring, but for Christopher Stone it was graphic. They saw all the towns and villages and had sight of the inhabitants who had endured the fighting. They ranged over the battlefields and viewed the countryside, now scattered with many military memorials and cemeteries. They conversed with all the officials and conferred with Lithuanian ministers and senior officers. They also met former senior officers from the Tsar's armies and did all of this to be able to analyse the quality of the troops and their leaders, as well as their weaponry and the nature of the land over which the battles were fought.

My father was firmly of the opinion that the Staff College was there to introduce up-to-date staff training and that the students should have access to original publications, instead of having to rely on theoretical values, half-truths and outdated practice. Having returned and written up his analysis of all that he had learned, he therefore set about turning his analysis into a book on the Tannenberg Campaign which could also be employed as a textbook for the students. There would also be a practical advantage on a personal financial level – or at least, he hoped there might be, particularly if it were to be used as a textbook.

His return to Britain saw him at last move into Staff College House and resume family life, which had been impossible due to the tardiness of the Department of Works in redecorating the residence. Unfortunately, the army threw further complications in his way by refusing to allow him to publish his book when it was completed. This was despite the fact that my father was lecturing other institutions on the campaign and openly gaining fees and expenses for his services. However, the refusal was not a personal slight on my father, but rather a reflection of Cavan's aversion to any serving officers publishing on military matters.[15] Consequently, he had to wait more than a year before he was able to win his case and see the book in print, finally putting his literary agent to work on securing publication in 1925.

The book was eventually released by Blackwoods, priced at 15s. The first 750 copies were to pay no royalties, but my father need not have worried about his sales and eventual profits. When publication day dawned, he had many applauds and a flood of favourable reviews in both the national dailies and institutional journals, and the book eventually ran on to three editions. By 1927 he was able to note that 874 copies had been sold and that he was starting to receive royalties.

By the end of November 1922, my father had achieved all the aims and objectives that he had set himself on arrival at the Staff College, except for having RAF instructors on his staff. Through army eyes, having RAF instructors at Camberley was seen as part of the solution to the modernisation programme, but in the eyes of the RAF this was seen as part of the problem. As Chief of the Air Staff, Trenchard had until now been flying high under the wings of Winston Churchill, who had put the RAF into the chair of Middle East Command, but when Churchill lost his seat in Parliament on 17 November, the RAF lost its champion at Westminster and Trenchard found himself obliged to fall into line with the War Office requirements to a far greater degree than before.

Much as he appreciated the ways in which air power had revolutionised warfare, my father continued to vocalise his concerns about the rifts that were developing between the RAF and the two older services. Although it was clear that it was the airmen who were at the greater fault, my father saw that problems on both sides of the argument were hindering its resolution in a way that would affect all concerned. Relationships with the RAF remained strained for some time after Winston Churchill left government, but even if the RAF may have seen my father as being part of the problem, he had nevertheless prescribed the right solution for the army.

At the start of 1923 he was in full swing with his own advanced training programme and he had two RAF officers, one Australian airman and two Royal Navy officers to top up the complement of first and second-year students. He was 43 years old, and all set for an active future in implementing change at the Staff College, influencing public opinion and developing imperial defence strategy, but it took him another three months to win over the RAF to his way of thinking.

In mustering the expert speakers for his lectures, he was able to pick up people he had met during the course of attending the meetings of the Central Asian Society and dining as an honoured guest with the Raleigh Club at All Soul's, Oxford; the Fellows of Corpus Christi College, Cambridge; the Royal Navy Club; and the Honourable Artillery Company in London. It was my father's intention to bring in expertise from outside whenever possible, and his collected experts were all as willing to speak to the students as he was to have them brightening the lecture halls at Camberley. However, the RAF remained unwilling to deliver their message to the students, notwithstanding the fact that, as the army's next generation of staff officers and commanders, these very men were being trained to command forces which could include air force personnel.

One way or another, my father was able to break through the barriers, either by direct approaches to the Chief of the Air Staff or indirectly through pressures being brought to bear on the RAF Staff College and letting his views be known through expert institutional circles. In any case, the RAF was being urged by the CIGS to agree to an interchange of instructors, but Trenchard refused to co-operate. Finally, he crossed swords with the Chief of the Air Staff at a meeting in the War Office on 13 March when he found the atmosphere less intimidating than he expected, so Trenchard must have been forewarned about the secretary of state's attitude towards the status of the RAF, even if he was not aware of what had been said in the debate at the House of Commons:

> I found that he was really frightened that we should regard the Air as a mere adjunct to the Army and that it should not be regarded as a power in itself. I told him quite straight that the Army required the modern invention of the aeroplane and that it could no more do without it than without artillery & that his policy of regarding the Air as something apart was delaying the training of the Army. I by no means considered that the sole duty of the air was to act with the Army It was the old old story of the Independent Cavalry again. There was only a certain proportion of cavalry & what there was had to be dished out to the best advantage.
>
> He asked me what staff work was required and I had to tell him that I must have an Airman for staff work. He didn't even know what staff work meant, organisation, administration, and General Staff work.
>
> In the end he decided that he saw my point, and would let me have an officer.[16]

So, by the end of the meeting he could actually say that he was walking on air:

> Brooke-Popham, Commandant of the Air Force Staff College and Higgins, who was in the Navy, and is now a sort of DSD [director of staff duties] of the

Air Ministry, were there but both were very quiet & frightened of Trenchard. Trenchard has no facility in expressing himself.[17]

On Friday, 13 April 1923 my father joined the party at the farewell dinner of two of his directing staff who were better known for their distinguished services in the 1939–45 war than their time spent as instructors at Camberley:

> Lieutenant Colonel Gort, VC, DSO and Lieutenant Colonel Neame, VC, DSO were two practical officers of outstanding merit. The students showed their appreciation by burying them in all the honours and they kept up an uproarious evening until the early hours of the morning. We don't often get two officers with VCs with so much brain or desire to work as these two.[18]

Gort, my father felt, was the most effective of all the lecturers, but in both Gort and Philip Neame – later Lieutenant General Sir Philip Neame who, as GOC Cyrenaica, would be Rommel's first opponent in the Western Desert – he saw evidence of a definite human touch that ensured them the devotion of their students.

With this in mind, it is interesting to note that the only flaw identified by Gort with relation to the Staff College syllabus under my father's charge was that insufficient attention was paid to what Gort called 'man-mastership'; that is to say, leadership on a personal level, which Gort saw as particularly essential for preventing a recurrence of what in the previous war had been characterised as 'shell-shock'.[19] While indicative of Gort's patrician care for the men under his command, this criticism does also emphasise one of the key flaws in a man who would rise to become one of my father's peers during the late 1930s, namely a tendency to become too much focused on fine detail. For while man-mastership was an essential attribute of the regimental officer, the successful staff officer needed to keep his mind on a far broader situation, beyond the confines of regimental soldiering: Gort, one feels, never entirely succeeded in making the distinction.

Being a student, or even an instructor, at the Staff College was one way of understanding the way of life on the staff in the army, but being commandant was a much more demanding experience, albeit one that my father relished. Nevertheless, he had his future in the army to consider as well as his present post. His future in the army was assured until the end of his term as commandant, still two years away, but the prospects of further advancement were diminished at the end of 1923 by the newly elected Labour Government of Ramsay MacDonald, the military outlook of which was, in the main, extremely short-sighted. In all events, however, the political shift and financial cuts set my father to seriously considering what form his future would take after he left Camberley in 1926.

In January 1925 there were twelve field marshals on the active list, which included the traditional eight who had been promoted to that rank along with three members of the royal household and a marshal of France. There were sixteen listed full generals, of whom only four held active commands, along with two more who were imperial governors. Out of the listed lieutenant generals, numbering thirty, only fourteen were employed and amongst all the budding and flowering major generals the prospects of further employment and advancement were sticky, as a smaller pool of talent was needed to keep the available posts filled. My father was now forty-eighth on the list and naturally those already employed were reluctant to give up their commands to join the half-pay lists and pensioned soldiery. To keep his name afloat in the minds of the selectors, some of whom he had just met, he wrote off to the adjutant general to alert him personally to his preference for command of a Regular division, knowing that the 1st and 3rd were going vacant in July 1926.

When General Sir George Milne, his former superior at Constantinople who had become CIGS in February 1926 in succession to Cavan, was attending the Combined Operations Conference at the Staff College the following month, my father refrained from mentioning his own predicament or what was happening in other commands. However, upon Milne's departure, 'he said, "I shan't say goodbye, as I shall soon be seeing you more often".'[20] The appointment of Milne had been wholeheartedly welcomed by my father, who wrote on hearing the identity of the new CIGS, 'I look upon today as the beginning of a new era for the Army. We shall now get expert guidance from a fine hand.'[21]

Being well aware that his time at the Staff College was drawing to an end made him think back for a moment to his being picked out as commandant:

> Somehow or other it does not seem as if I have done a full four years here. It has been a wonderful education for me and I can never bless Henry Wilson enough for having sent me here. [...] I have tried to make this place a human place and do away with any kind of abracadabra. All controversy has been reduced to facts and analysed at once. Any difficult point I have investigated and passed over nothing. [...] I have initiated the campaign for the reform of the Staff College and have apparently succeeded in effecting the reform which will be brought in pretty soon.[22]

For the most part, this is a fair analysis of his time at Camberley, but sadly, not all his reforms would last beyond his departure, with the integration of air power into the syllabus continuing through the interwar years in a manner that was patchy at best. My father's institution of lectures by outside experts, although it continued after his departure, was by the 1930s considered a distraction too far removed from the practical training that was necessary to prepare officers for the coming renewal of war.

Some criticism has also been made of the intellectual ethos of the interwar Staff College, in particular the fact that it was too easy for a lazy officer to get by doing the bare minimum, summed up by Fuller's 1923 instruction to that year's intake, 'During your course here no one is going to compel you to work, for the simple reason that a man who requires to be driven is not worth the driving'.[23] It may be inferred that neither Fuller nor my father would have done anything other than take full opportunity of all the intellectual opportunities afforded by Camberley's extensive library, but by failing to account for the fact that not all entrants would share their professional enthusiasm, the resulting educational mindset did perhaps lack the ethos that would have shaken the lazy and complacent sufficiently that they either buckled down or dropped out.

As well as feeling that he had done some good for the college, my father also felt that his time as commandant had been of great personal and professional utility. For him, at least, the intellectual opportunities had been gratefully grasped:

> Without reading and ample time in which to ponder and think, it is impossible to turn out a good leader. The greatest blessing that I have experienced at the Staff College has been the chance to ponder over the events of the war and to digest the lessons thoroughly. Had I continued to swash-buckle for years, as I was forced to do in 1919, 1920 & 1921, I should never have had time to collect my thoughts. The Staff College has also taught me how to write, talk and teach – all things which no other place could possibly have given me.[24]

At the beginning of April 1926, he had given his last lectures to the Senior Division at Camberley and on 19 April the directing staff and all the other officers at Camberley said their farewells to my father at a dinner in his honour.

This coincided with the Miners' Federation of Great Britain giving notice of their May Day intention to go on strike, which precipitated the General Strike of 4–13 May. The 1 May announcement that the strike would begin the following week found my father on his way to the family home in Norfolk to begin a spell on half pay, pending a further appointment. There was little trouble as he passed through London, albeit some militants were in evidence, and in rural Norfolk the strike barely made any impact. With the industrial unrest apparently quelled for the moment, he received a telegram on 27 May which gave him cause for much speculation, as he confided to his diary that night:

> When I got home I found a telegram from old Boney Fuller asking me to go up to London to see the CIGS at 3 p.m. tomorrow afternoon. As very few trains are available it means motoring. Old Uncle George has very little thought for anybody else apparently. Boney told me that he thought he had a swollen head. He certainly isn't considerate in any way. I can only think that they had their

meeting of the Selection Board on the 20th and that they have dished out their jobs in the way of Divisions and that Uncle George is now preparing to ask me if I would care to be DMO&I [director of military operations and intelligence]. He would have no cause to send for me on any other pretext as far as I can see. He would offer that through the Military Secretary. For a personal job acting under him he does not wish to run the risk of a refusal and so didn't want to write about it. One never knows and it may be something quite trivial in which case I shall be very angry indeed. I had a kind of feeling that he would not be able to do without me at the War Office.[25]

Fuller, it should be explained, was now serving as Milne's military assistant after his tenure at Camberley had come to its end earlier that year. He was therefore well placed to keep my father abreast of all that was going on at the War Office, where my father travelled the following day to visit Milne as requested:

He shook me by the hand and asked me to sit down and then he started straightaway saying that he was going to be quite frank with me. I had been tactless and complained that the 1st and 3rd Divisions had been given to other people. I didn't want to wait a minute to let him to go, but said it was a gross libel and demanded to know who had said it. He tried to brush the thing aside, but I wouldn't let him and made him take it back. At first he said that he would say no more about it and I said that I wouldn't have that – he must withdraw it. After about 20 minutes he did and I calmed down.

We then sat & went through the usual sort of affair & that he had now the 2nd Division to offer me. This I was happy to get and told him so. He then began again to say that I thought I had been forgotten and I had to go at him again and tell him that I had thought of retiring but that was because I had been offered a very good job but that whether I went or not was my own affair.[26]

In June, my father attended the Staff College reunion and visited Tonbridge School to inspect the Cadet Corps before moving in to Churchill House at Aldershot to take up command of 2nd Division on 1 September. Although, as he made clear to Milne, he had continued to be tempted by offers of a career outside the army, he was increasingly finding that he had a role and vocation within it as both a moderniser and an advocate of modernisation.

As he had earlier reflected, his time at Camberley had taught him how to teach, and he hoped for the opportunity to do more in that line of work. The Imperial Defence College was in the process of being set up as he left Camberley, with its intended remit being to facilitate greater understanding between senior military officers, diplomats, civil servants and officials. As such, it represented a further refinement, moving further into the realms of strategy, of what was being done for lower-ranking officers at Camberley and the other service colleges. While my father acknowledged that Vice Admiral Sir Herbert Richmond was an excellent choice as its first commandant, he considered that it would be a good thing if he himself could succeed Richmond in that role when it fell to the army to provide the next incumbent.

As a moderniser, my father's practical approach was expressed through a clear desire to incorporate new technology into the army's traditional roles without tying it up with excessive dogmatic doctrine. In terms of his general professional views at this stage in his career, much can be gained from a paper that he prepared in January 1923 for Major General James MacBrien in Ottawa. MacBrien had commanded 12th Canadian Brigade at Vimy and Passchendaele and was now Chief of General Staff (CGS) of the Canadian Militia – in effect, the C-in-C of Canada's land forces.

My father envisaged a world in which future warfare would be decided to a far greater extent by the application of air power, requiring an expansion of the RAF and a partial redefinition of roles for the other two services. Crucially, he saw no opportunity for an expeditionary force to be despatched from Britain so long as there was an air battle going on in the skies above, partly on practical grounds but primarily because, judging by 1914 when two divisions had been initially withheld from the BEF and used for home defence, it would be politically unacceptable. This, however, could be turned to advantage since it would allow time for the small peacetime army to be increased in size: like Kitchener in 1914, he saw the Regulars rather than the Territorials as the basis for any expansion of manpower. This was based, in part, on a prejudice against 'incompetent senior Territorial officers, who have to be employed because of their political or local influence', a view common amongst Regular officers of my father's generation, but also because of a belief that the depots of existing Regular units were the best place to train new recruits for whichever branches of the army required expansion to meet the enemy in question.

The Territorial units should, he felt, be structured entirely as a home defence force and their energies 'devoted firstly to the cult of anti-aircraft work, with guns and searchlights, barrages, balloons and aeroplanes, so that there may be defence against bombing'. Against the possibility of an invasion by air – which was not then practicable but which he feared may become a future threat – there was naturally a role for Regular formations in home defence but:

> [I]t would also appear that the secondary duty of the Territorial Force is the provision of quickly transportable units ready to move to any threatened point. This means motor cars, of which, with lorries and busses there are any amount. Fighting mobile machines, armoured cars and tanks, preferably the former owing to the good roads in England, would therefore seem indicated for the Territorial

Force backed up by a certain amount of moppers up in the way of Infantry and a few technical troops, artillery and sappers.[27]

In such a war, the RAF would take part in both the air defence of Britain and air attacks on the enemy, and the Royal Navy would likewise defend British coastal waters – my father felt that submarines would be of most use here, which would with hindsight prove a mistaken belief – and strike against enemy trade with its cruisers and large warships.

Having discussed home defence in the context of a major war, although noticeably without saying anything about what the army would do, or how it would do it, once an expeditionary force could safely be sent to Europe, my father then reviewed the options for the global employment of the army. In terms of small wars, the most likely theatres seemed to be in the Near and Middle East – Egypt, Palestine and Iraq – where 'a show may begin [...] at any moment', and 'India, which must always be maintained and though the question of a Bolshevik invasion is mere moonshine, still the state of the country is always a care to the British Government'.

Otherwise, however, he felt that the remainder of the Empire was safe in the event of anything short of an attack by a grouping of powers as part of major global war. This was a prospect 'so far out of practical politics that it cannot be considered at present', although the inevitable 'premonitory grumblings' that would accompany the establishment of such a threatening power bloc would allow countermeasures to be begun. My father therefore ended his paper by returning to the potential lesser conflicts that the army might face, and the means with which they might be fought:

> The Army then, for small wars in the Middle East and India remains the main implement. The advent of aeroplanes, tanks and armoured cars has definitely put the balance in favour of the Regular Army, despite the improved armament possessed by Egyptians and Arabs, and small wars will be much easier to run in every way. The composition of an Army for each small war will have to be thought out as the question arises, the main thing being whether mechanical transport can be substituted for camels, donkeys, horses and carriers.
>
> The internal defence of India has been still more simplified by the introduction of mechanical transport. Judging by the ease with which mechanical transport dealt with De Wet in South Africa and the counter revolution in Russia, I do not think that we have much to fear of a general insurrection there, taken in conjunction with the difference of creeds and so on.[28]

These ideas were well thought out and, for the most part, extremely prescient. The conversion of large swathes of the Territorial Army (TA) to the anti-aircraft role was still to come, although a start had been made in 1922 with the establishment of two air defence brigades in the London area, while the ideas relating to the use of armoured cars and other mobile forces to resist an invasion was essentially the doctrine that my father elected to employ as GOC Home Forces in 1940.

The use of mechanisation in small wars and in India was both reminiscent of what my father had done on a small scale in Persia, and a prefiguring of what he would later advocate as quartermaster general in India, a decade later. However, much of what was discussed in the paper was essentially theoretical and dealt with war at the strategic and operational levels. What he now needed, and was about to get as GOC 2nd Division, was the opportunity to gain practical experience with the army's new mechanised equipment and the tactics that went with it.

12

Command at Home

The headquarters of 2nd Division in Aldershot were to be found in a red-bricked house at the end of the Marlborough Lines, with one of the junior staff officers living in quarters at the end of it. Although my father took command at a slack period in the annual cycle of training and manoeuvres, it quickly became apparent that the tempo of life at Aldershot was rather less than that to which he had been accustomed at Camberley:

> Here am I in Command of 2nd Division and writing in the office. It is a curious sensation. All the training for the year has ceased and units have settled down to a leave season and individual training. In point of actual fact there is practically nothing for me to do. After commanding the Staff College I shall find work especially easy. [...] I am given a full Colonel as a GSO1[,] another as AA&G with a Staff-Captain to do the 'G'. They have a good deal of time in which to do little. They are all very civil and willing. The two Colonels are both considerably older than I am but do not show any ill-will about it.[1]

Although my father expressed no problem with the officer initially serving as his GSO1, it would not be long before he requested the services of 'Boney' Fuller to replace him, and Fuller would serve in that capacity for the remainder of my father's tenure as divisional commander. The circumstances that led to Fuller being available for this post, and their effect on the ongoing development of mechanisation in the army, are important and will be returned to later.

2nd Division had three brigades of infantry, all now back on the old four-battalion establishment, with Royal Artillery and Royal Engineer attachments, being constituted as follows:

Table VI: 2nd Division Order of Battle, 1926

4th Guards Brigade
   1st Grenadier Guards
   3rd Grenadier Guards
   1st Coldstream Guards
   1st Scots Guards
5th Infantry Brigade
   2nd Buffs
   1st King's Own Royal Regiment
   2nd Norfolk Regiment
   2nd Dorsetshire Regiment
6th Infantry Brigade
   1st Devonshire Regiment
   1st Northamptonshire Regiment
   2nd Queen's Own Royal West Kent Regiment
   2nd King's Royal Rifle Corps
Royal Artillery
   3rd Field Brigade
   4th Field Brigade
   8th Field Brigade
   3rd Pack Brigade
Royal Engineers
   5th Field Company
   11th Field Company
   38th Field Company

My father spent October settling into Churchill House – where the Ironside family now comprised myself, my mother and my sister – and getting to know his senior subordinates and staff. He also went out and about to inspect the various units under his command and organise the many training schemes being implemented by the brigade and regimental officers. He also attended the Motor Show at Olympia and joined the Selection Board at the University of London for choosing a Professor of Military Studies, as well as travelling up to Sheffield as a guest of the Cutlers' Company to dine at their hall and respond to their toast to 'imperial forces' on behalf of the army. In addressing the Cutlers, he made it clear to his audience that the army was mechanising and that the industrial resources of Sheffield had an important part to play in providing machines that could be adapted for war purposes and which would economise in the use of manpower. He also visited the Vickers Company works on the following day.

That mechanisation was taking root in the British Army was emphasised by a major demonstration of tanks, armoured cars and six-wheeled and tracked all-terrain vehicles which was staged for the Dominion Premiers at Aldershot that autumn. However, it was also clear that there remained considerable resistance to change, as he noted after the rehearsal on 8 November:

I thought it was the best show I have seen for years. I sat next [to] old Knox, the Director of Military Training and after it all his only remark was 'the horse is not done by a long chalk yet.' Personally I could hardly imagine that anybody would sit there and not be convinced that the horse was dead as far as the Army is concerned. It was a sad sight to see a smart Gunner Subaltern going past on a blood chestnut horse all looking round as if to say 'see what a smart pair we are' and a most magnificent team of eight Suffolk Punches pulling a 60-pdr team. Immediately behind them came their mechanical substitutes. Anybody could see how much more efficient these were. All the latest tanks from the great 30 tonner to the little two-man fellow made by Martell & turned out by Morris. The great improvement which was shown was the wheeled vehicles which had a track in their centre which they let down when they required it. Over 80% of the work will be done on wheels & only 20% on tracks. The pace is much increased with wheels and the running costs are of course much smaller.

They showed us the tanks and dragoons going down a hill at over 30 miles an hour. The momentum of 30 tons going at 30 miles is terrific & yet we are asked to tell the infantry not to be frightened of them. I am afraid I find it difficult to do myself.[2]

My father's resolve to promote mechanisation was reinforced by his experience of working with tanks during the closing months of the First World War, and the significance of this experience was underlined by the progress that had been made during the first decade of tank development. It is clear from my father's earlier written opinions that he was already a complete convert to mechanisation long before taking command of 2nd Division, but the 1926 demonstrations served to reinforce the opinions that he had already developed and demonstrated how much progress had been made in the all-arms mechanisation that made large mechanised formations a real and practical possibility:

Infantry really are no good against tanks and I cannot see the men waiting till they come. I saw the most stout-hearted of machine-gunners on the German side rolled up easily by tanks. All these things we saw at the mechanical demonstration are mere beginnings & yet they are sufficiently terrifying to infantry in themselves. The power to move on wheels on roads and on tracks across country has revolutionised things. There will be no infantry shortly except on lorries for use in very bad country – to be brought back to the mechanical transport as soon as their job is done. I must voice this opinion pretty strongly during the ensuing years. I am sure I shall get a good many people to rally round me.[3]

In the context of my father's closing assertion, it is interesting to note the historian Professor Brian Bond's categorisation of officer attitudes to mechanisation at this time, in which he lists five categories. The first were 'revolutionaries', mostly Royal Tank Corps officers, who envisaged an armoured army in which the tank would have the prime role and many of whom, like Fuller and his contemporary Major Percy Hobart, would harm their careers through their outspoken advocacy of their cause. Then came 'reformers', many of them a little more senior than the first group, with practical experience of working with tanks and armoured cars during the previous war and seeing the new arm as the dominant one within what would still remain an all-arms force.

Next, Professor Bond characterises the largest group – into which he places my father – as 'progressives', men who realised that improvement was needed but who were prepared to be pragmatic about it and work in small steps. What is interesting about this group is it contains not only some extremely senior figures from the last war, including Rawlinson and Milne, but also some rather more junior officers who would go on to great things after 1939, including Montgomery, Brooke, Auchinleck and Slim. Within this group, however, Professor Bond specifically marks out my father along with the future Earl Wavell – at that time a divisional GSO1 – as being particular converts to mechanisation; in the case of my father, after his wartime experiences and the chance to develop his ideas while at Camberley, this is not to be wondered at. The remainder of the army's senior officers, Professor Bond categorises as either 'conservatives', who might at best accept mechanisation as an adjunct to the existing arms, and 'reactionaries' who, largely on social grounds, looked down on the whole grubby affair from their position on horseback.[4]

The six-wheelers and trackers were the forerunners of today's all-terrain vehicles, which have been used in the most mountainous regions of the world, but at this early stage such performance was not a realistic expectation. Engines, transmissions and vehicle components were not capable of meeting present-day performance standards for armoured vehicles used by the infantry. The light tanks of the day were too slow for a scouting role, the medium tanks were verging on obsolete, there was no effective anti-tank gun, and although a prototype self-propelled artillery piece, the Birch Gun, had been introduced, the concept was never developed. This is not to belittle the progress that had been made, which was considerable, but the technological shortfalls do help to emphasise why a steady evolutionary approach was to be preferred over radical change. The fact that worthwhile projects like the Birch Gun were not proceeded with also underlines the extremely restrictive financial situation under which the interwar army was operating.

As an artilleryman himself, my father was naturally very taken with the Birch Gun, but also committed his thoughts with respect to the ongoing debate over the relative merits of wheels and tracks:

> It is interesting to see how the Quartermaster General and the Master General of the Ordnance fight over these questions. The MGO declares that a fighting vehicle must have tracks and the QMG would like to keep to wheels. Personally, I think that we shall have:–
> (i) Fighting vehicles with tracks and wheels which can be taken up and down at will. The wheels to do the ordinary work and the tracks only to come into action when the ground necessitates it.
> It is essential that fighting vehicles should have tracks.
> (ii) First-line transport of six-wheelers. These are ready practically to work at speed over even bad roads & can, if necessary, negotiate bad country at slow speed.
> (iii) Big heavy vehicles servicing the six-wheelers. Not to be required to move off road.[5]

The quarrels between these various factions, of which the differences between the QMG and MGO were but a minor example, were already becoming substantially entrenched, with strong words being used to defend strong opinions.

With Milne as CIGS a hesitant convert to the ideas of mechanisation, it seemed as if steady progress could be expected as far as the parlous state of interwar finances permitted, but this was not enough for Fuller and other 'revolutionaries', and Fuller in particular seems to have assumed that his access to Milne in his capacity as military assistant gave him rather more influence and independence than he in fact possessed. This led him to disastrously overplay his hand in a manner which, although it made him available to assist my father as GSO1 to 2nd Division, did great harm to the cause of mechanisation and to Fuller's own career. In short, it was planned for 1927 to create a brigade-sized Experimental Mechanised Force to push forward the development of doctrine for large-scale mechanisation, and Fuller was selected to command it. However, the command also included administrative responsibilities covering the garrison at Tidworth, which Fuller attempted to avoid. His logic was that he would need all his time to devote to the mechanisation project, but his high-handed attitude in presenting to Milne the conditions under which he would accept the post pushed the CIGS too far. Fuller found his appointment promptly cancelled, the Experimental Mechanised Force being instead placed under Colonel Jack Collins, a far less radical officer. Fuller tendered his resignation, which was refused, and his ally in the press, the military pundit Captain B.H. Liddell Hart, produced a scathing attack on the army's perceived failure to mechanise.

Although my father clearly retained great respect for Fuller and his ideas, as evidenced most obviously by the fact that he requested his services at Aldershot, Fuller's fall from grace provided a clear lesson as to the damage that a too enthusiastic championing of reform could have on one's career prospects. This in turn may help explain why, although the views that my father espoused at Camberley and retained when he first came to Aldershot might well be taken as qualifying him as one of Professor Bond's 'reformers', his ultimate realisation that mechanical practicalities and service politics would between them prevent any sort of overnight reform explains his eventual espousal of the 'progressive' standpoint.

As GOC 2nd Division, my father was directly subordinated to Aldershot Command which was intended to form the nucleus of any expeditionary force that might be mobilised for future hostilities. This placed him under the command of Lieutenant General Sir Philip Chetwode, a former cavalryman who had commanded XX Corps in Allenby's campaign against the Turks. Since the war, Chetwode had served as deputy CIGS and as adjutant general, and after leaving Aldershot would spend the remainder of his career in India where his path would again cross my father's.

In Professor Bond's characterisation of professional attitudes previously alluded to, Chetwode is placed with my father in the 'progressive' camp, but my father nevertheless detected some doubts in the mind of his superior officer, whose attitudes were at times a little too horsey for his taste and who did not share the same drive for modernisation that my father possessed. He also believed that to protect the tank against future armour-piercing weapons would render it so heavily armoured as to significantly reduce its mobility. To my father, this missed the point that, even if they were to be proved true, Chetwode's reservations did not prevent the use of existing tanks and armoured vehicles in the sort of small wars where the likely opponents would have no antidote to them. As well as saving lives, my father considered that such an employment of tanks would provide great experience in their use which would be invaluable in the future.

Because my father's command was headquartered at Aldershot, he was able to remain in the loop and further his reputation for introducing mechanisation and modernising staff training, which had now marked him out as a model for future high command. At the same time, he did not lose touch with leaders of industry and public affairs in London, who were just as eager to seek his opinions as he was to be seen in their company. In this, Chetwode's social contacts gave him a clear advantage over many of his peers, notably the inarticulate and unsociable Milne who had little political capital to deploy, and my father took good note of this contrast as an example of how the game should be played. He therefore took every opportunity of dining out with the great and the good to see and be seen by the leaders of government and industry. Such social activities were not purely intended as career furthering, however, for my father was determined to keep his mind active and to avoid the mental stagnation that he feared would ensue during a long spell of garrison duty.

As well as championing mechanisation, my father also kept up his interest in military aviation. In November 1926, No. 4 (Army Co-operation) Squadron, the RAF unit attached to 2nd Division, was the victim of two crash-landings in the area, which brought my father into closer contact with the airmen:

> I found quite an intelligent youngster called Slessor in charge. He walked very lame and had evidently had a crash. The Aerodrome at Farnborough is a bad one and they are having a good many crashes which mean the writing off of the machine. It always had an evil reputation. They still have these old Bristol fighters.
>
> One of them crashed just after I left the Aerodrome, both pilot & aircraftsman killed. [...] They are unavoidable, these crashes and they only prove that our people are really flying and not shirking.[6]

The Bristol Fighter was an early example of the fighter-bomber type, being a heavily armed two-seater with good manoeuvrability. However, the type had first flown in 1916 and, although modified post-war for the Army Co-operation role, the last 'Brisfits' were reaching the end of their useful life. After the accident, my father naturally expressed his concern to Squadron Leader John Cotesworth Slessor – who was destined to become a marshal of the RAF and, in 1950, Chief of the Air Staff – and the airman wrote back to say:

> Thank you very much for your kind note. We've just finished the Court of Inquiry; another case of error of judgement, I'm afraid. Impossible to discover why it happened. Worst of it is these darned newspapers always make such a song and dance about 'all them crashes' which makes it difficult to get an adequate supply of young officers of the right type.[7]

Then on 16 December a second Bristol Fighter crashed into one of the Norfolk Regiment's barrack rooms:

> [I]t took us twenty minutes to get the pilot out with axes and hacksaws. I thought he was particularly plucky and hardly a groan came out of him as they got him onto a stretcher. The petrol had burst and I was terrified that the whole thing would go up in flames.
>
> In the afternoon I walked up to the hospital and found that the pilot was not really so badly burned as had been expected. [...] It was another young temporary officer, but this time no idea that he was badly in debt or didn't mind what he was doing.
>
> I only hope that the papers will not make any more fuss.[8]

Shortly afterwards, my father found that his experience with these two crashes gave him a renewed contact with Sir Hugh Trenchard on the occasion of an invitation to dine with the Merchant Taylors on their schools' day. Held on 21 December, the headmasters of most of the well-known schools were present in their robes, and this provided a useful icebreaker for a discussion with the Chief of the Air Staff:

> He has a stepson at Eton and another at Stowe. He didn't agree with Eton at all and said that Alington was a rotter which I can well believe. Stowe he thought was much better. There are too many boys at Eton and they take not the slightest notice of parents' wishes as regards their boys' futures.
>
> Trenchard told me that he was getting every day anonymous letters and signed letters telling him that he was killing all the pilots by his behaviour. He remembered to me the time that Birkenhead and Winston tried to get him to down Haig by claiming all the men for the RAF. He said that they worked their hardest to estrange Haig and Wully Robertson by telling each bits of what the other had said. He warned each not to be influenced by any talk.
>
> We discussed the reasons for the high numbers of crashes and he pointed out that war flying would never get any safer. Civil flying naturally would, but war pilots had to fly in all weathers. I told him that I thought the short service was responsible for a good deal of it & he did not agree. The publication of casualty lists would serve no good purpose. He told me that he expected some 150 fatal casualties once the RAF had expanded to the required dimensions. I fancy the public will have something to say to that.[9]

It was clear that there was much upon which my father and Trenchard would never agree, but it is also clear that a mutual respect existed and the rest of the diary entry for this date contains an account of a wide-ranging discussion that took in Trenchard's own future prospects – he suspected at the time that he was being lined up as deputy CIGS, but would in fact remain in his current post for some time yet, with a promotion to Marshal of the Royal Air Force in the New Year – the recent death of Lord Rawlinson, and the somewhat farcical RAF career of T.E. Lawrence, who had enlisted in the ranks under an assumed name to escape from his post-war fame.

Back at Aldershot, both Chetwode and my father were now potentially in the running for promotion, and Chetwode was able to inform him that the situation for men of major general rank was now much improved. Chetwode, with whom he had developed a good, friendly working relationship that would last for many years, informed him that the Selection Board had been reduced in size, so that decisions were reached very much more quickly. As a result, jobs were being found both for officers coming to the end of their current postings and for those languishing on half pay.

Christmas gave some time off for reflection and, studying the top end of the Army List, my father noted that he was the youngest amongst the pool of sixteen officers who were likely to be in the running for CIGS to replace Milne if the latter retired as expected in 1930. This hardly put him in the serious running for the post, but assuming four-year tenures for Milne's successors, that pool would reduce to around thirteen by 1934 and to six in 1938:

> If I actually came up for CIGS in January 1938 at the same age or a little younger than Milne came up for it in 1926 I should have been a General Officer for just 20 years. Almost a record, I should say. I only hope I shall have passed on to something else by that time. In any case they must combine the head of some of the services by that time.[10]

The following day, he allowed himself some more general reflection:

> I look back on 1926 as not a very good year either for the country or for myself personally. We have lost enormous sums of money in the coal strike and it is all coming back to hit us taxpayers during 1927. Those of us who cannot make any money outside, cannot hope for any relief. My own year was spoilt by being five months on half-pay from 1 May to 1 October. I didn't really know which way to look for any money and I shall be short for another year. [...] I have now been given one of the four Regular Divisions in the country and have therefore been specially chosen. I think that means that if I do well here that I shall go on further.[11]

Although he was quite correct that he would see further advancement, this would not come without the further insecurity of another period on half pay, and although no career officer can be faulted for weighing up his chances of further advancement, it does seem that his preoccupation with his seniority and standing with respect to his peers was noted and commented upon by his contemporaries, some of whom would ultimately come to characterise him as overtly careerist. Indeed, it was commonly understood to be the case that he 'kept a large ledger in which he entered details of the service records of all the officers above him in the list, with his and other people's views on their performance, health, and prospects'.[12] It would seem that this 'ledger' was very likely no more than his daily diary, which most certainly does contain such observations, but it is clear from this alone that he kept a close eye on the Army List and on the standing and prospects of his peers and superiors.

In the British Army, divisional command was in peacetime a seat in the generals' waiting room for promotion, and the favourites in the race to the top were those whose wartime service and command ability outweighed their staff experience and, more often than not, those perceived by the government as suiting its political purpose. In 1927 the main governmental priority was to keep imperial defence at arms' length, while they sorted out the modernisation of the navy, army and air force at home. On 23 February 1927, he walked over to the headquarters in Aldershot to say goodbye to Sir Philip Chetwode, who was handing over to Lieutenant General Sir David Campbell, reviewing that day in his diary both Chetwode's prospects and those of the army's senior leadership more generally:

> He was considered for CIGS and Milne was given it, so that he is not likely to come up again. It is a pity, for he is a man of very strong character and who would always be straight and impartial. I think it is almost 1000-1 that Tim Harington is the next CIGS, which will be thoroughly bad for the Army. I simply cannot see how they will keep him out of it.[13]

General Sir Charles Harington – the 'Tim' nickname came from a coincidence of surnames with a notorious Irish politician active during his subaltern days – did not, in fact, succeed Milne, who would instead have his term as CIGS extended to run until 1933. It is not immediately clear quite why my father thought that Harington would have been so bad a choice as CIGS. He was another 'progressive' officer whose career progression had much resembled my father's own, including a stint as a staff officer with the Canadian Corps, but whose greater seniority in 1914 had seen him climb the ladder rather more quickly thereafter. That said, however, Harington's post-war career, which had seen him moved sideways through a series of command postings in a prime example of the 'Buggins' Turn' system that so bedevilled interwar career progression for men of my father's generation, certainly showed no great promise and my father would also later comment upon the apparent imbalance whereby the most senior jobs in the interwar years went to men whose experience in the First World War had been purely staff based, as Harington's had, at the expense of men who had experience as fighting leaders.[14]

Certainly, peacetime divisional command was about as far from fighting soldiering as it was possible to get. Returning from a levee at Buckingham Palace in February 1927, after five months in command, he confessed that he could hardly find a full day's work to do. This did, however, give him plenty of time to think about his profession:

> I am going to imagine a modern Force of 4 Divisions or so operating with the help of mechanical vehicles and to make a scheme on it. If I get down to anything satisfactory, I shall try and get it published in one of the military papers. It will be a good thing to get one's thoughts down on paper, as undigested ideas are not very much good.[15]

It was presumably with a view to getting his thoughts down on paper in just this manner that he drew up, later that month, some notes for his staff which took as their starting point the circumstances set out for the 1925 manoeuvres but approached them from the perspective of a modernised and mechanised force rather than the current organisation of divisions and brigades, which, in the present composition, were not suited for mobile warfare. He began by setting out his concepts and terms of reference:

Owing to the general use of the following instruments of war:

(i) Tanks & Armoured Cars
(ii) Mechanised Transport
(iii) Aircraft

the strategic and tactical marches of the future will be considerably modified.

(i) The proportion of infantry to other arms in a Division is far too high. Something like 2 brigades to the existing other arms will be nearer the mark.
(ii) Long infantry marching columns are too vulnerable and too slow to achieve success against a mobile enemy.
(iii) Strategical and tactical night marches will become much more general.
(iv) Winter will be chosen for fighting rather than summer. For preference the early winter.

In future, a general will have his troops disposed in fighting areas, not necessarily so close to each other as has been the case in late times – for they will be able to come up to support from a greater distance. He will no longer think in long marching columns, but in areas. So long as he knows how long it takes to fill one area from another – and this will be done mostly at night – that is all he requires. These fighting areas will have the troops of a given size and group ready for action – either to march or embus and they will be prepared to form front in any direction to face the attack of modern mobile forces.[16]

After sketching out an example of such a movement by areas, in which a force advanced by one or both of two parallel routes before converging to give battle, using mechanised transport until close to the enemy and then continuing with the infantry on foot, he returned to some of the problems that might need to be addressed, beginning with the importance of not taxing the infantry by lengthy pre-battle movements on foot, and then moving on to consider the threat posed by enemy mobile forces:

> Infantry must in future be used in country suitable to its nature. It cannot be used in open country suitable for the movement of fast tanks.
>
> Fighting areas must be made more or less tank-proof. One cannot afford to have mad elephants loose in one's camp even though one kills them later.
>
> The whole thing is most fascinating and I hope to be able to make accurate calculation as to the amount of transport and petrol that will be required.
>
> As regards vehicles for troops. There are large numbers of double-decker buses to take 50 men which have a radius of 100 miles and these are of course than those clumsy lorries built to carry heavy loads at a slower pace.
>
> We must get the infantry units much more handy in size. A coy. of 150 would be three busloads and 200 four busses. If we see to the firepower of these 200 men and abolish the Lewis Gun in favour of an [sic] universal automatic rifle we shall find a very handy unit. They could be no confusion between a battalion of 450 men supported with 9 busses and a bn. of 800 men marching along a road.
>
> The system of pooling buses would give one immense mobility. Resting units would not keep their buses.
>
> Would it be possible under these circumstances to have the 1st line transport of the new Bn. horsed or mechanical?
>
> What are the limits of the number of hours that the columns can usefully manipulate? What are the sizes of bus columns most suitable to movement? Will the size of the columns react on the size of the new Bn. and its organisation?[17]

It is interesting here, and perhaps somewhat surprising, that the one matter that is not addressed is the vulnerability of this system to attack from the air, with no measures listed to prevent air attacks beyond the desirability of moving at night. In other respects, however, the proposals seem a useful compromise between the ideals of mobile warfare and the continuing technological limitations.

The development and discussion of such schemes served a multitude of purposes, keeping his own professional wits sharp as well as – hopefully – sharpening those of his subordinates. He was not short of opportunities to lecture and speak about his thoughts and ideas, and this kept him abreast of all developments as well as in the sights of the selection boards. As well as his own book on Tannenberg, a short history of the Staff College had been dedicated to him and already published and he had written a foreword to *Basic Principles of Air Warfare (The Influence of Air Power on Sea and Land Strategy)*. Published under the pseudonym 'Squadron Leader', the author was in fact Major L.G. Burge, personal assistant to Sir Hugh Trenchard. To his diary, my father confided that it was 'not well written and it is difficult to follow at times, but it is a good beginning'.[18] In particular, he praised Burge's recognition of the fact that two opposing air forces must necessarily fight one another and could not simply be employed to act against enemy morale; this reflected his own view on the role of air power in a general war, which he had outlined at Camberley as part of his thoughts on the form of a future conflict.

In March 1927, he visited the old battlefields of Verdun and Vimy to scrutinise the scene again from a military point of view and he was not short of opportunities to meet his friends and colleagues at the sporting events and social gatherings within Aldershot Command, where career prospects were freely discussed and compared. Some prospect of active service briefly seemed likely when it became necessary to send British troops to China, where the armies of Chiang Kai-shek had occupied Hankow, where Britain had a trading concession, and were now menacing the international settlement at Shanghai. A division-sized Shanghai Defence Force was formed by taking a brigade from India and two from Britain, and my father entertained some hope of receiving the command.

Unfortunately, this was ruled out by the CIGS, who considered that it was sufficient to appoint a still-serving member of his old staff in Constantinople, Major General John Duncan, with Lord Gort as his GSO1. As the British Government were virtually acting as standard bearers on behalf of other nations who had their own trading interests to protect, the British military presence in China was organised to act in concert with the others to cover the vital entry ports along the 800-mile coastal strip. It was not war, but the situation warranted more than just a sideline command, particularly since the main points where intervention might be necessary – Peking, Shanghai and Canton – were so widely separated that it seemed to my father that if troops were sent there each force would need a commander, and a commander-in-chief to direct the three:

> Two of the key points are more or less just on the sea, whereas the northern one [Peking] is considerably inland. They are at this moment trying to run the business from London, a policy that can hardly go on for much longer. I fancy that we have tried to get the Japanese to run the new area at Peking and Tientsin and have failed and that is the reason for more troops being required.
>
> Every time I think of it all I get sicker and sicker about not being there in it all, instead of sitting here in Aldershot and being slowly denuded of all my troops and stores.[19]

The following day, having had one of his staff officers taken from him to go to China, he gave War Office policy in the theatre the benefit of further analysis:

> I have been thinking over this China question and it astounds me to find that we have sent out these thousands of infantrymen. We still think in the old terms of the Bn. Surely, it would have been better have sent modern tanks and armoured cars. Alas, we have so few of them and they might be required in the meantime

for a campaign in the meanwhile. For defence work in China we wanted less men and more machine-guns and aeroplanes.[20]

In fact, a small number of armoured cars did accompany Duncan's force and proved very useful, but my father was quite right to bemoan the lack of tanks and other trappings of mechanised warfare, the absence of which severely curtailed the effectiveness of the British force. Thankfully, however, the British role in China ended up being largely one of police work and holding the perimeter around Shanghai, for by the time Duncan's men had disembarked Chiang's forces had turned their attentions elsewhere.

Although thwarted in his hopes of getting the China command, my father continued to assess the opportunities for further advancement once his tenure as GOC 2nd Division came to an end. One option was to consider a stint in India, and the opportunity for such a posting seemed almost within his grasp after Field Marshal Sir Claude Jacob, military secretary to the India Office and so in effect the senior Indian Army representative in London, came to see him in Aldershot on 28 May 1927. Jacob explained that he was sounding out my father as a contender for the post of Chief of Staff of the Indian Army:

> The whole thing came as the greatest surprise to me and I pointed out to Jacob that I was still only a Major General, but he said that they would make me a Lieutenant-General at once. He pointed out that the pay was equivalent to £3,600 a year with a private railway carriage and that in actual fact I would be C-in-C of the Indian Army. He asked me if I was of the same opinion as the CIGS and I replied that, as far as I knew, I was. [...] I told Jacob that I would go willingly and at any time he required me.[21]

Lieutenant General Sir Andrew Skeen, the current post holder, had been a great disappointment and his position had become untenable in the rapidly changing programme of modernisation. There was a growing tendency towards separation between the army at home and the British Army in India, as the Army Council was stepping into the future while India was marking time, causing my father to remark that officers who came home from India with glowing reports often failed to live up to them when serving back in Britain. Also, social changes in India had made army life there less attractive for serving soldiers than had been the case in the past.

Understandably, however, the War Office could not let this upmarket verbal encounter pass by in silence and shortly after Jacob's visit, my father received a second call, this time from Sir George Milne:

> I walked down to the office to do a little office work and after I had been there a few minutes, who should walk in but the CIGS. He was staying with the C-in-C

and was going on to Ascot and the Tattoo tonight. He talked pleasantly enough and then I told him about Jacob's visit. I thought I had better do it because I wasn't going to have it said that I was intriguing or was discontented. He said first that it had nothing to do with Jacob who was in a false position – trying to do Chief of Staff from England. He said that he had had a lot of trouble with India and thought that they spent a lot of money there for very little result. He agreed with me that the question of Afghanistan and Russia was a bogey in that the Russians would never send Armies down that way. He thought that it was a good thing to have a bogey.

He then said that the CGS in India was a Lt. General's appointment and that they had refused to make any more temporary Lt. Generals. [...] He then said that I should not be promoted to Lt-General for some time. That now I had my Division in England it was better for me to stay here. He then finished up by saying, 'Of course you may have to go to India, in which case you will go.' He left me with the impression that he knew all about my name coming up for India, but I did not gather whether it came from Campbell or Jacob.[22]

This rebuff set my father to again weighing up his prospects. The June 1927 *Gazette* showed that the average age of the generals in employment was just over 60 and that of the lieutenant generals just over 59. It also showed that the retiring numbers would create some nine slots to be filled over the following three years:

One can see quite clearly that the average age of the Generals will increase fairly rapidly as we get further away from war. One has become so accustomed to so much movement that one gets bored when it slows down. Peace-time employment in most jobs is full of routine and apt to become very tiresome, especially after a life full of change. I cannot imagine myself commanding even a Regular Division for 4 years. What a Territorial Division for 4 years would have been like I really do not know. The Staff College offered so much change that 4 years were tolerable.[23]

Being suddenly faced with the dilemma of not knowing whether his future was at stake in the struggle between the India Office and the War Office over mechanisation, my father kept his ears open for opportunity. By meeting and talking to people in high places at social and professional gatherings, as well as to those he met during the ordinary course of work, he discovered exactly how to play his hand.

The current difficulty centred on the disappointing performance of Skeen as CGS in India and whether he should be replaced before completing his time. When Skeen addressed a divisional conference at Tidworth in July, the focus of which was on anti-aircraft gunfire, my father was easily able to sum up what sort of person he was:

> [A] tall well-built man of 55 or so with a blue eye of rather vague look. He is a Scot and pretty slow & deliberate. Being clean-shaven he looked more like a barrister than a soldier. He started off to the conference by that he had never seen an anti-aircraft gun fire since 1916 in Mesopotamia. No wonder he cannot initiate new things if that is his experience. I also found that he had never seen a tank. Almost a Soldier of medieval times in fact.
>
> He said that India had a long frontier to protect, but had little fear of intensive air attack. They had a few hired Russian pilots or perhaps inefficient oriental pilots against them. Machines would have a poor performance and they hoped to be able to compete with all enemy air action. He then said that there was no money and he proposed to use some old 18pdrs – by burying their trails in the ground – to protect the really dangerous target, Attock Bridge. I was horrified at such a suggestion, as India is a museum of ancient weapons of all sorts, which cost more and more to keep up every year. I was glad that Hill was all against anything but the 3' 20 cal[ibre] Service AA gun. As well have nothing as an old gun with no high firing and not sufficient muzzle velocity.
>
> Skene [sic] talked about protecting Attock Bridge with smoke and was surprised to hear how difficult smoke was to generate quickly and how difficult to get in the right place, more especially in a gorge like Attock.[24]

After an afternoon spent watching practical demonstrations of anti-aircraft fire control, the evening afforded my father the chance to have a long conversation with Skeen, which left him with a better idea of the man's professional qualities as well as of the situation in India at the time:

> He is certainly a man and a soldier, but not educated in a European sense. He cannot conceive what modern war is going to be like. I should say that he is very cautious and very obstinate.
>
> He certainly has absolutely no idea that there is a party who wish to push him out. His job finishes in Nov. 1928 and he has no intention of giving up on his own before that time. He is off back to India in November this year for a year. I do not believe that he will give up and I cannot see them actually kicking him out. What reason could they give? I would say that Birdwood would have a great say in any change that is contemplated. And yet, how can Jacob & Milne talk gaily of a successor to him, if he has no intention of leaving?[25]

At the same time as Skeen made it clear that he proposed to hang on to his post, his description of his duties also made the prospect of replacing him all the more appealing to my father. Nevertheless, as the demonstrations continued the following day it was again made clear to him why Skeen had incurred the wrath of those around him through his outdated views and also how the political aspects of the changing face of British India impacted upon the state of the Indian Army:

> Skeen was completely flabbergasted at the extent of intelligence required by all ranks in the field of anti-aircraft gunnery warfare. He couldn't see how the Indians were going to reach the required standard. He thought that we were trying to get the Indian Officers up to the 2nd class certificate standard. He thought that it would take 100 years to get Indians fit to take on such things. I thought it was all an argument against Indianisation. As regards this Indianisation, Skeen has obviously all the Indian politicians on his side and I should say that this is one of the factors against his being kicked out.
>
> The Indian politicians' idea is to keep the British Army in India as a kind of super Police Force to be called on when trouble has really begun.[26]

The storm that had blown up over the potential replacement of Skeen, by my father or anyone else, quickly subsided to my father's relief, as it directly affected his personal wellbeing in the army more than their relationships with the India Office:

> My meeting with Skene [sic] here has more or less put my mind at rest on going hurriedly to India. It seems that there will be no change until November [next] year and that is too far off to be contemplated. I shall then have been two years in command of a Division. Quite long enough. At the same time, I should very much like to go.[27]

Weighing things up, it seemed to him that on the one hand he had the advantage of having friends on the Selection Board that would decide on Skeen's replacement, including Milne and Campbell; on the other hand, he had some uncertainty as to whether the board would appoint anyone to the post whose last experience of Indian soldiering had been as a subaltern a quarter of a century previously.

In the middle of July, he stayed in Thame at the Spreadeagle Hotel to inspect the yearly manoeuvre area, designed to test out the divisional command and communications system and to exercise the brigades within the limits of the adjacent countryside. He considered the chosen area:

> ... quite a good one from the training point of view; hedgerow fighting with sufficient woodland to make it difficult. The only thing that we shall have to keep away from is the pheasant shooting cover, which makes it rather hard for us to have any wood fighting anywhere in England.

Clearly in terms of present-day standards, this training area was totally unsuitable and additionally such manoeuvres were, even in 1927, obliged to rely on outdated strategy and tactics, combined with outmoded equipment, to achieve their objectives. He went on to observe:

> This is a miserable business trying to train troops which one knows are obsolete and will not be used in the next war. The offensive power of infantry is no greater now than what it was in 1914, except for two things, namely smoke and mechanised fighting vehicles. Neither of these two things are we developing in any way whatever. If the infantry haven't got these two adjuncts they will simply go out & be murdered once more for no useful purpose. The infantrymen themselves, the senior ones more especially, are the men who are against any alteration in their arm of the Service and prejudice is hard to kill.
>
> Here we shall go and have the same old manoeuvres without the implements of war which we know to be necessary. I must try and make it quite clear that we are merely practising for war with the instruments that we have at the moment.[28]

The main purpose of the 1927 manoeuvres was to test the equipment and doctrines of the newly formed Experimental Mechanised Force under Colonel Jack Collins. Although the manoeuvres demonstrated that progress had been made towards mechanisation, and clearly showed the edge that a mechanised force had over conventional infantry, the cautious doctrine employed by Collins drew considerable criticism from the remaining disciples of Fuller's 'revolutionary' approach. In fairness, however, the technology did not yet exist to facilitate the employment of what would one day become the tactics of blitzkrieg.

A combination of vehicle types meant that performance varied hugely, something that was further complicated by the fact that the relative road speed of vehicles did not correspond to their relative off-road speed, which made movement of mixed forces problematic. Ideally, the manoeuvres should have identified these problems and given all concerned food for thought when it came to where best to direct such resources as were available to further the mechanisation process. Instead, however, and notwithstanding a positive endorsement of events by Milne, the presence of so many conflicting stances on mechanisation, and the incendiary effect of further newspaper articles by Liddell Hart in the *Daily Telegraph*, led to rifts and arguments into which my father was also drawn. Liddell Hart and the 'revolutionaries' intended to stir the government and the War Office into speeding up the plans to equip the army with the tanks and armoured vehicles fit for future conflict and provide the training grounds to suit their firepower and means of pursuit, but instead they risked provoking a reactionary backlash that would do more harm than good.

My father, for his own part, had clearly drawn his own lessons from the manoeuvres, emphasising in particular the case for giving the infantry tracked and wheeled vehicles with armoured protection. At the same time, he was keen to maintain a healthy debate within the forces under his own command, emphasising this in his summary of the conference that had concluded the manoeuvres:

> A most excellent Conference with the senior officers which has allowed me to lay down certain principles for our future study. I find that criticism can now be made in the Division without any ill-feeling. I think I have dissipated any kind of mistrust which certainly existed when I took over the command.
>
> We are advancing along the lines of the speech made by the CIGS to the Armoured Force and we now have authoritative policy behind us.[29]

Perhaps the curse of the thirteenth put a spell on these well-meant sentiments, for he soon discovered that he had incurred the immediate anger of Sir David Campbell, who took him to task for exercising his own judgement in contradiction of the training manuals and regulations. Without question, Campbell's missive was intended as a rebuke, and was recognised by my father as such:

> I have read your 'Notes' on the conference held at your Headquarters yesterday. After the conference several of my Staff were approached by officers in order to ascertain whether the views you expressed had been agreed to by me.
>
> In consequence, I wish you to make it known without any delay that the points discussed were never referred to me in any way and, in many ways, do not express my opinion. I also wish you to make it quite clear that training must be carried on strictly in conformity with our training manuals and is not to be based on anything you may have said which contravenes those regulations.
>
> Further, I feel very strongly that you had no justification for quoting what the CIGS is supposed to have said with your only authority – as far as I know – a newspaper report.
>
> I hope to deal with the points you have raised at my conference after the manoeuvres when I shall be in a position to put forward exactly what the CIGS's views really are.
>
> The only departure from regulations that can be allowed is the use of tanks with the advance guard. This the CIGS approved of at the War Office Staff Exercise and you were asked to try them out at your divisional training.[30]

Although on the face of it the horsiest of possible officer types – a 9th Lancer who had personally led two cavalry charges in 1914 and whose pre-war career as an amateur jockey had seen him win the 1896 Grand National – Campbell was, in fact, much in favour of mechanisation, so there was no question here of my father simply having offended the sensibilities of one of the army's conservatives. Indeed, Campbell had himself been reined in by Milne under similar circumstances when attempting to clarify CIGS' stance on mechanised warfare prior to assuming command at Aldershot, which leads one to suppose either that he had decided to pursue a by-the-book line thereafter, or possibly that he was in fact intervening to prevent my father similarly blotting his copybook with Milne. Indeed, both their copybooks would have been at risk, for had he done nothing Campbell would have made himself a party to my father's statements.

Nevertheless, whatever Campbell's motives, my father took the rebuke hard, for it carried with it an implicit criticism of his direction of 2nd Division and his work on its tactical doctrine:

> It is most profoundly discouraging to receive a letter of this nature during our manoeuvres. What am I to say to the troops at any conference? When we were down at the last War Office Exercise we were distinctly told that we were to try experiments and this is what I have been doing. [...] I cannot understand how the little man can have gone off at a tangent in such a way. I am quite sure that that little so-and-so Lewin, who commands the Artillery in our Command, has been putting his oar in and making misrepresentations. He is the one man in the Army for whom I have a strong feeling of disgust. I shall certainly not speak to him again, nor shall I have him inside my office again. I shall simply ignore him utterly.[31]

This Lewin, now Brigadier Royal Artillery with the Aldershot Command, was the same officer whose performance as a lecturer my father had found so uninspiring at Camberley.

On the following day, much to my father's surprise, Campbell wrote to say that the incident was now closed, but my father remained sensitive to the slight that had been implicit in Campbell's rebuke:

> How he can think it is closed I really don't know. I have no improper pride, but I can now have little authority to teach in the Division and it really strengthens my reasons for wanting to get out of it all. Nevertheless, I must look after my own interests for the time being.[32]

For the rest of the month he thought over his future in the army from every point of view and discussed it exhaustively with his friends, so that a broad spectrum of people became aware of what was going on. There had been much doubt in my father's mind as to where his career in the army was leading and it took him some time to put the attractions of commerce and industry aside, despite many hints from his friends and acquaintances that there was a more remunerative existence in the business world, where he had no fears of being short of offers of employment.

Unsurprisingly, this fed back to Campbell, leading to a meeting between the two men on 2 October:

In the evening I had my first interview with little Campbell and found him extremely civil and much regretting his outburst. He said he had mistaken my notes altogether. The whole thing was too ridiculous and does not make me think that he is very balanced. I expect he was very worried about something or other, but it upset me to think that I had to serve on in that way, as it is bad enough when people are sane. But, to run something that takes all one's energy to run properly and then to be brought up with a round turn, is too much of a good thing. I showed him my proposed Training Report and I left it with him to read. We talked about future training and I think he is prepared to look ahead and get rid of this Infantry fetish. However, I am afraid he is influenced by the last man who gets hold of him.

Thinking things over, I think that India as CGS is the best place for me if luck will only come my way, but I am afraid it will not. I must try and make a little more money with articles.[33]

When this storm in the Aldershot ranks had quickly blown over, he was overjoyed on 7 October to read Campbell's confidential report on him, which had ridden over the heat of argument and glowed brightly for his future:

I consider General Ironside fully qualified for the highest commands or appointments in the Army.

It has been a great pleasure and a very great assistance to me to have such a highly educated soldier and one possessing such wide and up to date views, serving under me. The importance of this is much emphasised at the moment when there is so much reorganisation to be considered and when in consequence it is essential to have higher Commanders who think ahead and who are not afraid to express their views. There is no need for me to enumerate General Ironside's high qualities as a soldier as they are already too well known. I should, however, like to say that General Ironside has proved himself to be a most loyal and helpful subordinate. I may add that he is a subordinate under whom I myself would serve with greatest confidence.[34]

Having been told by Campbell that it was odds on that he would go to India, my father decided to gear himself up to the probability and decided to purchase the latest version of the Owen Magnetic saloon car from Le Grice Elers Ltd in Winchester. He knew that this model of car, which had an extremely early example of the hybrid electrical drive, would cope with the road conditions and distances he would cover on the subcontinent. What was more, he could be confident in the knowledge that it was both mechanically reliable and eminently saleable in the local market – the more so, since he had himself managed to purchase the car for only £200.

After the saga of Thame had been shelved by Campbell, my father reflected:

> It is very nice of the little man to write such complimentary things about me in his Confidential Report, but one cannot help but think that it is rather as sop for having written me such an unbalanced reproof. I think as far as he is concerned it means that he is prepared to recommend me for India.[35]

Meanwhile, the mechanisation debate rumbled on with the press continuing to fan the flames. My father was still of the opinion that Milne would, in his quiet and methodical way, continue to champion mechanisation; the popular press did not think so. Until Parliament had debated the army's programme for change and Worthington-Evans, the minister, had sought powers to act, the plans for mechanisation would be brought to a standstill. Matters were not helped by the Cavalry Committee, chaired by Lieutenant General Sir Archibald Montgomery-Massingberd, GOC Southern Command, which argued against, and ultimately was successful in resisting, the large-scale reduction of the cavalry arm:

> It is quite within the bounds of possibility that Milne will get his back up and resign, in which case it means that Chetwode would take his place. He is much less mechanically minded than Milne and would be loath to do away with the Cavalry.
>
> Campbell told me that they had decided to reduce the Cavalry to 2 Brigades of 2 Regiments each, which will put a final end to the subsidised hunting and polo club which the Cavalry has really been for years.[36]

Thus did matters progress, or rather fail to progress, for the only major changes in the months to come were the conversion of two light cavalry regiments to the armoured car role and the provision of a small number of half-tracked carriers for 3.7in howitzers, to create some sort of mobile artillery to accompany the tanks.

The disbanding of the Experimental Mechanised Force after the 1928 manoeuvres, followed by financial retrenchment after the crash of the following year, meant that it would be the early years of the next decade before any serious progress was made. Then, after a promising start, this too would tail off so that by 1939 Britain had thrown away the lead in mechanised warfare that she had possessed twenty years previously. Although he remained an advocate of mechanised warfare, my father would play little further active part in its development, being away in India or on half pay until his appointment to Eastern Command in 1936 and thus in no position to exert any influence on the debate.

For the moment, however, India remained as yet part of an uncertain future, and my father was therefore relieved to have the routine of peacetime command interrupted by being chosen to represent the British Army at the *Cycle d'Information* being held by the French Army at Versailles in late November 1927. It was a summit assembly with lectures, visits and exhibitions, coupled with lunches, receptions and dinners for those who wished to carry on their relationships with the French military elite. For my father, moving on from finding a solution to the problems of fixing up his own future, the prospect of scrutinising the state of the French Army and renewing acquaintances with fellow modernisers on the other side of the Channel generated a spark of renewed interest and enthusiasm:

> I am really looking forward very much to this course and I ought to get a good insight into the Army of post-war France. I know so many French officers that I ought to be *personna grata* with the French authorities. I shall dig out my *Legion d'Honneur* and *Croix de Guerre*, which I prepared for my visit to Morocco, which never came off. Apparently, there is a Colonel coming with me, who is at present commanding a Territorial Brigade in Scotland. I hope he speaks French well, but I have never seen him before and know nothing about him or why he has been chosen.[37]

Besides the two British representatives there were two Poles, three Serbs, five Spaniards, one Swede, two Romanians and two Greeks, but – unsurprisingly – no Germans.

While he waited to go over to France, he attended the Motor Show at Olympia and he was attracted by the Mercedes Grand Prix Sports Supercharger car, which was, however, priced at £2,300. He lectured on fortification to the Sappers at Chatham and perused the books and papers prepared for the course of studies in Paris. He exchanged ideas with Major General Walter Kirke, then deputy CGS in India, who would later collaborate with him to defend Britain from invasion in 1940. Nevertheless, although he kept as busy as he could, it can still be said that when he crossed the Channel at the end of November 1927, he broke the spell of peacetime soldiering and phantom command to take the stage again – albeit briefly – in the theatre of the military play.

He first met Marie-Eugène Debeney, the long-serving French Chief of Staff who did much to shape the character of the French Army between the wars, and dined with him at the Restaurant Drouant near Les Invalides:

> Debeney made a short speech welcoming us and I then replied. After a glass or two of the Volnay I got going and I think I said the right things, as everybody was very pleased and all the French Generals came up and complimented me by saying that I had spoken well and absolutely without accent. Several of the foreigners also complimented me & thanked me for replying for them.
>
> We then had coffee and liqueurs and talked for a bit until Debeney approached me and said that he proposed to *Filer à l'anglaise* & then I also disappeared as a signal to the others to go.[38]

After a day or two the French opened their hearts and freely discussed the ways of war and their way of facing up to the problems of modernising and mechanising their army. The corps commanders and divisional generals lectured on the deployment of weapons and the methods of attack, while members of *Conseil de Guerre*, including General Maxime Weygand who would replace Debeney as Chief of Staff in 1931, attended the proceedings:

> They talk and think of nothing else in the French Army but the coming war with Germany. They sit and peer over the frontier and imagine a lot of what is going on in Germany. Germany is preparing a large air-fleet and her factories for a new chemical war. Whenever anything is mentioned they always say 'Oh, the Bosches do this or that & we must counter it'. Everything points towards the Bosche.[39]

When the course ended, Weygand came to say goodbye to him personally and he made his way back to England via Newhaven to reach home again on Christmas Eve.

13

The Raj that Was

After the partying spirits at Christmas had been poured back into the vats of working life again, my father walked back into his office with a sigh of despair at having to go on dealing with the routines of divisional command, where the focus of training now shifted towards preparing for the 1928 manoeuvres. Although it is evident that he appreciated the chance to get back in touch with actual soldiering after his time at Camberley, a year at Aldershot had sapped much of that initial enthusiasm and he was now seriously looking for an alternative to reinvigorate his career:

> With next manoeuvres I shall have got all I want of commanding a Peace Division. I hope I shan't have to face any more of it.
> This afternoon I seemed to be peculiarly dissatisfied with my lot here. I have now done nearly 6 years at home and it is time I got moving again whilst I am still young. I can do things now which I shall not be able to do later. It seems almost that I have got into a ruck of bad or medium Generals & one cannot get out of it quickly enough. Old George Milne said to Campbell 'one must employ the Lt. Generals' just as if it were not the right thing to choose the right man for a job, rather than a man because of his rank and the fact that he is unemployed at the time.[1]

To put the issue into better perspective, the CIGS was thinking more of himself being left on the generals' shelf than his divisional commanders being put out to grass. However, my father need not have worried, as on 21 February Milne was made a field marshal. He sent his congratulations by telegram and had an immediate reply from Milne, in which the CIGS expressed his hope that his promotion set the seal on the army being able to keep up with the times. My father was unsure, commenting that Milne's missive was:

> A curious letter and a little difficult to get at the real feelings of the writer. He takes his promotion as being a sign that the authorities approve of his policy. But, it looks to me as if he had been a little bit frightened of what he had done by way

of modernisation. Of course, I don't know what he has had to overcome in the way of opposition inside the Army itself. He may feel that his increased rank may now give him more authority to pursue his policy. It is possible that he doesn't know how eager the Army is for an advance.[2]

By the end of February 1928, rumours were again floating around that my father would be going to India as CGS. Meanwhile, he was particularly heartened by the fact that Lord Cavan, now in retirement but still with some influence in the Lords, had sought his advice about the new organisation that was being built up around the tanks and armoured vehicles that would be operating in the field:

> He said that Lord Haldane was going to speak in the House of Lords and he wished to talk also. It is curious that the late CIGS should not know anything at all on the subject and should want to be guided absolutely by what I said. I don't think the little man ever quite realised what was going on. He was always a little at sea over administration. I daresay that he filled the place better than would have done, say, Lord Horne. He was absolutely straight and he never favoured anyone unfairly.[3]

After receiving my father's notes on the subject, Cavan thanked him profusely but the House of Lords debate on 28 February ended leaving the matter of change in the army organisation on hold, following a persuasive speech by Lord Haldane:

> Not much of a Debate in the Lords yesterday. I don't seem to think it matters what they say or do in the Upper House. Nobody seems to take the slightest interest. Poor little Cavan dished out what I had sent him, but made the horrible mistake of saying that as C-in-C he would like to have a Deputy MGO there to tell him how to use the new weapons. The DMGO is there for purely administrative purposes.[4]

With respect to the last point, it should be understood that the Earl of Onslow, parliamentary undersecretary at the War Office, in declaring the changes from horse to mechanised traction as being akin to the Royal Navy's transition from sail to steam, made the case for the Master General of the Ordnance to manage the fighting field vehicles and the quartermaster general to handle the base-bound support vehicles.

The onset of spring brought no lift to my father's mood, and he began to feel that his current job was increasingly futile. Divisional training seemed pointless when the division that he commanded bore no resemblance to what would be its wartime establishment in a major war, or to the sort of more mobile formation that would be required in a lesser expedition. Seeing little hope of the Selection

Board choosing him for CGS India or for the Defence College, he decided that the best thing to do would be put himself forward for a district command in India, a prospect that Sir David Campbell had hinted the previous year was something for which my father was under consideration. In the hope of at least obtaining an interesting command, he expressed a strong preference for the Meerut District, in the north of India, but deliberately made no mention of the equivalent vacancy in the Deccan District to the south, which was not organised on a war-fighting basis.

On 3 April, my father received the fateful letter that asked whether he would accept command of either the Lahore or Meerut First Class Districts, and he decided to let his answer wait until after Easter when he had worked out the actualities:

> Naturally I have been considering the question of going to India. It is a nuisance, whatever anybody may say, to be separated. But I am quite sure that I should do right in not taking my family out to India. It is not the place in which to have children. One would never forgive oneself if they developed any diseases. You must give your children the very best start possible in health. The expense of running two establishments out in India, one in the hills and one in the plains, is just as much as running two shows, one in India and the other in England. Also, we have Longlands now, which is very comfortable and we might now be able to collect more furniture.
>
> I am sure that everybody will get after my wife and tell her that she ought to go out & that she would love it and that the boy could go and a whole lot of other nonsense. The whole thing will only be for such a short time that it really isn't worth the trouble. Moreover, the expense of fitting oneself out for India would be colossal. I can go out to India and live very cheaply and have done with it all very quickly.
>
> With a pay of 3,600 rupees a month and the rupee at 1/6 one would have to send home 1,600 rupees to find £120 a month. That would leave me with 2,000 rupees a month and surely I could live on that and save enough to pay off debts and what one would have to borrow to set oneself up in India. If I had to send £20 a month home to square the bank that would be 260 rupees only to get rid of things in a year. One is, however, never a millionaire.[5]

After further reflection, he decided to accept the Meerut District, providing that he did not have to go on half pay between appointments and that he would not have to leave for India until on or after 1 November, to obtain a month's leave before his departure. Reconciling the conflicting imperatives, he noted:

> I am really forced to go out to India for financial reasons. I cannot afford to go on as I am. It really suits me from two other reasons. The first being that Aldershot

has lost its importance and is doing no modern operations, and the second is that I am now assured of being on full pay till I am promoted.[6]

Having taken the plunge, mentally if not formally, he began to try and build up a picture of who the key players in the Indian military scene would be:

I had a long talk with [Brigadier Henry] Karslake who has been sent out to India as CRA [Commander Royal Artillery] Western Command. He was a little sarcastic about it, as he had hoped to get something in England. I didn't tell him that I was likely to go.

I had a talk with Gerry Boyd the Military Secretary [Major General Sir Gerald Boyd] and he told me that they have not decided on the new CGS in India. I told him that I hoped it would be [Major General] George Cory to be chosen and he did not seem to think it would be. He also told me that Romeo would be on ½ pay for a long time. It really is a damnable system that wastes the best years of a man's life & keeps him going until he reaches the age limit. The ludicrous rule that a General or Lt. General does not make a vacancy until he is 65 even if he retires keeps the list blocked with old men who are never going to be employed.[7]

'Romeo' was Major General John Cecil Romer, late GOC 1st Division, who would indeed spend the years 1928 to 1931 on half pay, highlighting the potential fate for my father unless he could secure another active posting. George Cory has already been encountered in this work, as the officer who took over from my father in North Persia. Since then he had served as deputy CGS India from 1922 to 1926, which on the face of it left him eminently qualified to be CGS: however, like my father, his lack of seniority left him at a crucial disadvantage under the 'Buggins' Turn' system.

Upon returning home, my father wrote to give formal notice to Boyd that he would accept the Indian appointment, glad to leave 2nd Division at the end of his two-year stint, and looking forward to promotion in 1931. As the days slipped by, my father took more account of the future, as it became generally known that he was going to India. When he saw General Sir Robert Whigham on 1 May he was told that he had bypassed the Selection Board and that the CIGS had personally selected him for India, which put the seal on his name, whatever might be decided by the board. This provided an explanation for Milne's surprise visit to my father's office during the previous year.

On 21 June, General Sir Philip Chetwode was appointed CGS India, the appointment of so senior an officer emphasising the lack of opportunity for men of my father and Cory's generation. The appointment did, however, ensure that the post would be filled by someone that my father held in high regard and who reciprocated that respect: as CGS and then C-in-C India, Chetwode would be a great source of support for my father over the coming decade.

My father pulled out of Churchill House on 14 August, having handed over command of 2nd Division to Major General Thomas Cubitt, and embarked for India from Birkenhead aboard SS *Ranpura* – with the Owen Magnetic stowed in the hold – on 26 October.

Although he had commanded Indian troops in Turkey and Persia, my father had only briefly served in India prior to this point, and that as a subaltern a quarter of a century previously. It is therefore helpful at this point to review the state of the Indian Army, and of British troops in India, during the years between the two world wars. The largest volunteer army in the world, the Indian Army had been in a state of slow evolution ever since the armies of the Honourable East India Company had been taken into the service of the Crown in the aftermath of the Indian Mutiny. With effect from 1895, the armies of the Madras, Bombay and Bengal Presidencies were united into a single Indian Army, and this unification was completed by further reforms over the following decade under the aegis of Lord Kitchener during his tenure as C-in-C India.

The Kitchener reforms created the Indian Army that fought with distinction in the First World War, but that conflict also demonstrated a need for further reform of manpower and organisation. One of the difficulties inherent in keeping Indian units up to strength had been the large number of single-battalion infantry regiments: in 1922, these were merged to form a smaller number of multi-battalion regiments and there was a similar, though less drastic, reorganisation of the cavalry arm with some regiments amalgamated and others disbanded. The presence of a strong mounted arm within the Indian Army was an increasingly marked anachronism as time went on and European armies turned to mechanisation, and naturally this was something that drew my father's attention.

Whereas little if anything had been done to mechanise the Indian Army in the decade between the end of the First World War and the arrival of my father to command the Meerut District, some progress at least had been made in its Indianisation. With the growing demands of the Indian National Congress for an end to imperial rule, it was inevitable that concessions had to be made insofar as the military career prospects open to Indians were concerned. From 1919, a limited number of Sandhurst places were reserved for Indian cadets who would, in due course, receive their commissions not from the viceroy, under whose writ were already commissioned the Jemadars, Subedars and Risaldars who commanded the infantry platoons and cavalry troops of Indian Army regiments, but by the king.

This was part of a process by which demands for independence would be headed off with a transition towards granting Indians 'responsible government' of the subcontinent. Indian officers who held the king's commission would be able to command British and Indian troops alike, and by the slow extension of this process of granting the king's commission to Indians it was calculated that by some time in the 1960s the Indian Army would have an all-Indian officer corps – which indeed it duly did, although not in quite the manner that had been planned.

Mechanisation and Indianisation, then, were the underlying themes of interwar service in India, and naturally my father had his views on both. His stance on mechanisation does not need repeating, although he would find the pace of change even more frustratingly slow than had been the case in Britain, but he clearly gave some thought to the process of Indianisation and of what might come after it. When he had been a few months in India, he was prompted by a discussion with a fellow officer who advocated immediate Home Rule as a means of avoiding Congress-inspired protests turning to bloodshed, to put down his own view on the result of the Indianisation process:

> Personally, I cannot see how we are to run the Army out here after there is Dominion status [as proposed by his colleague]. We should not be allowed a free hand as to money, nor even as to how we were to spend it. Again, if we give Dominion status quickly, there will be little likelihood of bloodshed in India.[8]

The latter hope, sadly, was a mistaken one, but at the time of his writing the assumption was that British India would move from imperial possession to self-governing dominion as a single entity: the concept of Pakistan had scarcely been voiced, never mind the idea of the Partition of India and the immense upheavals and tension that would come with it. Later, preparing to return to India for a second time in 1933, he would write that he went back out 'with the firm belief that we ought to give them their freedom as quickly as possible'.[9]

For the moment, however, upon taking up his duties as a district commander my father had to deal with the situation as it then existed, and not as it might be at some time in the future. The Indian Army was only one element of the military presence on the subcontinent, for alongside it were the Regular units of the British Army in India and it was from these two sources together that the Army of India was formed.

Under the Kitchener system, the role of the Army of India was focused on the North-West Frontier, which was to be kept at peace in the event of tribal difficulties and held if necessary against a Russian attack through Afghanistan. This required that all units be fit to serve on the frontier as required and meant that each of the territorial districts be organised along the lines of an active infantry division with attached cavalry brigade. However, in 1921 the Indian Legislative Assembly ruled that the Army of India had a dual role of protecting against external attack *and* the maintenance of internal order. This meant that a portion of the troops were downgraded to internal policing duties only and the old divisional system was dropped; instead, only four of the first class districts would maintain the ability to field an active division, of which the whole, or parts thereof, could be made ready for service either on the frontier or as an Imperial Reserve to be called upon to serve outside of the subcontinent.

The Meerut District, formed out of the old Meerut and Lucknow Divisions and known as the United Provinces District from its formation in 1920 until 1927, was one of the four districts to retain this capability, and would have furnished 3rd Indian Division in the event of a major war at this time. Administratively, the district came under Eastern Command, of which General Sir John Shea, an Indian Army veteran in his last posting before retirement, was GOC-in-C throughout my father's time at Meerut. Although they crossed swords at times over my father's modernising agenda, and although he regretted some of his senior's impulsive outbursts and decisions, Shea won my father's respect over the coming years for his quick mind.

My father arrived at Bombay on 16 November after an uneventful voyage with stops at Gibraltar, Marseilles and Malta, beginning the journey to Meerut by car two days later and arriving after a week on the road to take up residence in the Garden House, which was reserved for the district commander. He was immediately away to see the troops exercising on 28 November and later, after a tiring day of manoeuvres on 18 December, he and Shea met with senior members of the Indian staff. Philip Chetwode was now established in his new role as CGS and was able to bring them up to date on events at home as well as in India:

> Chetwode was very cheery and I am quite sure he will make a difference out here. He gave me the good news that the Armoured Force [in England] was to be broken up and that Collins was to go to Netheravon to run the machine-gun school. They are now going to take the older units and are going to see how the new weapons can be brought into line with the older units. This is what we have been fighting for all my time at Aldershot. I hope they give the experimenting to [Brigadier Richard] Oldman.
>
> I am to have what mechanisation is going and we may hope to get something like a mobilisation next year. As usual, I shall be away before anything really gets going.
>
> [Lieutenant General Sir Cyril] Deverell, the QMG, was also down & a General Price – who was at school with me. Ap Rhys Price [Major General Henry Edward ap Rhys Pryce, director of supplies and transport in India]. I thought Deverell looked very ill, very yellow about the face. He is not a nice person under whom to serve and has a nasty supercilious-looking face. He seemed to be more interested in oil-cookers than anything else. I was glad to find he has the proper idea of cooking things at the back and sending them up by six-wheelers.[10]

The comment about the break-up of the Armoured Force being 'good news' should be understood not as a sudden relapse into military conservatism on the part of my father, but rather as indicating that the experimental phase was now over and that the new ideas could be rolled out to the rest of the army. This, of course, would not in fact happen for some time to come.

While all this hinted at steady, if unspectacular, progress, Chetwode also had disquieting news with respect to events in Afghanistan:

> Chetwode told me that the situation in Afghanistan was bad and that it might get worse daily. Apparently the Mohmands have said that they propose to kill every Russian they find, because they bombed them. This might give the Russians a pretext for going in and punishing the Afghans. Chetwode said that he was considerably frightened. I didn't tell him that I didn't think that the Bol[shevik]s would ever dare to do anything like that. I think they are all imputing too much power and strength of character to the Bol[shevik] leaders.[11]

Chetwode's warning meant that there was little surprise in the news in January 1929 that the King of Afghanistan had abdicated, plunging the country into a convoluted civil war that went on for some time to come, but did not, as my father has correctly surmised, lead to Russian involvement. Although the deposed Afghan king fled to India, the conflict did not spread beyond Afghanistan's borders and the Meerut District remained calm; certainly calm enough for my father to take an admiring look at the real treasures of India at Fatehpur Sikri and at the Taj Mahal, as well as another look at his own future in the army:

> I had a long talk with Chetwode and he said that I would find myself going along too quickly, and I told him that I didn't want to go along as a pottering old man. He said he nearly finished his military career at 58 and that he had only been saved by a miracle. I have been thinking it out and I don't think I shall go too soon.

Promoted Lt. General	52
Half Pay	53
Army Council or War Office	56
Army Commander	60
CIGS or C-in-C India	65

> That will take me within reasonable distance of retiring and I cannot want more than that. C-in-C India will fall vacant for a British Service Officer in 1940 – if there is such an appointment and I should be just 60 then. The chances are good and age is very much in my favour. Personally, I should much rather have it all over quickly and then be able to enjoy myself as Jack Asses do. The thing is not to wear oneself out so that the harness falls off a dead man. I have seen that so often with Army Officers who had no sort of hobby outside their work. They soon fade away.[12]

Through his immediate commander, Shea, and even more so through Chetwode, my father could keep himself informed of the progress of events in Britain. The most important news was the announcement that Milne would stay in place as CIGS until February 1932. The announcement was widely sensed as being quite out of place with the times and with the plans for mechanisation and modernisation of the British Army. It was seen as an opaque and ill-judged Cabinet decision, which had a sting in the tail for some, but came as a promotional shot in the arm for others. Certainly, it altered the employment prospects of many senior officers, in particular my father, who recorded with some pleasure that of the men next in line for the post, he was the only one then eligible who would still be of a suitable age in 1940: thus, he would stand to reach the top of his profession in 1940, even if the job went to someone else in 1932 or 1936. He therefore wrote to congratulate Milne on his extension in post which, in the event, was to be followed by a second extension that gave him a third additional year and thus an unprecedented seven-year stint as CIGS.

Although my father was, as we have seen, rather despondent about the lack of modern resources available in India as opposed to back in Britain, he sought at least to train his command along modern lines and for modern warfare. In this he found himself at least to some extent thwarted by the set ideas of his subordinates, which proved hard to break even when their methods were shown in exercises to be flawed and which called into serious question the ability of the district to furnish an effective division for active service if called upon to do so. After three months in command, he wrote:

> This blooming War Division makes me laugh. A staff which is all but raw. Not a single Brigadier fit to command his Brigade and only one Bn. Commander fit to command a Brigade. The British Bns. are commanded, one by a mediocre man and the other two by complete duds. I haven't got the least idea who is going to officiate in any of the three Brigades and one of the Brigadiers has got the sack and will not come back. How can you have any continuity of training? I might as well just go off myself and leave the thing alone. I shall be heartily glad when I have finished training officers and men. I have done it for 7 years now and I was at it all through the war and yet I shall be at it most probably as a Lt. General.[13]

Nevertheless, he did receive some appreciation from an unlikely source, with his efforts to smarten up the training programme inspiring Mr Roshan Lall, so-called Poet Laureate of India, to write effusively about his efforts:

> Quite mad! He was the son of a Member of Council in the U.P. and had been sent to Exeter College, Oxford and then went off his head. He was shut up in the Seychelles Islands and now goes about touting his so-called poems. He

touched me for a food fat sum of money for it. I really ought to have been hard hearted and have kicked him out. I wrote him a letter thanking him. The burden of command.[14]

The McGonagall-esque offering ran as follows:

Give Wealth and give THEM honour in the World
Give Knowledge and give well-bred Progeny
Oh Gracious Lord oh Heed thou Prayer this day
Do Bless GENERAL & LADY IRONSIDE with Prosperity

Who Governs over the MEERUT DISTRICT in Full sway
Whom numerous BRIGADE COMMANDERS Humbly Homage pay
Who dreadful Terror is to enemy
That GENERAL OFFICER COMMANDING may Victorious be

Whose Kindness UNIVERSALLY is Known
By whom Full Mercy is to his WAR SOLDIERS Shown
Who's Pearl of Wisdom Ethic's Image Great
Victorious be that GREAT EUROPEAN WAR Potentate

Who to the POOR Protection's Hand Extends
With Patronage the HELPLESS Ones be Friends
Who treads the Path of Virtue Night and Day
Be glorious that GENERAL OFFICER COMMANDING Always

When he was in the GREAT EUROPEAN WAR was Terrific Fam'd and Brave
And in the KILLING THE ENEMIES Hero like Behave
On whom always attendeth Victory
Victorious be that MAJOR-GENERAL-WARRIOR Ever be

Where MEERUT DISTRICT is Grand like mighty INDRA'S own
And GOC in Chief SIR JOHN SHEA, Rich as Kuber's Own
And Glory like the Sun and Moon like Fame
Be Glorious that GENERAL OFFICER COMMANDING of Holy Name

To wool of the SOLDIERS' DISLOYALTY He was Fire
To Harvest of Injustice Lightening Dire
And Wind he's to Quench Disorder's Lamp
Victorious be MAJOR-GENERAL of Noble Stamp[15]

As well as providing patronage to Mr Lal's poetic endeavours, my father also made a rather more useful expenditure of time and money on picking up his linguistic studies where he had left them off a quarter of a century earlier, recording in February 1929 that he had had 'my first Urdu lesson for 25 years. I have really not forgotten very much, and the Munshi is very good indeed at teaching.'[16] His desire to economise while in India did place some restrictions upon his off-duty activities however, and although he tried his hand at tiger shooting, and enjoyed it very much, the expense prevented him from repeating the experience in the immediate future. There were, however, plenty of large-scale sporting events both at Meerut and at nearby Delhi, and my father was a spectator at everything from horse trials to a Highland Games, which enabled him to keep up with all the best social circles within political and military India.

In preparation for a planned trip to the North-West Frontier, my father renewed his acquaintanceship with the Mountain Artillery and was favourably impressed with their activity and intensive training regime, regretting that these troops were directly subordinate to Shea at Eastern Command rather than being assigned to the Meerut District. This was his first visit to the frontier, and he made an extensive trip of it, the narrative of which filled up most of a volume of his diaries. Reviewing that volume in 1949 when he began to look over his career in retrospect, he wrote:

> We have been accused of making too much fuss over the defence of the Frontier. Of maintaining an Army for Imperial purposes & not for the defence of India.
> It remains to be seen whether, now that Pakistan exists, the Frontier tribes will ever threaten India. Or whether the Afghans may be induced to do so by Russian propaganda and with Russian help. The rich plains of India are regarded with envy by the poverty-stricken hillmen.[17]

My father's trip occupied the summer hot season, during which military training was kept at a minimum, but he was back in time to oversee the training program in his district over the cooler winter months. It will be recalled that he had been promised the use of such mechanised assets as were available, and it had been grudgingly confirmed by the Inspector of Cavalry that this would indeed be the case, but these mechanised assets were depressingly few in number.

Although elements of the Royal Tank Corps had been serving in India for some years, these comprised only a small number of independent armoured car companies, equipped with a variety of vehicles of varying age and utility. These cars were of some use on the frontier simply by virtue of the fact that there was nothing at all to oppose them, but they had no off-road capacity and thus their employment was somewhat limited. Six-wheeled lorries had begun to be made available in India by this time – it will be recalled that my father commented favourably on their employment in the front-line logistic support role in the previous year's manoeuvres – and in 1927 an armoured car body had been experimentally mounted on a six-wheeler chassis to good effect.

The idea of tanks in India had also been mooted since the early 1920s, and a small number of light tanks had arrived in January 1925 for trials, but they had been unable to overcome resistance from the devotees of the horse and the experiment had not been proceeded with. Finally, and most recently, 1928 had seen the arrival of a small number of tracked Carden-Lloyd Carriers, which could mount a machine gun or – at the risk of overstraining their engines – be used as artillery tractors.[18]

The material, then, was beginning to become available, but its use was still restricted to the small Royal Tank Corps contingent and there were no moves to mechanise even the Regular British Army cavalry regiments serving in India, let alone the mounted arm of the Indian Army. The resistance to mechanisation from horse-minded officers has already been noted and, although far more openminded than might be expected from his cavalry pedigree, even Chetwode still advocated the employment of old-style horsed cavalry. Ahead of the 1929–30 winter training season, for example, a memorandum was circulated by Chetwode on the correct use of divisional cavalry – that is to say, the mounted units attached to each infantry division, which amounted to a whole regiment in the current Indian organisation.

Although recognising the value of mounted troops for reconnaissance, my father strongly felt, and outlined in his diary, that Chetwode seemed to grant far more theoretical autonomy to the commanders of divisional cavalry regiments than my father as a divisional commander would be prepared to countenance.[19] More generally, my father summed up the situation and the need for change in the Indian Army mindset as follows:

> It really makes me laugh at their continued fetish of Cavalry. I looked up my diary for 1927 and saw photographs of the various armoured and unarmoured machine-gun carriers which had been brought out then – two years ago. There is absolutely no reason why these things should not be swarming about in the next war. Why shouldn't we use ordinary common towing cars with machine-guns in them? Last war we were held up by barbed wire and machine guns and war became stationary. Why shouldn't we be held up by mobility and machine-guns? I cannot see how any reconnoitring force can get through a barrier of these mobile machine-guns. In their cars they can carry any amount of ammunition. How can a cavalry force attempt to penetrate such a screen of mobile machine guns unless it is supplied with armoured fighting vehicles capable of making a gap for their horsemen.
>
> I am quite in agreement that the first thing is to get all the 1st and 2nd line transport mechanised. Then, perhaps, the Young Cavalryman will begin to realise that he must get these mechanised fighting vehicles or he will be ousted.[20]

Here, then, was a model for the gradual mechanisation of the forces in India, clearly drawing on my father's own experiences in 1918 when his use of mobile machine guns helped stem the tide of the great German offensive. Clearly, British commanders in India would have to work for some time to come with considerable numbers of mounted troops, but this suggestion of integrating cavalry and mechanised vehicles was an excellent attempt at a compromise solution that maximised the utility of mounted troops and gave them some chance of still carrying out their assigned roles even on a modern battlefield.

Although he could do little from India to further the progress of mechanisation in the army as a whole, my father did continue to keep himself fully up to date with such changes as were being made, particularly when, as with the next news on that front, there were consequences for the promotion prospects of the army's senior officers:

> I am told that Milne has decided upon mechanising two more Cavalry Regts. That is the best way of getting rid of the backward spirit.
>
> Milne is not likely to give away his ideas before he thinks it is time to do so, but, if I read him correctly, he will not recommend a Cavalryman for CIGS. It will be all the easier for him to pass over Chetwode by getting him appointed to the command out in this country.[21]

If Chetwode were indeed to become the next C-in-C India, this would leave either 'Tim' Harrington or Archibald Montgomery-Massingberd as next in line to succeed Milne as CIGS. Since my father knew that Milne had a low opinion of Harrington due to the latter's courting of publicity, he assumed that the CIGS would use his political contacts to ensure that it would be Montgomery-Massingberd who would succeed him when he retired. This would, in turn, potentially work to my father's advantage, because if Montgomery-Massingberd – a fellow artilleryman – were to succeed Milne then it would leave my father, after his expected 1931 promotion, as one of the most senior staff-qualified Gunners in line to fill the post of Master General of the Ordnance when it became vacant in that year. My father had earlier identified that job, along with Southern Command back in Britain or Western Command in India, as the most likely vacancies to which he might succeed as a lieutenant general, although he also glumly noted that a stint on half pay was a more likely outcome.[22]

In almost all his predictions my father would be proved correct, including, sadly, his prediction of a spell on half pay for himself, although with Milne extending his tenure until 1933, Montgomery-Massingberd would have to wait for his chance to be CIGS. Only with regards to the post of Master General of the Ordnance was he mistaken, for not only did he miss out on the post himself but it went to a more junior officer whose name he had not even considered: Major General Sir Ronald Charles.

During the hot months of 1930, my father returned to Britain to spend leave with his family, returning overland by car as far as Basra. Re-joining his district in the autumn of that year, he was back in time to see Sir Philip Chetwode confirmed as C-in-C India and, a little later, to receive notification that he would be promoted on 1 March and that his successor at Meerut would be Major General C.A. Ker.

Back in England again in May 1931, he returned home to Longlands to sit and wait on a lieutenant general's half pay, unsure whether the next move would be a return to high command or to join the ranks of retirement. As if to make matters worse, the White Paper published on 11 September hit lieutenant generals with a pay reduction, effective from 1 October, as part of the financial retrenchment that followed the crash of two years previously. Luckily, my father had been posted to the lieutenant governorship of the Tower of London which came with a yearly stipend of £400, but he remained in a state of enforced idleness and limbo and even the £400, though welcome, troubled him as it was in effect earned by doing nothing.

On Christmas Day 1931, with Milne still in office and the identity of his eventual successor unknown, he reviewed his situation and prospects:

> I am afraid I sat or stood and dreamed of what the next year was likely to bring me. I have so many times thought I was going to get things and then found that I have not even been in the running for them. I suppose the best thing that could happen to me would be for Tim Harrington to be appointed CIGS and for me to get the Aldershot Command – all in February 1933. Far enough off even for that.
>
> If Chetwode comes home as CIGS then I might be made Chief of the General Staff in India. Considering my age and the way that people look at things I suppose it would be better for me to go out to India and then come home to Aldershot.
>
> What I am going to do with myself during the next 14 months I don't know. If I were certain that that were the limit of my waiting I shouldn't mind so much. But it doesn't follow in the least that I should be given a job then. Much more likely that the job should go to [Lieutenant General Sir Basil] Burnett-Hitchcock as he is the senior.[23]

At the end of the year, Philip Chetwode wrote with some timely advice and reassurance, reminding my father that he himself had been in much the same position all too recently:

> If you get a chance in the next year or two, it seems to me that you are perfectly certain to go to the top, but at the moment, at any rate, it looks on paper that you will have to wait till 'Uncle George' goes early in 1933. However, I have myself three times in my life felt that I was done for and that there was nothing else; but a death vacancy or something else happens to alter the whole outlook.

Personally, I can only hope very much that you will stick it out, at any rate for some time yet.[24]

During the coming months, his correspondence with Chetwode would prove something of a lifeline for my father, keeping him in touch with events in India – where the main concerns were budgetary, and little or no further progress towards modernisation and mechanisation proved possible – and giving him someone with whom he could discuss his own ideas. In turn, he kept Chetwode informed of events back in Britain which helped keep his mind actively applied to the military situation even while he was on half pay.

Still there were no signs of a return to duty, and although my father was pleased to be appointed Colonel Commandant of the Royal Artillery just before Christmas 1932, he was still left wondering whether he would have to spend another year on half pay. On 27 November of that year it had been announced that Montgomery-Massingberd would succeed the ageing and time-expired Milne as CIGS, taking office the following February. My father, however, saw little personal advantage in this: although he was, after his own fashion, a moderniser, the new CIGS was of the opinion that in any future war the initial brunt would be borne by the existing arms, and that mechanisation should therefore be focused on supporting cavalry and infantry units rather than on developing tank warfare through independent tank formations. As such, his views were somewhat out of step with my father's, who saw little opportunity for further employment under the new regime. Only two posts were due to become vacant for an officer of lieutenant general rank, namely director general Territorial Army in October 1933 and QMG in India in September 1934.

On 13 February 1933 Philip Chetwode was made a field marshal, which heralded promotion all round, and the first hint of a further reshuffle came in April 1933 when the military secretary, Lieutenant General Sir Sidney Clive, sounded out my father for the possibility of a four-year appointment as quartermaster general in India to replace General Sir Alexander Wardrop, who was coming home early to take over as GOC-in-C Northern Command. My father suspected skulduggery in the appointment, with an ulterior motive of getting him out of the way before the plum jobs at home came to be filled but, at the same time, he reflected that it would be most pleasant to 'be away from my friend Massingberd. I really couldn't kow-tow to a creature like that and he should be gone by the time I have to look round again.'

Sitting out the tenure of a detested CIGS under the congenial command of Sir Philip Chetwode had a certain appeal, therefore, but with his family growing up and his own mother growing old and infirm, there were also strong ties to keep him at home. The nature of the job was also an issue, and he thus had a lot to think on after receiving Clive's letter:

> I have taken the afternoon to consider matters. It almost seems a joke that they should make me QMG in my old age. I don't think I'm suited to the job – though I could do it better than our old friend Wardrop. I think I never even considered QMG for a minute. How did the W.O. come to think of it. I presume that Chetwode was offered a few names and made his choice. They didn't want me in this country, the swines. I'm not sure that it isn't all for the best as the carry-ons at home would have got on my nerves. Would any business run things as the W.O. does? I very much doubt if it is possible.
>
> I wonder what Mariot will say to it?[25]

Unsurprisingly, my mother was 'pretty upset' by the news of a potential four-year parting: at the end of the day, however, my father realised that to refuse the job would mean the end of his military career and since he was in no position to retire, he had better accept.

On 12 April, the day after he had received Clive's letter, my father's thoughts were more than allayed by Philip Chetwode writing from India imploring him, 'If you are offered an appointment out here I beg that you will not refuse it. You may not like it as well as others, but it is bound to lead to bigger things.'[26] This personal note, addressed to 'my dearest Tiny', certainly helped settle his mind, and led him to hope that Chetwode might have it in mind for him to eventually move across to CGS India or GOC-in-C Northern Command rather than serve out his full four years as QMG. In any case, as he wrote, 'the Army at home is dead for a long time to come. Interest has departed from it. India is in the melting-pot and there should be plenty of opportunity there in the years to come.'[27]

Having written back to Clive to accept the post, his appointment was duly rubber-stamped by the War Office, with an instruction for him to take up his duties on or about 12 October 1933. His posting to India forced him to vacate Longlands House and to buy Southernwood House at Hingham. It was nothing new for my mother to be left behind to manage house and home on her own, as she instinctively knew that in my father's mind the army came first and that she would dutifully follow him when the call came. Meanwhile, my father had the company of his bull terrier puppy Caesar to keep him occupied on the voyage out and in his spare time once he arrived in Delhi.

Domestic rearrangements in order, he finally set off for India on 21 September, travelling from Folkestone to Boulogne and on to Marseilles in his new model Owen Magnetic. From there he boarded the RMS *Viceroy of India* with crowds of other passengers for the journey to Bombay. On arrival, he drove to New Delhi to take up residence in King George's Avenue and set about his duties.

Relative to the equivalent post at the War Office in London, the QMG in India had a rather larger portfolio of responsibilities and, as my father discovered upon investigating the remit of the role when it was first offered to him, had superintendence of the following individuals or bodies:

1) Director of Movements & Quartering.
2) Director of Suppliers & Transport.
3) Director of Veterinary Services.
4) Director of Remounts.
5) Director of Farriers.
6) Embarkation Staff.[28]

The substantial focus on care of military animals, necessitated by their continued importance in the Indian military establishment, is noteworthy and reflects the fact that there had been little further progress towards mechanisation during my father's spell on half pay. These roles, however, were essential ones, and my father had not been long in his new post before he came to realise that the levels of animal transport were already maintained at the bare minimum necessary to keep the troops supplied during active operations. Moderniser though he was, there was no question that in the role of QMG he was obliged to work with logistical methods that, in their basic form, had little changed since the previous century.

Insofar as his approach to his duties was concerned, he wrote that he hoped to quickly obtain the confidence of his subordinates, facilitate the exchange of ideas and 'make the job a human one and stop people treating things in an academic fashion. There will be a devil of a lot of paper flying about.'[29] In this last prediction, my father was most assuredly correct, and he spent many long days during his first weeks in Delhi going through mountains of paperwork, much of which he felt was an unnecessary product of the sheer size of the bureaucracy involved. Many of these schemes related to planning for shifting the Army of India to a war footing, which would include the potential despatch of brigades to help hold Singapore and other imperial garrisons. With Germany announcing her withdrawal from the League of Nations only days after my father took up his new role, and with tensions brewing between Russia and Japan in Manchuria, it began to seem that these schemes needed to be considered as something that might be of more than theoretical importance.

More likely than a mobilisation to meet a global crisis, however, was the need to support operations on the North-West Frontier. Because of an increased establishment in machine guns and other support weapons for both British and Indian battalions, the logistical trail needed to support troops engaged in mountain warfare had grown larger. Mechanisation in place of mules was certainly a partial answer, but this in turn required a program of increased road building and other infrastructure improvements to enable vehicles to be used effectively in the tribal areas.

As QMG, my father would be heavily involved in the details of implementing these policies, and found that there was considerable resistance to new ideas. He pushed, for example, for the building of modern hard-surfaced roads designed for motor vehicles rather than horses, citing a report from a British newspaper which asserted that 100 miles of two-lane road could be had for 500 tons of bitumen. He decided to look into this further, irrespective of the views of the engineer-in-chief for India, Major General George Henry Addison. Having earlier reviewed the army's plans for operation in Afghanistan in the event that intervention was again required in that country, he was aware that the so-called 'Pink Plan' called for only modest advances by the available troops, and required reinforcements – unnecessary ones, he felt – from Britain at an early stage:

> Our [projected] advance from Kabul to Kandahar is so appallingly slow that something must be done to investigate things. The ground is so hard underneath in many places that it might be possible to do something like this. One would have to limit the pace of traffic of course. Given fine weather and proper control it might be possible to start off with one of these roads, banking upon finishing the early part of the campaign while a proper road was being built next to the 'skin' road. Surely there must be something in this statement I hear so often?
>
> I only wish I had some of my Canadian War Engineers here. I could then get a practical opinion. Why should Addison know anything more about roads than I do?[30]

My father's practical approach to getting things done won him the praise of the C-in-C, and Chetwode furnished him with a glowing confidential report when the time came for the annual review of all senior officers. It read as follows:

> I am fortunate in securing the help of Sir E. Ironside in the important post of QMG in India. His brains and his imagination are already transforming the policy of his great department and I am satisfied that the result will be increased efficiency at less cost. Some may think him unorthodox, if so, I can only wish there were more like him. Fully qualified for the highest appointments and commands.

My father was naturally pleased with the praise, believing that it reflected the success of his approach to the job he had been given. After recording Chetwode's words, he went on to write:

> This is a wonderful tribute to what I have done in my 5 months here as QMG. This due to the fact that I have wanted to know what was going on in my Dept. and to my having taken nothing for granted. I told my subordinates that I expected them to convince themselves of two things:–

(i) That their show was efficient.
(ii) That it was running as cheaply as possible.

If a show was running expensively, it was to be examined to see whether the efficiency gained could not be obtained at a lesser cost.[31]

Not all the QMG's duties were military, however. As a member of the Indian General Staff my father also attended the vice-regal garden parties in Delhi, one such gathering leading to a decidedly extracurricular mission after the viceroy, Lord Willingdon, asked him to set up a *machan* for the renowned Indian artist Archibald Herman Muller, who wished to portray a tiger on the prowl in its natural surroundings in the jungle. He was with the artist to make sure that the prowling beast provided exactly what the artist expected of his sitter and the result was duly exhibited and priced at 200 *annas*, which in those days was the equivalent of £50. My father did not make a purchase, but later secured the painting for £1 at one of the Harrods auctions in London in 1938. It is a masterpiece of animal art, which for many years has graced the walls of my own study.

Meanwhile, back in England, my mother looked after my schooling terms at Pinewood Preparatory School and my sister's presentation at Buckingham Palace, followed by her outing to Ascot at the end of the social season. This left time for her to prepare for the voyage to India with my sister Elspeth (Jane to all) accompanied by her first cousin Sarah (Sally) Tetley-Jones, in whose company she rejoined my father in Delhi in October 1934. All three were soon whisked off to be spectators to further tiger shooting — a baptism of fire in the dress circle of an Indian colosseum watching the gladiators of the forest fighting for their lives.

It is clear, notwithstanding his initial misgivings about taking on the QMG's role in India, that my father in fact found the post rewarding and interesting, so much so that in August 1934 he turned down the option to return to an active command at Quetta — it was, he remarked, the first time that he had ever refused a post that was offered to him. Furthermore, far from continuing to covet the post of CGS, he instead confided to his diary that he felt that General Sir William Bartholomew, who came out to assume that role in 1934, was far better suited to it than he was and would assuredly do a good job. Bartholomew was, however, a staff man at heart rather than a commander and this, with Chetwode due to vacate the post of C-in-C India in 1935 and General Sir Robert Cassels to take over, set him thinking on what these appointments might mean for his own future career:

> How funny it is that years ago — in 1928 — when Jacob approached me as to whether I would go to India as CGS I was quite keen to go, and now that I have seen it — 6 years later — I have come to the decision that I should prefer to be QMG for a short time than CGS for the full 4 years. I am made for commanding and

not for being a staff officer. I could be C-in-C in India far better than CIGS at the War Office. Thorpe [Major General Gervaise Thorpe, Deputy Adjutant General in India] said yesterday that I ought to be the C-in-C out here in relief of Cassels in Oct. 1940 when I should be just over 60 and Hugh Elles CIGS at home about the same age. It would suit me very well to have a programme rather as follows:

1. C-in-C Western Command India 15.6.35–2.2.37/12.10.37
2. C-in-C Southern Command 2.2.37–1.11.40
   or C-in-C Aldershot 12.10.37–1.11.40
3. C-in-C India 1.11.40–1.11.45

I should then have had 11 years in high positions and should certainly be the senior General in the Army if I can survive.[32]

Such planning was all well and good, however, but for the moment he was compelled to continue in his job as QMG in the face of considerable financial retrenchment as the army and the government of India both sought to make the economies necessitated by the economic depression. My father was required to fight his corner hard, as the Treasury sought to recoup its costs at India's expense:

> The W.O. want us to buy our 'warlike stores' through them. We refuse. The reason being that the W.O. add on anything from 4% to 15% for what they call 'Inspection and Packing'. If we ordered direct from the firms, we should escape these charges. The W.O. put forward the plea that they wish to ensure that all such stores are uniform in the Empire. As we have an Indian Stores Department in London and also keep Mechanical Transport experts at the India office, we naturally want to do our own inspection and packing. It is the Treasury, of course, which insists upon these charges being made. We are now to concoct a letter showing why we are to have a free hand.[33]

In a linked problem, the very issue of compatibility of equipment caused other problems when it came to planning for the potential despatch of the British Expeditionary Force to India in order to furnish the reinforcements deemed necessary under the Pink Plan for the completion of any hypothetical operations that might be required to keep the Russians out of Afghanistan and the Afghans out of India. It was all very well for the War Office to desire commonality of equipment, but this ran contrary to my father's efforts to make the logistical support for the Army of India more flexible and effective. For example, if units of the BEF were to deploy to India then they would 'bring the trailer cookers they have designed with them'. These had been designed with European conditions in mind:

> They cannot be taken off the trailers and are all for Coys. Ours are all for Platoons. We have no 3 tonners capable of pulling these things and they burn heavy oil for

which we have no facilities. The G.S. here are frightened to tell the W.O. what they think of the plan. Personally, I am in hopes that we shall never be so foolish as to pour troops into a place like Afghanistan, where they cannot be used. We want a place as a bogey to put up to the politicians & so ensure that we can have a mechanised force at home. The defence of India is naturally a good card to play and Quetta and Kandahar are reported as placed where the mechanised forces are definitely required.

One sees what difficulties the W.O. has in trying to keep up an Expeditionary Force that can go to Europe or to some mild part of the Empire. It is largely a matter of transport and I think we should be ready with plans for the British Ex. Force here, however unlikely it is for them to be employed here.[34]

My father hoped that Bartholomew, once established as CGS, would revise the plans for Afghanistan, but serious revisions to the Pink Plan did not begin until 1938. In the meantime, my father worked to perfect his plans for the logistical support of the Army of India, developing a system based on pushing a road head up close to the theatre of action, from where animal transport could be used to facilitate the distribution of supplies that would be brought up by lorry. Outlining his scheme in full to Chetwode shortly before that officer left India, he concluded by stating that his arrangements signified that considerable progress had been made towards increasing readiness for war, without overstretching the limited finances available:

> We are straightening out the ravages of the axe, with respect to our supply services, by reducing the heavy expenditure on M.T., and we are increasing our mobility without loss of efficiency.
>
> We have, I think, ample M.T. in our hands and in sight in the country to serve the Pink Plan, but we must avoid serving out M.T. to all and sundry, and where it cannot be given an economical day's work, this is what we are so prone to do.[35]

My father could take pride, therefore, in what he had achieved as QMG and, although his arrangements were not tested by war, they were sorely tried and not found wanting when the army was compelled to offer its humanitarian assistance in responding to the devastating Quetta earthquake of 31 May 1935. My father was on leave in Britain at the time, but the massive logistical support required for the relief effort was delivered where it was needed and my father paid great tribute in his diaries to the efforts of Henry Karslake, now a major general and GOC Baluchistan District, who oversaw the relief work. More generally, his diaries also pay tribute to the heads of department who worked under him, only one of whom had presented any trouble and that through personal conceit rather than any inefficiency in his job.

His leave in Norfolk gave him a well-deserved rest from his duties in India, and he and my mother spent their time meeting and seeing their friends and enjoying the many invitations to lunch and dine with them. I enjoyed the summer cricketing season in play at the family matches and my father was invited to shoot at the start of the autumn season. On 16 July, the *London Gazette* carried, along with the news that Montgomery-Massingberd was to be a field marshal, the announcement that my father was to be promoted to the rank of full general with seniority from 30 June of that year. At 55, this made him the youngest officer of his rank in the whole British Army, something which the newspapers picked up on.

For the moment, he continued with his preparations to return to India and resume his duties as QMG and in due course travelled out along with my sister, reaching Bombay on 7 October. It became increasingly clear, however, that he would not, after all, serve out his full four years in that post and that his promotion would bring with it an appointment to a command. Chetwode, indeed, had recommended exactly that in the conclusion to his last confidential report on my father, writing the previous year:

> I think he should go on to High Command soon. His experience in India will have fitted him all the better for it – but his true work lies in teaching men to make war, and in doing so to force out of his officers any originality and independence they have in their composition.[36]

For his own part, he was ready for a change, writing:

> I have been delighted by the work, but I have had enough of it in 2½ years and I am very glad to give it up. That is almost the limit that I like to go with a job. Only the infinite variety of the QMG work has kept me going.[37]

My father's new appointment was, in due course, announced as taking him back to Britain as GOC-in-C Eastern Command, which would place him back in the heart of matters just as things were starting to progress again with the resumption of moves towards mechanisation and the belated realisation that serious war preparations would again need to be considered in light of the deteriorating political situation in Europe. Refreshing himself as to the progress that had been made under Montgomery-Massingberd's tenure as CIGS, he was left unimpressed:

> I am more & more dissatisfied with the new attempt to bolster up the infantry arm [with additional machine guns]. We still seem to think that infantry can work forwards under the fire of its own arms. No other country believes that this is possible in modern war. You require either artillery or tanks. No number of machine-guns will make an infantry attack successful. For defence the infantry

is already sufficiently supplied with machine-guns and light automatics. To me, the new scheme smacks of compromise, but nobody wants this mass of subsidiary weapons in a small war or in Internal Security duties.

Further, the maintenance of the cavalry in the form of tanks and armoured cars is also a compromise – to attempt to enlist the same class of man as has been usual in the Cavalry. But, the Tank Corps has already attracted some of the best class of men in England. To attempt to keep up the same class of officer doesn't appear to me to be very necessary. I should have preferred to see the Tank Corps increased. Cavalry Regts. are not territorially connected and it seems to me that it was not necessary to perpetuate them.

It will be interesting to see how the experiment goes on. I have never had anything to do with the two mechanised cavalry regiments, the 11th Hussars and 12th Lancers. Reports say that they are very good, but one cannot tell.[38]

All in all, as he prepared to leave India my father's thoughts were positive and hopeful. He could depart as QMG with pride in a job well done and take up his new role in a spirit of enthusiasm for the ongoing modernisation of the army in which he now hoped to again play an active part.

14

Eastern Command

After completing his time as QMG in India, my father left Bombay in the opening month of 1936. My mother travelled back on the SS *Victoria* via Genoa, while his own passage home was designed to bring him step by step back to reality through Colombo, Hong Kong, Shanghai, Vancouver, Ottawa, Halifax and Greenock. All the way back to Britain he was in the sights of the press and was feted by officialdom, who wanted to know what he was doing and where he was going.

In Singapore he inspected the garrison, and from the virtually undefended Hong Kong he ventured into Canton. After dining with the governor, he realised that the inevitability of Japanese supremacy in China and the consequent threat to the security of Hong Kong stood out in everybody's minds. Nevertheless, he was astute enough to observe that Japanese imperialism was, at heart, motivated by the same concerns that had led to the establishment of the British in China:

> Has any body computed the theory that our objects & those of the Japanese are identical? To get China in order and to get the market for goods going? Why cannot we share with Japan? Why must we think that we must be kicked out? Japan has plenty to think of and would be glad to square with us. Cannot we square our Dominions that we must keep this trade going? I cannot see why we must champion China against Japan. Why should we? The long-sighted say that we are merely putting off the evil day & that Japan will go for us. I don't believe this. Japan is far too occupied with China & Russia and cannot afford to assault us. Our danger will come when Russia screams to us in the League of Nations to save her from Japan & to put in Sanctions. Then what will we do?[1]

The initial point was a fair one but, sadly, by 1936 things had moved on from the days of the early twenties when the League of Nations carried some weight and the old Anglo-Japanese alliance was still a fresh memory. Certainly, though, my father was quite correct in his military assessment of Hong Kong's vulnerability and he was glad, after touring the defences on the day before his departure, that it was neither his responsibility to hold the place nor to advise on the defence of Britain's eastern outposts. With words that would be proven sadly prophetic only six years later, he concluded, 'If the Fleet runs away to Singapore, then Hong Kong will be in for a quick and sticky end'.[2]

My father was being besieged with cables from Canada inviting him to dine, and he set off from Hong Kong to Victoria on 26 February aboard the RMS *Empress of Russia*. There was a tense atmosphere amongst the passengers as they passed by Nagasaki and Yokohama, sighting Fujiyama in the distance. As the ship crossed the dateline on 8 March, the tension hotted up on receipt of news from Europe:

> The fat is in the fire. Hitler has denounced The Treaty of Locarno and has occupied the Rhineland. France has called upon the powers signed up to the Treaty to employ sanctions against Germany – Italy, Belgium, and ourselves. What an unholy mess. We are left with Belgium again.
>
> Germany offers to re-join The League of Nations and non-aggression Pacts with all & sundry for 25 years.
>
> What an unholy mess.[3]

For the moment, all my father could do was speculate how things might turn out, and whether French action against Germany might bring Russia in on the French side and thereby in turn expose Russia to attack from Japan – that, he felt, would mean 'a dog-fight again'. More pertinently, he observed that a future European war would not only see Britain again obliged to commit herself in defence of Belgium but 'it may mean our being tied to the coat-tails of France once more'.[4]

Striking land again at Victoria after a 4,200-mile voyage across the calming seas of the Pacific Ocean, he commenced a three-week journey along the Canadian Pacific Railway to his eventual destination of Halifax. The trip might have been shorter but for the stops and starts to meet and enjoy the company of his Canadian compatriots. Seeing men who were once under his command on the Western Front now thriving as civilians in business, and discussing the economics and military standing of Canada, mobilised his thoughts on their readiness to pick up their weapons again to fight off future aggression. By the time he arrived at Greenock he felt retuned to the Greenwich Mean Time of his home habitat, which was now threatened by the hostile outlook on the European horizon.

His visit to Canada had left him with a sense of robust British sentiment and he hoped that this two-way emigrational feeling would be preserved for the future. Back at Hingham he immediately felt at home and spent his first day at the Fakenham Races, where he met all the Norfolk people and lunched with Lord Leicester, who was also entertaining the Queen of Norway.

He formally assumed his duties as GOC-in-C Eastern Command on 16 April 1936. His new office overlooked Horse Guards Parade, whereas the boundaries of his command covered England east of a line from Lincoln to Chichester. As well as the local elements of the Territorial Army amounting to three divisions, the Regular 4th Division was also under my father's orders. Thus established, he called on the CIGS at once, made sure that his bull terrier pet – Caesar – was in quarantine at Woolwich, chose a West End flat to be near his place of work, and engaged Captain Peter Labouchère as his ADC.

With Montgomery-Massingberd now in retirement, the post of CIGS was filled by the man who my father was replacing at Eastern Command, the newly promoted Field Marshal Sir Cyril Deverell. After two successive appointees who had served their time largely on the staff, the appointment of Deverell meant that post of CIGS was filled by a man who had cut his teeth as a fighting soldier; in Deverell's case, an infantryman who had successively commanded a battalion, brigade and division on the Western Front. My father, although he had not taken to Deverell when the two men had served alongside one another in India, and observed now that he would have to take special care to try and win his confidence, welcomed the change at the top and his own new appointment:

> I think I am going to enjoy myself vastly in this Command with plenty to do and plenty of moving about. I don't think I shall lose interest at all. Will anything come to disturb the even course of our way? Everybody says that it will, but I hope it won't. I don't think it will. I wonder what kind of Expeditionary Force we could scratch up and who the Commanders would be? If we could have Philip Chetwode as C-in-C it would be good, but I am afraid that he is already too old for a strenuous campaign. He would give the men an immense confidence. There isn't anybody else, with the exception of Jock Stuart under whom I should like to serve.[5]

On 6 May, my father's fifty-sixth birthday, Mussolini occupied Addis Ababa and four days later annexed Abyssinia, giving Italy and himself another lease of life. Meanwhile, my father attended Viscount Allenby's funeral at Westminster Abbey, finding himself seated next to Alfred Duff Cooper, secretary of state for war, with Milne and Montgomery-Massingberd acting as pall-bearers.

Dinner invitations were piling in faster and faster, and his staff and ADC were ready to take those matters off his shoulders to allow him freedom of thought for command. Certainly thought was needed, for as the novelty of his new appointment wore off, realisation sank in as to just how parlous Britain's military situation had now become:

> God, what a state we have been brought to by an invertebrate Government and backbenchers military advisers. It makes one quite sick. I can do absolutely nothing except go on with cadre training. We haven't a single Tank under a dozen years old & most of them are sixteen. All we do is to contemplate an increase of

4 Bns of Infantry, when we cannot even fill the ones we have. I suppose we are bolstering up the wretched Cardwell system.[6]

The Cardwell System, it will be remembered, was the Victorian hangover that kept one half of the army at home but reduced the function of homebased units to acting as depots for imperial commitments.

Feelings of despair did not stop him from travelling widely about the Eastern Command area, looking at every town and village, road and river to get to grips with keeping his commanders and their troops up to the mark. On 20 May he visited Hawkinge Aerodrome near Folkestone and saw the new autogiros at play with the RAF, where they were being tested in the observation and personal transport roles. The RAF officers were not impressed:

> It was unsafe on the ground and could be blown over easily. It gave away the position of an HQ very easily from the air. It had a very cramped position for the Army Officer being carried & it gave no possible chance of using a parachute owing to the great flippers overhead. It could land on any restricted piece of ground, but it required almost as much ground to start it as an ordinary aeroplane. The squadron leader told us that 8 had been bought by Army funds and had hardly been used. All the 8 were present on manoeuvres, but the total flying had been under 120 miles. The fact of the matter is that no machine is wanted for the transport of Army officers when the roads are good. In Europe this will almost always be so. The Army insisted on these machines because they wished to have something they could summon like a car.[7]

Nowadays we all know that the helicopter in all shapes and sizes has taken its place and we see that the US Osprey transporter has adopted the halfway solution, with engine twist taking the place of blades to give lift and propulsion that the autogiro lacked. In my father's day, however, as with the earliest tanks, the technology did not yet match the concept.

Although my father was well placed to form his own judgement on matters of military policy and technology, he also took care, as always, to cultivate those whose expertise in other areas might be of use to him. Very often those you know matter more than what you know, and this enabled him to gain some useful insights into the European diplomatic scene from John Cudahy, his one-time friend at Archangel in 1919, who was now the US ambassador in Poland and who flew to Norwich on 31 May to meet him again at Hingham. It was a visit of equal value to them both; to Cudahy, keeping in touch with the British Army, and to my father, keeping in tune with what was happening in Germany through the special relationship with his American friend:

I found Cudahy much the same as ever. He is still a rich man, but says that he finds being an Ambassador is expensive work. He has always belonged to Roosevelt's political party and when he found that the slump had taken some of his fortune, he thought he might do a little work outside his business. He was to have gone to Cuba, but was sent to Warsaw.

Cudahy went on to provide my father with his review of the situation and prospects in central Europe, giving 'his considered opinion that he didn't think Poland would be a nation in 10 years' time':

Then he told us of Germany, arranging the most mighty machine for war that there has ever been. Inculcating into the minds of all the young people that 'it was the finest thing in life to die for your country. It seemed to him that unless a miracle happened, there must be war in Europe within 10 years. I asked him what miracle might come and we could none of us imagine it. His advisers told him that Germany would be ready for war in 2 years, and I told him that I thought it would be longer than that.[8]

Cudahy's visit left my father more convinced than ever that Britain could hardly avoid war in the near future. At a later meeting on 13 December, shortly before Cudahy returned to Warsaw, he had him to lunch and the two men discussed whether Great Britain would support Russia against Germany. Cudahy reiterated his view that Poland was doomed as an independent state, but saw Russia as the greater threat and was undecided as to whether the Poles would go down fighting or turn towards Germany for help. For his own part, Cudahy told my father that he was hoping to go as ambassador to Berlin, but that Roosevelt wanted him in South America.

If war with Germany was coming closer, then this was made obvious on 3 July when the Zeppelin airship *Hindenburg* flew over the AA practise camp at Weybourne in Norfolk. My father noted:

One cannot imagine an airship of ours being allowed to fly over any coastline of Germany. We should have been arrested or even shot down. They flew at only a few hundred feet. Probably all the German intelligence people have reported that we are fortifying the North coast of Norfolk.[9]

This attitude of complacency was, at least in part, reinforced by the prime minister – Stanley Baldwin – in a speech to his constituents on 19 July, although it came with a warning that such complacency must come to an end. My father recorded that the prime minister had spoken as follows:

'We have ignored our defences for years in the hope of a general disarmament, which we have done our best to bring about. Our hopes have been disappointed. We have decided and the electors have decided, that we must repair our deficiencies.

'This has been forced upon us, though we have been reluctant to do it. We think the nations should have been able to avoid the madness, but as they have not done so I cannot, as Prime Minister, neglect the primary duty of government, which is the defence of the people.'[10]

As my father rather pungently commented when recording these remarks, 'He naively says that we have neglected our Defence Service for the last 4 years to see if others would disarm. He should have said something like 12 years instead of 4.'

As GOC-in-C Eastern Command, my father was left to wait and wonder what would come of this shift in policy and whether it came in time to redress the situation into which Britain had allowed herself to fall. At the same time, he did not neglect to keep his eye trained on all parts of his command to keep up the standards of the men under his control, before amusing himself by shooting, riding and mixing with his friends and acquaintances. He always attended meetings, conferences and dinners where he met and talked to ministers and officials. Included amongst those events was the installation of a new Lord Warden of the Cinque Ports on 30 July, where he witnessed Lord Willingdon, the former viceroy, assume the reins of office.

Recruitment into the army was at a very low level at this time, as my father had observed over the inability to fill the ranks of mooted new battalions, and morale was generally at a low ebb due in no small part to a lack of clear direction at the highest level. My father did his best to raise spirits in Eastern Command, writing on Trafalgar Day:

I think I have given a fillip to training in the Command. If I haven't restarted the enthusiasm, then I don't know how I can start it. Officers have become tired and cynical with the continuous lack of men and absence of modern weapons. Milne in the whole of his 7 years as CIGS never brought a single tank into service. Not a single one. And when Massingberd gave up 3 years later, he had not a single tank design, upon which he could go into production. A whole decade lost by these men who meant well. Could there be any greater weakness? I have told Deverell that he ought to withdraw Martell from the clutches of the MGO. To give him practically unlimited money and to tell him to design the best medium tank he can. It is maddening to think that we are in the state we are in. We invented Tanks, which won the war, and now we are behind most of the other nations. We are badly caught. And I cannot see how we can catch up under a period of years. The War Office is an inefficient machine, which moves too slowly. I have never served in it. What should I do, were I to be put in as CIGS tomorrow under some sudden casualty? Quite certainly I should have to sack the present Army Council.[11]

What my father had grasped was that it was all very well for Baldwin to belatedly and half-heartedly call for rearmament, but the army as it currently stood was not well set up, in terms of organisation or equipment, to serve as a basis for expansion. Even after Baldwin had publicly recognised the need to reform Britain's armed forces, continued penny-pinching from Neville Chamberlain at the Treasury limited what could be done and added to the lack of direction. Thus, while it was accepted – at least for the moment – that a European war would again require the despatch of a British Expeditionary Force to the Continent, and planning had now begun on how this would be formed and deployed, the force envisaged was to consist of only five divisions.

How such a force was to be sustained, let alone expanded, remained unclear. Duff Cooper, the minister, wanted to modernise the twelve standing divisions of the Territorial Army so that they could supplement the BEF in the field; Chamberlain, citing economy as much as anything else, wanted the TA formations retained at home and converted to the anti-aircraft role.

With respect to the latter concept, it will be recalled that my father had touted a similar idea in a paper, back at Camberley; the crucial difference, however, was that in my father's musings of 1923, such a use of the TA would be made possible by the simultaneous use of Regular cadres to raise a mass army on the lines of that fielded in the previous war. The latter concept, however, remained political anathema even as late as the mid-1930s, while amongst the generals Deverell, for one, believed that it would be unnecessary as he could not conceive of the dictator states being able to sustain a long war. Nor, for that matter, could Britain sustain a long war with her current resources, nor even equip her existing forces for a short one.

Baldwin's 1936 call to rearm meant, Deverell told my father, that the army could expect a 'trickle' of new equipment as the factories began to come on line in 1937, but the necessary 'torrent' of material needed would not make itself apparent until 1939. All this left my father wondering how Britain would cope in the intervening months, and the only comfort that he could find in an otherwise depressing situation was that he felt that the absence of a properly equipped expeditionary force during this time would prevent Britain's politicians engaging in any European intrigues.

As Britain took her first hesitant steps towards rearmament, other national and international events continued to dominate the headlines. On 4 November, Franklin Roosevelt was re-elected President of the USA for another four years with a big majority, while at the same time King Edward VIII had the whole of the Empire and youth at his feet, but was likely to throw away his inheritance for Mrs Simpson.

On 18 November, Italy and Germany recognised Franco's government in Spain and speculation over King Edward and Mrs Simpson rose to the point where Baldwin made it quite clear that there could be no such thing as a morganatic marriage for the king. Finally, the king announced his decision to abdicate on 12 December, after holding the world in thrall about his relationship with Mrs Simpson. My father's opinion on the abdication was succinctly expressed, 'It certainly is for the good of the country that he should go. He could have led the growth of the Empire, but he failed. To his credit be it that he has acknowledged it and made room for someone else.'[12]

In the middle of December, the CIGS sent my father a copy of his paper on the reorganisation of the army, which confirmed the concept of a five-division BEF as a long-term goal. More specifically, this force would consist of two corps each of two infantry divisions, plus the as yet unformed Mobile Division, which was to be an armoured formation comprising two mechanised cavalry brigades and one brigade of heavy tanks. To facilitate the formation of the new division, and to provide each of the infantry divisions with a light armoured regiment for the reconnaissance role, Deverell's paper announced the mechanisation of a further eight cavalry regiments. This was after the CIGS had earlier told my father in confidence that he intended to force through the mechanisation of additional cavalry regiments in India as well.

The infantry divisions, meanwhile, were to be reorganised so that some battalions took on the role of machine gun units, which were to be taken out of the brigades and deployed as divisional or corps-level assets; this had the effect of reducing the infantry brigades to the three-battalion organisation that had been resorted to in the closing months of the previous war. As well as receiving a mechanised cavalry regiment, the infantry divisions were also to have their artillery mechanised and re-equipped with the new 25-pdr field gun.

All this, however, was an eventual ideal: for the moment, the equipment was not available to furnish such a force, and even once it did reach the troops it would be necessary to institute an extensive training program to effectively complete the conversion process in those units that were being rerolled. All this would take time, so that if a BEF was required at the present time, the best that could be fielded would be two divisions of infantry, having some mechanised transport, but with horsed artillery of Great War vintage and no armoured support at all. As my father rightly observed, sending 'such a force to fight outside England is little short of criminal. There is no good having a force at all unless it is fit to fight.'[13]

Deverell's paper went on to outline how, by steady progression, the situation would improve as new equipment came out of the factories. However, as my father recognised, 'This forecast is based on the assumption that the personnel will be forthcoming. At present there is little hope of putting 4 Divisions and their ancillary troops into the field, much less keeping them in the field.'[14] Enumerating the various requirements, he came to the conclusion that there was a manpower deficit of 40,000 men, most of which fell on the infantry, and that the support arms had only the bare minimum necessary to meet their current commitments.

As if this was not bad enough, the concentration on Europe – which was politically essential to dispel the impression of Britain as militarily impotent and therefore of no consequence – meant that the Empire and other overseas commitments would necessarily be neglected. Having seen for himself the vulnerability of Hong Kong, he could at least report that there was to be a small acceleration in the defensive measures being taken there, and likewise at Singapore, but their scale – Singapore, for example, was to gain a third infantry battalion for its garrison – was hardly commensurate to the importance of these posts as centres of imperial communications and bases for the other two services. The British preoccupation with costs, he felt, stood out starkly in contrast to the attitude in Germany or Italy where labour would simply be drafted in to complete any necessary work.

It was all very well to identify the problems, but my father could no more supply the answers than could anyone else, and his final reflections on the implications of Deverell's report, and the consequences of neglecting the Empire, were gloomy:

> What will it all come to? I notice a slight change in opinions, but only a slight one. We have a higher standard of living in this country than in the rest of Europe. We live almost in luxury. So many luxury trades maintain a lot of people. I hope it is not too many.
>
> But, if we don't maintain the Empire, we shall not be able to maintain our position and certainly not our population at the same standard. It is up to us. If we allow the Empire to fall from us, we shall suffer at once. We shall get what we deserve. If only some of the working classes could realise what conditions are in France, Russia, Germany & Italy, they would see how incomparably better they are with us. In all European countries, whether they be the so-called Dictator or Democratic Countries there is no standard of luxury. In some of the smaller countries, such as Poland, Czechoslovakia & Roumania, there is widespread poverty.
>
> We are at a turning-point in our history. I am wondering if we shall turn the right way.[15]

A newspaper article the following day advocated conscription, and provoked a further train of thought. My father was in favour of the measure, which he believed was best suited to getting the Territorial Army up to strength. As recorded in a lengthy diary that reads almost as a stream of consciousness, his mind then moved from this to means of economising elsewhere in the service to facilitate the sort of reforms that were needed.

This in turn led to the conclusion that change was needed at the top and the establishment of generals thinning out. Too many of his senior colleagues – and he went through them one by one – were variously described as 'stout and grey', 'red-faced and grey', and 'a bit part-worn'. Only for Jock Stuart – properly speaking, General Sir John Burnett-Stuart, GOC-in-C Southern Command, who he clearly admired – did he have anything positive to say, but at the other end of the spectrum the adjutant general, Sir Harry Knox, was described as 'overweighted with the care of getting men. Large & stout and heavy in body and mind. With the slowness & obstinacy of a Northern Irishman.'[16]

He went on to reflect that he had been lucky in his own service in that he had never had to serve at the War Office, and it was perhaps this and a clear awareness of the unenviable position that Deverell was in, caught between the army and the government, that led him to suggest that a more appropriate climax to his own career might take him not to the War Office as CIGS but back to India as C-in-C:

> The more I think of it, the more I think that I should make a bad CIGS. I couldn't put in the number of hours that Deverell does. I should hate all the routine and should miss my horses. Can one compare the job of CIGS to the job of CinC Eastern Command? There isn't any comparison. I wonder if I shall have the courage to say that I am not the man for CIGS? Shall I let it be known that I would like India? I shall be lucky if I get India. I think that I ought to leave my future to fate, and be pleased with whatever I get.[17]

The future aside, however, he had good reason to be pleased with his situation at present, and in reviewing the year 1936 as it came to a close he could say to himself that it had been:

> … a most successful one. It is the first time in England that I have had sufficient money upon which to live. I have done 9 months & have lived and enjoyed myself very much. This Eastern Command is the pick of them all. […] I have had very few soldiers to train, but I have done something to impress my personality upon those that are here.[18]

As with his earlier musings, one can see the old ambition and desire to serve being tempered now with an awareness of advancing years and recognition of a desire to spend more time at home with his family. Along with more general speculation about what the coming year would bring, he mused in particular on the situation in the Middle East and the possibility of service in that theatre:

> Palestine is being emptied of troops and I am told that the Govt. is very dissatisfied with little Waucope [sic. General Sir Arthur Wauchope], now running Palestine.

> I wonder if my destiny is to go out there during 1937? I am sure that the Arab trouble will break out again the minute the Commission declares anything but an immediate stoppage of Jewish immigration. Then I might be sent out as a combined Commissioner & General? I would rather remain quietly at home enjoying myself. Still, as the years go on one will be more and more unsuited to rough Command. But, there are no other Generals near me in rank who are younger & none have my experience. I wonder? We have such a nondescript Army that I have no confidence in commanding it. To go out now must mean disaster for us. And yet, very few people know that. They cannot believe we are as bad as we are. Who could?[19]

It should not be assumed from this that my father was giving up on his career, or that he had lost his enthusiasm for the service in which he had spent most of his adult life. Nevertheless, one can see a genuine concern as to the state into which the army had fallen, combined with a certain slowing down that was only to be expected from a man now well into his fifties. Still, he ended his diary for the year on a positive note, looking forward to the coming year which, whatever else it brought, he felt was sure to be interesting.

In fact, particularly if one takes to heart the Chinese concept of 'interesting times', 1937 was to be extremely interesting indeed, both for the army and for my father personally. The year began much as the old one had ended, however, with further futile debate over the role of the army after Deverell published his paper on that topic in February.

My father, who had no part in the formulation of the paper, was not particularly impressed with its contents. Although it stated the need for a BEF of four infantry divisions plus the Mobile Division, backed up with twelve divisions of the Territorial Army equipped to the same standard, its focus remained towards imperial defence. Further, the paper was poorly structured and poorly argued, to the extent that my father felt that it would have little influence on the economy-minded Neville Chamberlain whose preference was to see defence spending focused on the RAF. However, his disappointment was to some extent abated by a statement from Stanley Baldwin, now only months away from retirement as prime minister, that a £400 million loan had been floated for defence purposes in advance of the White Paper published on 16 February, which called for a £1.5 billion expenditure over five years to put right eighteen years of neglect.

Then, on 8 March, having been invited to attend a dinner at the Carlton with Duff Cooper, in the presence of some 200 people, including various ministers and leading civil servants, he found himself sitting next to Lord Strathcona, the parliamentary undersecretary of state for war, with the permanent secretaries of the Home Office and the Air Ministry at the same table:

My grandfather, Surgeon Major William Ironside, who died when my father was only a year old.

My grandmother, Emma Marie Ironside (*née* Richards), taken at the time of her marriage when she was 28 years old.

My grandparents, photographed at Mhow in India, 1874.

The earliest known photograph of my father, believed to have been taken when he was around 5 years of age.

Although my father's first military experience was in the Tonbridge School cadet corps, he noted in later life that he never rose beyond the rank of lance corporal.

Edward Goldberg, the Tonbridge master who nurtured my father's growing skill at languages.

My father as a gentleman cadet at the Royal Military Academy, Woolwich.

Lieutenant Charles Vereker, shop subaltern, whose threat that my father would find himself in the Royal Garrison Artillery almost caused him to leave the army before he was even commissioned.

My father (front right) with friends at an Honourable Artillery Company sports day, around 1899, in which he won second prize in the wheel race.

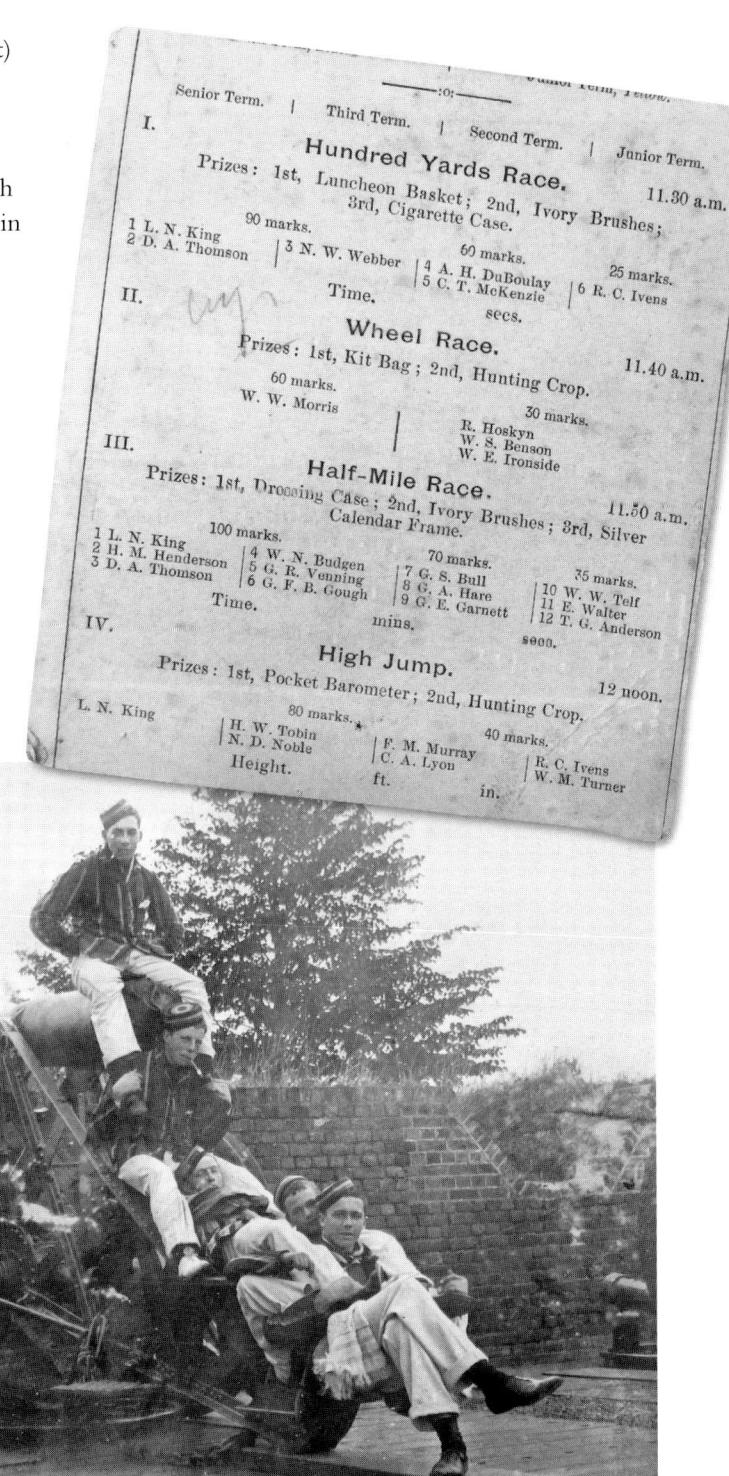

My father's battery on the move at Okehampton Artillery Practice Camp.

Officers of XIII Brigade Division, RA, at Okehampton Artillery Practice Camp. My father, newly joined 2nd lieutenant with 44th Field Battery, is second from the right of the back row.

The newly commissioned 2nd Lieutenant Ironside at Colchester Artillery Barracks, under orders for South Africa.

On active service out on the veldt.

A group photograph with fellow officers in South Africa. Seated, middle row, from left to right: my father; Vaughan, 13th Hussars; Eustace Crawley, 12th Lancers; Morrison, Royals; and Leslie, Bengal Lancers.

My father has captioned this 1901 photograph, 'Fetching in Fodder. Jeudwine's Column.' Good practice for his subsequent undercover work posing as a wagon driver in German South West Africa.

The faithful bulldog Bill, my father's companion during the Boer War and his subsequent undercover work.

A post-Boer War formal portrait of my father, proudly displaying the campaign medals for that conflict.

Another formal portrait, taken at Pretoria – most likely when my father was serving at Roberts Heights as brigade major on the staff of the Transvaal District from 1909 to 1912.

My mother, the then Miss Mariot Ysobel Cheyne, taken around 1907 – a year or so before she met my father.

My parents on their honeymoon on 26 June 1915.

The trenches around Hooge, site of the 6th Division's successful attack on 9 August 1915.

My father with Gibby in the trenches, and the cheque that was sent by a Connecticut schoolgirl to buy the dog a gas mask.

2nd October, 1917.

Dear Sir,
         With reference to your letter of the 8th. September, I return herewith the cheque for 1 Dollar which has been duly endorsed by Mr. Lloyd George. I am to regret that you have not received an earlier acknowledgement.
         Yours faithfully,

                    A. Stevenson

Lt.Col. E. Ironsides.

Staff officers of 4th Canadian Division at the time of the Vimy Ridge battle. Maj. Gen. Watson is in the centre of the front row, flanked by my father and Gibby; my future father-in-law, Thomas Morgan-Grenville, is on the far right of the back row.

Winter fashions in North Russia, 1919. The shuba fur coat was an essential adjunct to uniform clothing.

My father made journeys of many miles through the frozen wilderness, courtesy of Corporal Piskoff's sleigh-driving skills.

Senior Allied commanders at Archangel, including, from left to right: my father, US Brigadier General Wilds P. Richardson, Rear Admiral Sir John Green, and Brigadier General John Turner.

The Archangel–Vologda railway line was one of the main communication routes for my father's forces in North Russia.

A White Russian armoured train, complete with 6in naval gun.

Winter in Archangel.

PROCLAMATION.

To All Germans now serving with the Bolsheviks.

The Allied Command is prepared to receive all Germans, Czechs, and Letts, with all inhabitants of the Baltic Provinces of Russia who are prepared to come in and hand themselves over at our outpost lines. They should come forward unarmed under a White Flag. An armistice has been declared in Europe, and any of the above who come forward will be treated under the conditions of the armistice arranged in Europe. The desire of the Allies is merely to restore order to Russia, and it is the duty of all good European patriots to work for this object.

Brigadier-General.
Commanding Allied Forces in Northern Russia.

G. H. Q. ARCHANGEL.
8th November 1918.

Proclamation sent out by my father in both English and Russian in the hope of keeping German personnel out of the civil war in Russia following the end of the First World War (note that the Russian calendar was still several days behind that used by the rest of Europe, so this does in fact post-date the 11 November Armistice).

ПРОКЛАМАЦІЯ.

Всѣмъ нѣмцамъ, находящимся въ настоящее время на службѣ у большевиковъ.

Союзное командованіе готово принять всѣхъ нѣмцевъ, чеховъ, латышей и всѣхъ жителей Русскихъ Балтійскихъ провинцій, которые были бы согласны сдаться. Они должны будутъ явиться подъ бѣлымъ флагомъ на наши аванпосты. Перемиріе объявлено въ Европѣ, и съ тѣми, которые добровольно сдадутся, будетъ поступлено согласно условіямъ мирнаго договора, заключеннаго въ Европѣ. Единственное желаніе союзниковъ, возстановить порядокъ въ Россіи и долгъ каждаго европейскаго патріота содѣйствовать этому дѣлу.

Генералъ Бригады,
Командующій Союзными Силами въ Сѣверной Россіи.

Senior officers of the British mission to Archangel. From left to right: Walsh, Needham, my father, Perkins, and Crosbie. Perkins, commanding the Royal Artillery, had been one of my father's instructors at Woolwich and now found himself taking orders from his former pupil.

The handover at Archangel to the White Russian General Miller. The standing figures in the foreground are, from left to right: Colonel Pimorofsky, my father, General Miller, Colonel Thornhill, General Savitch, and Count Hamilton.

General Miller reviews the men of Dyer's Battalion prior to the handover of Archangel to White Russian control.

Greek troops during my father's stint commanding the British contingent at Ismid. He called them 'Black avised scoundrels. Well dressed but badly booted.'

Reza Khan, shown at the time of his coronation as Shah of Persia in 1925.

The assembled dignitaries at the Cairo Conference. First row, seated, from left to right: Sir Malcolm Stevenson, High Commissioner for Cyprus; Sir Walter Congreve, GOC Egypt; Sir Herbert Samuel, High Commissioner for Palestine; Winston Churchill MP, Secretary of State for the Colonies; Sir Percy Cox, High Commissioner for Iraq; Sir Aylmer Haldane, GOC Mesopotamia; my father, GOC Persia; and Sir Percy Radcliffe, Director of Military Operations. Second row, standing, left to right: Sir Geoffrey Archer, Governor of Somaliland; Miss Gertrude Bell, Oriental Secretary to the High Commissioner for Iraq; Sassoon Effendi, Minister of Finance, Iraq; E.H. Atkinson, General Staff, Mesopotamia; Colonel Stewart, General Staff Mesopotamia; Jafar Pasha al-Askari, Minister of Defence, Iraq; T.E. Lawrence, Special Advisor to the Colonial Office; Air Vice Marshal Sir Geoffrey Salmond, AOC Middle East; Colonel Trevor, Staff, Middle East; and Major Young, Staff, Persian Gulf. In the foreground are Archer's two lion cubs and their attendant; in the back row, second from left, is my father's ADC Lord Edward Hay.

My father with his great friend, the broadcaster Christopher Stone, during the tour taken by the two men to the battlefield of Tannenberg in preparation for my father's book on that campaign.

My father as GOC 2nd Division, photographed with some of his staff at Aldershot; the officer seated second from the right is J.F.C. Fuller, whose career my father helped foster and who was at this time serving as his GSO1.

Back at Tonbridge to inspect the cadet corps, 1 July 1926.

Wreck of a Bristol Fighter that crashed into the barracks housing the 2nd Norfolk Regiment, 16 December 1926.

Vickers Medium Mark I tanks on manoeuvres – product of the initial attempts to create an armoured fighting force during the mid-1920s.

Field Marshal Sir George Milne, CIGS 1926–23.

During my father's tour of the North West Frontier, he encountered what he described as 'an old Pathan Mullah trekking about in Waziristan'.

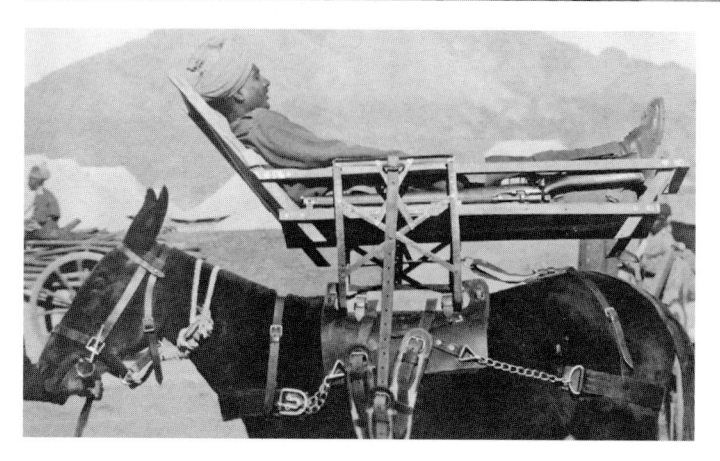

A mule-back stretcher for carrying wounded men during mountain operations, photographed during my father's tour of the North West Frontier.

Sir Philip Chetwode as C-in-C India with his staff, including my father as quartermaster general. Front row, left to right: Matheson, Cassels, Chetwode, Macmullan, and Jeffries. Second row, left to right: Leslie, Pryce, my father, Wigram, and Steel.

My father after a successful day's tiger shooting.

Archibald Herman Muller's painting of a hunting tiger, for which my father was asked to assist the artist in his search for suitable inspiration. My father later purchased the painting, which has for many years graced the walls of my own study.

My father's bull terrier Caesar, who accompanied him to India as a puppy and who remained his companion until sadly killed in a fall at Gibraltar.

My grandmother in later life, photographed at the age of 90.

Hitler and Mussolini observe the 1937 combined manoeuvres, to which my father was invited as the personal guest of *Generalfeldmarschall* von Blomberg.

The two dictators take the salute. My father recorded: 'the difference in the salute given by the two leaders. Hitler's is mild & the other man's fierce and uncompromising.'

My father in conversation with Marshal Pietro Badoglio (left) and Field Marshal Sir Cyril Deverell (right), at the German combined manoeuvres.

My father on his way to the War Office, accompanied by Caesar and Sir Herbert Creedy, Under Secretary of State for War.

The Spanish Republican destroyer *José Luiz Diez* aground after her failed attempt to escape from Gibraltar.

My elder sister, Elspeth, at the time of her presentation, aged 17½.

Myself, aged 13.

My father as CIGS returning from a conference at 10 Downing Street, with tin hat and gas mask in hand.

At work at the War Office, with bull terrier Caesarina in attendance.

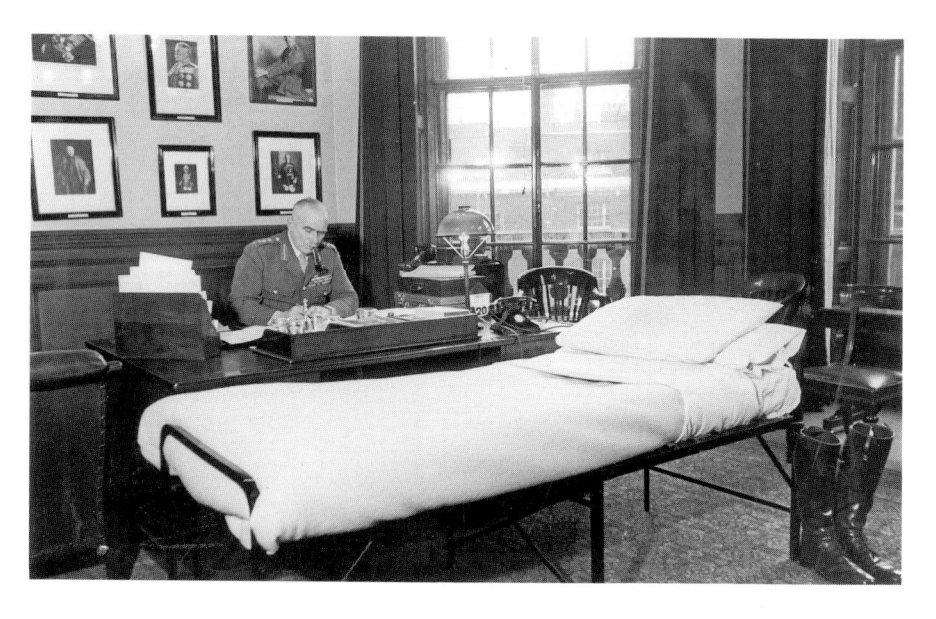

The demands of the role of CIGS in wartime meant that my father was required to sleep in his office on occasion.

On his way to or from one of the many conferences held during the winter of 1939–40 as the Chamberlain government struggled to take a grip on the course of events.

Riding provided some respite from the cares of office; my father is seen here on Mighty Atom.

The Chiefs of Staff Committee: my father, Air Chief Marshal Sir Cyril Newall, and Admiral of the Fleet Sir Dudley Pound.

An aerial photograph of the airfield at Stavanger following a successful naval bombardment – a rare positive moment from the doomed Norwegian campaign.

My father confers with Lord Gort, his predecessor as CIGS and the ill-fated commander of the BEF in France.

The investiture of Gort and my father with the Grand Cross of the Legion of Honour at Arras on 8 January 1940.

My father with Churchill, Gamelin and Gort prior to the fall of France.

My father and the Canadian Major General McNaughton fail to make an impression on Gamelin, who seems either detached or lost for words.

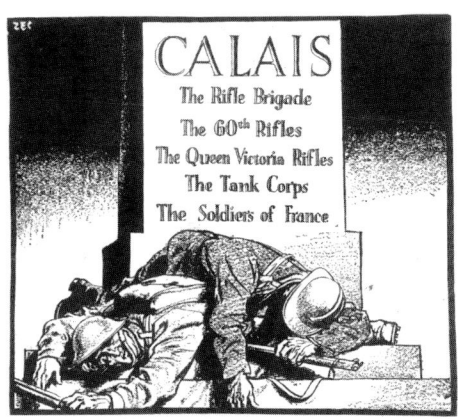

The fall of Calais left a deep impression on my father, who had been obliged to transmit the orders for the city to be held to the last. This image, which he pasted into his diary, was published in the *Daily Mirror*.

Men of the Local Defence Volunteers, soon to become the Home Guard, on parade in 1940. My father played an important role in building up the morale of this infant force.

General Alan Brooke, later Field Marshal Lord Alanbrooke; exemplar of the new generation of general officers with whom my father found himself increasingly at odds from the late 1930s onwards.

Back in uniform for the Coronation procession, where he rode with fellow field marshals Alexander, Auchinleck and Montgomery.

My parents in their Coronation robes.

Family members at a Buckingham Palace garden party *c.* 1950 – myself in the centre, with my wife and mother.

My father in late life, with his granddaughter Fiona (born 1954).

I had several talks with these people. With the Air Secretary I developed my theory that this bombing as a reply to bombing is a pernicious idea. That we have not the same targets given us as we give the enemy. Why, therefore, commence operations at a disadvantage of anything from 50% to 80%? We must therefore develop our own strategy. To my mind it is to destroy the enemy's Armadas, as and when they come. Our guns will break up their formations, already disorganised by bad weather, and they will then be chased by our fighters, exactly as the Armada was chased. All around our coasts. We have the young men ready to do this fighting. Why do we discourage this form of air-fighting by calling it defensive?

The Air Secretary told me that psychologically this 'bombing' complex was encouraged by the fact that technicians were trying to build bigger & bigger aeroplanes to carry more & more weight of bombs and to stay longer in the air. Thus, they are struggling to produce an aeroplane that will go all the way to Berlin. They forget that even if they do go to Berlin, Berlin isn't London. These people forget the human problem. A war of mutual bombing is far more likely to produce a deadlock than anything else. It is a principle of war that you must take advantage of any effect produced by military action.[20]

This dismissal of the bombing doctrine by my father was out of step with the times but would ultimately be proved to be correct. In his focus on home defence, however, he was simply reverting to ideas that had begun to be sketched out over a decade previously at Camberley, when he had made clear his view that a priority had to be made of the defence of the British Isles to provide a secure base for subsequent offensive operations.

The increased sophistication of fighter aircraft simply added another weapon to the home defence arsenal. In 1937, Supermarine and Rolls-Royce were ahead of the game and the Royal Aircraft Establishment (RAE) was intent on keeping ahead, despite having no way-leave for the 'Forced Air Farm' in their grounds. The vast roars of the wind tunnel farm blades caused a residential uproar in Farnborough. So, as a way of keeping the peace without upsetting the pace of vital fighter aircraft design, working hours were set for the days of the week that least annoyed the householders and best suited RAE. I personally have distinct memories of the occasion when, playing in a first eleven cricket match, we stopped play, when I was a boarder at Pinewood Preparatory School across the road from RAE, to watch the two-hour flight by Flight Lieutenant M.J. Adam on 3 June 1937, during which he hit a record height of 53,937ft.

Civil Aviation Schools came under contract to the Air Ministry to train pilots on four-year temporary attachments to the RAF without being commissioned and being terminated with a £350 gratuity to help them find jobs as airline pilots. Thus, with financial and technical support assured, the position of the

RAF seemed well assured, but the inability of the CIGS to adequately sketch out the role of the army led my father to commit to paper his own thoughts on this head. Only once the nature of the role could be understood could one begin to plan for what sort of army was needed to fulfil that role. His thinking worked out as follows:

1. Reinforcement of the garrisons of Imperial territories to deal with internal trouble.
2. Reinforcement of these garrisons to meet a foreign threat.
3. Reinforcement of the naval bases to meet a similar threat.
4. The seizure of hostile naval bases in war.
5. Offensive operations against the enemy's overseas territories, to counter or forestall the danger of a land or air attack being launched thence against our own territories.
6. The protection of air bases we may establish in an allied country.
7. Participation in the active operations of an ally's land forces.[21]

It will be noted that only the last of these points directly prefigured the hypothetical war with Germany on which planning now increasingly seemed to be based. My father saw this preoccupation as an error, believing that any of the three 'dictator powers' of the future Axis might potentially trigger a conflict into which the others would then be drawn. Therefore, moving on to consider the employment of British land forces in the event of a major European war, his observations were more generalised and could be applied to other theatres of war as well as to a BEF co-operating with the French and Belgians against Germany:

The dispatch of a force to operate with an ally is firstly important as a 'token'. It shows our ally that we are 'in' the business. The Navy is unseen & the Air Force would be almost equally so. The allied nation requires the support of seeing something solid. Out of sight, out of mind is peculiarly applicable to such conditions. The objections to sending an army to help an ally are really twofold:

1. It is difficult not to subordinate our strategy – the employment of our forces – to that of our ally.
   We will always have a different kind of army to Continental nations & they will wish to employ it as their own.
2. It is difficult to limit the amount to which you may be asked to augment your Army.

Both these difficulties can be got over by straight talking in all arrangements that are made. If we understand that the frantic yells for help from our ally, if things go hard, must be dealt with exactly as one would deal with those of a hard-pressed subordinate, then one can limit one's commitments.

It will be instructive to consider these remarks again when we look at the events of 1939 and 1940, when my father was obliged to practise what his younger self had preached.

As a senior member of the military establishment, my father naturally had a place at the coronation of King George VI on 12 May, which he recorded had gone off most successfully. He himself rode on horseback in the procession, which was marred only by a single light rain shower at the very end and was enlivened when 'the British Legion round the Gunner Memorial at Hyde Park Corner started singing "Old Soldiers never die, they simply fade away" when we Generals passed by'. However, while the day was very enjoyable for both my father and mother, the former noted that he could expect to 'be made an ADC General [to the king] in October and will have to attend more of the Courts, I suppose, which will not suit me at all'.[22]

On the next day, my parents attended a reception at the German Embassy, hosted by the ambassador, Joachim von Ribbentrop, later Hitler's foreign minister:

> I think that all the younger Germans were delighted that so many Britishers had come to their show in such numbers. In their heart of hearts they were frightened the show would be a frost. Ribbentrop is a champagne maker, they tell me, and very rich. He is said to be an arrogant Nazi, but I did not think that he showed any sign of that and we had none of that stupid Nazi salute. His wife looked somewhat nondescript. I had a long talk with Marshal von Blomberg, a biggish greying man of perhaps my own age. Covered with Iron Crosses as usual. His main theme was that the Germans & the British should understand each other better, that they no ideas about 'spoiling' the Franco-German Alliance. […] I told Blomberg that one of the main obstacles to friendship with Germany, for us, was the fact that the Germans insisted upon parading their Nazi faith abroad. Keep it in Germany. I understood that they had tried our democratic ideas in Germany, but that they had failed. That was their business and not ours. Then I got on to Italy and told him frankly that we looked upon Mussolini as we would a gnat biting us. It could be possible for Italy to incommode us, but in the end we would just crush the gnat. The withdrawal of the correspondents from England was merely infantile. The people of England knew nothing of Italy beyond the fact that Soho was full of Italian waiters. Our Empire was a peculiar one, but it could not be upset by a thing like Italy. When I finished, Blomberg bowed & said he quite understood our feelings.[23]

Werner von Blomberg was at that time the German minister for war and C-in-C of the armed forces, although his opposition to Hitler's plans for an early move towards war would see him ousted within the year. The same gathering introduced my father to a number of British Fascists and pro-Nazis, most notably George Pitt-Rivers, who informed him that the generals of his generation needed to enter politics or risk being replaced – unsurprisingly, my father dismissed him as 'a crank of the worst kind'.

On 15 May, he and the CIGS, together with the MGO, Lieutenant General Sir Hugh Elles, lunched with the French military attaché at his offices in Hyde Park Terrace, where they met General Gamelin, but none of them could have foreseen the shake-up that was about to upset the entire high command less than a fortnight later when it was announced that Duff Cooper, who was being shifted to the Admiralty, was to be replaced as secretary of state for war by Leslie Hore-Belisha. This appointment would turn out to have radical consequences for the careers of a number of senior officers, my father included, but the initial weeks of Hore-Belisha's tenure of office were relatively quiet and gave little indication of the storm that was about to break over the army.

Thus, the summer passed quietly enough, with my father's main military preoccupation being the development of a simplified form of foot drill to replace the parade ground 'form-fours'. On 3 July, he attended his nephew's wedding at Lexden in Colchester, and on 19 August he received an invitation to attend the German combined manoeuvres as the personal guest of von Blomberg. This was a useful opportunity to assess the rise of German military power, but raised an awkward question of protocol:

> I have written in at once to find out if Deverell is to go. I couldn't go as [the] personal guest of von Blomberg if Deverell is to be there too. It doesn't really matter very much, though I could probably give a better account of what there was to be seen than anybody else.[24]

At the same time, he heard from the War Office that the 'bear-leaders' for the British delegation to the German combined manoeuvres would be Lieutenant General Koch, General von Reichenau and General Freiherr von Fritsch, and that they would assemble at Warnemünde on 23 September with the week-long programme ending in Berlin on 29 September. Field Marshal Sir Cyril Deverell, in his role as CIGS, had decided to take advantage of flying out with the RAF representative, but my father felt that the safest route for him to take was by boat train and he arrived just in time for dinner on the night before the start:

> During the evening I got Richtman & Reichenau and Koch & got them drinking whisky. They were silly to think that they, who had never tasted it, could compete with an old Scotsman like me. I got them more than a little bit full and it was a question of 'in vino veritas'. In the end, Reichenau wanted to drink to 'Brotherhood with England, but only for two years'. Most amusing and

I don't think that any of the three villains saw any humour in their toast, which I drank enthusiastically. I wonder if there is anything prophetic in 1940 or 1941.[25]

The exercises with the German Navy organised by Admiral Raeder took place at Sassnitz, viewed by the dignitaries aboard the Admiralty Yacht *Grille*, and were followed by a massive 800-tank and 400-plane exercise attended by both Hitler and Mussolini who rolled by in an open six-wheeler car. During the exercise, the British delegation were ushered over to the official tent and introduced to the Führer:

> He came walking down to us in his long coat & I was at once struck by his vacuous looking grin – one can hardly call it a smile – and his watery weak-looking eyes. Mussolini had gone off to another corner. Reichenau told Hitler that I could speak German & I chatted for a minute with him in German. He complimented me & told me I spoke it like a German.
>
> The man struck me not at all. His voice was soft & his German of the south. He made no more impression on me than would have a somewhat wild professor whom I rather suspected of having a drop too much for the occasion.
>
> I must say that I was disappointed. The man must have the stuff in him, but he didn't make any impression on me.[26]

More impressive were the military vehicles of the rapidly expanding *Wehrmacht*, on which my father commented favourably due to their robust construction. It was clear, he wrote, that 'whatever else happens in Germany, the Army never goes short', and he was left in some doubt as to the viability of a French, or worse still, Franco-British attack on Germany if Hitler moved against France's Eastern European allies.

The next day was spent visiting a work camp which was designed to give boys their first insight into life outside the family and to prepare them for military service, as well as to instil a sense of devotion and enthusiasm into the young men for their immediate masters and *Arbeitsdienst*. At the end of the presentation the lecturer let off praise for the Führer from whom all good things came. The teaching was designed to give the German people a new outlook on service to the State and not for personal gain, but my father remained unconvinced:

> Can it last? Can the tempo be kept up? Is it really good in the end to be so very material, even if it is for the State & not for oneself? It is certainly designed to make the German boy think he is the salt of the earth & to look down upon the slip-shod methods of others.
>
> It would definitely be repulsive to me to live under such a system. It wouldn't suit our people. We want change of our 'out of work' system, but not in this way. It cannot be right.[27]

The last day of the manoeuvres was spent in Berlin watching a tattoo and the march past of all the services along the Charlottenburgweg with bands playing.

When he returned to London on 1 October he was bombarded by everybody with questions about his impressions and decided to write them out while they were fresh in his mind:

> Germany's idea of defence has always been the assumption of an offensive in order to prevent your opponent from advancing against you. I don't think their ideas have changed. They will probably take the offensive again with the Air Force she has collected. Her mobile forces will find greater and greater systems of fortification growing up against them. Short sharp wars cannot be counted upon.[28]

By 10 October he had completed his official report:

> I have finished writing my impressions of the German Combined Manoeuvres and it is difficult to concentrate upon the essentials amongst so much propaganda. I should sum up roughly as follows:–
> 1. Militarily speaking. Germany will not be ready for any big war for some three or four years.
>   (a) The men have not had the machines in their hands for long enough to enable them to handle them with ease.
>   (b) The Staff is not yet complete and a Staff is particularly necessary to the German Army.
>   (c) They have not had time to build up a big enough reserve of trained men.
>   (d) They are a long way from being militarily self-sufficient.
> 2. From a civil point of view the Führer is opposed to war.
> 3. The friendship between Germany and Italy is hardly skin-deep. Each of the Dictators wishes the other to create the opportunity for war. Which is the more astute?
> 4. I hazard a guess that Mussolini will create the opportunity in the Mediterranean and then Hitler will act.[29]

15

In Sight of the War Office

On returning from his trip to Germany, my father found himself again back in the throes of the political struggle over the future of the army. By the end of October 1937, the talk of the town amongst the various members of the War Office Selection Board centred on the secretary of state for war. As already mentioned, that post had been filled since May of that year by Leslie Hore-Belisha, a National Liberal MP who had previously made a great impact as minister of transport.

His appointment was part of the Cabinet reshuffle instituted when Neville Chamberlain succeeded Baldwin as prime minister, and Hore-Belisha was in many ways Chamberlain's man, having had his start in government as junior minister in the Treasury when Chamberlain was chancellor. He was, at 44, one of the youngest appointees to the role. He had served in uniform during the Great War, rising to the rank of major in the Royal Army Service Corps – and he was Jewish, a point which ought not have mattered but was in fact brought up again and again to reinforce his 'otherness'.

Coming into the role with no fixed plan and aware that his military knowledge needed bringing up to date, Hore-Belisha employed the same methodology that had brought him success in his previous post, namely good links with the press and a reliance on expert advisers. Both these methods led him, perhaps inevitably, to a close working relationship with Liddell Hart, to whom he had, in fact, been introduced by his predecessor, Duff Cooper. Liddell Hart would quickly come to be seen as the *éminence grise* of the War Office, to an extent that even men like my father, who initially welcomed the arrival of Hore-Belisha as a timely new broom, rapidly became suspicious about the political direction of the army

Hore-Belisha's initial reforms were largely directed towards changing conditions and terms of service with a view to helping solve the army's manpower problems. With considerable energy and flair, he was able to drive through to completion existing projects designed to solve this, which had been begun under Duff Cooper, along with some fresh initiatives of his own. None of this was particularly controversial, although his modern political tactics and courting of press attention were certainly out of step with the established ways of doing things at the War Office.

Next, Hore-Belisha turned his attention to the Territorial Army. The new focus on home defence meant that serious effort was at last put into properly equipping the Territorial anti-aircraft formations for their role, but this prioritisation meant that plans for a Territorial contribution to a field force available to go overseas had to be shelved, at least for the moment. My father was therefore caught between, on the one hand, pleasure that a measure that he had long advocated was at last being properly implemented and, on the other, concern over the effect that this would have on the army's ability to respond effectively to events outside of the British Isles.

Furthermore, feathers were ruffled by Hore-Belisha's preference for promoting senior Territorial officers to the command of Territorial divisions, such commands having previously only been given to Regular officers. In this, at least, my father was opposed to the secretary of state's views, writing that he was 'quite sure that no Territorial can be entrusted with the serious defence of London', when it was proposed that just such a candidate be made GOC of the division responsible for the capital's air defences.[1]

A similar prejudice against senior Territorial officers can be seen in his Camberley paper on home defence, written over a decade previously; in mitigation, one can only point out that the view that only Regulars could command divisions effectively, misguided though it doubtless was, was common amongst my father's peers and by no means peculiar to him.

Further controversy ensued when Hore-Belisha intervened to question the selection of the first GOC for the soon to be activated Mobile Division. Deverell had considered it most tactful to appoint an officer from a cavalry background, Major General John Blakiston-Houston, rather than give further offence to the cavalry – already mechanised and deprived of their horses – by putting them under a tank officer. Notwithstanding that Blakiston-Houston had already headed the divisional staff in an important tactical exercise without troops – of which more anon – Hore-Belisha wished instead to promote the leading tank advocate Brigadier Percy Hobart and give him the command when the division was properly constituted.

Hobart was not only a military radical but had been involved in a scandalous divorce case to boot: it was felt all round that he was too controversial a choice, and eventually Major General Alan Brooke, a Gunner, would be given the command as a compromise candidate. However, Hore-Belisha still managed to find a post for Hobart and brought him into the War Office as director of military training, a post which brought with it a promotion to major general. Undoubtedly, Hore-Belisha had picked a winner with the brilliant but unconventional Hobart, who would go on to raise and train the 7th and 11th Armoured Divisions and later oversee the strange collection of specialist armoured vehicles that were used to such good effect on D-Day, but by pushing his selection against the wishes of the army's high command he added to a growing wave of resentment of ministerial interference.

These difficulties over officer appointments served to convince Hore-Belisha that change was needed to the very top of the army's hierarchy. From the outset, he had made it clear that he had no intention of rubber stamping the officer appointments made by the Selection Board of senior generals. To facilitate the bringing on of younger men, he had already brought in Lord Gort to be his military secretary – which ensured Gort an accelerated promotion to lieutenant general – and, as may be seen with regards to the divisional command choices outlined above, thereafter took a close involvement in subsequent appointments. At the same time, he sought to revitalise the Army Council and have it meet on a regular basis in the manner of the French *Conseil Supérieur de la Guerre*.

The resistance of many generals to these points convinced Hore-Belisha of the view that too many of the army's senior officers were too hidebound by tradition and thought only in terms of fighting the previous war over again. My father, ingrained with the customs of the service but a long-term advocate of looking beyond the experience of 1914–18, was caught uncomfortably in the middle of much of this, and related a worrying conversation with Deverell at a meeting of the Selection Board shortly after the conclusion of the debate concerning the appointment of the first GOC Mobile Division. Matters on the day in question were not aided by the fact that Liddell Hart had just had a piece published in *The Times*, in which Deverell felt that he had been misrepresented:

> Poor devil, he looked tired and ill. He impressed upon us several times that he hoped we understood how difficult his situation was. Deverell ended by saying that he was prepared to give up his job at any moment if there was anybody who could make a greater success than he did. He would struggle on as best he could. That Liddell Hart controlled Belisha and actually saw him more times than he, the CIGS did. That he was engaged every day in giving interviews to all & sundry over every sort of question. The position seemed to me to be very bad and that we couldn't go on this way very much longer. I looked round at all the astonished faces of the senior officers of the Army. I think none of us could believe that we were really in for a row.[2]

My father had no great time for Blakiston-Houston, and none whatsoever for Hobart, whose personal life alone he felt rendered him ineligible for such a high-profile post, but the issue here was one of the relative powers of the secretary of state on the one hand versus the CIGS on the other. In that context, such political interference was unacceptable.

Deverell had already made little secret of the fact that he wished to step down, and my father suspected that his preference was to serve out his last years in uniform as C-in-C Gibraltar, a post that was traditionally seen as a comfortable stepping stone towards a dignified retirement.

Insofar as Hore-Belisha was concerned, my father's assessment of him up until this point, although in many ways personally critical, still saw him as a potential force for good in the army. Barely a fortnight prior to the stormy meeting of the Selection Board just described, he had written:

> All this new rebuilding of the Army that is going on is much too important for personal question to enter into the matter. Belisha may be specially sent to us to get us ready. They all say he is out for himself. If this is so, then he must make a success of the War Office or finish his career. How will he do this? How ought he do this? During this next year he should have a great chance of getting his own way. He might put Deverell into Gibraltar if he liked, Knox into the Chelsea Hospital. Elles is going, and May could be moved out.[3]

The last three officers named were then respectively adjutant general, Master General of the Ordnance, and quartermaster general: what my father was therefore hinting at was that Hore-Belisha might well replace all the senior members of the Army Council. As such, it was a remarkably prophetic remark.

It would be another month, however, before matters finally came to a head. By the end of November my father was speculating that it would only be a matter of time before Deverell, who had already clashed with Hobart in the few weeks since the latter had been appointed director of military training and thereby further strained his relationship with Hore-Belisha, would be driven to resign. Signs that change was in the wind were also indicated by the fact that both my father and Lieutenant General Sir John Dill, GOC-in-C Aldershot Command, had been called in to see the secretary of state. Deverell, speaking to my father on 1 December, felt that this indicated the two men were being sounded out as possible replacements for him as CIGS, but my father felt that this could not be the case and told Deverell so. Nevertheless, by that evening he had had second thoughts and was left musing over the situation and where it might lead:

> What about myself? Am I to be taken into the War Office? I have absolutely no idea. I am sure that Belisha will make a change. Was he looking Dill and I over? How will he manage to get rid of Deverell? I have a sort of idea that he wants to have a more junior Army Council. My feelings are mixed. I feel that I could do some good for the Army. It would be very hard work, but surely I should not to shirk that? I think that Belisha would be quite a different being if one had his trust. It is all very upsetting.[4]

In all events, he would not be left to speculate for long, as 2 December, which he rightly characterised as a 'fateful day' for himself and the army, saw the apparent dénouement of the power struggle that had been going on at the War Office and turned the future of the army into turmoil. Upon arriving at his office, my father was met with a message bidding him to see Hore-Belisha at 16.00 that afternoon. Suspecting that something big was happening, and no doubt impatient to resolve the issues that had troubled his thoughts the previous evening, he telephoned the CIGS in the hope of gaining more information:

> Deverell answered at once & said, 'I can tell you what it is for, if you like. I am going and Gort is to succeed me.' Rather a miserable voice, I thought, & then he added 'and he is going to tell you that you are not going to get it.' The whole thing was not a surprise. I knew Deverell was going. The indications were all that he was. I was not even much surprised by Gort being put in. A good choice, I think. A man of great prestige in the Army, who will enthuse life into the machine. A man of social position & strength of character. I think the Army will welcome the new CIGS with enthusiasm.[5]

This advance warning at least gave my father some time to take stock of the situation and to consider its implications for his own career. The crucial point that struck him was that the appointment of so junior an officer as CIGS meant that there would necessarily have to be a separation between the policy of the army on the one hand, clearly a matter for Gort as CIGS, and its training and preparation for active service which must necessarily fall to the heads of the various commands. As he noted while awaiting his meeting with Hore-Belisha, 'How could Gort, even if made a full General on the spot, run the training with so many men immeasurably senior to himself?'

One of those senior men was, of course, my father, and bearing in mind his own doubts as to his suitability for the role of CIGS he was left to speculate that he might instead be named as the commander designate of any future expeditionary force. Such a role was far more to his taste and, thanks to the warning that he obtained through his conversation with Deverell, he was able to go to his meeting with the secretary of state with some sort of plan in mind:

> I think I shall tell him straight away that he has done the right thing. Then I shall ask him as to my personal position. I shall tell him that I cannot earn a full pension however long I stay on. If he has no idea of making me the head of the training, then are there any other jobs which I might be recommended for? Governor of Gibraltar? High Commissioner in Palestine? A Governorship?[6]

C-in-C India was another possibility, but that appointment was three years away from falling vacant, and the possibility of being passed over for a top job but being obliged to remain on in the service was not a happy prospect. Reading the whole entry for this tumultuous day, one gets a very real sense of my father's impatience to know what his fate was to be. After all, and as he noted himself, an early end to his career, quite apart from being personally shaming, would have necessitated considerable personal financial retrenchment. Knowing how much rested on this meeting, he therefore resolved to 'beware of giving too much away to this clever man Belisha. I must ask my questions & then reserve my judgement until I know what my prospects are.'

Unsurprisingly, impatience carried my father early to the War Office. Seeking the ex-CIGS, he was told that he had gone for good. Gort, however, was present and although there was some initial awkwardness this was largely dissipated by my father's congratulations on his appointment and the two men spoke for a few minutes before it was time for my father to see the secretary of state:

> It was apparently a bombshell to [Gort] when he was asked to be CIGS. I told him that I was not so surprised & that I was very glad and wished him well. The method of telling Deverell was not the kindest, just a note to say that he had been superseded at once. The first news that came in was that [Major General Ronald] Adam had arrived from the Staff College as DCIGS [Deputy Chief of Imperial General Staff]. Gort didn't know then that he was to be CIGS. Deverell didn't know he had been superseded. I told Gort that I didn't want to stay in the Eastern Cmd if I had no future and that he ought to get in the Generals he wanted.
>
> Then, in to see Belisha. He started by asking me if I had heard of the changes and I said that I had seen Gort. I then told him that I thought he had chosen the right man & that the Army would be delighted. That I had never really pictured myself as CIGS and I was in no way disappointed. He then most surprisingly said, 'God bless you. I cannot tell you how I appreciate that.' He said that he had seen Dill, who had taken things very well, but 'not so well as you have done,' because he said he was disappointed he couldn't be CIGS. I told him that I had never thought I would make a good CIGS. Then he told me that he considered the halo which surrounded people at the War Office to be quite uncalled for. That he was reducing the authority of the War Office & increasing that of the Generals outside. That he considered myself, Dill and Wavell as his Generals ready to go wherever they were required for operations. He was going to make a *Conseil Supérieur* and take the Generals into his confidence. I then let him have a few ideas upon what I thought of his plans.[7]

In a sense, then, things had panned out in a way that left my father in a position that was more to his taste and better suited to his abilities than if he had been selected for the post of CIGS that had gone to Gort. Nevertheless, he had evidently been a serious contender for CIGS and it is therefore instructive to look briefly at the process by which the selection of Deverell's replacement was made, for it provides a useful review of my father's professional standing at this time.

From the perspective of Hore-Belisha, still at this point closely advised by Liddell Hart, the other possible candidates for CIGS, after Gort, seem to have been Wavell, Dill and my father. Indeed, this seems a likely order of preference, for while recognising my father as the only officer worth keeping from the older generation of full generals, it seems that Hore-Belisha was keen to appoint a younger man of lieutenant general's rank. Certainly, the inference that my father was the fourth man on the list may be drawn from the fact that he was not mentioned with the other three as a possible candidate when Hore-Belisha outlined his options to the prime minister. Of the possibilities eventually discounted, Wavell was perhaps too junior and 'though he has more brain than Gort, is, I fancy, not without calculation as to the effect of showing courage on his personal opinion'; Dill was perceived as being 'too conventional' and as potentially lacking in energy due to poor health after a recent riding accident. Gort, for his part, was seen as having attributes that the others lacked, in particular his social standing, and since it was Hore-Belisha's intention from the outset to delegate a portion of the duties previously carried out by the CIGS to the new DCIGS, Ronald Adam, it was also to Gort's advantage that he was expected to work well with that officer who was seen as a 'thinker' to complement Gort, the man of action.[8]

So much, then, for the merits and demerits of the other contenders for CIGS. As for my father, three things have been put forward to set against what was otherwise an excellent record. One was, as noted, the secretary of state's preference for a more junior candidate. The second was that my father was seen by those around him in much the way that he had come to see himself; a man more suited to an active role than to a post at the War Office. Indeed, Liddell Hart – who, for what it is worth, thought Wavell the best option for CIGS, something which in itself calls into question the popular assertion that he was the puppet master behind the secretary of state – saw my father as ideally suited to become the next C-in-C India, and told Hore-Belisha as much.

For these two points, there is evidence aplenty, but the third suggestion that has been presented is something of a red herring, although it has been made much of by historians. This concerns the fact that my father had made a poor showing during the major tactical exercise without troops held three months previously – the same exercise mentioned above with reference to the vexed issue of appointing the first GOC Mobile Division – and had been publicly criticised for this by Deverell. Such criticism, it has been argued, was perceived to call into question my father's professional standing amongst those who would have had to serve under him had he been appointed CIGS, and has been presented as a major reason why he was not selected.[9]

At first sight, this all sounds rather damning. It must be stressed, however, that a strong body of opinion at the time – Liddell Hart, for one – felt that the criticism of my father's performance was unfair. Since the exercise also cast my father as the commander of a force clearly modelled on the sort of BEF that Britain might expect to send to the Continent in the near future, a closer look at this ill-fated exercise also gives a fascinating insight into how he might have performed had he received such a command in reality.

The format of the operation was to simulate a multiday action between two large formations which, for the purposes of the exercise, were represented only by their staffs and signals organisations. Orders would be issued down the chain of command as if to real troops, but their results would be decided by umpires, and the results fed back up the chain as if from a real battlefield. The area chosen was a large swathe of south central England centred on Bedford, and the objective of the 'Anglian' force commanded by my father – a thinly disguised BEF of two two-division army corps and the new Mobile Division – was to mount an attack through a 40-mile-wide corridor representing the Aachen Gap between Belgium and the Ruhr. The defending forces had approximately half the number of troops available, comprising two infantry divisions reinforced by the addition of a tank brigade and some light forces.

The whole exercise, the largest to be attempted during the interwar years, was the brainchild of Major General Alan Brooke, who was then director of military training. Unfortunately for my father, Brooke had envisaged the Mobile Division, then still under its original commander designate, Blakiston-Houston, as filling a very different role to that in which my father elected to employ it, and this set the scene for the post-exercise criticism.

In brief, Brooke saw the Mobile Division, which was composed of the 1st and 2nd Light Armoured Brigades of mechanised cavalry regiments in light tanks and armoured cars and the 1st Army Tank Brigade with heavy infantry support tanks, as best employed in a fighting reconnaissance role much akin to the use of the old horsed cavalry divisions. Such employment, however, left no role for the slow heavy tanks, which needs must have been detached from the division and left behind. My father, on the other hand, preferred to keep the whole division concentrated, ready to mount a decisive blow once the opposing force had been worn down in a conventional battle. Ironically, this was not through any great faith in the ability of the division to perform at its best in this configuration, but because he felt it unwise from a command-and-control perspective to break up the divisional organisation. Even before the exercise got underway, my father bemoaned the fact that, unlike a real wartime commander, he had had no role in the organisation and training of the troops that came under his command and was therefore obliged to work with the organisational structure that he was handed.

As well as concerns over the realism of the concepts behind the exercise, my father also took issue with the way that it was umpired, believing that far too little information was being fed back up from the imagined battlefield. Three days in, for example, he was still complaining that he had not received any indication of what casualties his own notional troops had sustained. He was also, as is clear from the content of his diary entries, simultaneously preoccupied with his impending visit to the German manoeuvres and continued to devote a good portion of time to preparing for his trip to the Continent – considering the one-off opportunity that it represented to get a handle on a real enemy rather than an imagined one, this focus is hard to fault.

The opening days of the exercise went well for my father's 'Anglian' forces, which pushed the enemy steadily back all along the front, although to my father this was another indication of the unreality of the scenario, and he wrote, 'I don't think that in real life people can afford to abandon their territory in this way. Neither politically nor militarily is it good business.'[10] My father's surmise was that the enemy forces were attempting to trade space for time to put together a coherent defensive line. My father's response was to keep pushing forward with his infantry – I Corps in the south and II Corps in the north – while retaining the Mobile Division in reserve until the situation had clarified. Once the enemy forces had been properly located, the armoured forces could then be committed to the battle but, as of the second day of fighting, he noted that he was 'adhering to my policy of not using the Mobile Division until I know something'.[11]

Since cloud cover and drizzle prevented air reconnaissance and the light armour was being held in reserve along with the rest of the Mobile Division, a complete understanding of the enemy positions and intentions remained lacking. Nevertheless, based on the progress of the infantry, and notwithstanding the forced narrowness of the front due to the artificial borders to the exercise area, he had at this point good hopes of turning the enemy's southern flank. To this end, the Mobile Division was shifted to support I Corps in that sector with a view to a single envelopment of that flank. If II Corps also made good progress, a full-fledged double envelopment might also prove possible, so one of two II Corps brigades in the centre of the 'Anglian' line were shifted northwards, leaving only a single brigade to link the two wings of my father's forces.

The third day of the exercise saw a continued enemy retreat, with the enemy forces retreating in the face of II Corps being funnelled back through Bedford. The updated knowledge of enemy positions led to a further change of plans by my father:

> I came to the conclusion that our 1st Corps had no chance of making any turning movement & that the enemy would effect his escape to his second line. But, there appeared to me a chance of getting the Mobile Division in between my two Corps & right across the rear of the people withdrawing through Bedford. I am hoping that I may be able to get a good bit of débris moving back.
>
> I have never been able to get much information from my extreme right.

On the whole, I think my original plan was as good as I could have made it. There was so little chance of getting a flank with two enemy divisions together with light mobile forces operating in a funnel of barely 50 miles across, when a good deal of the country is intersected by canals and unsuitable for the operation of mobile forces.

The enemy had the easier task, but he seems to have carried it out very efficiently. I cannot hold up my Mobile Division any longer, for if I do I shall find the enemy quietly sitting in his new position. I think I have found a very good flank on my left for the Mobile Division to picket the enemy Heavy Armoured people who are being collected behind his new position.

It is so very easy to imagine that one has enveloped something, whereas one is merely striking into thin air.[12]

In the event, the situation continued to develop in a positive manner, with the enemy committing substantial reserves to check the Mobile Division, thus enabling the 'Anglian' I Corps to carry out an envelopment of the enemy southern flank after all and opening up opportunities for II Corps to attack in the north. Thus things stood at midnight on 20 September, at which point the exercise was brought to an end.

The conference to discuss the findings of the exercise was held the following morning at 11.00: unfortunately, because of a mix-up by his ADC, my father had to rush to be there on time and arrived feeling decidedly out of sorts and feeling unprepared for the discussion, which was kicked off by a report presented by Deverell but prepared by Brooke:

[W]e were thoroughly slated. The main reason being that I had not broken up the Mobile Division. But, I told the CIGS later that to break up an organisation before war begins is not to try things out. I think we have done good, for now the Mobile Division is to be broken up and the Tank Bde taken away from it. This I have always thought was the proper thing to do. My effort, criticised as it was, was the final touch in upsetting the organisation. Now we shall go back to a mechanised Cavalry and use it for the same service of reconnaissance and protection. At the end of the Conference, Deverell read out the conclusions arrived at during the trailing of the Mobile Div. I told Deverell that we ought to have had this before, and he agreed. I had never seen the Division and had never been told anything of its use. We must be given a doctrine.

I arrived back at the hotel at 4 p.m. thoroughly angry & disgruntled. My own arrangements had fallen down and I hadn't had much success. Deverell was not insulting in any of his criticism, which was mostly justified, though I had not been allowed to give any explanation. I am always preaching that I must take criticism & I hope that I did.[13]

With that summing-up, my father drew a line under things and set off for his trip to Germany. It is unlikely that the brief exercise preyed on his mind to any great degree afterwards, and it certainly did no harm to his working relationship with Deverell. Brooke, as we have seen, replaced Blakiston-Houston and became the first proper GOC Mobile Division. In due course, the composition of the division itself was altered to give it a more balanced and homogenous force in line with the lessons of the exercise: thus reorganised, it went to France in 1940 as 1st Armoured Division.

Ironically, the affair seems to have been seized upon by historians primarily because the defence of my father made by Liddell Hart in his memoirs – which blamed the concept of the exercise for its unsatisfactory ending, rather than any fault of my father's – introduced the idea that Deverell's criticism put my father out of the running for CIGS. In fact, as we have seen, the real reasons for his not being chosen in 1937 stem from Hore-Belisha's preference for a more junior candidate, and from the perception of my father primarily as a fighting general rather than a staff officer. Indeed, the fact that the latter perception remained the case even after the September exercise would tend to support the view that even if his performance in the exercise was faulted, his reputation did not suffer as a result.

As a window on his potential as a field commander at the highest level, the exercise also offers some useful insights. He certainly did not use his armoured forces in the way that Brooke would have liked or in which the German panzer generals did during the blitzkrieg years of the Second World War. On the other hand, his initial withholding of the Mobile Division from the battle and subsequent integration of attacks by armoured and infantry formations has some of the hallmarks, albeit in a very primitive form, of the more methodical operations carried out by British forces under Montgomery and other commanders in the later years of the war, in which 'crumbling' attacks by infantry were used to create opportunities that could be exploited by armour. One cannot read too much into a single theoretical exercise, particularly one in which the troop formations involved were to some extent experimental in their composition, but there is certainly nothing in my father's conduct of the 'Anglian' forces on this occasion that would imply unsuitability to command an equivalent force of British troops in real combat.

So much, in any case, for the logic behind the decision of who should replace Deverell. Whatever arguments one can present for and against my father as a possible contender for CIGS, the fact of the matter was that Gort was Hore-Belisha's chosen man and that was that. Insofar as this kept my father in line for an active command, this was no bad thing so far as his assessment of his future prospects was concerned. When he finally had the opportunity to speak to Deverell, on the evening after the news of Hore-Belisha's coup had broken, the departing CIGS confirmed the wisdom of his willingness to accept the new regime. My father recorded that he found Deverell 'very hurt and despondent':

His only remark was, 'Well, Tiny. I couldn't do any more'. He then thanked me for being such a tower of strength. He showed me his answer to Hore-Belisha's letter, calling upon him to resign. Most dignified and calm. He was very bitter at the way he had been treated, but he entreated me to stay on and stick it out.[14]

There is nothing here, one must also note, to suggest that there was any bad blood on either side in the aftermath of the September exercise. On the other hand, my father was exasperated in the extreme by Liddell Hart – 'more than ever pleased with himself' after Hore-Belisha's coup – who insisted on buttonholing him, after the two men had been guests at a lunch hosted by the German military attaché, for a discussion of military politics into which my father refused to be drawn. Failing to take the hint, Liddell Hart asserted that 'Deverell had ruined my chances of being made CIGS by his criticism – quite unthought out – of my efforts in the exercise run by the War Office', and then 'said that I must have patience – as if I hadn't had patience for 20 years. That I couldn't be spared. That I might have to go to India much earlier than I might expect.'[15] It was a most unsettling interview, from which my father was keen to escape.

Deverell's parting injunction to stay on, which my father in any case considered necessary for the good of the army now that he was its senior serving general, turned out to be wise advice. My father had already submitted his impressions of the German combined manoeuvres to Deverell, and had been asked in turn to set down and submit his ideas on ensuring that the British Army was better prepared for war and how this should be effected.

This report my father now delivered to Gort as the new CIGS, without realising that in making his recommendations there was nothing else that could have sealed his own fate so well. It will be recalled that one of the problems that my father had faced during the September exercise was that he had been pitched into command of the 'Anglian' forces without having had any prior involvement in their training and organisation for war. It may well be inferred, therefore, that it was as much from that experience as from his time in Germany that his report to Gort was formulated. He began by outlining the many and extensive duties of the CIGS who, he felt, was under the current system obliged to function as both the perfect staff officer and the perfect commander of the army as a whole, there being no other authority senior to heads of the various commands. He went on to voice his concerns over what this was leading to, and to suggest a solution:

> I feel very strongly that under the present system there has been and is a lack of clear policy and of single minded direction in training with the consequences that the army is drifting uncertainly – and cannot be expected to answer uniformly to the helm. Further this lack of uniformity in training has militated against prompt decisions as to the organisations required, or equipment needed. At present each

Commander-in-Chief is training and experimenting largely on his own ideas, and I consider that unless they are given an official lead not even consultive [sic] co-operation between them will produce the necessary homogeneity.

I therefore consider that a separate officer is required to be responsible for the preparation of the Army for war. I suggest that he might be called the Inspector General, and he should normally be the Commander-in-Chief designate of the Field Force. He would thus be best placed to understand its handling and the relative capabilities of its various parts and Commanders. I would recommend that this officer should not be a member of the Army Council or the War Office Staff to ensure his not being immersed in administrative detail. His duty would be to forge the instrument decided upon by the Army Council, and to advise the latter on changes which on his experience he deems necessary. He should of course have access to, and be liable to be called upon for advice by members of, the Council.[16]

The paper went on to define how the duties of CIGS and inspector general would be divided: for the most part, this was on a clear line of policy to the former and practice to the latter. However, he did suggest 'that the IG might be Chairman of the Selection Board and Staff Selection Board as he is in daily personal touch with officers of all ranks'. Nowhere did he directly suggest himself for the role, although his seniority clearly made him the obvious candidate, but he did somewhat let the cat out of the bag by remarking that he did 'not consider it advisable for the Inspector general also to be charged with the Command and Administration of a Command, certainly not one the size and complexity of Eastern Command'. Not for the first time, he had nevertheless just written the job description for a post that he himself would one day hold – but, as it would transpire, not just yet.

Getting away from London and down to Norfolk, where he was obliged to dodge dinner invitations from people who wished to hear at first hand about the changes at the War Office, gave him chance to think things over away from the centre of events:

Things are so serious that one must do nothing likely to hurt the Service. I mustn't make too much of this from a personal point of view because there are always people ready to come on. I am the last of the people who commanded in war and the others came nowhere. I have been running things for 20 years, whereas the next to me have been very few years at it. Then there is my own personal desires. They will always be to be in command. I am delighted not to have been faced with the problem of being saddled with CIGS. It would have been personally distasteful & I am more than doubtful whether I could have been a successful one. I am not made for routine. There is this to be said, that the upheaval of the War Office is not a routine job. How long would the upheaval have taken[?] A goodly term of years, I think.

We now have to think of India. Can they say that Cassels is inefficient[?] Would the Viceroy say that he had no confidence? I very much doubt it. There is no doubt that I could bring a new point of view to bear on matters military in India, but if I have to wait until I am 60 it will be too long. I shall perhaps have lost the wish to put things right. I shall never acquire the habit of sitting in an office and running things from there. But, one may become cynical, especially if things in this country continue to go slowly and badly. No one on earth can give one an understanding that one will get this or that appointment. These appointments are [word illegible] Cabinet prerogatives & Governments & Cabinets change easily enough.[17]

Some additional perspective on matters came on 6 December after a chance meeting with Winston Churchill in which, again, the discussion took a fatefully prescient turn. Churchill, then still in the political wilderness, was staying with the Earl of Cholmondeley at Houghton Hall, and this was one dinner invitation that was too good an opportunity to pass up:

Winston was most cordial & kept reiterating that he must see that I was not done down. He was horrified that Hore-Belisha had not seen me before he made his decision to change to Gort. He talked about the *Conseil Supérieur* and more than once said that he would see Belisha this next week & impress upon him that I was not to be thrown over. He told me that I should not go abroad and that I should resist being sent, because I was the man that would be called upon to lead the Army, were we unfortunate enough to have to go to war.[18]

Churchill went on to remind him that Sir John French had been apparently broken and passed over in the lead-up to the First World War, but had gone on to lead the BEF; both men agreed that it was as well to trust to the fates and see what was 'written' and that no good could come of seeking to advance one's career by intrigue. The conversation then turned to world affairs, and in particular to the situation in the Mediterranean where things remained extremely volatile as a result of Mussolini's invasion of Abyssinia. Churchill felt that if it came to war then the Royal Navy would be able to easily turn the balance in Britain's favour, and the army would be required, if at all, for mopping-up operations only. This view, my father felt, was overly optimistic, particularly if rising tensions with Japan drew naval forces out to the Far East. Matters then returned to more immediate concerns:

He reassured me about Liddell Hart. That Belisha had these ideas himself and was not led by anybody. I thought that he must have consulted Liddell Hart, but that he would not allow Liddell Hart to dictate to him for long. I told Winston to tell Belisha two things. He must allow the new Army Council to run their affairs. He cannot have a second upset. Not to do the Dictator over Gort. Also to dispel the idea from the Army that Liddell Hart had any influence over him.

Winston was most kind as regards myself. He was going to see that I was not to suffer from this change. Very nice of him. But, I really do not see how it is going to be translated into fact, or what line the help is to take. I cannot see much open at the moment.[19]

The final consequence of the lengthy discussion with Churchill was that the latter ended by encouraging my father to take his own views direct to Hore-Belisha as secretary of state, rather than dealing purely with the CIGS. This my father resolved to do, in a process that also helped him further codify his thinking.

His initial thinking, as confided to his diary, was broken down under the headings of:

(1) An Inspector General for Training in Peacetime
(2) A GOC Home Forces on the outbreak of war
(3) A C-in-C Expeditionary Force

Insofar as the nature of a future war was concerned, his views had not materially changed from those expressed in his 1923 paper in that the requirements of home defence would preclude the despatch of a major expeditionary force overseas in the early stages of a major European conflict. Small forces would likely need to be sent to Egypt and/or Palestine, but the bulk of the army would remain at home to keep order during the expected devastation of enemy bombing. For this reason, he advocated that upon the outbreak of hostilities the post of inspector general be merged with that of GOC Home Forces. 'He could then make it his business to train the troops in peace, get them ready in war, organise this country, and finally throw off an expeditionary force as required.'[20] In tending away from a commitment to sending a BEF straight to the Continent, my father's views were in fact now in line with many others at this time, including both Hore-Belisha and the minister for co-ordination of defence, Sir Thomas Inskip. Indeed, the latter presented a very similar focus of priorities to Parliament later that month, although this stemmed from the inability to finance such a force alongside the urgent rearmament of the Royal Navy and RAF.

The whole process of thinking through the army's roles and priorities certainly made my father think more seriously about his own future and whether he should take the initiative to seek out a particular job, rather than await events. The eventual structure of his paper for Hore-Belisha, which when completed was some seven foolscap pages long, dealt mainly with the duties that he envisaged for the post of inspector general, which was clearly sketched out with himself in mind. He made a clear case for the necessity of the post, but feared that it would be resisted as being 'too like the ap[pointmen]t of a C-in-C in peace';[21] that is to say, a reversion to the days prior to the institution of the post of CIGS.

Weighing up his options, he saw the case that he was making as the best opportunity for the continuation of his own career and the security of his finances:

> I have got my Paper ready, calling upon Belisha to make an Inspector General. It is really necessary. Will he appoint such a man & if he does will he appoint me? The odds are very much in my favour if he makes the appointment. It would give me a chance in the next 3 years of becoming a Field Marshal. It might even mean that I would get the command in India.
>
> I must see the effect of my paper in the next 3 months. If the appointment is not made it is more than ever imperative that I should do something to shape my fate.[22]

The remaining options seemed less promising to him. He might trust to his luck and to Churchill, but Churchill was out of office and unless war were to come in the next few years he considered that he would be too old for an active command. The Chichele Professorship of Military History at Oxford was shortly to become vacant and, assuming he could obtain the appointment, this would offer financial security and a chance to think and write at length, but would end his military career and necessitate a complete change in lifestyle. The latter concerns also applied to the option of pursuing contacts in business, which he doubted would more than defer the extra expense that such work would entail.

Lastly, the other appointment due to become vacant in 1938 was the governorship of Gibraltar:

> A safe employment for 5 years and a living wage which would take me on until Bing [the present author] was 19. A finisher as regards military service. A sedentary job where one would have simple enjoyments of sailing & riding. A certain amount of rather repulsive social entertaining, but interesting enough.[23]

In the aftermath of the removal of Deverell, it does seem as if Hore-Belisha and Gort made serious efforts to re-establish a sense of order and normality within the War Office. Certainly, Liddell Hart in his memoirs claimed that at this time he was very much frozen out of things and officers who had once freely consulted with him were close-mouthed now that they had obtained War Office posts in the aftermath of the December coup. On the other hand, a planned meeting between Gort and the heads of the various home commands was cancelled at the last minute, and this did not bode well for the willingness of the new CIGS to solicit or accept advice from his peers.

Although my father was not aware of it, differences also quickly emerged between Gort and Hore-Belisha that drove the latter into a renewed reliance on Liddell Hart's advice – up to and including the provision of notes to back up his speech to present the army estimates to Parliament in March 1938. In the mind of my father, still at this stage ambivalent in his view of his political master, Hore-Belisha had bought himself a useful breathing space by his radical personnel changes:

> I have been thinking of Belisha again. He is far too clever to make any mistake and be found out in a short period. At any rate he could not be worse than somebody like Duff Cooper, who was incredibly idle. If he doesn't produce the men needed for the Regular Army he will have failed, no matter what he says in the newspapers. But, he will be allowed to go on for a long time before anybody talks of failure. Certainly a year or more.[24]

On 23 January, *The Sunday Pictorial* published a front-page headline and long article on the disorganisation and conflict in the British Army and drew attention to the lack of up-to-date weapons, tanks and general equipment. It was said that the army was playing at soldiers, devoting too much time to foot drill on the parade ground while still training with the weapons of the last war. There was considerable sensationalism in this but, nevertheless, there had been a lot of widespread anxiety about the purpose and effectiveness of the army and my father naturally wished he had more influence over the reorganisation. It seemed to him that there was no clear policy and that ideas were being picked up without proper consideration, and just as soon discarded again.

Amidst all of this, my father remained unsatisfied with his position at Eastern Command, which gave him neither the scope nor the influence to exert much effect on things. Then, quite unexpectedly and overnight, the future changed for him through the offer of one of the posts that he had earlier considered as offering a way out of his current situation, namely the governorship of Gibraltar. The initial enquiry, sounding him out, came from a letter from the new military secretary, Lieutenant General Douglas Brownrigg, which he received on 29 January. After some consideration, he elected to accept, writing, 'my position would be quite impossible if I were to refuse it'.[25]

The result of acceptance was a three-year appointment as governor and C-in-C, which was officially announced at the end of March. He would take up the appointment as of August 1938, replacing 'Tim' Harrington, who was to retire, and until then would remain in post as GOC-in-C Eastern Command. Although this seemed to be the end of his active career, in the event, the Gibraltar appointment would serve to place my father conveniently on call as events continued to develop on both the domestic and European stages.

16

On Call at the Rock

As the implications of the apparent end of his military career sank in, and as my mother travelled out to Gibraltar to investigate their new domestic arrangements, my father became more and more convinced that his impending removal from Eastern Command was down to the machinations of the secretary of state. Towards the end of March, he wrote that he was:

> … quite prepared now to fizzle out. The only thing I am sad about is that I have not been given more time to fizzle. All the older men […] will go on longer than I have. They have had the luck not to be caught by this little swine Belisha. I have been caught by him.[1]

In fact, the move to Gibraltar seems to have been the initiative not of Hore-Belisha but of Gort, who argued that it was necessary to have an effective commander on hand to deal with any crisis in the Mediterranean and an officer of my father's calibre was needed at Gibraltar rather than someone who was serving out their final years before retirement. Hore-Belisha's biographer, R.J. Minney, asserts that there were those at the time who saw Gort's selection of my father to go to Gibraltar in less charitable terms, as being a means of removing an obvious rival.[2] Minney saw this in terms of my father having been a strong contender for the post of CIGS, but it would seem more likely that any envy on Gort's part – of which, it should be noted, Gort's own biographer makes no suggestion – was the result of my father's outspoken promotion of the idea of an inspector general whose powers would detract considerably from those of Gort as CIGS.

For his part, Hore-Belisha reinforced the 'official' logic of Gort's recommendation by suggesting to my father that this new appointment would place him in line to be C-in-C Mediterranean if war came. My father, however, did not believe that this promise held any validity and reasoned that although his financial prospects were now relatively secure his active military career was at an end, with only the prospect of 'a Peace Field Marshalship to carry me through to a better pension'.[3] My father's perception was that the government was responding at last to the threat posed by Mussolini's Italy, which remained to many eyes a greater threat than

Hitler's Germany at this juncture, and that this explained Hore-Belisha's suggestion, although he had no time at all for the secretary of state's simultaneous suggestion that my father might also find himself commanding British troops in Spain if it proved necessary to intervene against Franco. Insofar as Britain was in a position to commit any troops outside of the defence of the home islands and the Empire, these troops were earmarked for the Middle East, and this news my father welcomed.

Meanwhile, there was continued dissent and division within the War Office, as it quickly became apparent to Hore-Belisha that the men he had put in as part of the December 1937 reorganisation were not performing to his satisfaction. Matters were confused enough as it was, with Germany's annexation of Austria on 12 March, and the growing threat to Czechoslovakia raising again the likelihood of a war in northern Europe and resurrecting the idea of sending a BEF to the Continent, albeit a reduced one of only two divisions.

It therefore did not help that a clear split with regards to policy and personnel had opened up between the senior generals and their political master, but the fact of the matter remained that there was now a clear division between Gort and the majority of the generals on the one hand, and Hore-Belisha, advised by Liddell Hart and supported by a small clique of the army's more radical senior officers, on the other. The difficulty with this situation was that matters became so polarised that the reaction of the one group to the ideas of the other was immediate dismissal based simply on the origin of the idea, as a result of which my father found himself obliged to oppose, on principal, ideas and appointments to which, in his own more radical days a decade earlier, he would likely have lent his support.

A diary entry from late May, with the Czechoslovakia crisis that would end at Munich already rapidly building up, perfectly sums up the strained relations within the War Office:

> We spent the whole day yesterday on the Selection Board. I spoke very strongly against the way in which the Secretary of State had taken into his hands the complete power of the senior appointments. We were driven to every kind of subterfuge to circumvent him. That is not our business. It is in his charter that he is responsible for appointments, but we are responsible for recommendations as to fitness. If he overrides these, then it is for the Army Council to act.
>
> There is a 'salon' held in Liddell Hart's premises, where the promotion & appointment of officers is openly discussed. The officer culprits are Hobart, now DMT, Broad, MGA at Aldershot, Pile, now [GOC] 1st AA Div. They put their names down for every conceivable kind of appointment, chiefly with promotion. I told Gort that the Army was not prepared to accept Hobart as DMT and that he must be got out of it. He had upset the Army completely. I am glad that the Selection Board backed me up. Now it is for the Army Council to see that we have our authority back again.[4]

Having done his bit in the internal struggle at home, my father now turned his attention to his new appointment. In the week after his fifty-eighth birthday on 6 May 1938, my father was asked to be in Gibraltar as soon as possible after 24 October and was granted £210 towards his costs of travel.

The limited information available about the defences of Gibraltar shocked him when he discovered the poor state of the troops, weapons, ammunition and supplies held in stock there, after which he summarised the current 'scandalous' situation as follows:

1) There are two Bns. at Gibraltar with a total strength of 1020 all ranks. No 3rd Bn. is to be relied upon.
2) The Artillery defence against land attack consist of one 6' gun at Princess Caroline Battery. This is not even manned. Four mobile 6' How[itzer]s. These are manned by the personnel of the AA Bty. The upper 9.2' can bear with one gun at long range.

    War reserves of ammunition are 300 a gun.

    No firing could therefore be justified.
3) The situation with regard to the 9.2' and 6' gun ammunition is terrible. There are no modern shells in Gibraltar and the useful effect of those held is doubtful particularly against modern armed ships.

    It is believed that around 200 modern 6' shells will arrive in 1939.
4) There is no defence armament which will bear on the Eastern side of the Rock, though the Admiralty oil tanks on that side are described in the Defence Scheme as among the most likely objectives.

    The upper 9.2' can bear, but not at ranges under 5000 yards.

    The lower 9.2' is not manned.
5) The AA defences consist of 4 3' AA guns. Anything more modern is not expected until the Autumn of 1939 at the earliest.
6) There are 30 days reserves of meat, flour & biscuit for 3,000 men. A working margin of 18 days flour & biscuit for 2,000 men & nominally 180 days frozen meat.

All this shows into what a state we have allowed out fortunes to sink. One can hardly believe it oneself. None of the MPs would believe it. Nor would Belisha admit the weakness.[5]

Meanwhile, he remained at his post as GOC-in-C, Eastern Command. In the King's Birthday Honours, he was appointed an Ordinary Member of the Military Division of the Knights Grand Cross of the Order of the Bath, and on the strength of this and his forthright expressions about the way forward for the British Army at the time of the mounting threats of war, he was able to keep in touch with all the people in the institutional world, the civil service and Parliament to try and ensure that his own future in the army was safeguarded. At the same time, he had to fend off the unwelcome attention of foreign military attachés who, he feared, would not believe the truth about his appointment even if he told them, and would instead assume that Britain was sending one of her top generals to the Mediterranean for a good reason.

Alongside all this, the political infighting continued unabated and now took another new turn, into which my father was drawn by virtue of its connection to Eastern Command, with the breaking of what became known as the 'Sandys Affair':

> Back in London to find a nice kettle of fish. I had seen in the papers that a young MP, Winston Churchill's son-in-law, Sandys, had been threatened with the Official Secrets Act. He had sent a question to the Secretary of State for War, which he proposed to ask. This question contained all the latest information about the shortage of AA guns, down to the smallest detail. The Act gives power to the Govt. to force any men to give the name of the person from whom he obtained the information. Things seemed pretty hot in the House of Commons.
>
> On my return to my office I found an order from the WO to convene a Court of Enquiry to ascertain the name of the person communicating the information. Apparently, most improperly, Pile, the GOC-AA Division, had been sent for to the WO and had been given certain information. The HQ of the Command had been completely ignored.
>
> Apparently, the MP, who is also a 2nd Lieutenant in the AA Artillery, had asked the Adjutant for the information for private purposes. Absolutely appalled by the bareness of the cupboard, he lost his head and put the exact numbers on the paper he sent Belisha. The fat was then in the fire. Belisha wishes to hide the bareness of the cupboard by having a scandal in the Army, but I don't think he will throw dust into the eyes of MPs, who now have the complete evidence of our lack of defence.
>
> I have ordered a Court of Enquiry to investigate. I have put my best Major General on it, as I don't want to have any legal mistakes made.
>
> The whole fact of the matter is that the Territorials themselves are thoroughly dissatisfied with the progress made in AA Defence and they are complaining bitterly. That we should have 300 out of 1,000 light & 60 old guns for the defence of London – not one single new one – is more than scandalous. The appointment of Senior Officers to command such numbers is ludicrous & merely an expense for nothing. Paris has 900 guns & we have 60. A damning proof of our incompetence.[6]

While Hore-Belisha received criticism and even threats, my father, meanwhile, was feted by the press for the part he was playing in arranging the enquiry, and he recorded this in his diary entry for 30 June:

All the Evening Papers on the last day in June were filled with my pictures and the fact that I had ordered a Court of Enquiry to investigate what is now known as the 'Sandys Case'. The Army Council has done nothing but consider this stupid thing for several days. Belisha is in a ferment & has got very excited. In the House they had an uproar at the news that Sandys had been ordered to appear at the Court in uniform. He had been ordered to appear as a witness. Sandys appealed to the Speaker in a matter of privilege and was upheld in his appeal.

This morning all the officers of the Court assembled & finally, after a lot of chat, the Court was ordered not to sit until the Committee in the House had sat & given its decision.

I was besieged by Reporters & Camera men at my home & they followed me down the road taking my picture walking along with Caesar. At the Horse Guards there was another crowd of camera men & there was general excitement.

Belisha has been most stupid in getting excited and in ordering a Court of Enquiry. Apparently, he thought that we need not call Sandys. But, his ignorance of Military Law is so colossal, & he takes no advice, that he doesn't stop to think. Sandys is an officer in the Territorials and nothing can be said at a Court which may impugn an officer's character, except in his presence, so his name couldn't even be mentioned without his being there.

I now hear that there was a luncheon-party at the House of Commons, attended by many MP's, where Pile, the AA Divisional Commander, gave away the most secret information – in fact the identical paper which Sandys quoted was on the table. All this was given away without my knowledge, but probably with the knowledge of Belisha. It all comes about through Belisha using unconventional methods of getting publicity. He has no knowledge of the usages in the Services and does not stop to think. He takes no advice.

I walked to my office with [Sir Herbert] Creedy, the Permanent Under Secretary at the WO & he & I both agreed that Belisha overestimates his popularity in the House. It seemed to us that they were all after him & that he had been very unpopular. He had tried to treat the House in a cavalier fashion and had received a bad fall. Will the outcome of it all be his retirement as Swinton retired? Would it be a good thing for the Army to get him out of it? I am of the opinion that it would. He is a hopeless little opportunist and out for himself. He has not the sympathy of the Army behind him & will have to fight a lone hand.[7]

Before Parliament rose for the summer recess he was able to meet Hore-Belisha after a short briefing from the adjutant general, Lieutenant General Sir Clive Liddell:

He told me that Belisha was more than worried. That the papers were putting in stories of his dismissal & resignation & then withdrawing them. His Press, as he calls it, is getting worse & worse each day. He can think of nothing else & does no work in the War Office in consequence. He was 3½ hours under cross-examination by the Committee and finds it difficult to get away from some of the statements he has made in the House.[8]

When my father went to meet with the secretary of state, he was asked for his opinion as to what he should do:

> I told him that he ought to tell the natural truth and call me in to make my statement as the officer responsible for calling the Court of Enquiry. The silly ass began then to apologise to me. He then said that he knew that I should have been made CIGS long ago. That I – like him – had suffered from being unconventional. That he had tried to do me a good turn by sending me to Gibraltar. He had done it on his own initiative, thinking that I should be well placed in the coming business. He then added cryptically that a lot might happen before I went to Gibraltar. I told him that all that had nothing to do with the case in point. That I bore him no ill will and I then told him how he had overruled many of the recommendations of the Selection Board in the past. The poor little wretch then said, 'One lives and learns.' I told him that he had a physical coward in [Lieutenant General Robert] Haining in Palestine & that a Commander was needed there if ever there was, not only a good legal administrative officer. He gave me a long garbled story of how Haining had to be given a chance and I told him that Commands were very different things to Administrative Posts. How he made us send in many names for each job and he then made the choice. He said that a Secretary of State should not be passive in these matters and I agreed, but said that he had definitely ruled us out. I quoted to him [Lieutenant General Sir Guy] Williams, who was relieving me, and what a poor little man he was & quite unfit as a personality to do it.
>
> The man was hopelessly rattled and was thinking so much of his own future, that he could not think of his job – to get on with the running of the Army. I came away with the definite idea that he was weakening upon the idea of sending me to Gibraltar.[9]

The Sandys Affair was eventually concluded by a Parliamentary Select Committee, which managed to come to a conclusion that placed no particular blame on anyone. My father's initial assessment that Sandys had 'lost his head' by bringing the matter into the public domain was not far from the mark. Hore-Belisha was not deliberately concealing the parlous state of London's air defences, and he was, insofar as possible, attempting to improve them. Thus, by bringing the situation out into the open, Sandys in fact caused a substantial distraction of time and effort by the secretary of state and the War Office more generally – ironically for my father, one of the things that the affair prevented was a planned trip by Hore-Belisha to review the defences of Gibraltar.[10] More widely, the affair exposed the secretary of state to a certain amount of ridicule as, by ordering the Court of Enquiry, he ensured that he had to explain himself on the floor of the House of Commons, where he came in for a degree of criticism.

On 25 July, my father sent in his notice to the War Office that he was taking sixty-one days leave up to 4 October. Meanwhile, he held firmly on to his Royal Commission of Appointment as governor and C-in-C Gibraltar, dated 12 August 1938. However, he was unexpectedly called in to see the CIGS on 24 September, at the height of the Sudeten Crisis, and asked how he would look upon being sent to the Middle East:

> He said that he thought that Mussolini must be our trouble and that all the German troops had been withdrawn from the Italian frontier and that Mussolini had taken his line. I told Gort that I was ready to go anywhere he wanted me. I thought that he treated the whole thing in a most impossible way. [...] He finished up by saying, 'you will be cut off from us and have military charge of the whole of the Middle East. We shall expect you to win the war out there.'[11]

It was not very clearly explained, not least because Gort indulged in his well-known habit of going into the minutiae while neglecting the big picture, but apparently two brigades were already on their way out to Egypt, one from England and one from India. Major General Arthur Grasset had been appointed as his chief staff officer and the War Office, having been pushed into taking action at such short notice, was in a state of complete havoc having been given three days in which to draft my father's instructions and to arrange for his departure on 27 September.

His instructions from the War Office, enlisting his services for visiting Egypt on special duty, required him to review the general military situation in the Middle East, particularly in Egypt and Palestine and, if war were to break out, he would at once be nominated as GOC-in-C Middle East. His interim report on 2 October showed that the civil government in Palestine had broken down completely and that the Arabs were in open rebellion against it. British troops were overtaxed in their efforts to protect the civilian population in the towns and at other vital points.

After my father returned to London on 16 October, by which time Chamberlain had returned from Munich with his 'Piece of Paper' and war had been staved off for the moment, he sent in his final report to the CIGS in which he emphasised that the army and RAF should be under one command to avoid the belief that an enemy can be defeated by bombing alone.

From the various asides with Gort, my father quickly established that Gort and Hore-Belisha were apprehensive of operations against Hitler very shortly:

Gort said to me that Gibraltar was only a 'garage' as far as I was concerned and it didn't matter in the least whether I went there or not. I smiled to think what the Gibraltarians would say to this if they knew, paying their Governor a high salary.[12]

He sailed off for Gibraltar with my mother on 6 November while I stayed behind at Pinewood School. Upon landing, after a four-day passage, he was met by the colonial secretary, military secretary and his ADC, all in full dress and frock coats.

One of the first salutes he received was from the Spanish Republican destroyer *José Luiz Diez* moored up in the harbour and holed on the port side near the waterline. The vessel had an eight-week internment order placed on it to allow for repairs before having to sail away again by 6 January and, of course, it was being closely watched by Franco's warships patrolling up and down the Bay of Algeciras outside British waters. In these circumstances, he chaired his first Defence Committee meeting on 23 November in order to set all the officials thinking along the right lines on local defence issues. Meanwhile, the Spanish naval attaché from London, who had resigned himself to the hopeless future facing the *José Luiz Diez*, was forced to wait a couple of days for an audience. My father was obliged to enforce the letter of international law, but the unfortunate attaché told him that there were so many Franco observers in Gibraltar that the Republican command did not know what they were going to do to save the ship.

Being out of touch with London put my father very closely in touch with all the goings on at Gibraltar, and he very quickly became thoroughly acquainted with the lives and souls of all the inhabitants and how much they enjoyed living under British rule with the doorway to Spain down the road. It was a small world for him in Gibraltar, but within a week or two he knew everybody and everybody knew him. He hunted in Spain, as master of the Calpe, and polished up his Spanish.

For general amusement, there was a racecourse and football ground on the North Front, which also acted as an emergency landing ground for Fleet Air Arm aircraft. However, plans were already in hand to turn it into a modern airport in the propeller-driven world. An east–west directional take-off and landing ground had to be put in place for planes to fly clear of Spanish airspace after lift-off seawards from an extended North Front strip. Any attempt at that time to construct an air base on the British Neutral Ground without Anglo-Spanish agreement would have endangered the Rock for, as my father noted, it was no more possible to protect such an installation from an attack from Spain – either by a hostile Spain or a Spain harbouring potential enemies – than it was to protect the harbour or the naval dockyard.

Another concern for him as governor were the wells and water catchments, and he was well aware that these were the rain drains of life for all the inhabitants when he inspected the waterworks on 7 December:

We are down to our last few drops of water owing to the drought and have only 1 million gallons left out of 14 millions that we can store. At this time of year the whole storage area is usually full. We are at the moment pumping water from the two 16ft deep wells sunk at the very edge of the Neutral Ground. There is now a danger of running into brackish water and we have to go easy with these wells.[13]

Meanwhile the '*JLD*', as the stranded Republican destroyer was generally referred to, remained swinging at her buoy in the harbour. However, at 01.00 on 30 December, the last moonless night of 1938, she slipped moorings and made for the open sea, only to run into four waiting nationalist warships. My father, barely in bed when he heard the shots of the engagement between the *José Luiz Diez* and the nationalist flotilla, was initially told that the destroyer had got clear away, but this proved not to be the case:

At 2.45 a.m. an ADC came and woke me up with a note from the Brigadier saying that the Spanish destroyer had run aground at Catalan Bay & he was going there at once. I got up and went round at once and there I found the most hopeless confusion. Half Gibraltar streaming there on foot and by car. The narrow road, which has no turning place was jammed with cars and we couldn't have got any troops past. I managed to get the police functioning – so many are silly old things who speak little English – and cleared the road. I found Curry, the Brigadier, on the beach and the destroyer ashore quite close inshore. The *Vannock* [*sic* – HMS *Vanoc*], one of our destroyers standing by with her searchlight full on the destroyer. The Spanish flag was still flying. Some dead and wounded were brought ashore in the Catalan Bay fishermen's boats. Apparently some 5 dead and 10 hit. A mass of people thronging the beach who had to be cleared off.[14]

When the captain of the *José Luiz Diez* was ordered to haul down his flag, and told that force would be used if he did not obey orders, he just shrugged his shoulders and complied. Brigadier Curry reported that the Spaniard was not as upset by the turn of events as might have been expected, and it later transpired that a number of the crew had sought to escape rather than sail with her. My father arranged for the dead sailors to be buried at sea, for fear that a funeral ashore might turn into an unwelcome Communist demonstration, but could not intern the surviving crewmen due to the British Government not having recognised Franco's nationalist forces as legal belligerents. However, while the crew were repatriated, the *José Luiz Diez* was interned and remained at Gibraltar until the end of the Spanish Civil War after which she was reincorporated into the Spanish Navy under the new regime.

I still have a clear memory of this night, as my sister and I had sailed out to Gibraltar on the Orient Line SS *Oronsay* for Christmas and I stole a lift in my father's car to Catalan Bay to see what was happening. I remember seeing the

José Luiz Diez grounded in the glare of the *Vanoc*'s searchlight, and the crowds of people watching.

Although the internal strife within Spain was drawing to an end, Europe as a whole continued to move towards war and my father was compelled to again consider the defenceless situation of Gibraltar. As governor, my father was instrumental in persuading the Colonial Office and government to remedy the situation by installing anti-aircraft guns, modernising the water and power supplies, and above all sheltering the population from air attack. No consideration had been given to air-raid precautions for the Rock in case of bombing and he was quite clear in his mind about constructing shelters for the inhabitants, recognising that it was unrealistic to expect the garrison to fight to the last man in the event of an attack, if the inevitable consequence would be heavy losses of women and children. By the end of March 1939, the Colonial Office had agreed to cover payments and authorise some further expenditure, as they wanted to see the population shifted into the fabulous galleries which had recently been revealed in the Upper Rock. However, these had been reserved for storing petrol and other emergency supplies, so could not be used as shelters.

Very sadly for my father, he heard on 10 March that his mother, my elderly grandmother aged 97, living at Alassio in Italy, had been taken ill and he was urgently ferried by warship to Oran to be flown to Genoa to see her. She had been weakened by internal infection and was able to see and talk quietly to him before she died on 19 March. He returned to Genoa and sailed back to Gibraltar on the Italian liner *Rex* to find, firstly, that his bullterrier, Caesar, had been killed falling over the cliff at the Governor's Cottage after chasing a goat and, secondly, that Hore-Belisha was planning a visit. This, it will be recalled, represented a return to an earlier commitment by the secretary of state to review the Gibraltar defences but, in the event, it did not materialise as the deteriorating political situation in Germany with Hitler's annexation of Czechoslovakia forced him to cancel his visit.

In my father's role of C-in-C elect of the Middle East, he was obliged to involve himself in plans for the conduct of the war by British forces in Egypt, although he privately doubted that, if war did break out, he would be in any position to get away from Gibraltar and actually take up command. The lack of realism inherent in the assumption that he could move to the other end of the Mediterranean upon the outbreak of war seemed to confirm his view that the government at home had not given sufficient thought to the southern theatre, being preoccupied by the threat posed closer to home by Hitler's Germany and the consequent need to put troops into the field alongside the French.

Only in April did the War Office awaken to the impracticality of transferring my father from one end of his prospective command to the other, and that only after a report to that effect from the C-in-C Mediterranean Fleet, Admiral Sir Dudley Pound.[15] Nevertheless, planning had to take place for a potential outbreak of war in the Mediterranean and May 1939 saw a series of meetings that were intended to develop a common strategy that could be followed by my father and his French counterparts. The key player on the French side was General Charles Noguès, the French resident general in Morocco, to whom my father had the unenviable task of trying to explain exactly what plans were in hand for the defence of Egypt in case of attack by Italian forces controlling the Red Sea approaches and the Mediterranean.

Indeed, the defence of Egypt was all that could be reasonably contemplated, for the British troops in that part of the world would be completely cut off in the event of war with Italy, with even the option of reinforcement from British India negated by the strong Italian presence in Abyssinia, Eritrea and Somaliland. My father had no confidence in the ability of the Royal Navy to keep open the sea lanes against Italian interdiction, and could get no strategic commitments from Admiral Pound. All in all, with lack of material and lack of strategy, Britain's situation amounted to 'a poor damned hand to play in dealing with the French. A dreadful disclosure of weakness.'[16] The nation's military weakness relative to France was, he felt, even more unbalanced than it had been in 1914.

On 4 May my father met formally with Noguès in Rabat, Morocco, having met him in private the previous night where he pressed the Frenchman to ask London to make plans for a combined Allied offensive in North Africa. The discussions quickly drew out the fact that the strategic situation was complicated by the build-up of forces in Spanish Morocco, made possible by Franco's victory in the Civil War, which were of great concern to the French, particularly if fascist Spain were to throw in her lot with the other dictator powers. Noguès further informed him 'that the Spanish plan was to leave twenty thousand men opposite Gibraltar – *pour impressionner les Anglais* – and not with the idea of attacking'.[17]

My father realised that his masters in London had completely failed to take into account the French concerns over what Spain might do, and this now meant that the French, for all their numbers, were in no better position to mount an offensive in the Mediterranean than were the British. Although the need to resolve the Spanish situation – hopefully through diplomacy – now made the western Mediterranean more important than it had been, my father continued to feel that his remaining at Gibraltar had largely a symbolic value, underlining the fact that Britain had no intention to give up the Rock.

Reflecting after the discussions were over, my father made his diary entry for the day in a despondent mood. 'There is not the vestige of an offensive plan. We are to allow the enemy to attack, hope for the best and develop an attack when we have seen what modern war is like and where we can act.'[18]

While the theory held by the government might well be to defeat Italy while containing Germany, no practical planning had been done to facilitate this and there was no coherent strategy for the Middle East and Mediterranean. He went on to write:

I am more convinced than ever that we want somebody with offensive spirit in Egypt and ready to take up the struggle there. I feel that I could do it better than anybody we have at the moment. I am watching the opportunity slip through my fingers. Fate will decide. Perhaps someone else can do it better than I could.[19]

He became so worked up about the situation that he put his thoughts into a long letter to Winston Churchill, explaining the military situation and soliciting his help. He ended by saying:

I write to you as my old Chief who knows me well. You know most of the officers left in the British Army capable of commanding & I can assure you the supply is not promising. I do not write out of any desire for personal gain. I am in a well-paid job, but I feel that we are in a hole and that I could get us out of it if war comes.

You will not think this letter disloyal, for I know you must realise that we have a very inexperienced WO with very little vision. They are all untried and uncertain of their present leader, the Jew.

If you think I have written out of place, please tear this letter up & think no more of it than that I have the Empire dreadfully on my mind at the moment & have no personal axe to grind.[20]

Luckily for my father, he did not have to let Churchill tear up the letter as the opportunity to do it himself appeared on 7 May when he was offered the job of being inspector general of overseas forces, commencing on 1 July. His duties were to last for one year at least, being responsible to the Army Council for the higher training of troops who would join up with any field force proceeding abroad. This included consultation with foreign staffs and reporting on overseas garrisons, as well as arrangements with the military authorities in India. It also meant vacating his governorship of Gibraltar, but this, and the reason for his departure, was not publicly announced until the end of May, at which time he also found that General Sir Walter Kirke had been appointed to the companion post of inspector general of home forces.

My father's short tenure as governor of Gibraltar, from 12 August 1938 until 11 July 1939, saw him make a number of significant improvements, including constructing the underground air-raid shelters, pushing ahead with the airport developments on the British Neutral Territory, initiating the formation of what became the Gibraltar Defence Force and ultimately the Royal Gibraltar Regiment, and maintaining friendly relations with the French in Morocco. However, on his own doorstep, when the storeroom on one side of the inner courtyard was being renovated, he was fortunate in saving three illuminating letters hidden away in the heap of waste papers. One was from Admiral Collingwood, another from the

Spanish Army commander in Ceuta, and the third was from Lord Liverpool. In their relation of the military and naval significance of the Rock, and the difficulties with the Spanish – particularly at Ceuta, but also generally insofar as British possession of the Rock was concerned – these letters from over a century ago, which remain in my possession, strike a number of parallels with my father's own situation and, indeed, with more recent events.

17

Waiting in the Wings

The impetus for the reorganisation that brought my father home stemmed from Hore-Belisha having identified, and discussed with Liddell Hart, the need to have a C-in-C in readiness now that there was a definite commitment to send troops to the direct support of the French. Although Liddell Hart had made the unlikely alternative suggestions of Hobart or Pile – both too junior, apart from anything else – Hore-Belisha produced a shortlist composed entirely of future field marshals: Alexander, Maitland Wilson, Dill, Wavell and my father. Dill was a strong choice, and had some expectation of receiving the post since the two Regular divisions of his Aldershot Command would form I Corps in the event of war and this was earmarked as the first formation to go to France, but my father's appointment as inspector general was generally seen as indicating that the job would go to him. That this was not made explicit was symptomatic of the lack of interest from on high in the choice, Chamberlain having delegated the choice to Hore-Belisha, and set the scene for continued confusion and misunderstanding in the months to come.

It will also be noted that Gort's name did not appear in Hore-Belisha's list and that Gort himself seemingly played little or no role in the selection process. Relations between CIGS and secretary of state had by now degenerated, due to what the former perceived as the latter's meddling, to the point that the two men were barely on speaking terms. Indeed, there was some resentment of my father's appointment amongst Gort's circle at the return of the 'old gang' at the expense of the 'new blood' that Hore-Belisha had sought to bring in through his coup less than two years previously. The director of military operations and intelligence, Major General Henry Pownall, a Gort man through and through, thought my father a poor choice and confided to his diary a scathing assessment of his qualities:

> Ironside is entirely unsuited to be C-in-C on a modern battlefield. He would do alright bush-whacking or knocking the Middle East about but he is *not* intelligent, not enough so to deal with a first class enemy. It isn't enough to have a commanding presence and a reputation – not nearly enough. But this is what he gets the job on.[1]

Although my father likely had no idea of these mixed feelings about his return, it was clear that he was returning to an awkward position: CIGS and secretary of state at odds with one and other, and he with no great opinion of either, yet answerable to both.

Taking courage in both hands my father secured a pass from the *Coronel Gobernador Militar* in Algeciras on 20 June 1939 to drive through Spain with his ADC and chauffeur to San Sebastian. Without impediment, he reached the War Office on 1 July by way of Dieppe and Newhaven. He found that the game of 'Belisha-Bounce' was in full swing:

> I found Gort in his office & found him very cheery and certainly pleased to see me. I had had doubts. We went through the list of senior officers and I found that we had much the same ideas on their characters. The one thing that I found out was that the main reason of my coming home was to command in case of war. They were all complaining of the flightiness of Belisha, who had flown off to Paris to deliver a speech. They told me that <u>he</u> was the CIGS and a practical Dictator. If he did not like a man he at once tried to push him out. He had abolished the post of MGO because he didn't like Taylor, one of the most efficient officers he had in the War Office. Very few of them can stand up to Belisha for some reason or other.
>
> Then I saw Walter Kirke, who is my Co-Inspector. He gave me what was the probable story. When his job as DG [director general] of Territorials came to an end, Belisha didn't want him to go. He had realised that he couldn't get good advice from the young people he had put into the War Office and had begun to ignore the advice that they did give. He had to have Kirke and asked him what he should do. Kirke recommended the resuscitation of the two Inspector Generals. Belisha jumped at it and appointed Kirke to the Home Inspectorate. Kirke then told him that he must bring me home at once from Gibraltar for the other Inspectorate. Belisha jumped at this, but next morning propounded the theory that I might be made CIGS and Gort the Inspector General. He then realised that Gort would be junior to the generals in the Commands and that moving him from CIGS would look like a slight. So he rushed off to the King and got him to agree. The King asked Belisha if he had arranged this with the Committee of Imperial Defence. Belisha passed this over & went back to the Prime Minister & said that the King had agreed. He then told the Treasury, who held the thing up for some time. But, Belisha forced it through by sheer bounce. He is certainly unscrupulous enough. Unfortunately he has nobody to keep him straight at the War Office.[2]

Without an office or staff and living temporarily in a hotel, my father decided to visit the GOC-in-Cs of the Home Commands and find out what were their difficulties:

> My difficulty will be to get the WO to do what I want when I make up my mind what is wanted. But, I must do it through the War Office and the ordinary channels. I am sure that at the moment the Army is like a herd without a shepherd. They feel that they get nothing done at the War Office, where so much work is done for so little result. They all want a lead. Every body I have seen has been more than complimentary over what I have done already and say that now they are sure that things will get moving. I think that they really mean it.[3]

Nevertheless, he was very conscious that time was now at a premium and bitter over the delays to his taking up the appointment, by which a whole month had already been lost.

His first action was to write to Belisha to put a stop on shifting senior officers out of the expeditionary force without his knowledge, as such personnel changes would prevent the effective training of commanders and staffs. Since it had been made clear to him that the primary reason that he had been brought back from Gibraltar and given this appointment — for which, it will be recalled, he had himself written the brief only the year before — was so that he was on hand to command the expeditionary force in the event of hostilities, this was of personal as well as professional importance.

On 7 July, after Hore-Belisha had returned from France, he was able to meet with him and straighten out some of the misunderstandings that were circling the War Office and confronting the inspector generals:

> He had a splitting headache, he said, but we talked for an hour and a half. He greeted me back warmly. He also complimented me upon Gibraltar and said that the Colonial Office were pleased. He then told me that he was considering my charter and was trying to see that there should be no friction. I told him that I had never had any friction in my career and that only Milne and Massingberd had produced a kind of friction to that effect because they knew that I was too strong for them.
>
> He then asked where the future generals were coming from — he could see no talent. I told him that he had turned out good & bad together and that we must go warily in future. He promised me not to make any change in the BEF without my knowledge.
>
> He thought Danzig was very serious and he did not agree that it was something about which we could go to war. That Germany had a certain amount of right on her side. But, we had given an unqualified assurance to Poland and if she considered she was being menaced, then she could call on us. That Beck [Józef Beck, Polish foreign minister] would not say what Poland's plan was in case of Danzig declaring herself part of the Reich. I was required to go to Warsaw and extract this out of the Polish General Staff. I was to meet the PM and Halifax

at 12 noon on Monday to receive my instructions. Belisha had only the haziest idea of what was to happen if we were to carry out our guarantee to the Poles. I pointed out that I had no idea what happened & that I had seen the DMO&I [Henry Pownall] who was pretty vague himself.

Belisha told me that the French C-in-C would be Generalissimo in France, but the C-in-C of the British Expeditionary Force would have the 'right of appeal'. I at once asked him to whom the British C-in-C could appeal – to the Cabinet, to the Prime Minister, the War Office or what. Belisha said he didn't know. None of that had been considered. Nothing had been done as regards the probable employment of the BEF. Belisha had no idea what the French plan was – or said he didn't. He talked about the formation of a combined *Conseil Supérieur*. He had a hazy idea as to its formation from our point of view. I told him that we must not be tied to the cart tail of the French and dragged into action without any reconnaissance. He agreed.

He complained to me that the Navy had no plan, and I agreed with that. I told him that the principle was to hold Germany & attack Italy, but that I knew of no plan to implement this & the WO had not gone very deeply into this. I told him that this vitally concerned the British Army. He said that he thought that a plan was being made.

As far as I can see, we have nothing prepared with the French and I shall have to see to that. Even Gort had a lot of hazy ideas about our being in Belgium from an extemporised line across the North of France. He thought that the King of the Belgians was pro-German. I can see that I shall have to get down to the French plan very thoroughly.

Belisha said that he proposed to separate all the Inspectors from the War Office and hand them over to the Inspector-General.[4]

The problems over what to do in the event of war would continue to vex my father over the coming months, and the lack of forward planning that he identified would blight Britain's efforts once hostilities were opened. It is, therefore, interesting to see how swiftly he had identified these issues and begun to make plans to tackle them in such time as remained.

The concerns over Poland, however, suggested that there would be little further time available, and certainly gave my father another set of immediate concerns as he was pitched into Britain's belated efforts to make contact with her new ally on what was potentially going to become the Eastern Front in a new war with Germany. Since it was anticipated that Hitler's next move would be to press German claims on Danzig and the 'Polish Corridor', it was essential to obtain knowledge of the Polish plans for this eventuality. The political situation was complicated by the fact that the territory at stake was part of Prussia that had been ceded to Poland after the First World War, which gave German ambitions some claim to legitimacy and also provided an excuse for non-intervention to those who favoured appeasing Hitler in order to buy more time to prepare for war.

The selection of my father to be on standby for this mission was not surprising as he knew the Poles and they knew him. He could speak French, German and Russian and this would give him a vital voice in the proceedings. When he presented himself at Downing Street on the morning of 10 July, Chamberlain was there to meet him along with the foreign secretary, Lord Halifax. Although the purpose of the meeting was to discuss my father's trip to Poland, Chamberlain first asked him about Gibraltar:

> I told him the place was impregnable, though the town might be destroyed. The Dockyard might be damaged. If the full complement of guns was in position, even that might be difficult. [...] I told him that the population now had deep dug-outs and was safe from annihilation. He seemed relieved to hear that.[5]

After telling them more about relationships with Spain and the challenging nature of living next door to the Franco regime, the discussions concentrated on the Polish dilemmas:

> [Chamberlain] told me that they had no idea what the Poles were going to do and he wanted me to go there to find out. Beck had always put them off by saying that their action was dependent upon the amount of provocation they got. I told him that our chief card was that we had given a guarantee if Poland felt her independence was menaced & that they must therefore tell us what they intended to do under circumstances that the Poles thought might arise. Both Chamberlain and Halifax seemed to think that the Danzigers would declare themselves part of the Reich and that we wanted to know what then would happen. Would that mean a direct menace to their independence? Would they act? Our attitude had always been to the Poles that we should like Danzig settled. Chamberlain said that no undertakings by Hitler would be any use. We must have some definite practical guarantee that, with Danzig in the Reich, Poland would have practical rights equal to those she had now. It should not be beyond the brains of the allies to devise some guarantees that would bind Hitler. I must say that I was glad to see that he had no belief in Hitler's promises. I told him that I had seen and talked with Hitler and that I was not sure whether Hitler blew up spontaneously or whether he did it to impress his listeners. Chamberlain thought he did it spontaneously. I said if that were so there was more danger of war. He didn't agree, but said he agreed that something might always occur to overbalance him. He thought that Hitler had an acute political sense and didn't want war.
>
> I told them that Hitler would present us with a *fait accompli* & would then turn to us and say 'do you really want war over this trivial matter'? They agreed, but

said we must settle Danzig, so that Hitler could not say that he had had a success through threatening force.

Chamberlain asked me how long the Poles could stand up & I told him that they must be overrun unless Hitler chose the wrong moment. That you might take Poznania in a couple of months, but that you couldn't overrun the whole country in a couple of months. No one knew what a heavy air bombardment of Warsaw might bring. I didn't think it would bring the Poles to their feet. He asked me what all these horses were for, and I told him that it was because machines didn't work in snow & because there were large numbers of horses in the Middle East. This seemed new to him.

They then told me that they had no answer from the Poles as to my coming and were awaiting that.

My impression was that they both thought that war was almost inevitable or very nearly so. They did not express the optimism that Belisha expressed. They both knew that the so-called WO plan was to leave Germany alone and knock out Italy. I didn't tell them that so far I could see no signs of this policy being passed into a plan. If both Italy & Spain remained hostily [sic] neutral it would make our strategic arrangements very difficult and they agreed. There was no practical way of attacking Germany except through her western frontier and that was now protected by a Siegfried Line.

Chamberlain said that it seemed impossible to come to an understanding with Russia. Did I think it was right? I told him that much as it was against the grain, it was the only thing we could do. Chamberlain ejaculated 'the only thing we cannot do'. I told him that we must not expect too much from any Russian advance, that the Russians had never done well outside their own country and that their Army must be very badly commanded. They had shot 80% of their officers over the rank of colonel in 1936 and couldn't have many left.[6]

After his meeting with the prime minister, my father was summoned to see Belisha on 11 July at the House of Commons:

He told me that I had made a very favourable impression, which amused me a good deal. Then we walked down to the FO and had an hour's talk with [Halifax]. In the end, I had to draft my own instructions, which they signed. They are all dreamers & thinkers and cannot turn them into orders. Unpractical creatures. Not a good augury for war.[7]

Halifax also told my father that the Polish ambassador in London had told him that the Poles were delighted with the thought of his going to Poland, as they all knew him. Two days later, he met with Sir Howard Kennard, the British ambassador in Warsaw:

Quite the most completely wet person I have seen for years. He is home 'having his teeth done'. He told me that he had had no leave for a long time and that Danzig had 'got on his nerves'. Poor man, I suppose that he is quite useless and has come away.[8]

My father was well briefed for the visit by the military attachés, as well as the Polish ambassador in London. Although the Poles had what my father thought to be too low an opinion of the German Army, believing it over-mechanised, they considered it impossible for them to hold the Polish Corridor and Poznania in the face of the expected German offensive. They planned to maintain a central reserve, and ultimately launch a counter-offensive once a line had been stabilised. The difficulty, which he knew he would have to impress on the Poles, was that Britain could not provide the sort of immediate action that the Poles expected in support of this. Even with French help, an attack on the Siegfried Line would be a major undertaking that would take months to prepare. It was therefore difficult to see how Britain could actually fulfil her guarantee to Poland, or maintain her ally in the field when war came. What was therefore required was time, and this in turn required Polish restraint:

> The most dangerous thing to me is that the flag may go up through a Corporal of Sappers blowing up the single Danzig Bridge towards East Prussia. We are then committed to a European War. I must get the Poles to realise that haste is against them. We develop slowly and require warning if we are to help Poland. We must therefore hope for a slowly developing tension over Danzig and not a sudden coup. The Poles must therefore be absolutely open with us. The slower things go the better for the Poles.[9]

With this policy in mind, he left London on the 17th and flew to Warsaw via Copenhagen and Gdynia. He stayed at the Bristol Hotel and dined with our military attaché and Colonel Adrian Carton di Wiart VC, head of the British Military Mission to Poland. In order to secure the frankness that he hoped for from the Poles, he decided that his policy would be to be completely frank himself. He was, however, somewhat hamstrung by the fact that he had promised the foreign secretary that he would speak to the Poles purely from the military point of view, even though he would be meeting Beck, the foreign minister, General Kasprzycki, minister for war, General Stackiewicz, CGS, and Marshal Śmigly-Rydz, inspector general of the forces. His four-day visit was, as he expected, packed with talk:

> The little *chargé d'affaires*, [Clifford] Norton, seems quite intelligent and keen. He did not say much about his Ambassador, who is skulking in London and his third Attaché was a youngster with thinning hair called Robin Hankey. We all

discussed my long instructions. I see that the inclusion of Norton at some talks has led to the bringing in of Beck, which is going to slow up things considerably. Our diplomats cannot allow a soldier to interfere in their legitimate business. They are much too jealous for that. I shall get the Marshal by himself in order to induce confidence.

I am still strongly of opinion that Hitler will shift away from this Danzig business and that he will start some other hare – probably in Roumainia [sic] – which will divert our attention from the Poles.

My programme has been made up of too much ceremony. I go visiting all the morning of tomorrow & they return the visit all of the afternoon. I suppose this is all inevitable, but it hardly seems necessary to me in times like these. We are all very touchy still in spite of the danger.[10]

The round of visits enabled my father to meet all the main players on the Polish side, although it was clear that Śmigly-Rydz and Beck were the two most vital contacts. My father and Norton met the two men together and the four spoke briefly before Norton whisked Beck away and left my father with the marshal. The two men were of an age and had met before and their discussion was cordial, although matters turned swiftly political when Śmigly-Rydz brought up the subject of British loans to Poland and the conditions that the Treasury was attempting to apply to them. The Polish complaint was 'that they had been asked to tie this "crisis loan" on to the export of coal and the equalisation of the Zloty'. As my father observed in his diary, 'The two things had nothing to do with each other. Were we in a crisis or not? Was it worth supporting the Poles from a military point of view?'

It might have been hoped that the discussion with the marshal would have resolved the latter point, but it was only when Beck rejoined the discussion that real progress on that front was made. My father had come to Poland with mixed opinions of him, which cannot have been helped by the story passed to him by Lieutenant Colonel Edward Roland Sword, our military attaché in Warsaw, that Beck, while serving as Polish military attaché in Paris, 'got hold of papers from the French IIieme Bureau and communicated them to the Germans'. This was at a time when Poland was seeking a rapprochement with Germany, but my father still found the story hard to credit.

In person, however, my father found Beck altogether more likeable and helpful than he had expected:

A long thin dark man, speaking French almost like a Frenchman. I thought him a very different type to the others. Much more a man of the world and far from the 'twister' that they had called him in England. His refusal to discuss the military question was merely because he didn't really speak with authority. Both he and Smigly-Rydz were emphatic that they had decided to oppose the

Germans before we decided to come in behind them. We did not pressure them to oppose the Germans.[11]

After this series of meetings, my father composed a wire to the government back in London, noting the following points:

(i) That I am certain that the Poles will do nothing rash in a military sense.
(ii) That the military effort that they have made is nothing short of prodigious.
(iii) That we ought not to make so many conditions to our financial aid. That time is short.
(iv) That one of the ways of convincing Hitler that we are serious is by granting this monetary aid to Poland and showing him that we are behind the Poles.
(v) That the Poles are strong enough to resist.[12]

When he left Poland on 19 July, having taken part in all the ceremonial visits and much wining and dining, he had a complete understanding of the state of play in the country and the plans of its armed forces. In his report to the secretary of state for war he said, firstly, that the Poles did not wish to act hastily, whatever provocation they were given, and they realised fully the responsibility which rested upon them not to involve all the Allies in a needless war. They did not believe that any incident over Danzig could fail to bring on a larger confrontation. My father concluded with an assessment that the real direction of the country was coming from Beck and Śmigly-Rydz, and that the latter would be the de facto ruler of the country in time of war.

On 24 July, he went to the War Office and met Hore-Belisha, looking fresh and smiling on his way to a Committee of Imperial Defence meeting:

> He asked me whether I thought the world war was coming and I told him that I thought it was. Was it coming this year? I said probably, but nobody could tell. He then pulled down the map of Europe and showed the most amazing ignorance of Poland and what it was like.

My father could not understand how the secretary of state and CIGS could make decisions relative to the future war based only on his report, or why he, who had so recently visited Poland, was not invited to the meeting to brief in person on his findings. The fatalistic War Office mentality was alien and disconcerting to him, leading him to reflect that 'much as I should hate it, I ought to take the War Office in hand. Gort doesn't even begin to know how to run the bigger things.'[13]

For my father, whose belief that war was imminent was bolstered by Germany's declaration that Danzig need not be a cause of war but must be handed over, the signs of change came when Winston Churchill invited him to Westerham to talk and dine that evening:

I made a night of it with Winston Churchill at Chartwell. I dined with him and there we sat talking until 5 a.m. this morning.

What a man. Whisky and cigars all the time. A fascinating house overlooking the Weald of Kent. [...] Last September, had there been a war, he would have been given the Admiralty. Now he might even be Prime Minister.

It was clear that the two men were in many ways kindred spirits. They were of a generation, and it is clear that my father had a great deal of admiration for Churchill, which contrasted markedly with his views of Chamberlain, in whose abilities as a war leader he had no faith. The two men went on to discuss the prospects for the future:

Winston considered that it was now too late for any appeasement. The deed was signed and Hitler is going to make war. He walked about in front of the map and demonstrated his ideas, repeating 'You are destined to play a great part. You will be C-in-C. You must be clear what is going to happen:
(i) The crippling or annihilation of Poland.
(ii) The employment of Italy to create diversions Mussolini has sold his country for his job.
(iii) The capture of Egypt, chiefly by Italian forces.
(iv) A pressing on to the Black Sea via Roumania.
(v) An alliance with Russia, when the latter sees how the land lies.'

I told Winston that I was sure that we were in for a bad time and that we should have to have guts to withstand the first German & Italian rush. We had no considered plans. No plan to deal with the war in general. Even the hazy idea of attacking the Italians had not been put into a framework. He showed me a plan that he had written on the Mediterranean, pressing for action there and not a solemn bottling up of each end. I told him of my difficulties with Pound, now the First Sea Lord. He said that he was horrified of the appearance of Pound, limping around as lame as anything.

Winston then produced the idea of putting a squadron of battleships into the Baltic. It would paralyse the Germans and immobilise many German divisions. The submarine had been dealt with & would no longer be a menace. This idea of British ships in the Baltic was revolutionary and I was very surprised at how Winston was so navally-minded. All his schemes came back to the use of the Navy. It ran through my head that here was a grand strategist imagining things, and the Navy making no plans whatever. Quite definitely, the man who is now First Sea Lord had no plan for the Mediterranean Fleet when he was in command of it. He could give me no idea of any offensive plan for dealing with Italy. I am sure there is none now.[14]

There are a number of points of interest in this conversation, with reference to my father's future relations with Churchill in particular and with the wider political-military establishment more generally. The lack of faith in Sir Dudley Pound is particularly interesting when one considers that he and my father would shortly find themselves working closely together as two-thirds of the wartime Chiefs of Staff Committee, but also that Pound's tenure on that committee, and at the head of his service, would continue far longer under Churchill's premiership than would my father's.

It was some time since my father had had the chance to update his first-hand knowledge of naval warfare, and it must be inferred that it was this lack of up-to-date awareness of the realities of war at sea that allowed him to accept at face value Churchill's blithe assurances of the survivability of British warships in confined waters and in the face of German submarines and aircraft; assumptions that the opening months of the Second World War would prove to be disastrously flawed.

Interesting too, however, is the fact that both men favoured an indirect approach to the defeat of Germany, with an emphasis on the Mediterranean and Balkans. When one considers that Britain was struggling to meet her commitment to provide even a pocket-sized BEF to send to France, and that Churchill's career had almost been destroyed in the previous war through his promotion of a similarly indirect approach via the Dardanelles, this seems at first glance a perverse emphasis. However, one should also bear in mind that both men had served on the Western Front and had seen it in all its horrors, and that my father, in particular, was of the belief that Hitler would be drawn into southern Europe and the Balkans, most likely through a move against Poland's ally Romania. Exploiting this in order to avoid the heavy casualties consequent in directly attacking Germany was therefore by no means an illogical stance. However, advocacy of such indirect strategies – in particular some of Churchill's more extreme flights of naval fancy, not least the idea of British battleships in the Baltic – would cast both men together in the first months of the coming war as members of the 'Crazy Gang', looked at askance by those who sought to fight a more direct and conventional war against Germany.

Returning to more present concerns, my father's meeting with Churchill had not gone unnoticed. To his political superiors, the matter was not of great concern. Hore-Belisha told my father that he, personally, did not mind my father's consulting with Churchill, but that he had felt it necessary to mention the matter to Chamberlain, who for his part wished to make it clear that Churchill 'was in opposition and was a strong critic of the Government's doings'. My father in turn reassured Hore-Belisha 'that I had no intention of making any permanent liaison with Winston' but, at the same time, 'that I had always worked very well with him and would give nothing secret away'.[15] With this, my father's political masters seemed satisfied, but not so the War Office, where the issue was not just my father's discussions with Churchill but with Hore-Belisha and with the political leadership of the country in general.

My father's formal instructions as to his role as inspector general were finally issued to him on 27 July, which was, as he pointed out, a month after he had been in the post and three months after he was notified that he would receive the appointment. Thus formally briefed, he sought meetings with the inspectors of the various arms of the service and with senior figures from the War Office. Amongst the latter was Henry Pownall, and their discussion brought up the concerns from within the Gort circle as to my father's activities in the political and diplomatic spheres.

Considering that Pownall, as we have seen, shared the low opinion of my father common to the younger generation of officers who had entered the War Office under the patronage of Hore-Belisha and Gort, his account of the meeting is surprisingly fair. My father himself raised the issue of the difficulties in which he was placed, writing:

> I told him of my difficulties as regards being sent for by various politicians and asked questions which I cannot refuse to answer. I told him that if anything did happen I would always report the matter to the CIGS so that he would understand what people were driving it. I reiterated my determination not to be played off against the CIGS. If I took part in that I should make confusion worse.[16]

Pownall felt that my father protested too much insofar as his loyalty was concerned and believed that he had been giving advice to Hore-Belisha 'behind Gort's back', which was essentially true. Nevertheless, Pownall placed the blame for this primarily with Hore-Belisha, who seemed to the Gort circle to be actively seeking second opinions with which to confound the War Office, and he did sympathise with my father's situation, going on to write, 'It *is* difficult for him of course when the S of S, PM, or Halifax asks for his opinion to refuse to give it. Indeed he can't so refuse. But he *must* report to Gort what he has said, however much discretion he has shown.'[17]

The discussion then moved to my father's new instructions, and the remit of his post. Here, Pownall was rather less charitable, writing that he thought that my father did not understand them even though they were clear enough so far as Pownall himself could see. Pownall went on to assert of my father:

> In some muddled way he thought he had the power to intervene in the framing of policy. It is quite clear that he is not entitled to do so. But he must know what the policy is, otherwise he can't perform his duties of inspection to see that it is carried out. In order to see that training is on proper lines, he must also know

the presumed areas and methods of employment of the Field Force, i.e. he must know war plans (incidentally he has been going about saying there are none).[18]

On the last point, one can quite readily see Pownall and Gort hoist by their own petard: what other conclusion could my father, as de facto C-in-C-designate of the BEF, draw by the failure of the War Office to confide its plans in him than that there were no such plans to confide?

My father, in his own account of the discussion, outlined his case for acting on the assumptions that he had and, after all, without any formal instruction, assumptions were all that he had been able to work on. For all Pownall's derision of his thinking as muddled, it was based – other, perhaps, than treating the circumstances of 1914 as a rather more binding precedent than was justified – on a common-sense appraisal of the facts as my father understood them:

> The appointment of C-in-C designate of the Army in France is never made in our country until the last moment although it is tacitly understood. My seniority is so great that it is well known that I cannot be employed in war except as the C-in-C. If I am not employed as that I must remain as the Inspector for training while war is going on. Everybody in England has taken it for granted that I shall be C-in-C and I should not have been so stupid as to give up my command in Gibraltar for anything less than the C-in-C designate in war. I could not have been brought back otherwise.
>
> I pointed out that training and policy were so closely tied together that it was impossible to pull them apart. Unless I knew what the Army was intended for I couldn't train it efficiently. I had not been given all this information and I wanted it.[19]

My father left the meeting with the belief that all was now cleared up, and recorded that when, after leaving Pownall, he was approached by Major General Francis Nosworthy, DCGS India, who wanted his opinion on planned operations in the Red Sea, he made it clear to him that his own war role – assuming that it was confirmed – would be restricted to the command of a six-division BEF under French command and that the direction of the wider war was a matter for the CIGS. However, the War Office response as recorded by Pownall, who restricted his comments to my father's current role, confirmed that he was still only to be allowed the bare minimum of information relating to policy and strategy, and no voice in making it:

> I am to give him, and Kirke, in future all CID conclusions (and the relevant papers) *after* decisions have been taken. *Not* before, because that would give him the opportunity to advise on matters in which the CIGS is the proper and only

advisor. And I shall send him a paper showing what the position is at the present time so that he can stand fair.[20]

It may reasonably be divined from this that my father's exclusion from the decision-making process, even on questions such as that of Poland on which he had the ability to make a relevant contribution, stemmed from internal power struggles and that the Gort circle were prepared, at best, to tolerate his presence as inspector general but not to treat him as a C-in-C designate. A further argument in favour of the latter point can be taken from my father's own discovery, a few days prior to his meeting with Pownall, of a mooted plan for when war broke out to appoint him DCIGS and British representative on the Allied Supreme War Council which, in effect, would have amounted to a means of keeping him away from both the War Office and the front. On the other hand, Chetwode had written on 10 July to say that he believed Hore-Belisha wished to make my father CIGS in place of Gort, a rumour which might, in itself, have a great deal to do with the Gort circle's attitude towards my father.

Such infighting and muddle over policy did not create an enviable situation nor did it aid my father in his current role as inspector general or in his preparation for his assumed wartime role as commander of the BEF. In order to speed up the standardisation of training, he ordered the adaptation of the methods used by Dill's Aldershot Command which would form the BEF's I Corps when war came, but even this was not done because of the excellence of Dill's methods but because no comparable corps-level formation existed from which a template could be taken. It was none of it very inspiring stuff, and now, as the clock continued to tick down towards war, the British establishment prepared to go on holiday.

My father, meanwhile, spent much of the remaining weeks of summer visiting the troops – particularly at Aldershot – and observing their training. Much of what he saw pleased him, and he identified a number of promising officers at brigade level and below, but the command changes that he had protested about continued all the same. The Regular core of the army was, he felt, sound but basic training seemed to be suffering and the more so for the first militia conscripts coming into the army under the terms of the Military Training Act.

Newspaper headlines on 17 August stated that Hitler was making demands for a settlement in a fortnight. Three days later, my father recorded:

Halifax has been back at the Foreign Office studying the latest reports in the place. The Prime Minister remains fishing in Scotland. Parliament remains on holiday. There is nothing to do but wait the desire of Hitler. He keeps the whole of Europe on tenterhooks in his nerve-campaigning. A dreadful state of affairs.[21]

Only towards the end of the month, with news of Hitler's pact with Russia, did recognition come that war was inevitable, and even then the army was slow to mobilise. The newspapers all depicted my father as the man who would become C-in-C in wartime, but no formal notification came through of this appointment. My father pasted a number of these articles into his diary, writing:

> The papers are beginning to publish more and more articles about me, which are driving me into a position of importance. I can do nothing at the moment and feel futile. Walter Kirke, who has always been a great support to me, says that he thinks that if war breaks out, both Belisha & Gort will fade away & that I shall be sent for and put in a responsible position. He doesn't think that I shall be sent over to France to command the little Army we shall collect there.[22]

The idea seemed to be resurfacing that he might, after all, be appointed CIGS, but again nothing was confirmed. Kirke even told him that he had been Deverell's choice to succeed him as CIGS but that this had been quashed by Sir Herbert Creedy, the permanent undersecretary of state at the War Office, on the grounds that my father would turn the place upside down. My father reflected that this was perhaps for the best as he was not cut out to be a peacetime CIGS – but that 'I might be the man in war'.[23]

The fateful day for my father came on 1 September when Winston Churchill phoned him from Chartwell to say:

> 'They've started. Warsaw & Cracow are being bombed now'. I rang up Gort at the War Office, who said that he was off to a meeting. Didn't believe it. I urged him to tell Belisha. He did & Belisha was seen rushing off to Downing Street. I rang Winston again and he said he had the news definitely from the Polish Ambassador, who had told him ½ hour ago. So much for our hopeless optimism and the wretched little fourth form boys running us. How could the War Office possibly be ignorant of this?[24]

With the outbreak of war, my father's job as inspector general effectively ceased to exist but, for the moment, no orders came to confirm his new appointment even though his erstwhile staff quickly received notification of their new appointments:

> Two of my Inspectors have gone over to Aldershot to join GHQ. They are all receiving their orders. One of them asked me when I was going and he seemed surprised when I told him that I had received no appointment. I wonder. Can they afford not to appoint me? They may consider these 4 divisions which are now going over as not sufficient for me to take over. The papers would

probably kick up now after all they have said. I can only wait. Perhaps we may do something after the assembly of Parliament at 6 o'clock tonight.[25]

In fact, the waiting continued all that night and the following day. Germany had not responded to Chamberlain's ultimatum, and it seemed that any final decision of appointments was to wait until Britain was formally at war. My father was repeatedly reassured everywhere he went that he was sure to be appointed to command the BEF, but official confirmation remained unforthcoming.

On Sunday, 3 September, the day Chamberlain announced at 11.00 that the country was at war, my father was brought to the high table, although it was late in the day before he received his summons to the War Office:

> I was ushered in to Belisha and there he said to me at once 'I want you to come as CIGS'. Pretty devastating. I said to him, 'Why do you want to do this?' He then said that there were no ideas in the War Office and that I took a broader view of the war than anybody else. I said that I would do as I was ordered. That it was war & that I never picked or chose and neither asked for a job or refused one. He then said he would like to be quite frank with me. That he had a great fight in the new War Cabinet and had been backed by Winston Churchill [newly appointed First Lord of the Admiralty]. That it had been said that I talked too much and was unreliable. I told him that it was a most scandalous lying accusation. That if he thought that[,] I had no intention of taking the job. He said that he had complete trust in me and was quite satisfied to place his confidence in me. He also said that the report was Chief of Staff Conferences would be completely upset if I were in there. That he didn't believe that. I again told him that if he had the slightest doubt I wouldn't come. That I always spoke the truth, perhaps brutally, but once a decision was taken, there was nobody more loyal than I was. I always carried out any decision as if it were my own. Belisha then asked me to dismiss the conversation from my mind. Gort was to be C-in-C of the BEF.
>
> He then had Gort in and told him that he could have carte blanche as to officers for the BEF. I told him that we couldn't make that mistake. The war was being run from the War Office by the CIGS and we couldn't allow key positions to be mutilated. Gort agreed and I said that Belisha must leave me to settle that.
>
> Now, my own personal feelings. I felt annoyed that I should now be brought in to put right the show that had got out of hand. I had been passed over for an inferior man and had suffered oblivion, to be brought back in case of need. War is undoubtedly different from peace, but there it is. The running of the greatest war in our history is now in my hands. I have missed out so far in commanding a British Army and that cannot be helped.[26]

18

CIGS

Considering the surprise that he must have felt on receiving the news of what his and Gort's appointments were to be, my father's response was remarkably phlegmatic. Still, it was hardly an ideal situation for the nation to begin a major war with such a radical exchange of jobs amongst the army's most senior commanders. As is clear from his own published diaries, it was to Hore-Belisha that both my father and Gort owed their respective new appointments. Indeed, the secretary of state recorded that he had had to defend his choice of my father as CIGS to the War Cabinet, receiving considerable opposition to the idea from the secretary of state for air, Sir Kingsley Wood, but ultimately winning approval thanks in part to the intervention in my father's favour of Winston Churchill, newly back in office as First Lord of the Admiralty.[1]

It was because of this political wrangling that the appointments took so long to be confirmed, and this allowed for further intriguing within the War Office, as recorded on 3 September by my father's critic from the Gort camp, Henry Pownall:

> Finally the great argument as to who was to be C-in-C, a thorny subject which has been going to and fro for days. H-B having removed Tiny from his rock, finds he is saddled with him. In military opinion he is unfitted to be C-in-C in the field or CIGS. In H-B's opinion he can't be left out of one or the other for 'psychological' reasons, i.e. publicity and opinion, especially the opinion of some politicians, notably Winston, who do not know the man 'au fond'. And so it went on for days, with Grigg pulling all the strings he could find. But in vain for on Sunday the new War Cabinet decided on sending Gort as C-in-C, Tiny as CIGS.[2]

This combination of factors therefore both explains my father's appointment and the difficulties that he would face from a number of senior generals from the Gort and Pownall generation that would blight, and ultimately help end, his time as CIGS. However, it still begs the question of what was behind Hore-Belisha's volte-face and the apparent reversal of the roles that pre-war planning had seemingly assigned to Gort and my father. To explain this, we need to look at the relations between Gort and Hore-Belisha, which had degenerated through 1938 and 1939 to the point that the two men could hardly work together. While it is therefore true that Hore-Belisha had more than once voiced the opinion that he would like to see my father as CIGS, it is fairer to say that what he really wanted was to see the back of Gort.

For Hore-Belisha, giving Gort the BEF got him out of the War Office, but at the price of losing as a potential C-in-C an officer – my father – whose experience surely made him a better fit than the actual appointee and who would, in all likelihood, have made a better fist of things in 1940 than Gort did. Almost certainly, even my father's best would not have been sufficient to turn the tide of blitzkrieg in the face of German superiority and French defeatism, and so in retrospect it was as well for him that he avoided the poisoned chalice that command of the BEF would prove to be for Gort. However, the change of posts meant that he now had to find his feet in a job for which he had not prepared, and for which he had more than once expressed doubts over his fitness.

Ironically, in bringing him home from Gibraltar, Hore-Belisha may well have done both my father and himself a disservice, for in retrospect it is not at all unrealistic to imagine my father, had he stayed on at Gibraltar, stepping very effectively into the Mediterranean and Middle Eastern roles that fell in reality to Sir Henry Maitland Wilson. Such duties, one feels, might have been far more congenial to him, and better fitted to his abilities, than CIGS or command of the BEF.

It is, however, futile to dwell on what history might have been. Hore-Belisha had made his choice, and all concerned now had to make the best of it.

While the secretary of state had removed Gort from his immediate circle, however, he had done little to diminish the disregard in which he was held by the new C-in-C and his coterie of BEF staff officers. With my father's view of him ambivalent at best, Hore-Belisha was left with only a limited fund of credibility with the army's senior command and had, in fact, set the seeds for his own downfall. That he had allowed this situation to develop, combined with the extent to which his choices to fill key appointments were influenced by personal and political factors rather than the good of the service, must be counted serious black marks against what was otherwise a fine peacetime record as a reforming secretary of state.

In dealing with my father's tenure as CIGS, and with the spell as GOC-in-C Home Forces that followed on from it, it is important to recall that his collected wartime diary entries form, in themselves, sufficient material for a complete book and have been published as such. The records of the meetings of the War Cabinet and Chiefs of Staff Committee are even more voluminous. In these closing chapters, it is therefore necessary to take something of a selective view as to what is covered: the purpose of this volume as a whole is to furnish a full and rounded biography of my father, and not a scripted analysis of the first year of the Second World War. What follows, therefore, is first and foremost the personal history of my father's war service, and such analysis as has been attempted is focused very closely upon the decisions and actions with which he was personally concerned and their consequences for him, the nation, the army and the course of the war.

In the immediate aftermath of the declaration of war, once it became apparent that London was not, after all, to be completely destroyed by aerial bombardment, Britain's initial priorities turned towards the despatch of the BEF to France and to the course of events in Poland. The former went off well enough, no doubt due in part to the fact that Gort had been able to co-opt a number of senior staff officers from the War Office in order to make up his command team. Although the BEF in its initial form was composed of a single weak army of two infantry corps, its senior staff was structured from the outset for the far larger army group that it was eventually envisaged as forming once Britain's military build-up was complete.

The result of this was that some of the best available staff brains went off to France and found little to do, leaving the War Office on the back foot and ensuring a certain amount of discontinuity, just as my father picked up the reins as CIGS. Further dislocation took place because, initially, peacetime working practices were maintained, with the civilian staff clocking off punctually each night and many of the military staff commuting in from distant homes. My father, for his part, tried to set a standard by maintaining a bed in his office and beginning his day with a ride in the park followed by breakfast at the United Services Club. The rest of his morning was taken up by attending meetings first of the Chiefs of Staff (COS) Committee and then of the War Cabinet, and the papers from these form a vital supplement to his own diaries for this period.

Of the three chiefs of staff, the senior man, representing the senior service, was Admiral of the Fleet Sir Dudley Pound, in post since June 1939. Pound had previously commanded the Mediterranean Fleet where, as we have seen, his performance had not impressed my father. Although in worsening health, which would later dog his performance and ultimately compel his resignation only weeks before his death in October 1943, Pound at the outbreak of the war was at least able to serve as a useful counterbalance to Churchill as First Lord of the Admiralty, tempering the latter's more extreme ideas – such as the Baltic plans outlined to my father at Chartwell – with realism and judgement. The primary difficulty from the point of view of my father and the army was that the Royal Navy had its own plans and followed them with little awareness of, or interest in, what the other two services were doing – or so it seemed. The RAF was represented by Air Chief Marshal Sir Cyril Newall, whose grand-sounding rank in fact only placed him on a level with my father as a full general and who, with date of rank from April 1937, was in fact the junior member of the trio. He was, however, the longest-serving member, having assumed the post of Chief of the Air Staff in September 1937. In this guise, he had facilitated the introduction of the new monoplane fighters that would enable the RAF to face the Luftwaffe on equal qualitative terms, during the course of which process he became increasingly distanced from the conventional RAF policy of a war-winning strategic bombing offensive.

Although Newall would outlast my father on the committee, this rejection of received dogma made him a marked man in his own service and would ensure his removal on political grounds barely a year into the war. In the short term, since Allied bombing of Germany was forbidden on political grounds while the Luftwaffe, committed to Poland, lacked the aircraft to seriously threaten British airspace, the RAF had only a limited role.

Thus, with the navy disinclined to discuss its plans, the bulk of the concerns of the COS Committee were with matters pertaining to the army. After his first meeting on 4 September, my father summed up the two men, noting, 'Pound is very deaf and hardly says anything except on naval subjects. Newall is quick and sketchy.' He went on to observe that they had 'got through our work very quickly and I refused to have any endless talk'.[3]

Although the heads of the three services were not formally part of the War Cabinet, it became accepted practice that they functioned as its in-house military advisers on most occasions. Chamberlain had assembled a surprisingly small team to help him direct the war effort composed, in addition to himself, of only eight other ministers. Over and above the service ministers, these comprised Chancellor of the Exchequer Sir John Simon, and the foreign secretary, Lord Halifax, plus Sir Samuel Hoare and Lord Hankey, whose somewhat nebulous positions as lord privy seal and minister without portfolio respectively served to get their expertise into the Cabinet without tying them to a particular remit. The inclusion of the three service ministers, Churchill, Hore-Belisha and Wood, in the Cabinet rendered the post of minister for co-ordination of defence somewhat redundant, but for the time being this position was maintained and filled by the veteran former First Sea Lord Admiral of the Fleet Lord Chatfield.

My father was impressed with Chamberlain's calmness now that the war that he had tried so hard to avoid was upon him, but was less impressed with the rest of the Cabinet, registering his particular disgust after his second Cabinet session as follows:

> A futile meeting. Some of the Ministers sharpening their wits on each other, but it took us some hours to hear the situation from the fighting services. I felt like explaining things to a lot of old gentlemen. The only men in the room were Winston, Kingsley Wood, and Belisha, the rest were a nuisance and asked a lot of questions that we hadn't time to answer.[4]

My father had arrived at this particular meeting directly after a tiring and tiresome flying visit to Paris, of which more anon, but even allowing for the fact that this was unlikely to have left him in the best of tempers, it is a telling indictment of the rest of Chamberlain's team that even Hore-Belisha was deemed a better man than they. What was more, as time went on even Chamberlain himself failed to maintain the initial good impression he had made, with my father deploring his lack of vigorous leadership and observing that in meetings 'he initiates nothing but discussion of the most futile kind'.[5]

Insofar as the Polish situation was concerned, those directing Britain's war effort could do little more than watch. The Royal Navy could not operate in the Baltic in the face of German aircraft and submarines, and even flying from France British bombers could not reach Polish airspace. My father's initial reading of events was that the opening German attacks were intended to pin the Poles in place and that the main blow would come from the south, out of Hitler's puppet Slovak Republic. In fact, the reverse was the case, with only secondary attacks out of Slovakia, and this had become apparent by 5 September. Reports from Britain's diplomatic and military representatives in Warsaw were patchy, and such word as did get through was not positive. On 8 September, my father interviewed:

> ... a frantic young officer sent by Carton de Wiart, who has gone to Lyublin, to explain the agony of the Pole. The Polish Army have not been able to counterattack owing to the low-flying bombers, who have prevented them advancing. It is a thing I have been attempting in vain to put into the British officers in command here. I shall now try to do it again by sending for them and putting one last effort into them. We are, of course, far better armed than the Poles.[6]

All, it seemed, that could be gained from the Polish situation was an awareness of German military methods and whatever time that a Polish defence could buy before Hitler turned his divisions to the West, and the progress of the Polish campaign was summarised as part of the weekly résumés produced by the COS Committee for consideration by the War Cabinet. These summaries emphasised the advantages that had accrued to the German forces through their having obtained air superiority, but also attributed much of the success of the German armoured and mechanised units to the unusually dry conditions.

The Poles were credited with some isolated success against isolated German mechanised troops, but were critiqued for their overconfidence and failure to carry out tactical withdrawals to prevent troops being cut off.[7] Initial hopes that the Poles might at the least hold on through the winter – hopes that were already fading as Warsaw came under siege barely two weeks into the fighting – were dashed once and for all when the USSR joined in this 'fourth partition of wretched Poland'.[8] With the final Polish collapse, all attention could now be given to the war in the West, which had always been the theatre of primary concern so far as the British Army was concerned.

It was as a result of this priority that my father, along with Newall, had flown to France the day after Britain declared war to meet with the French C-in-C, General Maurice Gamelin. The two senior officers were flown over in an RAF plane from Hendon, taking a low and circuitous route to keep clear of barrage balloons and clouds:

> Landed at Le Bourget after 2hr 20 minutes & to Vincenees where we found Gamelin installed in the old fortress in a war HQ. A small dapper little man with dyed hair. The Air Commander of the NE, a big fat common man with a common accent. After some time I got Gamelin to explain his plan. He had finished mobilisation [on the] 5th and was commencing his concentration at once. He intended to start at once – if he had not done so already – to move up into the no man's land between the Maginot & Siegfried Lines. Still inside his own country in three salients from the NE corner to the Luxembourg frontier. He would squeeze out these pockets & by the 17th hoped to be facing the Siegfried Line. He would then bring up his heavy artillery & try his experiment on the line. All very steady and calm.
>
> He reported German concentrations – he thought they were defensive – against the Luxembourg frontier. He hoped that the Germans would attack him there. He was delighted at having completed mobilisation without any bombing. Was nervous of his concentration.[9]

As time went on and it became clear that nothing could be done to help the Poles either directly or indirectly, such French enthusiasm for the offensive as had initially existed quickly disappeared and the focus shifted instead to preparations to meet a German offensive in the West. Britain, too, focused her military attentions to the coming fight for France, which at least meant that planning for the possibility of sending British troops to the Balkans with a view to combined operations with the Turks – who, in fact, chose to remain neutral – against Germany's southern strategic flank could be shelved. Such an operation, as envisaged, would have enabled a link-up with the Polish forces fighting with their backs to the Romanian border, and also with any Czech resistance or uprising, and might well have served to bring Romania into the Allied camp as well.

On a wider level, such a scheme would also secure the eastern Mediterranean and the Suez Canal, and thus safeguard imperial lines of communication. My father had initially favoured these operations, harking back as they did to some of his pre-war thinking, and he argued strongly for them in a paper of 7 September. In this he predicted a static war on the Western Front which would allow surplus British troops and all available Indian and Dominion forces to be employed offensively in southern Europe. It was essential, he argued, that Britain retain the command of this theatre and he was therefore suspicious of the French having given command of their forces in the Levant to the very senior General Weygand as this smacked of an attempt to have their own man-in-waiting as Allied C-in-C in the theatre.

Had these schemes been pushed further then no doubt there would have been much unseemly inter-Allied wrangling, which would likely have been further complicated had the Turks been brought into the Allied camp as my father hoped. In the event, however, the intervention of the USSR in Poland and the complete collapse of Polish resistance eliminated the *raison d'être* of the whole scheme.

Although the idea of Turkey forming a bulwark against a German drive into the Middle East would linger for a little while yet, as early as 24 September my father was counselling in a second paper against any premature involvement in the Balkans, lest it provoke Italy and expose any new allies that Britain might acquire to being immediately overrun in the way that Serbia and Romania had been in the previous war.

Even without a potential second front to think about, those directing British strategic planning were quickly obliged to consider the requirements of a lengthy fight. At the end of the first week of war, my father observed:

> I have had time to audit the Army in the few days in which I have been in power and my main job is to get across [to France] the contingents envisaged. If I can do that, I can perhaps see how to accelerate the process. It is a young Army. The C-in-C only commanded a Bn. in the last war and has never commanded anything since. Even this first contingent has deficiencies of a very serious nature. It is only when one comes to the Bds. and Bns. that our strength is shown.
>
> Even this first Contingent has deficiencies of a very serious nature. To the Ministers only yesterday I gave the details in full. Winston & Coy. were horrified when I produced the figures.[10]

Churchill's dismay was due to the fact that he had been pushing for the despatch of twenty British divisions to France in the first six months of the war. Even when it was made clear that Britain did not have the resources to equip a force of that size in that timeframe, his response had been to hope that it would be possible to borrow equipment from French stocks, a 'solution' that obliged my father to point out that even if this could somehow be arranged the men would also require training. At length, in planning for a three-year war the decision was taken to build towards an active force of thirty-two divisions. Of these, twenty were to be in the line in France by September 1940. However, my father was later compelled in light of the need to maintain a force in the Middle East to reduce the latter figure to fifteen, of which one was to be a Canadian division, with four more on hand in Britain as a reserve and the equivalent of twelve more in the Middle East. This policy of a slow build-up was in line with the more generic strategic choice to stand on the defensive in Europe until sufficient strength had been assembled and only then to shift to an offensive strategy.

Almost from the outset, however, there were difficulties in working effectively with the French command. As early as 12 September, with the BEF still in the early stages of its deployment to France, my father was obliged to write directly and personally to Gamelin to request him to use his influence to prevent the French press publishing details of the British deployments which, further magnified by re-reporting through the US media, could well reveal details of BEF shipping and deployments.[11]

As time went on, and it was clear that the French proposed to sit tight behind the Maginot Line, the role, dispositions and security of the BEF continued to present concerns to which the French seemed unable to supply viable answers. To be sure, compared with the nine field armies in the French order of battle, the BEF contribution was relatively insignificant and its role magnified by political rather than military concerns. Major General Sir Richard Howard-Vyse, the head of British Military Mission with the French high command, found the French noncommittal when it came to assisting with material and equipment to help supply the BEF. He reported too that Gamelin showed no inclination to make offensive plans. The French did, however, continue to press for British reinforcements, which were deemed necessary to enable the BEF to hold the Allied left flank, north of the Maginot Line, facing the wide open frontier with neutral Belgium. Eventually, a number of Territorial divisions would be sent, without their heavy equipment, to complete their training in France – very much an empty gesture as the troops were of use only for labouring duties behind the lines.

My father reviewed these concerns, and others, in a lengthy diary reflection on the strategic situation in the aftermath of the fall of Poland and the Nazi-Soviet Pact:

> It will be interesting to see how this develops as the time goes on. There are really no indications that the Germans are going to invade Belgium and Holland. But we ought to be able to have timely information. There are many reports that Germany will invade Holland first. I am doubtful if the Dutch could put up much of a show if this was attempted. It is quite a possible move. It will naturally make it clear that the Germans intend to invade Belgium later. It will mean that the Belgian northern defences are already turned and that they will stand less time than ever. Even if Holland being invaded gave away the intention of the Germans as regards Belgium, we should hardly have the time to move up and come into line with the Belgian defences on the Albert Canal, the Maastricht Peninsula and Liege. We wouldn't get there in time. We must study our line in France on the Franco–Belgian frontier.

> The French are pressing us more & more to send out all we have to France. They seem to be adopting the usual attitude of all politicians – forgetting what was agreed in peace. They think we have any number of men available and that we are holding them up our sleeve. We agreed to send 4 Divisions and nothing more. Even that [sic] is not as well trained as they should be and, as I have so often told people, fighting & training are difficult things to do cheaply at the same time. We are now sending over to France all we can scrape up to augment this force – which by the way, only has half its strength in France by tomorrow, the 24th.[12]

Although my father was incorrect in his expectation that Germany would attack first the Netherlands and then Belgium in two separate operations, he had grasped the gist of the enemy planning and identified the main area of vulnerability on the Allied left flank. Indeed, at this stage of the war German planning was for a strike west hinged on a strong 'right hook' through the Low Countries. It was only after it was feared that this plan had been compromised through documents falling into Allied hands from a crashed aircraft, that the riskier Manstein Plan, with a weaker attack through the Low Countries and a main thrust by a reinforced left wing attacking through the Ardennes, was adopted.

Because the governments of both the Netherlands and Belgium positively refused to entertain the idea of Allied troops crossing their borders unless in response to an actual German attack, nothing could be done to resolve the awkward and potentially dangerous role assigned to the BEF by French planning. Under Gamelin's scheme, once the Germans had shown their hand, the 1st Army Group, under General Gaston Billotte and including the BEF, would advance into Belgium – initially to the line of the Escaut, but later to the River Dyle – to check the German advance. These operations, respectively 'Plan E' and 'Plan D', would come under the overall direction of the commander of the French northern armies, General Alphonse Georges. The question which remained unanswered was whether the Allies would be able to get there in time to secure these new positions: my father, as we have seen, feared that they would not.

As well as visiting Gort and the BEF troops in France, my father took part in a number of discussions with French and Belgian representatives during the autumn in which these options were developed and it seems from the historical records that he was briefly able to convince the mercurial Gamelin of his own accurate predictions of the intended German axis of advance. Both men were also trying to do their best to judge when the German blow might fall, each at different times expecting an attack in the autumn, although my father ultimately came round to the view that, German troop build-up notwithstanding, Hitler would wait until the spring.

Gamelin's appreciation was that an attack was likely in late October or early November. In fact, the Frenchman had guessed right and only bad weather thwarted Hitler's plans for an attack beginning on 12 November. However, German preparations for this abortive attack were sufficiently far advanced for the Dutch and Belgians to take fright and, although continued bad weather led to the German operations being delayed until the following year, the impetus of such obvious signs of an attack via the Low Countries sooner rather than later brought about another major Allied planning conference on 9 November at which Plan D was formally adopted. My father entered the conference with substantial doubts of the abilities of 1st Army Group to reach the line of the Escaut, let alone the Dyle, and so his subsequently recommending its adoption to the War Cabinet is something that requires further explanation, best furnished in his own words.

My father received Gamelin's call to attend the conference early in the afternoon of the 8th and travelled across that afternoon by destroyer from Dover and thence by special train. Upon arrival in Paris he went straight to bed, correctly anticipating a long and tiring day to come, which he subsequently recorded as follows:

> A full stage Conference with Gamelin. Newall is so uncertain that he eventually asked me to speak English, so that could understand what I was saying. I agreed – and then had to listen to a very bad interpreter repeating what I said. I had a bit with Gamelin afterwards and put our point of view. It is a dreadful pull on one's temper having an airman, who cannot speak French and doesn't understand military movement.
>
> Gamelin & Georges told us distinctly what was in their minds.
>
> Gamelin said that it was impossible for Hitler to remain doing nothing during the winter. That he was temperamentally not in a state to stay directing affairs without doing something. Therefore he was preparing something, though what that something was, he didn't know. He and Georges both thought it was a Blitzkrieg against Holland. They had been approached through their ambassador in Brussels to know what the French thought of this eventuality. They had been asked:
> (i)   Did they wish Belgium to remain neutral?
> (ii) Did they wish Belgium to join in?
>   In the second event
> (iii) What did the French propose to do?
>
> They had replied that they wished Belgium to join in and that they were studying what their action would be. Georges then took up the word and explained his plan. It was in general this:
> (i) A methodical advance into Belgium, based upon a definite knowledge of the situation at the moment & the time available for the advance.
> (ii) An advance to the line of the Scheldt [i.e. the Escaut; Plan E] as agreed already, from Maulde through Audenarde to Ghent & thence to the Dutch coast & the Scheldt.

(iii)   The sending forwards of light troops first to the line of the Dendre & then to the line Namur, Wavre, Louvain, Malines, Antwerp.
(iv)   There can be no question of fighting a battle on the Dendre. It must either be the line of the Scheldt or on the line in (iii).
He had no intention of being caught in a battle in the open as we had at Mons. The whole thing would be methodical and based upon the safe time available.
(v)   The occupation of the Dutch islands on the north and south of the Mouth of the Scheldt.

This was to be done by two Motorised Divisions moving up through Belgium, one to Kadsand, with the object of getting across to Walcheren & the other to move across the narrow neck leading into Beveland and Walcheren.

They also had a project of sending some men by sea from Dunkirk. This latter was, I thought, a project only & that it hadn't been considered carefully.

The operation for these islands would be one for the French, but they would gladly welcome a relief by British troops later.

I explained that we always wanted French troops on our left and might take this on as a temporary measure as the possession of the island was definitely of more use to us than to the French.

So far all had gone well.

Then we came to controversial question of the bombing of the Ruhr. I left Newall to do this himself and took practically no part. Twice Gamelin turned to Lelong & said 'je ne comprends pas'. In the end I was moved to pass across to him 'Oui moi non plus'. The French stated their case clearly.

(i)   They were not in any position to start unrestricted air war. They would be much better both from a fighter and a bomber point of view in March. Unless there was absolute necessity for it we should avoid it.
(ii)   That the bombing of the Ruhr would not have an immediate effect on the advance of the Germans through Belgium. It might produce a moral effect and it might produce a material effect within a fortnight or so, but no immediate, as the Germans would have collected all their stores well forward of the Ruhr.
(iii)   The French also expressed great doubt as to our ability to produce a stunning effect. The Ruhr was armed with 600 heavy AA guns & 2,500 light AA guns besides 280 fighter aeroplanes. Could we tackle all that?

Newall was very stupid & silly in putting his point. A heavy-heeled individual, who doesn't go down with the French at all. You can see their hackles going up every time he speaks.

The psychological moment to bomb the Ruhr is when the Germans enter Belgium and Holland. To do this one must have the machinery absolutely perfect or the moment will have passed. I don't believe that one could ever get the Machinery for this.

We then came back by train and destroyer, reaching London at 9.10 p.m.

Here I found a message saying that the cabinet was meeting at 9.30 p.m. & Belisha wanted me to see him before the meeting at his private house. This shows how little he thinks of other people. I telephoned him that I should not have time to come, far less explain all to him in 5 minutes. At the Cabinet meeting he was quite mild in saying 'I expected to see you before the meeting'. I told him that there was no time.

I found the Prime Minister was in bed with gout. [Sir John] Simon in the Chair. The cabinet not too well run as usual.

I explained what had happened and was at once asked if I thought the British Army ought to advance. I had to remind them twice that they had a C-in-C in France and that they had expressly put him under the orders of the French Commanders. The C-in-C had the right of protest to the Cabinet, but that until he protested – which he did not propose to do – they would be very ill-advised to step in. Gort had agreed and I had accepted the advance. This quietened them down completely.

I told them that we still had no communication with the Belgians and did not know what they were doing or when they would call upon us. Eventually a strong wire was sent to Brussels trying to get the Belgians to talk with us.

The British Army was to advance to the Scheldt between Maulde & Audenarde & thence to the line Wavre-Malines, if that is possible. It keeps us out of the way of the extreme left. I wondered how long we should be able to maintain that position and how soon we should find ourselves on the Albert Canal.

Then we had a go at the Ruhr. Impassioned speeches from all sides. The Supreme War Council is going to go over to France and try and make the French agree.

I got to bed thoroughly tired.[13]

One can see, therefore, that my father was placed in an impossible position with regards to his reservations about the plans for an advance into Belgium, being bound by political and diplomatic concerns to endorse – albeit on those grounds rather than military ones – a plan of operations regarding which he entertained considerable doubts. However, the Cabinet had chosen to subordinate the BEF to French command, and at BEF Headquarters Gort and Pownall were far more convinced of the validity of 'Plan D' than was my father. Caught in the middle, he had little ability to alter the decision. The War Cabinet, for its part, seemed more concerned with the air policy to be adopted in the event of German attack, and the minutes of the meeting at which my father made his report pass briefly over his comments in a manner that suggests that those present may not have appreciated the significance of the policy that they were being asked to endorse.[14]

It is unfortunate that, judging by Pownall's diaries, BEF Headquarters had now taken against both my father and Hore-Belisha, to the detriment of communications and co-ordination. Pownall, for example – who believed that my father's performance at the 9 November conference had come close to usurping Gort's authority as C-in-C – saw it as essential to the success of Plan D that all available air resources be thrown against advancing German troops rather than used for a blow against Germany itself, an appreciation which was clearly not fully shared back in London.[15] Equally, Pownall would have been less happy had he been aware of the complex and unworkable plans for air support of the troops being put forward by the RAF, which relied on the bombing of fixed points rather than attacks directed against identified troop concentrations, something that had my father seething within his diary in the aftermath of the November conference.

Nevertheless, the Allied armies were now awaiting the German attack committed to the plan that they would follow to disaster in May 1940. As they waited for the storm to break, over the winter of the aptly named 'Phoney War', the slowly growing BEF dug in along the Belgian frontier – a process which, in itself, would have unforeseen political consequences, as we shall see.

Along with political and strategic concerns, my father also had personal issues to deal with, one of which surrounded the attempted return to duty of 'Boney' Fuller. After his retirement from the army in 1933 as a major general, Fuller had become increasingly interested in the occult and in the politics of Fascism. Although unconnected, neither interest did anything for Fuller's credibility and standing in the eyes of the army, and before the war – ostensibly on the grounds that it would have upset the cycle of promotions, but no doubt because he was aware of how inappropriate the proposal would have sounded – my father had been obliged when GOC-in-C Eastern Command to block a background suggestion from Liddell Hart that he should use his place on the Selection Board to get Fuller back into the service.[16] Within a week of the outbreak of war, Fuller had sought out my father to investigate the possibility of his renewed employment, and the two men dined together on 8 September:

> Naturally, he was careful not to express his fascist feelings to me too strongly, because he wanted to know whether he would be employed or not. I wanted to see whether he had been tinged too much with German or Fascist sentiments. I have not seen him for a long time and I wanted to see what state he was in.
>
> I can only employ him as a brain with myself and under my control. I have to decide whether I could control him. Whether the rest of the Army would work with him, even under my protégé.

We have arranged to meet again. Had he not been away playing so long with these Mosley Fascists he might have been invaluable.[17]

Requests for employment from other retired officers – even one from Deverell – were easier to dismiss, but my father clearly had a great respect for Fuller's military abilities, as he had made clear when rebuffing Liddell Hart back in 1936, and saw them as an asset worth harnessing. Indeed, after a second meeting some weeks later my father, reservations about his politics notwithstanding, began to consider Fuller for a senior and central role at the War Office:

> I asked him if he was prepared to be brought back and if his political activities had been too deep for him to come back. As I expected, he said that his activities had been because he had nothing to do when he retired and wasn't going to remain idle. I am inclined to bring him back as DCIGS but I must first get Adam something to do. I might send him out as the new Corps Commander and so have his place vacant.
>
> Boney thought that we should make peace. Chiefly because he thought that France would give in. I don't believe in that. I think that we shall go on & that Germany shall be defeated. Then, will come the difficulty. Saving Germany from chaos if not bolshevism. Russia will be so strong that nobody can tackle her and she will in the end swallow up all the Baltic States and bolshevise them.[18]

My father had inherited Ronald Adam as DCIGS, and although nothing came of the idea to replace him with Fuller, Adam would in due course go to France to command the BEF's III Corps, composed of some of the first fully equipped Territorial divisions to go overseas. There is perhaps a touch of naivety – or, more generously, loyalty to an old friend – in my father's acceptance of Fuller's claims about his politics, particularly with his stated preference for making peace even now, but it would be hard to find more conclusive proof of my father's admiration for and support of Fuller as a military thinker. Nor was he the only senior general to consider Fuller sound: the future Lord Alanbrooke was another who gave Fuller a clean bill of political health and in fact actively defended him from investigation.[19] In the event, however, the risks of employing someone with Fuller's past and politics in such a position were deemed to represent too great a risk, and, although spared internment along with Mosely and other leading British Fascists, he remained the only retired officer of his rank not to be re-employed during the Second World War.

Another high-profile figure whose pre-war activities made him a potential security risk was the Duke of Windsor. However, ex-monarchs can deploy rather more clout than ex-major generals, and it was agreed that the duke should have an appointment and that his presence with the BEF in France would be an aid to morale. Facilitating this caused my father considerable difficulties, not least due to the attitude of the duke himself who, although agreeing to waive the honorary rank of field marshal that he had enjoyed as monarch and accept a major general's commission, balked at serving as a direct subordinate of Howard-Vyse, the head of the military mission. Having already spent more time than he cared to on facilitating the duke's whims, my father was less than pleased at this insubordination:

> Wretched little man. He gives me more bother than anybody else put together. I have written and told him that he has accepted an appointment in His Majesty's Army & must not regard himself as a free-lance. He is under General Howard-Vyse in his Mission. I haven't finished with the little devil yet. I suppose it is his wife that has put him up to this. He goes home and discusses everything with her.[20]

However, royal blood carried more weight in Republican France than might have been assumed, with Gamelin writing to my father that it was particularly agreeable to him '*de faciliter la tache de son Altesse Royale*' and appreciating the honour of having the duke assigned to liaise with his staff.[21] This opened the doors for the duke to have tête-à-tête talks with the French generals, which were denied to the members of Howard-Vyse's mission. As he carried out his tours of inspection, he was able to close the gap between protocol and practice and his formal reports were accompanied by candid private letters. In the first of these, he said:

> I have dealt at length in the first report with the obvious weaknesses and defects of the French defenses [sic] along the Belgian frontier to the NW of the Maginot Line on from where the main defence system stops, and the only remarks 'off the record' I have to add here concern the difference in the attitude of the French and ourselves to the gentle art of digging in. I have drawn attention to the fact that the French are not working against time; the fact is that they are not working at all as far as I could see, whereas I know that Gort has the 1st British Corps digging hard which not only strengthens the main defences but also has the advantage of getting the men fit.
> I think the French look at it this way. The word fitness does not exist in their vocabulary and they would agree what is the use of digging trenches that may never be used and anyway they are determined if possible to give the Germans battle in Belgium. Of course, they would burrow like rabbits at the sound of the first shell, but French logic says never dig until you have to.[22]

The letter concluded with a personal summary of the duke's opinion of the French senior command – noncommittal about Gamelin and Georges, but with more praise for Billotte and particularly for Corap of Ninth Army. The duke would remain in France, furnishing additional appraisals of this nature but still plagued with rumours about the extent of his pre-war relationship with the Nazis, until after the German invasion. Thereafter, he was shunted off to spend the rest of the war as governor of the Bahamas to keep him out of trouble.

The most significant of the personal problems facing my father, however, was the ongoing tension with Hore-Belisha. Whatever his merits as peacetime secretary of state, he seemed to my father increasingly unfit to fill the role in wartime and after less than a fortnight of hostilities my father had had enough:

> I woke up to think of Belisha. He is, of course, quite incompetent to run an Army either in peace or war. I have now had ten days of him and he cannot get on without me. He talks of me being a great combination with him. But he produces very little of the aforesaid combination but intrigue and answering in the House of Commons. How much the House of Commons will sit under heavy bombing, I do not know.

He went on to muse over a solution that had been employed in the previous war, when Kitchener had been brought into the Cabinet:

> I believe that the only solution is to put in a soldier instead of Belisha, with a very good Undersecretary of State to run the House of Commons thing & let the soldier get on with the work. I have been spat into funny places & might even be spat in there, but I am not going to try to produce such a job for myself. It is written. That is enough for me and I must do my best at the moment where I am to see that the Army doesn't fall down.[23]

No doubt my father was very wise not to put himself forward as a potential replacement for Hore-Belisha. Such an attempt would surely have been perceived as self-aggrandising and intriguing, and would almost certainly have proved counter-productive. However, Hore-Belisha's tenure at the War Office was almost up, although the manner of his fall would prove a fairly undignified experience for all concerned.

In brief, what brought things to a head was the unlikely matter of the defences being constructed along the Franco–Belgian border, which Hore-Belisha was taken to view when he paid a visit to the BEF in mid-November. He had paid a low-key visit two months previously, not long after the first troops had gone over, but this was a high-profile affair with the press in attendance and the BEF top brass out in force. For Gort, however, as even his own biographer admits, it was an excuse to belittle the secretary of state, who was deliberately subjected to 'every form of climatic and gastronomic discomfort that Gort's Spartan regime could provide'.[24]

At his own request, Hore-Belisha's itinerary had been designed so that he saw the troops rather than the defences and this focus, combined with a misunderstood reference to the speed with which the French were constructing pillboxes, led him to come away with the conclusion that the British were less efficient than their allies and were lagging behind in the construction of defences, whereas in fact, as the Duke of Windsor had noted, the reverse was the case. Worse still, this view was shared by the representatives of the Dominion powers who accompanied Hore-Belisha on his tour, and he passed this concern on, in conjunction with his own advice to take heed of the French methods, in an extremely tactless letter to Gort dated 22 November. He also raised the matter with the Army Council, which drew my father into the whole affair.

As my father observed in a diary entry for 28 November, which served somewhat as a summary of his recent activities, he had 'been hard put to it these last few days' attempting to force through the provision of equipment for the divisions serving in France and this affair was very much an unwelcome distraction:

> Then I have had what amounts to an attack on Gort for not having done enough work in the time. Our Belisha waited until I had left the Cabinet and then made a statement upon what he had seen in France. None of the Cabinet appears to have questioned what he said or to have thought of asking for professional advice. So, I told Belisha that he must not lower the prestige of the C-in-C in the eyes of the Cabinet without telling him. I told him that I would go over to France at once & inspect the line thoroughly and make a report. I have only seen it once some weeks ago and I shall be able to see the difference. What swine these people are. They have not the courage to say things straight out.[25]

My father left on 29 November, returning on 2 December. Unfortunately, the telegram sent to apprise Gort of my father's impending arrival included the phrase that he was 'to inspect defences in BEF area on War Cabinet instructions', something which, according to his biographer, Hore-Belisha deeply resented as he had given no such instructions. He had, however, impressed upon Gort's engineer-in-chief, Major General R.P. Pakenham-Walsh, that more work on defences must be done, so there was no question in BEF Headquarters but that the secretary of state was unhappy.

For his part, Hore-Belisha seemed oblivious to the offence caused by his intervention and apparently believed – as later reported by Major (later Major General Sir) Francis de Guingand, then serving as his military assistant – that he was offering helpful advice rather than criticism.[26] Only when my father arrived at Gort's headquarters did he realise how serious matters had become, noting that Gort was 'insisting to have the Prime Minister informed'.[27]

My father spent a day going over the line held by each of the two BEF corps, in the same awful weather conditions that had blighted Hore-Belisha's visit. After his day with Dill's I Corps, he wrote:

> One and all were cursing Belisha at being such a swine as to accuse them of not having done any work. This will be remembered against him for a long time and his name will stink in their nostrils. Dill said that he could hardly speak civilly to him.[28]

It was worse still with Brooke's II Corps, where the evidence from the generals seemed to suggest that Hore-Belisha had actively sought criticism of Gort from his subordinates, 'for he took Montgomery one of the Divisional Commanders, aside and asked him if the Commander-in-Chief came round often. This is pretty thick for a filthy little Jew.'[29] As is clear from the language that he employed, this revelation marked a serious drop in my father's already low estimation of Hore-Belisha.

For his part, my father was impressed with the progress of the defensive work and, more generally, with the conduct of the officers and troops, finding particular praise for Dill and noting of the brigade commanders that 'they are all young men well on their toes'. Together, my father and the generals put together a lengthy paper explaining the affair. It was, he thought, enough to secure Hore-Belisha's dismissal but suspected that it would never be used as such and that the secretary of state would 'oil out of it thoroughly as usual'.[30]

On his return, my father reported to Hore-Belisha in what quickly became a heated exchange. Hore-Belisha believed that my father should have calmed things down, while my father sought to impress upon him how deeply offended were the commanders of the BEF. More to the point, Hore-Belisha had lost their confidence and trust and, as he confided to his diary but did not tell the secretary of state to his face, that of my father also.

For the moment, things died down, but Gort's position was soon again under threat, this time because it was intimated that the French were dissatisfied with him and would prefer to see Dill in command of the BEF. This provoked an interesting and revealing summary from my father of the relative merits of the British Army's senior generals, himself included:

> It is curious how people intrigue against our Army Comdrs. Gort has not been tried, not at all. Dill is a staff officer & has not had any command in war. Gort did command a Bn. The best man we have is undoubtedly Wavell, but he has never been given a chance of commanding anything. But he is a soldier & a thinker. He is undoubtedly in the right place in the Middle East. He does not impress politicians because he never says anything. You can make him an impassioned speech & when you stop he says 'Yes' or 'No'.

The next best man we have is Brooke, in command of the 2nd Corps. He has great ability & has commanded all sorts of things in peace. He can think & talk, too, which makes him more acceptable to the politicians.

In the last war French & Haig were constantly being intrigued against. Politicians take violent fancies to men who express any ideas which they agree with.

Dill would make a good CIGS, far better than I am I have no doubt, but not a Comdr. I don't think he has the nerve. I know him intimately & he is a staff officer pure & simple.[31]

In fact, there was more intrigue afoot than my father knew, for as his diaries reveal Hore-Belisha was asked by Chamberlain on 14 December, only two days after my father had penned the above, whether he had confidence in Gort and my father. Notwithstanding the prime minister's heavy hint that both men could be replaced if the secretary of state thought it necessary, Hore-Belisha answered in the affirmative on both counts. Hore-Belisha's biographer calls this a serious error on the part of his subject, for it was clearly not viable for all parties to continue in their current roles when the CIGS and C-in-C lacked confidence in the secretary of state. By refusing to sack the generals, in whom he retained confidence, Hore-Belisha had effectively ensured the end of his tenure at the War Office.[32]

As the snowfall impeded any German winter advances on the Continent, the stately fall from office of the secretary of state for war puzzled the London press. Chamberlain was keen to keep Hore-Belisha in government, if not in the War Office, and was all for moving him to the Ministry of Information – in charge of our propaganda – until Lord Halifax pointed out what a boon it would be to Goebbels if Britain were to give such a post to a Jew. The Board of Trade was then offered, but this would have been a demotion and so Hore-Belisha instead elected to resign.

My father's reflection on his departure was curiously dispassionate considering how deeply he had come to loathe him, but the comparison that he drew between Hore-Belisha and his replacement, Oliver Stanley, perhaps does a lot to explain why Hore-Belisha had struggled to hold, and ultimately lost, the confidence of his generals. In his diary entry of 6 January, my father wrote:

At 8 p.m. last night when I went to see Belisha's secretary I was told he had resigned. I had no inkling that it was coming. Changing horses in mid-stream is always a bad thing, but I must say that I had a feeling of intense relief on the whole. The man had failed utterly in war to run his show & we should have had a disaster. He is much better out of it. Oliver Stanley I just know and the main thing is that he is a gentleman, although I know nothing about his energy & determination. It will be much easier to get on with him.[33]

In the case of Stanley, no doubt it helped that he had been a Gunner in the last war, rising to the rank of captain; certainly, my father had every expectation that his new political master would have a better awareness of practical military matters.

For some time after Hore-Belisha's departure, the papers were full of speculation regarding the reasons for his fall, and the Beaverbrook press was strident in its demands that he be reinstated. For the army and for my father personally this coverage was something of a distraction from the stage-managed presentation of the Grand Cross of the Legion of Honour to my father and Gort at Arras on 8 January 1940 in front of the assembled press contingents. This was in response to the award of high British honours to Gamelin and Georges the previous month, and was an elaborate affair carried out with great dignity, albeit that my father found it amusing to see a detachment from the Welsh Guards keeping pace with the quickstep of the Zouave contingent who made up the French portion of the guard of honour. Gort, my father recorded, seemed careworn and it was clear that he felt some guilt over his part in Hore-Belisha's ousting.

I had been included in the party at General Gamelin's request and I recall seeing the presentation, with the Zouaves on guard in their ceremonial uniform. Later, our party carried out an inspection of the French portion of the front and were taken to see the troops and defences, including a British brigade which had been placed under temporary French command in order to obtain some experience on an active front. I also accompanied my father when we were taken round the Maginot Line and we were shown into one of the underground gun emplacements in its fixed and immovable bastion.

After the last full day of our tour, which ended on 11 January with a return to Britain on the destroyer HMS *Basilisk*, my father recorded his impression of the French forces that we had visited:

> I tried in my mind to sum up the state of the French Army and its fighting value. I must say that I saw nothing amiss with it on the surface. The generals are all tried men, if a little old from our viewpoint. None of them showed any lack of confidence. None of the liaison officers, Swayne or the Duke of Windsor say that they have seen any lack of morale after the long wait they have had, after the excitement of mobilisation. I say to myself that we shall not know until the first clash comes. In 1914 there were many officers & men who failed, but old Joffre handled the situation with great firmness. Will the Blitzkrieg, when it comes, allow us to rectify things if they are the same. I don't know. But I say to myself we must have confidence in the French Army. It is the only thing in which we can have confidence. Our own Army is just a little one & we are dependent on the French. We have not even the same fine Army we had in 1914. All depends on the French Army & we can do nothing about it, but it is up to us to back it up & not to deny it. The only thing I can say is that the men are not doing the

amount of work in digging in which I should like to have seen. Gamelin is not downhearted & has breathed not one word of worry to me. I shouldn't have expected that he would. He is very anxious that the Boche should attack & I think he would welcome a trial of strength. The French air is frightfully weak and especially in fighter aircraft. Again we can do nothing about it.

Gort has given me no inkling that he finds anything seriously amiss with the French Army. None of his staff have even whispered doubts. Gammell the British Brigadier I found in the French line, made no mention of any doubts. His men had, of course, not mixed with the French troops but they showed no uneasiness. The issue is in the lap of the Gods & we can do nothing to alter things. We must remain loyal to the French.[34]

19

Scandinavian Sideshow

As my father left France and set foot again in England, the situation in Scandinavia was developing in a manner that made British involvement there an increasingly likely probability. Actions were already being taken to realise the risks before the fall of Hore-Belisha, so Oliver Stanley was not able to avoid taking account of the situation upon taking up his posting as secretary of state, thereby having to grasp the weapons of the diplomatic battle on a much wider front.

For both sides in the war, Scandinavia was of strategic importance for a number of reasons. For Germany, access to Swedish iron ore, mined in the far north of the country, was an important requirement for the running of its war machine, and Swedish neutrality served to ensure that the Baltic remained, in effect, a German lake and an open corridor for trade. For Britain, the denial of these resources to Germany was of paramount importance, and there was also the concern from a naval point of view with relation to German abuses of Norwegian neutrality as a means of circumventing the Allied naval blockade. This was particularly important during the winter months, when the Gulf of Bothnia froze over and prevented iron ore shipments by the Baltic route – the alternative was for the ore to be transported by train to the Norwegian port of Narvik, and thence shipped southwards to Germany. Unless Britain violated Norwegian territorial waters either by laying mines or by directly intercepting German ore ships – measures which Churchill at the Admiralty had proposed but which had been denied on diplomatic grounds – nothing could be done to prevent these shipments.

Since the Chamberlain government took an essentially reactive approach to the development of the war, those pressing for more assertive action had to wait on events. The situation was changed, however, by Russia's 30 November attack on Finland, which opened the so-called Winter War. Notwithstanding Russian expectations of a steamroller advance, the Finns put up a stout resistance and this created the option for a second front in Scandinavia. Although both Sweden and Norway reaffirmed their neutrality, it was hoped that they might at least be prevailed upon to allow the passage of British and French troops through their territory. By landing at Narvik, such troops would, by virtue of their presence, be able to prevent the use of that port for German ore shipments and would also be in a position if necessary to take control of the Swedish mines themselves.

Although a German response was deemed extremely likely, this would not in itself be a bad thing as it would divert German manpower away from future offensive operations. The response of the COS Committee to the Winter War was therefore to recommend that a small force sent to Scandinavia would exert an influence out of proportion to its size:

> There is a further important consideration which should be taken into account if Germany invades either Norway or Sweden. In order to dispute our control of the Northern Swedish ore fields Germany would have to despatch a considerable force and this would entail an appreciable dispersion of her effective strength. The force which we should be compelled to send to achieve this would be in comparison small and could be withdrawn if necessary.[1]

The danger, conversely, was that if Britain delayed then Germany might send troops to secure the resources itself, possibly by means of an invasion of Norway. In that eventuality, Britain would be caught on the back foot although my father entertained doubts as to the ability of the German armed forces to mount a successful amphibious operation of this scale.

With a strong case for intervention on both diplomatic and military grounds, the War Cabinet was generally favourable to the concept, albeit with concerns from the Air Ministry for the overstretching of their resources. Unsurprisingly, however, the overtures to the Swedish and Norwegian Governments were rejected and although British planning continued, it was not possible to send any effective aid to the Finns, let alone interfere with the ore shipments. Nevertheless, the diplomatic game continued, requiring Britain to have forces available to potentially deploy to the Scandinavian theatre: something which acted as a counterweight to French demands for more British troops in France, and necessitated a careful juggling of priorities.

This, then, was essentially the situation as it stood in January 1940. On 12 January, my father in his role as CIGS met with his new political master ahead of that day's War Cabinet meeting, at which the Scandinavian situation was high on the agenda. His impression of the secretary of state was favourable:

> The relief was literally immense not to have that little swine Belisha clogging up our work. Stanley had already read up all the papers on Scandinavia and I had about ½ hour with him. He was able to take the thing at the War Cabinet without any further coaching.

> Eventually, it was decided not to do the Narvik violation of Norwegian Territorial Waters [i.e. the laying of mines], much to the disgust of Winston. Two

factors which turned the PM against the project. First the violent reaction of Sweden at the idea and second a wire from Australia expressing mistrust in the advisability of doing anything so violent.

It was then decided that Sam Hoare, who is supposed to have special relations with Scandinavia, should go to Stockholm and try to arrange with the Swedish Govt. There seems to be little hope of our being able to anything with their consent, and we appear to be too weak to take a strong line. Buying the mines at Gällivare and getting Sweden to restrict the passage of ore to Germany were all put forward in turn. The position is most delicate, because Norway & Sweden are terrified of having war in their country.[2]

My father's initial favourable impression of Stanley, justified by this meeting, was sustained as their relationship developed, with the politician quick to grasp the information that my father gave him on the military situation and able to convey it effectively to his Cabinet colleagues. It was a refreshing change from the days of Hore-Belisha.

Later on the 12th, Brigadier Ling, who had been sent to report on the situation in Finland, returned with a personal letter from the Finnish commander, Field Marshal Mannerheim, asking for help and pleading, insofar as a proud and distinguished soldier could plead, that such help should not be long delayed. Even Mannerheim was aware, however, that nothing could be done without Swedish aid and asked that, above all, Britain should not act in such a way as to cause the Swedes to cut Finland off from the outside world.

With this additional intelligence, my father put together a paper on the options that Britain might now take, noting in particular the relative ease with which Germany could move against Gällivare and the mines by sea, whereas Britain would have to come in overland via Narvik and would need to move during winter to be in place to pre-empt a German occupation in the spring. This would require British troops trained and equipped for arctic conditions, and measures were set up to create such a force.

The other imperative for Britain to act before the ice melted was that Mannerheim had stated his opinion that, without help, the Finns would likely not be able to hold out beyond May. In order to prevent this eventuality, the concluding portion of my father's paper discussed the options for sending volunteers to fight alongside the Finns. This was no easy option, for Mannerheim anticipated the need for some 30,000 foreign volunteers if he was to stop the Russians and only 3,000 Swedes had come forward. If Britain were to assist in providing the balance, the army would have to be involved to a considerable degree. This would present further problems, as my father outlined:

To train such volunteers seems to me to be an impossible task and to equip them almost equally so. They will be from many different countries if such an appeal succeeds and we and the French must supply. Finland asks specifically that the men should be sent in small packets to Finland.

To demobilise some of our trained soldiers and ask them to volunteer seems to me to offer very many difficulties politically and militarily.[3]

In the event, small numbers of volunteers did go to aid the Finns, including some British Army personnel who notionally left the service before departure, but the total number of non-Scandinavian volunteers was relatively insignificant. Material aid, including aircraft, was also sent by Britain and France. The onset of spring would bring about renewed planning for overt military action but, for the moment, the main focus of attention reverted to France and the Low Countries where a new development served as a reminder of the impending German attack.

The steady shift of German forces from the Polish theatre to the Western Front was alarming in itself and clear sign that the storm was about to break, but the attention of both the Allied and neutral powers was sharply focused on the aftermath of the so-called Mechelen Incident of 10 January, in which documents relating to the German plans for an imminent offensive in the west fell into Belgian hands after an aircraft carrying a staff officer of airborne troops crash-landed in Belgium after losing their way. As noted in the previous chapter, this security breach was ultimately responsible for the delay to, and recasting of, German preparations to produce the Manstein Plan, which was eventually implemented in April 1940. In the short term, however, the main product of the incident was to test the patience of the Allied powers as the Belgians dithered over how best to respond.

The first indication to my father that something was amiss was in the early hours of 13 January, when news was received that the Belgians were expecting an attack on themselves and the Dutch. Although there was substantial dissent amongst the Allies as to whether the plans were genuine or part of a deception tactic, my father had little doubt in their validity, noting that although it was of course bad practice for a staff officer to travel by air with papers of such importance, 'the same thing happened to me in Turkey'.[4] More important in his mind was what ought to be done which, for a further twenty-four hours, amounted to not very much.

Then, at midnight on the night of 13–14 January, the British ambassador in Brussels was summoned to the Belgian foreign minister to be told that the Belgians expected to be attacked that morning and 'that he expected HM's Govt. and the French Govt. to give full support'. My father was awoken with this news at 4 in the morning on the 14th, and all preparations were set in motion to be ready to implement Plan D, but the attack never came:

I told Chatfield this morning that it was intolerable that the Belgians should treat us like this. Refusing to have any conversations so we can concert operations and then screaming for help. There is no doubt that the Belgians thought they were going to be attacked, for they recalled 40,000 men from leave and various duties. I have sent a wire to Gamelin asking him to bring matters with the Belgians to a head.

We have to undertake a movement from a prepared position across a very flat plain to lines of obstacles which have in no way been prepared. All to help a country resist invasion and a country which is so terrified of infringing its own neutrality that it will make no preparations. We risk an encounter battle for the sake of Belgium. It is indeed to our advantage to save the Belgian divisions from being destroyed, so that we may incorporate them in our army. And we keep the main force of the German airforce away from possible aerodromes on the Dutch & Belgian coasts.

It is thick mist over Belgium & it is freezing. I wonder how that would have suited:

(i) It facilitates movement off the roads in the country north of the Meuse – the Low Countries. It makes the crossing of frozen inundations possible. Though it is possible to lower the water level & so leave the ice without support.

(ii) The fog makes aeroplane action in support of marching columns almost impossible. It gives the columns a chance of marching unmolested and it certainly stops the field of view of the defence.

(iii) The fog must also make parachute landings out of the question.

(iv) With frozen roads the Ardennes, thus all the country in Belgium and Luxembourg south and east of the Meuse must be very difficult for troop movement.

The Germans have 44 divisions opposite Belgium and Luxembourg and they undoubtedly have an attack mounted. Nobody can tell how the Belgian troops will stand up to a German attack or how long they would be able to resist. The weakest part of this line is the Albert Canal which faces Holland to the north. If this goes, the whole of the back of the Liege & Meuse positions is exposed & the Belgian defence collapses. I have no knowledge of the nature of the defences on the Albert Canal, but I am sure that they are not in any way adequate. All digging must be at an end now & so no last minute works can be carried out.

Unless we can come up pretty close behind the Belgians I cannot believe that they would stand any heavy bombardment. We must advance methodically.[5]

Although there was no attack, the fallout from the Mechelen Incident indicated the clear existence of strained relations in a number of key areas. One, as we have seen, was the tension between the Allied powers and Belgium, but there was also tension between Britain and France over the issue of command of the BEF. Gamelin had difficulty accepting the fact that the inclusion of the BEF in the moves called for under Plan D – and therefore, in effect, his ability to implement the plan at all – was conditional on the approval of the British War Cabinet.

When it came to it, it took many hours and several meetings during the course of 14 January for the Cabinet to give that approval, which in itself showed the divisions within the Cabinet between Churchill – 'enthusiastic and full of energy', keen to act at once and seize the opportunity – and Chamberlain – 'negative and angry at the Belgians for making conditions'.[6] In the aftermath, however, Gamelin began to take steps to tighten his control over the BEF, having evidently decided that its saluting platform was made for him to stand on. At least in part this was motivated by infighting amongst the French generals, with suspicions in the high command of the BEF – noted by Pownall – that the real issue was not whether the BEF should be under French command, which Britain had already agreed to, but whether it should be subordinate to Georges as part of Billotte's First Army Group or directly under Gamelin's headquarters.

Since the British sector was directly sandwiched between two of Billotte's armies, it seemed to Gort and Pownall most appropriate for the BEF to remain subordinate to Georges and Billotte, at least until the summer of 1940 when, as additional forces became available, the headquarters of the British First and Second Armies would be activated and the BEF raised to the status of an army group in its own right. However, what seemed obvious to the men on the ground was less so to those playing politics, and my father was drawn into the situation at a time when his focus ought ideally to have been elsewhere. He visited the French high command at the end of January, but this was largely for the purposes of planning for intervention in Scandinavia and it was only at the end of the meeting that he noted a potential cause for concern after Gamelin confided in him:

> He told me that there were political things happening. That the Government might fall if nothing were done. I am told that Daladier is Gamelin's man and that Georges is Reynaud's. Perhaps Gamelin would be pleased if there were a change of PM.[7]

Paul Reynaud was then the minister of finance, and somewhat opposed to Prime Minister Édouard Daladier. When the issue of command was eventually broached, Gamelin had initially taken a hard line and declared that he had always considered the BEF in France as being under his orders, and not Georges', something that was made explicit in a letter that my father received on 19 February. My father, preferring to have the matter resolved once and for all, elected to refer the matter to the War Cabinet for a definitive answer. Pownall recorded that this was against the advice of Gort, who preferred to let things lie, but in the event it was Gort himself who, on 22 February, invited my father to come across to France and help resolve matters.[8]

The reticence at BEF Headquarters would seem to stem from the assumption, voiced by Pownall, that if matters were formally resolved then the BEF would end up under Gamelin rather than Georges. This would have been operationally difficult, but was surely better than the alternative solution of going to war without a defined chain of command and potentially have the BEF receiving conflicting orders from two different sources. It was, perhaps, more than Pownall could bear to credit my father with the tact required to resolve the situation in a manner favourable to the BEF, but in fact that is exactly what happened, albeit that it required a second trip to France before things were finally ironed out.

Taking passage by destroyer on 28 February with instructions from the Cabinet to get the matter settled, he spent the following day with Gamelin's Chief Staff Officer, Colonel Petibon, who explained the situation from the French point of view and noted that, as and when the Belgian Army came under Allied command, it too must necessarily come directly under Gamelin as Allied C-in-C. Both officers drew extensively on the command arrangements in force at the end of the First World War to further their arguments, but my father remained firm throughout that, while he personally would be happy to see the BEF remain directly under Gamelin, it was the wish of Gort and the War Cabinet that the BEF be subordinate to Georges and he was obliged to press for this outcome. He went to bed without, it would seem, any firm idea whether his arguments had been successful, but it soon became clear the following day that they had:

> I was over at Gamelin's HQ to find him in a good humour and ready to agree to leaving the Army under Georges. He went into a long description of how it was a matter '*d'aucune importance*'. He explained how he had arranged the Staff that he and Georges more or less shared in an extraordinary way. That Georges would succeed him, if he were to go. It was all over in 20 minutes and I left him to go off and see Daladier.[9]

If any rebuttal is needed of Pownall's criticisms of my father's abilities to represent the interests of the BEF, the above surely serves to supply it.

There matters apparently rested, but the collapse of Finnish resistance, leading to a peace treaty between Finland and the Soviets on 12 March, precipitated the fall of the Daladier government which was criticised for its refusal to send aid to the Finns while France was itself under threat. On 21 March, Reynaud was appointed to lead the French Cabinet and Daladier became minister of defence, which was thought to be a change for the better – it was certainly good for Gamelin, who remained under Daladier's protection and thus retained his post even though Reynaud lacked confidence in him.

In all events, things were certainly friendlier on 23 March when my father lunched with the French generals again, although the morning's conversation made it clear that there was an ongoing lack of confidence and understanding between the French generals and the new French Government:

> Georges laughed and talked away & was most affable. He wears a khaki glove over his left hand, owing to a wound & gets rheumatism in it if cold. It doesn't stop him using it. I saw only the most cordial relations between him and Gamelin. His staff told the liaison officers that our raising the question of command had cleared the air considerably for him, and they seemed grateful to us. So far, things have gone very well indeed, but there has been no adversity to try the relations. It is only in difficulty and in acute differences of opinion that one can test things out.[10]

However, the air of friendship was soured at the end of the month during General Gamelin's visit to Britain for talks. He stayed several nights in London and was taken by my father to review various troop formations undertaking training in England, including the new 1st Canadian Division which had arrived as the vanguard of a re-raised CEF:

> A secret paper from the Chief of Staff's bag was handed to the Manager of the Hyde Park Hotel late last night [29 March]. It was Gamelin's copy of all our intended operations. Really too appalling. Unbelievable. I got Kell and MI5 on to it at once. The story is roughly this: The paper was handed personally to Gamelin's Staff Officer on Thursday morning this was translated for him and he then left for the Embassy. Then on to the Supreme War Council, Gamelin having a French translation but not the original English copy. The French say they cannot believe it was left in their room. During Thursday morning [28 March] a Scots maid found it and consulted with a Scots waiter on the floor. Both are very confused in their statements but apparently it was found on a table. On the advice of the Scots waiter it was put on the back of a sofa. The next thing known is that it was handed to the Manager of the hotel late on Friday evening by the head waiter of the floor – an Italian. The Italian has been 3 years at the hotel. When cross-examined the Scotsman said that he had informed the Italian on the Thursday morning & the Italian says he never saw the paper till the Friday evening & that he reported the matter at once.
>
> MI5 are pursuing the matter, & meanwhile a French officer has gone off by aeroplane to see Gamelin & try to get his story of what happened.
>
> The thing looks bad as it gives away everything and couldn't have been more clear than if we had prepared it to hand to the enemy.[11]

The change of government in France reinvigorated the options for an Allied intervention in Scandinavia, where the need to deny Germany access to Swedish iron ore remained significant, even without the emotive but ultimately distracting requirement to assist the gallant Finns. This was one of the main topics of the conference attended by Gamelin, during the course of which the security breach took place, and led to an important development in that the decision was taken to begin mining operations in Norwegian coastal waters.

The instance of the German tanker *Altmark*, erstwhile supply ship to the pocket battleship *Admiral Graf Spee*, being allowed to transit Norwegian waters with a cargo of British POWs on board, indicated that the Norwegians were unable to effectively police their own neutrality and had necessitated the intervention of a Royal Navy boarding party from HMS *Cossack* to release the prisoners. This action was carried out on the direct instructions of Churchill as First Lord of the Admiralty, and he remained a keen advocate of such active schemes. However, great pressure was also placed upon Chamberlain's government by the French, who were keen to tie down German forces away from France and the Low Countries. Back in January, my father had employed the exact same argument in favour of the Finland option, noting that if sufficient German forces were diverted to Scandinavia, then not only France but southern Europe could be made safe from the threat of German invasion.[12]

Allied planning followed two routes. Firstly, in Operation Wilfred mines would be laid in two locations on the Norwegian coast, of which the most significant was off the mouth of the Vestfjorden, whereby access to Narvik would be blocked. Secondly, working on the assumption that Germany would react, Plan R4 called for Allied troops to be sent to secure Narvik and other key locations.

Although numbers would later increase, the initial landing scheme envisaged a brigade to secure Narvik and the iron ore railway, and battalions to hold Bergen, Trondheim and Stavanger. Forces that had been earmarked for intervention in Finland – mostly British, but including a brigade of *Chasseurs Alpins* – would be reassigned to furnish the land force: numbers were small, but represented all that could be spared from France. Matters were complicated by the fact that the French decided at the last minute to veto a supplementary plan – also Churchill's – to block the Rhine by aerial mines as a means of distracting and harassing the Germans, which had initially been approved at the London conference. However, they remained committed to the Scandinavian gambit and Operation Wilfred was therefore set in motion.

This is not the place for anything more than an outline of the Norwegian campaign, but it is necessary to appreciate both the extent and the limitations of my father's role in these operations. Notwithstanding that Operation Wilfred had been slated for 5 April, the French decision not to proceed with the parallel mining of the Rhine led to a three-day delay as attempts were made to convince them to reverse this decision. Without the distraction it was hoped that the Rhine operation would cause, my father feared that the neutral opinion would focus on the Allied violation of Norwegian waters and thus paint Britain and France in the worst light.

Neutral opinion was certainly something that was on his mind, as he had just had the unwelcome distraction of having to provide a positive 'spin' on Allied military prospects for the benefit of an American interviewer, something that had unexpected consequences when it was belatedly discovered that the interview was also syndicated to British newspapers. The result was that the British press gained a false opinion of my father's views on the course of the war and particularly of the confidence that he had in the French ability to resist in the face of a German attack. Otherwise, as time ticked by and Churchill flew to France in a final attempt to convince the French to allow the Rhine mining, the most pressing matter for the CIGS was dealing with the popular backlash against the decision that, in this war, Highland regiments would go to war in trousers rather than kilts.

The reason it was Churchill who was sent to France was because on 3 April Lord Chatfield had resigned as minister for co-ordination of defence, which post was then abolished. Even with this change, which saw Churchill take on some of Chatfield's responsibilities, my father remained unconvinced that Chamberlain had assembled a team fit to win the war:

> I cannot think that we have a War Cabinet fit to compete with Hitler. Its decisions are so slow and cumbersome. We still refer the smallest thing to a Committee. Halifax is much too good a man to compete with a lot of knaves. The Prime Minister is hopelessly unmilitary. I am sure that Sam Hoare is not a whit better than Kingsley Wood. The only advantage is the disappearance of Lord Chatfield. There is one less to talk at the Cabinet. Winston becomes a sort of Chairman of the Coordination Committee. We shall have more strength there if he can be kept upon the proper lines. But the whole show is ponderous & clumsy.[13]

Wood and Hoare, it should be explained, had recently exchanged portfolios.

The whole of the Norwegian campaign served as a case study of the ineffectuality of trying to run a war by committee, as my father had grasped from an early stage, but the resulting tensions saw a drastic breakdown in his previously effective working relationship with Winston Churchill now that the first lord was also de facto defence minister. As with the difficulties with the press after the American interview, this would have consequences later on.

Britain had not been alone in stepping up her plans for Norway in the aftermath of the *Altmark* Incident, and German preparations for an offensive into Scandinavia – to encompass the invasion of Denmark as well as Norway – were also set to come to fruition in the second week of April. Therefore, as the British warships sailed on their minelaying mission, they ran into elements of the German fleet carrying troops to secure the key Norwegian ports and a number of confused and confusing clashes took place in which both sides had ships damaged and sunk. Crucially, German forces were able to secure Narvik and its surrounding fiords and to land a strong force of mountain infantry to occupy the port. A naval attack on 10 April cost both sides two destroyers, but British gunfire and torpedoes also destroyed the German supply ships and tankers and as such effectively immobilised the German force and denied their troops ashore any chance of being resupplied.

Otherwise, the situation worsened day by day and the Germans occupied Bergen, Trondheim and Oslo. Denmark, meanwhile, had surrendered as early as 9 April and her administration had been taken over. My father suspected that this would be the precursor of a general offensive in the west and, indeed, France and the Low Countries remained the main strategic focus throughout the course of events in Norway:

> It seems to me that all this will be followed as soon as possible by an advance upon the Western Front. Holland will be overrun and Belgium as far as the point to which we arrive – probably the line of the Dyle.
>
> You cannot make war by referring everything to Committees and sitting wobbling and havering.
>
> The logical conclusion is an attack on the Western Front. Against both Belgium and Holland. There is nothing more we can now do. We have given the III Corps to France & we have 1 Regular Bde. and the 49th Division for Scandinavia. Nothing more. That cannot be said to be much with which to come and go.
>
> They will be fatal days, these next few.[14]

The Regular brigade in question was 24th Guards Brigade, which had previously been prepared for operations in Finland and was now posted to give some stiffening to the Yorkshire and North Midland Territorials of Major General Pierse Mackesy's 49th Division. III Corps, which had been the subject of some wrangling, remained in France but Gort was instructed to take the Regular 5th Division out of the BEF line and hold it in reserve for redeployment to Norway if required.

The main problems facing my father, however, related not so much to the availability of troops but to how they should be equipped – the lack of arctic clothing remaining a problem – and where they should be sent. Although troops had been embarked on board Royal Navy cruisers preparatory to implementing Plan R4, the development of a major naval campaign as a result of the German operations meant that they had been disembarked and the cruisers redeployed. The capture of the ports to which they ought to have been sent also necessitated a major rethink and the result was that strategic planning took place on the fly. It was eventually decided to make the initial objective the recapture of Narvik but, with intelligence suggesting that the place was held by up to 5,000 Germans, this was not the easy task that Churchill had initially presented to the Defence

Co-ordination Committee. My father identified the following points as essential to its success:

(i) That Narvik cannot be reinforced from the sea any more.
(ii) That we will require an advanced base near Narvik for the martialling [sic] of our forces.
(iii) That it would be of great value if we could seize the port of Tromsö to the North now and establish an oiling base for our destroyers.
(iv) That I get some officers into the country to find out what forces there are in Narvik with some certainty, so that we can make a plan.
(v) That we be given sufficient time in which to make our plans and carry them out.[15]

My father went on to note that he had set about planning for such an operation. Unfortunately, the time with which to do so was the one thing that the Allies did not have.

After an additional delay, and much resulting exasperation confided to my father's diary, Mackesy and the leading elements of his command sailed for Narvik on 12 April. However, even before their departure, moves were afoot to redirect a portion of the already limited land force to Trondheim. This was at the request of the Norwegian Government, but the idea was enthusiastically seized upon by the other two services and my father was faced with a midnight conference with Pound, Newall and their assistants in which he was pressed to divert part of Mackesy's command to Namsos with a view to thereby 'staking a claim' on nearby Trondheim. 'I am afraid', he wrote, 'that I lost my temper and banged on the desk.'[16]

Reflecting more calmly on things the following day, he recorded his belief that it would be best to secure Narvik as a bridgehead in the north, which would also secure the rail connection with Sweden and thereby facilitate combined operations if the Swedes could be persuaded to join the war. In all events, subsequent operations could be developed from this base as the situation allowed. No doubt this would have been the most sensible course of action, but it was not to be:

> We had a dreadful coordination meeting under Winston, where he was half-tight and so sleepy that he couldn't understand what we were saying. I couldn't get him to draft the orders under which we were to operate. We eventually decided on Namsos just north of Trondheim. Not before the 16th, four days from now. A meeting till midnight that could have been run in a few minutes if we had a man to give us our orders.
>
> When shall we leave the military men to run our own show?[17]

The result of this decision was that the already limited British contribution to the land campaign in Norway was split in two. After the Royal Navy attacked Narvik in overwhelming force on 13 April and eliminated the eight remaining German destroyers, the mood in the Admiralty was for a similar penetration of the fiords leading to Trondheim:

> They have put up a completely new plan – which has the disadvantage of taking some time to execute. I said that we must go on with our Namsos landing. Which can now be increased by one of the Bdes. from Narvik.
>
> The difficulty now is that we must have the generals with proper orders & we must have them on the spot. It means the cancelling of orders and various changes which may be difficult.
>
> Winston was less annoying, but still went into details which took up a lot of time and wore his & our tempers out.[18]

Amongst the difficulties was the fact that, since the ships had already sailed, a logical division of forces was not possible. In the new plan, 146th Brigade would go to Namsos and 24th Guards Brigade would go to Narvik; Mackesy would command the latter operation and Carton de Wiart, now underemployed at home as commander of a second-line Territorial division, would be flown out to command the Namsos operation.

However, the brigadier commanding 146th Brigade was embarked on the same Narvik-bound ship as Mackesy and his staff, and the brigade's heavy equipment could also not be diverted. The result was that the Namsos contingent was unable to achieve its objective and was eventually evacuated on 3 May.

A third force, under Major General Bernard Paget and built around 148th Brigade shipped out from England but also including some of the French troops, was landed at Åndalsnes on the night of 18–19 April with a view to attacking Trondheim from the south. Elements of 15th Brigade, withdrawn from 5th Division in France, were added to this contingent later, but the Trondheim operation never took place. Diverted instead to join the Norwegian resistance to a German force advancing from Oslo by way of Lillehammer to relieve the cut-off German troops at Trondheim, Paget's command was largely destroyed or dispersed in a series of running battles during the second half of April and the survivors evacuated by 2 May.

Throughout this frustrating process, my father was involved in an endless series of meetings and committees which attempted to direct operations by remote control from London. What was needed, he recognised, was a C-in-C who could direct operations from the spot, but the best that was achieved was the 19 April appointment of Major General Hugh Massy, previously DCIGS, to co-ordinate the troops under Carton de Wiart and Paget. Mackesy, in the north, remained independent but struggled with a polyglot command that included French and Free Polish troops and was further hamstrung by the Admiralty having appointed the very senior Admiral of the Fleet Lord Cork as their commander on the spot which, in due course, enabled him to assume command in chief of land and naval operations. Mackesy balked at the direct attack that Cork wished him to make against Narvik, and instead carried out a more deliberate campaign. As a result, he was eventually supplanted as land-force commander by Major General Claude Auchinleck, but he too pursued a deliberate course, quite aware after the disasters further south that the campaign as a whole was now lost. Narvik did not fall to the Allies until the night of 28–29 May, by which time the focus of events was very much elsewhere and the decision to evacuate had already been taken.

The Norwegian campaign was the only major operation by the British Army that took place in its entirety during my father's tenure as CIGS. Strictly speaking, the last forces were not withdrawn until after his relief, but the major decisions took place under his tenure. In that the campaign was a failure that brought down the Chamberlain government, it seems legitimate to question the level of accountability that my father should bear for that failure. The answer, however, would seem to be that there is little that can be directly laid at his door. At BEF Headquarters, it was feared that he was stripping troops from France to go to Norway, but in fact it can be seen that he took the minimum that was possible from Gort's command and, in truth, the existing political commitment to the defence of France took this decision out of his hands.

Like the rest of the War Cabinet, he was caught out by the fact that Germany launched its own operation against Norway ahead of the British intervention: all planning presupposed that Germany would only react to a British operation and thus there were no contingency plans for an opposed landing in Norway. More specifically, he was taken aback by the effective use of air power in the campaign – particularly by the Germans, although there were some impressive feats by Allied airmen too – and it is a legitimate criticism of the campaign as a whole that Allied planning did not take the air threat into sufficient account. On both these points, however, the collective nature of strategic decision-making means that one must also accept a collective shouldering of the burden of guilt.

In the most recent study of the operational conduct of the war in Norway, the only major criticism laid at my father's door is the suggestion that he made poor choices in his appointment of senior commanders. This, however, would seem to be unfounded. Carton de Wiart was a commander of proven merit, and Paget – who in any case only received the Åndalsnes command at the last minute after the initial choice, Major General F.E. Hotblack, was felled by a stroke – certainly demonstrated by his later record that he was a perfectly capable officer. Massy, perhaps, showed less ability but, then again, he was dropped into a near-impossible situation. Mackesy did prove unsatisfactory at Narvik, and his initial choice for a command in Norway seems to have stemmed as much as anything from the fact that he was commanding the division that provided the bulk of the troops that were to be sent.

No doubt the decision to send Auchinleck out as a more senior officer was the right one, and could have been made earlier, but on that count the elevation of Lord Cork to be Allied C-in-C at Narvik had already muddied the waters of command and the insertion of yet another cog into the mechanism could well have had adverse consequences. In all events, considering that none of the officers sent out in command had been tested at that level in a major war, it is hard to see how anyone could have been expected to pick the best men for the jobs based solely upon peacetime records. This charge against my father's record can therefore also be dismissed.

At the end of the day, the primary cause of the failure of British arms in the Norwegian theatre came from a lack of strategic direction from the very top. My father was quite correct to assert that wars could not be fought and won by committee, and his frustration during these weeks at political meddling and insistence on interfering in detail is palpable from his diaries. With limited forces, and beginning with Germany in possession of the strategic initiative, it is doubtful that the intervention in Norway could ever have ended with an Allied success.

Poor strategic decision-making threw away such opportunities as existed. Crucial in the failure of the land campaign was the division of forces and objectives inherent in the attempt to operate against Narvik and Trondheim with insufficient forces. This, it will be recalled, was pushed through against my father's wishes and over his protests, albeit that once the decision was made he did his best to ensure that it was carried out.

However, just as he grew increasingly dissatisfied with the politicians – saving, perhaps, Oliver Stanley – there were also signs that they were growing dissatisfied with him and that he was no longer as secure in the role of CIGS as he once had been. The increased difficulties that he experienced with Churchill, whose working methods as the chair of the Defence Co-ordination Committee drove my father to distraction even while he continued to admire his energy and resolve, cost him the support of his most significant ally in the War Cabinet. Although his personal relationship with Gort remained sound enough, if distant, his relations with the BEF staff were often strained, although by no means justifying the vitriol poured out by Pownall. He was, therefore, an increasingly isolated figure within the political and military establishment.

An early hint that he might be assigned to a new role came even before the commencement of the Norwegian campaign, when he was approached about the possibility of going out to India as C-in-C to replace General Sir Robert Cassels. This was a post that he had once coveted but it now had echoes of banishment, notwithstanding the inherent compliment of choosing him for a situation which required, in light of the volatile political situation, 'a man of standing and prestige'.[19] Reflecting further on the prospect, he wrote:

> It seems a pity to give up on CIGS at a critical moment but I am sure that India is going to give us trouble and I suppose I am the man who has the most experience of the country. I understand the people and I like them, though I have had nothing to do with the politicians. I think I could compete with them. There is literally no one else with my prestige in India.[20]

If he were to go, he reflected, he would at least make it a *sine qua non* that he received his field marshal's baton before he went. The service would be hard, but it would be a fitting end to his career, for 'if I am made C-in-C India I shall be the only officer who has been promoted CIGS and C-in-C India both. A record. How angry people like Milne and Massingberd will be.' Still, on balance, he preferred not to go – which was just as well, for the matter was dropped and Cassels' tenure extended for a further year.

More suggestive that change was afoot was the posting of Sir John Dill from France back to London to take up the newly created post of Vice Chief of the Imperial General Staff (VCIGS). At BEF Headquarters, it was generally assumed, and gleefully recorded by Pownall, that Dill's posting was a first step to his replacing my father as CIGS, but my father did not see things that way, at least at first, noting the original proposal as follows:

> It is now an idea to have a second DCIGS & it was suggested to bring Dill back from France to act under me & that I should become a kind of super CIGS. A difficult business & might bring a clash of personalities.[21]

Dill arrived in London on 19 April and briefly met with my father before leaving to visit his terminally ill wife. Two days later, he was summoned to see Oliver Stanley, and this seems to have caused my father to consider the possibility that he might, after all, be expected to step aside. He had, he recorded, given Dill 'a paper of notes so that we can talk with one voice. I hope that [Stanley] is not going to take advice from two people. That is impossible. I have asked to get in and see him as soon as I know what he has discussed with Dill.'[22] After further reflection, he wrote:

> I hope that we are not going to have divided counsels. I may have to stand down if [Stanley] thinks that Dill can run it better than I can. When Dill came over he gave me a direct understanding that I was to remain in supreme control. One never knows dealing with politicians. That is the danger of Dill coming in here. Still, with a war on, one must not stand in the way of any operation that the Government wish carried out.[23]

In the event, however, it was the politicians who were the first to go, as the failure of the Norwegian campaign caused Chamberlain to lose the confidence of Parliament. The final day of his administration began with farce:

> We were summoned at 7 a.m. to the Admiralty for a Chiefs of Staff meeting. I had great difficulty in getting in from Whitehall and then we sat for ½ hour listening to rumours that were coming in & they began telephone to the French. Then I got away & could not get out again. All the night-watchmen had gone away and the day's men not there. Doors double and treble locked. I walked up to one of the windows & opened it and climbed out. So much for security.[24]

Before the day was out, Winston Churchill was made prime minister, and also assumed the mantle of minister of defence. Anthony Eden replaced Oliver Stanley at the War Office, but the service ministers were no longer included in the new slimmed down War Cabinet which was announced on 12 May. If it had been intended to remove my father as well, however, any such move was overtaken by events, when the night of 9–10 May saw the opening of the German offensive against France and the Low Countries.

20

Desperate Days

The long-awaited German offensive triggered the Allied implementation of Plan D, sending the BEF into the Low Countries with the French Seventh Army to their north and First Army to their south. My father's direct involvement in the early days of operations was limited. This was Gamelin's battle so far as the strategy was concerned, and Gort's when it came to the operational deployment of the BEF. As CIGS, his main role was to try and keep the War Cabinet abreast of what was happening – no easy task in the confused early days of the fighting, as the situation in the Low Countries went from bad to worse.

For both Gamelin and Gort, the Allied response to the German attack was dictated by the requirements of Plan D, and the BEF rolled forward to the Dyle largely as planned. For the first few days the atmosphere at Gort's headquarters, as recorded by Pownall, showed a certain amount of cautious optimism. The main difficulty was with the Belgians not being integrated into the Allied command structure, which caused difficulties at all levels. Only on 14 May did the true situation become apparent, when news broke of the German thrust through the Ardennes and the consequent rupture of the French lines around Sedan.

Although my father had commented from an early stage as to his puzzlement that the German drive into the Low Countries represented far less of an effort than could be expected from the full power of their forces on the Western Front, he seems to have been caught as much by surprise as the rest of the Allied command at the eventual main German strike through the Ardennes. Until the full extent of the Manstein Plan was revealed and the French line broken, his thinking seems to have been predicated on the idea that Holland would collapse but that the Allies – including the Belgians as they fell back and linked up with the British and French – would be able to hold a static position on the Dyle line.

For those in London, the difficulty was keeping abreast of just what was happening in France. Only on the afternoon of the 14th did it begin to become apparent that a crisis was being faced and the French high command was struggling to resist the breakthrough and restore the line. On the morning of the 15th, having been up half the previous night with a toothache that had required an extraction to resolve it, my father received a further update that brought home the gravity of the situation. Though the extent of the German offensive was alarming enough, the effect it had on the French leadership was worse:

> This morning at 8 a.m. just as I was talking to Gort, the PM rang up and told me that he had been talking to Reynaud, who was thoroughly demoralised. He had said that the battle was lost. That the road to Paris was open. Couldn't we send more troops. Winston told him to keep calm, that these incidents happened in a war. We have no extra demands from Gamelin and Georges, both of whom were calm, though they both considered the situation serious. I told him this. Apparently the French are giving back at Namur & may bend back to Charleroi, still keeping a hold on us at Wavre.
>
> I shouldn't be surprised if the line was back again upon the French frontier before long.
>
> The Germans are using mechanised troops with very few infantry columns. The German tanks are very good and I think that there can be no doubt that the French have been caught unawares and that they have not fought well. That happened in the last war. Drastic steps had to be taken to put things right.
>
> Winston told Reynaud that even if the French gave in we should fight on alone. He was quite calm and very firm.[1]

For all the bleakness of the picture – made bleaker still by bad news from Norway as the campaign around Narvik wound down – my father could still take considerable confidence in the resolve of Churchill and the new War Cabinet. Weighing up the options for an unpredictable future gave him few certainties, with neither side looking likely to impose a peace of its choosing on the other:

> Now as regards a peace without victory. That seems to me to be very possible. The longer it goes on the less is a lasting peace likely. Is such a peace possible from the 'lasting' point of view? With two such differing theories of life as 'democracy' & 'Hitlerism' it seems to me that it must be a fight to the death. There can be no compromise. Indeed 'Hitlerism' must disappear if it is not victorious or it will merely try again.[2]

As if of a mind with this no-compromise policy, the War Cabinet authorised the RAF to begin striking back directly at Germany and bombing targets on the Ruhr, a policy that my father heartily endorsed even though he was aware that it would invite inevitable retribution. Little could be done, however, to influence the air battle over France, where the dominance of the Luftwaffe exerted a baleful effect on all Allied movements. Every fighter sent to France was one fighter less to defend Britain once Germany transferred her bomber fleet to Dutch airfields and put them in effective range of British cities.

As the German Army advanced into France the fate of the BEF became the most important issue facing the War Cabinet and the CIGS was the one and only person on hand with the knowledge, experience, ability and, above all, understanding of the military dimensions of the task. Churchill returned from France on 17 May, having made provision for a limited amount of further air support to be sent, but the meeting of the War Cabinet that day was gloomy. From my father's telephone calls with Gort, too, it was apparent that cracks were starting to develop in the confident message being put out by BEF Headquarters.

A withdrawal to the line of the Escaut had been ordered and the BEF was pulling back in good order, but some of the French troops on their right were beginning to crumble. As my father noted, if Billotte could not plug the breach, 'we shall find ourselves cut from our L[ines] of C[ommunication] in Amiens. This means that we shall be trying to evacuate the BEF from Dunkerque, Calais & Boulogne. An impossible proposition.'[3] Interestingly, considering the negative tone of this note, the editors of my father's published diaries record that on this day he recommended to the Admiralty that measures be taken to assemble small craft to help evacuate the BEF.[4] Undoubtedly this comes from the recollections of Colonel Macleod, who was on my father's staff at the time. My father, however, makes no mention of this in his own diary. Perhaps, at the time, he did not appreciate the significance of the suggestion, or the importance of the role that the 'little ships' would play in the eventual successful evacuation. Indeed, my father would repeat the opinion several times in the days to come that evacuation was unlikely to save more than a fraction of the BEF's manpower – let alone its equipment or any of its allies – but it is important to distinguish doubts as to whether an evacuation would be feasible from an opposition to the concept itself. Quite simply, the idea of getting the BEF back to Britain – although he recognised that its preservation was very likely the hinge on which hung Britain's ability to resist alone – was not yet foremost in his mind, nor in those of the members of the War Cabinet. As Colonel Macleod observed, with reference to the assembly of small craft, evacuation was still only being considered as a worst-case scenario.

In London, the priority remained, as my father put it, getting the BEF 'line back to something reasonable to cover our communication', without which, he felt, an evacuation would likely be impossible anyway.[5] This would shape his analysis of the situation for some days to come, eventually crystallising into the concept of a counterstroke that would shift the BEF to the south, restoring the line and hopefully striking a blow against the German offensive at the same time.

What my father had noted, and what underpinned his eventual proposal, was that the German offensive had relied almost exclusively for its success on armoured and mechanised spearheads supported by air power, which were now operating some way in advance of the main infantry force of the German Army.

While the panzers had created a gap in the Allied line, so too had they opened one up between themselves and their supports. Initially, his thinking was based on an extension of the BEF line to the south to restore a link with the French and to cover the lines of communication which were now by way of Abbeville and Arras. As he was well aware, Gort's options for more radical mobile operations were limited by the fact that he had only slow-moving infantry tanks available – 1st Armoured Division, with fast cruiser tanks, was only just in the process of being shipped to France.

Nevertheless, by 19 May the seriousness of the situation led him to propose a more radical option to the War Cabinet in a meeting that he described as 'very serious' and lacking in the usual 'useless talk':

> I told them of the dangers which existed to the BEF through the cutting of their communications. I did not think that the French had enough troops available to stop the threat now coming against Peronne and Abbeville. I am quite sure that the French will always think more of Paris than anything else. I spoke to Gort & told him that he must arrange with his tactical trains to get some large proportion of his reserves down in to the area Douai–Béthune–Arras so as to have something there. If the worst comes to the worst the BEF must be prepared to turn south and cut its way through to the Abbeville–Amiens line & eventually to the Seine to cover Havre. What is to happen to the Belgians I really don't know. They have the longest wheel to make and are very unwilling to evacuate Belgium completely. I daresay that they will never get out at all. In any case we must think of the BEF whose feeding is becoming very difficult already.
>
> The Armoured Division will not commence landing at Havre till tonight. They may be very useful in the extrication of the BEF in the last resort.
>
> I am told that the French staff are very despondent. I don't know what they can do more than they are doing. But, I am quite sure that the German main columns will be coming up pretty soon towards this big gap in the Douai–Amiens area.[6]

The last point is significant. If the Germans were to get their infantry up and close the gap, the opportunity would be lost. The result was that after a series of further Cabinet meetings the decision was taken that evening to send my father across to France in person and visit Gort 'with what was practically an order to be prepared to draw southwards on his LofC'.[7] There could be no question of a direct order to implement the scheme that my father had envisaged – that would be an operational matter for Gort, who would clearly be far more au fait with the situation on the ground than anyone in London – but the time had clearly passed when the future of the BEF could be trusted to the interests of foreign powers and the indecision of foreign generals. My father's instructions made it implicit that Gort was no longer to be tied to the Belgians and, by sending my father out with orders, the Cabinet had in effect pulled the BEF out of the French command structure. In all of this, my father considered them entirely justified.

After an overnight journey, my father reached BEF Headquarters at Wahagnies at 06.00 on the morning of the 20th:

> I found Gort in good heart in a magnificent château belonging to a sugar magnate. He quite understood & we arranged to get the 50th Div. & 5th Div. down towards Arras. Also, the 44th Div. is on our extreme left to be relieved by the Belgians. This would make a beginning towards facing the gap in the South.[8]

This was far from the major redeployment that my father had suggested to the War Cabinet, but it was the best that could be done under the circumstances. As Gort and Pownall explained to my father, the bulk of the BEF was now committed to the line of the Escaut where an attack was expected imminently. It would therefore be impossible to make the wholesale move to the south that had been envisaged in London. However, as related, two divisions were available for active operations and Gort was already working up a plan to use them in a spoiling attack around Arras.

Recognising that the situation was far worse than had been appreciated in London, all that my father could manage was to suggest the expansion of the attack in order to do the most damage to the German forces and thereby obtain some breathing space for the Allies. Even the usually critical Pownall, who had no time at all for the plan that my father brought from London, was impressed by the speed with which he was able to revise his ideas in light of the more up-to-date information available.

Gort had strongly impressed during their conference that since the bulk of the German offensive power was held by their southern wing – the troops that had broken through the Ardennes – and that the danger was greatest for those Allied forces, including the BEF, who were north of the gap and who risked being encircled and thrown back against the Channel coast, the troops with the best chance of effectively striking against the German forces in the gap were those to its south. Most immediately, this meant the French V Corps, part of Blanchard's First Army. If the attack was to be expanded as my father wanted, it was from these troops that support must be obtained.

With Gamelin having been dismissed the previous day, direction of the French forces was now in the hands of the elderly but fiery Weygand, who had been appointed commander-in-chief and under whose leadership better things could be hoped for from the French command. Accordingly, accompanied by Pownall to represent the BEF, my father now attempted to make contact with the French high command:

> The roads are an indescribable mass of refugees, both Belgian and French moving down in every kind of conveyance. Poor women pushing perambulators, horsed wagons with all the family & its goods in it. Belgian units all going along aimlessly, Poor devils. It was a horrible sight and it blocked the roads, which was the main difficulty.
>
> I then found Billotte & Blanchard at Lens (1st Army). All in a state of complete depression. No plan, no thought of a plan. Ready to be slaughtered. Defeated at the head without casualties. Trés fatigués & nothing doing.
>
> I lost my temper & shook Billotte by the button of his tunic. The man is completely beaten. I got him to agree [to support the attack] and Blanchard accepted to take Cambrai. There is absolutely nothing in front of them. They remain quivering behind the water line, north of Cambrai, while the fate of France is in the balance. Gort told me, when I got back to his HQ, that they would never attack.
>
> I spoke to Weygand on the phone, told him that there was no resolution here and that there was no co-ordination. I told him that Billotte should be relieved.[9]

Again, even the critical Pownall thought that my father had done just what was required, noting in his own diary, 'Tiny was quite good in speaking to them firmly', and that he had added his own voice to my father's argument.[10]

The result of this day's planning was the Battle of Arras. Elements of the 5th and 50th Divisions and 1st Army Tank Brigade, under the overall command of Major General Harold Franklyn, attacked on the afternoon of the 21st, with some flank support from the French 3rd Light Armoured Division. The battlefield lay immediately to the south of Vimy Ridge, overlooked by the monument to the Canadians who had fallen there in the previous war.

Initial gains against Rommel's 7th Panzer Division were good, and a Waffen-SS detachment was completely routed. German forces were driven back over 6 miles and Rommel reported that he was under attack by several divisions rather than, as was the reality, two reinforced brigades. However, the supporting attack from the south never materialised, eventually going in a day late, and co-operation by the French troops in the area was poor. Ultimately, therefore, Franklyn was obliged to pull his men back to their starting positions.

By the time the attack went in, my father was already back in Britain. After leaving Gort he motored back to the Calais aerodrome at Saint-Inglevert and found an empty space with no planes, virtually left ready for landings by troop carriers at any moment. He spent the night in the local hotel, the Excelsior, which was straddled by a stick of bombs in the night. 'The end of my room blown up & I was blown up off my bed. I was asleep again in 5 minutes'.[11]

He returned to Hendon on 21 May in a forty-minute flight, escorted by six fighters:

> I saw Winston, who persists in thinking that the position is no worse.
>
> Enemy tanks have entered Amiens & passed on to Abbeville. Nobody to stop them & they are supposed to be going to Boulogne.
>
> How can one think the thing is not serious?
>
> I begin to despair of the French fighting at all. The great army defeated by a few tanks.[12]

In fact, the French were preparing for a final effort to restore the situation – or, rather, their new commander-in-chief was preparing. Weygand's plan was for a counter-attack southward towards the line of the Somme, in effect my father's original conception writ large. However, the fighting spirit of Weygand was not matched by that of his immediate subordinates, and the whole affair collapsed into farce and misunderstanding before it was properly begun.

A conference was scheduled for the 21st, to take place at Ypres, but Gort was misinformed as to the timing and arrived only after Weygand had left. Billotte, who did attend the conference, was involved in a car accident on the way back to his own headquarters. After two days in a coma, he died on 23 May: Blanchard stepped up to replace him, but only with effect from 25 May.

Although the Ypres conference resulted in the approval of Weygand's plan for a counter-attack, in Gort's case against his better judgement, the need to pull the BEF and flanking Allied forces back to the line of the French frontier in order to free sufficient divisions for mobile operations meant that the attack was scheduled for 26 May. In the event, because Blanchard was not aware that Gort had been permitted to fall back prior to redeploying, the withdrawal of the BEF was interpreted as an abandonment of allies and led to much distrust and ill feeling. By the 25th, with the Belgian defences beginning to crumble, Gort, after consulting with Dill who had visited his headquarters, took the unilateral decision to withdraw from the planned counter-attack and use the available troops to shore up his line. Upon learning of this, Blanchard, who had been confirmed that day as commander of First Army Group, ordered his whole command to withdraw northwards in order to secure the Dunkirk bridgehead.

My father tracked these momentous events from London, recording his impressions in a series of diary entries. His preoccupation, as quickly becomes evident, was the holding of the Channel ports – Boulogne, Calais, Dunkirk – in the hope of extricating as much of the BEF as possible. This, at last, gave him the sort of positive role that was far more to his taste than passively following the course of affairs on the Continent, and it also enabled him to actively support the BEF without directly interfering in Gort's command of it.

Nevertheless, as with many who would be taken by surprise by the eventual success of Operation Dynamo, my father for many days continued to fear the worst and worried that only a fraction of the British troops trapped with their backs to the Channel could be safely brought out. However, for all his fearing of the worst, my father was ahead of most contemporaries in anticipating that even a portion of the BEF might be got out by sea. As late as 24 and 25 May, Gort, Brooke and Dill were all of the opinion that little could be saved at all and that such of the BEF as might make it to safety would have to break out towards the Somme rather than be brought out by sea, a stance which makes that of my father – in effect, that an evacuation by sea was unlikely to save much but must be tried – seem positively optimistic.

Only Churchill remained seemingly unaffected by the reverses, and on 22 May my father contrasted his own attitude with that of the prime minister, recording:

> Winston came back again from Paris at 6.30 p.m. and we had a Cabinet at 7.30 p.m. He was almost in buoyant spirits, having been impressed by Weygand. Said that he looked like a man of 50.
> But when it came down to things, it was still all 'projects'. The BEF has lost a chance of extricating itself and is very short of food and ammunition. I am trying to square up things this end to clear the Channel Ports for Gort.[13]

My father's hopes, however, and perhaps even Churchill's buoyancy, were soon to be hit by further blows, as the former wrote in his diary for 23 May:

> Things are not good.
> Boulogne was isolated by German tanks this morning at 8 a.m. and I have only just got my 3 Bns. of Motorised Inf. & the Tank Regt. into Calais on time.
> I am now pushing in the Canadians under their Div. Cmdr McNaughton. He may be able to do a little to open up the communications to St Omer, but it doesn't look much as if he could.
> Meanwhile the BEF is short of food & ammunition.
> Damned bad.[14]

At Boulogne, the hope had only ever been to deny the port to the Germans, and for that purpose a static garrison built around 20th Guards Brigade had been despatched. Upon arrival on the morning of 22 May they linked up with a pioneer detachment belonging to the BEF's rear echelon and a ragtag French force under General Lanquetot.

Calais, on the other hand, was seen as a port from which a supply line to the BEF might be established in order to redress the growing concerns about Gort's shortages of food and ammunition. It was for this reason that a mobile force – stripped largely from the support units of 1st Armoured Division and formed into a new 30th Infantry Brigade – was sent to that port. With tanks and motorised infantry, it was hoped that a convoy could be fought through to the BEF even though German mobile forces were operating in the intervening area. 1st Canadian Division was to prepare a brigade group to reinforce the initial contingent.

By late afternoon on the 23rd, however, my father was recording more bad news:

> Boulogne has definitely gone. The Germans entered the French fort north of the town and have taken the guns and have now prevented any chance of ships coming into the port. So goes all the people in Boulogne including the two Guards Bns. there. A rotten ending indeed.[15]

In fact, the situation was not as dire as he had been informed. For the loss of one of their number, British and French destroyers were able to take off the bulk of the Guards during the course of the day. Through confusion, the pioneers were almost left behind, but a daring night-time passage by HMS *Vimeira* plucked a further 1,400 men to safety. However, a number of British troops were left behind to be taken captive on the 25th, and the French garrison of the old town, cut off from the harbour, was also compelled to surrender. Aspersions were cast in some French quarters that the British were too quick to cut and run, triggering a mindset of suspicion that would have serious consequences for the troops that my father had sent to hold Calais.

With Boulogne gone and clear evidence that the whole of the German Armoured Force was now in action, with at least four panzer divisions driving northwards towards the coast around Calais and St Omer, the situation seemed grim indeed and it became increasingly difficult for those in London to exert any control over events. Accordingly, authority was devolved to the man on the spot. Closing his diary entry for the 23rd, my father wrote:

> We have sent complete discretion to Gort to move his Army as he likes to try and save it. The French are doing nothing with their 1st Army and I don't think their Government has any connection with Blanchard, who has replaced Billotte.
>
> Gort is very nearly surrounded and there is just the possibility that he may be able to withdraw through Ypres to Dunkerque. I have directed some food there for him. That may help if he attempts to withdraw.
>
> I cannot see much hope of getting any of the BEF out. The only chance is that Weygand's manoeuvre may be carried out. We have lost faith in the French power of attack. Whether it will come again is impossible for a foreigner to say. Only a Frenchman can make a difference.[16]

The manoeuvre in question was the joint attack southwards by the BEF and northwards by the French: as we have already seen, this came to naught under circumstances that strained the crumbling alliance yet further. My father, meanwhile, continued with his efforts to keep the Channel ports open and to supply Gort, reporting that a certain amount of food and ammunition had been landed at Dunkirk and more, or so he understood, at Ostend. Contact, too, had been made with the senior French officer in the area:

> McNaughton, the Canadian General, who went over to spy out the Dunkerque–Calais position, found [General Robert] Fagalde, the French Corps Comdr in Dunkerque. He had been appointed C-in-C in the North. His first order was to our people in Calais to stand fast. A good sign. The first order of co-ordination, which has been given by the French Command in the north for 10 days. Let us hope that it is the beginning.
>
> The German Mobile Columns have definitely been halted for some reason or another. Rather similar to the halt they made before. It is quite certain that there has been very little movement about. They must have got quite a lot of petrol at Boulogne.
>
> I have been cursing my Brigadier in Calais for conducting such a supine defence. Our men don't fight either.[17]

In the light of the subsequent epic defence by Brigadier Claude Nicholson and his men, for which my father had only praise, the closing comment in the passage quoted above should be taken as indicative of the frustration that my father must have felt after the failure of the operation on the night of 22–23 May, by which it was hoped to fight supplies through to Gort. For the moment, the decision was taken that Calais would be evacuated, but this would soon be overturned.

My father's diary for much of this period is far less detailed than the norm, and the handwriting shows some indication of its having been composed in some haste. Although he never made any record in his diary of the crucial decision taken by Winston Churchill to reverse the evacuation order, my father told me that when he was dining with Churchill and Eden that evening he was told to issue the orders for the defence of Calais. It has been argued that the primary purpose of this volte-face was to draw attention away from the soon to be crucial beaches and harbour of Dunkirk, but this seems to be *ex post facto* justification.

As the text of the War Office operational order to Brigadier Nicholson made clear, the main purpose was to show solidarity with the French in conformity with Fagalde's order to keep up the fight. After the British pull-out from Boulogne, the alliance could not stand another withdrawal that would be seen as leaving French troops in the lurch. The message to Nicholson read as follows:

> In spite of the policy of evacuation given you this morning, fact that British forces in your area now under Fagalde who has ordered no repeat no evacuation means that you must comply for sake of Allied solidarity. Your role is therefore to hold on, harbour being for present of no importance to BEF. Brigade Group

48 Div started marching to your assistance this morning. No reinforcements but ammunition being sent by sea. Should this fail RAF will drop ammunition. You will select best position and fight on.[18]

Churchill, with his love of the dramatic, was displeased with the uninspiring tone of the message and followed up this order with an exhortation for the garrison to do their utmost, but this too emphasised that the objective was to demonstrate solidarity with France. My father also sent his own personal orders to Nicholson, reiterating the same points and concluding with an understated appeal of his own, 'Yours are all regular troops, and I need not say more'.[19] This was a slight misrepresentation, as one of Nicholson's battalions was a Territorial unit, Queen Victoria's Rifles, but the import, that Nicholson was to fight to the last, was clear. These instructions, although of military and political necessity, can hardly have been easy to send.

In conveying the Calais order, my father completed his last significant role insofar as the Battle of France was concerned. On the 25th, after the news that Gort had abandoned any hopes of attacking southwards and had instead begun his retreat to the Dunkirk perimeter, he recorded his thoughts on the progress of the campaign and the prospects for the future:

> The final debacle cannot be long delayed and it is difficult to see how we can help. It cannot mean the evacuation of more than a minute portion of the BEF and the abandonment of all the equipment of which we are so short in this country.
>
> Horrible days to have to live through.
>
> I wish I could have seen the dire destruction of all these damned armoured divisions, which have done all the trouble. They have taken years to make and train & they have carried out their purpose.
>
> The question now is what we shall do. We shall have the most appalling pressure to send an Army over to France to keep things going and we shall have the people here shouting for protection against invasion. What proportion we shall come to in the end is difficult to say. We must lay down a minimum for Home Defence. Then a small BEF as a token. We shall have lost practically all our trained soldiers by the next few days – unless a miracle appears to help us.[20]

Evidently, his thinking at this stage was based on the assumption that the French forces south of the breakthrough would be able to stabilise their line and that a static front could be established. This could potentially be anchored on the line of the Somme where 1st Armoured Division and 51st (Highland) Division were already deploying, along with various rear-echelon formations, to continue the fight independently of the main body of the BEF falling back on Dunkirk.

The direction of these hypothetical future operations, however, and the strategic choices that they entailed, seemed likely to fall to another. As my father went on to observe, his focus had now been redirected elsewhere:

> I am now concentrating upon the Home Defence. The Cabinet are still wondering about what they will do about appointing a Commander-in-Chief. They have lost confidence in Kirke and want a change to some man well-known in England. They are considering my appointment. I have said I am prepared to do anything they want. Obviously, when one considers how the Germans have worked out their plans for the conquest of other countries, they must have considered how to get at us. Parachutists, troop-carrying aeroplanes, tanks in flat-bottomed boats and the like. Given perhaps foggy weather they might get a footing. The essence of the problem is information and instant action. Delay is fatal. Attack every body of men seen irrespective of loss. Only extreme energy from the top will allow us to deal with this menace.[21]

Here, one sees an energy and resolution that had for some time been rather less to the fore in my father's diary entries. There is little doubt that here was a task that he relished far more than the role of CIGS and, what was more, a task to which he was by temperament and experience far better suited.

The next day was, as he recorded it, a 'memorable' one that saw the beginning of the miracle that he had hoped for in the form of the formal instruction to Gort 'to withdraw to the coast with a view to making an attempt to get out'. Although my father still doubted that much could be saved – noting, 'It will be a matter of getting as many men out as possible with very little equipment. They will want a lot of putting right when they are landed and will have to be reconstituted.' – this was the beginning of the process that would lead to Operation Dynamo and the lifting of some 338,000 British and French troops from the beaches and harbour of Dunkirk. The day was, however, no less memorable for the professional changes that it brought for him:

> I was told I had to take over the Command in England and organise that. I am to be made a Field-Marshal later. Not at once, because the Public may think that I am being given a sop and turned out. An honour for me and a new and most important job. One much more to my liking than CIGS in every way. The next few months may show whether we can stand in England by ourselves. All a matter of the Air Force. If we can keep that in being, all is well.[22]

Such was the vulnerability of Britain's infrastructure to air attack, particularly by night, pending the introduction of what my father referred to as homing devices – in fact, the first airborne interception radar – for the RAF's night fighters, that he feared Germany might well attempt to bring Britain to her knees by air attack alone. Alternatively, an invasion might follow German attainment of air superiority, and it was against this eventuality that my father's new role would require him to plan.

In contrast with the confused political dynamics surrounding his appointment as CIGS, my father's replacement by Sir John Dill and reassignment to an active command was a straightforward and transparent process. At least as far back as 16 April when its likelihood was recorded by the diarist Sir Henry 'Chips' Channon MP,[23] my father's impending departure from the War Office was an open secret, just as it was generally understood within the army that bringing Dill back from France to be VCIGS was a precursor to his stepping into my father's shoes.

As we have seen from the previous chapter, a distance had emerged between Churchill and my father during the Norwegian campaign and it seems most likely that the change was already intended to take place as part of the general shake-up consequent on Churchill's replacement of Chamberlain, being delayed only by the sudden onset of blitzkrieg The new situation, with Britain directly under threat, clearly required a man of action to organise the forces on the ground, just as it required a first-class staff brain at the War Office to 'infuse a disorientated department with purpose and authority'.[24]

My father had previously stated his belief that Dill was the better staff officer of the two of them, just as he had little doubt that he himself was the better commander, and when viewed in this light the new assignments placed each man in the position best suited to their respective abilities. However, Dill's brief stint as VCIGS had left my father with doubts over the fitness of the man who would replace him in the top job, writing that he left the War Office 'with the feeling that Dill will not do the work either physically or mentally of CIGS. He seemed to me to be whacked already. He simply cannot do the work necessary.' There was clearly no thought that this might pave the way for his own return as CIGS in due course, however. If Dill failed, 'they will just have to find someone else'.[25] For his part, he had a more important role to concentrate on.

The task facing my father was one to challenge even his abilities and experience. Planning under his predecessor, Sir Walter Kirke, had concentrated primarily upon defence against an airborne landing, with the focus on being able to round up parachutists before they could consolidate on the ground or, worse still, capture a port that could then be used to bring in reinforcements by sea. Up until the fall of the Low Countries and their coastline there had been no option for a direct landing by sea after a short passage, but with German troops now extending their control westwards along the Channel coast, this situation had changed radically and my father had to prepare for an invasion by sea — albeit potentially incorporating, or preceded by, an airborne landing — and cast his plans accordingly.

Aside from the army's contribution to the Air Defence of Great Britain which took the form of seven AA divisions, my father had a pitifully small force at his disposal composed for the most part of divisions that were still unfit for deployment due to lack of manpower, training and/or equipment. Although over coming days he would watch with increasing astonishment and pleasure the return of far more of the original BEF than he had ever expected to see safely back in the country, the formations that came home were lacking all their transport, equipment and heavy weapons. This meant the material shortfall was, if anything, rendered more acute and was further strained by the need to arm the men of the Local Defence Volunteers (LDV, Home Guard from 22 July). The decision to send forces to Western France – the 2nd BEF under Brooke, built largely around 52nd (Lowland) Infantry Division along with a Canadian brigade group – removed some of the best that was available from his grasp, although these troops were back in the country by mid-June following the final collapse of France.

In view of the extreme threat, the authority of the post was expanded to give my father, unlike his predecessor, complete operational control of all troops in the country except those assigned to the Air Defence of Great Britain, which remained under the Air Ministry. Major General Bernard Paget was appointed to be my father's Chief of Staff, 'a very able man, besides being a cheery one, in whose company one could never be downhearted'.[26]

Headquarters were established at Kneller Hall, just outside London near Richmond-on-Thames and in happier times home to the Royal Military School of Music. Setting aside divisions still undergoing training, deployed in the north and west of the country away from the threatened sector, or in Northern Ireland, the forces immediately available to resist a German landing stood as follows:

Table VII: Troops Available to Resist Invasion, May–June 1940

Home Forces – General Sir Edmund Ironside GOC-in-C
Eastern Command – Lt Gen. Sir G. Williams
Northern Sector (East Anglia)
    15th (Scottish) Infantry Division – Maj. Gen. R. Le Fanu
    18th (East Anglian) Infantry Division – Maj. Gen. L.H.K. Finch (from 9 June)
    55th (West Lancashire) Infantry Division – Maj. Gen. V.H.B. Majendie
Southern Sector (Kent)
    45th Infantry Division – Maj. Gen. E.C.A. Schreiber
    1st London Division – Maj. Gen. C.F. Liardet
Command Reserve
    2nd London Division – Maj. Gen. H. Willans
    20th Armoured Brigade – Brig. E.D. Fanshawe[27]

GHQ Reserve
2nd Armoured Division – Maj. Gen. J.C. Tilly[28]
IV Corps – Lt Gen. F. Nosworthy[29]
    43rd (Wessex) Infantry Division – Maj. Gen. R. Pollok
    52nd (Lowland) Infantry Division – Maj. Gen. J. Drew
    1st Canadian Division – Maj. Gen. A. McNaughton[30]

The above does not include static defences such as coast defence guns, nor the additional three brigades of infantry assigned to the London District for the defence of the capital. As well as the two armoured formations listed, 8th Royal Tank Regiment was also available, having been left behind when the rest of 1st Army Tank Brigade deployed with the BEF.

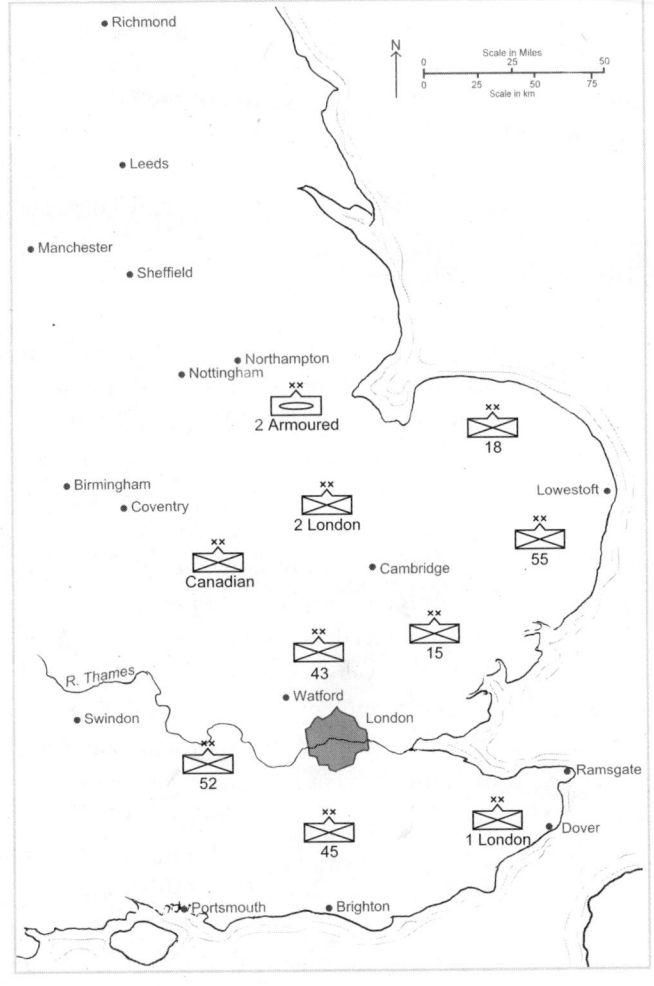

Anti-invasion deployments, May–June 1940.

On paper, this sounds like an impressive force but, as noted, there were substantial deficiencies in weapons and equipment. As of 1 June, a total of 963 tanks were available in the whole of the British Isles, including depots and training units, but 132 of these were obsolete models and a further 618 were obsolescent light tanks armed only with machine guns. There were only 103 cruiser tanks and 110 infantry tanks. The infantry divisions lacked transport and would have needed to requisition civilian vehicles in order to move rapidly. They were also severely lacking in artillery and anti-tank weapons.

On 31 May, even after counting in the artillery component of 12th Division, the infantry of which had gone to France with the BEF, Eastern Command's six infantry divisions had between them only thirty-nine of the modern 25-pdr field guns, when there should have been seventy-two per division, backed up by a further 120 guns of older patterns. Each division should have had forty-eight 2-pdr anti-tank guns – which happened to be the most effective available counter to German tanks – but there were only fourteen in the whole command, and no division had more than half its allocation of the far less effective Boys anti-tank rifle. 43rd Division, the only GHQ Reserve formation for which complete figures are available, was slightly better off with forty-eight field guns, all of them 25-pdrs, and a full complement of 307 anti-tank rifles, but only eight anti-tank guns.[31]

A slightly later set of figures, prepared by my father himself, confirm that the Canadians were in a better position, still having sixty-four field guns (types unspecified) and, thanks to an attached anti-tank regiment, sixty anti-tank guns. 52nd Division, however, was less well off with sixteen field and twelve anti-tank guns. All three divisions in GHQ Reserve, along with 15th and 45th Divisions from Eastern Command, are also shown as having their full complement of 590 Bren guns, but only the first three had their full allocation of ninety carriers.[32]

In common with the rest of those directing Britain's war effort, my father shared the – thankfully erroneous – belief that an invasion of Britain formed part of the existing German operational plans and that detailed preparations would already have been set in train. He was convinced, he wrote, 'that the Germans will make a determined landing, the minute they are able to do so, in England. It will be no amateur affair. It will be well and carefully prepared.'[33] In fact, as we now know, planning for Operation Sealion was put together on the fly and was never truly satisfactory. He was also firmly convinced of the dangers posed by a Fifth Column operating within Britain although, again, fears to this effect would prove to be groundless. Nevertheless, these assumptions, along with the nature and limitations of the troop formations under his command, all helped shape his planning for the defence of the country.

Upon relieving Kirke, he reviewed the general situation and priorities as he saw them:

(i) Enemy aliens. They must be cleared out of the Coast area at once.
(ii) All troops must be filled up with men and material at once.
(iii) The petrol situation is not good. There is far too much petrol in the Coast areas, most of it unguarded.
(iv) There is unrestricted movement at week-ends in the Coast areas, offering the Germans any amount of transport for the taking.
(v) There must be much more realisation of the serious nature of the position in England.
(vi) There is a very scratch staff here in the Home Forces.
(vii) The Civil Depts are very slow in their methods and do not realise the value of time in military operations.[34]

He considered the fight for the coastal areas to be the matter of prime importance. With only a limited force available for a counter-attack, it was imperative that the invasion be contained on the coast if at all possible. Bearing in mind some of the later criticisms of my father's defensive arrangements, it is important to stress that he noted this at an early stage, writing on 30 May as follows:

If the Germans ever attempt a landing here they will put the utmost energy into establishing what might be called a 'bridge-head' in England. All our energies must be put into stopping this. No waiting for more troops to come up. Our mobile forces must attack at once regardless of losses and nip the landing in the bud. We cannot inculcate that idea too much into everybody concerned.[35]

The difficulty, of course, was that the mobility of the forces under my father's command was decidedly limited. For this reason, common sense required that measures should also be taken for hindering the advance of the enemy in the event that he was able to break through the coastal defences and establish himself ashore, and therefore preparations to this end also became a significant part of my father's role.

That said, my father recognised that anything that could be done to increase the mobility of his troops was a vital priority. With added mobility, it would be easier for the coastal divisions to concentrate and resist an attack, but mobile forces would also be essential in delaying and harassing any enemy troops that were able to move inland – either as a result of a break-out from a bridgehead, or an aerial landing. One of his early initiatives was recorded as follows:

I have decided to form troops of 3 motor cars with Brens in them, commanded by a young Tank Corps officer and to christen them 'Ironsides'. They will be given to each Division to the tune of 3 troops.[36]

By 29 May, he was planning for some 400 such cars, a substantial increase on the original concept, and developing it further, he looked to mount light field guns on lorries – a precursor of the gun portee system employed to great effect in the Western Desert later in the war:

> I hope to have a good many of these 6pdr and 12pdr guns mounted on light lorries. They may not be tanks, but they may get a shot and knock the gentleman out. Our people must act just as the Germans do and go straight in and attack whatever the casualties. Gradually perhaps I shall get some tanks.[37]

For anything less than a full-scale invasion, armoured cars – once they became available – should be sufficient to deal with motorboat landings, while requisitioned civilian buses would hopefully give infantry the means to round up parachutists.

As he toured the Kent countryside, which was clearly the most vulnerable sector, he also looked at the options for static defences to inflict further delays upon any invaders who managed to fight their way inland. This role, he recognised, was a perfect way to utilise the newly formed LDV:

> Static defence in every village by blocks and information going out from there. And thousands of Molotov Cocktails thrown down from the windows of houses. That might well settle tank columns. We just want the courage of the men. Nothing else matters. No defence is any good if the men behind it leave it and run away. The old LDVs won't do that.[38]

By using the LDVs as a blocking and intelligence-collection force, he hoped to seriously impede enemy mobility and thereby 'avoid the spectacle of France having her guts torn out without any effort being made to deal with the aggressor'.[39]

After a few days in his new post, my father was gratified to learn that he still had the prime minister's good opinion. The day after the two men dined together on 29 May, he wrote:

> Winston said to me last night: 'We all depend upon you, because you don't lose your head in a crisis & have shown that during the last few months.' He also repeated the fact that I was going to be made a Field Marshal in a few days. That will give me a good deal of added authority.[40]

Certainly, some added authority would have been of great utility since dealing with the various civilian authorities, and with the enthusiastic but disorganised LDV, was a trying business. The Home Defence Executive, with which he met for the first time on 28 May, consisted of some fifty people, including ten ministers, and was classed by Colonel Macleod as a 'debating society' through which little could be achieved. Cutting through the red tape, Macleod records that my father had this replaced with a far smaller core executive, chaired by Sir Findlater Stewart and with its only other permanent members being Wing Commander Eric Hodsoll, the Home Office's senior Civil Defence expert, and Macleod himself as representative of the staff of GOC-in-C Home Forces. Other ministerial representatives would be co-opted as necessary.[41]

While such unnecessary meetings could be dispensed with to give my father the time needed to deal with more important matters, it was also necessary for him to take an active and public role in events so that his name and reputation could be tied to the defence effort. Therefore, 6 June saw him meeting with senior officers and officials involved in the setting up of the LDV. A complete transcript of his speech to this gathering, and of the subsequent question and answer session, survives in the National Archives and provides insights into the way in which he approached the incorporation of the LDV into home defence plans and the bluff, no-nonsense approach that he brought to the post of GOC-in-C Home Forces.

A large part of the initial speech was reassurance that the volunteers were valued and formed an integral part of the defence plan. A desire to be useful and to make a contribution had to be balanced with a need to avoid duplicating, and perhaps even impeding, tasks that were already being filled by Regular forces. There had been, he said, 'examples where somebody has come edging in and has said "I am an LDV" they have said "Go to hell out of it; we do not want you here". I hope we shall have no more of that.'[42] He reiterated that the main roles of the LDV in the event of an invasion would be intelligence gathering and static defence through local road blocks. Weapons and uniforms were in short supply and he explained that priority for rifles was being given to troops in rural areas, since a shotgun was just as effective and far safer in the sense of preventing civilian casualties in a residential area. Shotguns he also recommended as the best means of dealing with parachutists in bad light or in woodland; again, the concern regarding the use of rifles was with respect to where a stray shot might end up.

He made it clear throughout that he had faith in the men who were organising the LDV, the majority of whom had served in the previous war. He deliberately drew on this parallel, suggesting that, if necessary, LDV men would work as effectively under conditions of aerial bombardment as the BEF of the Great War, when it had 'walked up through Ypres' amidst the German shell bursts. He noted that 'this time the Bosche has produced bombs from aeroplanes with a whistle on them', of which he had been on the receiving end 'at Calais the other day when they blew me out of my bed'. He said this was clearly intended to break morale, but he made it clear that he expected his audience to take this in their stride and, more importantly, to maintain morale amongst their men and local civilians.[43]

Other potential threats were dealt with in a similar direct fashion: parachutists, for example, would be less of a threat than might be expected because the effectiveness of the German airborne forces had been degraded by the heavy casualties – estimated at 50 per cent – that they had sustained in the invasion of the Low Countries. Presumably to prevent erroneous scare reports of parachute landings, he stressed that parachutists would only be committed to secure an important objective and were unlikely to be dropped in rural areas where there was no obvious military target. This provoked one of the most robust responses during the question and answer session when an interlocutor attempted to question the last assumption on the grounds that his locality, though rural, had had war industry relocated to it. He was bluntly told, 'Now don't argue with me'.[44]

Otherwise, the questions raised a number of points that made it clear there were many administrative and operational issues regarding the LDV that still needed to be worked out. Chains of command were not always clear; defence plans did not exist for all towns and cities; LDV units in the London commuter belt could not function during the working day as their men were all at their City desks; and LDV coast watchers were defecting to Admiralty-organised Coast Guard units because the latter were paid. If the points could be answered there and then, they were – for the rest, they were referred to the relevant bodies for further decision.

The penultimate question and answer exchange, however, made it clear that my father had made the right impression on his audience and that his appointment as GOC-in-C Home Forces had been well judged, insofar as its effect on morale was concerned:

QUESTION: May I suggest if you could give us a short broadcast?
GENERAL IRONSIDE: Myself?
QUESTION: Yes, it would have an extraordinary effect. There is a slight drop in enthusiasm. What these men want to know and you can tell them is they are an integral part as you have told us and their job is static defence and observation and information.
GENERAL IRONSIDE: If I do broadcast something it goes over to the Bosche just the same.
QUESTION: That is so but you have no idea what the effect would be.[45]

Judging by a slightly flustered response and a request for any further questions to be sent up on paper or via liaison officers, this praise and endorsement may have left my father for once lost for words.

All this planning, of course, took place against the backdrop of the conclusion of the Dunkirk evacuation and the extrication of the bulk of the BEF. Although they were no longer his direct concern – other than in the sense that every man brought back home was one more man to help defend the British Isles – my father naturally followed these events with a keen eye, although admitting that he did not envy Dill the responsibility for co-ordinating operations. His delight when it became apparent that far more men were being brought out than he had imagined possible was evident. On the afternoon of 30 May, he 'heard that 40,000 men were off last night, which puts a completely different complexion upon the picture of 4,000, as they gave me at first. It is wonderful what you can do with any number of small boats.'[46]

Then, on 2 June, two days before the evacuation operations were brought to a close, he recorded that he had met with the newly returned Major General Giffard Martel, GOC 50th Division, who informed him:

> [W]e haven't more than 2,000 men on shore [at Dunkirk]. The rest are French. Many of the French fighting very well. It is most extraordinary what we have been able to get off. I would never have believed it possible. Of course no equipment, but the bodies of trained men are almost as precious.[47]

As might be expected, he had particular praise for the defenders of Calais:

> A great effort, which I hope we shall never forget. It would have been impossible to have used Dunkirk as a point from which to evacuate the BEF & the 1st French Army without this stand. The most famous Regts. in the Army. They fought it out to the end. When I sent them to Calais I was sure they would do their duty and they did it. A fitting finish to their history. Requiscant. The historic name of Calais should be written once more on British hearts.
> One wonders how many survived.[48]

One officer who did survive the fall of Calais, it might be noted, was a certain 2nd Lieutenant Hugo Ironside of the 3rd Royal Tank Regiment. A number of secondary sources suggest that he was a cousin of my father, but this does not seem to have been the case. Certainly, if there was a relationship then it was a very distant one indeed. Still, the coincidence of names was such that the unfortunate subaltern was identified as a possible bargaining chip by the Nazis on the assumption that a family connection did exist and, after a series of unsuccessful escape attempts, he ended up in Colditz Castle.

With the BEF back home, the priority now became re-equipping its formations and integrating them into the Home Defence Plan. 4th and 50th Divisions went to Southern Command, being formed into V Corps under Auchinleck, while others were posted to Northern Command, thereby in both cases extending the coastal defences outwards from the key central sector covered by Eastern Command. Battle-experienced officers from the BEF were moved into command positions to disseminate that experience: Brooke, after his second return from France, eventually took over Southern Command in place of the unsatisfactory Lieutenant General Sir Bertie Fisher, while Ronald Adam, late GOC III Corps, went to Northern

Command to replace Lieutenant General Sir William Bartholomew with whose performance my father was unhappy.

As more senior officers returned to Britain and his command grew, another thing about which my father was unhappy was the lack of fulfilment of the promise that he would be made a field marshal. As he noted on the day after his meeting with the LDV, at which the retired Montgomery-Massingberd had turned up in full uniform, he felt 'that it would have given me added authority to be one. The only one serving in an active capacity. I wonder if they will wriggle out of their promise?'[49]

Meanwhile, although there was a continued question mark over the potential need to make troops available for the 2nd BEF – something my father resisted beyond the approved despatch of 52nd and 1st Canadian Divisions, although he was eventually obliged to concede that 3rd Division would go as well once it had been re-equipped – the twin priorities remained of equipping the available troops and formulating a detailed plan for their employment in the event of invasion. The former was largely out of his hands, being down to industrial capacity and the prioritisation, on political grounds, of those units earmarked to go back to France. However, as far as the latter was concerned, good progress was being made, beginning with an appreciation of just what the German threat was likely to consist of:

> The first effort will be an air one against our Air Industry, aerodromes, and Air Force generally. The RAF say that we may expect 4,800 tons of bombs a day. This is a total calculated upon the initial carrying capacity of the planes available.
>
> The initial effort of the Bosches against our Navy will be to mine our fleet into its bases, then to attempt a diversion to draw off our naval forces.
>
> As regards air-borne expedition, the Bosches have sufficient aircraft to transport 9,750 lightly-equipped men in one flight. The number of flights per day will vary from 1½ per day to East Anglia to three for Kent. Taking into account air opposition and ground opposition it is thought that the numbers can be calculated upon a basis of 10,000 for East Anglia and 20,000 for Kent. These only after a large measure of air superiority had been achieved.
>
> Such air-borne expeditions will be followed by sea-borne expeditions pushed forward with the utmost brutality.
>
> This is a dismal enough picture as regards numbers and takes little account of weather and opposition from the Navy & Air Force.
>
> Probably it can be very much reduced.
>
> All we can do at the moment is to speed up our Information and our Mobility on land. Instant and brutal action is required at once. Attack to the last man 'out all you can' as Cromwell said.[50]

Over the coming weeks, as Italy joined the war and France dropped out of it, my father continued to address the problems that he faced and work on a defensive plan, continuing all the while with his morale-boosting tours and visits. He remained concerned at the huge imbalance in terms of armoured and mobile forces in the event that the Germans were able to establish themselves ashore, and frustrated at the lack of resources available to counter it:

> My main fear is the penetration by armoured fighting vehicles. I am very lacking in gun power and I can see no immediate prospect of reinforcement at the moment. I have called into being every available gun that I can find and I have mounted them as both static and as mobile units. I can do no more at the moment.[51]

He remained confident that the LDV, now under Kirke's direction, would perform well and delay the invader, but this was not enough and mobile forces were essential if delay was to be turned into defeat:

> The key question is mobility, mobility and not too many troops tied up in static positions. We must have some tied up owing to the small amount of territory we have to play with. Also, so many of our troops are incapable of attacking through lack of training and lack of equipment.
>
> I know very well what is coming. I shall be tempted to dissipate my reserves. I must have mobility to save me.[52]

By the end of June, a more definite plan had been prepared, taking into account expected enemy intentions, the state of the available forces and my father's own concerns about how the military operations in the aftermath of an invasion were likely to play out. The first stage was based on a strong defensive crust on the coast itself, which might not stop the invasion but would serve as an outpost line to buy time for the defenders. If the enemy could not be stopped on the beaches, then certainly he could be delayed and heavy casualties inflicted by the initial defenders and localised counter-attacks by mobile divisional assets. However, if the enemy did establish himself ashore and begin to move inland, it was essential to limit his progress until a major counter-attack could be mounted.

The second stage of the defensive plan was therefore based on trading space for time, in order to allow such reserves as were available to be brought into action. At the last resort, defending formations would fall back to a final position – GHQ stop-line – which ran nearly due east from Bristol before kinking southwards towards Basingstoke to cover London and running east again to a point just short of Maidstone. From there, it turned northwards to run through Cambridge to the Wash. An extension ran north from the Wash to a point near Richmond, North Yorkshire, to cover the industrial cities of the Midlands and Yorkshire.

Between the coast and GHQ stop-line, a number of lesser stop-lines were instituted at divisional and corps level where stands could be made in order to buy time and delay an advance; potentially, the attack might even be turned back at one of these intermediate lines. All lines followed where possible the line of waterways or escarpments, and were reinforced with concrete pillboxes. Without sufficient mobile reserves to mount a major counter-attack at command or corps level, this plan at least gave some chance for an effective response to be mounted by elements of GHQ Reserve, even if the coastal defensive crust was pierced. In its basic form, this plan was approved by the chiefs of staff and the War Cabinet on 25 June.

Despite this approval, however, not everyone was happy with the way in which the defences had been arranged. Nor did the War Office help matters, for my father was constantly left wondering which of his formations might be called upon for other purposes – 3rd Division, for example, was taken from his command into War Office Reserve, returned to him and then removed again, all in the space of a single day. Also he, and his chief assistant Paget even more so, were forever being called up to London for conferences and meetings. My father began to develop doubts about the regard in which he was held by Churchill and Eden, observing that his promised promotion had still not come through and Gort remained unemployed but on hand as a potential replacement for him. In fact, his worries were misdirected: his political stock remained high, and it was his military colleagues who posed the threat to his position.

As soon as the day after their approval by the chiefs of staff, my father's defensive plans were being critically analysed by the vice chiefs, whose professional opinions found considerable fault with the fact that the GHQ stop-line was set so far back from the coast and so much territory would be given up if it became necessary to pull back to it. My father was acquainted with these criticisms, but remained firm in his belief that while it would indeed be preferable to fight an offensive battle much closer to the landing beaches, the means were not yet available with which to do so. His plan was not the best way to defeat an invasion, but it was the best way to do so with the resources available – the coat was being cut to suit the cloth.

Both Dill and Air Chief Marshall Newall supported this stance, emphasising to the critics that the GHQ stop-line existed as a final point to fall back upon, not as a position to be assumed as soon as the defensive crust was penetrated.

More pertinently, the holding of divisions in GHQ Reserve behind the GHQ stop-line was criticised for placing these formations too far from the battlefront. However, it was possible to nullify this criticism by the reorganisation of GHQ Reserve into two corps, McNaughton being promoted to corps command alongside Nosworthy. This was made possible by the assignment of 1st Armoured Division, to which 1st Army Tank Brigade and 20th Armoured Brigade were attached to bring it swiftly back up to strength after its return from France, as a GHQ Reserve formation. Since the assumption was still being followed that the

Germans were likely to make their main landings in Kent and East Anglia, the creation of two mobile reserves, one to be placed north and the other south of the Thames, facilitated a swifter response to either threatened sector.

Notwithstanding this refinement of arrangements, and a reiteration of instructions that the beaches were to be defended at all costs, matters came to a head on 29 June when my father was called in for a meeting with the COS Committee and presented with a summary of the various criticisms, including a memorandum from Lord Hankey emphasising that the fight must be made and won on the coast, as well as another from Churchill that was far more open to the idea of mobile forces resisting the enemy inland. My father was understandably frustrated both by the continued interference and the mixed messages:

> I spent an unsatisfactory day with the Chiefs of Staff. They are not clear in their minds as to what they want as to our defence. At one time they say that we must defeat the enemy on the beaches when he lands & that we must hold a sufficient reserve. That the teaching of the war is that we must hold lines. The whole thing is very difficult & I have given them my views:
>
> (i) The coast line is terrific in length and we may be attacked at any point of it owing to the fact that the Germans might start from Norway, the Baltic, Holland, Belgium or France. They might even take Ireland first and so extend the probability of landing still further to the west. The veil of secrecy in Germany is complete. We have no secret service at all this war and know little of preparations.
> Very few preparations had been made to prepare beaches & possible landing-points and work is still very incomplete.
> (ii) Air landings can take place anywhere in the UK or Ireland with even less warning than in the case of sea-borne landings. With the means at Germany's disposal, large forces – up to 20,000 can be transported by air.
> (iii) The forces we have available in the UK are both untrained and armed insufficiently, especially in tanks and guns, & anti-tank weapons.
>
> And so we have decided to hold the coast as a 'crust'. Work is proceeding fast on anti-tank obstacles at beaches, wire & pill-boxes. The idea is to inflict all the losses we can and to attack at once with our mobile forces at the beaches or at any point to which they have penetrated. For this we have what local reserves we have, and two Reserves each of a Mobile Division and an Armoured Division.
> We are also creating a local static defence of armed riflemen, using blocks and pill-boxes all over the country.[53]

Again, the point was emphasised that if this was not the best plan, it was the best plan for the resources at hand, and this the chiefs of staff seem to have accepted.

At the beginning of July 1940, after the defensive plans had undergone their final refinements in light of the War Office critique, the forces now available to my father were organised and deployed as follows. Training formations and troops deployed away from the invasion zone are omitted, but the vast increase that had been achieved during his tenure as GOC-in-C is apparent:

Table VIII: Troops Available to Resist Invasion, July 1940

Home Forces – General Sir Edmund Ironside GOC-in-C
Northern Command – Lt Gen. Sir R. Adam
I Corps – Lt Gen. H.R.L.G. Alexander
    1st Infantry Division – Maj. Gen. K. Anderson
    2nd Infantry Division – Maj. Gen. N. Irwin
    44th (Home Counties) Infantry Division – Maj. Gen. A.E. Perceval
X Corps – Lt Gen. W.G. Holmes
    54th (East Anglian) Infantry Division – Maj. Gen. J.H.T. Priestman
    59th (Staffordshire) Infantry Division – Maj. Gen. F.V.B. Witts
    42nd (East Lancashire) Infantry Division – Maj. Gen. H.B.D. Wilcox
Command Reserve
    24th Army Tank Brigade – Brig. K.E.S. Stuart
    2nd Motor Machine Gun Brigade – Brig. T.D. Murray

Eastern Command – Lt Gen. Sir G. Williams
II Corps – Lt Gen. E. Osborne
    18th (East Anglian) Infantry Division – Maj. Gen. L.H.K. Finch
    52nd (Lowland) Infantry Division – Maj. Gen. J. Drew
XI Corps – Lt Gen. H. Massy
    15th (Scottish) Infantry Division – Maj. Gen. R. Le Fanu
    55th (West Lancashire) Infantry Division – Maj. Gen. V.H.B. Majendie
XII Corps – Lt Gen. A. Thorne
    45th Infantry Division – Maj. Gen. E.C.A. Schreiber
    1st London Division – Maj. Gen. C.F. Liardet
    1st Motor Machine Gun Brigade – Brig. M.B. Burrows

Southern Command – Lt Gen. Sir A. Brooke
V Corps – Lt Gen. C. Auchinleck
    4th Infantry Division – Maj. Gen. R. Eastwood
    50th (Northumbrian) Infantry Division – Maj. Gen. W.H.C. Ramsden[54]

VIII Corps – Lt Gen. Sir H. Franklyn
  48th (South Midland) Division – Maj. Gen. R.L. Petre
  70th Independent Infantry Brigade – Brig. P. Kirkup
Command Reserve
  21st Army Tank Brigade – Brig. G.P.L. Drake-Brockman

GHQ Reserve
IV Corps – Lt Gen. F. Nosworthy
  2nd Armoured Division – Maj. Gen. J.C. Tilly
  43rd (Wessex) Infantry Division – Maj. Gen. R. Pollok
  1st Armoured Reconnaissance Brigade – Brig. C.W. Norman
VII Corps – Lt Gen A. McNaughton
  1st Armoured Division – Maj. Gen. R. Evans
  1st Canadian Division – Maj. Gen. G.R. Pearkes
  New Zealand Imperial Force – Maj. Gen. Sir B. Freyberg[55]

VIII Corps, deployed in the West Country, and elements of X Corps, deployed along the North Sea coast, fell outside of the obvious invasion area but are included for completeness as they formed part of the coastal defensive crust. Additional forces under my father's control, not listed above, were posted to Western and Scottish Commands. Elements of the Australian Imperial Force had begun to disembark, but were held as a War Office Reserve at Aldershot and placed outside of my father's command.

After the conference on 29 June, the criticisms of my father's command and planning seemed to him to have dropped – in part because many began to doubt that the invasion would come, although my father maintained that it would – and he continued with his round of inspections and visits as, all the while, the air raids multiplied and intensified. In fact, although the War Office and the War Cabinet were happy, dissent continued at a lower level.

Brooke, at Southern Command, felt that he had too few resources and too much attention was being placed on the North Sea coast as opposed to his own sector along the English Channel. Brooke also disliked the investment of time and effort in pillboxes and stop-lines, preferring that it be devoted to building up a reserve of mobile troops, although it is hard to see how curtailing the one could have aided the other. In this latter point he was backed up by Major General Bernard Montgomery, GOC 3rd Division, whose command, although comprehensively re-equipped and capable of mobile operations, was now assigned to a static coastal defence role in Kent. Far better, felt Montgomery, that it be added to the mobile reserves.

Of course, for all their future eminence, neither of these commanders had the full picture that my father possessed, but they did both have the political nous to further their cases and both men appealed to Churchill when the prime minister

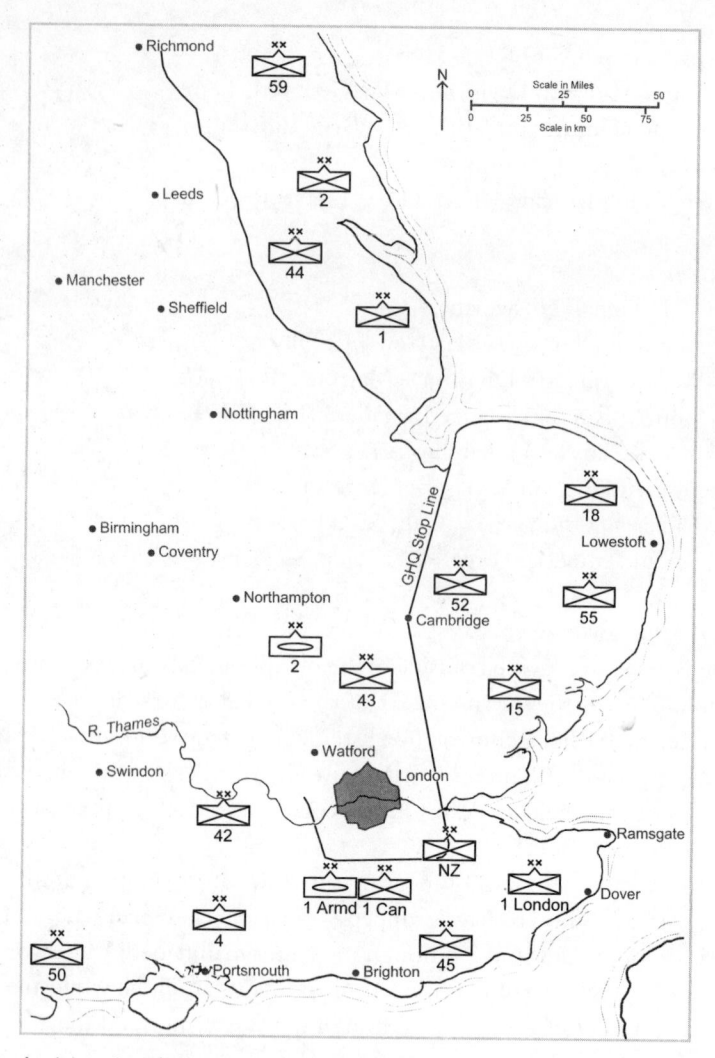

Anti-invasion deployments, July 1940.

visited their commands. In the case of Montgomery's intervention, the result was my father receiving from Churchill 'an order, or what is practically an order, to withdraw two divisions from the beach-line'. My father sought compromise and had two divisions reduced to one, but the end result was that 3rd Division was reassigned to GHQ Reserve with effect from 11 July, leaving my father fuming that it was 'difficult to tackle Winston when he is in one of his go-getter humours'.[56]

Montgomery's intervention caused my father annoyance, but Brooke's intervention, which took place when Churchill visited Southern Command on 17 July, had more drastic consequences. On the afternoon of 19 July, two days after Churchill had visited Brooke, my father was summoned to see the secretary of state:

[I was] told that I was to be replaced by Alan Brooke as C-in-C Home Forces. Eden told me that the Cabinet wished to have someone with the late experience of war. I told Eden that he needn't worry and that I was quite prepared to be released. I had done my best. In order that the matter should be placed on a good footing, I was to be made a Field Marshal.

And so, my military career comes to an end in the middle of a great war. I have had 41 years and 1 month's service and I have reached the very top. I can't complain. Cabinets have to make decisions in times of stress. I don't suppose Winston liked doing it, for he is always loyal to his friends.

Now I must settle down to live in Hingham and working in the garden, where I can amuse myself with simple things.[57]

After waiting in vain for most of the following day for Brooke to relieve him in person, my father left his headquarters for the last time at 4 in the afternoon of 20 July 1940. Notwithstanding his promotion, he did so still in the uniform of a general. His servant 'said to me "shall I change the badges on your coat" and I said "no" for it seems hardly worth it. I shan't be wearing any more khaki for a long time, if ever.'[58]

Eight days later, Churchill wrote to him in a letter that demonstrated his personal loyalty and the regard in which he continued to hold my father, even after their differences over the previous months:

Although the fortune of war has for the time being ended our collaboration, I hope you will allow me to thank you for all the work that you have done during these just grievous ten months of the struggle. It would be a pleasure to me if you would allow me to submit your name to the King for the dignity of a barony. A seat in the House of Lords could offer your services to the nation in the same way as is done by Lords Trenchard & Milne. It will not bar any further opportunities of service which may present themselves and allow you to offer your council to the nation.

PS – I had to delay sending this letter in order to ascertain whether such a submission on my part would be in accordance with HM's pleasure. It is thought that the next Honours List will be the most suitable time. Please therefore let me know your wishes.[59]

In due course, the 1941 New Year's Honours List included his ennoblement as Baron Ironside of Archangel and of Ironside in the County of Aberdeen, and he was introduced into the House of Lords on 26 February by Lord Hastings and Field Marshal Lord Birdwood.

Epilogue

After his induction into the House of Lords, in which he never subsequently spoke, my father retreated to Norfolk, wondering whether he would ever be employed again. The Foreign Office pleaded with him to write to Reza Shah in Teheran, who had become increasingly unapproachable but, having been out of touch for ten years, he felt that there was no point in intervening.

He attended War Weapons Week and National Savings Week gatherings and, in March 1941, he was invited to inspect the troops stationed in Iceland to boost the morale of the men who had become thoroughly disgruntled at being based on this tiny isolated island so far from the centre of things. Expecting to be away for at least two weeks in June of that year, he prepared himself for the trip, only to be told that his presence was no longer needed due to the withdrawal of the troops and the handover of the garrison to US forces.

The world's attention had by now turned to the struggle between Germany and Russia, where the German advances had been halted in the region of Kiev. Rumours swirled in the newspapers about the strengths and weaknesses of the German Army, while the Russians continued with their withdrawal from the Odessa area and fears of the crisis spreading to Iran – as Persia had officially been renamed on 21 March 1935 – were paramount. Naturally, my father's feelings about affairs in Iran were aroused. He knew that the country, still under the rule of Reza Shah, wanted no foreign influence within her borders but he feared that she would be left with little choice.

The news that Iran had been invaded by British troops from the south and by Russia from the north came on 25 July. My father speculated that this might mean a role for him, but recognised that with the British part of the operation being directed from India this was unlikely. The Iranian Government resigned a few days later and the new prime minister settled for peace with Lieutenant General Edward Quinan, GOC Persia and Iraq Command. By 17 September, Reza Shah had abdicated and my father gained some publicity by lending his name to the *Daily Telegraph* through the Ministry of Information. While acknowledging that the former Shah had been an autocrat and dictator, he felt that Reza had done well by his country and clearly never had any regrets over his own part in his rise to power.

A leading article on the Russian winter campaign also appeared in the *Daily Telegraph*, so my father was able to keep his name before the Ministry of Information, who then commissioned him to write weekly commentaries for publications in the South American press. This made a useful addition to his army pay as well as keeping him in touch with public life, as was expected for a person of his standing. He was on call to represent or celebrate the army's position and he maintained his profile by putting himself at the disposal of all those fighting to safeguard the nation.

However, the call to duty of a more active kind never came. It was not that his name was not put forward, but rather that nothing more ever came of it. A 1944 Foreign Office telegram sent from the newly liberated Brussels by Sir Hughe Knatchbull-Hugessen, ambassador extraordinary and plenipotentiary to Belgium, succinctly identifies the problem:

> While I personally would have nothing against proposed appointment of Lord Ironside, I am certain that it would cause serious difficulty with military element both SHAEF and 21st Army [Group]: nor do I think it would be advisable to appoint in any capacity here a Field-Marshal who is senior to present Commander-in-Chief of 21st Army [Group]. I must ask most urgently that my views be not quoted as coming from me.[1]

It is unfortunately unclear what post my father was being considered for, as the telegram is seemingly an orphan within the archives with no additional correspondence to provide a context.

However, my father's seniority as a field marshal was only part of the problem. Not only did he outrank the officers now commanding Britain's forces in the field, but they came for the most part from a group of men who had been opposed to many of his policies in the late 1930s and during his war service as CIGS and GOC-in-C Home Forces. Pownall, perhaps his most persistent critic, had gone to the Far East as Chief of Staff to Wavell and then Mountbatten, but Brooke was now CIGS in succession to Dill and a field marshal to boot, as was Montgomery, who was commanding the Anglo-Canadian forces in northern Europe as GOC-in-C 21st Army Group. To have my father return to the military stage would not have sat well with men of this stamp, all of whom had to some extent sought to undermine him when he had held high office.

To my father's immense credit, he took this lack of military employment with great dignity, although doing so meant that his final years were passed almost completely cut off from the service in which he had made his life and career.

To watch over his own future in old age, he purchased Morley Old Hall in Norfolk and the 30 acres of farmland surrounding it with the aim of building a family hub for the future. However, the mansion was moated and outdated and he could not secure planning permission to make it habitable. After the war ended he was still not able to achieve his aims and, following a serious car accident at Scotch Corner while en route to Scotland, he had to call a halt to his plans and seek respite at Hingham.

In 1959, after a fall which led to a broken femur, he was taken to the Millbank Army Hospital in London where he became the victim of a post-operative thrombosis. This ended his life in his seventy-ninth year, on 22 September 1959.

He received a funeral service in Westminster Abbey and was, in due course, commemorated by a memorial plaque in the Nelson Vault at St Paul's Cathedral. In keeping with his post-1940 detachment from public life, the funeral in the great abbey was followed by a more modest thanksgiving service and burial at Hingham in a simple soldier's grave. His death was the signal for my mother to seek preferment by the queen to spend the remaining years of her life in one of the grace-and-favour residences at Hampton Court Palace.

My father's reputation since his death has suffered somewhat, thanks to the publication of diaries such as Pownall's with their negative comments on his abilities, and historians have seemingly taken these judgements at face value rather than seeking to place them in the balanced context that I have striven for here. It perhaps does not help that my father's own diaries are so voluminous that to publish more than a tiny selection from them would be almost impossible. Even those in print covering 1918–22 and 1937–40 are mere extracts.

Yet it is only by reading his diaries in full and studying them at length, as I have done in the years since my father's death, that one can gauge the full measure of the man. Certainly, such an understanding leads one to offer rebuttal of many of the claims made against my father's character and record: that he was careerist and an intriguer; that he pursued a personal campaign against Hore-Belisha; that he lacked intelligence; that he did not understand the modern warfare of the 1930s and 1940s; and that he advocated unwise strategic choices during his time as CIGS.

Tellingly, none of these criticisms have ever been applied to my father's early career. Prior to the time of his departure for India, there is little or nothing which can be levelled against him and, on this, even the most critical of historians are in agreement. His early experiences as a subaltern and intelligence operative in Africa marked him out for staff training. His progression thereafter through the successive grades of staff officer was exemplary, to the point that, as we have seen, he was the de facto commander of 4th Canadian Division for much of his time as its GSO1, and this experience left him well placed to exercise effective command in his own right from 1918 onwards.

He distinguished himself further on the Western Front, in Russia, Turkey and Persia, as much a plenipotentiary as a soldier. In these roles, the ingredients of his success can be characterised as follows: he had the ability to get on with troops and get the best out of them; he had an outstanding physique and stood out amongst his troops and superiors; he spoke foreign languages easily and he was capable of getting things done. Thereafter, with youth on his side, diplomatic experience under his belt and a certainty that the future lay in armoured and mechanised warfare, he was evidently the right man for modernising staff training at Camberley. Any suggestion that he lacked intelligence can surely be rebutted by this record alone.

Those who encountered him later in his career – Pownall in particular – would have done well to look past the bluff exterior and the 6ft 4in frame and consider that it was brain as well as brawn that had won my father his accelerated promotion, knighthood and unequalled record during the years immediately after the First World War.

It was only after leaving Camberley that the situation began to change for him and his progress through the ranks slowed. Writing shortly after his relief as CIGS, he identified this moment as a major turning point in his life and career:

> My outlook on life altered very much from the moment that I had finished my command at the Staff College in 1926, when I was 46 years old. Everything seemed in front of me and I was full of personal ambition. That disappeared gradually under Milne and Massingberd for the 10 years that ensued. I began to realise that I was no longer the man that was going forward rapidly to do things. Neither of these two men wanted me and I began to lose confidence in myself – or rather in my future. Gradually I realised that time was slipping away and I don't think that I ever lost interest in what I was doing. But, I began to feel an irritation that I was in no way responsible for the organisation and training of the Army.[2]

If during the 1920s and 1930s he came to dwell more upon furthering his own career, it is hardly surprising, for this was a time when money was tight for himself and the army. He needed to remain in active employment to be financially secure but also to retain some measure of influence over the development of the army and to see the continuation of the modernising plans that he advocated. It is hardly to be wondered, then, that he kept close tabs on the careers of his seniors and peers and sought the best possible appointments.

That he had the support of senior officers such as Cavan, Chetwode and – more equivocally – Milne, and intelligent and able subordinates like Fuller, meant that he was able to rise in accordance with his abilities and spend less of the interwar period on half pay. Being Churchill's man also helped a great deal, although this support could never be entirely relied upon as Churchill's power waxed and waned.

My father might not have driven the modernising agenda as far or as fast as the likes of Liddell Hart wanted, but realistically he did not personally have the means to force the pace. Liddell Hart might have done well to remember, for all his accusations of careerism, that my father protected and sought to find employment for 'Boney' Fuller, long after that officer had become a liability due to his extreme politics. Apolitical himself, and with a serviceman's distaste for politicians as a class, my father was interested only in Fuller's military brain.

That same distaste for politicians, however, meant that the advent of Hore-Belisha with his reforming agenda and unconventional methods was always going to prove problematic and set up an awkward relationship. In fairness to my father, he seems to have done his best to give the man the benefit of the doubt, notwithstanding his dislike and distrust, but it is also clear that he took the army's side when matters became polarised. Undoubtedly there is an anti-Semitic tone to some of my father's comments about his political master. However, the point is that my father did not dislike Hore-Belisha because he was Jewish, but because he came to believe that he was unfit to do his job. Hore-Belisha's Jewishness, therefore, became a stick with which to beat him, not a cause for dislike in itself. This may be unpalatable to twenty-first-century eyes, but it does reflect the views and mores of my father's times, upbringing and class.

The irony is that just as my father was accused of entering into intrigues, so too did he find himself on the receiving end of the intrigues of others. Behind-the-scenes manoeuvrings by Alan Brooke to obtain the post of GOC Mobile Division, his critique of my father's conduct of the 1937 exercises, and replacing him as GOC-in-C Home Forces should all be noted, as should Pownall's cultivation of an anti-War Office clique in the staff of the BEF. Indeed, Montgomery's going over my father's head to Churchill regarding the role of 3rd Division in July 1940 should also be marked.

We must therefore consider much of the criticism of my father from these sources as a consequence of the intrigues against him, rather than being solidly grounded in actual appraisal of his abilities. Certainly, he was no more out of touch with modern warfare than any of his contemporaries. Indeed, his tactical instructions as GOC Meerut District and GOC-in-C Eastern Command – the last postings before 1940 in which he had direct command of troops – show a continued awareness of the requirements of mobile and mechanised warfare. He had kept abreast of military developments on the Continent and, thanks to his attendance of the pre-war German manoeuvres, was better informed than most of his peers about the enemy's capabilities and methods. Even as Germany gained the upper hand in France, he remained able to adapt to a fluid situation, recast his plans as necessary and play an important role in the holding of the Channel ports to facilitate the eventual evacuation of the BEF.

The Battle of France, however, was not his to fight. Hore-Belisha's political manoeuvring had placed him in the position of CIGS, for which he was the first to admit he was not ideally suited and in which, in all but the final weeks, he was almost completely hamstrung by the wavering and indecision of the Chamberlain War Cabinet. He recognised this immediately after vacating the post. His time as CIGS, he wrote, was:

Intensely interesting but marred by too many committees and too much explanation to all & sundry. Military decision delayed and criticised before they can be executed. One's own decision feels weakened by the amount of talk to which it is subjected. It is bad enough to leave 3 Chiefs of Staff to settle something, but when their hard-earned decision is subject to committee rulings the running of war is well-nigh impossible.[3]

The above might stand as an epitaph for the Norwegian campaign, in particular – the one major operation conducted in its entirety, at least so far as all the important decisions were concerned, under the aegis of Chamberlain's leadership team.

All that my father could do as CIGS – and indeed, as GOC-in-C Home Forces – was the best that he could with what he had available, and within the political and military command framework in which he was tasked to operate. In the case of Norway, he did not agree with the strategic choices being made – in particular, the division of forces – but once those choices were made, he did his best to implement them.

The case has been made that, in truth, no British general in the first half of the Second World War truly had the chance to shine in these 'lean years'. Material weaknesses that stemmed from years of political neglect between the wars simply did not provide the army with the tools that its commanders needed to do their jobs to their best ability. My father, in this sense, joins Gort, Wavell and Auchinleck as one of the men who never got the chance to prove what they could do, had they been given the resources that were later provided to the likes of Montgomery, Alexander and Slim. Criticism of his counter-invasion plans for the summer of 1940 must therefore be understood in this context: he knew that they were not ideal, but he lacked the men and material to enact the sort of schemes that Brooke and Montgomery put forth. All he could do was build up his forces, redeploy additional reserves as they became available and focus on the hands-on, morale-boosting direct command that had made his name two decades before.

At the end of the day, it is not for me to offer the final verdict on the military record of Field Marshal Lord Ironside. The closeness to the subject and his written record that has enabled me to assemble this book debars me from making a definitive judgement of a man who, while an important figure in the history of the British Army, was also my own father. At the outset, I stated my intention to give my father and his career the historical prominence that they deserve and to allow his story to be told from his own perspective and using his own words and reflection. This is what I have done. It is now for others to take these new insights into my father's life and career and to make their own judgements on the man and his place in history. It is my firm hope that when they do so, they will see, as I do, a man and a soldier for whom the priority was always duty, never glory, and – most importantly of all – victory, no matter at what personal cost.

Notes

References to Chapter 1
For the most part, this chapter is a synopsis of the first of five memoir volumes which precede my father's diary proper. Historical background on the Second Boer War is taken from the following works:

Arthur, Sir George, *Life of Lord Kitchener* (London: Macmillan, 1920).
Pakenham, Thomas, *The Boer War* (London, Weidenfeld & Nicolson, 1979).
Surridge, Keith Terrence, *Managing the South African War, 1899–1902: Politicians v. Generals* (Martlesham: Boydell & Brewer, 1998).

1. For his elaboration of this, see Ironside, Edmund (ed.), *High Road to Command: The Diaries of Major General Sir Edmund Ironside 1920–22* (London: Leo Cooper, 1972) pp.8–10.
2. Ironside Diaries, 1880–1902, pp.72–74.
3. Ironside Diaries, 1880–1902, p.80.
4. Ironside Diaries, 1880–1902, p.79.
5. Ironside Diaries, 1880–1902, p.82.
6. Bond, Brian, *The Victorian Army and the Staff College, 1854–1914* (London: Eyre Methuen, 1972) p.3.
7. Bond, *Victorian Army and the Staff College*, p.123.
8. Ironside Diaries, 1880–1902, p.108.
9. Ironside Diaries, 1880–1902, p.168.
10. Ironside Diaries, 1880–1902, pp.172–73.
11. Ironside Diaries, 1880–1902, p.174.
12. For a summary of these operations as a whole, see Surridge, Keith Terrence, *Managing the South African War, 1899–1902: Politicians v. Generals* (Martlesham: Boydell & Brewer, 1998) pp.79–80; Arthur, Sir George, *Life of Lord Kitchener* (London: Macmillan, 1920) Vol. I, pp.294–301.
13. Ironside Diaries, 1880–1902, pp.164–65.
14. Ironside Diaries, 1904–14, Vol. I, p.47.

References to Chapter 2
The majority of this chapter is summarised from my father's memoir. I have attempted to piece together additional details from my contact with the von Estorff family and experts at the headquarters of United Kingdom Support Command Germany, who have helped me to authenticate parts of the military background in German South West Africa. My contact with Gerhard von Estorff at Teyendorf in 2002 revealed that Ludwig was his great-uncle and he very kindly let me see Ludwig's privately published reminiscences of his soldiering in Africa. Other than my father's own writings, which form the backbone of the narrative, the other main source was Christoph-Friedrich Kutscher (ed.), *Ludwig von Estorff. Wanderungen Und Kämpfe in Südwestafrika, Ostafrika Und Südafrika, 1894–1910* (Wiesbaden: Wiesbadner Kurier Verlag, 1968).

Background on the Vereeniging Conference and post-war settlement are from Thomas Pakenham, *The Boer War*, as cited in the notes to the previous chapter.

1. Ironside Diaries, 1904–14, Vol. I, p.41.
2. *London Gazette*, 10 September 1901, pp.5927–32.
3. McGregor, Gordon, *The German South West Africa Commemorative Medal Issued to Non-German Military Personnel* (Windhoek: Privately Published, undated).
4. Kutscher, Christoph-Friedrich (ed.) *Ludwig von Estorff. Wanderungen Und Kämpfe in Südwestafrika, Ostafrika Und Südafrika, 1894–1910* (Wiesbaden: Wiesbadner Kurier Verlag, 1968).

References to Chapter 3
My father's early memoir yet again forms the backbone of this chapter, but I have also drawn on his later diary entries from the early twenties when, back at Staff College as commandant, he reflected on his time there as a student. Detailed background on Camberley comes from Brian Bond, *The Victorian Army and the Staff College, 1854–1914* (London: Eyre Methuen, 1972).

An overview of service on the Western Front comes from Richard Holmes, *Tommy. The British Soldier on the Western Front 1914–1918* (London: Harper Collins, 2004) and David Stevenson, *1914–1918: The History of the First World War* (London: Penguin, 2004).

The organisation and structure of 6th Division are sourced from Richard A. Rinaldi, *Order of Battle of the British Army 1914* (Takoma Park, MD: Tiger Lily Books, 2008) and Major General T.O. Marden, *A Short History of the 6th Division August 1914–March 1919* (London: Hugh Rees Ltd, 1920). The latter is also invaluable in providing detail of the division's operations during my father's time as part of its staff.

1   Strictly speaking, his appointment was to the staff of the Potchefstroom Sub-District.
2   The six First Class Interpreterships were in German, Dutch, Afrikaans (Cape Dutch), Danish, Norwegian and Urdu.
3   Bond, *Victorian Army and the Staff College*, p.3. See this work more generally for background on the Staff College and the evolution of Britain's General Staff.
4   Ironside Diaries, 1904–14, Vol. II, p.2.
5   Ironside Diaries, 1904–14, Vol. II, p.4.
6   Ironside Diaries, 1904–14, Vol. II, p.6.
7   Ironside Diaries, 1904–14, Vol. II, pp.89–90.
8   Ironside Diaries, 1904–14, Vol. II, p.90. 'Hayward' was actually Captain Cecil Percival Heywood, Coldstream Guards.
9   Ironside Diaries, 1904–14, Vol. II, p.160.
10 For Mentions in Despatches, see the National Archive (TNA), WO372/24/32640.
11 Marden, Major General T.O., *A Short History of the 6th Division August 1914–March 1919* (London: Hugh Rees Ltd, 1920) p.15.
12 Ironside Diaries, 1904–14, Vol. II, p.177.
13 Ironside Diaries, 1904–14, Vol. II, pp.179–80.
14 Ironside Diaries, 1904–14, Vol. II, p.197.

References to Chapter 4

For his time with the Canadian Corps, I was lucky enough to be able to draw on my father's original memoir and extracts from *High Road to Command*, in which he reflected on his time on the Western Front during a return visit to the battlefields in peacetime.

As well as the general sources relating to trench warfare referenced in the previous chapter, the following works relating to the Canadian Corps and its battles were of great use:

Berton, Pierre, *Vimy* (Barnsley: Pen & Sword, 2003).
Cook, Tim, *No Place to Run: The Canadian Corps and Gas Warfare in the First World War* (Vancouver: University of British Columbia Press, 2000).
Harris, Stephen J., *Canadian Brass: The Making of a Professional Army 1860–1939* (Toronto: University of Toronto Press, 1998).
Nicholson, Colonel G.W.L., *Canadian Expeditionary Force 1914–1919* (Ottawa: Queen's Printer, 1962).
Radley, Kenneth, *Get Tough Stay Tough: Shaping the Canadian Corps 1914–1918* (Solihull: Helion, 2014).

1. It will be recalled that an artillery brigade was the command equivalent of an infantry battalion.
2. Ironside Diaries, 1904–14, Vol. II, p.198.
3. See Holmes, *Tommy*, p.201. Of course, in the event, my father had risen higher still by the time the four years had passed.
4. It should here be explained that the CEF consisted of all Canadian forces overseas. The majority of those deployed to the Western Front – though not all – were also part of the Canadian Corps, which was a combat formation. The two terms are therefore not interchangeable.
5. Harris, Stephen J., *Canadian Brass: The Making of a Professional Army 1860–1939* (Toronto: University of Toronto Press, 1998) p.116.
6. Nicholson, Colonel G.W.L., *Canadian Expeditionary Force 1914–1919* (Ottawa: Queen's Printer, 1962) pp.126.
7. Ironside Diaries, 1936, Vol. I, entry for 7 April 1936, p.188. Note, therefore, that this entry post-dates by two decades the events described, being penned whilst my father was travelling through Canada on his return from India.
8. Ironside (ed.), *High Road to Command*, p.72.
9. Ironside (ed.), *High Road to Command*, p.72.
10. Ironside Diaries, 1904–14, Vol. II, p.221.
11. Quoted in Cook, Tim, *No Place to Run: The Canadian Corps and Gas Warfare in the First World War* (Vancouver: UBC Press, 2000), p.256.
12. Ironside (ed.), *High Road to Command*, p.73.
13. Ironside Diaries, 1904–14, Vol. II, p.245.
14. Ironside Diaries, 1904–14, Vol. II, p.243.
15. A newly arrived unit. Used to support 11th Canadian Brigade during the attack on 9 April; later assigned to 12th Canadian Brigade.
16. Ironside (ed.), *High Road to Command*, p.73.
17. Ironside Diaries, 1904–14, Vol. II, pp.252–53.
18. Ironside Diaries, 1904–14 Vol. II, pp.261–62.
19. Ironside Diaries, 1904–14, Vol. II, pp.262–64.
20. Ironside Diaries, 1904–14, Vol. II, p.276.
21. Ironside (ed.), *High Road to Command*, pp.77–78.
22. Ironside Diaries, 1904–14, Vol. II, pp.129–30.
23. Ironside (ed.), *High Road to Command*, pp.78–79.
24. Ironside Diaries, 1904–14, Vol. II, pp.132–33.
25. Ironside Diaries, 1904–14, Vol. II, pp.134–35.

References to Chapter 5

In addition to the general sources used for the last two chapters, context and background for my father's involvement in training commanding officers for the Machine Gun Corps, and his subsequent tactical employment of these weapons, came from Paul Cornish, *Machine Guns and the Great War* (Barnsley: Pen & Sword, 2009).

The war experience of 2nd Division is related in Everard Wyrall, *The History of the Second Division 1914–1918* (London: Thos. Nelson & Sons, undated), of which the second volume covers the period in which my father held command of 99th Brigade.

The real gems with reference to this period, however, are the brigade War Diaries, which now form part of series WO95 in the National Archives (TNA). These contain vast amounts of detail not only of the daily activities of the troops under my father's command, but also his own activities and movements. Further detail is added by the inclusion as appendices of reports and memoranda relating to the period, some of which have also been quoted above.

Lastly, my father's departure from the Western Front suddenly means that we have a positive plethora of his own words on the events that he experienced. In his unpublished papers, an overlap means that we have both the first surviving entries of the daily diary that he would keep for the rest of his life, but also his draft memoir of the period up to the end of his command in Russia. In addition, however, there is also his published account of his Russian service: Edmund Ironside, *Archangel 1918–1919* (London: Constable, 1953).

1. Ironside Diaries, 1914–18, Vol. I, p.140.
2. Ironside Diaries, 1914–18, Vol. I, p.140.
3. Ironside Diaries, 1914–18, Vol. I, p.141.
4. Ironside Diaries, 1914–18, Vol. I, p.142.
5. Ironside Diaries, 1914–18, Vol. I, p.143.
6. Ironside Diaries, 1914–18, Vol. I, p.144. This was, of course, not the first action by the Machine Gun Corps, which had been in existence for over two years, but it was one of its first solo efforts.
7. Ironside Diaries, 1914–18, Vol. I, pp.143–44.
8. Holmes, *Tommy*, p.177. The tenth battalion in the new system, or thirteenth in the old, was the divisional pioneer battalion.
9. Ironside Diaries, 1914–18, Vol. I, p.148.
10. 99th Infantry Brigade No. B.M. (S)215, 25 May 1918, marked 'SECRET' and attached as Appendix VII to 99th Brigade War Diary for May 1918, in TNA, WO95/1370/2.
11. 99th Brigade War Diary, 30 July 1918, in TNA, WO95/1370/3.
12. 99th Brigade War Diary, 26 August 1918, in TNA, WO95/1370/4.
13. 99th Brigade War Diary, 29 August 1918, in TNA, WO95/1370/4.
14. 99th Brigade War Diary, 1 September 1918, in TNA, WO95/1370/4.
15. 99th Brigade War Diary, 6 September 1918, in TNA, WO95/1370/4.
16. Ironside Diaries, 1914–18, Vol. II, p.127.

17 Ironside Diaries, 1918, Vol. I, 21 September 1918, p.2.
18 Ironside Diaries, 1918, Vol. I, 21 September 1918, p.3.
19 Ironside, Edmund, *Archangel 1918–1919* (London: Constable, 1953) p.22.

References to Chapter 6
From his time in Russia onwards, my father kept a detailed daily diary and this forms the main source for most of the rest of this work. Insofar as his time in Russia was concerned, however, it is also possible to drawn upon his later reflections as put down on paper towards the end of his life in Edmund Ironside, *Archangel 1918–1919*, as cited in the notes to the previous chapter. It is interesting to see which of his judgements had mellowed over the intervening decades, and which remained as strong at the end of his life as they had in its prime.

It is, of course, necessary to place my father's experiences in some sort of context, and in this the following works were of great use:

Crownover, Roger, *The United States Intervention in Russia 1918, 1919: The Polar Bear Odyssey* (Lewiston: Edwin Mellen Press, 2001).
Jackson, Robert, *At War with the Bolsheviks* (London: Tom Stacey, 1972).
Kinvig, Clifford, *Churchill's Crusade: The British Invasion of Russia, 1918–1920* (London: Bloomsbury, 2007).

1 Ironside Diaries, 1918, Vol. I, 1 October 1918, p.15.
2 Ironside Diaries, 1918, Vol. I, 2 October 1918, p.18.
3 Ironside Diaries, 1918, Vol. I, 2 October 1918, p.19.
4 Ironside Diaries, 1918, Vol. I, 7 October 1918, p.51.
5 Ironside Diaries, 1918, Vol. I, 14 October 1918, p.61.
6 Ironside Diaries, 1918, Vol. I, 14 October 1918, p.61. 'Maynard' was Brigadier General Charles Maynard, commanding at Murmansk.
7 Ironside Diaries, 1918, Vol. I, 18 October 1918, p.64.
8 Ironside Papers, Ironside to Stone, 20 November 1918.
9 Ironside Diaries, 1918, Vol. I, 26 November 1918, p.178.
10 Quoted in Kinvig, Clifford, *Churchill's Crusade: The British Invasion of Russia, 1918–1920* (London: Bloomsbury, 2007) p.44.
11 Ironside Diaries, 1918, Vol. I, 7 December 1918, pp.212–13.
12 Ironside Diaries, 1918, Vol. II, 21 December 1918, pp.20–21.
13 Ironside Diaries, 1918, Vol. II, 25 January 1919, pp.84–85.
14 On my father's appreciation of air warfare see in particular Ironside Diaries, 1918, Vol. II, 11 December 1918, pp.5–9.
15 Ironside Diaries, 1918, Vol. I, 10 December 1918, p.224.
16 Ironside Diaries, 1918, Vol. I, 11 December 1918, pp.224–26.

17 Quoted in Jackson, Robert, *At War with the Bolsheviks* (London: Tom Stacey, 1972) p.94.
18 Ironside Diaries, 1918, Vol. I, 11 December 1918, p.227.
19 Ironside Diaries, 1918, Vol. II, p.51.
20 Ironside Diaries, 1918, Vol. II, 26 January 1919, p.85. The Canadian officer was Captain Mowatt CFA.
21 Ironside Diaries, 1918, Vol. II, 31 January 1919, pp.89–90.
22 See Powell, Geoffrey, *The History of the Green Howards. Three Hundred Years of Service* (Barnsley: Pen & Sword, 2015) p.167, which records that the two men were eventually released in 1931.

References to Chapter 7

Other than extracts from my father's correspondence with Christopher Stone, and from the printed correspondence of Field Marshal Sir Henry Wilson – for which see Keith Jeffery (ed.), *The Military Correspondence of Field Marshal Sir Henry Wilson, 1918–1922* (London: Army Records Society, 1985) – all sources used for this chapter are those listed in the references for Chapter 6.

1 Ironside Diaries, 1919, Vol. I, 26 May 1919, p.63.
2 Ironside Diaries, 1919, Vol. I, 27 May 1919, p.70.
3 Ironside Diaries, 1919, Vol. I, 28 May 1919, pp.72–73.
4 Ironside Diaries, 1919, Vol. I, 28 May 1919, p.73.
5 Ironside Diaries, 1919, Vol. I, 10 June 1919, pp.94–95.
6 Ironside Diaries, 1919, Vol. I, 3 June 1919, p.82.
7 Ironside Diaries, 1919, Vol. I, 30 May 1919, p.76.
8 Ironside Diaries, 1919, Vol. I, 10 June 1919, pp.93–94.
9 Wilson to Churchill, 16 June 1919, in Jeffery, Keith (ed.), *The Military Correspondence of Field Marshal Sir Henry Wilson, 1918–1922* (London: Army Records Society, 1985) pp.112–14.
10 Ironside Diaries, 1919, Vol. I, 11 June 1919, p.95.
11 Ironside Diaries, 1919, Vol. I, 22 June 1919, pp.115–16.
12 Kelly quoted in Kinvig, *Churchill's Crusade*, pp.194–95. Kinvig offers an alternative narrative to set against my father's version of events, but even if one were to accept all of his points at face value it is hard to escape the conclusion that Kelly was his own worst enemy and would have enjoyed a far more successful career if only he had learned to keep his mouth shut.
13 Ironside Diaries, 1919, Vol. I, 11 June 1919, p.95.
14 Radcliffe to Ironside, quoted in Ironside, *Archangel*, pp.154–55.
15 Ironside Diaries, 1919, Vol. II, 1 August 1919, p.1.
16 Ironside Diaries, 1919, Vol. II, 4 August 1919, p.11.
17 Ironside Diaries, 1919, Vol. II, 9 August 1919, p.22.

18 Ironside Diaries, 1919, Vol. II, 11 August 1919, pp.23–24.
19 Kinvig, *Churchill's Crusade*, pp.248–50, 333–34.
20 Ironside Papers, Ironside to Stone, 30 June 1919.
21 Ironside Diaries, 1919, Vol. II, 27 September 1919, pp.116–17. 'Altham', was Captain Edward Altham RN, who had commanded the flotilla on the Dvina.
22 Ironside Diaries, 1919, Vol. I, 9 June 1919, p.93.
23 Ironside, *Archangel*, p.67.
24 Ironside Diaries, 1919, Vol. II, 27 September 1919, pp.125–26.
25 Ironside Papers, Ironside to Stone, 30 June 1919.

References to Chapter 8

Other than the quoted correspondence from the papers of Gertrude Bell and Sir Henry Wilson, the bulk of the material in this chapter is summarised from my father's memoir, *High Road to Command*, and from his diaries.

Background material on the political situation in the Middle East in the aftermath of the collapse of the Ottoman Empire is taken from James Barr, *A Line in the Sand. Britain, France, and the Struggle for the Middle East* (London: Simon & Schuster, 2011).

1 Ironside (ed.), *High Road to Command*, p.88.
2 Ironside (ed.), *High Road to Command*, p.89.
3 Ironside Diaries, 1920, Vol. I, 20 July 1920, p.184.
4 Ironside Diaries, 1920, Vol. I, 21 July 1920, pp.186–87.
5 Ironside Diaries, 1920, Vol. I, 21 July 1920, pp.186–87.
6 Ironside Diaries, 1920, Vol. I, 23 July 1920, pp.190–92.
7 Ironside Diaries, 1920, Vol. I, 7 August 1920, p.232.
8 Ironside Diaries, 1920, Vol. I, 10 August, p.240.
9 Ironside Diaries, 1920, Vol. I, 14 August, p.260.
10 Ironside Diaries, 1920, Vol. I, 21 August, p.284.
11 Bigany to Ironside, 26 August 1920, pasted into Ironside Diaries, 1920, Vol. I, p.296.
12 Ironside Diaries, 1920, Vol. II, 2 September, pp.10–11.
13 Ironside Diaries, 1920, Vol. II, 15 September, p.20.
14 Ironside Diaries, 1920, Vol. II, 14 September, p.18.
15 Ironside Diaries, 1920, Vol. II, 16 September, pp.25–26.
16 Ironside Diaries, 1920, Vol. II, 28 September, p.46.
17 Ironside Diaries, 1920, Vol. II, 29 September, p.48.
18 Bell to Father, 10 October 1920, in Burgoyne, Elizabeth (ed.), *Gertrude Bell: Her Personal Papers 1914–1926* (London: Ernest Benn, 1961), p.172.
19 Wilson to Haldane, 24 August 1920, in Jeffery, (ed.), *Military Correspondence of Field Marshal Sir Henry Wilson*, pp.197–99.

References to Chapter 9

Again, the bulk of this chapter has been assembled from my father's diaries and papers, and from material contained within *High Road to Command*.

A number of histories of Iran were consulted, notably Michael Axworthy, *Empire of the Mind: A History of Iran* (London: Hurst, 2007) and Cyrus Ghani, *Iran and the Rise of Reza Shah: From Qajar Collapse to Pahlavi Power* (London: I.B. Tauris, 2001). Of these, only the former is able to make any valid judgements as to my father's involvement in events, having drawn directly upon his papers and memoirs, and that only briefly due to the breadth of material covered by the title.

1. Ironside (ed.), *High Road to Command*, p.135.
2. Ironside Diaries, 1920, Vol. II, 28 September 1920, pp.46–47.
3. Ironside Diaries, 1920, Vol. II, 4 October 1920, p.65.
4. Ironside Diaries, 1920, Vol. II, 6 October 1920, pp.66–68.
5. Ironside Diaries, 1920, Vol. II, 7 October 1920, p.71.
6. Ironside Diaries, 1920, Vol. II, 10 October 1920, p.77.
7. Ironside Diaries, 1920, Vol. II, 10 October 1920, p.79.
8. Ironside Diaries, 1920, Vol. II, 23 October 1920, p.101.
9. Ironside Diaries, 1920, Vol. II, 24 October 1920, pp.101–02.
10. Ironside Diaries, 1920, Vol. II, 27 October 1920, p.105.
11. Ironside Diaries, 1920, Vol. II, 28 October 1920, p.106.
12. Ironside (ed.), *High Road to Command*, p.146.
13. Ironside Diaries, 1920, Vol. II, 29 October 1920, pp.110–11.
14. Ironside Diaries, 1920, Vol. II, 29 October 1920, p.112.
15. Ironside Diaries, 1920, Vol. II 31 October 1920, p.113.
16. Ironside Papers, Ironside to Stone, 4 January 1921.
17. Ironside Diaries, 1921, Vol. I, 18 January 1921, p.26.
18. Ironside Diaries, 1921, Vol. I, 14 January 1921, pp.21–22.
19. Ironside Diaries, 1921, Vol. I, 19 January 1921, pp.27–28.
20. Ironside Diaries, 1921, Vol. I, 29 January 1921, pp.34–36.
21. Ironside Diaries, 1921, Vol. I, 31 January 1921, p.40.
22. Ironside Diaries, 1921, Vol. I, 12 February 1921, pp.61–62.
23. Ironside Diaries, 1921, Vol. I, 15 February 1921, pp.66–69.
24. Ironside Diaries, 1921, Vol. I, 23 February 1921, p.93.

References to Chapter 10

In addition to directly cited correspondence, much of this chapter has been condensed from material in *High Road to Command*, which contains, amongst other things, a far more detailed account of my father's naval cruise. Background on the Cairo Conference is predominately from Barr, *Line in the Sand*, as previously cited.

1 Ironside Diaries, 1921, Vol. I, 25 February 1921, p.96.
2 Ironside Diaries, 1921, Vol. I, 25 February 1921, p.97.
3 Ironside Diaries, 1921, Vol. I, 8 March 1921, p.120.
4 Ironside Diaries, 1921, Vol. I, 8 March 1921, p.121.
5 Ironside Diaries, 1921, Vol. I, 12 March 1921, p.126.
6 Ironside Diaries, 1921, Vol. I, 13 March 1921, p.127.
7 Ironside Diaries, 1921, Vol. I, 14 March 1921, p.129.
8 Ironside (ed.), *High Road to Command*, pp.194–95.
9 Bell to Father, written aboard the *Hardinge*, Burgoyne, (ed.), *Gertrude Bell*, Vol. II, p.212.
10 Ironside Diaries, 1921, Vol. II, 8 April 1921, pp.2–4. It is evident that this entry was written up as a summary after the fact, presumably on 23 April, the date on which regular entries again commence.
11 Ironside Diaries, 1921, Vol. II, 8 April 1921, p.5.
12 Ironside Diaries, 1921, Vol. II, 12 August 1921, pp.108–09.
13 Ironside Papers, Churchill to Ironside, 4 September 1921. A full copy of this letter is reproduced in Ironside (ed.), *High Road to Command*, plate facing p.217.
14 Ironside (ed.) *High Road to Command*, p.208.
15 Ironside (ed.) *High Road to Command*, p.232.
16 Ironside (ed.) *High Road to Command*, p.208.

References to Chapter 11

Although its role had not altered since my father's time as a student, a good overview of Camberley in the interwar years can be had from Edward Smalley, 'Qualified, but Unprepared: Training for War at the Staff College in the 1930s' in *British Journal for Military History*, Volume 2, Issue 1, November 2015, pp.55–72. Although the focus of the piece is on the era immediately after my father's tenure as commandant, it is easy to trace his legacy through the history of the college in the subsequent years.

Commentary on the state of the army in the period is drawn largely from Brian Bond, *British Military Policy Between the Two World Wars* (Oxford: Clarendon, 1980) and B.H. Liddell Hart, *The Memoirs of Captain Liddell Hart* (London: Cassel, 1965).

The biographies of two of my father's subordinates at Camberley also provide useful material:

Colville, J.R., *Man of Valour. The Life of Field-Marshal the Viscount Gort, VC, GCB, DSO, MVO, MC* (London: Collins, 1972).

Trythall, Anthony John, *'Boney' Fuller: The Intellectual General* (London: Cassel, 1977).

1. Ironside Papers, Ironside to Stone, 11 August 1921.
2. Ironside Diaries, 1922, Vol. I, 24 April 1922, p.284.
3. Bond, Brian, *British Military Policy Between the Two World Wars* (Oxford: Clarendon, 1980), p.74.
4. Ironside Diaries, 1922, Vol. II, 21 May 1922, p.54.
5. Ironside Diaries, 1922, Vol. II, 9 June 1922, p.78.
6. Ironside Diaries, 1922, Vol. II, 16 May 1922, p.42, emphasis as original.
7. Cavan to Ironside, 8 May 1922, pasted into Ironside Diaries, 1922, Vol. II, p.34.
8. Ironside Diaries, 1922, Vol. II, 9 May 1922, p.34.
9. Ironside Diaries, 1923, Vol. I, 16 October 1922, p.4.
10. Ironside Diaries, 1919, Vol. I, 9 June 1919, p.92.
11. Ironside Diaries, 1923, Vol. I, 20 November 1922, p.64.
12. Ironside Diaries, 1922, Vol. II, 22 June 1922, p.105.
13. Ironside Diaries, 1922, Vol. II, 22 July 1922, p.134.
14. Ironside Papers, Byng to Ironside, 21 October 1922.
15. For which, see Liddell Hart, B.H., *The Memoirs of Captain Liddell Hart* (London: Cassel, 1965), Vol. I, p.64.
16. Ironside Diaries, 1923, Vol. I, 13 March 1923, pp.221–22.
17. Ironside Diaries, 1923, Vol. I, 13 March 1923, pp.222–23.
18. Ironside Diaries, 1923, Vol. I, 13 April 1923, p.268.
19. Colville, J.R., *Man of Valour. The Life of Field-Marshal the Viscount Gort, VC, GCB, DSO, MVO, MC* (London: Collins, 1972), pp.54–55.
20. Ironside Diaries, 1926, Vol. I, 19 March 1926, p.61.
21. Ironside Diaries, 1926, Vol. I, 19 February 1926, p.21.
22. Ironside Diaries, 1926, Vol. I, 22 March 1926, pp.72–73.
23. Quoted in Smalley, Edward, 'Qualified, but Unprepared: Training for War at the Staff College in the 1930s' in *British Journal for Military History*, Vol. 2, Issue 1, November 2015, p.62.
24. Ironside Diaries, 1926, Vol. I, 22 March 1926, p.73.
25. Ironside Diaries, 1926, Vol. I, 27 May 1926, p.145.
26. Ironside Diaries, 1926, Vol. I, 28 May 1926, p.146.
27. Ironside to MacBrien, 27 January 1923, pasted into Ironside Diaries, 1923, Vol. I, pp.138–42.
28. Ironside to MacBrien, 27 January 1923, pasted into Ironside Diaries, 1923, Vol. I, pp.138–42.

References to Chapter 12

For the most part, the sources for this chapter replicate those employed in the previous one. As well as its treatment by Bond, the role of India and the Indian Army in British military thinking, which will become of greater significance in the following chapter, is outlined in Philip Mason, *A Matter of Honour. An Account of the Indian Army, its Officers and Men* (London: Jonathan Cape, 1974).

1   Ironside Diaries, 1926, Vol. II, 6 October 1926, pp.55–56.
2   Ironside Diaries, 1926, Vol. II, 8 November 1926, pp.103–04.
3   Ironside Diaries, 1926, Vol. II, 15 November 1926, p.111.
4   Bond, *British Military Policy*, pp.130–32.
5   Ironside Diaries, 1926, Vol. II, 13 November 1926, p.108.
6   Ironside Diaries, 1926, Vol. II, 9 November 1926, p.104.
7   Slessor to Ironside, 10 November 1926, pasted into Ironside Diaries, 1926, Vol. II, p.105
8   Ironside Diaries, 1926, Vol. II, 16 December 1926, pp.143–44.
9   Ironside Diaries, 1926, Vol. II, 21 December 1926, pp.151–52.
10 Ironside Diaries, 1926, Vol. II, 25 December 1926, p.160.
11 Ironside Diaries, 1926, Vol. II, 26 December 1926, pp.161–62.
12 Liddell Hart, *Memoirs*, Vol. I, p.81.
13 Ironside Diaries, 1927, Vol. I, 23 February 1927, pp.2–3. Note that the diary for 1927 is physically bound as a single volume but is numbered internally as if in two parts, the page numbering beginning again from 1 for entries September–December, and is therefore cited as two volumes.
14 Bond, *British Military Policy*, p.52.
15 Ironside Diaries, 1927, Vol. I, 22 February 1927, p.2.
16 Ironside Diaries, 1927, Vol. I, 28 February 1927, pp.10–11.
17 Ironside Diaries, 1927, Vol. I, 28 February 1927, pp.12–13.
18 Ironside Diaries, 1927, Vol. I, 28 March 1927, p.66.
19 Ironside Diaries, 1927, Vol. I, 3 April 1927, p.77.
20 Ironside Diaries, 1927, Vol. I, 4 April 1927, p.79.
21 Ironside Diaries, 1927, Vol. I, 28 May 1927, pp.133–35.
22 Ironside Diaries, 1927, Vol. I, 16 June 1927, pp.156–57.
23 Ironside Diaries, 1927, Vol. I, 22 June 1927, p.163.
24 Ironside Diaries, 1927, Vol. I, 7 July 1927, pp.182–83.
25 Ironside Diaries, 1927, Vol. I, 7 July 1927, p.184.
26 Ironside Diaries, 1927, Vol. I, 8 July 1927, p.188.
27 Ironside Diaries, 1927, Vol. I, 8 July 1927, p.190.
28 Ironside Diaries, 1927, Vol. I, 17 July 1927, p.201.
29 Ironside Diaries, 1927, Vol. II, 13 September 1927, p.2.
30 Campbell to Ironside, 15 September 1927, pasted into Ironside Diaries, 1927, Vol. II, p.28.
31 Ironside Diaries, 1927, Vol. II, 15 September 1927, p.28.
32 Ironside Diaries, 1927, Vol. II, 16 September 1927, p.34.
33 Ironside Diaries, 1927, Vol. II, 2 October 1927, pp.43–46.

34 Ironside Diaries, 1927, Vol. II, 7 October 1927, p.47.
35 Ironside Diaries, 1927, Vol. II, 7 October 1927, p.47.
36 Ironside Diaries, 1927, Vol. II, 7 October 1927, p.48.
37 Ironside Diaries, 1927, Vol. II, 9 October 1927, p.49.
38 Ironside Diaries, 1927, Vol. II, 29 November 1927, p.105. *Filer à l'anglaise* being the French equivalent of 'To take French leave'!
39 Ironside Diaries, 1927, Vol. II, 20 December 1927, p.186.

References to Chapter 13

General background on the military situation in India and the Indianisation of the Indian Army is taken largely from Mason, *Matter of Honour*, already cited in the notes to the previous chapter, with additional detail from Frederick William Perry, *The Commonwealth Armies: Manpower and Organisation in Two World Wars* (Manchester: Manchester University Press, 1988) pp.98–102.

Progress towards mechanisation on the subcontinent is dealt with in David Fletcher, *Mechanised Force: British Tanks between the Wars* (London: Stationary Office, 1991), specifically the chapter spanning pp.68–78.

On the 'Pink Plan' see Lorne J. Kavic, *India's Quest for Security: Defence Policies, 1947–1965* (Los Angeles: University of California Press, 1967) pp.14–16.

1 Ironside Diaries, 1928, Vol. I, 18 February 1928, p.37.
2 Ironside Diaries, 1928, Vol. I, 23 February 1928, p.41.
3 Ironside Diaries, 1928, Vol. I, 26 February 1928, p.44; Cavan to Ironside, pasted into diaries, p.45.
4 Ironside Diaries, 1928, Vol. I, 29 February 1928, p.49.
5 Ironside Diaries, 1928, Vol. I, 4 April 1928, pp.97–98.
6 Ironside Diaries, 1928, Vol. I, 10 April 1928, p.98.
7 Ironside Diaries, 1928, Vol. I, 11 April 1928, p.99.
8 Ironside Diaries, 1929, Vol. II, 10 July 1929, p.118.
9 Ironside Diaries, 1933, Vol. I, 12 April 1933, p.188.
10 Ironside Diaries, 1928, Vol. II, 18 November 1928, pp.45–46.
11 Ironside Diaries, 1928, Vol. II, 18 November 1928, p.46.
12 Ironside Diaries, 1928, Vol. II, 18 November 1928, p.116.
13 Ironside Diaries, 1928, Vol. II, 14 February 1929, p.207.
14 Ironside Diaries, 1928, Vol. II, 25 January 1929, p.144.
15 Ironside Diaries, 1928, Vol. II, 27 January 1929, pp.157–58.
16 Ironside Diaries, 1928, Vol. II, 12 February 1929, p.204.
17 Ironside Diaries, 1929, Vol. I, note written on title page and dated August 1949.
18 See Fletcher, David, *Mechanised Force: British Tanks between the Wars* (London: Stationary Office, 1991) pp.68–72.

19 Discussed in Ironside Diaries, 1929, Vol. I, 13 July 1929, pp.123–26.
20 Ironside Diaries, 1929, Vol. I, 11 July 1929, p.120.
21 Ironside Diaries, 1929, Vol. I, 11 July 1929, pp.120–21.
22 This is discussed in Ironside Diaries, 1928, Vol. II, 16 March 1929, pp.254–55.
23 Ironside Diaries, 1931, Vol. II, 25 December 1931, p.243.
24 Chetwode to Ironside, 28 November 1931, pasted into Ironside Diaries, 1931, Vol. II, p.215.
25 Ironside Diaries, 1933, Vol. I, 11 April 1933, pp.182–84.
26 Chetwode to Ironside, 27 March 1933, pasted into Ironside Diaries, 1933, Vol. I, p.187.
27 Ironside Diaries, 1933, Vol. I, 12 April 1933, pp.187–88.
28 Ironside Diaries, 1933, Vol. I, 12 April 1933, p.186.
29 Ironside Diaries, 1933, Vol. I, 13 April 1933, p.189.
30 Ironside Diaries, 1934, Vol. I, 2 January 1934, p.5.
31 Ironside Diaries, 1934, Vol. I, 21 March 1934, p.129.
32 Ironside Diaries, 1934, Vol. II, 22 May 1934, p.11.
33 Ironside Diaries, 1934, Vol. II, 4 September 1934, p.203.
34 Ironside Diaries, 1934, Vol. II, 4 September 1934, p.203.
35 Closing paragraphs of report to Chetwode, pasted into Ironside Diaries, 1934, Vol. III, pp.25–36.
36 Confidential Report for 1934, pasted into Ironside Diaries, 1935, Vol. I, p.190.
37 Ironside Diaries, 1935, Vol. III, 6 November 1935, p.13.
38 Ironside Diaries, 1935, Vol. III, 16 January 1936, pp.189–90.

References to Chapter 14

As with the coverage of military affairs in Britain prior to my father's departure for India, much background material for this chapter comes from Bond, *British Military Policy*, as previously cited. Also of use were books by, or about, two of the men who would become key players in the coming years:

Liddell Hart, B.H., *The Memoirs of Captain Liddell Hart* (London: Cassel, 1965).
Minney, R.J., *The Private Papers of Hore-Belisha* (New York: Doubleday, 1961).

1 Ironside Diaries, 1936, Vol. I, 20 February 1936, p.40.
2 Ironside Diaries, 1936, Vol. I, 25 February 1936, p.62.
3 Ironside Diaries, 1936, Vol. I, 8 March 1936, p.94.
4 Ironside Diaries, 1936, Vol. I, 8 March 1936, p.94.
5 Ironside Diaries, 1936, Vol. I, 10 May 1936, p.246.
6 Ironside Diaries, 1936, Vol. II, 18 May 1936, p.19.

7   Ironside Diaries, 1936, Vol. II, 20 May 1936, pp.23–24.
8   Ironside Diaries, 1936, Vol. II, 31 May 1936, pp.42–43.
9   Ironside Diaries, 1936, Vol. II, 3 July 1936, p.104.
10 Ironside Diaries, 1936, Vol. II, 19 July 1936, pp.137–38.
11 Ironside Diaries, 1936, Vol. III, 21 October 1936, pp.39–40.
12 Ironside Diaries, 1936, Vol. III, 12 December 1936, p.116.
13 Ironside Diaries, 1936, Vol. III 19 December 1936, p.188.
14 Ironside Diaries, 1936, Vol. III, 19 December 1936, p.189.
15 Ironside Diaries, 1936, Vol. III, 19 December 1936, pp.191–92.
16 Ironside Diaries, 1936, Vol. III, 20 December 1936, pp.193–94.
17 Ironside Diaries, 1936, Vol. III, 20 December 1936, pp.195–96.
18 Ironside Diaries, 1936, Vol. III, 31 December 1936, pp.215–16.
19 Ironside Diaries, 1936, Vol. III, 31 December 1936, p.216.
20 Ironside Diaries, 1937, Vol. I, 9 March 1937, pp.146–47.
21 Ironside Diaries, 1937, Vol. I, 9 March 1937, pp.147–48.
22 Ironside Diaries, 1937, Vol. II, 12 May 1937, pp.24–27.
23 Ironside Diaries, 1937, Vol. II, 14 May 1937, pp.31–33.
24 Ironside Diaries, 1937, Vol. II, 19 August 1937, p.231.
25 Ironside Diaries, 1937, Vol. III, 25 September 1937, p.80.
26 Ironside Diaries, 1937, Vol. III, 26 September 1937, pp.88–90.
27 Ironside Diaries, 1937, Vol. III, 27 September 1937, pp.94–95.
28 Ironside Diaries, 1937, Vol. III, 1 October 1937, p.118.
29 Ironside Diaries, 1937, Vol. III, 10 October 1937, p.143.

References to Chapter 15

Sources for this chapter are largely as for that preceding it, with additional material from Colville's biography of Gort, *Man of Valour*, as previously cited.

Now that this narrative has caught up with the period covered by the published extracts from my father's diaries, useful context is also to be had from the editorial notes to Colonel Roderick Macleod and Denis Kelly (eds), *The Ironside Diaries 1937–1940* (London: Constable, 1962).

1   Ironside Diaries, 1937, Vol. III, 26 October 1937, p.170.
2   Ironside Diaries, 1937, Vol. III, 27 October 1937, pp.171–72.
3   Ironside Diaries, 1937, Vol. III, 10 October 1937, p.142.
4   Ironside Diaries, 1937, Vol. III, 1 December 1937, p.229.
5   Ironside Diaries, 1937, Vol. III, 2 December 1937, pp.229–30.
6   Ironside Diaries, 1937, Vol. III, 2 December 1937, pp.230–31.
7   Ironside Diaries, 1937, Vol. III, 2 December 1937, pp.232–33.
8   Minney, R.J., *The Private Papers of Hore-Belisha* (New York: Doubleday, 1961) pp.68–76. The quotations concerning Wavell and Dill are from

Hore-Belisha to Chamberlain, 23 November 1937, p.70. See also Liddell Hart, *Memoirs*, Vol. II, pp.55, 63, 67.
9   For more on this line of argument, see Brian Bond's essay in Keegan, John (ed.), *Churchill's Generals* (New York: Grove Weidenfeld, 1991) p.19; the original case is made in Liddell Hart, Memoirs, Vol. II, pp.21–23.
10 Ironside Diaries, 1937, Vol. III, 19 September 1937, p.55.
11 Ironside Diaries, 1937, Vol. III, 19 September 1937, p.57.
12 Ironside Diaries, 1937, Vol. III, 20 September 1937, pp.59–60.
13 Ironside Diaries, 1937, Vol. III, 21 September 1937, pp.63–64.
14 Ironside Diaries, 1937, Vol. III, December 1937, p.234.
15 Ironside Diaries, 1937, Vol. III, 3 December 1937, p.235.
16 'Notes on Higher Organisation to ensure a better preparation of the Army for War', pasted into Ironside Diaries, 1937, Vol. III, p.237.
17 Ironside Diaries, 1937, Vol. III, 5 December 1937, pp.240–41.
18 Ironside Diaries, 1937, Vol. III, 6 December 1937, pp.241–42.
19 Ironside Diaries, 1937, Vol. III, 6 December 1937, p.245.
20 Ironside Diaries, 1937, Vol. III, 7 December 1937, p.250.
21 Ironside Diaries, 1937, Vol. III, 13 December 1937, p.262.
22 Ironside Diaries, 1937, Vol. III, 16 December 1937, pp.266–67.
23 Ironside Diaries, 1937, Vol. III, 16 December 1937, p.267.
24 Ironside Diaries, 1938, Vol. I, 2 January 1938, p.3.
25 Ironside Diaries, 1938, Vol. I, 20 February 1938, p.106.

References to Chapter 16

Again, sources for this chapter are largely as for that preceding it, with the Hore-Belisha papers providing a counterpoint and supplement to my father's own recording of events.

1 Ironside Diaries, 1938, Vol. I 28 March 1938, p.179.
2 Minney, *Hore-Belisha*, p.210.
3 Ironside Diaries, 1938, Vol. I, 20 February 1938, p.106.
4 Ironside Diaries, 1938, Vol. II, 26 May 1938, pp.52–54.
5 Ironside Diaries, 1938, Vol. II, 23 May 1938, pp.47–48.
6 Ironside Diaries, 1938, Vol. II 28 June 1938, pp.121–22.
7 Ironside Diaries, 1938, Vol. II, 30 June 1938, pp.126 & 128; p.127 is filled up with press cuttings showing my father and Caesar, along with clipping to the effect that Hore-Belisha had had to be assigned a police protection officer after receiving threats to his person.
8 Ironside Diaries, 1938, Vol. II, 14 July 1938, p.155.
9 Ironside Diaries, 1938, Vol. II, 14 July 1938, pp.157–58.
10 On this point see Minney, *Hore-Belisha*, p.128.

11 Ironside Diaries, 1938, Vol. III, 24 September 1938, pp.4–5.
12 Ironside Diaries, 1938, Vol. III, 17 October 1938, p.108.
13 Ironside Diaries, 1938, Vol. III, 7 December 1938, p.229.
14 Ironside Diaries, 1938, Vol. III, 30 December 1938, pp.271–72.
15 Ironside Papers, Gort to Ironside, 17 April 1939 (marked 'SECRET').
16 Ironside Diaries, 1939, Vol. II, 1 May 1939, p.4.
17 Ironside Diaries, 1939, Vol. II, 4 May 1939, p.16.
18 Ironside Diaries, 1939, Vol. II, 4 May 1939, p.18.
19 Ironside Diaries, 1939, Vol. II, 4 May 1939, p.20.
20 Ironside Diaries, 1939, Vol. II, 4 May 1939, p.24.

References to Chapter 17

Once more, sources for this chapter are largely as for those preceding it. There is little in the Hore-Belisha papers or in biographical treatments of Gort about the time of my father's tenure as inspector general of overseas forces and their attitude to it. However, a useful insight into the views held by Gort's circle can be found in the diary of Henry Pownall, published as Brian Bond (ed.), *Chief of Staff. The Diaries of Lieutenant General Sir Henry Pownall* (London: Leo Cooper, 1972).

1 Diary entry of 1 May 1939 in Bond, Brian (ed.), *Chief of Staff. The Diaries of Lieutenant General Sir Henry Pownall* (London: Leo Cooper, 1972) Vol. I, p.203, emphasis as original.
2 Ironside Diaries, 1939, Vol. II, 1 July 1939, pp.184–85.
3 Ironside Diaries, 1939, Vol. II, 1 July 1939, pp.185–86.
4 Ironside Diaries, 1939, Vol. II, 7 July 1939, pp.190–92.
5 Ironside Diaries, 1939, Vol. II, 10 July 1939, p.198.
6 Ironside Diaries, 1939, Vol. II, 10 July 1939, pp.199–202.
7 Ironside Diaries, 1939, Vol. III, 11 July 1939, p.4.
8 Ironside Diaries, 1939, Vol. III, 13 July 1939, p.12.
9 Ironside Diaries, 1939, Vol. III, 13 July 1939, p.15.
10 Ironside Diaries, 1939, Vol. III, 17 July 1939, p.35.
11 Ironside Diaries, 1939, Vol. III, 18 July 1939, p.36.
12 Ironside Diaries, 1939, Vol. III, 18 July 1939, p.38.
13 Ironside Diaries, 1939, Vol. III, 24 July 1939, pp.58–60.
14 Ironside Diaries, 1939, Vol. III, 25 July 1939, pp.64–65.
15 Ironside Diaries, 1939, Vol. III, 29 July 1939, p.72.
16 Ironside Diaries, 1939, Vol. III, 31 July 1939, pp.85–86.
17 Diary entry of 31 July 1939 in Bond (ed.), *Chief of Staff*, Vol. I, pp.215–16; emphasis as original.
18 Diary entry of 31 July 1939 in Bond (ed.), *Chief of Staff*, Vol. I, p.215.
19 Ironside Diaries, 1939, Vol. III, 31 July 1939, p.86. It is hard to see what

other precedent than that of Sir John French in 1914 was being drawn on to justify my father's beliefs relating to the appointment of a wartime C-in-C.
20 Diary entry of 31 July 1939 in Bond (ed.), *Chief of Staff*, Vol. I, p.216; emphasis as original.
21 Ironside Diaries, 1939, Vol. III, 20 August 1939, p.133.
22 Ironside Diaries, 1939, Vol. III, 25 August 1939, p.147.
23 Ironside Diaries, 1939, Vol. III, 26 August 1939, p.152.
24 Ironside Diaries, 1939, Vol. III, 1 September 1939, p.167.
25 Ironside Diaries, 1939, Vol. III, 1 September 1939, p.169.
26 Ironside Diaries, 1939, Vol. III, 3 September 1939, pp.181–82.

References to Chapter 18

The majority of this chapter is again sourced from the diaries, papers and biographies of the main participants: those of Gort, Pownall and Hore-Belisha have all already been cited in previous chapters, and to these must be added the diaries of Sir Alan Brooke, as he then was – Lord Alanbrooke (Alex Danchiv and Daniel Todman, eds), *War Diaries 1939–1945* (London: Weidenfeld & Nicolson, 2001).

Additional context on the strategic situation in France and the Low Countries comes from Brian Bond, *France and Belgium 1939–1940* (London: Davis Poynter, 1975) and Hugh Sebag Montefiore, *Dunkirk: Fight to the Last Man* (London: Viking, 2006).

1 Minney (ed.), *Hore-Belisha*, pp.229–30.
2 Bond (ed.), *Chief of Staff*, Vol. I, pp.223–24.
3 Ironside Diaries, 1939, Vol. III, 4 September 1939, p.183.
4 Ironside Diaries, 1939, Vol. III, 5 September 1939, p.185.
5 Ironside Diaries, 1939, Vol. III, 16 September 1939, p.227.
6 Ironside Diaries, 1939, Vol. III, 8 September 1939, pp.195–96.
7 See Résumés of 7, 14 and 21 September, TNA, CAB66/1/13, CAB66/1/30, and CAB66/1/46. See also CAB/1/31 'Supply of Arms to Poland', dated 15 September, which makes it plain that even by that date the Polish cause had been all but given up on.
8 Ironside Diaries, 1939, Vol. III, 23 September 1939, p.251.
9 Ironside Diaries, 1939, Vol. III, 4 September 1939, pp.184–85.
10 Ironside Diaries, 1939, Vol. III, 8 September 1939, pp.195–97.
11 Ironside to Gamelan, 18 September 1939, pasted into Ironside Diaries, 1939, Vol. III, p.218.
12 Ironside Diaries, 1939, Vol. III, 23 September 1939, pp.251–52.
13 Ironside Diaries, 1939, Vol. IV, 9 November 1939, pp.112–16.
14 TNA, CAB65/2/11 'Conclusions of a Meeting of the War Cabinet held at 10 Downing Street SW1, November 9, 1939, at 9.30 p.m.'.

15 For Pownall's version of events, see diary entry for 10 November 1939 in Bond (ed.), *Chief of Staff*, Vol. I, pp.252–54.
16 For which, see Liddell Hart, *Memoirs*, Vol. I, p.231.
17 Ironside Diaries, 1939, Vol. III, 8 September 1939, p.193.
18 Ironside Diaries, 1939, Vol. III, 27 September 1939, p.271.
19 Lord Alanbrooke (Alex Danchev and Daniel Todman, eds), *War Diaries 1939–1945* (London: Weidenfeld & Nicolson, 2001) entry for 20 November 1941, p.201.
20 Ironside Diaries, 1939, Vol. III, 25 September 1939, p.263.
21 Gamelin to Ironside, 22 September 1939, pasted into Ironside Diaries, 1939, Vol. III, p.260.
22 Ironside Papers, Windsor to Ironside, 13 October 1939.
23 Ironside Diaries, 1939, Vol. III, 14 September 1939, p.222.
24 Colville, *Man of Valour*, p.158.
25 Ironside Diaries, 1939, Vol. IV, 28 November 1939, p.155.
26 Minney (ed.), *Hore-Belisha*, pp.262–63.
27 Ironside Diaries, 1939, Vol. IV, 29 November 1939, p.158.
28 Ironside Diaries, 1939, Vol. IV, 30 November 1939, pp.158–59.
29 Ironside Diaries, 1939, Vol. IV, 1 December 1939, p.159.
30 Ironside Diaries, 1939, Vol. IV, 1 December 1939, p.160.
31 Ironside Diaries, 1939, Vol. IV, 12 December 1939, p.193.
32 Minney (ed.), *Hore-Belisha*, pp.266–67.
33 Ironside Diaries, 1940, Vol. I, 6 January 1940, p.7.
34 Ironside Diaries, 1940, Vol. I, 10 January 1940, p.23.

References to Chapter 19

There is not a great deal of material in print on the Norwegian debacle, but one recent study, in particular, has been of great use as it focuses on the strategic and operational decision-making in which my father was involved. This is Joseph Moretz, *Towards a Wider War. British Strategic Decision-Making and Military Effectiveness in Scandinavia, 1939–40* (Solihull: Helion, 2017). Otherwise, supplementary material for this chapter comes from the various diaries and memoirs already cited, and the developing situation in France as outlined in Bond, *France and Belgium* and Sebag Montefiore, *Dunkirk*.

1 TNA, CAB 66/4/19, 'Stoppage of the Export of Swedish Iron Ore to Germany', dated 20 December 1939.
2 Ironside Diaries, 1940, Vol. I, 12 January 1940, p.31.
3 Paper entitled 'Operations in Scandinavia', pasted into Ironside Diaries, 1940, Vol. I, p.35; emphasis as original.
4 Ironside Diaries, 1940, Vol. I, 13 January 1940, p.32.

5 Ironside Diaries, 1940, Vol. I, 14 January 1940, pp.36–38.
6 Ironside Diaries, 1940, Vol. I, 16 January 1940, p.46.
7 Ironside Diaries, 1940, Vol. I, 31 January 1940, p.76.
8 Gamelin to Ironside, 16 February 1940, pasted into Ironside Diaries, 1940, Vol. I, p.123; for the affair as viewed at BEF Headquarters, see diary entry for 22 February 1940 in Bond (ed.) *Chief of Staff*, pp.284–86.
9 Ironside Diaries, 1940, Vol. I, 1 March 1940, pp.130–31.
10 Ironside Diaries, 1940, Vol. I, 23 March 1940, p.181.
11 Ironside Diaries, 1940, Vol. I, 30 March 1940, p.200.
12 This is discussed in Ironside Diaries, 1940, Vol. I, 31 January 1940, p.75.
13 Ironside Diaries, 1940, Vol. II, 7 April 1940, p.14.
14 Ironside Diaries, 1940, Vol. II, 9 April 1940, pp.18–19.
15 Ironside Diaries, 1940, Vol. II, 10 April 1940, p.22.
16 Ironside Diaries, 1940, Vol. II, 11 April 1940, p.28.
17 Ironside Diaries, 1940, Vol. II, 12 April 1940, p.29.
18 Ironside Diaries, 1940, Vol. II, 13 April 1940, p.34.
19 Ironside Diaries, 1940, Vol. I, 20 March 1940, p.174.
20 Ironside Diaries, 1940, Vol. I, 23 March 1940, pp.181–82.
21 Ironside Diaries, 1940, Vol. II, 13 April 1940, p.34.
22 Ironside Diaries, 1940, Vol. II, 21 April 1940, p.69.
23 Ironside Diaries, 1940, Vol. II, 21 April 1940, p.70.
24 Ironside Diaries, 1940, Vol. II, 10 May 1940, p.122.

References to Chapter 20

The general background on the course of events on the Continent is taken from the previously cited Bond, *France and Belgium* and Sebag Montefiore, *Dunkirk*. On the particular case of the Channel ports, see also Michael Glover, *The Fight for the Channel Ports. Calais to Brest 1940: A Study in Confusion* (London: Leo Cooper, 1985), and respecting Calais, Airey Neave, *The Flames of Calais* (London: Hodder and Stoughton, 1972).

On the defence of Great Britain against the threat of invasion, there is some good material in the relevant volume of the official history by Basil Collier, *The Defence of the United Kingdom* (London: HMSO, 1957). However, far and away the best source, combining operational and organisational history with a solid and balanced account of the intrigue going on behind the scenes, is David Newbold's unpublished doctoral thesis, 'British Planning and Preparation to Resist Invasion on Land, September 1939–September 1940' (King's College London).

1 Ironside Diaries, 1940, Vol. II, 15 May 1940, p.142.
2 Ironside Diaries, 1940, Vol. II, 15 May 1940, p.146.
3 Ironside Diaries, 1940, Vol. II, 17 May 1940, p.150.

4   See footnote to Macleod and Kelly (eds.), *Ironside Diaries*, p.314.
5   *Ironside Diaries*, 1940, Vol. II, 17 May 1940, p.151.
6   *Ironside Diaries*, 1940, Vol. II, 19 May 1940, p.155.
7   *Ironside Diaries*, 1940, Vol. II, 19 May 1940, p.156.
8   *Ironside Diaries*, 1940, Vol. II, 20 May 1940, p.156.
9   *Ironside Diaries*, 1940, Vol. II, 20 May 1940, pp.156–57.
10 For this and Pownall's account of the rest of my father's visit, see diary entry for 20 May 1940 in Bond (ed.), *Chief of Staff*, pp.323–24.
11 *Ironside Diaries*, 1940, Vol. II, 21 May 1940, p.157.
12 *Ironside Diaries*, 1940, Vol. II, 21 May 1940, p.157.
13 *Ironside Diaries*, 1940, Vol. II, 22 May 1940, pp.158–59.
14 *Ironside Diaries*, 1940, Vol. II, 23 May 1940, p.159.
15 *Ironside Diaries*, 1940, Vol. II, 23 May 1940, p.159.
16 *Ironside Diaries*, 1940, Vol. II, 23 May 1940, pp.159–60.
17 *Ironside Diaries*, 1940, Vol. II, 24 May 1940, p.160.
18 Quoted in Glover, Michael, *The Fight for the Channel Ports. Calais to Brest 1940: A Study in Confusion* (London: Leo Cooper, 1985) p.101. 48th Division, part of the BEF, did not in fact send any troops towards Calais – the War Office had evidently been misinformed on this head.
19 Quoted in Sebag Montefiore, *Dunkirk*, p.228.
20 *Ironside Diaries*, 1940, Vol. II, 25 May 1940, p.162.
21 *Ironside Diaries*, 1940, Vol. II, 25 May 1940, p.163.
22 *Ironside Diaries*, 1940, Vol. II, 26 May 1940, p.166.
23 Rhodes James, Robert (ed.), *Chips: The Diaries of Sir Edward Channon* (London: Penguin 1970) diary entry for 16 April 1940, p.296.
24 Danchev, Alex, 'Dill', in Keegan (ed.) *Churchill's Generals*, p.55.
25 *Ironside Diaries*, 1940, Vol. II, 27 May 1940, p.167.
26 *Ironside Diaries*, 1940, Vol. II, 30 May 1940, p.175.
27 A Yeomanry formation equipped only with light tanks and armoured cars.
28 Administratively assigned to Northern Command.
29 Detached to France with 2nd BEF until mid-June, then shifted to Eastern Command Reserve.
30 Elements detached to France with 2nd BEF until mid-June.
31 Figures from Collier, Basil, *The Defence of the United Kingdom* (London: HMSO, 1957) pp.124–25.
32 *Ironside Diaries*, 1940, Vol. II, table forming part of entry for 1 June 1940, p.185.
33 *Ironside Diaries*, 1940, Vol. II, 28 May 1940, p.172.
34 *Ironside Diaries*, 1940, Vol. II, 27 May 1940, pp.167–68.
35 *Ironside Diaries*, 1940, Vol. II, 30 May 1940, pp.176–77.
36 *Ironside Diaries*, 1940, Vol. II, 27 May 1940, p.168.

37 Ironside Diaries, 1940, Vol. II, 30 May 1940, p.178.
38 Ironside Diaries, 1940, Vol. II, 29 May 1940, p.174.
39 Ironside Diaries, 1940, Vol. II, 30 May 1940, p.176.
40 Ironside Diaries, 1940, Vol. II, 30 May 1940, p.175.
41 Note by Macleod, in Macleod and Kelly (eds), *Ironside Diaries*, p.344.
42 'Notes on a meeting between General Ironside and leaders of the Local Defence Volunteers, 5 [sic] June 1940' TNA, WO199/3244A, pp.4–5.
43 'Notes on a meeting between General Ironside and leaders of the Local Defence Volunteers, 5 [sic] June 1940' TNA, WO199/3244A, p.5.
44 'Notes on a meeting between General Ironside and leaders of the Local Defence Volunteers, 5 [sic] June 1940' TNA, WO199/3244A, p.8.
45 'Notes on a meeting between General Ironside and leaders of the Local Defence Volunteers, 5 [sic] June 1940' TNA, WO199/3244A, p.14.
46 Ironside Diaries, 1940, Vol. II, 30 May 1940, p.178.
47 Ironside Diaries, 1940, Vol. II, 2 June 1940, p.187.
48 Ironside Diaries, 1940, Vol. II, 5 June 1940, p.197.
49 Ironside Diaries, 1940, Vol. II, 7 June 1940, p.202.
50 Ironside Diaries, 1940, Vol. II, 8 June 1940, pp.206–08.
51 Ironside Diaries, 1940, Vol. II, 9 June 1940, p.216.
52 Ironside Diaries, 1940, Vol. II, 23 June 1940, p.253.
53 Ironside Diaries, 1940, Vol. II, 29 June 1940, pp.263–64.
54 Replaced by Maj. Gen. J.S. Nichols as of 7 July 1940.
55 Redesignated as 2nd New Zealand Division once all assigned units had arrived.
56 Ironside Diaries, 1940, Vol. III, 9 July 1940, p.22.
57 Ironside Diaries, 1940, Vol. III, 19 July 1940, p.38.
58 Ironside Diaries, 1940, Vol. III, 20 July 1940, p.39.
59 Churchill to Ironside, 28 July 1940 (postscript added 4 August), pasted into Ironside Diaries, 1940, Vol. III, p.67.

References to Epilogue

1 Knatchbull-Hugessen to Hall, 12 December 1944, TNA, FO954/1B/349.
2 Ironside Diaries, 1940, Vol. II, 15 June 1940, pp.235–36.
3 Ironside Diaries, 1940, Vol. II, 27 May 1940, p.169.

Select Bibliography

Archival Sources

Ironside Papers
  Ironside Diaries.
  Ironside–Stone correspondence.
  Miscellaneous correspondence.
The National Archives (TNA)
  CAB65 – War Cabinet and Cabinet: Minutes 1939–45.
  CAB66 – War Cabinet and Cabinet: Memoranda 1939–45.
  FO954/1B/349 – Knatchbull-Hugessen to Hall, 12 December 1944.
  WO95/1370/1-4 – 99th Brigade War Diaries, 1918.
  WO199/3244A – Notes on a meeting between General Ironside and leaders of the Local Defence Volunteers, 5 [sic] June 1940.

Printed Primary Sources and Memoirs

Alanbrooke, Lord (Alex Danchev and Daniel Todman, eds), *War Diaries 1939–1945* (London: Weidenfeld & Nicolson, 2001).
Bond, Brian (ed.), *Chief of Staff: The Diaries of Lieutenant General Sir Henry Pownall* (London: Leo Cooper, 1972).
Burgoyne, Elizabeth (ed.), *Gertrude Bell: Her Personal Papers 1914–1926* (London: Ernest Benn, 1961).
Ironside, Edmund, *Archangel 1918–1919* (London: Constable, 1953).
Ironside, 2nd Baron (ed.), *High Road to Command: The Diaries of Major General Sir Edmund Ironside 1920–22* (London: Leo Cooper, 1972).
Jeffery, Keith (ed.), *The Military Correspondence of Field Marshal Sir Henry Wilson, 1918–1922* (London: Army Records Society, 1985).
Kutscher, Christoph-Friedrich (ed.), *Ludwig von Estorff. Wanderungen Und Kämpfe in Südwestafrika, Ostafrika Und Südafrika, 1894–1910* (Wiesbaden: Wiesbadner Kurier Verlag, 1968).

Liddell Hart, B.H., *The Memoirs of Captain Liddell Hart* (London: Cassel, 1965).
Macleod, Colonel Roderick, and Denis Kelly (eds), *The Ironside Diaries 1937–1940* (London: Constable, 1962).
Minney, R.J. *The Private Papers of Hore-Belisha* (New York: Doubleday, 1961).
Rhodes James, Robert (ed.), *Chips: The Diaries of Sir Edward Channon* (London: Penguin 1970).

Secondary Sources

Arthur, Sir George, *Life of Lord Kitchener* (London: Macmillan, 1920).
Axworthy, Michael, *Empire of the Mind: A History of Iran* (London: Hurst, 2007).
Barclay, C.N., *On Their Shoulders. British Generalship in the Lean Years 1939–1942* (London: Faber and Faber, 1964).
Barr, James, *A Line in the Sand. Britain, France, and the Struggle for the Middle East* (London: Simon & Schuster, 2011).
Berton, Pierre, *Vimy* (Barnsley: Pen & Sword, 2003).
Bond, Brian, *British Military Policy Between the Two World Wars* (Oxford: Clarendon, 1980).
—*France and Belgium 1939–1940* (London: Davis Poynter, 1975).
—*The Victorian Army and the Staff College, 1854–1914* (London: Eyre Methuen, 1972).
Collier, Basil, *The Defence of the United Kingdom* (London: HMSO, 1957).
Colville, J.R., *Man of Valour: The Life of Field-Marshal the Viscount Gort, VC, GCB, DSO, MVO, MC* (London: Collins, 1972).
Cook, Tim, *No Place to Run: The Canadian Corps and Gas Warfare in the First World War* (Vancouver: University of British Columbia Press, 2000).
Cornish, Paul, *Machine Guns and the Great War* (Barnsley: Pen & Sword, 2009).
Crownover, Roger, *The United States Intervention in Russia 1918, 1919: The Polar Bear Odyssey* (Lewiston: Edwin Mellen Press, 2001).
Fletcher, David, *Mechanised Force: British Tanks Between the Wars* (London: Stationery Office, 1991).
Ghani, Cyrus, *Iran and the Rise of Reza Shah: From Qajar Collapse to Pahlavi Power* (London: I.B. Tauris, 2001).
Glover, Michael, *The Fight for the Channel Ports. Calais to Brest 1940: A Study in Confusion* (London: Leo Cooper, 1985).
Harris, Stephen J., *Canadian Brass: The Making of a Professional Army 1860–1939* (Toronto: University of Toronto Press, 1998).
Holmes, Richard, *Tommy: The British Soldier on the Western Front 1914–1918* (London: Harper Collins, 2004).
Jackson, Robert, *At War with the Bolsheviks* (London: Tom Stacey, 1972).

Kavic, Lorne J., *India's Quest for Security: Defence Policies, 1947–1965* (Los Angeles: University of California Press, 1967).

Keegan, John (ed.), *Churchill's Generals* (New York: Grove Weidenfeld, 1991).

Kinvig, Clifford, *Churchill's Crusade: The British Invasion of Russia, 1918–1920* (London: Bloomsbury, 2007).

McGregor, Gordon, *The German South West Africa Commemorative Medal Issued to Non-German Military Personnel* (Windhoek: privately published, undated).

Marden, Major General T.O., *A Short History of the 6th Division August 1914–March 1919* (London: Hugh Rees Ltd, 1920).

Mason, Philip, *A Matter of Honour: An Account of the Indian Army, its Officers and Men* (London: Jonathan Cape, 1974).

Moretz, Joseph, *Towards a Wider War: British Strategic Decision-Making and Military Effectiveness in Scandinavia, 1939–40* (Solihull: Helion, 2017).

Neave, Airey, *The Flames of Calais* (London: Hodder and Stoughton, 1972).

Newbold, David, 'British Planning and Preparation to Resist Invasion on Land, September 1939–September 1940' (unpublished doctoral thesis, King's College London).

Nicholson, Colonel G.W.L., *Canadian Expeditionary Force 1914–1919* (Ottawa: Queen's Printer, 1962).

Pakenham, Thomas, *The Boer War* (London: Weidenfeld & Nicolson, 1979).

Perry, Frederick William, *The Commonwealth Armies: Manpower and Organisation in Two World Wars* (Manchester: Manchester University Press, 1988).

Powell, Geoffrey, *The History of the Green Howards: Three Hundred Years of Service* (Barnsley: Pen & Sword, 2015).

Radley, Kenneth, *Get Tough Stay Tough: Shaping the Canadian Corps 1914–1918* (Solihull: Helion, 2014).

Rinaldi, Richard A., *Order of Battle of the British Army 1914* (Takoma Park, MD: Tiger Lily Books, 2008).

Sebag Montefiore, Hugh, *Dunkirk: Fight to the Last Man* (London: Viking, 2006).

Smalley, Edward, 'Qualified, but Unprepared: Training for War at the Staff College in the 1930s' in *British Journal for Military History*, Volume 2, Issue 1 (November 2015) pp.55–72.

Stevenson, David, *1914–1918: The History of the First World War* (London: Penguin, 2004).

Surridge, Keith Terrence, *Managing the South African War, 1899–1902: Politicians v. Generals* (Martlesham: Boydell & Brewer, 1998).

Trythall, Anthony John, *'Boney' Fuller: The Intellectual General* (London: Cassel, 1977).

Wyrall, Everard, *The History of the Second Division 1914–1918* (London: Thos Nelson & Sons, undated).

Index

Addison, Major General George Henry 240
Aden 174
Adye, Colonel John 31–32, 34
Afghanistan 20, 151, 213, 228, 230, 240, 242–3,
Alanbrooke, Field Marshal Lord *see* Brooke, Field Marshal Alan
Aldershot 8, 14, 55, 74, 142, 185, 195, 199, 201, 204, 206, 208, 211–2, 218–9, 223, 225, 229, 236, 242, 266, 281, 295, 306–7, 373
Arbuthnot, Captain Dalrymple 'Dally' 27
Archangel *see* Russia
Australia and New Zealand Army Corps (ANZAC) 86–8, 94, 126
Austria 281

Baghdad *see* Iraq
Baldwin, Prime Minister Stanley 250–3, 256, 263
Bateman Champain, Brigadier General Hugh 157–8
Beaverbrook, Lord 72–3, 328
Beck, Józef 295, 297, 299–301
Belgium 51, 56, 247, 270, 296, 316–20, 323, 333–4, 336, 340, 350, 371, 377
Bell, Gertrude 152, 174, 177, 176
Bingham, Hon. Francis 52
Blakiston-Houston, Major General John 264–5, 270, 273
Blomberg, Werner von 15, 259–60
Boer War 14, 28–34, 54–55, 71, 125, 152, 182
Bond, Professor Brian 202, 204
Botchkareva, Madame 118–9
British Armed Forces
    Brigades
        1st Armoured Reconnaissance Brigade 373

1st Army Tank Brigade 352, 361, 370
1st Light Armoured Brigade 270
1st Motor Machine Gun Brigade 372
2nd Light Armoured Brigade 270
2nd Motor Machine Gun Brigade 372
2rd Pack Brigade 200
3rd Field Brigade 200
3rd Rifle Brigade 60
4th Field Brigade 200
4th Guards Brigade 200
5th Infantry Brigade 200
6th Brigade 67
6th Infantry Brigade 200
8th Field Brigade 200
15th Brigade 342
17th Infantry Brigade 60–1, 66
18th Infantry Brigade 62, 65–6
19th Infantry Brigade 59–61
20th Armoured Brigade 360, 370
20th Guards Brigade 354
21st Armoured Tank Brigade 373
24th Guards Brigade 340, 342
30th Infantry Brigade 354
70th Independent Infantry Brigade 373
71st Infantry Brigade 61–62
99th Infantry Brigade 95–103
140th Brigade 342
238th Special Brigade 124
XIII Brigade Division 30
XVI Brigade 104
Rifle Brigade 67
Regiments
    1st Buffs/East Kent 60–61
    1st Devonshire Regiment 200
    1st King's Liverpool Regiment 100
    1st King's Own Royal Regiment 200

1st Leicestershire 60, 62
1st Middlesex Regiment 61
1st North Staffordshire 60
1st Northamptonshire Regiment 200
1st Royal Berkshire Regiment 96, 154
1st West Yorkshire Regiment 60, 62, 66
2nd Dorsetshire Regiment 200
2nd East Yorkshire Regiment 150
2nd Gurkha Rifles Regiment 154, 162
2nd Hampshire Regiment 125
2nd Leinster Regiment 60
2nd Norfolk Regiment 200
2nd Queen's Own Royal West Kent Regiment 200
2nd Sherwood Foresters Regiment 61–62
2nd West Yorkshire Regiment 60
2nd Yorkshire and Lancashire 60–61, 154
3rd Royal Tank Regiment 367
8th Bedfordshire Regiment 61
8th Royal Tank Regiment 361
9th Norfolk Regiment 62
9th Suffolk Regiment 62
11th Essex Regiment 62
Leinster Regiment 55
Royal Gibraltar Regiment 291
Royal Scots Regiment 109, 118, 128–9
Divisions
   1st Armoured Division 273, 350, 354, 357, 370, 373
   1st Division 226
   1st London Division 360, 372
   2nd Armoured Division 361, 373
   2nd Division 8, 95–103, 113, 194, 198–205, 212, 218, 226–7
   2nd London Division 360
   3rd Division 373–4, 380
   4th Division 60, 143, 367
   4th Infantry Division 372
   5th Division 85, 352
   6th Division 59–70, 76, 143
   7th Armoured Division 264
   9th (Scottish) Division 69
   11th Armoured Division 264
   12th Division 362
   15th (Scottish) Infantry Division 360, 362, 372
   18th (East Anglia) Infantry Division 360, 372
   24th Division 82, 85
   27th Division 61
   29th Division 64
   33rd Division 96
   34th Division 62
   37th Division 100
   42nd (East Lancashire) Infantry Division 372
   43rd Wessex Infantry Division 361, 373
   45th Infantry Division 360, 362, 372
   48th (South Midlands) Division 373
   49th Division 340
   50th (Northumbria) Infantry Division 372
   50th Division 352
   51st (Highland) Division 357
   52nd (Lowland) Infantry Division 360–2, 368, 372
   55th (West Lancashire) Infantry Division 360, 372
   59th (Staffordshire) Infantry Division 372
   Guards Division 100
   Mobile Division 256, 264–5, 269–73, 370, 380
   Regular 4th Division 248
   Regular 5th Division 240, 242
Infantry
   1st King's Shropshire Light Infantry 60–1
   1st Oxfordshire and Buckinghamshire Light Infantry 125
   2nd Duke of Cornwall's Light Infantry 150
   2nd Durham Light Infantry 61–2
   2nd Highland Light Infantry 136
   6th Royal Marine Light Infantry 108
   14th Durham Light Infantry 62
Company
   5th Field (Royal Engineers) Company 200
   11th Field (Royal Engineers) Company 200
   16th Machine Gun Company 61
   18th Machine Gun Company 62

Index

38th Field Company 200
71st Machine Gun Company 62
King's Royal Rifle Corps Company
Battery
   'A' Battery RHA 155
   'I' Battery RHA 39, 49, 51
   'Y' Battery 52
   15th Light Armoured Motor Battery 155
   24th Heavy Battery RGA 61
   44th Field Battery 26–34, 39, 49
   63rd Battery 28
   90th Battery 52
Corps
   1st King's Royal Rifle Corps 96, 98
   2nd King's Royal Rifle Corps 200
   I Corps 271–2, 293, 306, 326, 372
   II Corps 76–77, 271–2, 326–7, 372
   III Corps 60, 322, 340, 367
   IV Corps 361, 373
   VI Corps 64, 97, 99, 101
   VII Corps 373
   VIII Corps 372
   X Corps 372–3
   XI Corps 372
   XII Corps 372
   XX Corps 204
   Machine Gun Corps 92, 94, 98–9, 102, 187
   Royal Army Service Corps 263
   Royal Army Service Corps 62
   Royal Air Force 115, 141, 155, 173–6, 178, 182, 186–8, 109–1, 196–7, 205–6, 249, 256–8, 260, 277, 286, 311–2, 314, 321, 348, 357–8, 368
Royal Flying Corps 64–5
Royal Navy 20, 129, 145, 181, 187, 190–1, 197, 224, 258, 261, 276–7, 290, 296, 302, 311, 313, 338, 340, 342, 368,
Territorial Army 197, 237, 247, 252, 254, 256, 264
British Government 51, 110, 146, 149, 166, 192, 197, 211, 248, 276, 288
Colonial Office 166, 172, 176, 186, 289, 295
Foreign Office 111–2, 159, 165, 306,
House of Commons 191, 283–4, 286, 298, 324
House of Lords 166, 224, 375–6

War Office 15, 52, 65, 71, 101–4, 107, 109, 119, 122, 124, 129, 132–4, 146–7, 159–61, 164, 179, 184–5, 189–91, 195, 211–3, 216–8, 224, 230, 238, 242, 251, 255, 260, 263–6, 268–9, 274–6, 278, 281, 285–6, 289, 294–6, 301, 304, 305–6, 307–13, 322, 327, 343, 346, 348, 359, 370, 372, 373, 380
Brooke, Brigadier General Lord 72–73, 75–6
Brooke, Field Marshal Alan 7, 13, 202, 264, 270, 272–3, 326–7, 354, 360, 367, 372–5, 377, 380–1
Brownrigg, Lieutenant General Douglas 279
Buchan, John 7, 13, 37, 47
Buller, General Sir Redvers 29–30
Byng, Lieutenant General the Hon. Julian 72, 85, 92, 99, 103, 189

Cairo *see* Egypt
Callwell, Colonel Charles 37
Camberley *see* Staff College at Camberley
Campbell, Lieutenant General Sir David 208, 216–20, 223, 225
Canadian Armed Forces 70–3, 75–80, 82–3, 85–90, 104, 247, 352, 354–6, 361–2, 368
   5th Canadian Brigade 73
   10th Canadian Brigade 73, 77–78, 82–83
   10th Canadian Machine Gun Company 78
   10th Canadian Infantry Brigade 78
   10th Canadian Light Trench Mortar Battery 78
   10th Canadian Machine Gun Company 78
   11th Canadian Brigade 77–78, 80, 82–83
   11th Canadian Light Trench Mortar Battery 78
   11th Canadian Machine Gun Company 78
   11th Canadian Infantry Brigade 78
   11th Canadian Light Trench Mortar Battery 78
   12th Canadian Light Trench Mortar Battery 78
   12th Canadian Machine Gun Company 78
   12th Canadian Infantry Brigade 78

12th Canadian Light Trench Mortar
    Battery 78
38th (Ottawa) Battalion 78
44th (Manitoba) Battalion 78
46th (Regina and Moose Jaw) Battalion
    78
47th (British Columbia) Battalion 78
50th (Calgary) Battalion 78
54th (Kootenay) Battalion 78
67th Canadian Pioneer Battalion 78
72nd Battalion (Seaford Highlanders of
    Canada) 78
73rd Battalion (Royal Highlanders of
    Canada) 78
75th (Mississauga) Battalion 78
78th Battalion (Winnipeg Grenadiers) 78
2nd Canadian Division 71, 90
85th Battalion (Nova Scotia Highlanders)
    78
87th Battalion (Canadian Grenadier
    Guards) 78
102nd (Northern British Columbia)
    Battalion 78
124th Canadian Pioneer Battalion 78
3rd Canadian Division 71, 88–90
12th Canadian Brigade 78, 83, 89, 196
4th Canadian Division 14, 70, 72–3,
    75–86, 88–90, 102
1st Canadian Division 71, 90, 337, 355,
    368, 361, 373
Canadian Gunners 118
Canadian Field Artillery 119, 121
Cape Colony *see* South Africa
Carson, Major General John Wallace 72
Cavan, General the Earl of 185, 187, 190,
    193, 224, 379
Chamberlain, Neville 169, 252, 256, 263,
    286, 293, 297–8, 302–3, 308,
    312–3, 327, 330, 335, 338, 343,
    346, 359, 380–1,
Chetwode, Lieutenant General Sir Philip
    140, 204, 206, 208, 220, 226–7,
    229–30, 231, 234–8, 241, 243–4,
    248, 306, 379
China 109, 211–2, 246
Churchill, Winston 14–5, 130, 133–5,
    142, 166, 172, 174–6, 179–80,
    190, 195, 276–8, 283, 291,
    302–4, 307–9, 311–2, 315, 330,
    335, 338–40, 344, 346, 348–49,

354, 356–7, 359, 370–1, 373–5,
    379–80
Collins, Colonel Jack 203, 216, 229
Congreve VC, Sir Walter 62, 66, 148
Cooper, Duff 248, 252, 256, 260, 263, 279
Cory, Major General George 168, 226
Cotesworth Slessor, Squadron Leader John
    205
Cowan, Vice Admiral Sir Walter 182
Cox, Sir Percy 148–9, 151–2, 158, 160,
    173–7
Creedy, Sir Herbert 284, 307
Cudahy, John 249–52
Cummins, Brigadier General H.A.V 146
Curzon, Lord George 141, 151, 157–8, 164,
    166,
Czechoslovakia 254, 281, 289

Daladier, Prime Minister Édouard 335–6
Debeney, Marie–Eugène 221–2
Denmark 339–40
Deverell, Field Marshal Sir Cyril 229, 248,
    251–6, 260, 264–9, 272–4, 277–8,
    322
Dickson, Brigadier General William E.R.
    159, 164
Dill, Captain Sir John 13, 55, 266, 268–9,
    293, 306, 326–7, 345, 353–4, 359,
    366, 370, 377
Dowding, Captain H.C.T. 55–6
Drake, Major Bernard Francis 27–8, 33–4

Eden, Anthony 346, 356, 370, 375
Edward VIII, King 37, 252–3
Egypt 31, 172, 175, 197, 277, 286, 289–91,
    302
Estorff, Major Ludwig Gustav Adolph Von
    45–50

Fascism in Britain 260, 321–3
Finland 107, 330, 332–3, 336–8, 340
First World War 7, 15, 30, 48, 52, 54, 56, 65,
    70, 95, 105, 125, 172, 184–5, 201,
    208, 227, 276, 296, 336, 379
    Battle of Albert 94, 99–101
    Battle of Amiens 96–7, 99, 101
    Battle of Ancre 77
    Battle of Ancre Heights 76
    Battle of Cambrai 86, 125
    Battle of Passchendaele 75, 85–90, 92, 96

Index

Battle of Vimy Ridge 77–86
Flanders 85–6, 90
Tannenberg Campaign 188–9
Ypres 64–7, 86–8
France 58, 70–6, 85, 92, 96, 101–5, 113, 141, 143, 148, 181, 221, 247, 273, 293, 305, 307, 311, 314–7, 320, 322–5, 331, 333–40, 342–3, 362, 347–60, 364, 366–7, 369, 380
    French Armed Forces 221–2, 290, 314–9, 328–9, 334–5, 337, 351, 353, 354–60
Franco, Francisco 253, 281, 287–8, 290, 297
Fuller, Colonel J.F.C. 8, 14, 56, 184, 187, 194–5, 199, 202–4, 216, 321–2, 379–80
Furse, Lieutenant General Sir William 63, 69

Gamelin, General Maurice 260, 314, 316–9, 323, 328–9, 334–8, 347–8, 351–2
Gatacre, Major General Sir William 26
George VI, King 259
Germany 9, 14, 43–4, 47–9, 55, 58, 106, 222, 239, 247, 249–50, 253–4, 258–9, 261–3, 273–4, 281, 289–90, 295–6, 298, 300–1, 303, 308, 312, 314, 316–7, 321–2, 330–2, 337–8, 343–4, 348, 359, 371, 376, 380
    German Armed Forces
        First World War 40, 42–8, 65–6, 92–4, 96, 99, 101, 103
        Russia 104, 106–7
        Second World War 250, 259–62, 281, 299, 302, 307–8, 313, 317–8, 321, 330–1, 333–4, 336, 338–40, 342, 347–55
Gibraltar 8, 15, 21, 181–2, 229, 265–7, 278–80, 282, 285–92, 294–5, 297, 305, 310
Gordon, Brigadier General Hon. Frederick 61–2
Gordon-Finlayson, Brigadier General Robert 109–12, 119
Gort VC, General Lord 8, 13, 183, 192, 211, 265–9, 273–4, 276–81, 286–7, 293–4, 296, 301, 304–11, 317, 320–1, 323–9, 335–6, 340, 343–4, 348–58, 370, 381
Gough, Sir Hubert 76–7, 92–3,
Graham, Colonel C.A.L 119–21, 128, 130–1

Greek Armed Forces 142–3, 145, 148
Grogan, Brigadier General George 124–7, 131

Haig, Sir Douglas 72, 85, 88, 92–93, 96, 206, 327
Haldane, Lieutenant General Sir Aylmer 101–3, 146, 148–9, 152, 160, 164–5, 168, 173–6
Haldane, Lord Richard 224
Halifax, Lord Edward 295, 297–8, 304, 306, 312–3, 327, 339
Hitler, Adolf 247, 259, 261, 281, 286, 289, 296–8, 300–3, 306–7, 313, 317–8, 339
Home Guard *see* LDV
Hong Kong 246–7, 254
Hore-Belisha, Leslie 260, 263–7, 269, 273–4, 276–81, 283–6, 289, 293, 295, 301, 303–6, 309–10, 312–3, 321, 324–8, 330, 332, 378, 380
Horthy, Admiral Miklós 141
Hughes, Major General Sir Sam 71–4, 76
Hungary 14, 19, 21, 140–1

India 8, 14, 49–51, 136, 146, 148–50, 165–6, 170, 173, 175, 180, 184, 197–8, 204, 211–5, 219–20, 223–31, 233–46, 248, 253, 255, 267, 269, 274, 276, 278, 286, 290, 305, 344–5, 376, 378
    Indian Armed Forces 51, 146, 149, 215, 226–30, 233–5, 238–43
        36th Indian Brigade 154
        42nd Deoli Regiment 154
        122nd Rajput Regiment 154
        2nd and Lahore Division 78
        3rd Indian Division 229
        31st Indian Pack Battery 155
Iraq 148–52, 172, 176–7, 179, 197, 376
Ironside *née* Cheyne, Lady Mariot Ysobel 53, 58–9, 65, 104–5, 138, 140, 176, 185, 200, 225, 238–9, 241, 244, 246, 259, 280, 287, 379
Ironside, Field Marshal the Lord William Edmund
    Army Mechanisation 198, 201–3, 209–10, 216–8, 220, 227–9, 234–5, 237, 252–3
    Death 378

Early Life 19–24
First World War 58–68, 70–6, 80–90,
    93–6, 98–103
Gibraltar 279–80, 282, 287–92
Hungary 140–1
India 225–30, 233–5, 239–41
Iraq 150, 152
Marriage 53, 58, 65, 138, 140, 185, 241
Medals and Honours 36–7, 49, 65,
    90,169, 283, 375
Persia 151, 154–7, 159–60, 165
Royal Military College 24–5
Russia 103–4, 109–24
Second World War 307–75
South Africa 27–50, 52
Staff College at Camberley 24, 54–8,
    180–7, 190–4
Turkey 143–8
Ironside, Surgeon Major William 19

Jacob, Field Marshal Sir Claude 76, 212–4, 241
Jafar Pasha al–Askari 174, 176
Japan 239, 246–7, 276, 108
Jardine, Captain James 36
Jeudwine, Major Hugh 37

Keir, Major General Jack 60, 62, 64
Kelly, Lt Colonel John Sherwood 124–6,
    130–1, 135–6
Kemal, Mustafa 143
Kemp, Rear Admiral T.W. 107
Khan, Kutchik 122, 150, 155, 157, 166, 168
Kiggell, Brigadier General Launcelot 56, 180
Kitchener, Major General Lord 29, 31–2, 59,
    105, 182, 196, 227–8, 324
Knox, Major General Alfred 119
Knox, Sir Harry 201, 255, 266
Kolchak, Admiral Alexander 119, 124

Lall, Roshan 231–2
Lavie, Lieutenant Colonel H.E 122–3, 145
Lawrence, T.E. 172
Lenin, Vladimir 106
LDV 360, 264–6, 368–9
Ludendorff, *General der Infanterie* Erich 92,
    96, 189
Leutwein, *Major* Theodor 43–44
Liddell Hart, Captain Basil 27–7, 204, 216,
    263, 265, 268–9, 273–4, 278, 281,
    293, 321–2, 379

Lindley, Sir Francis 111–2, 122, 129
Lloyd George, Prime Minister David 14, 67,
    129, 142,
Lynden-Bell, Major General Arthur 103

MacBrien, Major General James 78, 80, 82,
    89, 196
MacDonald, Prime Minister Ramsay 192
Madden, Admiral Sir Charles 181–2, 187
Malta 182, 229
Marushevsky, General 116, 118–9
Mesopotamia 146–9, 152, 156–8, 166, 170,
    172–6, 187–8, 214
Miller, General Yevgeny 122, 127–8, 132–7
Milne, Field Marshal Sir George 142–4, 146,
    148–9, 193, 195, 202–4, 207, 212,
    214–8, 220, 223, 226, 231, 235–237,
    248, 251, 295, 345, 375, 379
Milner, Sir Alfred 31
Montague–Bates, Brigadier General 144–6
Montgomery–Massingberd, Field Marshal
    Sir Archibald 220, 235, 237, 244,
    248, 268, 295
Montgomery, Field Marshal Sir Bernard
    Law 202, 273, 326, 373–4, 377,
    380–1
Morgan-Grenville, Hon. Thomas 66–67, 76,
    113, 118
Mosley, Oswald 321–2
Muller, Archibald Herman 241
Muspratt, Colonel Sydney 149
Mussolini, Benito 248, 259, 261–2, 276, 280,
    286, 302

Needham, Brigadier General Henry 113,
    136
Newall, Air Chief Marshal Sir Cyril 311–2,
    314, 318–9, 341, 370
Norman, Herman 158–64, 167, 169, 170
Norway 247, 330–2, 339–44, 348, 371, 381
Nosworthy, Major General Francis 305, 361,
    370, 373
Nogués, General Charles 290

Odlum, Brigadier General Victor 75–8,
    80–83
Okehampton Artillery Practise Camp,
    Dartmoor 26
Ossipov, Constantine 'Kosti' 114–5, 137–8,
    149, 141, 171

Perley, Sir George 72
Persia 14, 149, 151–62, 164–167, 169–71, 198, 376, 378
  Kazvin 154, 156–7, 159–60, 162, 165–166, 168, 171
  North Persia Force 154–6
  Persian Cossack Brigade 155, 157, 159–64, 166–9, 171
  Persian Coup 171
  Teheran 151, 156, 158–63, 166, 171, 376
Pereira, Cecil 113, 96
Plumer, General Sir Herbert 86, 58
Poland 249–50, 254, 295–302, 307, 312–3, 315–6
Poole, Major General Frederick 103, 107–9, 111–2
Pound, Admiral of the Fleet Sir Dudley 289–90, 302–3, 311, 341
Pownall, Lieutenant General Sir Henry 293, 299, 304–5, 309, 320–1, 335–6, 344–5, 351–2, 377–80

Qajar, Ahmad Shah 151, 154–5, 158–9, 161–3, 167–71

Radcliffe, Brigadier General Percy 88–9, 104
Rawlinson, Sir Henry 56, 99, 133–6, 142, 146, 150, 166, 202, 206
Red Army *see* Russia, Bolshevik Armed Forces
Reza Khan 164, 167–71, 376
Reza Shah *see* Reza Khan
Ribbentrop, Joachim von 259
Richmond, Vice Admiral Sir Herbert 196
Roberts, Field Marshal Lord 29, 31
Robertson, Major General William Robertson 56, 85, 180
Romanian Armed Forces 14, 140–1
Roosevelt, Franklin 250, 252
Royal Aircraft Establishment 257–8
Royal Air Force *see* British Armed Forces
Royal Artillery *see* British Armed Forces
Royal Military Academy at Woolwich 20–1, 23–5, 54, 58, 174
Royal Military College at Sandhurst 22–3, 54, 227
Royal Navy *see* British Armed Forces
Russia 103–7, 108–12, 128, 130, 132–3, 135, 137–8, 155, 187, 213, 239, 246–7, 250, 254, 298, 302, 307, 322, 331–2, 378
  Archangel 103–10, 112–3, 115–6, 118–9, 123–4, 128–9, 132–5, 138, 165
  Bolshevik Armed Forces 103, 106–108, 115, 117–8, 120–1, 123–4, 127, 130–3, 157, 162, 165, 197
  Dvina River 109–12, 114–15, 118, 120–21, 124, 129–30, 132, 135
  Kotlas *110*, 123, 129, 132–3
  Murmansk 104, 106–8, 112, 119, 122, 128, 134, 136
  Russian Revolution 103, 106–7, 122, 151
  Shenkursk *110*, 118–21, 128
  Siberia 119, 124
  Troitsa *110*, 130–2, 135–6

Sadleir-Jackson, Brigadier General Lionel Warren de Vere 126–7, 130, 132–3, 135–7
Salmond, Air Vice Marshal Sir Geoffrey 148, 173–4, 182
Second World War 7, 71, 138, 184, 273, 303, 310, 322, 381
  Battle of Arras 352–3
  Battle of France 257, 280
  British Coastal Defence 361–4, 369, 371–4
  Dunkirk Evacuation 15, 353, 356–8, 366–7
  Mechelen Incident 333–4
  Outbreak of War 307–8
  'Phoney War' 321
  'Plan D' 317–21, 333, 335, 347
  Norwegian Campaign
    Narvik 331, 340–1
    Iron Ore 330–2, 337–8
    Admiral Graf Spee 338
    Operation Wilfred 338
    Altmark Incident 338–9
    Plan 'R4' 338, 340
  War Office Politics 308, 312–3, 322, 324–5, 327, 343, 348, 350–1, 359, 370, 373
  Western Front 303, 314–315, 333, 340, 347, 350, 378
Settle, Major General Sir Henry 38
Shea, General Sir John 63, 229, 231, 233
Singapore 239, 247–6, 254

Skeen, Lieutenant General Sir Andrew 212–5
Smuts, Jan 30, 36–7, 141
Soames, 2nd Lieutenant Arthur H.L. 52, 64–5
South Africa 21–2, 26–31, 33–7, 45, 50–6, 67, 71, 125–6, 197
  Bechuanaland 29, 38, 40, 42, 45
  Bechuanaland Border Police 25–6
  Bloemfontein 29
  Boer War 27–34, 36–52, 55, 125
  Cape Colony 29–32, 37–8, 40, 42, 49
  Cape Town 27–9, 31, 37–9, 42, 44, 47–9, 52
  Ladysmith 29–30, 37
  Natal 29, 49
  Potchefstroom 52–53, 126
  Pretoria 29–30, 52
  Prieska 29, 31–4
  Vereeniging 29, 36, 38, 52
  Queen's South Africa Medal 36
  South West Africa Commemorative Medal 49–50
Spain 281, 287–90, 292, 297–8
Staff College at Camberley 24, 45–58, 62, 69, 101, 179–81, 183–5, 189–96, 213, 268, 279
Stanley, Oliver 327–8, 330–2, 344–6,
St Salvator's School 20

Starosselsky, Colonel Vsevolod Dmitryevich 155, 157, 159, 161–4, 170
Stone, Christopher 15, 113, 136, 138, 165–6, 183, 189
Strathcona, Lord 256–7
Sweden 330–2, 341

Tchaikovsky, President Nikolai 108
Tonbridge School 21–3, 195
Trenchard, Air Marshal Sir Hugh 172–3, 175, 182, 186, 190–2, 206, 375,
Turkey 142–8, 315, 333

United States Armed Forces 98–9, 107, 109, 112, 120, 122, 126, 128, 249

Vaida-Voevod, Prime Minister Alexandru 141
Vanier, Major George 189
Voulichevitch, Colonel 130

Watson, Major General David 73–6, 78, 83–4, 88–9, 102
Wilson, Brigadier General Sir Henry 56–7, 129–30, 144, 179–80, 185, 188, 193, 310
Winter War 330–1, 336
Wood, Sir Kingsley 309, 312, 339

You may also enjoy …

A CLEAR CASE OF GENIUS

ROOM 40'S CODE-BREAKING PIONEER

ADMIRAL SIR REGINALD 'BLINKER' HALL

WITH COMMENTARY BY PHILIP VICKERS

978 0 7509 8265 8

'This is a most interesting book, both for its content and the way in which the autobiography has been salvaged and updated by Vickers' commentary. Blinker Hall was one of the great heroes of WWI but almost totally unknown because he was Director Naval Intelligence – Most Highly Recommended.' – Firetrench.com

The History Press

The destination for history
www.thehistorypress.co.uk

You may also enjoy …

NIGEL WEST
CHURCHILL'S SPY FILES
MI5'S TOP-SECRET WARTIME REPORTS

978 0 7509 8549 9

Acclaimed intelligence expert Nigel West unravels tales of hitherto unknown spy missions, using ground-breaking research and Churchill's personal spy reports to paint a fresh picture of the worldwide intelligence scene of the Second World War.

The History Press
The destination for history
www.thehistorypress.co.uk